CONTENTS UNITS 7–8

	Aims and Objectives	4
1	A Note on Reading Eliot's Poetry	5
2	Biographical Note 1888–1925	7
3	The Early Poems 1909–12	9
4	*The Waste Land*	23
	Further Reading and References	41

AIMS AND OBJECTIVES

The aim of Units 7–8 is to introduce you to Eliot's poetry up to 1925, concentrating on three poems: 'Portrait of a Lady', 'The Love Song of J. Alfred Prufrock', and *The Waste Land*. You should also try to read at least 'Gerontion' and *The Hollow Men*, though there is no detailed consideration of them in the units. The discussion will direct you from time to time to comments on Eliot's work in F. R. Leavis, *New Bearings in English Poetry*, C. K. Stead, *The New Poetic* and the Course Reader,[1] and to information about the poems in B. C. Southam, *A Student's Guide to the Selected Poems of T. S. Eliot*. The edition of Eliot's poems used is *Collected Poems 1909–1962* published as a Faber paperback in 1974.

For broadcasts associated with these units see the Broadcast Notes (television programme 7 and radio programmes 4 and 5) and the *Broadcast and Assignment Calendar*.

[1] Graham Martin and P. N. Furbank (eds.) (1975) *Twentieth Century Poetry: Critical Essays and Documents*, The Open University Press.

THE OPEN UNIVERSITY

Arts : A Third Level Course
Twentieth Century Poetry

Units 7-8

T S ELIOT'S POETRY

Prepa[illegible] n

Cover The Hanged Man, one of the Tarot cards mentioned in *The Waste Land* (Courtesy A. G. Müller C.I.E./U.S. Games Systems Inc.)

The Open University Press
Walton Hall Milton Keynes
MK7 6AA

First published 1976. Reprinted 1977, 1980

Designed by the Graphic Design Group of The Open University.

Printed in Great Britain by
EYRE AND SPOTTISWOODE LIMITED
AT GROSVENOR PRESS PORTSMOUTH

ISBN 0 335 05104 9

This text forms part of an Open University course. The complete list of units in the course appears at the end of this text.

For general availability of supporting material referred to in this text please write to: Open University Educational Enterprises Limited, 12 Cofferidge Close, Stony Stratford, Milton Keynes, MK11 1BY, Great Britain.

Further information on Open University courses may be obtained from the Admissions Office, The Open University, P.O. Box 48, Walton Hall, Milton Keynes, MK7 6AB.

1.3

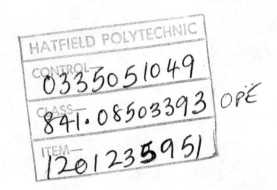

T. S. ELIOT'S POETRY 1909–25

1 A NOTE ON READING ELIOT'S POETRY

1.1 Coming to terms with a poem of any substance, and most of Eliot's poems come into that category, is a longish, a cumulative process. There is a first stage of tentative impressions, variously intense, variously accurate, as if you were looking at a painting in patchy light. You might take away a sense of striking metaphors, or descriptions, unexpected turns of phrase, pleasure or bewilderment over the rhythms, along with a rough idea of the 'subject', of 'what it's about', but with blanks to be filled, elusive or simply puzzling details, even areas that you dislike or are bored by or have no feeling about at all, except that for reasons you cannot put your finger on they 'don't make sense'. A second stage of conscious study now follows. Two or three more readings may be enough to fill out the blanks, to get the details right, to grasp the structure, though with difficult and complex poems – and again Eliot's tend to be both – you will probably need a bit of help from expert commentators. But when you have made this kind of sustained effort, you may then feel that you do now 'understand' the poem as far as you can, or want to. And not unreasonably. Yet there is a third stage beyond that which makes me put the term 'understand' in inverted commas. This is the point when you take personal possession of the poem, when you begin to 'realize' it as an element in your own imaginative life. Matthew Arnold is responsible for a famous definition of a work of literature that it is 'a criticism of life', and that is one way of thinking about this third stage. You cannot really claim to have 'understood' a poem till it has had that sort of personal meaning. But that may make the process sound more intellectual than it actually is, and Eliot's own account is in one way more suggestive. He once compared the 'meaning' of a poem – what you arrive at, or at least aspire to, during the stage of conscious study – to the juicy steak the burglar uses to keep the watchdog quiet while he gets on with burgling the house. The implication is that the reader's consciously questing mind (the watchdog) needs to be diverted while the poem (the burglar) does its proper – and stealthy – work. Or again, more explicitly, he once faulted a friend's essay on Henry James because 'you don't really criticize any author to whom you have never surrendered yourself, . . . you have to give yourself up, and then recover yourself, and the third moment is having something to say, before you have wholly forgotten both surrender and recovery. Of course the self recovered is never the same as the self before it was given'. (Tate *T. S. Eliot: The Man and His Work* p 59.)

1.2 That outlines a high ideal, one you might think applies only to professional critics. But this third stage of coming to terms with a poem involves something on these lines, a process more complex and personal – 'the self recovered is never the same as the self before it was given' – than accumulating information about it, or pondering the usefulness of tips from the writers of critical essays. Now this creates a considerable problem for the authors of introductory course units, which is why I mention it here. A written commentary necessarily reflects an advanced stage in the long process of 'understanding' the poem. The first tentative reactions have long ago been gathered up, sifted, re-organized, corrected, developed into something resembling a coherent statement, and by definition, coherent statements are exactly what the first readings of poems do not produce. So, when you work your way through these units, it matters very much that you start from your own impressions of *the poems*, as you are asked to read them, and not from the developed comments which the paragraphs marked 'Discussion' will so often include, nor – even more importantly – from any critical essays you happen to consult. These warnings do not apply to the same extent to information for the elucidation of difficult, deliberately allusive passages. The units will provide some of this, and direct you where to find more. But here again keep in mind the story about the young student who asked Eliot what he meant by the line in *Ash Wednesday*: 'Lady, three white leopards sat under a juniper-tree'. Eliot replied, deadpan: 'I mean, "Lady, three white leopards sat under a juniper-tree".' Information alone, that is, is useless, often misleading, unless it is taken into an effort to move beyond 'understanding' the poem to the third stage of personal relationship with it.

1.3 These units have been planned accordingly. They aim to take you through the first stage of immediate impressions, and well into the second stage of conscious attention to difficulties and problems: what they do not, and could not, attempt is to reach the third stage, which depends on you. Yet having divided the whole process into three separate stages, it is then too easy to forget the degree of overlap between them, that the third stage begins, though in rudimentary form, during the first. Here is a brief example.

Prelude IV

His soul stretched tight across the skies
That fade behind a city block,
Or trampled by insistent feet
At four and five and six o'clock;
And short square fingers stuffing pipes,
And evening newspapers, and eyes
Assured of certain certainties,
The conscience of a blackened street
Impatient to assume the world.

I am moved by fancies that are curled
Around these images, and cling:
The notion of some infinitely gentle
Infinitely suffering thing.

Wipe your hand across your mouth, and laugh;
The worlds revolve like ancient women
Gathering fuel in vacant lots.

1.4 Now read the poem again.

1.5 First impressions will surely somewhere touch on the different feelings expressed in the last two 'verses'. 'I am moved by fancies . . . etc.' offers one feeling about the situation evoked in the opening lines (whatever you decide that is), and 'Wipe your hand across your mouth . . . etc.' offers another. Let's say tenderness, compassion followed – perhaps it is cancelled? – by cynical dismissal. Now no amount of second-stage enquiry by the watchdog of the conscious mind into the relationship between the 'he' and the 'I' of the poem; into the connection between 'his soul' and 'the conscience of the street'; into the exact force of 'assume'; or into the question whether 'the infinitely suffering thing' is the soul, or the city crowds evoked by the 'insistent feet' and the 'short square fingers' – none of this conscious probing of meaning and structure should overlay that first impression of the poem's duality of feeling. If it does, if the sense of unresolved conflict does not survive into the third stage of personal realization, then something has gone very wrong during the second. In this case perhaps the likelihood is small. The poem does not offer much in the way of stimulus to the commentator. But the general warning is of the first importance. With Eliot's major poems, difficult, in places obscure, often densely allusive, the business of accumulating, well, yes, necessary information very easily smothers the first impressions, and comes to seem the only interesting thing. It takes sustained energy to conserve one's original feelings about the poem, to let them change and develop as the process of conscious study takes over, but not to lose them beneath the cartloads of auxiliary learning that are easier to accept as 'understanding' the poem than the real thing, the third stage. Eliot's poetry, not undeservedly, has a reputation for being 'intellectual', 'learned', yet in his own criticism he speaks repeatedly of 'feeling' and 'emotion', as C. K. Stead's chapters in *The New Poetic* most relevantly insist, and for the reader exploring his work for the first time, feeling is the more reliable guide. What, in the first instance, does the poem make you feel? It is round that question that your initial fragmentary half-articulated impressions should begin to form.

T. S. Eliot c. 1918 (Radio Times Hulton Picture Library)

2 BIOGRAPHICAL NOTE 1888–1925

1888 Thomas Stearns Eliot, born in St Louis, Missouri. His grandfather, a Unitarian minister, moved there from Massachusetts in 1834. His father went into business. His mother was active in social work, and also wrote poetry on religious themes. Eliot was the youngest of seven children.

1897 Eliot's father had a house built for summer vacations on the New England coast, near the fishing port of Gloucester, Massachusetts.

Eliot wrote of his childhood: 'In New England I missed the long dark river [the Mississippi], the ailanthus trees, the flaming cardinal birds, the high limestone bluffs where we searched for fossil shell-fish; in Missouri I missed the fir trees, the bay and goldenrod, the song-sparrows, the red granite and the blue sea of Massachusetts.' (E. A. Mowrer *This American World* p xiv.)

1906–9 Undergraduate at Harvard University, Cambridge, Massachusetts.

1908 Learns Italian by studying Dante's *Divine Comedy*. Reads Arthur Symons' *The Symbolist Movement in Literature* (1899), which introduced him to the poetry of Jules Laforgue.

He later wrote: 'the form in which I began to write, in 1908 or 1909, was directly drawn from the study of Laforgue together with the later Elizabethan drama'. (Ezra Pound *Selected Poems* p 8.) |

1910–11 Postgraduate study. Spends a year in Paris studying French literature and philosophy. Writes several of the poems eventually published in the *Prufrock* volume.

1912–14 Further postgraduate work at Harvard. Studies Sanskrit, Indian metaphysics, and the English idealist philosopher, F. H. Bradley. Considers an academic career in the Philosophy Department at Harvard.

1914 Visits Germany where he planned to study philosophy at Marburg, but moves to England on account of the war, hoping to study at Oxford where F. H. Bradley taught. Writes 'The Death of Saint Narcissus' (not published till 1967).

Meets Ezra Pound, and shows him his early poems. Pound wrote: '[Eliot] is the only American I know of who has made what I can call adequate preparation for writing. He has actually trained himself *and* modernised himself *on his own* . . . It's such a comfort to meet a man and not have to tell him to wash his face, wipe his feet, and remember the date [1914] on the calendar'. (Pound *Selected Letters* p 40.)

1915 Marries Vivien Haigh-Wood, and lives in London. Earns his living as a schoolteacher and lecturer for adult education classes.

1916 Completes doctoral dissertation on the philosophy of F. H. Bradley.

1917 Joins the Foreign Department of Lloyd's Bank in the City of London. Publishes *Prufrock and Other Observations*. Becomes Assistant Editor of *The Egoist*, a small *avant-garde* magazine which published Joyce's early work. Eliot publishes his first literary criticism here.

1918–19 Writes poems collected in *Ara Vos Prec* (1920), including 'Gerontion'. Also, early drafts of material incorporated in *The Waste Land*; and a number of seminal critical essays, including 'Tradition and the Individual Talent', and 'Hamlet', later collected in *The Sacred Wood* (1920).

He wrote in a memorial essay on Henry James: 'It is the final perfection, the consummation of an American to become, not an Englishman, but a European – something which no born European, no person of European nationality, can become.' (*The Egoist* 1918.)

1921 Suffers a nervous breakdown, and in recuperating, first at Margate, then at Lausanne, completes *The Waste Land*. Publishes essay on 'The Metaphysical Poets'.

1922 Publishes *The Waste Land*. Starts a new literary and intellectual journal, *The Criterion*.

1925 Leaves Lloyd's Bank, and becomes director of publishing firm Faber & Gwyer (now Faber & Faber). Publishes 'The Hollow Men', and begins the (unfinished) play *Sweeney Agonistes* printed in 1926–7 as *Wanna Go Home Baby?*

3 THE EARLY POEMS 1909–12

3.1 Eliot's first volume, *Prufrock and Other Observations*, published in 1917, contained two groups of poems, one written in 1909–12 when he was still at Harvard, the other in 1915–16 after his arrival in England. The first group is the more substantial, being made up of 'Portrait of a Lady', 'The Love Song of J. Alfred Prufrock', 'Preludes', 'Rhapsody on a Windy Night' and 'La Figlia Che Piange'. We have already looked briefly at two of these poems, 'La Figlia' (Unit 1, Section 2), and 'Prelude IV' (paras. 1.3–1.5). In this section, we will discuss 'Portrait of a Lady' and 'The Love Song of J. Alfred Prufrock' in detail. Will you please read the first of these now?

'PORTRAIT OF A LADY'

According to Conrad Aiken, a friend of Eliot's in those years, the 'Portrait' was based on a real acquaintance, a fact useful in indicating the kind of society available to a literary young man in pre-1914 Boston, Mass.

■ After you have read the poem, make notes on these points:
(a) your feelings about the lady, the speaker, and their relationship;
(b) the different ways Eliot chooses to present the two characters;
(c) whether it's reasonable to think of the poem as a 'short-story-in-verse', a kind of compressed narrative, or whether that formula leaves something out of account.

Discussion

3.2 (a) I have two impressions of the lady. The first is that she's affected, precious, cultivated in an enervating and snobbish way (her comments on Chopin), and, though claiming to be experienced about feelings and true friendship remarkably banal as well ('youth is cruel . . . Paris in the Spring . . . Achilles' heel' etc.). The little mannered repetitions and insistences of her speech aim at an effect of urbane subtlety that never succeeds. We are told that she arranges the first meeting as if it were a 'scene', and it is in keeping that she seems to act out feelings she wants to have rather than experience real ones. But a second impression soon grows – qualifying my initial feeling of hostility. The lady is also a figure of considerable pathos. Beneath her strained and artificial effort at a highminded aesthetic friendship with her younger admirer, there is a touching and pitiful need for affection.

> The voice returns like the insistent out-of-tune
> Of a broken violin on an August afternoon:
> 'I am always sure that you understand
> My feelings, always sure that you feel,
> Sure that across the gulf you reach your hand.

I am absolutely convinced about that gulf. The lady's manner both creates and tries to bridge it in the same gesture. Her very insistence makes a response difficult. It is easy to share the speaker's discomfort at being appealed to in terms that effectively silence him. His comparison of her voice with a broken violin neatly illustrates this interplay of distaste and sympathy. It is harsh and mocking, as well as painfully sad. Something valuable, capable of eloquence and beauty, has been broken.

The young man I find considerably more elusive. What does he want from the lady? Does he visit her simply out of politeness? Why then does his self-possession 'flare up' at their last meeting when she suggests they correspond, if not because he wants some further relationship with her? Yet, evidently, he is stifled by the kind of friendship she has been offering. One possibility is that he wants the kind of relationship she would be outraged by (or so he feels) – an 'affair'. Hence the 'false note' of his inner reaction to their first meeting. But then what does he do? 'Let us take the air, in a tobacco trance . . . ' I take this to mean that he retreats into the anaesthesia of a correctly conventional and meaningless routine, discussing public matters, correcting his watch, and so forth. It seems that if the lady is trapped in one kind of artifice, he is helpless before the claims of another. After the second meeting, he is ashamed of his inability either to respond in her terms, or to establish terms of his own. But then again, he declares his detachment and 'self-possession' before the facts of a more passionate kind of life (murder, fraud), except when he is stirred by some popular romantic cliché of a song, and the 'smell of hyacinths across the garden'. Is it that he is too coldly self-controlled to respond to the real feelings he nevertheless senses beneath the lady's explicit ones? Yet the last section points to a different reason for his failure (if indeed that is what it is).

> And I must borrow every changing shape
> To find expression . . . dance, dance
> Like a dancing bear,
> Cry like a parrot, chatter like an ape.

Would you agree that this unexpected outburst sounds a note of desperation not unlike that of the lady's? What pressure forces him to 'borrow' his sense of identity? It seems unlikely to be the lady. Surely he is the stronger of the two. Yet if it is something in himself, we are not told what. In the final lines, his feelings are vague and unsure, half-critical of his mannered posing, yet also still caught up in it, as he tries and fails to decide what the experience amounts to. Are his thoughts about the lady's death tenderly elegiac or callously superficial? 'And should I have the right to smile?' Is that somewhat shockingly jejune, or a genuine 'placing' of his own satirical smiling throughout the poem? My uncertainty about the young man springs not just from a sense of unexplored complexities in his character, but from not knowing quite how to take him in these final confessional lines.

(b) We know the lady mainly through her speech, and it is worth noting how skilful Eliot is in suggesting what she cannot say and hardly knows about herself, without having to move beyond her threadbare restrictive idiom. Look at the way the rhymes give these bare lines a note of sad drooping finality.

> We must leave it now to fate.
> You will write, at any rate.
> Perhaps it is not too late.

There are also one or two key actions, highlighted by their relative isolation: the twisting of the lilac stalks in the second section, for instance. And then there are the mutely critical attitudes of the speaker. It is, in fact, a dramatic *presentation*. We don't know what the lady looks like. We know only her voice, a movement or two, her impact on her visitor. From these few moments in her life, Eliot leaves us to construct her character for ourselves. 'Dramatic', too, seems the way to describe the presentation of the young man. The poem is a soliloquy, a monologue, partly his imaginary address to the lady, partly his argument with himself. He reports actions that reflect his outer behaviour:

I smile, of course,
And go on drinking tea.

I mount the stairs and turn the handle of the door
And feel as if I had mounted on my hands and knees.

We do not hear what he says to the lady (polite conventionalities, I would imagine) but we have some access to his private thoughts, his unsatisfied protest and searching, his vague guilt and self-reproach. Some of this monologue, though, is enigmatic, using a language of condensed and suggestive metaphors that remain strikingly inexplicit.

  Among the windings of the violins
And the ariettes
Of cracked cornets
Inside my brain a dull tom-tom begins
Absurdly hammering a prelude of its own,
Capricious monotone
That is at least one definite 'false note'.

A few lines earlier the violins were 'attenuated' and the cornets 'remote'. Later as we've seen, the lady's voice seems to him like a 'broken violin', and in the last lines he calls the whole poem 'this music'. Or again:

I feel like one who smiles, and turning shall remark
Suddenly, his expression in a glass.
My self-possession gutters; we are really in the dark.

The last line ('gutters') picks up the candle motif introduced in the opening scene, and reminds us that the first meeting occurred 'among the smoke and fog of a December afternoon'. Smoke occurs again in the final lines.

Can these metaphors be interpreted? I would suggest that they can, up to a point. The speaker himself links these physical darknesses with the final state of the abortive friendship. The candles lit in the first section are (metaphorically) extinguished in the third. The musical metaphors are more problematic. I will return to them in a minute. Meanwhile, you might now like to ask yourself what light, if any, they throw on the young man's inner state.

(c) I asked you to consider a third point – whether it is enough to think of this poem as a 'short-story-in-verse'. Clearly there is a story of sorts. We meet two characters trying and failing to establish a relationship; we hear their voices, we have a sense of their social world; there is even a narrator, the speaker of the poem, brooding about what has actually happened between them. We could add, too, that their situation is not unfamiliar to readers of nineteenth-century novels. Both move in a society that constrains them, whose conventions inhibit, and may even nullify, their search for fruitful relationship. The title alludes to a novel by Eliot's elder compatriot, Henry James (1843–1916), whose *The Portrait of a Lady* (1881) is about a young American girl's disastrous marriage to a man of stiflingly aesthetic tastes. The conversation between Eliot's characters with its hidden 'velleities and carefully caught regrets' has something of the indirection of Jamesian exchanges. Yet when all that is said, some central effect seems to me to be unaccounted for. One point I imagine you will have made yourself is the cumulative effect of the poetic 'techniques' of rhythmic language, of rhyme, of imagery. For example:

My smile falls heavily among the bric-à-brac.

That hardly belongs to narrative prose. It is too condensed, too sudden. It is informative about the young man in a way peculiar to poetic language. At first sight, a witty way of describing the disappointment he conceals behind a wandering effortsome social smile, it also expresses the dislocation of his outward from his inner self, that indeterminate shifting lack of identity he goes on to speak about. His smile falls off. What better way to suggest a distintegrated personality? And in falling *heavily*, as if damaging the genteel appurtenances of the room, the image also conveys something of his dangerously unlocated hostility towards the lady's suffocating pretensions.

This example should remind us that the poem's language is a form of expression for the speaker, that the poem is as much a portrait of him, as of the lady. Would it not be true to say then that the story element is not primary, but a way of allowing the speaker to declare what he *is*, to reveal his very peculiar state of mind, the strange distance that seems to keep him apart from his own experience? He seems both sadder, more exasperated, more puzzled and more searching than the 'story' requires. Take these lines, for example.

> You will see me any morning in the park
> Reading the comics and the sporting page.
> Particularly I remark
> An English countess goes upon the stage.
> A Greek was murdered at a Polish dance,
> Another bank defaulter has confessed.
> I keep my countenance,
> I remain self-possessed
> Except when a street-piano, mechanical and tired
> Reiterates some worn-out common song
> With the smell of hyacinths across the garden
> Recalling things that other people have desired.
> Are these ideas right or wrong?

What ideas is he asking about? Those, presumably, that move the English countess, the Greek victim and the Polish murderer, the bank defaulter, and other people's common-or-garden romances. This vein of serious – unanswered – questioning suggests an altogether different person than the coolly polite young satirist who wryly, cruelly, recounts his experiences with the lady. To put the point another way, the poem conveys a complex mood (romantic, melancholy, frustrated, self-critical, intent) that speaks beyond the story as such, over and above the heads of the two characters whom, in a novel, we would be primarily interested in.■

3.3 ■ The poem, as well as the title, contains a number of allusions to other works of literature. I'd like you now to ask what difference, if any, they make to the poem. Using Southam's *Student's Guide* look up the allusions in these lines:

(a) And four wax candles in the darkened room,
Four rings of light upon the ceiling overhead,
An atmosphere of Juliet's tomb

(b) 'Yet with these April sunsets, that somehow recall
My buried life, and Paris in the Spring,
I feel immeasurably at peace. . .'

Do they add anything to the poem that it hasn't already conveyed?

Discussion

3.4 (a) It is natural to begin by thinking that the reference to Juliet is satiric. This lady is no Juliet, her suitor no Romeo, and their situation ludicrously unlike that of the star-crossed lovers. What could be less absolute, less deathwards-tending, than these politely lukewarm exchanges about a friendship that fails to materialize? That is to say, if we set the events of Shakespeare's play against those of Eliot's poem, the effect must seem sardonic. But isn't there another effect as well? Do the lines containing the allusion *sound* sardonic? Don't they rather convey an impressively ominous gloom, recreating a momentary feeling appropriate to Juliet's tragic death? The lady arranges a scene genuinely tomb-like, and the poem goes on to show how, in fact, she stifles the possible growth of real feelings. I am suggesting that the implied comparison between Juliet and the lady is, yes, mocking at one level, but serious at another. Or perhaps, to avoid trying to be too specific, that it brings into Eliot's poem an unexpected dimension of feeling, a notion of intense passionate romance, adding its own impact to the other impressions these opening lines make on us. (This perhaps, is the point to ask yourself why it is Chopin's *Preludes* they've been to hear.)

(b) The allusion to Matthew Arnold's *The Buried Life* works differently in one sense. Shakespeare's play is common knowledge; Arnold's poem is not. Here Eliot is more clearly speaking over the head of his character, hinting at something about her he wants us to know, that despite appearances she *has* a buried life. Yet this is something we might already have sensed. Think back to the incident of the lilacs. At the very moment the lady is talking about youth and life, we are told that her hands are, unconsciously, 'twisting the lilac stalks'. That should at least prepare us for the serious implications of 'my buried life'. So although it is not crucial to know about Arnold's poem, it does help to spell out Eliot's point that the lady's predicament is not confined to her. Arnold's lines – 'the mystery of this heart which beats so wild, so deep in *us*' – apply to human nature. This line of argument can be supported by taking the Shakespeare and Arnold allusions together. If the lady's emotional life *is* buried, then the tomb-like scene she arranges for the first rendezvous is something more than play-acting, and that opens up the possibility that the 'Romeo' of this poem may be in a similar plight. Has he also got a 'buried life'? We have seen that he is affected by the 'smell of hyacinths across the garden'. Admittedly, he tells us that in the face of 'things that other people have desired' he keeps his self-possession, but is he genuinely pleased about that? His tone seems complacent. Yet that could also mean a division from his 'buried self' more thorough than the lady's. Inability to grasp his whole experience is, we've seen, the note on which the poem ends. ■

There is no general rule about the length to which we should pursue allusions in Eliot's, or indeed in any other, poetry. One often feels that critics take such discussions too far, that the force of the allusions becomes more fascinating to them than the poem they contribute to. When that happens, it is right to become sceptical about the 'meanings' being extracted from the text. On the other hand, Eliot is a poet who uses allusion as a regular procedure. It is, for him, a kind of shorthand, sometimes precise and definable, sometimes more loosely introducing extra reverberations of feeling, sometimes backing up in one way what he has already suggested in another. Above all, it is a language of implication, putting much of the onus on the reader for deciding how it works. One of the problems in the 'second stage' of understanding his poetry is the question of how the allusions work. But don't make too much of it, and always consider the allusions in terms of your sense of the whole poem. If the meaning is not, in some sense, 'there', before you have found out about any allusions, then knowledge of them will not help it to be much of a poem.

3.5 In 3.2 (b) I left open the question of interpreting the metaphors drawn from music. What did you make of them? Some interpretation seems to me possible, for instance, of the kind of music played by violins – lyrical and romantic – and by cornets – military and heroic. Like a 'broken violin', a 'cracked cornet' is ludicrous and sad.

Both suggest lost potentialities. This reinforces the idea suggested by the reference to *Romeo and Juliet*, of an intense and tragic love which neither character in the poem can achieve. I'd be reluctant to go beyond that (and perhaps not as far). My reason involves some of the literary history surveyed by Nick Furbank in *Modernism and Its Origins*, especially in the section on the *Symboliste* view of poetic language (Units 4–5, Part 1 paras. 3.13.–3.17). You will remember that *Symboliste* poets took the view that a poem was like an expressive gesture, self-justifying and self-sufficient. It was not really *about* something. It itself created the thing it was about. Poetry's ideal should then be music, not in the normal metaphorical sense that it should sound well. It should resemble music more profoundly in the sense that its meanings should be undefinable. Or perhaps, 'untranslatable' would be a better term. Feeling and thought should be present, but in such a way as prevented the reader from saying exactly what feelings and what thoughts. Which is, isn't it, the way one does experience a great deal of music? The ideal even affects the structure of *Symboliste* poems which use motifs, like musical phrases, enigmatic in themselves, but whose repetition both builds to something approaching a meaning, and supplies internal coherence. This, I think, is the way we should take the pattern of reference to music in the 'Portrait', as an attempt at *Symboliste* writing.

3.6 ■ The point may be clearer if we turn to a poem of Pound's, also about a cultured lady as seen by a literary friend, also a 'dramatic monologue'. It's called 'Portrait d'une Femme'. Read it now. How chiefly does Pound's language differ from Eliot's?

Your mind and you are our Sargasso Sea,
London has swept about you this score years
And bright ships left you this or that in fee:
Ideas, old gossip, oddments of all things,
Strange spars of knowledge and dimmed wares of price.
Great minds have sought you – lacking someone else.
You have been second always. Tragical?
No. You preferred it to the usual thing:
One dull man, dulling and uxorious,
One average mind – with one thought less, each year.
Oh, you are patient, I have seen you sit
Hours, where something might have floated up.
And now you pay one. Yes, you richly pay.
You are a person of some interest, one comes to you
And takes strange gain away:
Trophies fished up; some curious suggestion;
Fact that leads nowhere; and a tale or two,
Pregnant with mandrakes, or with something else
That might prove useful and yet never proves,
That never fits a corner or shows use,
Or finds its hour upon the loom of days:
The tarnished, gaudy, wonderful old work;
Idols and ambergris and rare inlays,
These are your riches, your great store; and yet
For all this sea-hoard of deciduous things,
Strange woods half sodden, and new brighter stuff:
In the slow float of differing light and deep,
No! there is nothing! In the whole and all,
Nothing that's quite your own.
    Yet this is you.

(*Ezra Pound: Selected Poems, 1908–1959*, pp 34–5.)

Discussion

3.7 Pound's poem is, clearly, straightforward compared with Eliot's. Both speaker and lady are simpler, so is their situation. The speaker is little more than a robustly self-confident voice. There is no hesitation here about what he is judging, or about his right to do so. The poem's language is consequently definite and clear, sharp-edged.

> You have been second always. Tragical?
> No. You preferred it to the usual thing:
> One dull man, dulling and uxorious,
> One average mind – with one thought less, each year.

And this holds for the extended comparison of the lady's mind to the Sargasso Sea. Notice how little suggestive power its detail has, for all the potential exoticism. Mainly it impresses me with its cleverness – 'Can he really get away with comparing her mind to the Sargasso Sea? well, yes he does!' If Eliot had used such a metaphor, I doubt whether he would have elaborated it like this. His method is to concentrate, to select, to juxtapose image upon image, to leave each to reverberate in the imagination, in the way of the lines about Juliet's tomb. Or look again at the way the closing lines of the 'Portrait', suggest so much more than they state, of mood, of situation.

> Well! and what if she should die some afternoon,
> Afternoon grey and smoky, evening yellow and rose;
> Should die and leave me sitting pen in hand
> With the smoke coming down above the housetops;

Visually, that seems to me brilliant, offering one or two details out of which the mind creates a whole possible scene, controlled only by the underlying mood of elegy, by the sense of arrested life, and of the continuing patterns suggested by afternoon moving into evening, by sunsets, by the existence of houses, and the smoke from fires. Is the speaker sad or not about the lady's envisaged death? He doesn't know, and Eliot convers this uncertainty, even disengagement from his feelings, by shifting attention away from him to what he is observing, yet at the same time making that scene express the sadness the speaker *might* be feeling. That, again, is a *Symboliste* use of language. ■

3.8 A final point about these two poems. They are both dramatic monologues, as we've seen. Both poets express themselves through an invented character, who speaks directly to us, whose use of 'I' must not lead us to confuse him with the author. This is an example of the 'modernist' fondness for 'masks', for creating *personae*. (In Pound's case, as you will remember from Unit 6, he developed by donning and discarding a series of 'masks'.) If we want to know what Eliot is saying, we must listen not to the speaker of the 'Portrait', but to the whole poem. There are very few poems in which Eliot does not use a 'mask'.

'THE LOVE SONG OF J. ALFRED PRUFROCK'

3.9 Eliot wrote this poem over a number of years, some of it in Harvard, some in Paris where he studied in 1910–11. Back in America in 1912, he tried and failed to get it published there. Arriving in England in the autumn of 1914, he met Ezra Pound, who liked the poem, and through his contacts with an American *avant-garde* 'little magazine' called *Poetry* (Chicago), succeeded in having it printed in 1915.

■ Read the poem now, and make notes on these points. Your impressions of the speaker, and his situation. Whether the poem's events take place, or are only imagined by the speaker. Whether it is enough to read it as a 'character study'. Pound for example, seemed to have this impression. He wrote to the editor of *Poetry* (Chicago): 'Mr Prufrock does not "go off at the end". It is a portrait of failure, or of a character which fails, and it would be false art to make it end on a note of triumph . . . a portrait satire on futility can't end by turning that quintessence of futility, Mr P., into a reformed character breathing out fire and ozone'. (*Letters* p 50) Does such an account of the poem satisfy you? Finally, too, does the language of the poem ever suggest the *Symboliste* method of writing? If you know 'Prufrock' already, you may feel you can quickly formulate your ideas on some of these points. In that case, a useful starting point would be to try to decide on the identity of the 'you' Prufrock keeps referring to. When you have gained a general impression of the whole poem, look up in Southam's *Student's Guide* the notes about John the Baptist and Lazarus. What do these references contribute?

Discussion

3.10 I have two main impressions of the speaker. Outwardly, he is a nervously conventional man, fussy about his dress, sensitive to criticism, real or imagined, not in his first youth, solitary, but also involved in a routine of cultivated and fashionable social life. But in contrast to that, he has a lively and varied 'inner' life. He is reflective, wryly, sadly self-aware, romantic, serious in a way that never quite clarifies itself, resigned to the certainty of his failure to do what he really wants. His situation seems to be that his customary life bores him, that he has a range of more or less obscure feelings that he cannot voice, that he knows this but cannot, or will not, do anything about it. Certain details, together with the partly-mocking title, suggest something more specific: that he wants, yet fears romantic-sexual love, that he considers, or perhaps makes, an amorous proposal to one of the ladies he meets in the cultivated houses he visits, though his most nearly explicit avowal ('I am Lazarus come from the dead . . . ') fits oddly with the notion of a love-song, the language of an aspiring lover. As to whether the poem's events 'really' take place, or are merely evoked in Prufrock's mind, I think it is a crucial question, and despite the tenses of the verbs that suggest an actual journey, and the vividness of several scenes, the poem seems to me an event in Prufrock's mind, composed of memories and imaginings, untested possibilities. Does the poem 'tell a story'? The opening lines suggest that it will, and bits and pieces of stories are touched on, but the movement does not seem to me helpfully called 'narrative'. We have a speaker, certainly, and 'events' of some kind seem to be taking place, but one's uncertainty about whether they are in the past or the present, and how they are connected within the poem, makes 'story' an inappropriate description.

I don't know what you thought of this way of approaching the poem, or of Pound's energetic definition of Prufrock as 'the quintessence of futility'. You will have recognized, I hope, that the poem's method is that of the 'dramatic monologue'. It differs from the 'Portrait of a Lady' mainly in being so much more completely about the speaker. It would be natural to Pound, on first reading it, to see it as 'a character study', like so many of Browning's poems with a single speaker, and certainly it is a good way into the poem. But critics have objected to this approach as being too 'novelistic'. Hugh Kenner, for example, begins his comments by stressing simply, the intrinsic force of the poem's verbal texture

> Eliot deals in effects, not ideas; and the effects are in an odd way wholly verbal, seemingly endemic to the language . . . Every phrase seems composed as though the destiny of the author's soul depended on it, yet it is unprofitable not to consider the phrases as *arrangements of words before considering them as anything else*. (Kenner *The Invisible Poet* p 4. My italics.)

That is to say, instead of assembling the phrases into anything as definitive as Prufrock's 'character' or 'situation' or 'story', we should look at them in their own right. Nevertheless I want to pursue the other approach a bit further.

Our impression of Prufrock as resembling a fictional person in a novel with a history, a describable way of life, clothes, money, friends and so forth, depends for its first real evidence on the lines beginning 'And indeed there will be time', when he goes on to imagine what the society ladies might be saying about him. But by that point we have already read some forty lines, or nearly a quarter of the poem. What happens in this long 'introduction'? Assume for the moment that the 'you' of that energetic and amiable first line is a friend of Prufrock's (what did you decide about that 'you'?), where does he propose that they go? Straightforwardly enough, 'through certain half-deserted streets' which are, he tells us,

> The muttering retreats
> Of restless nights in one-night cheap hotels
> And sawdust restaurants with oyster shells:

This undoubtedly conveys the impression of a route, of actual streets with hotels and restaurants in them, but there is another, to me more striking effect. Look again at the first six words. What do you make of them?

The streets are seemingly the places the nights retreat to. These 'nights' are remarkably human, surely. Actually, of course, the people in the cheap hotels experience 'restless nights', and by implication, they have found a 'retreat' there. So what is evoked by these lines seems to me less an actual route for the journey Prufrock proposes than the off-stage presence (faintly sinister? rather shabby?) of other human lives. And this then leads into an altogether different version of the streets:

> Streets that follow like a tedious argument
> Of insidious intent
> To lead you to an overwhelming question . . .
> Oh, do not ask, 'What is it?'
> Let us go and make our visit.

Instead of Prufrock and his friend following the streets, the streets (like potential pickpockets?) are following them, tediously, but also insidiously, rehearsing a familiar argument. And more strangely still, as well as following, they turn out to be *leading* . . . The syntax allows you to connect 'lead' both with 'argument' and 'streets'. It is as if they have taken human form, like the 'nights', and with pedagogic beckonings have begun to draw us towards the 'overwhelming question'. What about? But here Prufrock breaks off in exasperation, or perhaps sheer boredom, as if his companion were the tedious presence, and once more proposes the visit.

Then follows the enigmatic couplet:

> In the room the women come and go
> Talking of Michelangelo

How did you relate this to the previous lines? Is it the place they are going to visit? That seems the natural meaning. Perhaps they have already reached it? Looking ahead though, the couplet is repeated after the lines about fog, which rather suggests that it reflects a thought, presumably a memory, in Prufrock's mind. Yet the more we dwell on the lines the more the questions multiply. Do 'I' speak these words, or 'you?' The shift in tone, from the winding syntax of the opening lines, the questions, the exclamatory emphases, the sense of somebody talking to somebody else, to the flat rhythm and the dead-pan note of the couplet, could suggest a new speaker. Or does it reflect a shift in Prufrock's mood? Again, what point is being made about the women in the room? Is it merely an observation in a 'by-the-way' sort of voice? Is the speaker impressed by the fact that the women are talking about a great Renaissance artist? Or is he suggesting that it's a case of trivial cultural chat? How you answer these questions I don't know. I'm struck myself by the way the rhyme enforces a contrast between the purposeless movement of 'come and go' and the magnificent reverberation of the name 'Michelangelo'. But whether that amounts to a point against the women, whether they are to be admired for their earnestness, or whether – more distant possibility – 'Michelangelo' represents a world of splendour and energy which the women are trying, vainly, to escape into from the pointless routine of their social lives, I would be hard put to decide.

The general point beginning to emerge from this kind of verse is that it allows several, overlapping, even contradictory, meanings at once, and yet doesn't – surely? – give an impression of confusion. We sense underlying currents of feeling, as it were below the words, connecting them in a way that matters more than their a-logical surface implications.

In the next lines about the fog, things at first seem quite straightforward. A night-time urban scene belongs well enough to the proposed journey through streets. But it is a highly imaginative rendering. The fog is seen as a cat rubbing its back on the windows, yet also an odd sort of cat, since it has a muzzle. And as the metaphor develops, the fog idea is almost displaced by the animal associations.

> Slipped by the terrace, made a sudden leap,
> And seeing that it was a soft October night,
> Curled once about the house, and fell asleep.

Notice how well these lines 'mimic' the cat's physical agility. Yet there are strange side-effects in the movement from the first line to the suggestion of thoughtful deduction in the second, and in the menace of the third – this cat is big enough to curl up round a house. Though, of course, we immediately reassure ourselves by remembering that it is 'really' fog. The passage is also quite different from the sort of writing we have met so far: neither conversation nor internal monologue, more an accomplished exercise in a 'poetic' manner, based on, though also departing from, a traditional metre, the iambic pentameter. Yet its emotional tone, the hints of mystery and fear, fit well with those of the 'half-deserted streets'.

In the next lines, we move more certainly into Prufrock's thoughts. His uncertainty, his ennui, the withdrawn identity that always 'prepares a face to meet the faces that you meet', provide the immediate context for the second occurrence of the couplet about Michelangelo. Here, it is far less enigmatic, emerging as one cause of his mood of indecision and boredom. And then, at last, we meet Prufrock as he appears, or as he imagines he appears, to other people, the 'quintessence of futility', the timid, conventional, bachelor. Yet don't we now have to see that aspect of Prufrock as only one factor in the total effect? If we confine the poem to its novelistic element – Prufrock's 'character' and 'story' – we have to forget about the elusive yet powerful emotional undertones that haunt so many passages, the way the detail of the verse is always moving in unexpected directions, leaving unexplained puzzles and obscurities. Of these, the most obvious is the identity of 'you'. I began by suggesting he might be a friend of Prufrock. Another possibility is that he might be the reader, Prufrock's imaginary audience. Or again, we might think of Prufrock as self-divided, as having a conversation with himself. I incline to that notion myself, but the poem, in the end, gives us no clear reason to choose.

Is the poem *Symboliste* in method? I think you will have seen that its indirection, its refusal to declare, as Pound's 'Portrait d'une Femme' declares, what it is about, reveal the *Symboliste* influence. And there is a more general reason. The poem is Prufrock's love-song, says the title, Prufrock's dramatic soliloquy, but when we look at his situation it seems that 'love' is not the problem. What Prufrock is incapable of doing is asking the mysterious 'overwhelming question', which seems altogether more serious, more general, than an amorous proposal. There is no single reason for his reticence. He thinks at one point that it might be in bad taste ('how should I presume'); at another he is afraid; at another, he thinks he would sound ridiculous; at another, he thinks nobody would understand him. And he is not even very clear what question it is he wants to ask.

> And would it have been worth it, after all,
> Would it have been worth while,
> After the sunsets and the dooryards and the sprinkled streets,
> After the novels, after the teacups, after the skirts that trail along the floor –
> And this, and so much more? –
> It is impossible to say just what I mean!

The comedy in all this – Prufrock's rueful, uneasy, *awareness* of the comedy – co-exists with an underlying and serious urgency. He does want an answer to his question, and the sense in which it is 'overwhelming' may be gauged by his self-identification with both John the Baptist and Lazarus. That view of Prufrock has – as he knows – its ludicrous side, but it is the clearest hint Eliot gives that he has something profound to say – *if only he could get it out*! So the centre of the poem, I'm suggesting, is about having feelings, impulses, thoughts that resist formulation in language. Prufrock's monologue dramatizes his inability to bring his ideas to the surface, to utter them to another human being. Certainly, the lady, or ladies, he thinks of speaking to are not his ideal listeners. That feared languid reply, 'That is not what I meant at all. That is not it at all' is very funny from one point of view, extraordinarily painful from another. (Perhaps like a lot of good comedy?) And certainly, too, Prufrock half-considers another more congenial audience, the 'lonely men in shirt-sleeves' well outside his social orbit. But while this more than suggests that his difficulty has something to do with the world he moves in where 'women come and go/Talking of Michelangelo', where he is observed and demolished by the 'eyes that fix you in a formulated phrase', his predicament goes deeper than that. So deep, in fact, that he cannot find words for it. The poem, on the other hand, does exactly this. It finds words, subtle, haunting, eloquent, for a wordless condition. So the monologue is internal, addressed to nobody, and its most convinced and moving moments, those where the social dimension and the comedy disappear completely, amount to a giving up of the struggle to speak, a final withdrawal.

> I should have been a pair of ragged claws
> Scuttling across the floors of silent seas.

Or, again, the more developed statement of this feeling in the closing lines.

Such an account of the poem would also fit the way Prufrock uses language, which keeps slipping away from his grasp to suggest things quite other than those he began by saying. There are other interpretations, of course, but I offer this one as taking more fully into account the texture and variety of its language, which is our immediate reading experience, without going so far as Hugh Kenner, who, as we have seen, wants to treat it as a pure word-mosaic. ■

3.11 ■ A final point, to bring some of the relevant literary history into focus. Eliot said that his early poems owed much to two models: Elizabethan drama, and the poetry of Jules Laforgue. The connection with the Elizabethan dramatic soliloquy in both 'Portrait of a Lady' and 'Prufrock' I need not elaborate. What of Laforgue? You will be able to read one or two of his poems in translation in Unit 12. For the moment you will get some notion of what he meant to Eliot by re-reading Part 1, para 4.11 of Units 4–5, *Modernism and Its Origins*, the comments on the 'Modernist' interest in 'masks'. How does this apply to Eliot's early poems?

Discussion

3.12 Prufrock, like the young man in the 'Portrait of a Lady' (you might later work out what they have in common) is an invented 'persona', a 'mask'. The method attracted Eliot, as it did Pound and Yeats, because, though like all poets since the Romantic period, they directly drew on inner autobiography for the material of their poems, they wanted to escape from what Keats accused Wordsworth of, 'the egotistical sublime', the direct assertion of the Romantic Ego. The 'mask' allows a form of indirect self-expression. Prufrock is not Eliot, but Eliot's way of saying what he has to say. The method also helped Eliot avoid Romantic solemnity. When, for example, Shelley writes in 'Ode to the West Wind':

> I fall upon the thorns of life, I bleed!

the very earnestness of the claim is self-defeating. It asserts, rather than conveys, intensity of feeling. It is like a friend saying to you that he is suffering from a bad migraine attack: you sympathize with, but you do not share his plight. The 'mask' offers a way of getting the reader to share the experience, rather than have it thrust at him. Prufrock's sadness, his frustration and longing, are the more affecting because they are not thrust at us as directly belonging to the poet. We contemplate them as general human experiences given a particular expression in Prufrock. And that is one way in which Laforgue was helpful to Eliot. He works, again and again, through a 'persona'.

But there is more to it than that. Browning could be said to have used 'masks' in his development of the dramatic monologue, to have achieved eloquent indirection for the expression of, say, the relationship of the artist to the man in his own life. What Laforgue offered was a much subtler form of expression. His 'mask' was more urbane – Eliot spoke admiringly of the 'inflexible politeness' with which the 'personae' of the Laforgue's poems met their emotional disasters – more self-aware, and it allowed a more complex account of the feelings. This last seems to me the key issue. Laforgue's method helped Eliot to create a form of expression more adequate to the nature of human feelings: to their interdependence and (from the 'rational' point of view) their contradictoriness; to their sources in direct sensation, on the one hand, and on the other, to the way they overlap with, or feed into, 'thoughts'. When we come to poems like Eliot's 'Portrait' and 'Prufrock' from much Romantic and Victorian poetry, I think it is hard not to feel that here is a *truer* account of how the mind (which of course includes the 'feelings') works.

Eliot insists again and again in his criticism that 'technical' inventions, and *not* new kinds of experience, are the marks of the truly creative poet, though the emphasis can be misleading since what he means by 'technical' is not superficial gadgetry, but arrangements of poetic language, of idiom, of rhythm, of verse form, which are freshly *expressive*. So a third point to notice about his debt to Laforgue is the 'technical' source of his urbane and varied tone: delicately expressive contrasts in both idiom and rhythm. Here are the opening lines of a Laforgue poem translated by Pound which you will meet again in Unit 12.

Your eyes! Since I lost their incandescence
Flat calm engulphs my jibs,
The shudder of *Vae soli* gurgles beneath my ribs.

You should have seen me after the affray,
I rushed about in the most agitated way
Crying: My God, my God, what will she say?!

My soul's antennae are prey to such perturbations,
Wounded by your indirectness in these situations
And your bundle of mundane complications.

Your eyes put me up to it.
I thought: Yes, divine, these eyes, but what exists
Behind them? What's there? Her soul's an affair
  for oculists.

(*Vae soli*, a Latin phrase, means 'woe to the solitary man'.)

(*The Translations of Ezra Pound,* p 438.)

The first verse uses the most heightened and dramatic language to express the lover's desolation: terms like 'incandescence' for the effect of the lady's eyes, the developed metaphor of a becalmed and lonely ship, and the Latin phrase. In the second verse, the tone is of ordinary speech, though the feeling is still excited. In the third, the language is more abstract, intellectual, the feeling about the lady more critical. The colloquial directness of the fourth verse, especially of the opening line, marks another shift of feeling into a kind of scorn: the lady has beautiful eyes, but what else? The range of diction, and the bold variants of the basic rhythm are neatly illustrated by comparing these lines:

Your eyes! Since I lost their incandescence

Your eyes put me up to it

This lover is capable of traditionally intense feeling, but he is also self-aware, even sardonic about the source of such feeling, just as Prufrock both feels, and is self-critically aware of his feelings. ■

3.13 ◪ We have already seen from the opening lines of 'Prufrock' how much our sense of the complexity and elusiveness of his predicament is conveyed to us by unexpected verbal shifts and turns. As a concluding exercise, you might like to try your hand at an analysis of these lines:

  I grow old . . . I grow old . . .
I shall wear the bottoms of my trousers rolled.

  Shall I part my hair behind? Do I dare to eat a peach?
I shall wear white flannel trousers, and walk upon the beach.
I have heard the mermaids singing, each to each.

I do not think that they will sing to me.

I have seen them riding seaward on the waves
Combing the white hair of the waves blown back
When the wind blows the water white and black.

(In the third line, your set text misprints, omitting 'to' after 'dare'.)

How does the total effect of these lines depend on contrasts in poetic idiom, of rhythm, of rhyme scheme? You should be able to name the basic rhythmic pattern, which is fully illustrated on record 1.[2] The key to this use of it is provided in Eliot's essay 'Reflections on *Vers Libre*' (Course Reader, pp 98–103), where he remarks:

> . . . the ghost of some simple metre should lurk behind the arras in even the 'freest' verse; to advance menacingly as we doze, and withdraw as we rouse. Or, freedom is only truly freedom when it appears against the background of an artificial limitation.

Discussion

3.14 The underlying rhythmical pattern is the iambic pentameter, the staple of Elizabethan dramatic verse, which as we know, helped Eliot when he began to write these poems. His use of the pentameter here is not regular, but 'free' (in the sense defined in Units 4–5 *Modernism and Its Origins,* Section 6), and the same is true of the rhymes which mainly give rhymed 'heroic' couplets, but irregularly, and here and there, move into blank verse. To illustrate: a 'regular' iambic line is:

> I do not think that they will sing to me.

Earlier ones offer more or less bold variants. The second line, for example, though it has eleven syllables, can easily be scanned as having five stresses – 'I', 'wear', 'bót-toms', 'tróusers', 'rolled'. The next line has fourteen syllables, and can just be scanned with five stresses – 'part', 'hair', 'behind', 'dare', 'peach', but the extra syllables make the movement brisker, more energetic, and a possible stress on 'eat' has to be rushed over. The next line too has fourteen syllables, and is the most 'irregular' line: it is impossible to avoid six stresses – 'wear', 'white', 'flánnel', 'trousers', 'walk', 'beach'. Then comes the more regular line about the mermaids, and finally the straightforward one already quoted. Now the crucial thing here is the placing of these lines. 'I do not think that they will sing to me' is, rhythmically speaking, not only regular, but dull and flat. But that is not the effect in context. The earlier lines reflect Prufrock's dream of becoming a fashionably-dressed lady-killer, the mounting energy that takes us through to his romantic claim about the mermaids, as if to say, 'I am not the dull timid fellow some people think I am: I am well-dressed, bold and imaginative and I've actually *heard* mermaids.' But then he drops back to reality. The collapse into a regular iambic pentameter, and one might add too, the visual placing of the line, reflect a sudden access of self-knowledge, a final resignation. The vision is not, in the end, for him.

The clearest example of expressive rhyme is:

> I grow old . . . I grow old . . .
> I shall wear the bottoms of my trousers rolled.

The rhyme enforces the juxtaposition of two contrasting feelings, each in its own way, as well as in the contrast with the other, expressive of Prufrock's state of mind. The contrast also works as a joke. Prufrock is deciding to wear turned-up trousers, then

[2] *Rhythms of Poetry*, OU 21.

becoming fashionable, as an answer to the problem of age. It's funny, has its admirable as well as its ludicrous side (he will not go down without a fight), and at the same time, as the rest of the passage shows, pointless. Age is not really what Prufrock is fretting over.

Marked contrasts in idiom are perhaps less emphatic here than in, say, the opening lines. But in the couplet about the trousers, there is the abrupt shift from inner feeling to outward social detail, while the deliberately low-key 'I do not think that they will sing to me' contrasts with the romantic suggestion of the previous line, and more strikingly with the lines that follow, where a strong rhythmic pulse co-operates with the merging of mermaids and seascape to make a wonderfully eloquent statement of Prufrock's dream of a fuller, but unobtainable, life.

I am aware that analysis of this kind cannot do justice to the flowing seamless character of the verse. They are, are they not, marvellous lines? But it is useful now and again to look at these effects 'technically', if only as a way of making oneself listen to them more carefully, to develop one's 'auditory imagination'. (See Course Reader, p 50) ■

3.15 I hope you will find time to follow up some of these general points in connection with other early poems. The second group of poems in the *Prufrock* volume show Eliot moving away from his achievements in the years 1909–12, trying a flatter, more simply satirical style of writing. The next phase of his development is expressed in the so-called 'quatrain' poems in the volume he published in 1920, where he adopts a tighter verse form, and a packed allusive manner. You might like to read 'The Hippopotamus', 'Whispers of Immortality' and 'Sweeney Among the Nightingales', as examples of this phase. C. K. Stead's comments are interesting and should be looked up. But these poems, though influential at the time, and greatly admired for their wit and intellectuality, are less important than 'Gerontion', a development of the 'mask' type of poem, and the preliminary drafts Eliot wrote for what became *The Waste Land*, to which I want now to turn.

4 THE WASTE LAND

4.1 Eliot first mentioned *The Waste Land*, late in 1919, when he referred in a letter to 'a long poem I have had on my mind for a long time'. (Valerie Eliot *T. S. Eliot: The Waste Land: A Facsimile . . .* p xviii.) It was written during the next two years, much of it in the autumn and winter of 1921. In January 1922, he showed a first draft to Ezra Pound, who recommended large excisions, as well as many changes of detail. Indeed, Pound's contribution to the structure of the published text was substantial, a debt Eliot recognized in his dedication of the poem to Pound as 'il miglior fabbro', the better craftsman. We will come back later to the poem's genesis and Pound's part in it. *The Waste Land* was published late in 1922, in *The Dial*, an American *avant-garde* literary journal, and in the first number of *The Criterion*, a new English quarterly of which Eliot had just become editor. It also appeared in book form in New York, and this edition included, for the first time, Eliot's Notes, which were to play a significant part in the poem's reputation. Early reviews reflected the bewilderment experienced by many of its first readers. Amy Lowell, the proponent of Imagism, or Amy-gism as Pound had mockingly re-named her movement, was not impressed. 'I think it is a piece of tripe', she wrote. The Notes, or rather, the bookish learned quality they seemed to confer on the poem, were much criticized. Nevertheless, by 1926, I. A.

Richards, the influential English critic then teaching at Cambridge, hailed it as a work peculiarly fitted to speak for the true condition of post-war Europe (see Course Reader, p 143n), and despite some fluctuations of reputation, a recent critic has argued that it is still Eliot's strongest claim to greatness, as being the finest and most truly 'modernist' poem (Walton Litz *Eliot in his Time,* p 145).

4.2 Yet even today, when Eliot's kind of poetry is less dauntingly unfamiliar than in 1922, *The Waste Land* is still not an easy poem. In reading it for the first time, don't be put off by a sense of bewilderment, and don't worry about not grasping a lot of the detail. That will come. The first thing is to get a direct feeling for the poem's prevailing mood: Section V, 'What the Thunder said', might be a good place to begin, or Section III, 'The Fire Sermon'. Secondly, you will need to get some feeling for how, as a whole, the poem works, that is to say, of its structure. Here, you could look at the account of the poem in your set book, F. R. Leavis, *New Bearings in English Poetry,* before reading more of this unit – though not, remember, before first tackling the poem. What I intend to do here is to suggest an approach to the poem by looking closely at a few passages in detail, to see what we can expect to find on a first reading.

4.3 ■ Please now read 'The Burial of the Dead', Section I, lines 1–42. Keep in mind that this is a 'modernist' poem, without explicit 'plot' or 'narrative', without logical connections between part and part. The method has sometimes been called 'cinematic', a cutting from scene to scene, a juxtaposing of image upon image, leaving the reader to work out the emotional and imaginative links for himself. A general question to ask from point to point is about the speaker of the poem. Who is he? What sort of feeling does he convey? For example, what attitude towards spring and rebirth does he express in lines 1–7? What sort of world does he evoke in lines 8–18? Is there a new note to his voice in the next section, lines 19–30, and how would you describe it? What sort of situation is evoked in lines 31–42? For the German quotations, look up the notes in Southam's *Student's Guide*, but at this stage do not burden yourself with too much ancillary information. Make what you can of Eliot's lines, as they stand, as the readers of the poem in *The Dial* and *The Criterion* originally had to.

Discussion

4.4 First, lines 1–18. The speaker's feeling about spring is clear enough. He resents it as a painful disturbance, rousing 'memory and desire', as life begins to stir again after the winter. Following this general statement, he shifts without warning or preamble into a fragment of what seems to be autobiography, a social occasion in Germany or Austria, the details suggesting a fashionable, leisured world. Did you notice that at line 13, a different voice speaks, an aristocratic lady called Marie? Or are her words a memory of the speaker's, something he overheard? The question is left open. What impression did you have of Marie? Perhaps what we're given is too slight to leave much trace, but I have the suggestion of a solitary person, lacking direction or purpose. Her talk is touchingly inconsequential, as she drifts from point to point. And did you notice any connection with the opening lines? I think there are at least links of association by means of imagery.

> Summer surprised us, coming over the Starnbergersee
> With a shower of rain;

Summer follows naturally upon 'cruellest' April. Then Marie talks of winter, and going south in search of sun. Sun and rain are the agents of the new life that disturb the speaker. Perhaps then we can take the fragmentary memory as an example of the state of mind that finds April cruel.

At line 19, a new tone sounds, severe, denunciatory, as of some Old Testament prophet.

> What are the roots that clutch, what branches grow
> Out of this stony rubbish? Son of man,
> You cannot say, or guess, for you know only
> A heap of broken images,

Unlike the opening lines, these directly address the reader, implicating him in some general human plight. 'Stony rubbish' seems to refer back to the reminiscence of lines 8–19. Mankind, the 'son of man', is accused of living in a similar state, parched, sterile and monotonous, with only the thought of death, 'fear in a handful of dust', as the grim alternative to pointless life.

At line 31, the speaker switches again to personal memory, and we are made aware of another voice than his, the speech of the 'hyacinth girl'. What impression did this episode make on you? Putting aside the German quotations for a moment, the main point is fairly accessible, I think. The speaker recalls a moment of intense personal meaning, a moment between lovers, unlike any other kind of experience. Look at the paradoxes: he is neither 'living nor dead', he 'knew nothing' (i.e. it was not a flash of insight, or ordinary knowledge about the girl), and though his eyes 'failed' he was looking into the 'heart of light' (was he blinded, or did he fail to understand something?) It is an erotic moment, but it goes beyond eroticism. Yeats sometimes writes about things he sees only 'in the mind's eye', by the light of imagination. In contrast, this visionary moment rises out of direct sensory experience. How, then, do the fragments of German fit in? Both come from Wagner's opera *Tristan and Isolde*, a classic of erotic romanticism. In the first quotation, a sailor longs for his sweetheart, while the second phrase is spoken to the dying Tristan, as he looks, vainly, for Isolde across the sea separating Cornwall from Ireland: 'desolate and empty the sea'. The first thing to notice about these quotations is, I think, that they tell us something about the speaker. He is a person who expresses his own feelings by remembered snatches from music or literature or painting. Does this make him a pedant? Perhaps like Eliot's early readers, you might feel this. Why, you may be inclined to ask, can't the speaker (and since we've seen from earlier poems that the habit is also Eliot's perhaps we should add, the poet) find his own words for his own experience? Isn't there something second-hand about taking over people's words? Here I want only to raise the issue. I will come back to it when we discuss Eliot's critical thought in Unit 9. But on Eliot's side, we can surely say this. One turns to poems, to music, to art, for an expression of feeling precisely because in them human experience is more completely, more sensitively, and more powerfully rendered than one's own efforts could ever achieve. In the Wagner quotations, we can think of the speaker as saying, as much to himself as to anybody else (the 'son of man' tone having entirely dropped away): 'The kind of thing I'm trying to say has been completely said by Wagner in parts of *Tristan and Isolde*.' And if this leads to the thought that the speaker is not altogether articulate about his deepest feelings, then that surely is a crucial thing to know about him.

The second thing to recognize is that Eliot makes new meaning out of the interaction between the Wagner allusions, and the speaker's memories. Why, of all the many phrases he might have selected, does he pick 'desolate and empty the sea'? Because Isolde did not come, Tristan died, and their great romantic love did not last. Doesn't this emphasis throw light on that strange phrase 'my eyes *failed*'? As a whole, the passage questions as well as evokes the traditional value set on an intense romantic love. The speaker's memories are vivid. I feel no question about the power of his feeling, yet in evoking the memory, he can hardly be said to affirm it, joyfully, confidently. The lines leave me with a sense of failure, of desolating loss.

How are the 'son of man' lines connected with what follows? Well, there is again the imagery: the contrasts of parching sun, desert, and stone, with the wind, the sea, the flowers and rain of the hyacinth episode. If the speaker addresses himself as well as the reader when he says that man knows nothing but a 'heap of broken images' and a fear of death, perhaps the personal memories are his attempt to find a positive alternative to the grim picture he has set before us. I do not want to turn the poem into an argument, but with statements like 'April is the cruellest month', and 'What are the roots that clutch, what branches grow/Out of this stony rubbish?' it is clear that the speaker is meditating very general questions about human life, about its sources and ending in the energies of nature, and about what makes it worth having. Romantic love is, isn't it, supposed to give life heightened meaning and value? The sharp contrast of imagery raises the possibility that the relationship with the 'hyacinth girl' might have made the speaker's life something more than a 'heap of broken images'. Did the vision fail because to him 'April is the cruellest month'? Or is it because the romantic vision, of necessity, fails, and so makes no kind of answer to the sombre warning of the Old Testament prophet? ■

4.5 I have spoken of the 'speaker of the poem' as if there were a single character whom we might come to know. It is a convenient term if only because the tone of the poem is often 'spoken', and many episodes are in the vein of reminiscence, direct and intimate. Yet it can be misleading. The speaker is often a mere medium, a voice for others like Marie, sometimes he is no more than the anonymous presenter of episodes, and his tone can veer with such alarming abruptness as to make the notion of somebody speaking *to* us difficult to sustain. It is rather that we overhear a man both thinking to himself, and addressing an imaginary audience. The poem, to use Leavis's helpful term, dramatizes a state of consciousness (see *New Bearings*, p 74), rather than anything so definite as 'a person' like, say, Prufrock, a 'character' with a history. Nevertheless, the notion of the poem's speaker is useful, and with these reservations, I will go on using it here.

4.6 ■ I want now to move on to Section II 'A Game of Chess'. It is more straightforward than Section I, but you should look up two allusions in Southam's *Student's Guide*: line 77 to *Antony and Cleopatra*, and line 99 to the Greek fable about Philomela. Then as before, briefly note your impressions. What effect is conveyed by the description of the lady's bedroom? Does one's feeling about it change as the passage develops? What of the lady herself, and her relationship with her visitor, the silent partner of their conversation? What do the allusions contribute to the total effect? Have the two episodes anything in common, and what do you make of the contrast in speech style of the lady in the first episode and the raconteur of the pub scene that follows?

Discussion

4.7 In the first section (lines 77–138), my immediate impression is of luxurious magnificence. The opening lines blaze with light ('burnished . . . glowed . . . candelabra . . . glitter'). Precious things are strewn about ('jewels . . . ivory'). The supports for the mirror are made of worked gold. The lady sits on a throne-like chair, which itself stands on marble. The ceiling is panelled and decorated, the fireplace large, formal with a carved stone mantelpiece, and above that, a classical painting, or perhaps the wall itself is painted. The scene, too, is made up (composed?) of beautiful objects: the chair, the 'fruited vines', the 'seven-branched' candleholder; and even the perfumes, which introduce an intimate erotic note to set off against the formal splendour, are 'synthetic'. The language is elaborate, composed, stately; the sentences extend through several lines with clause opening out of clause, creating a slow deliberate rhythm, as the attention is moved from one detail to another. But when I look more closely, I notice also a gradually increasing sense of oppression. There is the fact that the lady herself does not at first appear, but only the objects that surround her, and when she does appear (lines 108–10) she is not what the setting leads you to expect. Then, the scene is static. Even the fire becomes a 'framed' visual effect, beautiful and exotic, but frozen:

> Huge sea-wood fed with copper
> Burned green and orange, framed by the coloured stone,
> In which sad light a carvèd dolphin swam.

Its light, strangely, is 'sad'. And notice that 'carvèd dolphin' suggests tamed energies; as, earlier, do the 'fruited vines', and the perfumes that instead of exciting 'drown the sense in odours'. Despite the sensuous richness of the scene, it is as if direct sensory experience has been overwhelmed, captured, transformed by the art that represents it. Towards the end, the sense of enclosure becomes explicit. Some of the pictures are described, menacingly as 'staring forms/[that] Leaned out, leaning, hushing the room enclosed'. We are even given a clue to the source of menace in the lines about Philomela. Art here, it is clear, speaks of primitive impulses of terror and cruelty, though again, at a distance, indirectly, through a fable.

The change of feeling throughout lines 77–110 prepares for the lady's nervy jagged speech, her anxious clutching at the attention of her visitor – whether a husband or a lover is left unclear. His spoken reaction to her questions is, presumably, polite, soothing, compliant, but what the poet gives us are his unspoken thoughts, melancholy and despairing. There is 'nothing' between these two. The lady has no insight into his state of feeling, and his feeling for her is reluctant, forced, habitual. The magnificent promise of the opening lines shrinks and dwindles to the routine misery of a loveless couple, linked only by an external bond.

What about the allusions? In line 77, the close parallel with the passage from *Antony and Cleopatra* invites us to compare Eliot's lady with Shakespeare's. It is a developed example of the technique used in the 'Portrait of a Lady' and 'Prufrock'. Shakespeare's description begins:

> The barge she sat in, like a burnished throne
> Burned on the water: the poop was beaten gold;
> Purple the sails, and so perfumed that
> The winds were love-sick with them;

Clearly, in this case, we are faced with more than simple allusion. Eliot's lines are directly indebted to Shakespeare's, yet the indebtedness is of a kind that we have to call 'creative'. Eliot builds on Shakespeare, incorporating in his own verse the kind of experience Shakespeare has so marvellously expressed, but towards an effect entirely his own. The richness and magnificence of Eliot's lines is distinct – to take the obvious point, his lady is in her bedroom, Cleopatra is outside, displayed to the whole world – and they have, as we've seen, their own non-Shakespearean direction. The point of this deliberately invited contrast is, I would suggest, that Eliot's luxurious setting is nothing more than that. It conspicuously lacks a Cleopatra. The lady in his poem is at her dressing table, but with what effect, to what ultimate purpose?

> Under the firelight, under the brush, her hair
> Spread out in fiery points
> Glowed into words, then would be savagely still.

With this culmination, isn't the suggestion that the lady's sexual and emotional energies that might have given point, meaning, human actuality to the implied promise of the opening lines, have been deadlocked, suppressed? The poem does not tell us why. It simply presents us with the fact. So the comparison with Cleopatra is not, as it might at first appear to be, sardonic but pitiful. And though the more shadowy comparison of her visitor to Antony verges on satire – 'footsteps shuffled on the stair' suggests a lover neither ardent nor heroic – here again, as the next section shows, the dominant feeling is one of tragic failure, some inward horror that can hardly be spoken.

> 'I never know what you are thinking. Think.'
>
> I think we are in rats' alley
> Where the dead men lost their bones.

The allusions to the Greek fable about Philomela (line 99) works rather differently. The speaker uses it to introduce a feeling and an idea that do not directly arise from the situation of the lady, which up to this point he has presented dramatically. The picture showing the transformation of the raped and mutilated Philomela is at first simply another of the appointments in the lady's room. The qualifying emphasis comes from the lines that follow:

> . . . yet there the nightingale
> Filled all the desert with inviolable voice
> And still she cried, and still the world pursues,
> 'Jug Jug' to dirty ears.

With the mention of the nightingale, we no longer observe the picture, we move into it. 'Yet *there*': even in that situation the nightingale's voice rises above the barbarism of sexual appetite, 'inviolable', giving expression to something indestructibly beautiful. The full and poignant rhythm of these lines underwrites the lyrical romanticism traditionally associated with the bird's song. But the qualifications are equally felt. Just as the 'barbarous king' destroyed, yet failed to destroy, Philomela, so the world still pursues the beauty of the song, which it hears, but fails to hear. The world's listening ears are 'dirty' because it gives only dirty-minded attention to Philomela's story. Here is the point where the speaker insinuates a direct moral judgement on human nature. Though perhaps 'judgement' is too rational a term. Notice how the movement from 'Jug Jug' (the traditional phrase for the nightingale's beautiful song) to 'dirty ears' suddenly resolves into a disgusted rejection the more detached, even forgiving attitude of the previous lines, where the barbarousness of the king is partly rescued from condemnation by the inviolability of what he tries to violate. Here is a case of a pattern in *The Waste Land*, much argued over by critics, that we'll come back to, which juxtaposes the past, seen in terms of art and literature, usually in beautiful, or at least dignified terms, with a drearily actual present, deserving only of contempt.

The second episode, the pub scene, is a case of this unattractive contemporary actuality. What it seems to have in common with the first is a sterile or meaningless sexuality. 'What you get married for if you don't want children?' sneers the raconteur. Albert, back from the war (another modern Antony?) will want sex from his wife, and will get it elsewhere if he has to. There are no romantic trappings here, nor does the speaker show any sympathy for the wife's clumsy and inexpert attempts at abortion. She is seen as a pitiful victim of the sexual appetite, and if she cannot satisfy it, well, 'others will'. The empty marriage, the pointless but determined sexuality, these seem to be the links with the first episode, while the point of the contrasting voices underlines a fundamental connection between two different social levels, and so suggests a general human malaise. ■

4.8 Looking back to 'The Burial of the Dead', what connections, however, tentative and undeveloped, can you suggest? We saw the poem's speaker adopt the tone of an austere moralist in the 'son of man' passage. Is there any hint of that tone in 'A Game of Chess'? Does the theme of romantic love in the lines about the 'hyacinth girl' recur? Or again, despite the fact that in 'The Burial of the Dead' the speaker shifts from voice to voice, and in 'A Game of Chess' is nearly anonymous, a mere dramatic presenter of two espisodes from contemporary life, has any unified impression of him begun to emerge? Think about these points before going any further.

4.9 ■ Please now read Section III, 'The Fire Sermon'. You will find that Eliot combines here the different methods used in the two previous sections. Much of it is self-communing reminiscence, though the speaker is a more definite presence than in 'The Burial of the Dead', in the sense that when he changes identity he tells us; but there are also dramatically presented episodes, as in 'A Game of Chess', where he offers glimpses of contemporary life. What are the connecting threads? And what is the topography of this section? Where do the episodes take place? Do you get any sense of movement, of shadowy narrative progress? There are, as usual, various allusions. After a first reading, I suggest you look up in Southam's *Student's Guide*, those to Spenser's poem in line 176, to Marvell's in lines 185–6, to Tiresias in line 218, and to St Augustine and Buddha in lines 307 and 308. There also is a specific reference back to Section II. Where is it, and what is its effect?

Discussion

4.10 The opening lines of 'The Fire Sermon' seem to me to illustrate very well the detailed texture of Eliot's writing in *The Waste Land*. They make a powerful immediate impression, and are not in that sense at all 'difficult', though they need careful reading especially for the shifts and turns of the feeling. The opening lines offer much more than a standard reaction to a standard scene: a river bank, late autumn, leafless trees.

> The river's tent is broken; the last fingers of leaf
> Clutch and sink into the wet bank. The wind
> Crosses the brown land, unheard. The nymphs are departed.

'Tent' gives the visual appearance of the river canopied over by summer foliage, and as a metaphor, a 'broken' tent introduces an unexpected note of violence to the passage from summer to winter, which is sustained in the notion of the leaves clutching and sinking, like somebody vainly trying to escape drowning, slithering down the river bank. You will remember from 'Prufrock' Eliot's development of a poetic language rich in elusive, yet powerful, suggestion. These lines seem to me such an example. The next two sentences are more simply elegiac in feeling, and with 'nymphs', a word of literary association, we move, or seem to move, towards a conventional lament. But then what happens?

> Sweet Thames, run softly, till I end my song.
> The river bears no empty bottles, sandwich papers,
> Silk handkerchiefs, cardboard boxes, cigarette ends
> Or other testimony of summer nights. The nymphs are departed.
> And their friends, the loitering heirs of City directors;
> Departed, have left no addresses.
> By the waters of Leman I sat down and wept . . .

The first line maintains the 'literary' note introduced by 'nymphs': only in poems do people address rivers, or describe what they are saying as a 'song'. But at once, we move into a contemporary world of picnics, stubbed-out cigarettes, outings with girls, observed with a kind of hopeless disdain. Notice how 'testimony of summer nights' crystallizes the feeling that what these encounters add up to is a pointless messiness, rubbish left lying about, nothing achieved or sustained. Yet again the feeling shifts. 'The nymphs are departed.' That reads satirically, if we take it in the context of the immediately preceding lines. *These* nymphs are neither figures in Greek mythology, nor the literary personifications of traditional poetry. They are good-time girls picked up by the 'loitering heirs' for occasional sex. But if we take it with what follows, it also reads elegiacally. These are the only nymphs now associated with the river, and what they represent, the emptiness, the casual nomadic quality of contemporary 'love', leads the poet on to the unambiguous lament, with its full biblical rhythm (notice the allusion to the psalm) of the line:

> By the waters of Leman I sat down and wept . . .

We now see that the 'literariness' of the address to the Thames was a conscious tactic, because when the line returns, it has accumulated sardonic force. The cultural and literary conventions that made for that kind of innocent artifice are no longer valid.

> Sweet Thames, run softly till I end my song,
> Sweet Thames, run softly, for I speak not loud or long.

Contemporary 'love' being what it is, this poet's song will soon be over as if he were saying to the river, 'I won't waste your time with my irrelevant poetising, just a minute or two longer'. And then finally that opening mysterious suggestion of violence, of subdued horror, reappears:

> But at my back in a cold blast I hear
> The rattle of the bones, and chuckle spread from ear to ear.

Notice how condensed that last phrase is. You hear a chuckle, but what spreads across the face is something you see, a smile or grin. The coalescence gives a nightmarish effect, as of something whose smiles can be heard and whose chuckles seen.

You will have discovered from Southam's *Student's Guide* that the 'Sweet Thames' line is a refrain from a poem by Edmund Spenser, celebrating the marriage of Renaissance aristocratic ladies, and invoking a pastoral scene with the Thames at its centre. Some critics argue that it is another example of Eliot contrasting the idyllic past with the sordid present. My own feeling is that the line illustrates the habit in the poem's speaker we have already noticed: his thinking in quotations. Here he thinks of himself for a moment as being like a Renaissance poet in his feeling about the river, about elegies to autumn, about poems in praise of nymphs. It is important to catch this traditional literary flavour of the line, its lyric feeling, but while it helps to know the actual source (even two or three stanzas of the poem, which you will find in the *Oxford Book of English Verse*, will sketch in the context Eliot is invoking), it is not essential to an understanding of the *structure* of Eliot's verse, which as I hope I've convinced you, has primarily to do with an accumulating complex of feeling, rather than with historical contrast. The other allusion is to Andrew Marvell's 'To His Coy Mistress'. (If you took A100 *Humanities: A Foundation Course* you may remember this poem; it too is in the *Oxford Book of English Verse*.) [3] Again, that it's a love, or rather, a seduction, poem in a particular tradition clearly fits in, but the main point is that, as in the lines from *Antony and Cleopatra*, Eliot builds on Marvell's stanza.

[3] The Open University (1971) A100 *Humanities: A Foundation Course*, The Open University Press.

But at my back I always hear
Time's wingèd chariot hurrying near,
And yonder all before us lie
Deserts of vast eternity.

Marvell uses the thought of mortality as an argument for making the most of life, but Eliot moves in the opposite direction. He excerpts the feeling of impending death, which he then reinforces. *That*, in his lines, is the underlying reality, the point of rest to which the whole passage moves. (Indeed, the phrase 'rattle of the bones' introduces a very un-Marvell-like note of gothic horrors, and echoes a phrase in 'A Game of Chess', which you might look for now. If you do not spot it, it was quoted in para 4.7.)

There is not space to look in detail at more of this first section, except to notice the way the Marvell poem appears again, but to strike a different note.

But at my back from time to time I hear
The sound of horns and motors, which shall bring
Sweeney to Mrs Porter in the spring.
O the moon shone bright on Mrs Porter
And on her daughter
They wash their feet in soda water

Here Marvell's courtly and urbane poem is played off, with satirical effect, against this modern seduction. But would you agree that it is not a sordid scene? There seems to me a kind of mad jazz-age gaiety in the lines, quite unlike the earlier passage about the nymphs. (It has been said of a good satirist that he has to love his subject as well as to hate it, and with Eliot, who has a strong satirical bent, the feeling about the objects of his attack is rarely simple.) What now immediately follows is, as I hope you discovered, an explicit reminiscence of the Philomela passage in 'A Game of Chess', which thus connects Sweeney with the 'barbarous king'. And looking back to the 'river's tent' lines, we can now see that we have moved through the seasonal round, from the evocation of summer, the presence of early winter, into spring again, a pattern already set up in 'The Burial of the Dead'. These are the kind of connections to look for in this poem: associative links through imagery, recurrent patterns, motifs.

You will have noticed that so far in this section, the river Thames has dominated. With 'Unreal City' the scene changes to London (which is also the locale of the second half of 'The Burial of the Dead'). The episodes speak clearly for themselves: loveless, melancholy, sexual encounters. In the one about the clerk and the typist, the speaker takes on a specific identity. He is Tiresias, the sage of Greek legend, bi-sexual, capable of understanding the experience of both men and women. When he speaks in his own voice he introduces a sadder, deeper note into the mainly satirical tone of the episode.

And I Tiresias have foresuffered all
Enacted on this same divan or bed;
I who have sat by Thebes below the wall
And walked among the lowest of the dead.

That is to say, the contemporary scene is viewed, its emptiness and pain immediately suffered, by a mythical figure. (You might consider whether the past, as represented by the city of Thebes, is here being favourably contrasted with the present.)

Eliot's own Note tells us that:

> Tiresias, although a mere spectator and not indeed a 'character', is yet the most important personage in the poem, uniting all the rest . . . all the women are one woman, and the two sexes meet in Tiresias. What Tiresias *sees*, in fact, is the substance of the poem.

There is a perhaps unintentional paradox in the claim, since Tiresias is blind, but we can then say that through him, Eliot has found an indirect way of generalizing the feeling about life diffused throughout the earlier sections and emerging with particular clarity in the seduction (if that is not too energetic a term) of the typist by the clerk. In 'A Game of Chess', the speaker is the anonymous presenter of two loveless marriages, of a sexuality both cruel and sterile, but despite an implication or two he makes no general judgement. 'The Fire Sermon' makes the point again, and this time, with the speaker taking on the identity of Tiresias, a general moral begins to emerge.

I asked whether you noticed any suggestion of narrative in this section. What I had in mind was the movement, first from the Thames of the opening scene into the 'Unreal City', and now the passage that follows the clerk/typist episode.

> And along the Strand, up Queen Victoria Street.
> O City city, I can sometimes hear
> Beside a public bar in Lower Thames Street,
> The pleasant whining of a mandoline
> And a clatter and a chatter from within
> Where fishmen lounge at noon: where the walls
> Of Magnus Martyr hold
> Inexplicable splendour of Ionian white and gold.

(The set book misprints 'fishmen' as 'fishermen'.) The speaker is walking through London streets, and a new feeling enters the poem, a brief moment of happiness, even exaltation: the sound of music from the Billingsgate pub, and the glimpse of the church interior. Then the scene goes back to the Thames, two journeys down river, one the romantically splendid wooing of Elizabeth I by the Earl of Leicester, the other the occasion of a characteristically joyless, though not un-tender, modern affair. Wagnerian motifs sound again during these episodes.

Now I do not want to make too much of the topographical detail in itself. What I suggest it represents is the speaker's mental and emotional journey through different kinds of experience. We have seen from 'The Burial of the Dead' both that an austerely moralistic attitude to human life comes easily to him, and that his romantic vision failed. 'A Game of Chess' catalogues further failures and desolation. In 'The Fire Sermon', after the sombre opening meditation, he moves first of all to the point of view of Tiresias who, though he makes no overt judgement, formulates a profound general pessimism. Then there are the river scenes, which conclude, as you will have seen from Southam's *Student's Guide*, in quotations from St Augustine and Buddha, which Eliot says he chose because they recommended asceticism as the only solution to human passions.

> To Carthage then I came
>
> Burning burning burning burning

It has fairly said that these quotations differ from the references to Shakespeare, Spenser and Marvell, because here, instead of building on the effects of another poet, Eliot falls back, rather helplessly, on gestures, that verse so threadbare and gnomic wholly fails to convey the *experience*, as distinct from the idea, of asceticism. What we might say in their defence is that they represent the speaker's tentative *effort towards* the severely confident, wholly articulated moral point of view of persons like Buddha and St Augustine. His state of mind can offer nothing more impressive precisely because he has not experienced their moral certainty, only the need for some alternative to his own confusion. Remember that if the speaker is at one point Tiresias, he is also the clerk and the typist, and all the other men and women. He has no single identity. ■

4.11 ■ Please now read 'Death by Water'.

(a) Working on the idea that *The Waste Land* hangs together (if it does) by reiterating and developing themes and motifs, how might this section link with, *and develop*, aspects of its predecessors?

Then move on to 'What the Thunder said', looking at Southam's introductory note, and his notes on Himavant (line 397), and the Sanskrit quotations (lines 399–401).

(b) The structure of this last section turns on a journey. How might it develop the implications of the end of 'The Fire Sermon'?

Discussion

4.12 (a) In earlier sections, death has been felt as terrible, an underlying menace that makes nonsense of life. 'Death by Water', an elegy for the physical dissolution of the body, develops the theme because of its different attitude towards it. The grave elegiac tone asks the reader to face the fact, without histrionics or self-regarding excitement, that death is not just his own, but every man's fate.

> Gentile or Jew
> O you who turn the wheel and look to windward,
> Consider Phlebas, who was once handsome and tall as you.

Notice also that it is death by drowning: the body is dissolved into the water which, in other contexts, is also associated with renewed life: the rain and the Hyacinth girl, the Thames with its various courtings. The imagery links once more with the pattern of natural life.

(b) 'What the Thunder said' develops 'The Fire Sermon' by pursuing a metaphorical journey that ends in certain explicit moral recommendations: 'Give, Sympathise, Control'. The journey begins after a memory of Christ's crucifixion, the speaker seemingly now one of the disciples.

> He who was living is now dead
> We who were living are now dying

His state of mind is presented with memorable power in the exhausting struggle through the rocky mountainous scenery and the futile search for water. The next lines allude to the journey to Emmaus of two disciples to whom Christ appears after his resurrection, though it is left uncertain whether the ambiguous, and indeed slightly menacing, third figure who accompanies the speaker and his friend really is Christ. Then we are briefly reminded of 'The Fire Sermon', of the dismal life of the 'Unreal City' which is not only London:

> What is the city over the mountains
> Cracks and reforms and bursts in the violet air
> Falling towers
> Jerusalem Athens Alexandria
> Vienna London
> Unreal

The journey continues, again in nightmarish form, and ends in a final emptiness

> There is the empty chapel, only the wind's home.
> It has no windows, and the door swings,
> Dry bones can harm no one.

But the chapel suggests a Christian building, and this is supported in Eliot's Note, which tells of an allusion to the Grail Quest. Again, though, the feeling is ambiguous. The details suggest that the quest failed, yet the next allusion to the cock that crowed when Peter denied Christ could imply that it only failed because of the seeker's cowardice. In striking contrast, the subsequent utterances of the thunder from Himavant, the holy mountain, are clear, detailed and authoritative, and what is even more striking, confidently underwritten by the speaker, who expounds the meaning of each statement for himself, and by implication, for his reader. The close of the poem finds the speaker thinking over his experiences, still uncertain of his future direction.

> I sat upon the shore
> Fishing, with the arid plain behind me
> Shall I at least set my lands in order?

Notice again how the imagery sustains the earlier pattern. The water longed for by the speaker arrives in the gust of rain preceding the thunder. The desert scenery of earlier lines and sections returns, though it is left uncertain whether the speaker has crossed it, or is trying to decide whether he should. ■

4.13 My intention so far has been to suggest one way through the poem's difficulties and obscurities, on a first reading. As you will have seen, I have said nothing about some parts of it, and I have to some extent pre-empted your response to the poem's structure by proposing the notion of a quest, a metaphorical journey, that ends in a tentative moral and religious affirmation. I have also omitted comment on two general aspects. One is Eliot's use of the myth of the Fisher King, and of other fertility myths about a dying and resurrected God who represents the natural vitality of the earth. You will find that clearly set out in Southam's *Student's Guide* (see the introductory note on pp 69–70, and detailed references *passim*); and it is taken as the key to the poem's structure by Leavis in his analysis in *New Bearings*. Eliot's own Note (*Collected Poems*, p 80) is the ultimate source of these interpretations. We can connect the fertility myth with the pattern of imagery, to which it adds a *generalizing story*: the natural cycle of generation, flowering, seeding, and death is embodied in such myths. I have also said nothing about the poem's social and cultural dimension – for most commentators, certainly the early ones, its outstanding feature. You might now like to register your own impressions. What does Eliot seem to be saying in this poem about his world? Southam claims, for example, that

> Eliot's immediate Waste Land is the world, as he saw it, after the 1914–18 war. The 'waste' is not, however, that of war's devastation and bloodshed, but the emotional and spiritual sterility of Western man, the 'waste' of our civilization. (Southam *Student's Guide*, p 69.)

■ What would you point to in the text to support such a view? When you have thought about that, you could usefully look through David Craig's essay 'The defeatism of *The Waste Land*' (see Course Reader, pp 290–302). Craig roundly attacks Eliot for the poem's pessimistic attitude towards the challenges and difficulties of modern life, and suggests that many of Eliot's interpreters (he instances Leavis' account in *New Bearings*) have far too readily accepted this pessimism as self-evidently justified. Whether or not you agree with Craig's view, the essay is vigorously argued, and it should help you to form your own ideas.

Discussion

4.14 We have already looked at parts of the poem – 'A Game of Chess' and 'The Fire Sermon' – which offer, clearly enough, cameos of modern life, as Eliot saw it, and a melancholy scene they certainly depict. But I hope you noticed that the contemporary note sounds much earlier, in the second half of 'The Burial of the Dead', in the lines I did not directly discuss. Madame Sosostris, for example, can be seen as the contemporary exponent of a false religion, battening on the human fear of death and the uncertain future, a figure both sinister and comic ('If you see dear Mrs Equitone, / Tell her I bring the horoscope myself: / One must be so careful these days'). Or more explicitly:

> Unreal City,
> Under the brown fog of a winter dawn,
> A crowd flowed over London Bridge, so many,
> I had not thought death had undone so many.
> Sighs, short and infrequent, were exhaled,
> And each man fixed his eyes before his feet.
> Flowed up the hill and down King William Street,
> To where Saint Mary Woolnoth kept the hours
> With a dead sound on the final stroke of nine.

The scene is, despite the realistic details of place and time, 'unreal' because the commuting crowd has no significant life (notice how the metaphor, 'flowed', dissolves the separate identities of its members). An allusion to Dante indicates that we are to think of the crowd as resembling certain spirits in the Inferno who 'in life knew neither good or evil, who never learnt to care for anyone but themselves', (Southam *Student's Guide*, p 76.) Throughout the poem, the speaker moves through a comparably spectral world, its realistic detail repeatedly invaded and undermined by the surreal presences in his mind. He is both within, and without, the 'Unreal City'. Within, in the sense that he dramatizes and participates in the different episodes; and without, because he brings to bear on them criteria and perspectives that he alone seems to know: that of the Old Testament prophet, those deriving from the allusions to past stages of European culture, or from the wisdom of the Upanishads. The clearest reference to the post-war condition of Europe comes in 'What the Thunder said':

> What is that sound high in the air
> Murmur of maternal lamentation
> Who are those hooded hordes swarming
> Over endless plains, stumbling in cracked earth
> Ringed by the flat horizon only

Eliot's Note (Southam *Student's Guide*, p 89) tells us that he alludes here to the Russian Revolution of 1917, and comparable upheavals in Eastern Europe in the immediate post-war years. But notice again that the imagery is generalized – one might fairly think of the Tartars invading Eastern Europe under Genghis Khan in the thirteenth century – that the activities of the 'hooded hordes' seem to lead nowhere, and that the next lines of the poem open up a long historical perspective, the creation and destruction of successive centres of civilization: Jerusalem, Athens, Alexandria, Vienna, London. Again, the contemporary event is linked with similar events from the past. It is not just London, but all these cities which are dismissed as 'unreal'.

Perhaps the strongest evidence for the account of the poem summarized by Southam is that contemporary readers took it that way. I. A. Richards believed that the poem expressed the spiritual crisis of modern man for whom science and history had disposed of the possibility of absolute beliefs (see Course Reader, pp 136–49). You have seen that Leavis, in his different way, believed the poem spoke eloquently to the modern condition. Again, we find the American critic F. O. Matthiesen writing in 1935:

> [Eliot] wanted to present here the intolerable burden of his 'Unreal City', the lack of purpose and direction, the inability to believe really in anything and the resulting 'heap of broken images' that formed the excruciating contents of the post-War state of mind. (Matthiesen *The Achievement of T. S. Eliot*, p 21.)

Or if we wanted more exactly contemporary evidence, there is Yeats's poem 'The Second Coming' (1919) with its apocalyptic vision of the end of the Christian era; and Pound's *Hugh Selwyn Mauberley* (1918), directly linking cultural decay with the catastrophe of the war. Eliot shared with Pound a vision of European cultural unity, perhaps only possible to Americans detached from the nationalistic antagonisms dividing European nations with especial virulence in the years before the war. (See Eliot's comment on Henry James, in Section 3.) Eliot refers in his seminal essay 'Tradition and the Individual Talent' to the importance for the poet of maintaining contact with 'the mind of Europe', and in *The Waste Land* that idea is strongly present as a possible cultural order against which the speaker sets the chaotic meaninglessness of contemporary life.

Yet having said that, we also have to take into account Eliot's own remark of 1931 in an essay called 'Thoughts after Lambeth':

> when I wrote a poem called *The Waste Land* some of the more approving critics said that I had expressed 'the disillusionment of a generation', which is nonsense. I may have expressed for them their own illusion of being disillusioned, but that did not form part of my intention. (*Selected Essays*, p 368.)

I think we have seen that there is evidence in the poem to support him, that he does repeatedly set the contemporary condition in a very general context. To take the clearest example: if the speaker *is* like the blind Greek prophet Tiresias, and London *is* like Thebes, then the poem must be claiming to speak about something in human life more persistent, more deep-seated than any contemporary disillusionment occasioned by the condition of post-war Europe.

As to David Craig's argument, I would like to pinpoint some issues which you can then mull over for yourself. First, the use of allusion. Does Eliot invoke an idealized past as a method of judging the contemporary scene, or does he intend to contrast a world of ideal possibilities with human actuality? (Remember that different allusions may yield different implications.) Second, does the poem strike you as defeatist, and if it does, is Craig right in thinking this a defect? Craig's argument implies that great literature conveys a positive attitude about human life, so there is a general point to think about, as well as the specific interpretation that *The Waste Land* conveys a sense of defeat. In thinking about this, keep in mind the movement of the poem (at least, as it seems to me) towards 'What the Thunder said', as well as the bleak and sombre tone of the different episodes. Third, there is the poem's account of sexuality, out of which its pessimistic tone seems so largely to rise. Craig discusses the clerk/typist episode, which has a fair claim to being the central event in the poem (it is the one witnessed by Tiresias), as follows:

> The unfeeling grossness of the experience is held off at the finger-tips by the analytic, unphysical diction – 'Endeavours to engage her in caresses' – and by the movement, whose even run is not interrupted by the violence of what is 'going on' . . . When we come to 'carbuncular' – an adjective which, placed after the noun and resounding in its slow movement and almost ornamental air, is deliberately out of key with the commonplace life around it – I think we begin to feel that Eliot's conscious literariness, whatever his intention, is working more to hold at arm's length something which he personally shudders at than to convey a poised criticism of behaviour. There is a shudder in 'carbuncular'; it is disdainful, but the dislike is disproportionately strong for its object; queasy emotions of the writer seem to be at work. The snobbery is of a piece with this. 'He is a nobody – a mere clerk, and a clerk to a *small* house agent at that. What right had *he* to look assured?' That is the suggestion. (Course Reader, p 295.)

Do you agree with this analysis of the passage?

The general point Craig raises is, I think, whether such episodes, dominated by feelings either not fully under control (uneasiness about the physical basis of life), or social attitudes evidently shallow and vulnerable to criticism, can be accepted as performing the role allotted to them in the poem. Can a deep pessimism about the value of human life be adequately conveyed unless we feel that the poem reflects a deep immersion in experience? You may find that some parts of the poem are, in that respect, more convincing than others. ■

4.15 Is *The Waste Land* a complete poem, or is it a collection of poems, or parts of poems, which do not in the end cohere? From the traditional standpoint, the poem was both chaotic and fragmentary. It is understandable then that much early criticism concentrated attention on explaining what kind of structure the poem had. As a 'modernist' poem it dispensed with narrative and action, substituting a myth (the Fisher King and the Grail Quest), brought into play by allusion rather than by explicit statement; and by an analogy with music, it was built up out of thematic motifs, whose repetition and variation established equivalences, contrasts and development between and within the different parts. The only familiar structure the poem could be said to use, and then in a drastically new version, was that of the 'dramatic monologue', as developed in the 'Portrait', 'Prufrock' and 'Gerontion'. Looking back at these poems from the vantage point of *The Waste Land*, it seems clear that Eliot had been trying to find a way round the constraints imposed by a monologue uttered by a single character with a personal story. One can think of *The Waste Land* as the dramatic monologue of a character who has no character, no particular history, who inhabits several identities, both past and present, both human and mythical. If he is a mere spectator of the human scene from one point of view, from another he is the single, if many-sided, protagonist. He is a kind of judge or critic of what he reports, yet his hold on any standards of judgement is uncertain, and he delivers his most forceful verdict against himself: 'These fragments I have shored against my ruins'. He is a person trying not to be a person, to feel and think and speak 'impersonally' (this would be

An escape from the Joycean 'nightmare of history' or more firmly ensconced within it?

Eliot's term). Or as Leavis put it, the poem's 'rich disorganization . . . is an effort to focus an inclusive human consciousness . . . characteristic of the age'. (Leavis *New Bearings*, pp 70, 74.) Yet such an account of the poem, the majority verdict of its interpreters, has never been unanimously accepted. In 1943, Yvor Winters maintained that *The Waste Land*, far from being a completed poem, was radically disorganized, that in writing about chaos Eliot had failed to create an adequate poetic form:

> Eliot, in dealing with debased and stupid material, felt himself obliged to seek his form in his matter: the result is confusion and journalistic reproduction of detail . . . Eliot suffers from the delusion that he is judging [his material] when he is merely exhibiting it. He has loosely thrown together a collection of disparate and fragmentary principles . . . the romantic on the one hand and on the other the classical and the Christian; and being unaware of his own contradictions, he is able to make a virtue of what appears to be private spiritual laziness; he is able to enjoy at one and the same time the pleasures of indulgence and the dignity of disapproval. (Winters *In Defense of Reason*, pp 499–500.)

More recently, in *Image and Experience* (1960), Graham Hough has proposed a comparable objection to the mosaic-like character of 'modernist' poetry, its practice of making random juxtaposition a substitute for intelligent connection, which is as much as to say of *The Waste Land* that by leaving the relationship of the parts ambiguous, if not thoroughly obscure, Eliot has ducked his responsibility to the reader. Even Eliot himself seemed to incline to such a view when, in 1959, asked about the form of the poem before Pound's editing of the original drafts, he replied: 'I think it was just as structureless, only in a more futile way'. (*Writers at Work*, p 83.)

I quote these dissentient voices to show that if, for you, the poem does not finally hold together, you are not on your own. Remember though that *the kind* of unity the poem exhibits may, as its defenders have always argued, resist developed intellectual formulation. Arguing this point of view in *The New Poetic*, C. K. Stead quotes with approval a statement of I. A. Richards:

> . . . the items are united by the accord, contrast, and interaction of their emotional effects, not by an intellectual scheme that analysis must work out. The value lies in the unified response which this interaction creates in the right reader. The only intellectual activity required takes place in the realization of the separate items. We can, of course, make a 'rationalization' of the whole experience, as we can of any experience. If we do, we are adding something which does not belong to the poem. (Cited in Stead *The New Poetic*, p 162.)

Pound, too, read the poem as 'an emotional unit', and wittily attacked overly intellectual interpretations:

> This demand for clarity in every particular of a work, whether essential or not, reminds me of the Pre-Raphaelite painter who was doing a twilight scene but rowed across the river in day time to see the shape of the leaves on the further bank, which he then drew in with full detail. (Cited in Kenner *The Invisible Poet*, p 131.)

I think that is a warning to keep in mind, especially if you find yourself consulting the more detailed commentaries.

4.16 Finally, a word about the genesis of the poem. The original drafts of *The Waste Land* amounted to a loose collection of poems[4] in a variety of styles, which Eliot had accumulated over several years, some from as early as 1914. In seeking Pound's advice, it seems clear that Eliot was at first uncertain about the nature of the 'long poem' he had mentioned in 1919. But it would be a mistake to think that the poem's published text was a creation of Pound's alone. Eliot accepted many, but not all, of Pound's suggestions, and a year after the poem appeared he wrote in an essay called 'The Function of Criticism' about 'the labour of sifting, combining, constructing, expunging, correcting, testing: this frightful toil is as much critical as creative'. (*Selected Essays*, p 30.) We may assume then that every one of Pound's proposals about *The Waste Land* was only agreed to by Eliot after a long and strenuous consideration. Pound's suggestions fall into three groups: (a) detailed verbal changes, (b) major cuts of long narrative passages, (c) smaller cuts of passages in which the speaker makes explicit judgements. The first, though always of interest, need not concern us here. The main items in the second group were: a low-life episode located in Boston, Mass., about a visit to a music hall and a brothel, preceding the present opening of the poem; a satirical account in the style of Pope about Fresca, a fashionable lady of contemporary London, with easy morals and a superficial interest in modern literature, which provided the opening of 'The Fire Sermon'; and the tale of the last voyage of a fishing vessel in the waters off New England, ending in shipwreck, preceding the present version of 'Death by Water'. In proposing that these episodes should go, Pound was really asking for compression, for intensity of effect. Each offered an independent and narrative interest, distracting attention from the main emotional centre. The first and third introduced places other than London, and the second was, one may guess, too overtly satirical in manner. Eliot seems to have regretted its loss, however: he wrote later that 'Pound induced me to destroy what I thought an excellent set of couplets' (Ezra Pound *Selected Poems*, 1928, p 18). The third kind of proposed excision is perhaps the most interesting, since it made the poem more enigmatic, less explicitly personal. There is an example in 'The Fire Sermon', immediately before the clerk/typist episode, where these lines occurred:

> London, the swarming life you kill and breed,
> Huddled between the concrete and the sky,
> Responsive to the momentary need,
> Vibrates unconscious to its formal destiny,
>
> Knowing neither how to think, nor how to feel,
> But lives in the awareness of the observing eye.
> London, your people is bound upon the wheel!
> Phantasmal gnomes, burrowing in brick and stone and steel!
> Some minds, aberrant from the normal equipoise
> (London, your people is bound upon the wheel!)
> Record the motions of these pavement toys
> And trace the cryptogram that may be curled
> Within these faint perceptions of the noise
> Of the movement, and the lights!
>
> (Valerie Eliot *T. S. Eliot: The Waste Land, A Facsimile* . . . p 43.)

This overt stepping-back from the life of ordinary Londoners, the speaker declaring himself an outsider who sees the truth about the 'Unreal City' is occasionally suggested in the published text, but these lines give him a confidence and detachment, a settled didacticism about London that is foreign to *The Waste Land* as we know it. Moreover, a couplet like

[4] Recently published as *T. S. Eliot: The Waste Land, A Facsimile . . .*, ed. Mrs Valerie Eliot, Faber, 1971.

Some minds aberrant from the normal equipoise
(London, your people is bound upon the wheel!)

might easily provide the reader with a shortcut. Instead of taking imaginative possession of the way the poem registers experience, of its rich and complex emotional tone (what I called stage three in 'understanding' the poem), the reader could take these lines as representing Eliot's 'point-of-view', and the poem as a series of exemplary illustrations of it. In accepting Pound's proposal to cut the lines, Eliot was acting on that principle of 'impersonality' that he set out in 'Tradition and the Individual Talent', whereby the poet's personal view of life was the least important thing about him.

4.17 Eliot's two other important poems of this period, 'Gerontion' and 'The Hollow Men', I will leave you to explore for yourself. Once you have gained some familiarity with individual poems, there is one general point to be considered – the pattern of Eliot's development as a poet. What changes do you notice in tracing his poetic achievement from 'Portrait of a Lady' to 'The Hollow Men'? Does he go on writing the same kind of poem, or continue to create new poetic forms? Would you agree that 'Prufrock', compared with 'The Hollow Men', is a young man's poem? Or do you think that despite the ten or twelve years separating their composition, they reflect the same kind of theme? Stead remarks of 'Gerontion' that it reveals 'the dark stain of some intense suffering which carries over into *The Waste Land*' (Stead *The New Poetic*, p 157). Do you agree with him?

FURTHER READING AND REFERENCES

There are any number of books about Eliot's work, and if you have time, and find his poetry interesting, you may want to consult more than your set books. The main thing, of course, is to concentrate on the poems, but some of these titles may be helpful.

Bergonzi, Bernard (1972) *T. S. Eliot,* Macmillan.
This is a short general survey of his life and work.

Matthiesen, F. O. (1935) *The Achievement of T. S. Eliot*, Oxford University Press.
Of the older books on Eliot, this is still the best. There is a revised and enlarged 1958 edition. You will find it helpful in the way it sets Eliot's poetry in the context of his general thinking about literature and culture.

Wilks, A. J. (1971) *T. S. Eliot's 'The Waste Land'*, Macmillan (Critical Commentary Series).
An introductory discussion of *The Waste Land*.

Here are the full titles of books other than set books referred to in the units:

Eliot, T. S. (1935) *Selected Essays*, Faber.
Eliot, Valerie (ed.) (1971) *T. S. Eliot: The Waste Land, A Facsimile of the Original Drafts including the Annotations of Ezra Pound,* Faber.
Hough, Graham (1960) *Image and Experience*, Duckworth.
Kenner, Hugh (1959) *The Invisible Poet*, Routledge and Kegan Paul.
Kenner, Hugh (ed.) (1970) *The Translations of Ezra Pound*, Faber.
Litz, A. Walton (1973) *Eliot in his Time*, Oxford University Press.
Mowrer, E. A. (1928) *This American World,* Faber.
Paige, D. D. (ed.) (1950) *Selected Letters of Ezra Pound*, Faber.
The Translations of Ezra Pound (1971) (ed. Hugh Kenner), Faber.
Pound, Ezra (1928) *Selected Poems*, Faber.
Richards, I. A. (1929) *Principles of Literary Criticism*, Routledge and Kegan Paul.
Tate, Allen (ed.) (1971) *T. S. Eliot: The Man and His Work*, Penguin.
Winters, Yvor (1960) *In Defense of Reason*, Routledge and Kegan Paul.

Set books referred to in the units:

Eliot, T. S. (1974) *Collected Poems 1909–1962*, Faber.
Leavis, F. R. (1972) *New Bearings in English Poetry*, Penguin.
Martin, Graham and Furbank, P. N. (1975) *Twentieth Century Poetry: Critical Essays and Documents*, The Open University Press. (Course Reader)
Pound, Ezra (1975) *Ezra Pound: Selected Poems 1908–1959,* Faber.
Stead, C. K. (1964) *The New Poetic*, Hutchinson.
Southam, B. C. (1968) *A Student's Guide to the Selected Poems of T. S. Eliot,* Faber.

ACKNOWLEDGEMENTS

Grateful acknowledgement is made to the following for material used in these units:

Faber and Faber and Harcourt Brace Jovanovich for extracts from T. S. Eliot, 'Portrait of a Lady', 'Prelude IV', *The Waste Land* and 'The Love Song of J. Alfred Prufrock', copyright 1936 Harcourt Brace Jovanovich, copyright 1963, 1964 T. S. Eliot; Faber and Faber and New Directions Publishing Corp, New York for extracts from Ezra Pound, 'Portrait d'une Femme' in *Collected Poems* and in *Personae,* and 'Pierrots' in *Collected Shorter Poems* and in H. Kenner (ed.) *The Translations of Ezra Pound,* copyright 1926, 1954 Ezra Pound.

TWENTIETH CENTURY POETRY

Unit 1	English Poetry in 1912
Units 2–3	Thomas Hardy
Units 4–5	Modernism and Its Origins
Unit 6	Ezra Pound
Units 7–8	T. S. Eliot's Poetry 1909–25
Unit 9	T. S. Eliot: Criticism
Units 10–11	T. S. Eliot's Poetry 1926–44
Unit 12	Poetry in Translation
Unit 13	Guillaume Apollinaire
Units 14–17	W. B. Yeats
Units 18–19	William Empson and F. R. Leavis
Unit 20	R. M. Rilke *Duino Elegies*
Units 21–22	Poetry and Politics
Units 23–24	W. H. Auden
Unit 25	Hugh MacDiarmid
Unit 26	Dylan Thomas
Unit 27	Robert Lowell
Unit 28	Philip Larkin
Unit 29	Ted Hughes Sylvia Plath
Unit 30	Robert Graves John Betjeman
Unit 31	Donald Davie Charles Tomlinson Geoffrey Hill
Unit 32	Poetry in Public East European Poets

de Gruyter Studies in Mathematics 5

Editors: Heinz Bauer · Peter Gabriel

Gerhard Burde · Heiner Zieschang

Knots

Walter de Gruyter
Berlin · New York 1985

Authors

Dr. Gerhard Burde
Professor of Mathematics
Universität Frankfurt/Main

Dr. Heiner Zieschang
Professor of Mathematics
Ruhr-Universität Bochum

With numerous figures

Library of Congress Cataloging in Publication Data

Burde, Gerhard, 1931–
Knots.
(De Gruyter studies in mathematics ; 5)
Bibliography: p.
Includes index.
1. Knot theory. I. Zieschang, Heiner. II. Titlc.
III. Series.
QA612.2.B87 1985 514'.224 85–7064
ISBN 0-89925-014-9 (U.S.)

CIP-Kurztitelaufnahme der Deutschen Bibliothek

Burde, Gerhard:
Knots / Gerhard Burde ; Heiner Zieschang. – Berlin ;
New York : de Gruyter, 1985.
(De Gruyter studies in mathematics ; 5)
ISBN 3-11-008675-1 geb.
NE: Zieschang, Heiner:; GT

3 11 008675 1 Walter de Gruyter · Berlin · New York
0 89925 014 9 Walter de Gruyter, Inc., New York

Cover design: Rudolf Hübler, Berlin. Typesetting and Printing: Tutte Druckerei GmbH, Salzweg-Passau. Binding: Lüderitz & Bauer, Berlin.

Preface

The phenomenon of a knot is a fundamental experience in our perception of three dimensional space. What is special about knots is that they represent a truly intrinsic and essential quality of 3-space accessible to intuitive understanding. No arbitrariness like the choice of a metric mars the nature of a knot – a trefoil knot will be universally recognizable wherever the basic geometric conditions of our world exist. (One is tempted to propose it as an emblem of our universe.)

There is no doubt that knots hold an important – if not crucial – position in the theory of 3-dimensional manifolds. As a subject for a mathematical textbook they serve a double purpose. They are excellent introductory material to geometric and algebraic topology, helping to understand problems and to recognize obstructions in this field. On the other hand they present themselves as ready and copious test material for the application of various concepts and theorems in topology.

The first nine chapters (excepting the sixth) treat standard material of classical knot theory. The remaining chapters are devoted to more or less special topics depending on the interest and taste of the authors and what they believed to be essential and alive. The subjects might, of course, have been selected quite differently from the abundant wealth of publications in knot theory during the last decades.

We have stuck throughout this book mainly to traditional topics of classical knot theory. Links have been included where they come in naturally. Higher-dimensional knot theory has been completely left out – even where it has a bearing on 3-dimensional knots such as slice knots. The theme of surgery has been rather neglected – excepting Chapter 15. Wild knots and algebraic knots are merely mentioned.

This book may be read by students with a basic knowledge in algebraic topology – at least the first four chapters will present no serious difficulties to them. As the book proceeds certain fundamental results on 3-manifolds are used – such as the Papakyriakopoulos theorems. The theorems are stated in Appendix B and references are given where proofs may be found. There seemed to be no point in adding another presentation of these things. The reader who is not familiar with these theorems is, however, well advised to interrupt the reading to study them. At some places the theory of surfaces is needed – several results of Nielsen are applied. Proofs of these may be read in [ZVC 1980], but taking them for granted will not seriously impair the understanding of this book. Whenever possible we have given complete and self-contained proofs at the most elementary level possible. To do this we occasionally refrained from applying a general theorem but gave a simpler proof for the special case in hand.

There are, of course, many pertinent and interesting facts in knot theory – especially in its recent development – that were definitely beyond the scope of such a textbook. To be complete – even in a special field such as knots – is impossible today and was not aimed at. We tried to keep up with important contributions in our bibliography.

There are not many textbooks on knots. Reidemeister's "Knotentheorie" was published in 1932. The book of Crowell and Fox "Introduction to Knot Theory" was conceived for a different purpose and level; Neuwirth's book "Knot Groups" and Hillman's monography "Alexander Ideals of Links" have a more specialised and algebraic interest in mind. In writing this book we had, however, to take into consideration Rolfsen's remarkable book "Knots and Links". We tried to avoid overlappings in the contents and the manner of presentation. In particular, we thought it futile to produce another set of drawings of knots and links up to ten crossings – or even more. They can – in perfect beauty – be viewed in Rolfsen's book. Knots with less than ten crossings have been added in Appendix D as a minimum of ready illustrative material. The tables of knot invariants have also been devised in a way which offers at least something new. Figures are plentiful because we think them necessary and hope them to be helpful.

Finally we wish to express our gratitude to Colin Maclachlan who read the manuscript and expurgated it from the grosser lapsus linguae (this sentence was composed without his supervision). We are indebted to U. Lüdicke and G. Wenzel who wrote the computer programs and carried out the computations of a major part of the knot invariants listed in the tables. We are greatful to U. Dederek-Breuer who wrote the program for filing and sorting the bibliography. We also want to thank Mrs. A. Huck and Mrs. M. Schwarz for patiently typing, re-typing, correcting and re-correcting abominable manuscripts.

Frankfurt (Main)/Bochum, Gerhard Burde
Summer 1985 Heiner Zieschang

Contents

Preface V

Chapter 1: Knots and Isotopies 1

A Knots 1
B Equivalence of Knots 4
C Knot Projections 8
D Global Geometric Properties 11
E History and Sources 13
F Exercises 13

Chapter 2: Geometric Concepts 15

A Geometric Properties of Projections 15
B Seifert Surfaces and Genus 17
C Companion Knots and Product Knots 19
D Braids, Bridges, Plats 22
E Slice Knots and Algebraic Knots 24
F History and Sources 26
G Exercises 27

Chapter 3: Knot Groups 29

A Homology 29
B Wirtinger Presentation 31
C Peripheral System 38
D Knots on Handlebodies 40
E Torus Knots 44
F Asphericity of the Knot Complement 46
G History and Sources 47
H Exercises 47

Chapter 4: Commutator Subgroup of a Knot Group 49

A Construction of Cyclic Coverings 49
B Structure of the Commutator Subgroup 52

C A Lemma of Brown and Crowell 53
D Examples and Applications 56
E Commutator Subgroups of Satellites 58
F History and Sources 61
G Exercises 62

Chapter 5: Fibred Knots 65

A Fibration Theorem 65
B Fibred Knots 68
C Applications and Examples 70
D History and Sources 75
E Exercises 75

Chapter 6: A Characterization of Torus Knots 77

A Results and Sources 77
B Proof of the Main Theorem 79
C Remarks on the Proof 85
D History and Sources 87
E Exercises 87

Chapter 7: Factorization of Knots 89

A Composition of Knots 89
B Uniqueness of the Decomposition into Prime Knots: Proof 94
C Fibred Knots and Decompositions 97
D History and Sources 99
E Exercises 99

Chapter 8: Cyclic Coverings and Alexander Invariants 101

A Alexander Module 101
B Infinite Cyclic Covering and Alexander Module 102
C Homological Properties of C_∞ 107
D Alexander Polynomials 109
E Finite Cyclic Coverings 113
F History and Sources 118
G Exercises 119

Chapter 9: Free Differential Calculus and Alexander Matrices 121

A Regular Coverings and Homotopy Chains 121
B Fox Differential Calculus 123
C Calculation of Alexander Polynomials 125
D Alexander Polynomials of Links 129
E Finite Cyclic Coverings Again 133
F History and Sources 135
G Exercises 135

Chapter 10: Braids 139

A The Classification of Braids 139
B Normal Form and Group Structure 147
C Configuration Spaces and Braid Groups 151
D Braids and Links 156
E History and Sources 161
F Exercises 162

Chapter 11: Manifolds as Branched Coverings 163

A Alexander's Theorem 163
B Branched Coverings and Heegard Diagrams 168
C History and Sources 178
D Exercises 178

Chapter 12: Montesinos Links 181

A Schubert's Normal Form of Knots and Links with Two Bridges 181
B Viergeflechte (4-Plats) 185
C Alexander Polynomial and Genus of a Knot with Two Bridges 190
D Classification of Montesinos Links 195
E Symmetries of Montesinos Links 202
F History and Sources 208
G Exercises 208

Chapter 13: Quadratic Form of a Knot 211

A The Quadratic Form of a Knot 211
B Computation of the Quadratic Form of a Knot 219
C Alternating Knots and Links 225

D Comparison of Different Concepts and Examples 230
E History and Sources 237
F Exercises................ 238

Chapter 14: Representations of Knot Groups 239

A Metabelian Representations 239
B A Class of Homomorphisms of $\mathfrak{G}$ into the Group of Motions of the Euclidean Plane 244
C Linkage in Coverings 250
D Periodic Knots 255
E History and Sources 266
F Exercises................ 267

Chapter 15: Knots, Knot Manifolds, and Knot Groups 271

A Examples 271
B Property P for Special Knots 274
C Prime Knots and their Manifolds and Groups 284
D Groups of Product Knots 296
E History and Sources 299
F Exercises................ 300

Appendix A: Algebraic Theorems 301
Appendix B: Theorems of 3-dimensional Topology 307
Appendix C: Tables 311
Appendix D: Knot Projections 0_1–9_{49} 341

Bibliography 345
List of Code Numbers................ 381
List of Authors According to Codes................ 382
Glossary of Notations................ 393
Author Index 395
Index 397

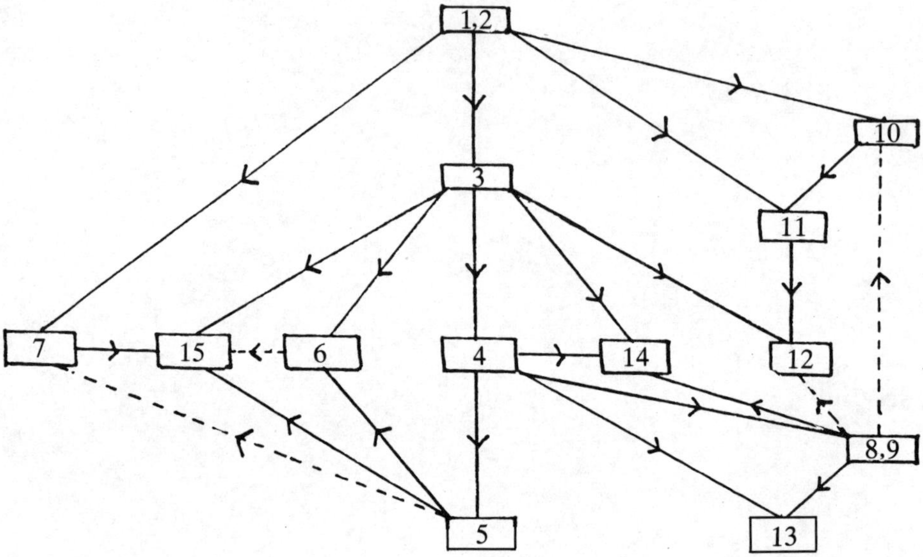

The diagram indicates how the different chapters depend on each other. An arrow from A to B means that results of A are essential for B. A broken arrow expresses that results of A are used in B but not at a vital point.

Chapter 1: Knots and Isotopies

The chapter contains an elementary foundation of knot theory. Sections A and B define and discuss knots and their equivalence classes, and Section C deals with the regular projections of knots.

Section D contains a short review of [Pannwitz 1933] and [Milnor 1950] intended to further an intuitive geometric understanding for the global quality of knotting in a simple closed curve in 3-space.

A Knots

A knot, in the language of mathematics, is an embedding of a circle S^1 into Euclidean 3-space, $\mathbb{R}^3$, or the 3-sphere, S^3. More generally embeddings of S^k into S^{n+k} have been studied in "higher dimensional knot theory", but this book will be strictly concerned with "classical" knots $S^1 \subset S^3$. (On occasion we digress to consider "links" or "knots of multiplicity $\mu > 1$" which are embeddings of a disjoint union of 1-spheres S_i^1, $1 \leqq i \leqq \mu$, into S^3 or $\mathbb{R}^3$.)

A single embedding $i: S^1 \to S^3$, is, of course, of little interest, and does not give rise to fruitful questions. The essential problem with a knot is whether it can be disentangled by certain moves that can be carried out in 3-space without damaging the knot. The topological object will therefore rather be a class of embeddings which are related by these moves (isotopic embeddings).

There will be a certain abuse of language in this book to avoid complicating the notation. A knot $\mathfrak{k}$ will be an embedding, a class of embeddings, the image $i(S^1) = \mathfrak{k}$ (a simple closed curve), or a class of such curves. There are different notions of isotopy, and we start by investigating which one of them is best suited to our purposes.

Let X and Y be Hausdorff spaces. A mapping $f: X \to Y$ is called an *embedding* if $f: X \to f(X)$ is a homeomorphism.

1.1 Definition (isotopy). Two embeddings, $f_0, f_1: X \to Y$ are *isotopic* if there is an embedding

$$F: X \times I \to Y \times I$$

such that $F(x, t) = (f(x, t), t)$, $x \in X$, $t \in I = [0, 1]$, with $f(x, 0) = f_0(x)$, $f(x, 1) = f_1(x)$.

F is called a *level-preserving isotopy connecting f_0 and f_1*.

We frequently use the notation $f_t(x) = f(x, t)$ which automatically takes care of the boundary conditions. The general notion of isotopy as defined above is no good as far as knots are concerned. Any two embeddings $S^1 \to S^3$ can be shown to be isotopic although they evidently are different with regard to their knottedness. The idea of the proof is sufficiently illustrated by the sequence of pictures of Figure 1.1. Any area where knotting occurs can be contracted continuously to a point.

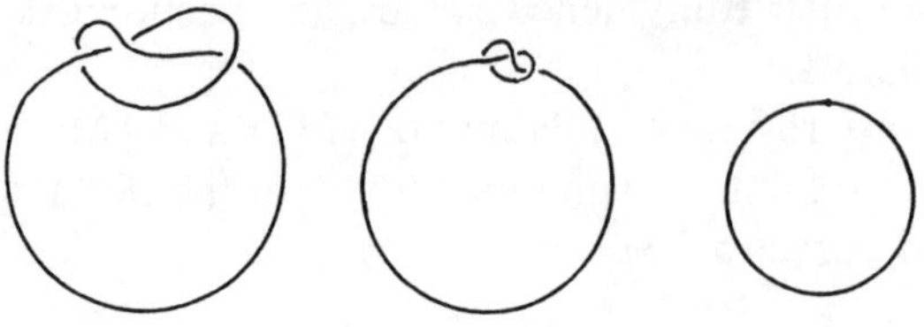

Fig. 1.1

1.2 Definition (ambient isotopy). Two embeddings $f_0, f_1: X \to Y$ are *ambient isotopic* if there is a level preserving isotopy

$$H: Y \times I \to Y \times I,\ H(y, t) = (h_t(y), t),$$

with $f_1 = h_1 f_0$ and $h_0 = id_Y$. H is called an *ambient isotopy.*

An ambient isotopy defines an isotopy F connecting f_0 and f_1 by $F(x, t) = (h_t f_0(x), t)$. The difference between the two definitions is the following: An isotopy moves the set $f_0(X)$ continuously over to $f_1(X)$ in Y, but takes no heed of the neighbouring points of Y outside $f_t(X)$. An ambient isotopy requires Y to move continuously along with $f_t(X)$ such as a liquid filling Y will do if an object ($f_t(X)$) be transported through it.

The restriction

$$h_1 \mid Y - f_0(X) \to Y - f_1(X)$$

of the homeomorphism $h_1: Y \to Y$ is itself a homeomorphism of the complements of $f_0(X)$ resp. $f_1(X)$ in Y, if f_0 and f_1 are ambient isotopic. This is not necessarily true in the case of mere isotopy and marks the crucial difference. We shall see in Chapter 3 that the complement of the *trefoil* knot – see the first picture of Figure 1.1 – and the complement of the unknotted circle, the *trivial knot* or *unknot*, are not homeomorphic.

We are going to narrow further the scope of our interest. Topological embeddings $S^1 \to S^3$ may have a bizarre appearance as Figure 1.2 shows. There is an infinite sequence of similar meshes converging to a limit point L at which this knot is called *wild.* This example of a wild knot, invented by R.H. Fox [Fox 1949], has indeed remarkable properties which show that at such a point of wildness something extraordinary may happen. In [Fox-Artin 1948] it is proved that the complement of the curve depicted in Figure 1.2 is different from that of a trivial knot. Nevertheless the knot can obviously be unravelled from the right – at least finitely many stitches can.

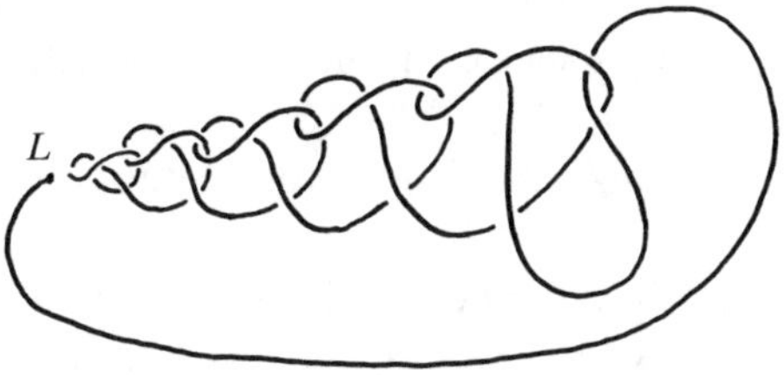

Fig. 1.2

1.3 Definition (tame knots). A knot $\mathfrak{k}$ is called *tame* if it is ambient isotopic to a simple closed polygon in $\mathbb{R}^3$ resp. S^3. A knot is *wild* if it is not tame.

If a knot is tame, any connected proper part α of it is ambient isotopic to a straight segment and therefore the complement $S^3 - \alpha$ is simply connected. Any proper subarc of the knot of Figure 1.2 which contains the limit point L can be shown [Fox-Artin 1948] to have a non-simply connected complement. From this it appears reasonable to call L a point at which the knot is wild. Wild knots are no exceptions – quite the contrary. Milnor proved: *"Most" knots are wild* [Milnor 1964]. One can even show that almost all knots are wild at every point [Brode 1981]. Henceforth we shall be concerned only with tame knots. Consequently we shall work always in the p.l.-category (p.l. = piecewise linear). All spaces will be compact polyhedra with a finite simplicial structure, unless otherwise stated. Maps will be piecewise linear. We repeat Definitions 1.1 and 1.2 in an adjusted version:

1.4 Definition (p.l. isotopy and p.l.-ambient isotopy). Let X, Y be polyhedra and f_0, f_1: $X \to Y$ p.l.-embeddings. f_0 and f_1 are *p.l. isotopic* if there is a level-preserving p.l.-embedding

$$F: X \times I \to Y \times I, \quad F(x, t) = (f_t(x), t), \ 0 \leqq t \leqq 1.$$

f_0 and f_1 are *p.l.-ambient isotopic* if there is a level-preserving p.l.-isotopy

$$H: Y \times I \to Y \times I, \quad H(y, t) = (h_t(y), t),$$

with $f_1 = h_1 f_0$ and $h_0 = id_Y$.

In future we shall usually omit the prefix "p.l.".

We are now in a position to give the fundamental definition of a knot as a class of embeddings $S^1 \to S^3$ resp. $S^1 \to \mathbb{R}^3$:

1.5 Definition (equivalence). Two (p.l.)-knots are *equivalent* if they are (p.l.)-ambient isotopic.

As mentioned before we use our terminology loosely in connection with this definition. A knot $\mathfrak{k}$ may be a representative of a class of equivalent knots or the class itself. If the knots $\mathfrak{k}$ and $\mathfrak{k}'$ are equivalent, we shall say they are the same, $\mathfrak{k} = \mathfrak{k}'$ and use the sign of equality. $\mathfrak{k}$ may mean a simple closed finite polygonal curve or a class of such curves.

The main topic of classical knot theory is the classification of knots with regard to equivalence.

Dropping "p.l." defines, of course, a broader field and a more general classification problem. The definition of tame knots (Definition 1.3) suggests appyling the Definition 1.2 of "topological" ambient isotopy to define a topological equivalence for this class of knots. At first view one might think that the restriction to the p.l.-category will introduce equivalence classes of a different kind. We shall take up the subject in Chapter 3 to show that this is not true. In fact two tame knots are topologically equivalent if and only if the p.l.-representatives of their topological classes are p.l.-equivalent.

We have defined knots up to now without bestowing orientations either on S^1 or S^3. If S^1 is oriented (oriented knot) the notion of equivalence has to be adjusted: *Two oriented knots are equivalent*, if there is an ambient isotopy connecting them which respects the orientation of the knots. Occasionally we shall choose a fixed orientation in S^3 (for instance in order to define linking numbers). Ambient isotopies obviously respect the orientation of S^3.

B Equivalence of Knots

We defined equivalence of knots by ambient isotopy in the last paragraph. There are different notions of equivalence to be found in the literature which we propose to investigate and compare in this paragraph.

Reidemeister [Reidemeister 1926′] gave an elementary introduction into knot theory stressing the combinatorial aspect, which is also the underlying concept of his book "Knotentheorie" [Reidemeister 1932], the first monograph written on the subject. He introduced an isotopy by moves.

1.6 Definition (Δ-move). Let u be a straight segment of a polygonal knot $\mathfrak{k}$ in $\mathbb{R}^3$ (or S^3), and D a triangle in $\mathbb{R}^3$, $\partial D = u \cup v \cup w$, u, v, w 1-faces of D. If $D \cap \mathfrak{k} = u$, then $\mathfrak{k}' = (\mathfrak{k} - u) \cup v \cup w$ defines another polygonal knot. We say $\mathfrak{k}'$ *results from* $\mathfrak{k}$ *by a* Δ*-move* (or Δ*-process*). If $\mathfrak{k}$ is oriented, $\mathfrak{k}'$ is to carry the orientation induced by that of $\mathfrak{k} - u$. The inverse process is denoted by Δ^{-1}. (See Figure 1.3)

Remark: We allow Δ to degenerate as long as $\mathfrak{k}'$ remains simple. This means that Δ resp. Δ^{-1} may be a bisection resp. a reduction in dimension one.

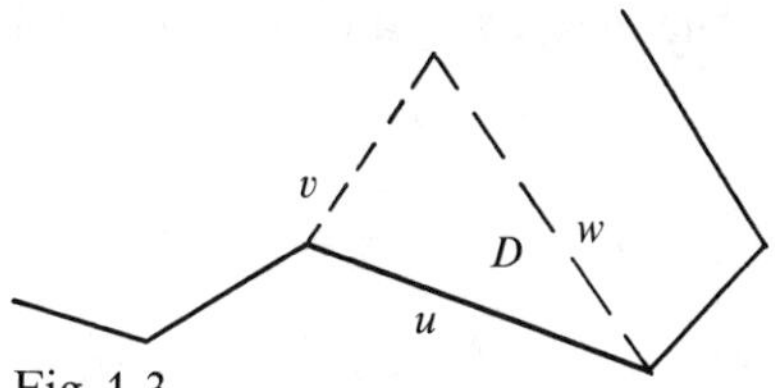

Fig. 1.3

1.7 Definition (combinatorial equivalence). Two knots are *combinatorially equivalent* or *isotopic by moves*, if there is a finite sequence of Δ- and Δ^{-1}-moves which transforms one knot to the other.

There is a third way of defining equivalence of knots which takes advantage of special properties of the embedding space, $\mathbb{R}^3$ or S^3. Fisher [Fisher 1960] proved that an orientation preserving homeomorphism h: $S^n \to S^n$ is isotopic to the identity. (A homeomorphism with this property is called a *deformation.*) We shall prove the special case of Fisher's theorem that comes into our province with the help of the following theorem which is well known, and will not be proved here.

1.8 Theorem of Alexander-Schönflies. *Let i: $S^2 \to S^3$ be a (p.l.) embedding. Then*

$$S^3 = B_1 \cup B_2,\ i(S^2) = B_1 \cap B_2 = \partial B_1 = \partial B_2,$$

where B_i, $i = 1, 2$, is a combinatorial 3-ball (B_i is p.l. – homeomorphic to a 3-simplex).

The *proof* can be found in [Graeub 1950], [Moise 1952, 1977]. □

The theorem corresponds to the Jordan curve theorem in dimension two where it holds for topological embeddings. In dimension three it is not true in this generality [Alexander 1924], [Brown 1962].

We start by proving

1.9 Proposition (Alexander-Tietze). *Any (p.l.) homeomorphism f of a (combinatorial) n-ball B keeping the boundary fixed is isotopic to the identity by a (p.l.)-ambient isotopy keeping the boundary fixed.*

Proof. Define

$$H(x, t)|\partial(B \times I) = \begin{cases} id,\ t = 0 \\ id,\ x \in \partial B \\ f \times 1,\ t = 1. \end{cases}$$

Every point $(x, t) \in B \times I$, $t > 0$, lies on a straight segment in $B \times I$ joining a fixed interior point P of $B \times 0$ and a variable point X on $\partial(B \times I)$. Extend $H(x, t)|\partial(B \times I)$ linearly on these segments to obtain a p.l. level-preserving mapping $H(x, t)$: $B \times I \to B \times I$, in fact, the desired ambient isotopy (*Alexander trick*, [Alexander 1923], Fig. 1.4). □

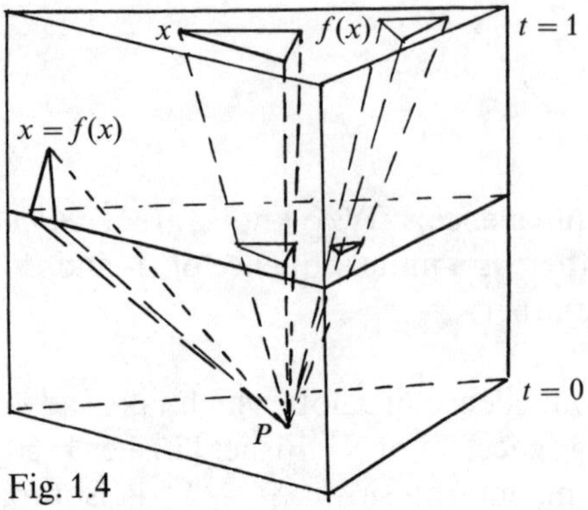

Fig. 1.4

We are now ready to prove the main theorem of the paragraph:

1.10 Proposition (equivalence of equivalences). *Let $\mathfrak{k}_0$ and $\mathfrak{k}_1$ be p.l.-knots in S^3. The following assertions are equivalent.*

(1) There is an orientation preserving homeomorphism $f: S^3 \to S^3$ which carries $\mathfrak{k}_0$ onto $\mathfrak{k}_1$, $f(\mathfrak{k}_0) = \mathfrak{k}_1$.

(2) $\mathfrak{k}_0$ and $\mathfrak{k}_1$ are equivalent (ambient isotopic).

(3) $\mathfrak{k}_0$ and $\mathfrak{k}_1$ are combinatorially equivalent (isotopic by moves).

Proof. (1) ⇒ (2): We begin by showing that there is an ambient isotopy $H(x, t) = (h_t(x), t)$ of S^3 such that $h_1 f$ leaves fixed a 3-simplex $[P_0, P_1, P_2, P_3]$. If $f: S^3 \to S^3$ has a fixed point, choose it as P_0; if not, let P_0 be any interior point of a 3-simplex $[s^3]$ of S^3. There is an ambient isotopy of S^3 which leaves $S^3 - [s^3]$ fixed and carries P_0 over to any other interior point of $[s^3]$. If $[s^3]$ and $[s'^3]$ have a common 2-face, one can easily construct an ambient isotopy moving an interior point P_0 of $[s^3]$ to an interior point P_0' of $[s'^3]$ which is the identity outside $[s^3] \cup [s'^3]$ (Fig. 1.5).

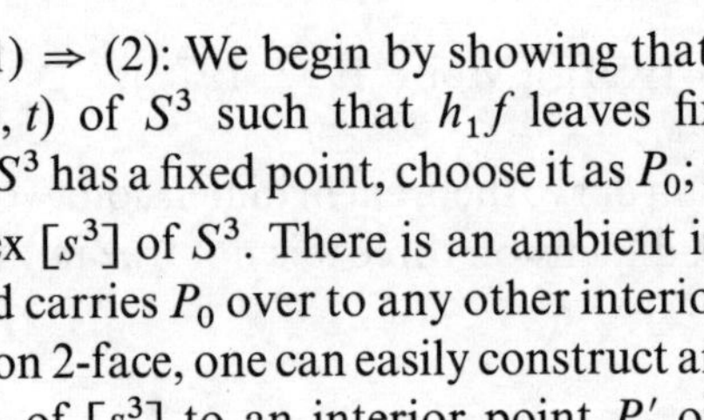

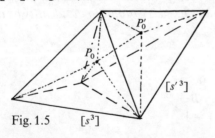

Fig. 1.5

So there is an ambient isotopy H^0 with $h_1^0 f(P_0) = P_0$, since any two 3-simplices can be connected by a chain of adjoining ones. Next we choose a point $P_1 \neq P_0$ in the simplex star of P_0, and by similar arguments construct an ambient istotopy H^1 with $h_1^1 h_1^0 f$ leaving fixed the 1-simplex $[P_0, P_1]$. A further step leads to $h_1^2 h_1^1 h_1^0 f$ with a fixed 2-simplex $[P_0, P_1, P_2]$. At this juncture the assumption comes in that f is required to preserve the orientation. A point $P_3 \notin [P_0, P_1, P_2]$, but in the star of $[P_0, P_1, P_2]$, will be mapped by $h_1^2 h_1^1 h_1^0 f$ onto a point P_3' in the same half-space with regard to the plane spanned by P_0, P_1, P_2. This ensures the existence of the final ambient istotopy H^3 such that $h_1^3 h_1^2 h_1^1 h_1^0 f$ leaves fixed $[P_0, P_1, P_2, P_3]$. The assertion follows from the fact that $H = H^3 H^2 H^1 H^0$ is an ambient isotopy, $H(x, t) = (h_t(x), t)$.

By Theorem 1.8 the complement of $[P_0, P_1, P_2, P_3]$ is a combinatorial 3-ball and by 1.9 there is an ambient isotopy which connects $h_1 f$ with the identity of S^3.

(2) $\Rightarrow$ (1) follows from the definition of an ambient isotopy.

Next we prove (1) $\Rightarrow$ (3): Let h: $S^3 \to S^3$ be an orientation preserving homeomorphism and $\mathfrak{k}_1 = h(\mathfrak{k}_0)$. The preceding argument shows that there is another orientation preserving homeomorphism g: $S^3 \to S^3$, $g(\mathfrak{k}_0) = \mathfrak{k}_0$, such that hg leaves fixed some 3-simplex $[s^3]$ which will have to be chosen outside a regular neighbourhood of $\mathfrak{k}_0$ and $\mathfrak{k}_1$. For an interior point P of $[s^3]$ consider $S^3 - \{P\}$ as Euclidean 3-space $\mathbb{R}^3$. There is a translation τ of $\mathbb{R}^3$, which moves $\mathfrak{k}_0$ into $[s^3] - \{P\}$. It is easy to prove that $\mathfrak{k}_0$ and $\tau(\mathfrak{k}_0)$ are isotopic by moves (see Fig. 1.6). We claim that $\mathfrak{k}_1 = hg(\mathfrak{k}_0)$ and $hg\tau(\mathfrak{k}_0) = \tau(\mathfrak{k}_0)$ are isotopic by moves also, which would complete the proof. Choose a subdivision of the triangulation of S^3 such that the triangles used in the isotopy by moves between $\mathfrak{k}_0$ and $\tau(\mathfrak{k}_0)$ form a subcomplex of S^3. There is an isotopy by moves $\mathfrak{k}_0 \to \tau(\mathfrak{k}_0)$ which is defined on the triangles of the subdivision. hg: $S^3 \to S^3$ maps the subcomplex onto another one carrying over the isotopy by moves, (see [Graeub 1949]).

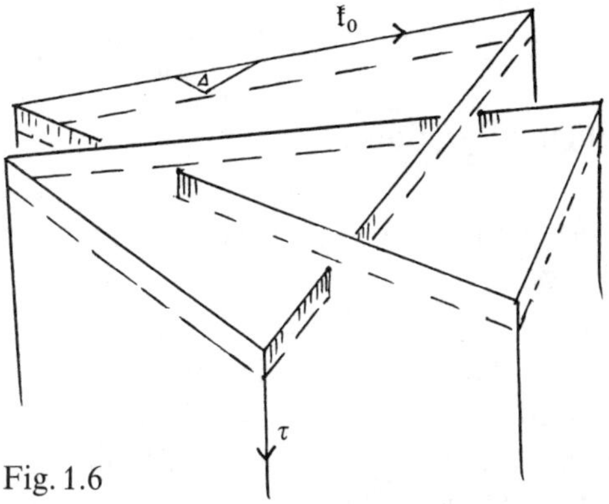

Fig. 1.6

(3) $\Rightarrow$ (1). It is not difficult to construct a homeomorphism of S^3 onto itself which realizes a $\Delta^{\pm 1}$-move and leaves fixed the rest of the knot. Choose a regular neighbourhood U of the 2-simplex which defines the $\Delta^{\pm 1}$-move whose boundary meets the knot in two points. By linear extension one can obtain a homeomorphism producing the $\Delta^{\pm 1}$-move in U and leaving $S^3 - U$ fixed. □

Isotopy by Δ-moves provides a means to formulate the knot problem on an elementary level. It is also useful as a method in proofs of invariance.

C Knot Projections

Geometric description in 3-space is complicated. The data that determine a knot are usually given by a *projection of* $\mathfrak{k}$ *onto a plane* E (projection plane) in $\mathbb{R}^3$. (In this paragraph we prefer $\mathbb{R}^3$ with its Euclidean metric to S^3; a knot $\mathfrak{k}$ will always be thought of as a simple closed polygon in $\mathbb{R}^3$.) A point $P \in p(\mathfrak{k}) \subset E$ whose preimage $p^{-1}(P)$ under the projection $p: \mathbb{R}^3 \to E$ contains more than one point is called a *multiple* point.

1.11 Definition (regular projection). A projection p of a knot $\mathfrak{k}$ is called *regular* if

(1) there are only finitely many multiple points $\{P_i \mid 1 \leqq i \leqq n\}$, and all multiple points are *double points*, that is, $p^{-1}(P_i)$ contains two points;

(2) no vertex of $\mathfrak{k}$ is mapped onto a double point. (The minimal number of double points or *crossings* n in a regular projection of a knot is called the *order* of the knot.) A regular projection avoids occurences as depicted in Figure 1.7.

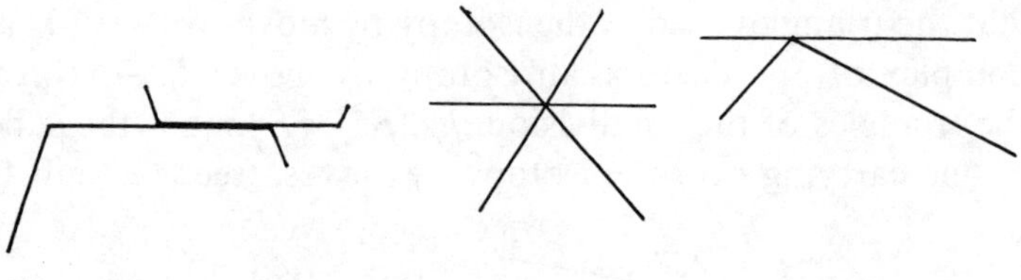

Fig. 1.7

There are sufficiently many regular projections.

1.12 Proposition. *The set of regular projections is open and dense in the space of all projections.*

Proof. Think of directed projections as points on a unit sphere $S^2 \subset \mathbb{R}^3$ with the induced topology. A standard argument (general position) shows that singular (non-regular) projections are represented on S^2 by a finite number of curves. (The reader is referred to [Reidemeister 1926′] or [Burde 1978] for a more detailed treatment.) □

The projection of a knot does not determine the knot, but if at every double point in a regular projection the overcrossing line is marked, the knot can be reconstructed from the projection (Fig. 1.8).

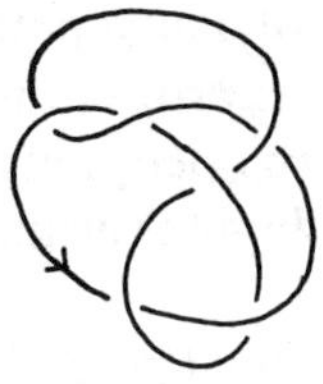

Fig. 1.8

If the knot is oriented, the projection inherits the orientation. The projection of a knot with this additional information is called a *knot projection* or *knot diagram*. Two *knot diagrams* will be regarded as *equal* if they are isotopic in E as graphs, where the isotopy is required to respect overcrossing resp. undercrossing. Equivalent knots can be described by many different diagrams, but they are connected by simple operations:

1.13 Definition (Reidemeister moves). Two *knot diagrams* are called *equivalent*, if they are connected by a finite sequence of Reidemeister moves Ω_i, $i = 1, 2, 3$ or their inverses Ω_i^{-1}. The moves are described in Figure 1.9.

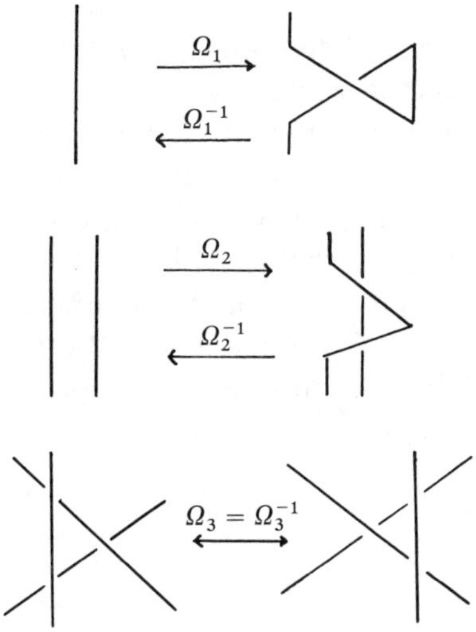

Fig. 1.9

The operations $\Omega_i^{\pm 1}$ effect local changes in the diagram. Evidently all these operations can be realized by an ambient isotopy of the knot; equivalent diagrams therefore define equivalent knots. The converse is also true:

1.14 Proposition. *Two knots are equivalent if and only if all their diagrams are equivalent.*

Proof. The first step in the proof will be to verify that any two regular projections p_1, p_2 of the same simple closed polygon $\mathfrak{k}$ are connected by $\Omega_i^{\pm 1}$-moves. Let p_1, p_2

again be represented by points on S^2, and choose on S^2 a polygonal path s from p_1 to p_2 in general position with respect to the lines of singular projections on S^2. When such a line is crossed the diagram will be changed by an operation $\Omega_i^{\pm 1}$, the actual type depending on the type of singularity corresponding to the line that is crossed.

It remains to show that for a fixed projection equivalent knots possess equivalent diagrams. According to Proposition 1.10 it suffices to show that a $\Delta^{\pm 1}$-move induces $\Omega_i^{\pm 1}$-operations on the projection. This again is easily verified (Fig. 1.10). □

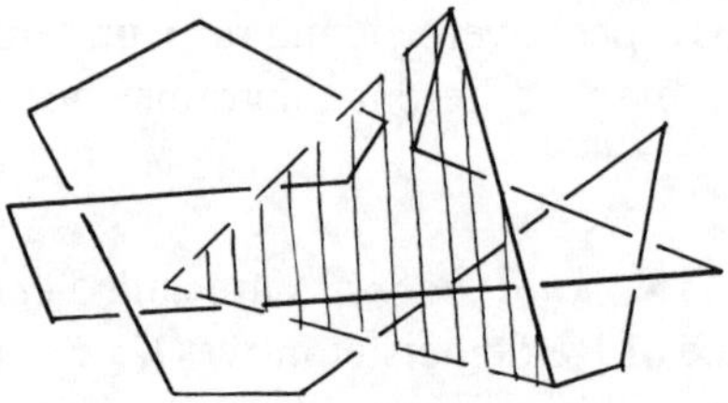

Fig. 1.10

Proposition 1.14 allows an elementary approach to knot theory. It is possible to continue on this level and define invariants for diagrams with respect to equivalence [Burde 1978]. One might be tempted to look for a finite algorithm to decide equivalence of diagrams by establishing an a priori bound for the number of crossings. Such a bound is not known, and a simple counterexample shows that it can at least not be the maximum of the crossings that occur in the diagrams to be compared. The diagram of Figure 1.11 is that of a trivial knot, however, on the way to a simple closed projection via moves $\Omega_i^{\pm 1}$ the number of crossings will increase. This follows from the fact, that the diagram only allows operations Ω_1^{+1}, Ω_2^{+1} which increase the number of crossings.

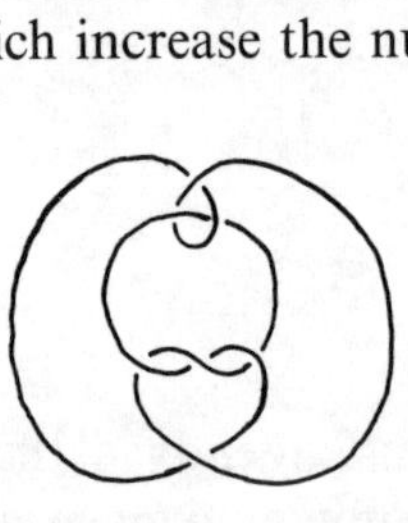

Fig. 1.11

Figure 1.11 demonstrates one thing more: The operations Ω_i, $i = 1, 2, 3$ are "independent" – one cannot dispense with any of them (Exercise E 1.5), [Trace 1984].

D Global Geometric Properties

In this section we will discuss two theorems (without giving proofs) which connect the property of "knottedness" and "linking" with other geometric properties of the curves in $\mathbb{R}^3$. The first is [Pannwitz 1933]:

1.15 Theorem (Pannwitz). *If $\mathfrak{k}$ is a non-trivial knot in $\mathbb{R}^3$, then there is a straight line which meets $\mathfrak{k}$ in four points.*

If a link of two components $\mathfrak{k}_i$, $i = 1, 2$ is not splittable, then there is a straight line which meets $\mathfrak{k}_1$ and $\mathfrak{k}_2$ in two points A_1, B_1 resp. A_2, B_2 each, with an ordering A_1, A_2, B_1, B_2 on the line. (Such a line is called a four-fold chord of $\mathfrak{k}$).

It is easy to see that the theorem does not hold for the trivial knot or a splittable linkage. (A link *is splittable or split* if it can be separated in $\mathbb{R}^3$ by a 2-sphere.)

What Pannwitz proved was actually something more general. For any knot $\mathfrak{k} \subset \mathbb{R}^3$ there is a singular disk $D \subset \mathbb{R}^3$ spanning $\mathfrak{k}$. For example one such disk can be constructed by erecting a cone over a regular projection of $\mathfrak{k}$ (Fig. 1.12). If $D \subset \mathbb{R}^3$ is immersed in general position, there will be a finite number of singular points on $\mathfrak{k}$ (boundary singularities).

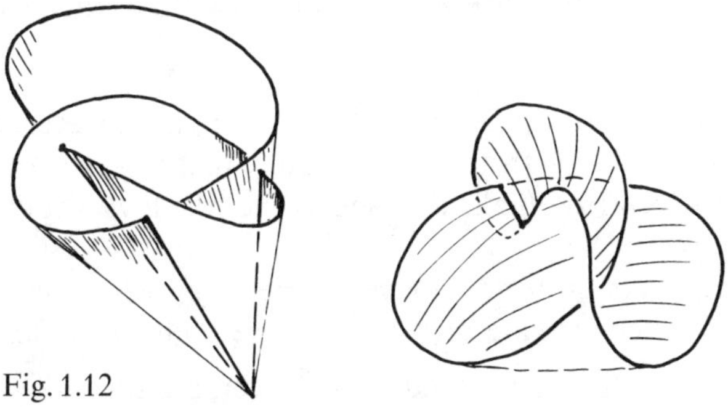

Fig. 1.12

1.16 Definition (knottedness). The minimal number of boundary singularities of a disk spanning a knot $\mathfrak{k}$ is called the *knottedness k* of $\mathfrak{k}$.

1.17 Theorem (Pannwitz). *The knottedness k of a non-trivial knot is an even number. A knot of knottedness k possesses $\frac{k^2}{2}$ four-fold chords.*

The *proof* of this theorem – which generalizes the first part of 1.15 – is achieved by cut-and-paste techniques as used in the proof of Dehn's Lemma. □

Figure 1.12 shows the trefoil spanned by a cone with 3 boundary singularities and by another disk with the minimal number of 2 boundary singularities. (The apex of the cone is not in general position, but a slight deformation will correct that.)

Another global theorem on of a knotted curve is due to J. Milnor [1950]. If $\mathfrak{k}$ is smooth ($\mathfrak{k} \in C^{(2)}$), the integral

$$\kappa(\mathfrak{k}) = \int_{\mathfrak{k}} |\mathfrak{x}''(s)|\, ds$$

is called the *total curvature* of $\mathfrak{k}$. (Here $s \mapsto \mathfrak{x}(s)$ describes $\mathfrak{k}$: $S^1 \to \mathbb{R}^3$ with $s =$ arclength.) $\kappa(\mathfrak{k})$ is not an invariant of the knot type. Milnor generalized the notion of the total curvature so as to define it for arbitrary closed curves. In the case of a polygon this yields $\kappa(\mathfrak{k}) = \sum_{i=1}^{r} \alpha_i$, where the α_i are the angles of successive line segments (Fig. 1.13).

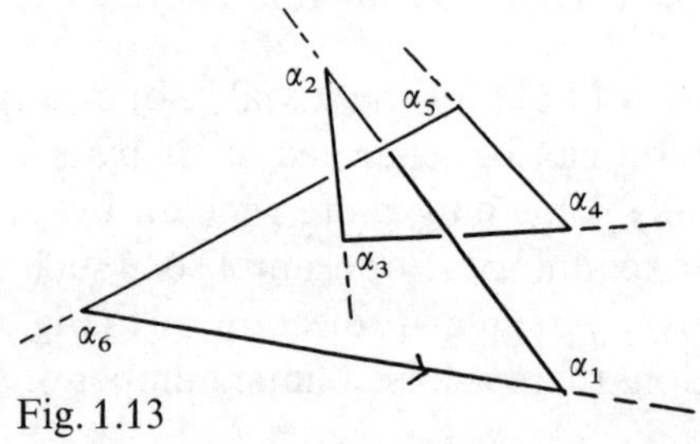

Fig. 1.13

1.18 Theorem (Milnor). *The total curvature $\kappa(\mathfrak{k})$ of a non-trivial knot $\mathfrak{k} \subset \mathbb{R}^3$ exceeds* 4π. □

We do not intend to copy Milnor's proof here. As an example, however, we give a realization of the trefoil in $\mathbb{R}^3$ with total curvature equal to $4\pi + \delta(\varepsilon)$, where $\delta(\varepsilon) > 0$ can be made arbitrarily small. This shows that the lower bound, 4π, is sharp.

In Figure 1.14 a diagram of the trefoil is given in the (x, y)-plane, the symbol at each vertex denotes the z-coordinate of the respective point on $\mathfrak{k}$. Six of eight angles α_i are equal to $\frac{\pi}{2}$, two of them, α and β, are larger, but tend to $\frac{\pi}{2}$ as $\varepsilon \to 0$.

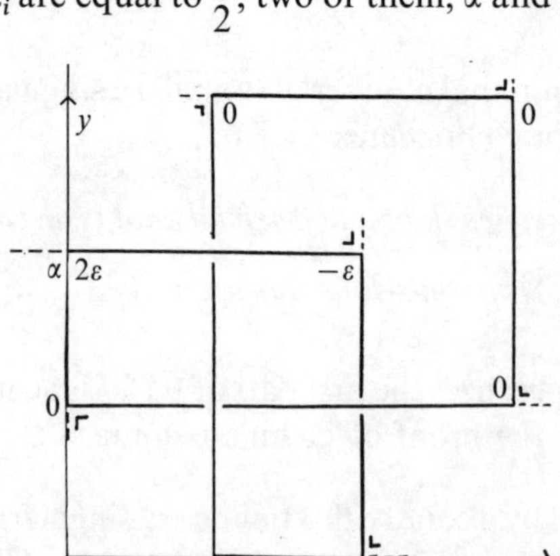

Fig. 1.14

E History and Sources

A systematic and scientific theory of knots developed only in this century when combinatorial topology came under way. The first contributions [Dehn 1910, 1914], [Alexander 1920, 1928] excited quite an interest, and a remarkable amount of work in this field was done which was reflected in the first monograph on knots, Reidemeister's Knotentheorie, [Reidemeister 1932]. The elementary approach to knots presented in this Chapter stems from this source.

F Exercises

E 1.1 Let $\mathfrak{k}$ be a smooth oriented simple closed curve in $\mathbb{R}^2$, and let $-\mathfrak{k}$ denote the same curve with the opposite orientation. Show that $\mathfrak{k}$ and $-\mathfrak{k}$ are not isotopic in $\mathbb{R}^2$ whereas they are in $\mathbb{R}^3$.

E 1.2 Construct explicitly a p.l.-map of a complex K composed of two 3-simplices with a common 2-face onto itself which moves an interior point of one of the 3-simplices to an interior point of the other while keeping fixed the boundary ∂K of K (see Fig. 1.5).

E 1.3 The suspension point P over a closed curve with n double points is called a *branch point of order* $n+1$. Show that there is an ambient isotopy in $\mathbb{R}^3$ which transforms the suspension into a singular disk with n branch points of order two [Papakyriakopoulos 1957′].

E 1.4 Let $p(t)$, $0 \leqq t \leqq 1$, be a continuous family of projections of a fixed knot $\mathfrak{k} \subset \mathbb{R}^3$ onto $\mathbb{R}^2$, which are singular at finitely many isolated points $0 < t_1 < t_2 < \ldots < 1$. Discuss by which of the operations Ω_i the two regular projections $p(t_k - \varepsilon)$ and $p(t_k + \varepsilon)$, $t_{k-1} < t_k - \varepsilon < t_k < t_k + \varepsilon < t_{k+1}$, are related according to the type of the singularity at t_k.

E 1.5 Prove that any projection obtained from a simple closed curve in $\mathbb{R}^3$ by using $\Omega_1^{\pm 1}$, $\Omega_2^{\pm 1}$ can also be obtained by using only Ω_1^{+1}, Ω_2^{+1}.

E 1.6 Let $p(\mathfrak{k})$ be a regular projection with n double points. By changing overcrossing arcs into undercrossing arcs at $k \leqq \dfrac{n-1}{2}$ double points, $p(\mathfrak{k})$ can be transformed into a projection of the trivial knot.

Chapter 2: Geometric Concepts

Some of the charm of knot theory arises from the fact that there is an intuitive geometric approach to it. We shall discuss in this chapter some standard constructions and presentations of knots and various geometric devices connected with them.

A Geometric Properties of Projections

Let $\mathfrak{k}$ be an oriented knot in oriented 3-space $\mathbb{R}^3$.

2.1 Definition (symmetries). The knot obtained from $\mathfrak{k}$ by inverting its orientation is called the *inverted knot* and denoted by $-\mathfrak{k}$. The *mirror-image* of $\mathfrak{k}$ or *mirrored knot* is denoted by $\mathfrak{k}^*$; it is obtained by a reflection of $\mathfrak{k}$ in a plane.

A knot $\mathfrak{k}$ is called *invertible* if $\mathfrak{k} = -\mathfrak{k}$, and *amphicheiral* if $\mathfrak{k} = \mathfrak{k}^*$.

The existence of non-invertible knots was proved only relatively recently [Trotter 1964]. The trefoil was shown to be non-amphicheiral in [Dehn 1914]; the trefoil is invertible. The *four-knot* 4_1 is both, invertible and amphicheiral. The knot 8_{17} is amphicheiral but it is non-invertible [Kawauchi 1979], [Bonahon-Siebenmann 1979]. For more refined notions of symmetries in knot theory, see [Hartley 1983′].

2.2 Definition (alternating knot). A *knot projection* is called *alternating*, if upper-crossings and under-crossings alternate while running along the knot. A *knot* is called *alternating,* if it possesses an alternating projection; otherwise it is *non-alternating*.

The existence of non-alternating knots was first proved by [Bankwitz 1930], see Proposition 13.30.

Alternating projections are frequently printed in knot tables without marking undercrossings. It is an easy exercise to prove that any such projection can be furnished in exactly two ways with undercrossings to become alternating; the two possibilities belong to mirrored knots. Without indicating undercrossings a closed plane curve does not hold much information about the knot whose projection it might be. Given such a curve there is always a trivial knot that projects onto it. To prove this assertion just choose a curve $\mathfrak{k}$ which ascends monotonically in $\mathbb{R}^3$ as one runs along the projection, and close it by a segment in the direction of the projection.

A closed plane curve defines a tesselation of the plane by simply connected *regions* bounded by arcs of the curve, and a single *infinite region*. (This can be avoided by substituting a 2-sphere for the plane.) The regions can be coloured by two colours like a chess-board such that regions of the same colour meet only at double points (Fig. 2.1, E 2.2). The proof is easy. If the curve is simple, the fact is well known; if not, omit a simply closed partial curve s and colour the regions by an induction hypothesis. Replace s and exchange the colouring for all points inside s.

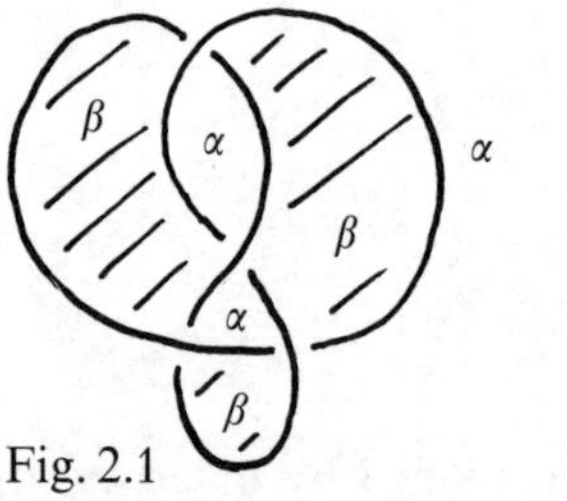

Fig. 2.1

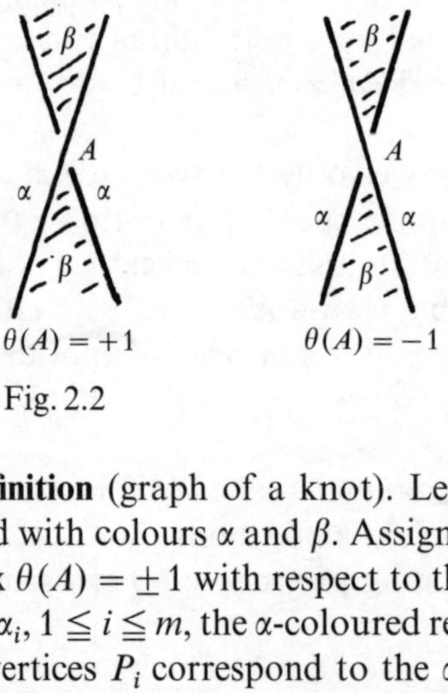

Fig. 2.2

2.3 Definition (graph of a knot). Let a regular knot diagram be chess-board coloured with colours α and β. Assign to every double point A of the projection an index $\theta(A) = \pm 1$ with respect to the colouring as defined by Figure 2.2. Denote by α_i, $1 \leqq i \leqq m$, the α-coloured regions of a knot diagram. Define a graph Γ whose vertices P_i correspond to the α_i, and whose edges a_{ij}^k correspond to the double points $A^k \subset \partial\alpha^i \cap \partial\alpha^j$, where a_{ij}^k joins P_i and P_j and carries the index $\theta(a_{ij}^k) = \theta(A^k)$.

If β-regions are used instead of α-regions, a different graph is obtained from the regular projection. Equivalent knot projections define "equivalent" graphs. (Compare 1.13 and 1.14.) It is easy to prove (E 2.5) that the two graphs of a projection belonging to α- and β-regions are equivalent [Yajima-Kinoshita 1957]. Another Exercise (E 2.3) shows that a projection is alternating if and only if the index function $\theta(A)$ on the double points is a constant (Fig. 2.3).

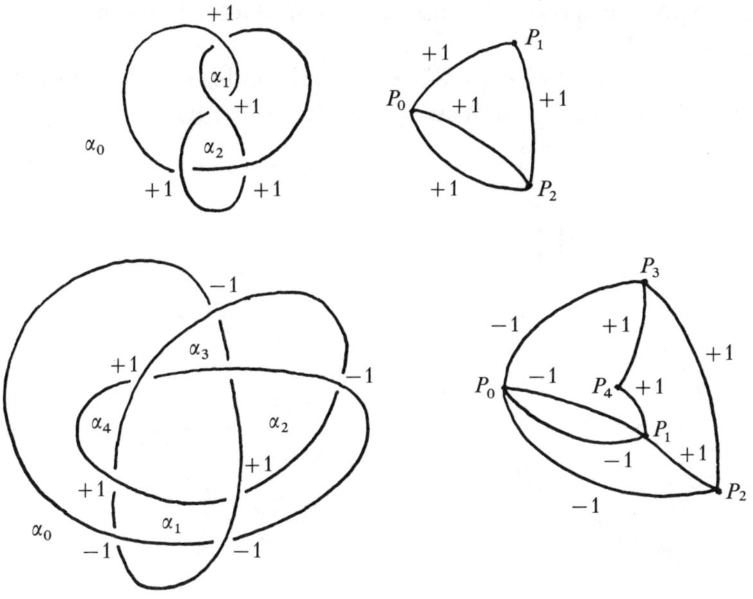

Fig. 2.3

Graphs of knots have been repeatedly employed in knot theory [Aumann 1956], [Crowell 1959], [Kinoshita-Terasaka 1957]. We shall take up the subject again in Chapter 13 in connection with the quadratic form of a knot.

B Seifert Surfaces and Genus

A geometric fact of some consequence is the following:

2.4 Proposition (Seifert surface). *A simple closed curve $\mathfrak{k} \subset \mathbb{R}^3$ is the boundary of an orientable surface S, embedded in $\mathbb{R}^3$. It is called a* Seifert surface.

Proof. Let $p(\mathfrak{k})$ be a regular projection of $\mathfrak{k}$ equipped with an orientation. By altering $p(\mathfrak{k})$ in the neighbourhood of double points as shown in Figure 2.4, $p(\mathfrak{k})$ dissolves into a number of disjoint oriented simple closed curves which are called *Seifert cycles*. Choose an oriented 2-cell for each Seifert cycle, and embed the 2-cells in $\mathbb{R}^3$ as a disjoint union such that their boundaries are projected onto the Seifert cycles. The orientation of a Seifert cycle is to coincide with the orientation induced by the oriented 2-cell. We may place the 2-cells into planes $z = \text{const}$ parallel to the projection plane ($z = 0$), and choose planes $z = a_1$, $z = a_2$ for corresponding Seifert cycles c_1, c_2 with $a_1 < a_2$ if c_1 contains c_2. Now we can undo the cut-and-paste-process described in Figure 2.4 by joining the 2-cells at each double point by twisted bands such as to obtain a connected surface S with $\partial S = \mathfrak{k}$ (see Fig. 2.5).

Since the oriented 2-cells (including the bands) induce the orientation of $\mathfrak{k}$, they are coherently oriented, and hence, S is orientable. □

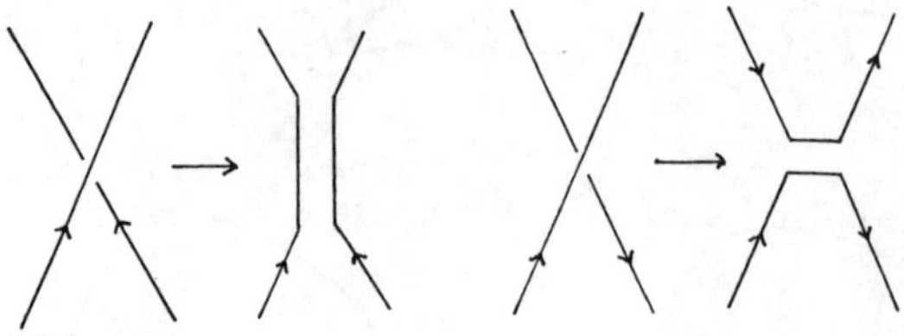

Fig. 2.4

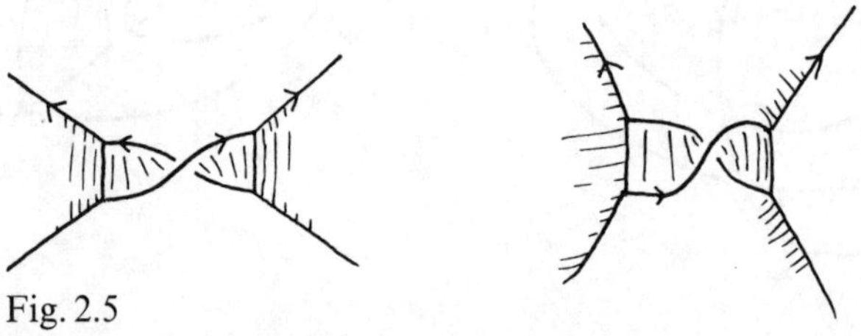

Fig. 2.5

2.5 Definition (genus). The minimal genus g of a Seifert surface spanning a knot $\mathfrak{k}$ is called the *genus of the knot* $\mathfrak{k}$.

Evidently the genus does not depend on the choice of a curve $\mathfrak{k}$ in its equivalence class: If $\mathfrak{k}$ and $\mathfrak{k}'$ are equivalent and S spans $\mathfrak{k}$, then there is a homeomorphism $h: S^3 \to S^3$, $h(\mathfrak{k}) = \mathfrak{k}'$ (Prop. 1.5), and $h(S) = S'$ spans $\mathfrak{k}'$. So the genus $g(\mathfrak{k})$ is a knot invariant. $g(\mathfrak{k}) = 0$ characterizes the trivial knot, because, if $\mathfrak{k}$ bounds a disk D which is embedded in $\mathbb{R}^3$ (or S^3), one can use Δ-moves over 2-simplices of D and reduce $\mathfrak{k}$ to the boundary of a single 2-simplex.

The notion of the genus was first introduced by H. Seifert in [Seifert 1934], it holds a central position in knot theory.

The method to construct a Seifert surface by Seifert cycles assigns a surface S' of genus g' to a given regular projection of a knot. We call g' the *canonical genus associated with the projection.* It is remarkable that in many cases the canonical genus coincides with the (minimal) genus g of the knot. It is always true for alternating projections (13.26(a)). In our table of knot projections up to nine crossings only the projections 8_{20}, 8_{21}, 9_{42}, 9_{44} and 9_{45} fail to yield $g' = g$; in these cases $g' = g + 1$.

This was already observed by H. Seifert; the fact that he lists 9_{46} instead of 9_{44} in [Seifert 1934] is due to the choice of different projections in Rolfsen's (and our table) and Reidemeister's.

There is a general algorithm to determine the genus of a knot [Schubert 1961], but its application is complicated. For other methods see E 4.10.

2.6 Definition and simple properties (meridian and longitude). A tubular neighbourhood $V(\mathfrak{k})$ of a knot $\mathfrak{k} \subset S^3$ is homeomorphic to a solid torus. There is a simple closed curve m on $\partial V(\mathfrak{k})$ which is nullhomologous in $V(\mathfrak{k})$ but not on $\partial V(\mathfrak{k})$; we call m *meridian* of $\mathfrak{k}$. It is easy to see that any two meridians (if suitably oriented) on $\partial V(\mathfrak{k})$ are isotopic. A Seifert surface S will meet $\partial V(\mathfrak{k})$ in a simple closed curve ℓ, if $V(\mathfrak{k})$ is suitably chosen; ℓ is called a *longitude* of $\mathfrak{k}$. We shall see later on (Proposition 3.1) that ℓ, too, is unique up to isotopy on $\partial V(\mathfrak{k})$. If $\mathfrak{k}$ and S^3 are oriented, we may assign orientations to m and ℓ: The longitude ℓ is isotopic to $\mathfrak{k}$ in $V(\mathfrak{k})$ and will be oriented as $\mathfrak{k}$. The meridian will be oriented in such a way that its linking number $lk(m, \mathfrak{k})$ with $\mathfrak{k}$ in S^3 is $+1$ or equivalently, its intersection number $int(m, \ell)$ with ℓ is $+1$. From this it follows that ℓ is not nullhomologous on $\partial V(\mathfrak{k})$.

C Companion Knots and Product Knots

Another important idea was added by H. Schubert [1949]: the *product* of knots.

2.7 Definition (product of knots). Let $\mathfrak{k} \subset \mathbb{R}^3$ meet a plane E in two points P and Q. The arc of $\mathfrak{k}$ from P to Q is closed by an arc in E to obtain a knot $\mathfrak{k}_1$; the other arc (from Q to P) is closed in the same way and so defines a knot $\mathfrak{k}_2$. The knot $\mathfrak{k}$ is called the *product of* $\mathfrak{k}_1$ *and* $\mathfrak{k}_2$, and it is denoted by $\mathfrak{k} = \mathfrak{k}_1 \# \mathfrak{k}_2$; $\mathfrak{k}$ is also called a *composite knot*. $\mathfrak{k}_1$ and $\mathfrak{k}_2$ are called *factors* of $\mathfrak{k}$.

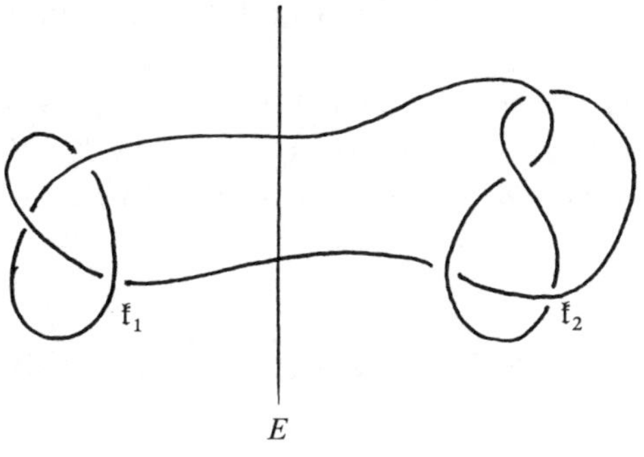

Fig. 2.6

It is easy to see that for any given knots $\mathfrak{k}_1$, $\mathfrak{k}_2$ the product $\mathfrak{k} = \mathfrak{k}_1 \# \mathfrak{k}_2$ can be constructed; the product will not depend on the choice of representatives or on the plane E. A thorough treatment of the subject will be given in Chapter 7.

There are other procedures to construct more complicated knots from simpler ones.

2.8 Definition (companion knot, satellite knot). Let $\tilde{\mathfrak{k}}$ be a knot in a 3-sphere $\tilde{S}^3$ and $\tilde{V}$ an unknotted solid torus in $\tilde{S}^3$ with $\tilde{\mathfrak{k}} \subset \tilde{V} \subset \tilde{S}^3$. Assume that $\tilde{\mathfrak{k}}$ is not contained in a 3-ball of $\tilde{V}$. A homeomorphism $h\colon \tilde{V} \to \hat{V} \subset S^3$ onto a tubular neighbourhood $\hat{V}$ of a non-trivial knot $\hat{\mathfrak{k}} \subset S^3$ which maps a meridian of $\tilde{S}^3$-$\tilde{V}$ onto a longitude of $\hat{\mathfrak{k}}$, maps $\tilde{\mathfrak{k}}$ onto a knot $\mathfrak{k} = h(\tilde{\mathfrak{k}}) \subset S^3$. The knot $\mathfrak{k}$ is called a *satellite* of $\hat{\mathfrak{k}}$, and $\hat{\mathfrak{k}}$ is its *companion* (Begleitknoten). The pair $(\tilde{V}, \tilde{\mathfrak{k}})$ is the *pattern* of $\mathfrak{k}$.

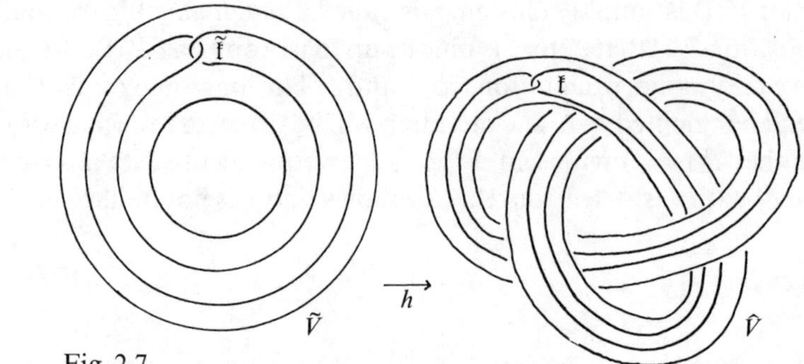

Fig. 2.7

2.9 *Remarks:* The companion is the simple knot, it forgets some of the tangles of its satellite. Each factor $\mathfrak{k}_i$ of a product $\mathfrak{k} = \mathfrak{k}_1 \# \mathfrak{k}_2$, for instance, is a companion of $\mathfrak{k}$. There are some special cases of companion knots: if $\tilde{\mathfrak{k}}$ is ambient isotopic in $\tilde{V}$ to a simple closed curve on $\partial \tilde{V}$, then $\mathfrak{k} = h(\tilde{\mathfrak{k}})$ is called a *cable knot* on $\hat{\mathfrak{k}}$. A cable knot on the trivial knot is called a *torus knot*. As an example consider $\tilde{\mathfrak{k}} \subset \tilde{V}$ as in Figure 2.7. Here the companion $\hat{\mathfrak{k}}$ is a trefoil, the satellite is called the *doubled knot* of $\hat{\mathfrak{k}}$. Doubled knots were introduced by J.H.C. Whitehead in [Whitehead 1937] and form an interesting class of knots with respect to certain algebraic invariants.

There is a relation between the genera of a knot and its companion.

2.10 Proposition (Schubert). *Let $\hat{\mathfrak{k}}$ be a companion of a satellite $\mathfrak{k}$ and $\tilde{\mathfrak{k}} = h^{-1}(\mathfrak{k})$ its preimage (as above). Denote by $\hat{g}, g, \tilde{g}$ the genera of $\hat{\mathfrak{k}}, \mathfrak{k}, \tilde{\mathfrak{k}}$, and by $n \geqq 0$ the linking number of $\tilde{\mathfrak{k}}$ and a meridian $\hat{m}$ of a tubular neighbourhood $\hat{V}$ of $\hat{\mathfrak{k}}$ which contains $\mathfrak{k}$. Then*

$$g \geqq n\hat{g} + \tilde{g}.$$

$g_s \geq n.g_c + g_p$

This result is due to H. Schubert [1953]. We start by proving the following lemma:

2.11 Lemma. *There is a Seifert surface S of minimal genus g spanning the satellite $\mathfrak{k}$ such that $S \cap \partial \hat{V}$ consists of n homologous (on ∂V) longitudes of the companion $\hat{\mathfrak{k}}$. The intersection $S \cap (S^3 - \hat{V})$ consists of n components.*

Proof. Let S be an oriented Seifert surface of minimal genus spanning $\mathfrak{k}$. We assume that S is in general position with respect to $\partial \hat{V}$; that is, $S \cap \partial \hat{V}$ consists of a system of simple closed curves which are pairwise disjoint. If one of them, γ, is nullhomologous on $\partial \hat{V}$, it bounds a disk δ on $\partial \hat{V}$. We may assume that δ does not contain another simple closed curve with this property, $\delta \cap S = \gamma$. Cut S along γ and glue two disks δ_1, δ_2 (parallel to δ) to the curves obtained from γ. Since S was of minimal genus the new surface cannot be connected. Substituting the component containing $\mathfrak{k}$ for S reduces the number of curves. So we may assume that the curves $\{\gamma_1, \dots, \gamma_r\} = S \cap \partial \hat{V}$ are not nullhomologous on the torus $\partial \hat{V}$, hence, they are parallel. The curves are supposed to follow each other on $\partial \hat{V}$ in the natural ordering $\gamma_1, \gamma_2, \dots, \gamma_r$, and to carry the orientation induced by S. If for some index $\gamma_i \sim -\gamma_{i+1}$ on $\partial \hat{V}$ we may cut S along γ_i and γ_{i+1} and glue to the cuts two annuli parallel to one of the annuli on $\partial \hat{V}$ bounded by γ_i and γ_{i+1}. The resulting surface S' may not be connected but the Euler characteristic will remain invariant. Replace S by the component of S' that contains $\mathfrak{k}$. The genus g of S' can only be larger than that of S, if the other component is a sphere. In this case γ_i spans a disk in $\overline{S^3 - \hat{V}}$, and this means that the companion $\hat{\mathfrak{k}}$ is trivial which contradicts its definition. By the cut-and-paste process the pair $\gamma_i \sim -\gamma_{i+1}$ vanishes; so we may assume $\gamma_i \sim \gamma_{i+1}$ for all i. It is $\mathfrak{k} \sim r\gamma_1$ in $\hat{V}$, and $r\gamma_1 \sim 0$ in $\overline{S^3 - \hat{V}}$. We show that $S \cap (\overline{S^3 - \hat{V}})$ consists of r components. If there is a component $\hat{S}$ of $S \cap S^3 - \hat{V}$ with $\hat{r} > 1$ boundary components then there are two curves $\gamma_i, \gamma_j \subset \partial \hat{S}$ such that $\gamma_k \cap \hat{S} = \emptyset$ for $i < k < j$. Connect γ_i and γ_j by a simple arc α in the annulus on $\partial \hat{V}$ bounded by γ_i and γ_j, and join its boundary points by a simple arc λ on $\hat{S}$. A curve u parallel to $\alpha \cup \lambda$ in $S^3 - \hat{V}$ will intersect $\hat{S}$ in one point (Fig. 2.8), $int(u, \hat{S}) = \pm 1$. Since u does not meet $\hat{V}$, we get $\pm 1 = int(u, S) = lk(u, \partial S) = k \cdot \hat{r}$, $k \in \mathbb{Z}$; hence $\hat{r} = 1$, a contradiction.

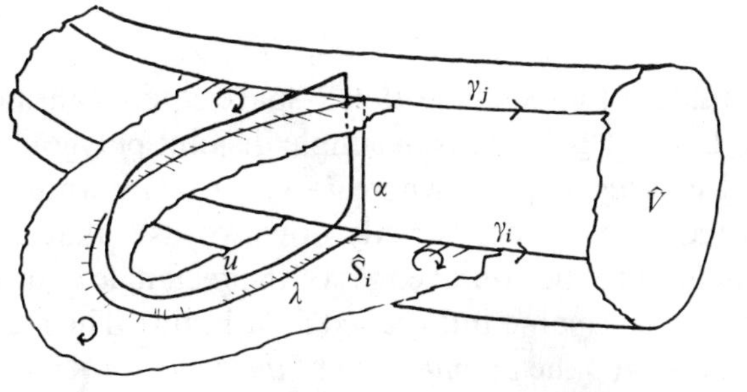

Fig. 2.8

It follows that the γ_i are longitudes; moreover

$$n = lk(\hat{m}, \mathfrak{k}) = lk(\hat{m}, r\gamma_i) = r \cdot lk(\hat{m}, \gamma_i) = r. \qquad \square$$

Proof of Proposition 2.10. Let S be a Seifert surface of $\mathfrak{k}$ according to Lemma 2.11. Each component $\hat{S}_i$ of $S \cap (S^3 - \hat{V})$ is a surface of genus $\hat{h}$ which spans a longitude γ_i of $\hat{\mathfrak{k}}$, hence $\hat{\mathfrak{k}}$ itself. The curves $\tilde{l}_i = \mathrm{h}^{-1}(\gamma_i)$ are longitudes of the unknotted solid torus $\tilde{\mathrm{V}} \subset \tilde{\mathrm{S}}^3$ bounding disjoint disks $\tilde{\delta}_i \subset \tilde{\mathrm{S}}^3 - \tilde{\mathrm{V}}$. Thus $\mathrm{h}^{-1}(\mathrm{S} \cap \hat{\mathrm{V}}) \cup (\bigcup_i \tilde{\delta}_i)$ is a Seifert surface spanning $\tilde{\mathfrak{f}} = \mathrm{h}^{-1}(\mathfrak{k})$. Its genus $\tilde{\mathrm{h}}$ is the genus of $S \cap \hat{V}$. As $S = (S \cap \hat{V}) \cup \bigcup_{i=1}^{n} \hat{S}_i$ we get

$$g = n\hat{h} + \tilde{h} \geqq n\hat{g} + \tilde{g}. \quad \square$$

D Braids, Bridges, Plats

There is a second theme to our main theme of knots, which has developed some weight ot its own: *the theory of braids*. E. Artin invented braids in [Artin 1925], and at the same time solved the problem of their classification. (The proof there is somewhat intuitive, Artin revised it to meet rigorous standards in a later paper [Artin 1947].) We shall occupy ourselves with braids in a special chapter but will introduce here the geometric idea of a braid, because it offers another possibility of representing knots (or links).

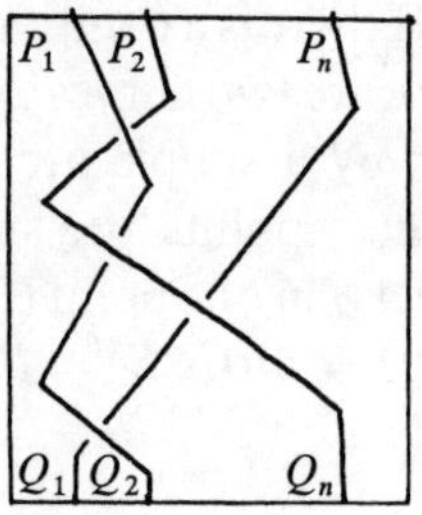

Fig. 2.9

2.12. Place on opposite sides of a rectangle R in 3-space equidistant points P_i, Q_i, $1 \leqq i \leqq n$, (Fig. 2.9). Let f_i, $1 \leqq i \leqq n$, be n simple disjoint polygonal arcs in $\mathbb{R}^3$, f_i starting in P_i and ending in $Q_{\pi(i)}$, where $i \mapsto \pi(i)$ is a permutation on $\{1, 2, \dots, n\}$. The f_i are required to run "strictly downwords", that is, each f_i meets any plane perpendicular to the lateral edges of the rectangle at most once. The strings f_i constitute a *braid* $\mathfrak{z}$ (sometimes called an n-braid). The rectangle is called the *frame* of $\mathfrak{z}$, and $i \mapsto \pi(i)$ the *permutation of the braid*. In $\mathbb{R}^3$, *equivalent*

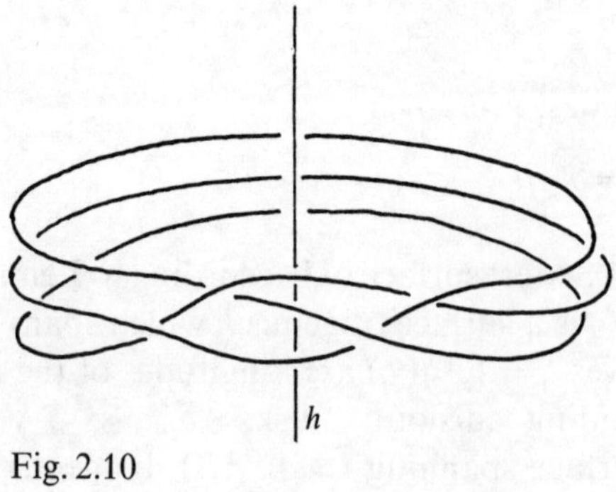

Fig. 2.10

or *isotopic braids* will be defined by "level preserving" isotopies of $\mathbb{R}^3$ relative to the endpoints $\{P_i\}$, $\{Q_i\}$, which will be kept fixed, but we defer a treatment of these questions to Chapter 10.

A *braid* can be *closed* with respect to an *axis* h (Fig. 2.10). In this way every braid $\mathfrak{z}$ defines a *closed* braid $\hat{\mathfrak{z}}$ which represents a link of μ components, where μ is the number of cycles of the permutation of $\mathfrak{z}$. We shall prove that every link can be presented as a closed braid. This mode of presentation is connected with another notion introduced by Schubert: the bridge-number of a knot (resp. link):

2.13 Definition (bridge-number). Let $\mathfrak{k}$ be a knot (or link) in $\mathbb{R}^3$ which meets a plane $E \subset \mathbb{R}^3$ in $2m$ points such that the arcs of $\mathfrak{k}$ contained in each halfspace relative to E possess orthogonal projections onto E which are simple and disjoint. $(\mathfrak{k}, E)$ is called an *m-bridge presentation* of $\mathfrak{k}$; the minimal number m possible for a knot $\mathfrak{k}$ is called its *bridge-number.*

A regular projection $p(\mathfrak{k})$ of order n (see 1.11) admits an n-bridge presentation relative to the plane of projection (Fig. 2.11a). (If $p(\mathfrak{k})$ is not alternating, the number of bridges will even be smaller than n). The trivial knot is the only 1-bridge knot. The 2-bridge knots are an important class of knots which were classified by H. Schubert [1956]. Even 3-bridge knots defy classification up to this day.

2.14 Proposition (J.W. Alexander [1923′]). *A link* $\mathfrak{k}$ *can be represented by a closed braid.*

Proof. Choose $2m$ points P_i in a regular projection $p(\mathfrak{k})$, one on each arc between undercrossing and overcrossing (or vice versa). This defines an m-bridge presentation, $m \leqq n$, with arcs s_i, $1 \leqq i \leqq m$, between P_{2i-1} and P_{2i} in the upper halfspace

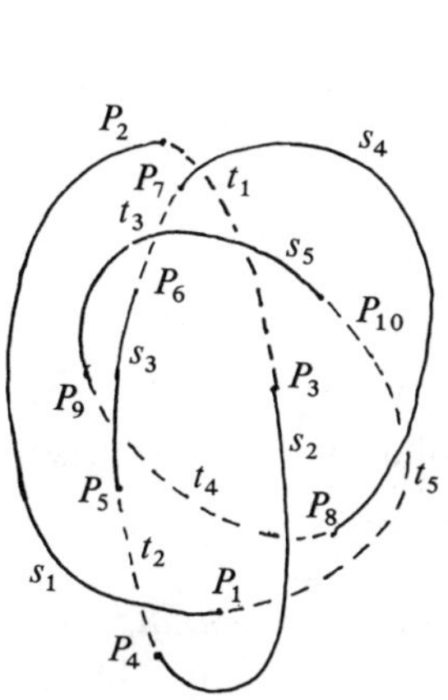

Fig. 2.11 a

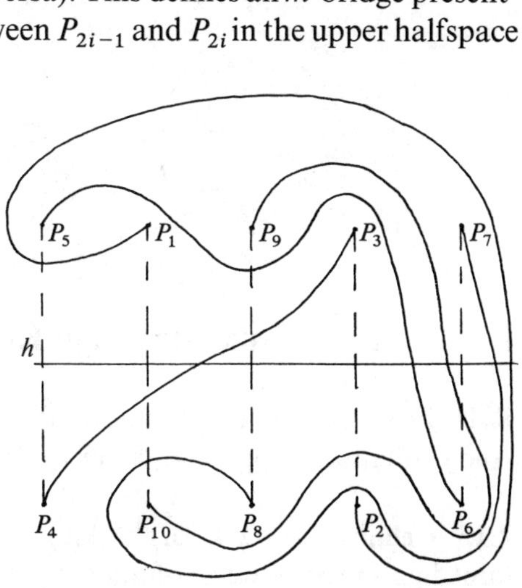

Fig. 2.11 b

and arcs t_i, $1 \leqq i \leqq m$, joining P_{2i} and P_{2i+1} ($P_{2m+1} = P_1$) in the lower halfspace of the projection plane (see Fig. 2.11a).

By an ambient isotopy of $\mathfrak{k}$ we arrange the $p(t_i)$ to form m parallel straight segments bisected by a common perpendicular line h such that all P_i with odd index are on one side of h (Fig. 2.11b). The arc $p(s_i)$ meets h in an odd number of points $P_{i1}, P_{i2}, \ldots$.

In the neighbourhood of a point P_{i2} we introduce a new bridge – we push the arc s_i in this neighbourhood from the upper halfspace into the lower one. Thus we obtain a bridge presentation where every arc $p(s_i)$, $p(t_i)$ meets h in exactly one point. Now choose s_i monotonical ascending over $p(s_i)$ from P_{2i-1} until h is reached, then descending to P_{2i}. Equivalently, the t_i begin by descending and ascend afterwards. The result is a closed braid with axis h. □

A $2m$-braid completed by $2m$ simple arcs to make a link as depicted in Figure 2.12 is called a *plat* or a *2m-plat*. A closed m-braid obviously is a special $2m$-plat, hence every link can be represented as a plat. The construction used in the proof of Proposition 2.14 can be modified to show that an m-bridge representation of a knot $\mathfrak{k}$ can be used to construct a $2m$-plat representing it. In Lemma 10.4 we prove the converse: *Every 2m-plat allows an m-bridge presentation. The 2-bridge knots (and links) hence are the 4-plats (Viergeflechte).*

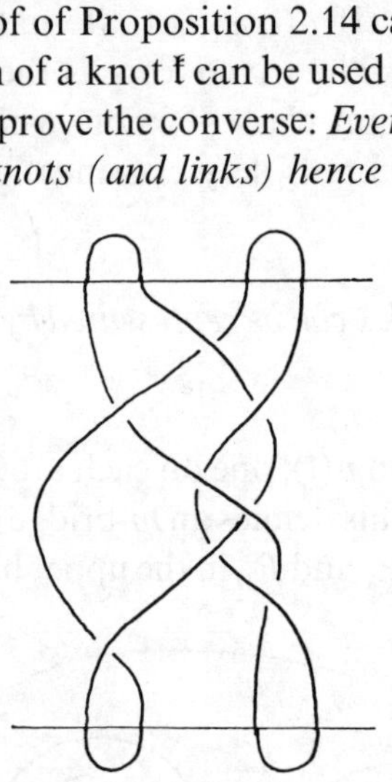

Fig. 2.12

E Slice Knots and Algebraic Knots

R.H. Fox and J. Milnor introduced the notion of a slice knot. It arises from the study of embeddings $S^2 \subset S^4$ [Fox 1962].

2.15 Definition (slice knot). A knot $\mathfrak{k} \subset \mathbb{R}^3$ is called a *slice knot* if it can be obtained as a cross section of a locally flat 2-sphere S^2 in $\mathbb{R}^4$ by a hyperplane $\mathbb{R}^3$. ($S^2 \subset \mathbb{R}^4$ is *embedded locally flat*, if it is locally a Cartesian factor.)

The local flatness is essential: Any knot $\mathfrak{k} \subset \mathbb{R}^3 \subset \mathbb{R}^4$ is a cross section of a 2-sphere S^2 embedded in $\mathbb{R}^4$. Choose the double suspension of $\mathfrak{k}$ with suspension points P_+ and P_- respectively in the halfspace $\mathbb{R}^4_+$ and $\mathbb{R}^4_-$ defined by $\mathbb{R}^3$. The suspension S^2 is not locally flat at P_+ and P_-, (Fig. 2.13).

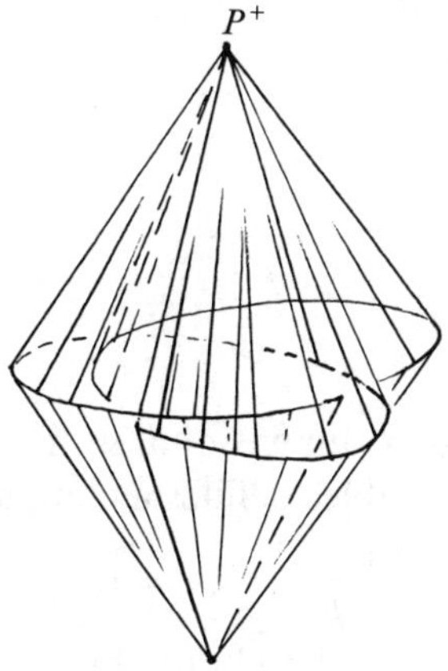

Fig. 2.13

There is a disk $D^2 = S^2 \cap \mathbb{R}^4_+$ spanning the knot $\mathfrak{k} = \partial D^2$ which will be locally flat if and only if S^2 can be chosen locally flat. This leads to an equivalent definition of slice knots:

2.16 Definition. A knot $\mathfrak{k}$ in the boundary of a 4-cell, $\mathfrak{k} \subset S^3 = \partial D^4$, is a *slice knot*, if there is a locally flat 2-disk $D^2 \subset D^4$, $\partial D^2 = \mathfrak{k}$, whose tubular neighbourhood intersects S^3 in a tubular neighbourhood of $\mathfrak{k}$.

The last condition ensures that the intersection of $\mathbb{R}^3$ and D^2 resp. S^2 is transversal. We shall give some examples of knots that are *slice* and of some that are not.

Let $f: D^2 \to S^3$ be an immersion, and $\partial(f(D)) = \mathfrak{k}$ a knot. If the singularities of $f(D)$ are all double lines σ, $f^{-1}(\sigma) = \sigma_1 \cup \sigma_2$, such that at least one of the preimages σ_i, $1 \leqq i \leqq 2$, is contained in $\mathring{D}$, then $\mathfrak{k}$ is called a *ribbon knot*.

2.17 Proposition. *Ribbon knots are slice knots.*

Proof. Double lines with boundary singularities come in two types: The type required in a ribbon knot is shown in Figure 2.14 while the second type is depicted in Figure 1.12. In the case of a ribbon knot the hatched regions of $f(D)$ can be pushed into the fourth dimension without changing the knot $\mathfrak{k}$. □

It is not known whether all slice knots are ribbon knots. – There are several criteria which allow one to decide that a certain knot cannot be a slice knot [Fox-Milnor 1966], [Murasugi 1965]. The trefoil, for instance, is not a slice knot. In fact, of all knots of order $\leqq 7$ the knot 6_1 of Figure 2.14 is the only one which is a slice knot.

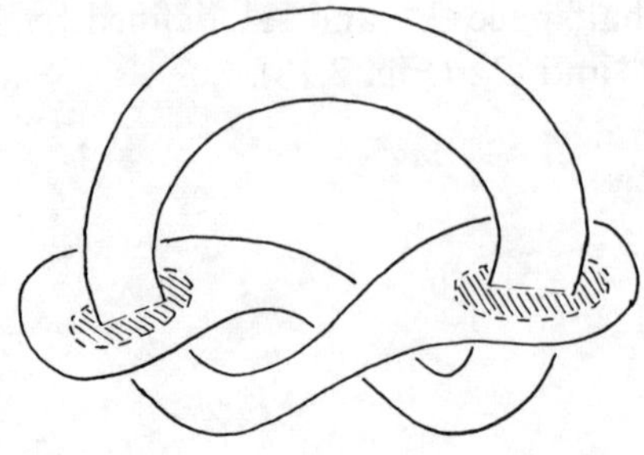

Fig. 2.14

Knots turn up in connection with another higher-dimensional setting: a polynomial equation $f(z_1, z_2) = 0$ in two complex variables defines a complex curve C in $\mathbb{C}^2$. At a singular point $z_0 = (\mathring{z}_1, \mathring{z}_2)$, where $\left(\frac{\partial f}{\partial z_i}\right)_{z_0} = 0$, $i = 1, 2$, consider a small 3-sphere S_ε^3 with centre z_0. Then $\mathfrak{k} = C \cap S_\varepsilon^3$ may be a knot or link. (If z_0 is a regular point of C, the knot $\mathfrak{k}$ is always trivial.)

2.18 Proposition. *The algebraic surface* $f(z_1, z_2) = z_1^a + z_2^b = 0$, $a, b \in \mathbb{Z}$, $a, b \geqq 2$, *intersects the boundary* S_ε^3 *of a spherical neighbourhood of* $(0, 0)$ *in a torus knot (or link)* $\mathfrak{t}(a, b)$, see 3.26.

Proof. The equations

$$r_1^a e^{ia\Phi_1} = r_2^b e^{ib\Phi_2 + i\pi}, \quad r_1^2 + r_2^2 = \varepsilon^2, \quad z_j = r_j e^{i\Phi_j},$$

define the intersection $S_\varepsilon^3 \cap C$. Since $r_1^2 + r_1^{\frac{2a}{b}}$ is monotone, there are unique solutions $r_i = \varrho_i > 0$, $i = 1, 2$. Thus the points of the intersection lie on $\{(z_1, z_2) \mid |z_1| = \varrho_1, |z_2| = \varrho_2\}$, which is an unknotted torus in S_ε^3. Furthermore $a\Phi_1 \equiv b\Phi_2 + \pi \bmod 2\pi$ so that $S_\varepsilon^3 \cap C = \{(\varrho_1 e^{ib\Phi}, \varrho_2 e^{ia\Phi + \frac{\pi i}{b}})\} = \mathfrak{t}(a, b)$. □

Knots that arise in this way at isolated singular points of algebraic curves are called *algebraic knots*. They are known to be *iterated torus knots*, that is, knots or links that are obtained by a repeated cabling process starting from the trivial knot. See [Milnor 1968], [Hacon 1976].

F History and Sources

To regard and treat a knot as an object of elementary geometry in 3-space was a natural attitude in the beginning, but proved to be very limited in its success.

Nevertheless direct geometric approaches occasionally were quite fruitful and inspiring. H. Brunn [1897] prepared a link in a way which practically resulted in J.W. Alexander's theorem [Alexander 1923′] that every link can be deformed into a closed braid. The braids themselves were only invented by E. Artin in [Artin 1925] after closed braids were already in existence. H. Seifert then brought into knot theory the fundamental concept of the genus of a knot [Seifert 1934]. Another simple geometric idea led to the product of knots [Schubert 1949], and H. Schubert afterwards introduced and studied the theory of companions [Schubert 1953], and the notion of the bridge number of a knot [Schubert 1954]. Finally R.H. Fox and J. Milnor suggested looking at a knot from a 4-dimensional point of view which produced the slice knots [Fox 1962].

During the last decade geometric methods have gained importance in knot theory – but they are, as a rule, no longer elementary.

G Exercises

E 2.1 Show that the trefoil is symmetric, and that the four-knot is both symmetric and amphicheiral.

E 2.2 Let $p(\mathfrak{k}) \subset E^2$ be a regular projection of a link $\mathfrak{k}$. The plane E^2 can be coloured with two colours in such a way that regions with a common arc of $p(\mathfrak{k})$ in their boundary obtain different colours (chess-board colouring).

E 2.3 A knot projection is alternating if and only if $\theta(A)$ (see 2.3) is constant.

E 2.4 Describe the operations on graphs associated to knot projections which correspond to the Reidemeister operations Ω_i, $i = 1, 2, 3$.

E 2.5 Show that the two graphs associated to the regular projection of a knot by distinguishing either α-regions or β-regions are equivalent. (See Definition 2.3).

E 2.6 A regular projection $p(\mathfrak{k})$ (onto S^2) of a knot $\mathfrak{k}$ defines two surfaces F_1, $F_2 \subset S^3$ spanning $\mathfrak{k} = \partial F_1 = \partial F_2$ where $p(F_1)$ and $p(F_2)$ respectively cover the regions coloured by the same colour of a chess-board colouring of $p(\mathfrak{k})$ (see E 2.2). Prove that at least one of the surfaces F_1, F_2 is non-orientable.

E 2.7 Construct an orientable surface of genus one spanning the four-knot 4_1.

E 2.8 Give a presentation of the knot 6_3 as a 3-braid.

E 2.9 In Definition 2.7 the following condition was imposed on the knot $\tilde{\mathfrak{k}}$ embedded in the solid torus $\tilde{V}$:

(1) There is no ball $\tilde{B}$ such that $\tilde{\mathfrak{k}} \subset \tilde{B} \subset \tilde{V}$.

Show that (1) is equivalent to each of the following two conditions.

(2) $\tilde{\mathfrak{k}}$ intersects every disk $\delta \subset \tilde{V}$, $\partial\delta = \delta \cap \partial\tilde{V}$, $\partial\delta$ not contractible in $\partial\tilde{V}$.

(3) $\pi_1(\partial\tilde{V}) \to \pi_1(\tilde{V} - \tilde{\mathfrak{k}})$, induced by the inclusion, is injective.

Chapter 3: Knot Groups

As one would expect, the complement of a knot is a strong invariant of the knot. A classification could be attempted using the tools of algebraic topology but, unfortunately, homological methods are not helpful. The fundamental group, however, is very effective and we will develop methods to present and study it. In particular, we will use it to show that there are non-trivial knots.

A Homology

$V = V(\mathfrak{k})$ denotes a tubular neighbourhood of the knot $\mathfrak{k}$ and $C = \overline{S^3 - V}$ is called the *complement* of the knot. H_j will denote the (singular) homology with coefficients in $\mathbb{Z}$.

3.1 Theorem (homological properties).

(a) $H_0(C) \cong H_1(C) \cong \mathbb{Z}$,

$H_n(C) = 0$ *for* $n \geqq 2$.

(b) There are two simple closed curves m *and* ℓ *on* $\dot{V}$ *with the following properties:*

(1) m *and* ℓ *intersect in one point,*

(2) $m \sim 0$, $\ell \sim \mathfrak{k}$ *in* $V(\mathfrak{k})$,

(3) $\ell \sim 0$ *in* $C = \overline{S^3 - V(\mathfrak{k})}$,

(4) $lk(m, \mathfrak{k}) = 1$ *and* $lk(\ell, \mathfrak{k}) = 0$ *in* S^3.

These properties determine m *and* ℓ *up to isotopy on* $\dot{V}(\mathfrak{k})$. *We call* m *a* meridian *and* ℓ *a* longitude *of the knot* $\mathfrak{k}$. *The knot* $\mathfrak{k}$ *and the longitude* ℓ *bound an annulus* $A \subset V$.

Proof. For (a) there are several proofs. Here we present one based on homological methods. We use the following well known results:

$$H_n(S^3) = \begin{cases} \mathbb{Z} & \text{for } n = 0,3, \\ 0 & \text{otherwise}, \end{cases}$$

$$H_n(\dot{V}) = \begin{cases} \mathbb{Z} & \text{for } n = 0, 2, \\ \mathbb{Z} \oplus \mathbb{Z} & \text{for } n = 1, \\ 0 & \text{otherwise}, \end{cases}$$

$$H_n(V) = H_n(S^1) = \begin{cases} \mathbb{Z} & \text{for } n = 0, 1, \\ 0 & \text{otherwise}; \end{cases}$$

they can be found in standard books on algebraic topology, see [Spanier 1966], [Stöcker-Zieschang 1985].

Since C is connected, $H_0(C) = \mathbb{Z}$. For further calculations we use the Mayer-Vietoris sequence of the pair (V, C) where $V \cup C = S^3$, $V \cap C = \dot{V}$:

$$\begin{array}{ccccccccc} 0 = H_3(\dot{V}) \to & H_3(V) \oplus H_3(C) & \to & H_3(S^3) & \to & H_2(\dot{V}) & \to & H_2(V) \oplus H_2(C) \\ & \| & & \wr\| & & \wr\| & & \| \\ & 0 & & \mathbb{Z} & & \mathbb{Z} & & 0 \end{array}$$

$$\begin{array}{cccccc} \to H_2(S^3) & \to & H_1(\dot{V}) & \to & H_1(V) \oplus H_1(C) & \to H_1(S^3) = 0. \\ \| & & \wr\| & & \wr\| & \\ 0 & & \mathbb{Z} \oplus \mathbb{Z} & & \mathbb{Z} & \end{array}$$

It follows that $H_1(C) = \mathbb{Z}$. Since $\dot{V}$ is the boundary of the orientable compact 3-manifold C, the group $H_2(\dot{V})$ is mapped by the inclusion $\dot{V} \hookrightarrow C$ to $0 \in H_2(C)$. This implies that $H_2(C) = 0$ and that $H_3(S^3) \to H_2(\dot{V})$ is surjective; hence, $H_3(C) = 0$.

Since C is a 3-manifold it follows that $H_n(C) = 0$ for $n > 3$; this is also a consequence of the Mayer-Vietoris sequence.

Consider the isomorphism

$$\mathbb{Z} \oplus \mathbb{Z} \cong H_1(\dot{V}) \to H_1(V) \oplus H_1(C)$$

in the Mayer-Vietoris sequence. The generators of $H_1(V) \cong \mathbb{Z}$ and $H_1(C) \cong \mathbb{Z}$ are determined up to their inverses. Choose the homology class of $\mathfrak{k}$ as a generator of $H_1(V)$ and represent it by a simple closed curve ℓ on $\dot{V}$ which is homologous to 0 in $H_1(C)$. These conditions determine the homology class of ℓ in $\dot{V}$; hence, ℓ is unique up to isotopy on $\dot{V}$. A generator of $H_1(C)$ can be represented by a curve m on $\dot{V}$ that is homologous to 0 in V. The curves ℓ and m determine a system of generators of $H_1(\dot{V}) \cong \mathbb{Z} \oplus \mathbb{Z}$. By a well known result, we may assume that m is simple and intersects ℓ in one point, see e.g. [Stillwell 1980, 6.4.3], [ZVC 1980, E 3.22]. As m is homologous to 0 in V it is nullhomotopic in V, bounds a disk, and is a meridian of the solid torus V. The linking number of m and $\mathfrak{k}$ is 1 or -1. If necessary we reverse the direction of m to get (4). These properties determine m up to an isotopy of $\dot{V}$. A consequence is that ℓ and $\mathfrak{k}$ bound an annulus $A \subset V$.

Since $\ell \sim 0$ in C, ℓ bounds a surface, possibly with singularities, in C. (As we already know, see Proposition 2.4, ℓ even spans a surface without singularities: a Seifert surface.) □

Theorem 3.1 can be generalized to links (E 3.2). The negative aspect of the theorem is that complements of knots cannot be distinguished by their homological properties.

3.2 On the characterization of longitudes and meridians by the complement of a knot. With respect to the complement C of a knot the longitude ℓ and the meridian m have quite different properties: The longitude ℓ is determined up to isotopy and orientation by C; this follows from the fact that ℓ is a simple closed curve on $\dot{C}$ which is not homologous to 0 on $\dot{C}$ but homologous to 0 in C. The meridian m is a simple closed curve on $\dot{C}$ that intersects ℓ in one point; hence, ℓ and m represent generators of $H_1(C) \cong \mathbb{Z}^2$. The meridian is not determined by C because simple closed curves on $\dot{C}$ which are homologous to $m^{\pm 1}\ell^r$, $r \in \mathbb{Z}$, have the same properties (see E 3.3(a)).

If we attach a solid torus W to C identifying the boundaries of C and W by a homeomorphism such that a meridian of W is mapped onto $m^{\pm 1}\ell^r$, we obtain an orientable closed manifold M. Is $M \cong S^3$? If so, for some $r \neq 0$, we might obtain 'essentially' different knots with homeomorphic complements. For $r = 0$ there are the cases where the orientation of the knot is inverted or the knot is replaced by its mirror – image (see Definition 2.1). Other examples of knots with homeomorphic complements are not known. However, there are examples of different links with homeomorphic complements. For many knots (torus knots, twist knots, product knots, satellites) it is known that the complement determines the knot type. We will discuss this problem in Chapter 15.

B Wirtinger Presentation

The most important and effective invariant of a knot $\mathfrak{k}$ (or link) is its *group*: the fundamental group of its complement $\mathfrak{G} = \pi_1(S^3 - \mathfrak{k})$. Frequently $S^3 - \mathfrak{k}$ is replaced by $\mathbb{R}^3 - \mathfrak{k}$ or by $\overline{S^3 - V(\mathfrak{k})}$ or $\overline{\mathbb{R}^3 - V(\mathfrak{k})}$, respectively. The fundamental groups of these various spaces are obviously isomorphic, the isomorphisms being induced by inclusion.

There is a simple procedure, due to Wirtinger, to obtain a presentation of a knot group.

3.3 Embed the knot $\mathfrak{k}$ into $\mathbb{R}^3$ such that its projection onto the plane $z = 0$ is regular. The projecting cylinder Z has self-intersections in n projecting rays a_i corresponding to the n double points of the regular projection. The a_i decompose Z into n 2-cells Z_i (see Fig. 3.1) where Z_i is bounded by a_{i-1}, a_i and the overcrossing arc σ_i of $\mathfrak{k}$. Choose the orientation of Z_i to induce on σ_i the direction of $\mathfrak{k}$. The complement of Z can be retracted parallel to the rays onto a halfspace above the knot; thus it is contractible.

To compute $\pi_1 C$ for some base point $P \in C$ observe that there is (up to a homotopy fixing P) exactly one polygonal closed path in general position relative to Z which intersects a given Z_i with intersection number ε_i and which does not intersect the other Z_j. *Paths of this type, taken for* $i = 1, 2, \ldots, n$ *and* $\varepsilon_i = 1$, *represent generators* $s_i \in \pi_1 C$. To see this, let a path in general position with respect to Z represent an arbitrary element of $\pi_1 C$. Move its intersection points with Z_i into the intersection of the curve s_i. Now the assertion follows from the contractibility of the complement of Z. Running through an arbitrary closed polygonal path ω yields the homotopy class as a word $w(s_i) = s_{i_1}^{\varepsilon_1} \dots s_{i_r}^{\varepsilon_r}$ if in turn each intersection with Z_{i_j} and intersection number ε_j is put down by writing $s_{i_j}^{\varepsilon_j}$.

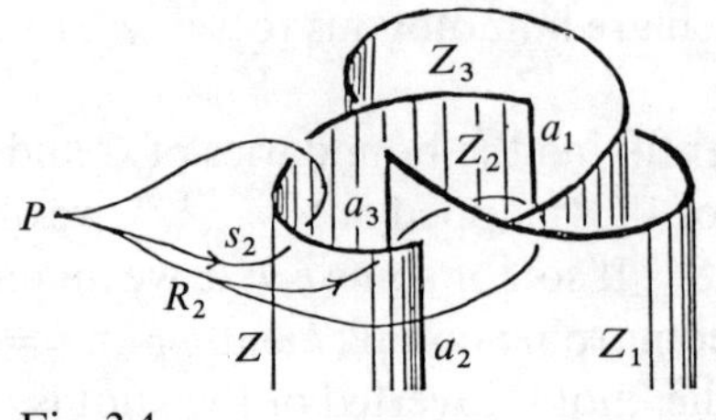

Fig. 3.1

To obtain relators, consider a small path ϱ_j in C encircling a_j and join it with P by an arc λ_j. Then $\lambda_j \varrho_j \lambda_j^{-1}$ is contractible and the corresponding word $l_j r_j l_j^{-1}$ in the generators s_i is a relator. The word $r_j(s_j)$ can easily be read off from the knot projection. According to the caracteristic $\eta \in \{1, -1\}$ of a double point, see Figure 3.2, we get the relator

$$r_j = s_j s_i^{-\eta_j} s_k^{-1} s_i^{\eta_j}.$$

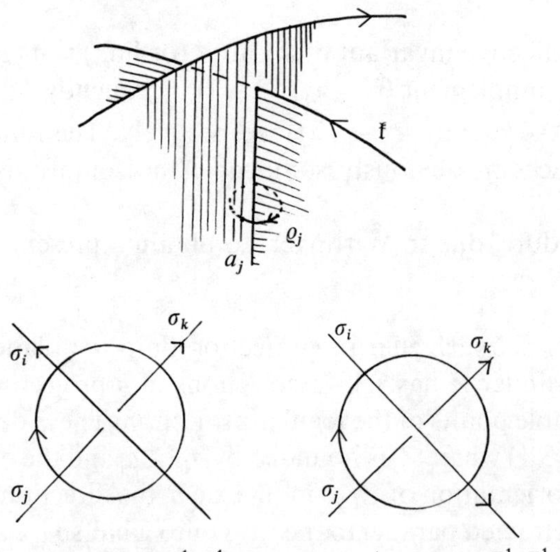

$\eta_j = +1 \quad r_j = s_j s_i^{-1} s_k^{-1} s_i \qquad \eta_j = -1 \quad r_j = s_j s_i s_k^{-1} s_i^{-1}$

Fig. 3.2

3.4 Theorem (Wirtinger presentation). *Let σ_i, $i = 1, 2, \dots, n$, be the overcrossing arcs of a regular projection of a knot (or link) $\mathfrak{k}$. Then the knot group admits the following so-called* Wirtinger presentation:

$$\mathfrak{G} = \pi_1(\overline{S^3 - V(\mathfrak{k})}) = \langle s_1, \ldots, s_n | r_1, \ldots, r_n \rangle .$$

The arc σ_i corresponds to the generator s_i; a crossing of characteristic η_j as in Figure 3.2 gives rise to the defining relator

$$r_j = s_j s_i^{-\eta_j} s_k^{-1} s_i^{\eta_j} .$$

Proof. It remains to check that $r_1, \ldots, r_n$ are defining relations. Consider $\mathbb{R}^3$ as a simplicial complex Σ containing Z as a subcomplex, and denote by Σ^* the dual complex. Let ω be a contractible curve in C, starting at a vertex P of Σ^*. By simplicial approximation ω can be replaced by a path in the 1-skeleton of Σ^* and the contractible homotopy by a series of homotopy moves which replace arcs on the boundary of 2-cells σ^2 of Σ^* by the inverse of the rest. If $\sigma^2 \cap Z = \emptyset$ the deformation over σ^2 has no effect on the words $w(s_i)$. If σ^2 meets Z in an arc then the deformation over σ^2 either cancels or inserts a word $s_i^\varepsilon s_i^{-\varepsilon}$, $\varepsilon \in \{1, -1\}$, in $w(s_i)$; hence, it does not effect the element of $\pi_1 C$ represented by ω. If σ^2 intersects a double line a_j then the deformation over σ^2 omits or inserts a relator: a conjugate of r_j or r_j^{-1} for some j. □

In the case of a link $\mathfrak{k}$ of μ components the relations ensure that generators s_i and s_j are conjugate if the corresponding arcs σ_i and σ_j belong to the same component. By abelianizing $\mathfrak{G} = \pi_1(S^3 - \mathfrak{k})$ we obtain from 3.4, see also E 3.2:

Proposition 3.5 *$H_1(S^3 - \mathfrak{k}) \cong \mathbb{Z}^\mu$ where μ is the number of components of $\mathfrak{k}$.* □

Using 3.5 and duality theorems for homology and cohomology one can calculate the other homology groups of $S^3 - \mathfrak{k}$, see E 3.2.

3.6 Corollary. *Let $\mathfrak{k}$ be a knot or link and $\langle s_1, \ldots, s_n | r_1, \ldots, r_n \rangle$ a Wirtinger presentation of $\mathfrak{G}$. Then each defining relation r_j is a consequence of the other defining relations r_i, $i \neq j$.*

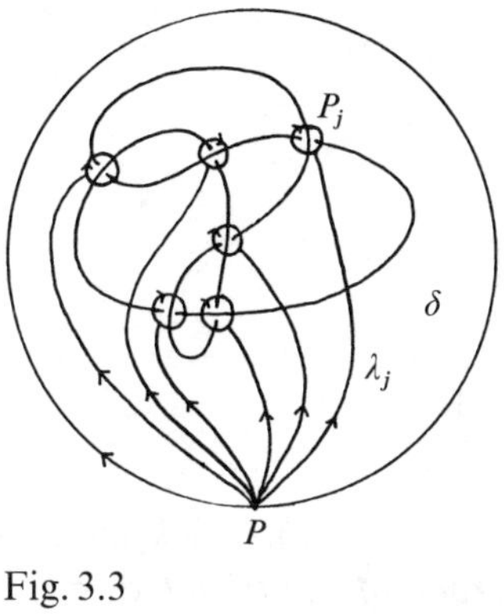

Fig. 3.3

Proof. Choose the curves $\lambda_j \varrho_j \lambda_j^{-1}$ (see the paragraph before Theorem 3.4) in a plane E parallel to the projection plane and "far down" such that E intersects all a_i. Let δ be a disk in E such that $\mathfrak{k}$ is projected into δ, and let γ be the boundary of δ. We assume that P is on γ and that the λ_j have only the basepoint P in common. Then, see Figure 3.3,

$$\gamma \simeq \prod_{j=1}^{n} \lambda_j \varrho_j \lambda_j^{-1} \quad \text{in } E - (\bigcup_j a_j \cap E).$$

This implies the equation

$$1 \equiv \prod_{j=1}^{n} l_j r_j l_j^{-1}$$

in the free group generated by the s_i, where l_j is the word which corresponds to λ_j. Thus each relator r_j is a consequence of the other relators. □

3.7 Example (trefoil knot = clover leaf knot).

From Figure 3.4 we obtain Wirtinger generators s_1, s_2, s_3 and defining relators

$$\begin{aligned} &s_1 s_2 s_3^{-1} s_2^{-1} && \text{at the vertex } A,\\ &s_2 s_3 s_1^{-1} s_3^{-1} && \text{at the vertex } B,\\ &s_3 s_1 s_2^{-1} s_1^{-1} && \text{at the vertex } C. \end{aligned}$$

Since, by 3.6, one relation is a consequence of the other two the knot group has the presentation

$$\begin{aligned} \langle s_1, s_2, s_3 \mid s_1 s_2 s_3^{-1} s_2^{-1}, s_3 s_1 s_2^{-1} s_1^{-1} \rangle &= \langle s_1, s_2 \mid s_1 s_2 s_1 s_2^{-1} s_1^{-1} s_2^{-1} \rangle \\ &= \langle x, y \mid x^3 y^2 \rangle \end{aligned}$$

where $y = s_2^{-1} s_1^{-1} s_2^{-1}$ and $x = s_1 s_2$. This group is not isomorphic to $\mathbb{Z}$, since the last presentation shows that it is a free product with amalgamated subgroup $\mathfrak{A}_1 *_{\mathfrak{B}} \mathfrak{A}_2$ where $\mathfrak{A}_i \cong \mathbb{Z}$ and $\mathfrak{B} = \langle x^3 \rangle = \langle y^{-2} \rangle$ with $\mathfrak{B} \subsetneq \mathfrak{A}_i$. Hence it is not commutative. This can also be shown directly using the representation

$$\mathfrak{G} \to SL_2(\mathbb{Z}), \quad x \mapsto \begin{pmatrix} 0 & 1 \\ -1 & 1 \end{pmatrix}, \quad y \mapsto \begin{pmatrix} 0 & 1 \\ -1 & 0 \end{pmatrix}$$

since

$$\begin{pmatrix} 0 & 1 \\ -1 & 1 \end{pmatrix} \cdot \begin{pmatrix} 0 & 1 \\ -1 & 0 \end{pmatrix} = \begin{pmatrix} -1 & 0 \\ -1 & -1 \end{pmatrix}$$
$$\neq \begin{pmatrix} -1 & 1 \\ 0 & -1 \end{pmatrix} = \begin{pmatrix} 0 & 1 \\ -1 & 0 \end{pmatrix} \cdot \begin{pmatrix} 0 & 1 \\ -1 & 1 \end{pmatrix}.$$

The reader should note that here for the first time in this book the existence of non-trivial knots has been proved, since the group of the trivial knot is cyclic.

We can approach the analysis of the group of the trefoil knot in a different manner by calculating its commutator subgroup using the Reidemeister-Schreier method. It turns out that $\mathfrak{G}'$ is a free group of rank 2, see E 4.2. We will use this method in the next example.

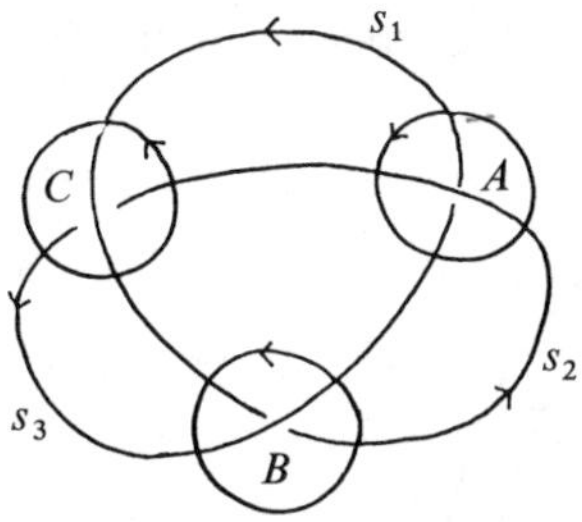

Fig. 3.4

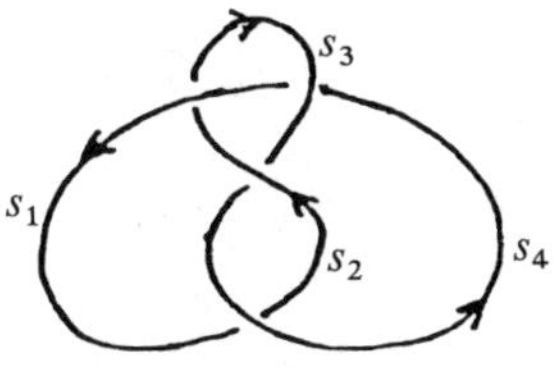

Fig. 3.5

3.8 Example (four-knot or figure eight knot), (Figure 3.5).

$$\begin{aligned}\mathfrak{G} &= \langle s_1, s_2, s_3, s_4 \mid s_3 s_4^{-1} s_3^{-1} s_1, s_1 s_2^{-1} s_1^{-1} s_3, s_4 s_2^{-1} s_3^{-1} s_2\rangle \\ &= \langle s_1, s_3 \mid s_3^{-1} s_1 s_3 s_1^{-1} s_3^{-1} s_1 s_3^{-1} s_1^{-1} s_3 s_1\rangle \\ &= \langle s, u \mid u^{-1} s u s^{-1} u^{-2} s^{-1} u s\rangle, \quad \text{where} \quad s = s_1 \quad \text{and} \quad u = s_1^{-1} s_3.\end{aligned}$$

The abelianizing homomorphism $\mathfrak{G} \to \mathfrak{Z}$ maps s onto a generator of $\mathfrak{Z}$ and u onto 0. Hence, $\{s^n \mid n \in \mathbb{Z}\}$ is a system of coset representatives and $\{x_n = s^n u s^{-n} \mid n \in \mathbb{Z}\}$ the correponding system of Schreier generators for the commutator subgroup $\mathfrak{G}'$ (see [ZVC 1980, 2.2]). The defining relations are

$$r_n = s^n (u^{-1} s u s^{-1} u^{-2} s^{-1} u s) s^{-n} = x_n^{-1} x_{n+1} x_n^{-2} x_{n-1}, \quad n \in \mathbb{Z}.$$

Using r_1, we obtain

$$x_2 = x_1 x_0^{-1} x_1^{+2};$$

hence, we may drop the generator x_2 and the relation r_1. Next we consider r_2 and obtain

$$x_3 = x_2 x_1^{-1} x_2^{+2}$$

and replace x_2 by the word in x_0, x_1 from above. Now we drop x_3 and r_2. By induction, we get rid of the relations $r_1, r_2, r_3, \ldots$ and the generators $x_2, x_3, x_4, \ldots$ Now, using the relation r_0 we obtain

$$x_{-1} = x_0^{+2} x_1^{-1} x_0;$$

thus we may drop the generator x_{-1} and the relation r_0. By induction we eliminate $x_{-1}, x_{-2}, x_{-3}, \ldots$ and the relations $r_0, r_{-1}, r_{-2}, \ldots$. Finally we are left with the generators x_0, x_1 and no relation, i.e. $\mathfrak{G}' = \langle x_0, x_1 \mid \rangle$ is a free group of rank 2. This proves that the figure eight knot is non-trivial. □

The fact that the commutator subgroup is finitely generated has a strong geometric consequence, namely that the complement can be fibered locally trivial over S^1 and the fibre is an orientable surface with one boundary component. In the case of a trefoil knot and the figure eight knot the fibre is a punctured torus. It turns out that these are the only knots that have a fibred complement with a torus as fibre, see Proposition 5.14. We will develop the theory of fibred knots in Chapter 5.

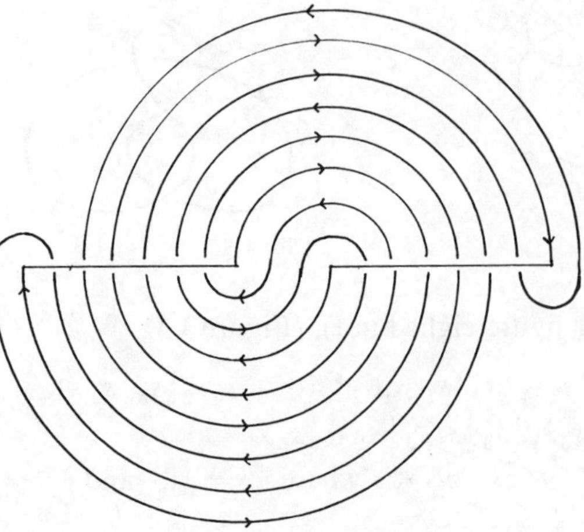

Fig. 3.6

3.9 Example (2-bridge knot $\mathfrak{b}(7,3)$).

From Figure 3.6 we determine generators for $\mathfrak{G}$ as before. It suffices to use the Wirtinger generators u, v which correspond to the bridges. One obtains the presentation

$$\begin{aligned}\mathfrak{G} &= \langle v, w \mid vwvw^{-1}v^{-1}wvw^{-1}v^{-1}w^{-1}vwv^{-1}w^{-1}\rangle \\ &= \langle s, u \mid susu^{-1}s^{-1}usu^{-1}s^{-1}u^{-1}sus^{-1}u^{-1}\rangle\end{aligned}$$

where $s = v$ and $u = wv^{-1}$. A system of coset representatives is $\{s^n | n \in \mathbb{Z}\}$ and they lead to the generators $x_n = s^n u s^{-n}$, $n \in \mathbb{Z}$, of $\mathfrak{G}'$ and the defining relations

$$x_{n+1} x_{n+2}^{-1} x_{n+1} x_{n+2}^{-1} x_n^{-1} x_{n+1} x_n^{-1}, \quad n \in \mathbb{Z}.$$

By abelianizing we obtain the relations $-2x_n + 3x_{n+1} - 2x_{n+2} = 0$, and now it is clear that this group is not finitely generated (E 3.4(a)).

(From the above relations it follows that

$$\mathfrak{G}' = \ldots *_{\mathfrak{B}_{-2}} \mathfrak{A}_{-1} *_{\mathfrak{B}_{-1}} \mathfrak{A}_0 *_{\mathfrak{B}_0} \mathfrak{A}_1 *_{\mathfrak{B}_1} \cdots,$$

where $\mathfrak{A}_n = \langle x_n, x_{n+1}, x_{n+2}\rangle$ and $\mathfrak{B}_n$ are free groups of rank 2 and $\mathfrak{A}_n \neq \mathfrak{B}_n \neq \mathfrak{A}_{n+1}$. Proof as E 3.4 (b).) A consequence is that the complement of this knot cannot be fibred over S^1 with a surface as fibre, see Theorem 5.1. This knot also has genus 1, i.e. it bounds a torus with one hole.

The background to the calculations in 3.8,9 is discussed in Chapter 4.

3.10 Groups of satellites and companions. Recall the notation of 2.8: $\tilde{V}$ is an unknotted solid torus in a 3-sphere $\tilde{S}^3$ and $\tilde{\mathfrak{k}} \subset \tilde{V}$ a knot such that a meridian of $\tilde{V}$ is not contractible in $\tilde{V} - \tilde{\mathfrak{k}}$. As, by definition, a companion $\hat{\mathfrak{k}}$ is non-trivial the homomorphisms $i_{\#}\colon \pi_1 \dot{V} \to \pi_1 V, j_{\#}\colon \pi_1 \dot{V} \to \pi_1 (\overline{S^3 - V})$ are injective, see 3.17. By the Seifert-van Kampen Theorem we get

3.11 Proposition. *With the above notation:*

$$\mathfrak{G} = \pi_1(S^3 - \mathfrak{k}) = \pi_1(\tilde{V} - \tilde{\mathfrak{k}}) *_{\pi_1(\partial \tilde{V})} \pi_1(S^3 - \hat{\mathfrak{k}})$$
$$= \mathfrak{H} *_{\langle \hat{t}, \hat{\lambda} \rangle} \hat{\mathfrak{G}},$$

where $\hat{t}$ *and* $\hat{\lambda}$ *represent meridian and longitude of the companion knot and* $\mathfrak{H} = \pi_1(\tilde{V} - \tilde{\mathfrak{k}})$. □

Remark: A satellite is never trivial.

3.12 Proposition (longitude). *The longitude ℓ of a knot $\mathfrak{k}$ represents an element of the second commutator group of the knot group* $\mathfrak{G}$:

$$\ell \in \mathfrak{G}^{(2)}.$$

Proof. Consider a Seifert surface S spanning the knot $\mathfrak{k}$ such that for some regular neighbourhood V of $\mathfrak{k}$ the intersection $S \cap V$ is an annulus A with $\partial A = \mathfrak{k} \cup \ell$. Thus $\ell = \partial(S - A)$ implies that $\ell \sim 0$ in $C = \overline{S^3 - V}$. A 1-cycle z of C and S have intersection number r if $z \sim r \cdot m$ in C where m is a meridian of $\mathfrak{k}$. Hence, a curve ζ represents an element of the commutator subgroup $\mathfrak{G}'$ if and only if its intersection number with S vanishes. Since S is two-sided each curve on S can be pushed into $C - S$, and thus has intersection number 0 with S and consequently represents an element of $\mathfrak{G}'$. If $\alpha_1, \beta_1, \ldots, \alpha_g, \beta_g$ is a canonical system of curves on S then

$$\ell \simeq \prod_{n=1}^{g} [\alpha_n, \beta_n], \quad \text{hence, } \ell \in \mathfrak{G}^{(2)}. \qquad \square$$

3.13 Remark. The longitude ℓ of a knot $\mathfrak{k}$ can be read off a regular projection as a word in the Wirtinger generators as follows: run through the knot projection starting on the arc assigned to the generator s_k. Write down s_i (or s_i^{-1}) when

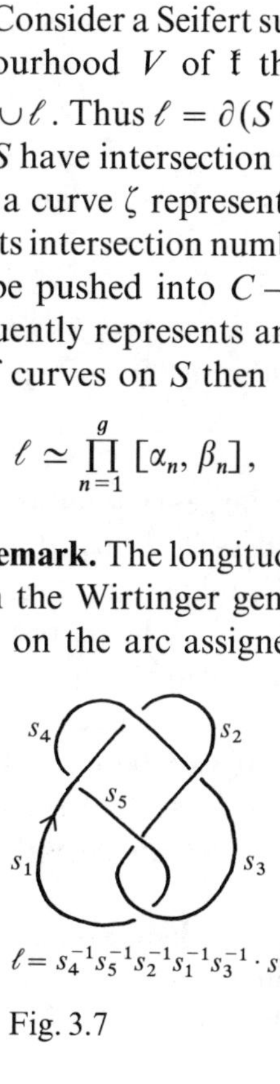

$\ell = s_4^{-1} s_5^{-1} s_2^{-1} s_1^{-1} s_3^{-1} \cdot s_1^5$

Fig. 3.7

undercrossing the arc from left to right (or from right to left) corresponding to s_i. Add s_k^α such that the sum of all exponents equals 0. See Figure 3.7, $\mathfrak{k} = 5_2$, $k = 1$, $\alpha = 5$.

C Peripheral System

In Definition 3.2 we assigned meridian and longitude to a given knot $\mathfrak{k}$. They define homotopy classes in the knot group. These elements are, however, not uniquely determined, but only up to a common conjugating factor. Meridian and longitude can be chosen as free abelian generators of $\pi_1 \dot{V}$. (In this section C always stands for the compact manifold $C = \overline{S^3 - V}$.)

3.14 Definition and Proposition (peripheral system). *The* peripheral system of a knot $\mathfrak{k}$ *is a triple* $(\mathfrak{G}, m, \ell)$ *consisting of the knot group* $\mathfrak{G}$ *and the homotopy classes* m, ℓ *of a meridian and a longitude. These elements commute:* $m \cdot \ell = \ell \cdot m$. *The pair* (m, ℓ) *is uniquely determined up to a common conjugating element of* $\mathfrak{G}$.

The peripheral group system $(\mathfrak{G}, \mathfrak{P})$ *consists of* $\mathfrak{G}$ *and the subgroup* $\mathfrak{P}$ *generated by* m *and* ℓ, $\mathfrak{P} = \pi_1 \dot{V}$. *As before, the inclusion* $\dot{V} \subset C$ *only defines a class of conjugate subgroups* $\mathfrak{P}$ *of* $\mathfrak{G}$. □

The following theorem shows the strength of the peripheral system; unfortunately, its proof depends on a fundamental theorem of F. Waldhausen on 3-manifolds which we cannote prove here.

3.15 Theorem (Waldhausen). *Two knots* $\mathfrak{k}_1, \mathfrak{k}_2$ *in* S^3 *with the peripheral systems* $(\mathfrak{G}_i, m_i, \ell_i)$, $i = 1, 2$, *are equal if there is an isomorphism* $\varphi\colon \mathfrak{G}_1 \to \mathfrak{G}_2$ *with the property that* $\varphi(m_1) = m_2$ *and* $\varphi(\ell_1) = \ell_2$.

Proof. By the theorem of Waldhausen on sufficiently large irreducible 3-manifolds, see Appendix B7, [Waldhausen 1968], [Hempel 1976, 13.6], the isomorphism φ is induced by a homeomorphism $h'\colon C_1 \to C_2$ mapping representative curves μ_1, λ_1 of m_1, ℓ_1 onto representatives μ_2, λ_2 of m_2, ℓ_2. The representatives can be taken on the boundaries $\dot{C}_i$. Waldhausen's theorem can be applied because $H_1(C_i) \cong \mathbb{Z}$ and $\pi_2(C_i) = 0$; the second condition is proved in Theorem 3.27. As h' maps the meridian of V_1 onto a meridian of V_2 it can be extended to a homeomorphism $h''\colon V_1 \to V_2$ mapping the 'core' $\mathfrak{k}_1$ onto $\mathfrak{k}_2$, see E 3.14. Together h' and h'' define the required homeomorphism $h\colon S^3 \to S^3$ which maps the (directed) knot $\mathfrak{k}_1$ onto the (directed) $\mathfrak{k}_2$.

The orientation on S^3 defines orientations on V_1 and V_2, hence on the boundaries $\dot{V}_1$ and $\dot{V}_2$. Since $h(\mu_1) = \mu_2$ and $h(\lambda_1) = \lambda_2$ it follows that $h|\dot{V}_1\colon \dot{V}_1 \to \dot{V}_2$ is an orientation-preserving mapping. This implies that $h|V_1\colon V_1 \to V_2$ is also orientation-preserving; hence $h\colon S^3 \to S^3$ is orientation preserving. Thus $\mathfrak{k}_1$ and $\mathfrak{k}_2$ are the 'same' knots. □

A direct consequence is the assertion 1.10, namely:

3.16 Corollary. *If two tame knots are topologically equivalent then they are p.l.-equivalent.* □

3.17 Proposition. *If $\mathfrak{k}$ is a non-trivial knot the inclusion $i\colon \dot{V} \to C = \overline{S^3 - V}$ induces an injective homomorphism $i_{\#}\colon \pi_1 \dot{V} \to \pi_1 C$.*

In particular, if $\pi_1 C \cong \mathbb{Z}$ then the knot $\mathfrak{k}$ is trivial.

Proof. Suppose $i_{\#}$ is not injective. Then the Loop Theorem of Papakyriakopoulos [1957], see Appendix B5, [Hempel 1976, 4.2], guarantees the existence of a simple closed curve κ on $\dot{V}$ and a disk δ in C such that

$$\kappa = \partial\delta \text{ (hence } \kappa \simeq 0 \text{ in } C), \ \delta \cap V = \kappa \text{ and } \kappa \not\simeq 0 \text{ in } \dot{V}.$$

Since κ is simple and $\kappa \sim 0$ in C it is a longitude, see 3.2. So there is an annulus $A \subset V$ such that $A \cap \dot{V} = \kappa$, $\dot{A} = \kappa \cup \mathfrak{k}$, as has been shown in Theorem 3.1. This proves that $\mathfrak{k}$ bounds a disk in S^3 and hence is the trivial knot. □

The two trefoil knots can be distinguished by using the peripheral system. We will give a proof of this fact in a more general context in 3.29, but we suggest carrying out the calculations for the trefoil as an exercise.

The peripherical group system $(\mathfrak{G}, \langle m, \ell\rangle)$ has not – at first glance – the same strength as the peripheral system $(\mathfrak{G}, m, \ell)$ since it classifies only the complement of the knot [Waldhausen 1968]. The question arises whether different knots may have the 'same' complement C. To look for such knots one can procede as follows: Let C be the complement of a knot, m the meridian and ℓ the longitude. Attach a solid torus W to C by identifying $\dot{W}$ and $\dot{C}$ in such a way that a meridian of W is identified with a simple closed curve $\kappa \sim m\ell^a$ on $\dot{C}$, $a \in Z$. This yields a closed orientable 3-manifold, its fundamental group is isomorphic to $\mathfrak{G}/\mathfrak{N}$ where $\mathfrak{N}$ is the normal closure of $m\ell^a$ in $\mathfrak{G}$.

A necessary condition for finding a knot as required is $\mathfrak{G}/\mathfrak{N} = 1$. However, as long as the Poincaré conjecture is not positively decided, this condition is not sufficient. The following definition avoids the Poincaré conjecture.

3.18 Definition (Property P). A knot $\mathfrak{k}$ with the peripheral system $(\langle s_1, \ldots, s_n | r_1, \ldots, r_n\rangle, m, \ell)$ has *Property P* if $\langle s_1, \ldots, s_n | r_1, \ldots, r_n, m\ell^a\rangle \neq 1$ for every integer $a \neq 0$.

Whether all knots have Property P is an open question. For this problem see E 3.12 and Chapter 15.

An immediate consequence of the proof of 3.15 is the following statement 3.19 (a); the assertion 3.19 (b) is obtained in the same way taking into account that $h|\dot{V}_1$ is orientation reversing:

3.19 Proposition (invertible or amphicheiral knots). *Let* $(\mathfrak{G}, m, \ell)$ *be the peripheral system of the knot* $\mathfrak{k}$.

(a) $\mathfrak{k}$ *is invertible if and only if there is an automorphism* $\varphi\colon \mathfrak{G} \to \mathfrak{G}$ *such that* $\varphi(m) = m^{-1}$ and $\varphi(\ell) = \ell^{-1}$.

(b) $\mathfrak{k}$ *is amphicheiral if and only if there is an automorphism* $\psi\colon \mathfrak{G} \to \mathfrak{G}$ *such that* $\psi(m) = m^{-1}$ *and* $\psi(\ell) = \ell$. □

The only knot with the minimal number 4 of crossings, the four-knot is invertible and amphicheiral. The latter property is shown in Figure 3.8.

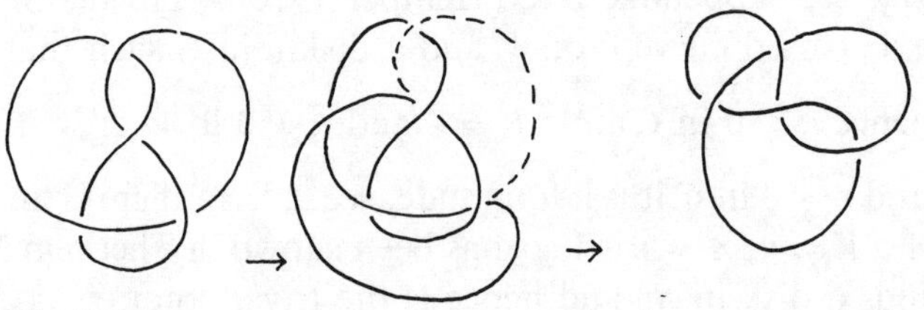

Fig. 3.8

D Knots on Handlebodies

The Wirtinger presentation of a knot group is easily obtained and it is most frequently applied in the study of examples. It depends however, strongly on the knot projection and, in general, it does not reflect geometric symmetries of the knot nor does it afford much insight into the structure of the knot group as we have seen in the preceding sections *B* and *C*. In this section, we describe another method. In the simplest case, for solid tori, a detailed treatment will be given in section *E*.

3.20 Definition (handlebody, Heegaard splitting). (a) A *handlebody* V of *genus* g is obtained from a 3-ball $\mathbb{B}^3$ by attaching g handles $\mathbb{D}^2 \times I$ such that the boundary $\dot{V}$ is an orientable closed surface of genus g, see Figure 3.9:

$$V = \mathbb{B}^3 \cup H_1 \cup \ldots \cup H_g,\ H_i \cap H_j = \emptyset \quad (i \neq j),$$
$$H_i \cap \mathbb{B}^3 = D_{i1} \cup D_{i2},\ D_{i1} \cap D_{i2} = \emptyset,\ D_{ij} \cong \mathbb{D}^2,$$

and $cl(\dot{\mathbb{B}}^3 - \bigcup_{i,j} D_{ij}) \cup \bigcup_i cl(H_i - (D_{i1} \cup D_{i2}))$ is a closed orientable surface of genus g.

Another often-used picture of a handlebody is shown in Figure 3.10.

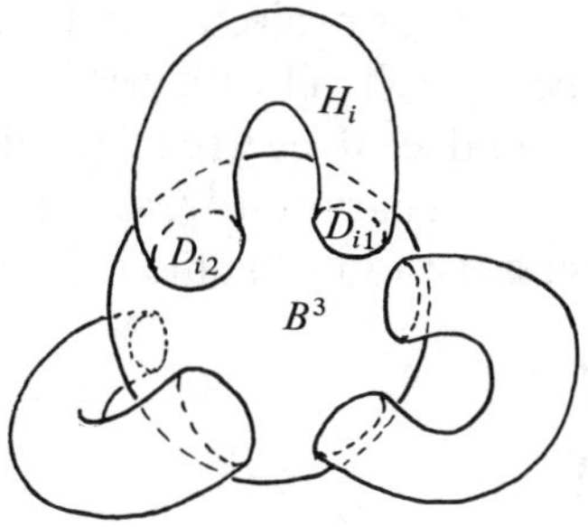

Fig. 3.9

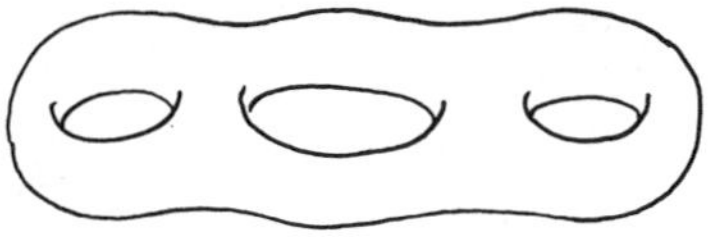

Fig. 3.10

(b) The decomposition of a closed orientable 3-manifold M^3 into two handlebodies V, W: $M^3 = V \cup W$, $V \cap W = \dot{V} = \dot{W}$, is called a *Heegaard splitting* or *decomposition of M^3 of genus g*.

A convenient characterization of handlebodies is

3.21 Proposition. *Let W be an orientable 3-manifold. If W contains a system $D_1, \ldots, D_g$ of mutually disjoint disks such that $\dot{W} \cap D_i = \dot{D}_i$ and $\overline{W - \cup_i U(D_i)}$ is a closed 3-ball then W is a handlebody of genus g. (By $U(D_i)$ we denote a regular neighbourhood of D_i with $U(D_i) \cap U(D_j) = \emptyset$ for $i \neq j$.)*

Proof as exercise E 3.9. □

Each orientable closed 3-manifold M^3 admits Heegaard splittings; one of them can be constructed as follows: Consider the 1-skeleton of a triangulation of M^3, define V as a regular neighbourhood of it and put $W = \overline{M^3 - V}$. Then V and W are handlebodies and form a Heegaard decomposition of M. (Proof as exercise E 3.10; that V is a handlebody is obvious, that W is also can be proved using Proposition 3.21.) The classification problem of 3-manifolds can be reformulated as a problem on Heegaard decompositions, see [Reidemeister 1933], [Singer 1933]. F. Waldhausen has shown in [Waldhausen 1968′] that Heegaard splittings of S^3 are unique. We quote his theorem without proof.

3.22 Theorem (Heegaard splittings of S^3). *Any two Heegaard decompositions of S^3 of genus g are homeomorphic; more precisely: If (V, W) and (V', W') are Heegaard splittings of this kind then there exists an orientation preserving homeomorphism $h: S^3 \to S^3$ such that $h(V) = V'$ and $h(W) = W'$.* □

Next a direct application to knot theory:

3.23 Proposition. *Every knot in S^3 can be embedded in the boundary of the handlebodies of a Heegaard splitting of S^3.*

Proof. A (tame) knot $\mathfrak{k}$ can be represented by a regular projection onto S^2 which does not contain loops (see Fig. 3.11). Let Γ be a graph of $\mathfrak{k}$ with vertices in the α-coloured regions of the projection (comp. 2.3), and let W be a regular neighbourhood of Γ. Obviously the knot $\mathfrak{k}$ can be realized by a curve on $\dot{W}$, see Figure 3.12. $\mathfrak{k}$ can serve as a canonical curve on $\dot{W}$ – if necessary add a handle to ensure $\mathfrak{k} \nsim 0$ on $\dot{W}$.

Fig. 3.11

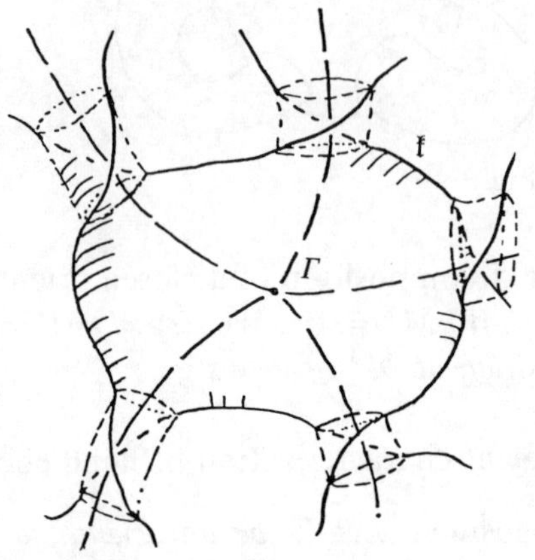

Fig. 3.12

W is a handlebody. To see this choose a tree T in Γ that contains all the vertices of Γ. It follows by induction on the number of edges of T that a regular neighbourhood of T is a 3-ball B. A regular neighbourhood W of Γ is obtained from B by attaching handles; for each of the segments of $\Gamma - T$ attach one handle.

$\overline{S^3 - W}$ also is a handlebody: The finite β-regions represent disks D_i such that $D_i \cap W = \dot{D}_i$. If one dissects $\overline{S^3 - W}$ along all the disks D_i one obtains a ball, see Figure 3.13. □

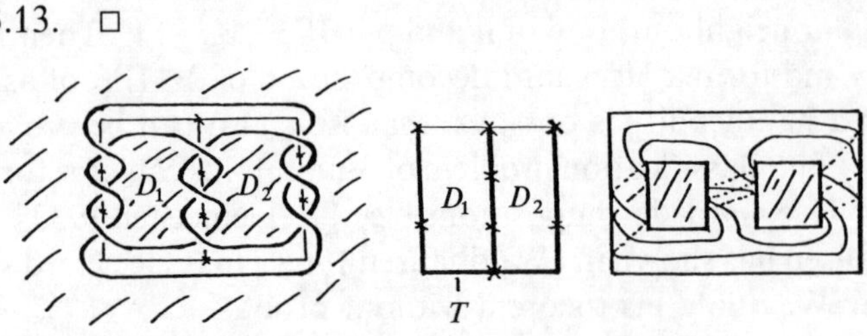

Fig. 3.13

We can now obtain a new presentation of the group of the knot $\mathfrak{k}$:

3.24 Proposition. *Let W, W' be a Heegaard splitting of S^3 of genus g. Assume that the knot $\mathfrak{k}$ is represented by a curve on the surface $F = \dot{W} = \dot{W}'$. Choose free generators s_i, s_i', $1 \leqq i \leqq g$, $\pi_1 W = \langle s_1, \ldots, s_g | - \rangle$, $\pi_1 W' = \langle s_i', \ldots, s_g' | - \rangle$, and a canonical system of curves κ_l, $1 \leqq l \leqq 2g$, on $F = W \cap W'$ with a common base point P, such that $\kappa_2 = \mathfrak{k}$. If κ_i is represented by a word $w_i(s_j) \in \pi_1 W$ and by $w_i'(s_j') \in \pi_1 W'$, then* *(a)* $\mathfrak{G} = \pi_1(S^3 - V(\mathfrak{k})) = \langle s_1, \ldots, s_g, s'_1, \ldots, s'_g \mid w_i(w'_i)^{-1},\ 2 \leqq i \leqq 2g \rangle$.

(b) $w_1(s_j)(w'_1(s'_j))^{-1}$ *can be represented by a meridian, and* $w_2(s_j)(w_1(w'_1)^{-1})^r$ *can be represented by a longitude for some (well defined) integer r, if the base point is suitably chosen.*

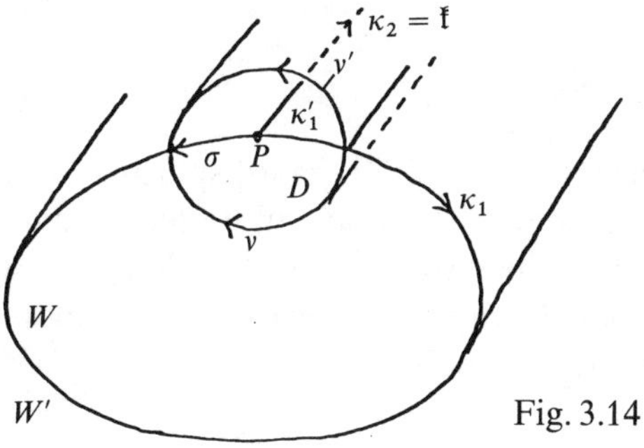

Fig. 3.14

Proof. Assertion (a) is an immediate consequence of van Kampen's theorem (see Fig. 3.14). For the proof of (b) let D be a disk in the tubular neighbourhood $V(\mathfrak{k})$, spanning a meridian $\mathscr{m}$ of $\mathfrak{k}$, and let D meet κ_1 in a subarc κ'_1 which contains the base point P.

The boundary $\dot{D}$ is composed of two arcs $\nu = \dot{D} \cap W$, $\nu' = \dot{D} \cap W'$, $\dot{D} = \nu^{-1}\nu'$, such that $\sigma\nu^{-1}\nu'\sigma^{-1}$ represents a Wirtinger generator. For $\kappa''_1 = \kappa_1 - \kappa'_1$ the paths $\sigma\nu^{-1}\kappa''_1\sigma^{-1}$ resp. $\sigma\nu'^{-1}\kappa''_1\sigma^{-1}$ represent $w_1(s_j)$ resp. $w'_1(s_j)$, hence $w_1(w'_1)^{-1} = \sigma\nu^{-1}\nu'\sigma^{-1}$. A longitude ℓ is represented by a simple closed curve λ on $\dot{V}$, $\lambda \sim \kappa_2$ in V, which is nullhomologous in $C = \overline{S^3 - V}$. Hence $\sigma\lambda\sigma^{-1}$ represents $w_2(s_j) \cdot (w_1(w'_1)^{-1})^r$ for some (uniquely determined) integer r (see Remark 3.13). If the endpoint of σ is chosen as a base point assertion (b) is valid. □

3.25 Corollary. *Assume* $S^3 = W \cup W'$, $W \cap W' = F \supset \mathfrak{k}$ *as in 3.24. If the inclusions* $i\colon \overline{F - V} \to W$, $i'\colon \overline{F - V} \to W'$ *induce injective homomorphisms of the corresponding fundamental groups, then:*

$$\mathfrak{G} = \pi_1(\overline{S^3 - V(\mathfrak{k})}) = \pi_1 W *_{\pi_1(F-V)} \pi_1 W' = \mathfrak{F}_g *_{\mathfrak{F}_{2g-1}} \mathfrak{F}_g$$

There is a finite algorithm by which one can decide whether the assumption of the corollary is valid. In this case the knot group $\mathfrak{G}$ *has a non-trivial centre if and only if* $g = 1$.

Proof. Since $F - V$ is connected, it is an orientable surface of genus $g - 1$ with two boundary components. $\pi_1(\overline{F - V})$ is a free group of rank $2(g-1)+1$.

There is an algorithm due to Nielsen [1921], see [ZVC 1980, 1.7], by which the rank of the finitely generated subgroup $i_{\#}\pi_1(\overline{F - V})$ in the free group $\pi_1 W = \mathfrak{F}_g$ can be determined. The remark about the centre follows from the fact that the centre of a product with amalgamation must be contained in the amalgamating subgroup. □

We propose to study the case $g = 1$, the torus knots, in the following paragraph. They form the simplest class of knots and can be classified. For an intrinsic characterization of torus knots see Theorem 6.1.

E Torus Knots

Let $S^3 = \mathbb{R}^3 \cup \{\infty\} = W \cup W'$ be a 'standard' Heegaard splitting of genus 1 of the oriented 3-sphere S^3. We may assume W to be an unknotted solid torus in $\mathbb{R}^3$ and $F = W \cap W'$ a torus carrying the orientation induced by that of W. There are meridians μ and ν of W and W' on F which intersect in the basepoint P with intersection number 1 on F, see Figure 3.15.

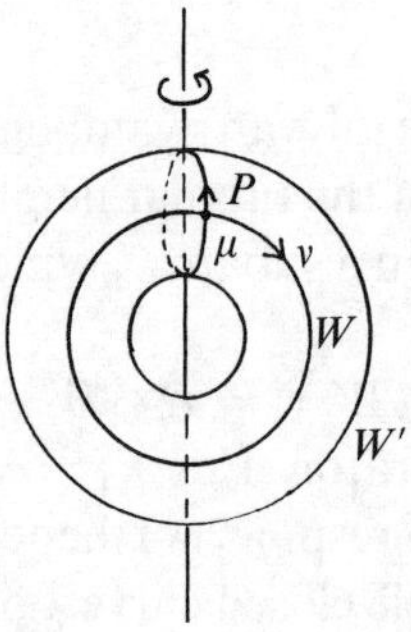

Fig. 3.15

Any closed curve κ on F is homotopic to a curve $\mu^a \cdot \nu^b$, $a, b \in \mathbb{Z}$. Its homotopy class on F contains a (non-trivial) simple closed curve if a and b are relatively prime. Such a simple curve intersects μ resp. ν exactly b resp. a times with intersection number $+1$ or -1 according to the signs of a and b. Two simple closed curves $\kappa = \mu^a \nu^b$, $\lambda = \mu^c \nu^d$ on F intersect in a single point if and only if $\begin{vmatrix} a & b \\ c & d \end{vmatrix} = \pm 1$, where the exact value of the determinant is the intersection number of κ with λ.

3.26 Definition (torus knots). Let (W, W') be the Heegaard splitting of genus 1 of S^3 described above. If $\mathfrak{k}$ is a simple closed curve on F with the intersection numbers a, b with ν and μ, respectively, and if $|a|, |b| \geqq 2$ then $\mathfrak{k}$ is called a torus knot, more precisely, *the torus knot* $\mathfrak{t}(a, b)$.

3.27 Proposition. *(a)* $\mathfrak{t}(-a, -b) = -\mathfrak{t}(a, b)$, $\mathfrak{t}(a, -b) = \mathfrak{t}^*(a, b)$ *(see Definition 2.1).*

(b) $\mathfrak{t}(a, b) = \mathfrak{t}(-a, -b) = \mathfrak{t}(b, a)$: *torus knots are invertible.*

Proof. The first assertion of (a) is obvious. A reflection in a plane and a rotation through π illustrate the other equations, see Figure 3.15. □

3.28 Proposition. *(a) The group $\mathfrak{G}$ of the torus knot* $\mathfrak{t}(a, b)$ *can be presented as follows:*

$$\mathfrak{G} = \langle u, v \,|\, u^a v^{-b} \rangle = \langle u | \rangle *_{\langle u^a \rangle = \langle v^b \rangle} \langle v | \rangle, \ \mu, \nu \text{ representing } u, v.$$

The amalgamating subgroup $\langle u^a \rangle$ is an infinite cyclic group; it represents the centre $\mathfrak{Z} = \langle u^a \rangle \cong \mathbb{Z}$ of $\mathfrak{G}$ and $\mathfrak{G}/\mathfrak{Z} \cong \mathbb{Z}_{|a|} * \mathbb{Z}_{|b|}$.

(b) The elements $m = u^c v^d$, $\ell = u^a m^{-ab}$, where $ad + bc = 1$, describe meridian and longitude of $\mathfrak{t}(a, b)$ for a suitable chosen basepoint.

(c) $\mathfrak{t}(a, b)$ and $\mathfrak{t}(a', b')$ have isomorphic groups if and only if $|a| = |a'|$ and $|b| = |b'|$ or $|a| = |b'|$ and $|b| = |a'|$.

Proof. The curve $\mathfrak{t}(a, b)$ belongs to the homotopy class u^a of W and to v^b of W'. This implies the first assertion of (a) by 3.24(a). From 3.24(b) it follows that the meridian of $\mathfrak{t}(a, b)$ belongs to the homotopy class $u^c v^d$ with $\begin{vmatrix} a & -b \\ c & d \end{vmatrix} = 1$. A longitude is described by $u^a(u^c v^d)^{-ab}$, because this element is mapped to the trivial element by the abelianizing homomorphism. This implies (b).

It is clear that u^a belongs to the centre of the knot group $\mathfrak{G}$. If we introduce the relation $u^a = 1$ we obtain the free product

$$\langle u, v \,|\, u^a, v^b \rangle = \langle u | u^a \rangle * \langle v | v^b \rangle.$$

Since this group has a trivial centre, see [ZVC 1980, 2.3.9], it follows that u^a generates the centre. Moreover, $\mathfrak{G} = \langle u | \rangle *_{\langle u^a \rangle} \langle v | \rangle$ implies that each of the factor subgroups is free.

(c) is a consequence of the fact that u and v generate non-conjugate maximal cyclic subgroups in the free product $\mathbb{Z}_{|a|} * \mathbb{Z}_{|b|}$, comp. [ZVC 1980, 2.3.10]. □

3.29 Theorem (classification of torus knots). *(a) $\mathfrak{t}(a, b) = \mathfrak{t}(a', b')$ if and only if (a', b') is equal to one of the following pairs: (a, b), (b, a), $(-a, -b)$, $(-b, -a)$.*

(b) Torus knots are invertible, but not amphicheiral.

Proof. Sufficiency follows from 3.27. Suppose $\mathfrak{t}(a, b) = \mathfrak{t}(a', b')$. Since the centre $\mathfrak{Z}$ is a characteristic subgroup, $\mathfrak{G}/\mathfrak{Z}$ is a knot invariant. The integers $|a|$ and $|b|$ are in turn invariants of $\mathbb{Z}_{|a|} * \mathbb{Z}_{|b|}$; they are characterized by the property that they are the orders of maximal finite subgroups of $\mathbb{Z}_{|a|} * \mathbb{Z}_{|b|}$ which are not conjugate. Hence, $\mathfrak{t}(a, b) = \mathfrak{t}(a', b')$ implies that $|a| = |a'|$, $|b| = |b'|$ or $|a| = |b'|$, $|b| = |a'|$.

By 3.27(b) it remains to prove that torus knots are not amphicheiral. Let us assume $a, b > 0$ and $\mathfrak{t}(a, b) = \mathfrak{t}(a, -b)$. By 3.14 there is an isomorphism

$$\varphi\colon \mathfrak{G} = \langle u, v \,|\, u^a v^{-b} \rangle \to \langle u', v' \,|\, u'^a v'^b \rangle = \mathfrak{G}^*$$

mapping the peripheral system $(\mathfrak{G}, m, \ell)$ onto $(\mathfrak{G}^*, m', \ell')$:

$$m' = \varphi(u^c v^d) = u'^{c'} v'^{d'},\ \ell' = \varphi(u^a(u^c v^d)^{-ab}) = u'^a(u'^{c'} v'^{d'})^{+ab}$$

with $ad + bc = ad' - bc' = 1$.

It follows that

$$d' = d + jb \quad \text{and} \quad c' = -c + ja \quad \text{for some } j \in \mathbb{Z}.$$

The isomorphism φ maps the centre $\mathfrak{Z}$ of $\mathfrak{G}$ onto the centre $\mathfrak{Z}^*$ of $\mathfrak{G}^*$. This implies that $\varphi(u^a) = (u'^a)^\varepsilon$ for $\varepsilon \in \{1, -1\}$. Now,

$$\begin{aligned} u'^a(u'^{c'} v'^{d'})^{ab} &= \varphi(u^a(u^c v^d)^{-ab}) = \varphi(u^a)\,\varphi(u^c v^d))^{-ab} \\ &= (u'^a)^\varepsilon\,(u'^{c'} v'^{d'})^{-ab}; \end{aligned}$$

hence, $(u'^a)^{1-\varepsilon} = (u'^{c'} v'^{d'})^{-2ab}$. This equation is impossible: the homomorphism $\mathfrak{G}^* \to \mathfrak{G}^*/\mathfrak{Z}^* \cong \mathbb{Z}_a * \mathbb{Z}_b$ maps the term on the left onto unity, whereas the term on the right represents a non-trivial element of $\mathbb{Z}_a * \mathbb{Z}_b$ because $a \nmid c'$ and $b \nmid d'$. This follows from the solution of the word problem in free products, see [ZVC 1980, 2.3.3]. □

F Asphericity of the Knot Complement

In this section we use some notions and deeper results from algebraic topology, in particular, the notion of a $K(\pi, 1)$-space, π a group: X is called a *$K(\pi, 1)$-space* if $\pi_1 X = \pi$ and $\pi_n X = 0$ for $n \neq 1$. (X is also called *aspherical.*)

3.30 Theorem. *Let $\mathfrak{k} \subset S^3$ be a knot, C the complement of an open regular neighbourhood V of $\mathfrak{k}$. Then:*

(a) $\pi_n C = 0$ for $n \neq 1$; in other words, C is a $K(\pi_1 C, 1)$-space.

(b) $\pi_1 C$ is torsionfree.

Proof. $\pi_0 C = 0$ since C is connected. Assume that $\pi_2 C \neq 0$. By the sphere theorem [Papakyriakopoulos 1957′], see Appendix B6, [Hempel 1976, 4.3], there is an embedded p.l.-2-sphere $S \subset C$ which is not nullhomotopic. By the theorem of Schoenflies, see [Moise 1977, pg. 117], S divides S^3 into two 3-balls B_1 and B_2. Since $\mathfrak{k}$ is connected it follows that one of the balls, say B_2, contains V and $B_1 \subset C$. Therefore S is nullhomotopic, contradicting the assumption. This proves $\pi_2 C = 0$.

To calculate $\pi_3 C$ we consider the universal covering $\tilde{C}$ of C. As $\pi_1 C$ is infinite $\tilde{C}$ is not compact, and this implies $H_3(\tilde{C}) = 0$. As $\pi_1 \tilde{C} = 0$ and $\pi_2 \tilde{C} = \pi_2 C = 0$ it follows from the Hurewicz Theorem, see [Spanier 1966, 7.5.2] [Stöcker-Zieschang 1985], that $\pi_3 \tilde{C} = \pi_3 C = 0$. By the same argument $\pi_n C = \pi_n \tilde{C} = H_n(\tilde{C}) = 0$ for $n \geq 4$.

This proves (a). To prove (b) assume that $\pi_1 C$ contains a non-trivial element x

of finite order $m > 1$. The cyclic group generated by x defines a covering $p: \bar{C} \to C$ with $\pi_1 \bar{C} = \mathbb{Z}_m$. As $\pi_n \bar{C} = 0$ for $n > 1$ it follows that $\bar{C}$ is a $K(\mathbb{Z}_m, 1)$-space hence, $H_n(\bar{C}) = \mathbb{Z}_m$ for n odd, see [Maclane 1963]. This contradicts the fact that $\bar{C}$ is a 3-manifold. □

G History and Sources

The knot groups became an important tool in knot theory very early. The method presenting groups by generators and defining relations has been developed by W. Dyck [1882], pursuing a suggestion of A. Cayley [1878]. The best known knot group presentations were introduced by W. Wirtinger; however, in the literature only the title "Über die Verzweigung bei Funktionen von zwei Veränderlichen" of his talk at the Jahresversammlung der Deutschen Mathematiker Vereinigung in Meran 1905 in Jahresber. DMV 14, 517 (1905) is mentioned. His student K. Brauner later used the Wirtinger presentations again in the study of singularities of algebraic surfaces in $\mathbb{R}^4$ and mentioned that these presentations were introduced by Wirtinger, see [Brauner 1928]. M. Dehn [1910] introduced the notion of a knot group and implicitly used the peripheral system to show that the two trefoils are inequivalent in [Dehn 1914]. (He used a different presentation for the knot group, see E 3.15.) O. Schreier [1924] classified the groups $\langle A, B \mid A^a B^b = 1 \rangle$ and determined their automorphism groups; this permitted to classify the torus knots. R.H. Fox [1952] introduced the peripheral system and showed its importance by distinguishing the square and the granny knot. These knots have isomorphic groups; there is, however, no isomorphism preserving the peripheral system.

Dehn's Lemma, the Loop and the Sphere Theorem, proved in [Papakyriakopoulos 1957, 1957′], opened new ways to knot theory, in particular, C.D. Papakyriakopoulos showed that knot compliments are aspherical. F. Waldhausen [1968] found the full strength of the peripheral system, showing that it determines the knot complement and, hence, the knot. New tools for the study and use of knot groups have been made available by R. Riley and W. Thurston discovering a hyperbolic structure in many knot complements.

H Exercises

E 3.1 Compute the relative homology $H_i(S^3, \mathfrak{k})$ for a knot $\mathfrak{k}$ and give a geometric interpretation of the generator of $H_2(S^3, \mathfrak{k}) \cong \mathbb{Z}$.

E 3.2 Calculate the homology $H_i(S^3 - \mathfrak{k})$ of the complement of a link $\mathfrak{k}$ with μ components.

E 3.3 Let $\mathfrak{k}$ be a knot with meridian m and longitude ℓ. Show:
(a) Attaching a solid torus with meridian m' to the complement of $\mathfrak{k}$ defines a homology sphere if and only if m' is mapped to $m^{\pm 1}\ell^r$.
(b) If $\mathfrak{k}$ is a torus knot then the fundamental group of the space obtained above is non-trivial if $r \neq 0$. (Hint: Use Proposition 3.28.)

E 3.4 Let $\mathfrak{G}' = \langle \{x_n, n \in \mathbb{Z}\} \mid \{x_{n+1} x_{n+2}^{-1} x_{n+1} x_{n+2}^{-1} x_n^{-1} x_{n+1} x_n^{-1}, n \in \mathbb{Z}\}\rangle$. Prove:
(a) $\mathfrak{G}'$ is not finitely generated.
(b) The subgroups $\mathfrak{A}_n = \langle x_n, x_{n+1}, x_{n+2}\rangle$, $\mathfrak{B}_n = \langle x_{n+1}, x_{n+2}\rangle$ of $\mathfrak{G}'$ are free groups of rank 2, and

$$\mathfrak{G}' = \ldots *_{\mathfrak{B}_{-2}} \mathfrak{A}_{-1} *_{\mathfrak{B}_{-1}} \mathfrak{A}_0 *_{\mathfrak{B}_0} \mathfrak{A}_1 *_{\mathfrak{B}_1} \ldots .$$

(For this exercise compare 3.9 and 4.6.)

E 3.5 Calculate the groups and peripheral systems of the knots in Figure 3.16.

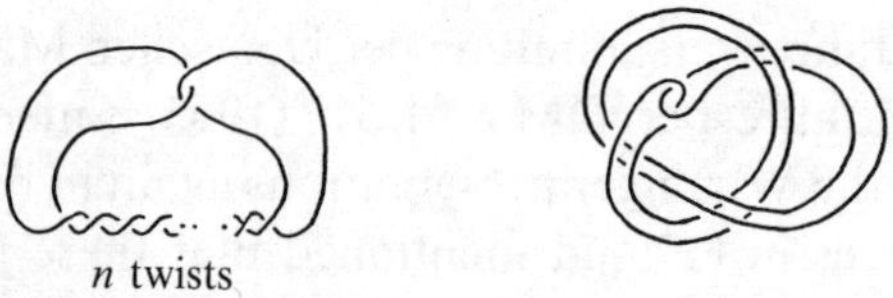

Fig. 3.16

E 3.6 Express the peripheral system of a product knot in terms of those of the factor knots.

E 3.7 Let $\mathfrak{G}$ be a knot group and $\varphi\colon \mathfrak{G} \to \mathbb{Z}$ a non-trivial homomorphism. Then $\ker \varphi = \mathfrak{G}'$.

E 3.8 Show that the two trefoil knots can be distinguished by their peripheral systems.

E 3.9 Prove Proposition 3.21.

E 3.10 Show that a regular neighbourhood V of the 1-skeleton of a triangulation of S^3 (or any closed orientable 3-manifold M) and $\overline{S^3 - V}$ ($\overline{M - V}$, respectively) form a Heegaard splitting of S^3 (or M).

E 3.11 Prove that $\mathfrak{F}_g *_{\mathfrak{F}_{2g-1}} \mathfrak{F}_g$ has a trivial centre for $g > 1$. (Here $\mathfrak{F}_g$ is the free group of rank g.)

E 3.12 Show Property P for torus knots.

E 3.13 Let $h\colon S^3 \to S^3$ be an orientation preserving homeomorphism with $h(\mathfrak{k}) = \mathfrak{k}$ for a knot $\mathfrak{k} \subset S^3$. Show that h induces an automorphism $h\colon \mathfrak{G}'/\mathfrak{G}'' \to \mathfrak{G}'/\mathfrak{G}''$ which commutes with $\alpha\colon \mathfrak{G}'/\mathfrak{G}'' \to \mathfrak{G}'/\mathfrak{G}''$, $x \mapsto t^{-1}xt$ where t represents a meridian of $\mathfrak{k}$.

E 3.14 Let V_1, V_2 be solid tori with meridians m_1, m_2. A homeomorphism $h\colon \dot{V}_1 \to \dot{V}_2$ can be extended to a homeomorphism $H\colon V_1 \to V_2$ if and only if $h(m_1) \sim m_2$ on $\dot{V}_2$.

E 3.15 (*Dehn presentation*) Derive from a regular knot projection a presentation of the knot group of the following kind. Assign a generator to each of the finite regions of the projection, and a defining relator to each double point.

Chapter 4: Commutator Subgroup of a Knot Group

There is no practicable procedure to decide whether two knot groups, given, say by Wirtinger presentations, are isomorphic. It has proved successful to investigate instead certain homomorphic images of a knot group $\mathfrak{G}$ or distinguished subgroups. The abelianized group $\mathfrak{G}/\mathfrak{G}' \cong H_1(C)$, though, is not helpful, since it is infinite cyclic for all knots, see 3.1. However, the commutator subgroup $\mathfrak{G}'$ together with the action of $\mathfrak{Z} = \mathfrak{G}/\mathfrak{G}'$ is a strong invariant which nicely corresponds to geometric properties of the knot complement; this is studied in Chapter 4. Another fruitful invariant is the metabelian group $\mathfrak{G}/\mathfrak{G}''$ which is investigated in the Chapters 8–9. All these groups are closely related to cyclic coverings of the complement.

A Construction of Cyclic Coverings

For the group $\mathfrak{G}$ of a knot $\mathfrak{k}$ the property $\mathfrak{G}/\mathfrak{G}' \cong \mathfrak{Z}$ implies that there are epimorphisms $\mathfrak{G} \to \mathfrak{Z}$ and $\mathfrak{G} \to \mathfrak{Z}_n$, $n \geqq 2$, such that their kernels $\mathfrak{G}'$ and $\mathfrak{G}_n$ are characteristic subgroups of $\mathfrak{G}$, hence, invariants of $\mathfrak{k}$. Moreover, $\mathfrak{G}$ and $\mathfrak{G}_n$ are semidirect products of $\mathfrak{Z}$ and $\mathfrak{G}'$:

$$\mathfrak{G} = \mathfrak{Z} \ltimes \mathfrak{G}' \quad \text{and} \quad \mathfrak{G}_n = n\mathfrak{Z} \ltimes \mathfrak{G}',$$

where $n\mathfrak{Z}$ denotes the subgroup of index n in $\mathfrak{Z}$ and the operation of $n\mathfrak{Z}$ on $\mathfrak{G}'$ is the induced one.

The following Proposition 4.1 is a consequence of the general theory of coverings. However, in 4.4 we give an explicit construction and reprove most of 4.1.

4.1 Proposition and Definition (cyclic coverings). *Let C denote the complement of a knot $\mathfrak{k}$ in S^3. Then there are regular coverings*

$$p_n\colon C_n \to C, \quad 2 \leqq n \leqq \infty,$$

such that $p_{n\#}(\pi_1 C_n) = \mathfrak{G}_n$ and $p_{\infty\#}(\pi_1 C_\infty) = \mathfrak{G}'$. The n-fold covering is uniquely determined.

The group of covering transformations is $\mathfrak{Z}$ for $p_\infty\colon C_\infty \to C$ and $\mathfrak{Z}_n$ for $p_n\colon C_n \to C$ $(2 \leqq n < \infty)$.

The covering $p_\infty\colon C_\infty \to C$ is called the infinite cyclic covering, *the coverings*

$p_n: C_n \to C, 2 \leq n < \infty$, *are called* the finite cyclic coverings of the knot complement *(or, inexactly, of the knot* $\mathfrak{k}$*).* □

The main tool for the announced construction is the *cutting of the complement along a surface*; this process is inverse to pasting parts together.

4.2 Cutting along a surface. Let M be a 3-manifold and S a two-sided surface in M with $\partial S = S \cap \partial M$. Let U be a regular neighbourhood of S; then $U - S = U_1 \cup U_2$ with $U_1 \cap U_2 = \emptyset$ and $U_i \cong S \times (0,1]$. Let M'_0, U'_1, U'_2 be homeomorphic copies of $\overline{M-U}$, $\bar{U}_1$, $\bar{U}_2$, respectively, and let $f_0: \overline{M-U} \to M'_0$, $f_i: \bar{U}_i \to U'_i$ be homeomorphisms. Let M' be obtained from the disjoint union $U'_1 \cup M'_0 \cup U'_2$ by identifying $f_0(x)$ and $f_i(x)$ when $x \in \overline{M-U} \cap \bar{U}_i = \partial(\overline{M-U}) \cap \partial U_i$, $i \in \{1, 2\}$. *The result M' is a 3-manifold* and we say that *M' is obtained by cutting M along S.* There is a natural mapping $j: M' \to M$.

Cutting along a one-sided surface can be described in a slightly more complicated way (exercise E 4.1). The same construction can be done in other dimensions; in fact, the classification of surfaces is usually based on cuts of surfaces along curves, see Figure 4.1. A direct consequence of the definition is the following proposition.

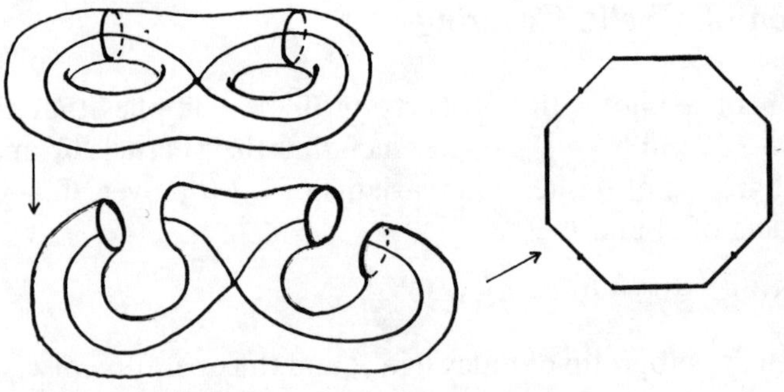

Fig. 4.1

4.3 Proposition. *(a) M' is a 3-manifold homeomorphic to $\overline{M-U} = M'_0$.*

(b) There is an identification map $j: M' \to M$ which induces a homeomorphism $M' - j^{-1}(S) \to M - S$.

(c) The restriction $j: j^{-1}(S) \to S$ is a two-fold covering. When S is two-sided $j^{-1}(S)$ consists of two copies of S; when S is one-sided $j^{-1}(S)$ is connected.

(d) When S is two-sided an orientation of M' induces orientations on both components of $j^{-1}(S)$. They are projected by j onto opposite orientations of S, if M' is connected. □

4.4 Construction of the cyclic coverings. The notion of cutting now permits a convenient description of the cyclic coverings $p_n: C_n \to C$: Let V be a regular neighbourhood of the knot $\mathfrak{k}$ and S' a Seifert surface. Assume that $V \cap S'$ is an annulus and that $\lambda = \partial V \cap S'$ is a simple closed curve, thus a longitude of $\mathfrak{k}$. Define $C = \overline{S^3 - V}$ and $S = S' \cap C$. Cutting C along S defines a 3-manifold C^*. The boundary of C^* is a connected surface and consists of two disjoint parts S^+ and S^-, both homeomorphic to S, and an annulus R which is obtained from the torus $\partial V = \partial C$ by cutting along λ:

$$\partial C^* = S^+ \cup R \cup S^-,\ S^+ \cap R = \lambda^+,\ S^- \cap R = \lambda^-,\ \partial R = \lambda^+ \cup \lambda^-,$$

see Figure 4.2. (C^* is homeomorphic to the complement of a regular neighbourhood of the Seifert surface S.) Let $r\colon S^+ \to S^-$ be the homeomorphism mapping a point from S^+ to the point of S^- which corresponds to the same point of S. Let $i^+\colon S^+ \to C^*$ and $i^-\colon S^- \to C^*$ denote the inclusions.

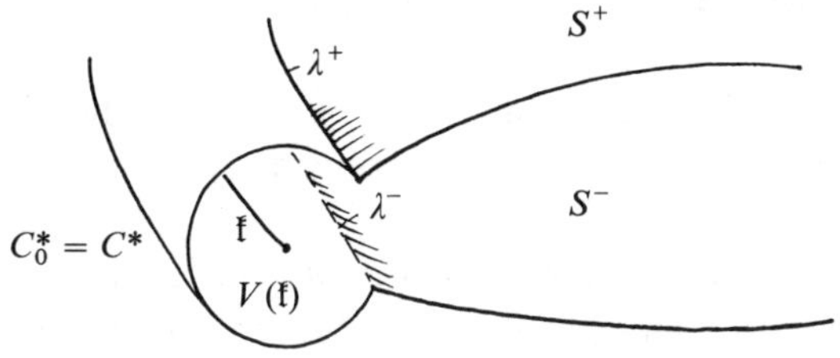

Fig. 4.2

Take homeomorphic copies C_j^* of C^* $(j \in \mathbb{Z})$ with homeomorphisms $h_j\colon C^* \to C_j^*$. The topological space C_∞ is obtained from the disjoint union $\bigcup_{j=-\infty}^{\infty} C_j^*$ by identifying $h_j(x)$ and $h_{j+1}(r(x))$ when $x \in S^+$, $j \in \mathbb{Z}$; see Figure 4.3. The space C_n is defined by starting with $\bigcup_{j=1}^{n} C_j^*$ and identifying $h_j(x)$ with $h_{j+1}(r(x))$ and $h_n(x)$ with $h_1(r(x))$ when $x \in S^+$, $1 \leqq j \leqq n-1$. For $2 \leqq n \leqq \infty$ define $p_n(x) = \iota(h_i^{-1}(x))$ if $x \in C_i^*$; here ι denotes the identification mapping $C^* \to C$, see 4.3(b). It easily follows that $p_n\colon C_n \to C$ is an n-fold covering.

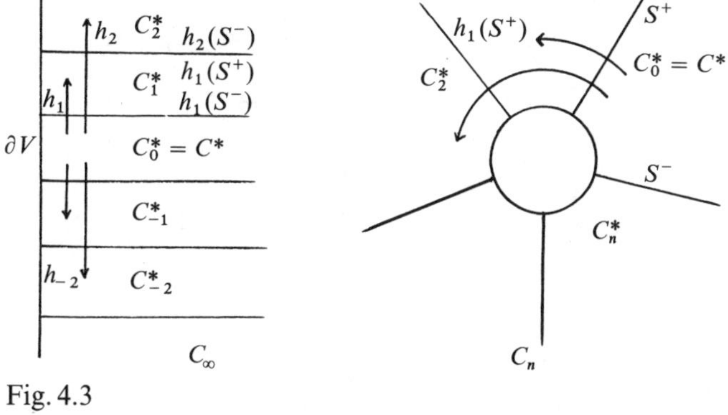

Fig. 4.3

By $t|C_j^* = h_{j+1}h_j^{-1}, j \in \mathbb{Z}$, a covering transformation $t\colon C_\infty \to C_\infty$ of the covering $p_\infty\colon C_\infty \to C$ is defined. For any two points $x_1, x_2 \in C_\infty$ with the same p_∞-image in C there is an exponent m such that $t^m(x_1) = x_2$. Thus the covering $p_\infty\colon C_\infty \to C$ is regular, the group of covering transformations is infinite cyclic and t generates it. Hence, $p_\infty\colon C_\infty \to C$ is *the* infinite cyclic covering of 4.1. In the same way it follows that $p_n\colon C_n \to C$ $(2 \leqq n < \infty)$ is *the* n-fold cyclic covering. The generating covering transformation t_n is defined by

$$t_n|C_j = h_{j+1}h_j^{-1} \quad \text{for } 1 \leqq j \leqq n-1,$$
$$t_n|C_n = h_1 h_n^{-1}.$$

B Structure of the Commutator Subgroup

Using the Seifert-van Kampen Theorem the groups $\mathfrak{G}' = \pi_1 C_\infty$ and $\mathfrak{G}_n = \pi_1 C_n$ can be calculated from $\pi_1(C^*)$ and the homomorphisms $i_\#^\pm\colon \pi_1 S^\pm \to \pi_1 C^*$.

4.5 Lemma (Neuwirth). *When S is a Seifert surface of minimal genus spanning the knot $\mathfrak{k}$ the inclusions $i^\pm\colon S^\pm \to C^*$ induce monomorphisms $i_\#^\pm\colon \pi_1 S^\pm \to \pi_1 C^*$.*

Proof. If, e.g. $i_\#^+$ is not injective then, by the Loop Theorem (see Appendix B 5), there is a simple closed curve ω on S^+, $\omega \not\simeq 0$ in S^+, and a disk $\delta \subset C$ such that $\partial\delta = \omega = \delta \cap \partial C = \delta \cap S^+$. Replace S^+ by $S_1^+ = (S^+ - U(\delta)) \cup \delta_1 \cup \delta_{-1}$ where $U(\delta) = [-1, +1] \times \delta$ is a regular neighbourhood of δ in C with $\delta_i = i \times \delta$, $0 \times \delta = \delta$. Then $g(S_1^+) + 1 = g(S^+)$, g the genus, contradicting the minimality of $g(S)$, if S_1^+ is connected. If not, the component of S_1^+ containing ∂S^+ has smaller genus than S^+, since $\omega \not\simeq 0$ in S^+; again this leads to a contradiction to the assumption on S. Compare Figure 4.4. □

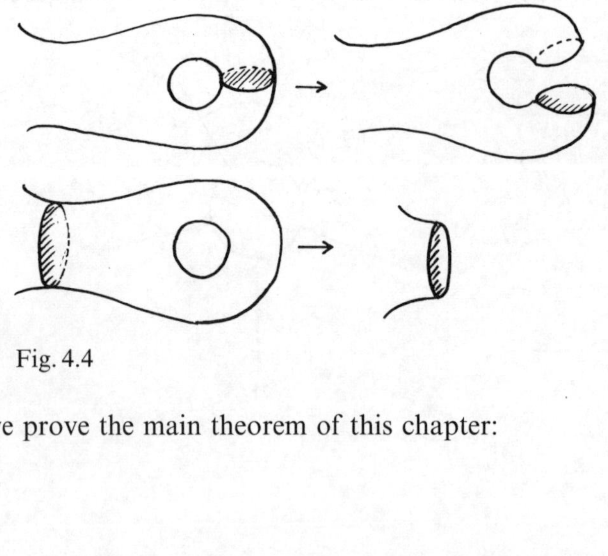

Fig. 4.4

Next we prove the main theorem of this chapter:

4.6 Theorem (structure of the commutator subgroup). *(a) If the commutator subgroup* $\mathfrak{G}'$ *of a knot group* $\mathfrak{G}$ *is finitely generated* $\mathfrak{G}'$ *is a free group of rank 2g where g is the genus of the knot.*

(b) If $\mathfrak{G}'$ *cannot be finitely generated then*

$$\mathfrak{G}' = \ldots \mathfrak{A}_{-1} *_{\mathfrak{B}_{-1}} \mathfrak{A}_0 *_{\mathfrak{B}_0} \mathfrak{A}_1 *_{\mathfrak{B}_1} \mathfrak{A}_2 \ldots$$

and the generator t of the group of covering transformations of $p_\infty\colon C_\infty \to C$ *induces an automorphism* τ *of* $\mathfrak{G}'$ *such that* $\tau(\mathfrak{A}_j) = \mathfrak{A}_{j+1}$, $\tau(\mathfrak{B}_j) = \mathfrak{B}_{j+1}$. *Here* $\mathfrak{A}_j \cong \pi_1 C^*$, $\mathfrak{B}_j \cong \pi_1 S \cong \mathfrak{F}_{2g}$ *and* $\mathfrak{B}_j$ *is a proper subgroup of* $\mathfrak{A}_j$ *and* $\mathfrak{A}_{j+1}$. *(The subgroups* $\mathfrak{B}_j$ *and* $\mathfrak{B}_{j+1}$ *do not coincide.)*

Proof. We apply the construction of 4.4, for a Seifert surface of minimal genus. By 4.5, the inclusions $i^\pm\colon S^\pm \to C_\infty$ induce monomorphisms $i^\pm_\#\colon \pi_1 S^\pm \to \pi_1 C_\infty$. By the Seifert-van Kampen Theorem (Appendix B3), $\mathfrak{G}' = \pi_1 C_\infty$ is the direct $\lim\limits_{n\to\infty} \mathfrak{P}_n$ of the following free products with amalgamation:

$$\mathfrak{P}_n = \mathfrak{A}_{-n} *_{\mathfrak{B}_{-n}} \mathfrak{A}_{-n+1} * \ldots * \mathfrak{A}_{-1} *_{\mathfrak{B}_{-1}} \mathfrak{A}_0 *_{\mathfrak{B}_0} \mathfrak{A}_1 * \ldots *_{\mathfrak{B}_{n-1}} \mathfrak{A}_n;$$

here $\mathfrak{A}_j$ corresponds to the sheet C^*_j and $\mathfrak{B}_j$ to $h_j(S^+)$ if considered as a subgroup of $\mathfrak{A}_j$ and to $h_{j+1}(S^-)$ when considered in $\mathfrak{A}_{j+1}$. Thus for different j the pairs $(\mathfrak{A}_j, \mathfrak{B}_j)$ are isomorphic and the same is true for the pairs $(\mathfrak{A}_{j+1}, \mathfrak{B}_j)$.

When $\mathfrak{G}'$ is finitely generated there is an n such that the generators of $\mathfrak{G}'$ are in $\mathfrak{P}_n$. This implies that $\mathfrak{B}_n = \mathfrak{A}_{n+1}$ and $\mathfrak{B}_{-n-1} = \mathfrak{A}_{-n-1}$; hence, $\pi_1 S^+ \cong \pi_1 C^* \cong \pi_1 S^- \cong \mathfrak{F}_{2g}$ where g is the genus of S (and $\mathfrak{k}$). Now it follows that $\pi_1 C_\infty \cong \pi_1 C^* \cong \pi_1 S \cong \mathfrak{F}_{2g}$.

There remain the cases where $i^+_\#(\pi_1 S^+) \neq \pi_1 C^*$ or $i^-_\#(\pi_1 S^-) \neq \pi_1 C^*$. Then $\mathfrak{G}'$ cannot be generated by a finite system of generators. Lemma 4.7, due to [Brown-Crowell 1965], shows that these two inequalities are equivalent; hence, $i^+_\#(\pi_1 S^+) \neq \pi_1 C^* \neq i^-_\#(\pi_1 S^-)$, and now the situation is as described in (b). (That $\mathfrak{B}_j$ and $\mathfrak{B}_{j+1}$ do not coincide can be deduced using facts from the proof of Theorem 5.1) □

Section *C* is devoted to the proof of the Lemma 4.7 of [Brown-Crowell 1965] and can be neglected at first reading.

C A Lemma of Brown and Crowell

The following lemma is a special case of a result in [Brown-Crowell 1965]:

4.7 Lemma (Brown-Crowell). *Let M be an orientable compact 3-manifold where* ∂M *consists of two surfaces* S^+ *and* S^- *of genus g with common boundary*

$$\partial S^+ = \partial S^- = S^+ \cap S^- = \bigcup_{i=1}^{r} \kappa_i \neq \emptyset,\ \kappa_i \cap \kappa_j = \emptyset \quad \textit{for } i \neq j.$$

If the inclusion $i^+ : S^+ \to M$ *induces an isomorphism* $i^+_\# : \pi_1 S^+ \to \pi_1 M$ *so does* $i^- : S^- \to M$.

Proof by induction on the Euler characteristic of the surface S^+. As $\partial S^+ \neq \emptyset$ the Euler characteristic $\chi(S^+)$ is maximal for $r = 1$ and $g = 0$; in this case $\chi(S^+) = 1$ and S^+ and S^- are disks, $\pi_1 S^-$ and $\pi_1 S^+$ are trivial, hence, $\pi_1 M$ too, and nothing has to be proved.

If $\chi(S^+) = \chi(S^-) < 1$ there is a simple arc α on S^- with $\partial\alpha = \{A, B\} = \alpha \cap \partial S^-$ which does not separate S^-, see Figure 4.5. We want to prove that there is an arc β on S^+ with the same properties such that $\alpha^{-1}\beta$ bounds a disk δ in M.

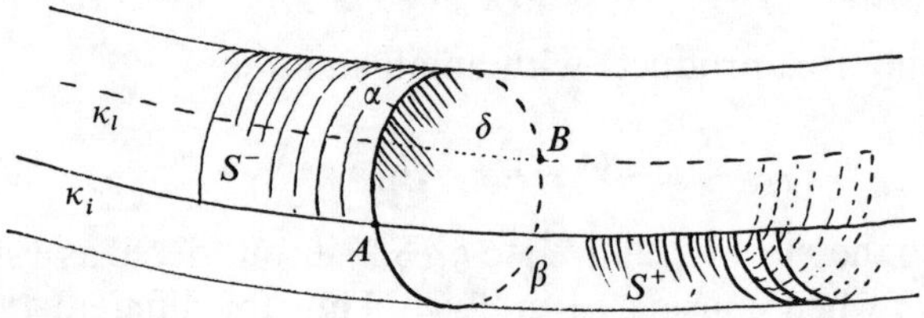

Fig. 4.5

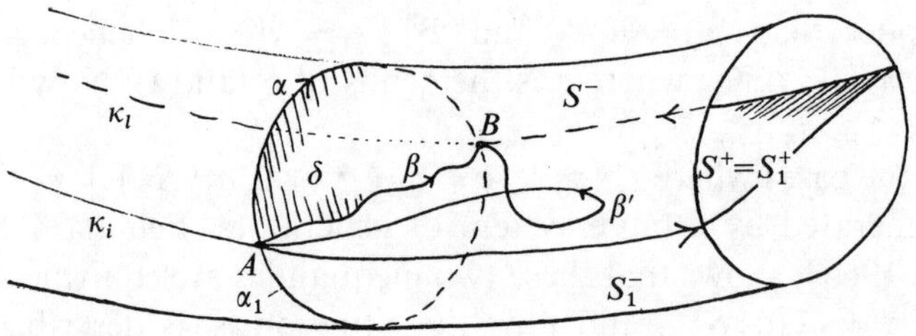

Fig. 4.6

$i^+_\#: \pi_1 S^+ \to \pi_1 M$ is an isomorphism by assumption, thus there is an arc β' in S^+ connecting A and B such that $(\alpha, A, B) \simeq (\beta', A, B)$ in M. In general, the arc β' is not simple. The existence of a simple arc is proved using the following *doubling trick*: Let M_1 be a homeomorphic copy of M with $\partial M_1 = S_1^+ \cup S_1^-$. Let M' be obtained from the disjoint union $M \cup M_1$ by identifying S^+ and S_1^+ and let $\alpha_1 \subset M_1$ be the arc corresponding to α. In M', $\alpha\alpha_1^{-1} \simeq \beta'\beta'^{-1} \simeq 1$. By Dehn's Lemma (Appendix B4), there is a disk δ' in M' with boundary $\alpha\alpha_1^{-1}$. We may assume that δ' is in general position with respect to $S^+ = S_1^+$ and that $\delta' \cap \partial M' = \partial\delta' = \alpha\alpha_1^{-1}$. The disk δ' intersects S^+ in a simple arc β connecting A and B and, perhaps, in a number of closed curves. The simple closed curve $\alpha\beta^{-1}$ is null-homotopic in δ', hence in M'. By the Seifert-van Kampen Theorem

$$\pi_1 M' = \pi_1 M *_{\pi_1 S^+} \pi_1 M_1 \cong \pi_1 M;$$

thus the inclusion $M \hookrightarrow M'$ induces an isomorphism $\pi_1 M \to \pi_1 M'$. Since $\alpha\beta^{-1} \subset M'$ it follows that $\alpha\beta^{-1} \simeq 0$ in M. By Dehn's Lemma, there is a disk $\delta \subset M$ with $\delta \cap \partial M = \partial\delta = \alpha \cap \beta$, see Figure 4.6.

The arc β does not separate S^+. To prove this let C and D be points of S^+ close to β on different sides. There is an arc λ in M connecting C and D without intersecting δ; this is a consequence of the assumption that α does not seperate S^-. Now deform λ into S^+ by a homotopy that leaves fixed C and D. The resulting path $\lambda' \subset S^+$ again connects C and D and has intersection number 0 with δ, the intersection number calculated in M; hence, also 0 with β when the calculation is done in S^+. This proves that β does not separate S^+.

Cut M along δ, see Figure 4.7. The result is a 3-mainfold M_*. We prove that the boundary of M_* fulfils the assumptions of the lemma and that $\chi(\partial M_*) > \chi(\partial M)$. Then induction can be applied.

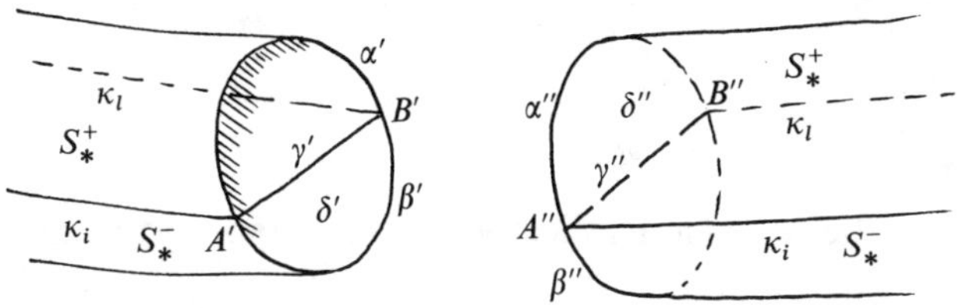

Fig. 4.7

Assume that $A \in \kappa_i$, $B \in \kappa_l$. Let γ be a simple arc in δ such that $\gamma \cap \partial\delta = \partial\gamma = \{A, B\}$. By cutting M along δ, γ is cut into two arcs γ', γ'' which join the points A', B' and A'', B'' corresponding to A and B. The curves κ_i and κ_l of ∂S^+ are replaced by one new curve κ_i' if $i \neq l$ or by two new curves $\kappa_{i,1}$, $\kappa_{i,2}$ if $i = l$. These new curves together with those κ_m that do not intersect δ decompose ∂M_* into two homeomorphic surfaces. They contain homeomorphic subsets S_*^+, S_*^- which result from removing the two copies of δ in ∂M_*. The surfaces S_*^+, S_*^- are obtained from S^+ and S^- by cutting along $\partial\delta$. It follows that

$$\chi(S_*^+) = \chi(S^+) + 1,$$

since for $i = \ell$ the number r of boundary components increases by 1 and the genus decreases by 1: $r_* = r + 1$, $g_* = g - 1$, and for $i \neq \ell$ one has $r_* = r - 1$ and $g_* = g$.

The inclusions and identification mappings form the following commutative diagrams:

$$\begin{array}{ccc} S_*^+ & \xrightarrow{j^+} & S^+ \\ {\scriptstyle i_*^+}\downarrow & & \downarrow{\scriptstyle i^+} \\ M_* & \xrightarrow{j} & M \end{array} \qquad \begin{array}{ccc} S_*^- & \xrightarrow{j^-} & S^- \\ {\scriptstyle i_*^-}\downarrow & & \downarrow{\scriptstyle i^-} \\ M_* & \xrightarrow{j} & M \end{array}$$

From the second version of the Seifert-van Kampen Theorem, see Appendix B3(b), [ZVC 1980, 2.8.3], [Stöcker-Zieschang 1985], it follows that

$$\pi_1 M = j_\#(\pi_1 M_*) * \mathfrak{Z},$$
$$\pi_1 S^+ = j_\#^+(\pi_1 S_*^+) * \mathfrak{Z},\ \pi_1 S_*^- = j_\#^-(\pi_1 S_*^-) * \mathfrak{Z},$$

where $\mathfrak{Z}$ is the infinite cyclic group generated by κ_i. By assumption the inclusion $i^+\colon S^+ \to M$ induces an isomorphism $i_\#^+$ which maps $j_\#^+(\pi_1 S_*^+)$ to $j_\# i_{*\#}^+(\pi_1 S^+) \subset j_\#(\pi_1 M_*)$ and $\mathfrak{Z}$ onto $\mathfrak{Z}$. From the solution of the word problem in free products, see [ZVC 1980, 2.3], it follows that $i_\#^+$ bijectively maps $j_\#^+(\pi_1 S_*^+)$ onto $j_\#(\pi_1 M_*)$; hence, $i_{*\#}^+$ is an isomorphism.

As induction hypothesis we may assume that $i_{*\#}^-$ is an isomorphism. By arguments, similar to those above, it follows that $i_\#^-$ can be described by the following commutative diagram.

$$\begin{array}{ccc} j_\#^-(\pi_1 S_*^-) * \mathfrak{Z} & = & \pi_1 S^- \\ {\scriptstyle i_{*\#}^- * (i_\#^- | \mathfrak{Z})}\downarrow \cong & & \downarrow {\scriptstyle i_\#^-} \\ j_\#(\pi_1 M_*) * \mathfrak{Z} & = & \pi_1 M. \end{array}$$

Since the mapping on the left side is bijective, $i_\#^-$ is an isomorphism. □

D Examples and Applications

Theorem 4.6 now throws some light on the results in 3.7–9: the trefoil (E 4.2) and the figure eight knot (3.8) have finitely generated commutator subgroups. The 2-bridge knot $\mathfrak{b}(7,3)$ has a commutator subgroup of infinite rank; in 3.9 we have already calculated $\mathfrak{G}'$ in the form of 4.6(b) using the Reidemeister-Schreier method.

We will prove that all torus knots have finitely generated commutator subgroups. Let us begin with some consequences of Theorem 4.6.

4.8 Corollary. *Let the knot $\mathfrak{k}$ have a finitely generated commutator subgroup and let S be an orientable surface spanning $\mathfrak{k}$. If S is incompressible in the knot complement (this means that the inclusion $i\colon S \hookrightarrow C$ induces a monomorphism $i_\#\colon \pi_1 S \to \pi_1 C = \mathfrak{G}$) then S and $\mathfrak{k}$ have the same genus.* □

In the following $\mathfrak{G}$ always denotes a knot group.

4.9 Corollary. *The centre of $\mathfrak{G}'$ is trivial.*

Proof. If $\mathfrak{G}'$ cannot be finitely generated, there are by 4.6 groups $\mathfrak{A}$ and $\mathfrak{B}$ with $\mathfrak{G}' = \mathfrak{A} *_{\mathfrak{F}_{2g}} \mathfrak{B}$ where g is the genus of $\mathfrak{k}$ and $\mathfrak{A} \neq \mathfrak{F}_{2g} \neq \mathfrak{B}$. From the solution of the word problem it follows that the centre is contained in the amalgamated subgroup and is central in both factors, see [ZVC 1980, 2.3.9]. But $\mathfrak{F}_{2g}$ has trivial centre ([ZVC 1980, E 1.5]). The last argument also applies to finitely generated $\mathfrak{G}'$ because they are free groups. □

4.10 Proposition. *(a) If the centre $\mathfrak{C}$ of $\mathfrak{G}$ is non-trivial $\mathfrak{G}'$ is finitely generated.*

(b) The centre $\mathfrak{C}$ of $\mathfrak{G}$ is trivial or infinite cyclic. When $\mathfrak{C} \neq 1$, $\mathfrak{C}$ is generated by an element $t^n \cdot u$, $n > 1$, $u \in \mathfrak{G}'$. (The coset $t\mathfrak{G}'$ generates the first homology group $\mathfrak{G}/\mathfrak{G}' \cong \mathfrak{Z}$).

Proof. (a) Assume that $\mathfrak{G}'$ cannot be generated by finitely many elements. Then, by Theorem 4.6, $\mathfrak{G}' = \ldots * \mathfrak{A}_{-1} *_{\mathfrak{B}_{-1}} \mathfrak{A}_0 *_{\mathfrak{B}_0} \mathfrak{A}_1 * \ldots$ where $\mathfrak{A}_j \supsetneqq \mathfrak{B}_j \subsetneqq \mathfrak{A}_{j+1}$. Denote by $\mathfrak{H}_r$ the subgroup of $\mathfrak{G}'$ which is generated by $\{\mathfrak{A}_j | j \leqq r\}$. Then $\mathfrak{H}_{r+1} = \mathfrak{H}_r *_{\mathfrak{B}_r} \mathfrak{A}_{r+1}$ and $\mathfrak{H}_r \neq \mathfrak{B}_r \neq \mathfrak{A}_{r+1}$; hence $\mathfrak{H}_r \subsetneqq \mathfrak{H}_{r+1}$ and

(1) $\qquad \mathfrak{H}_r \subsetneqq \mathfrak{H}_s \quad \text{if } r < s.$

Let $t \in \mathfrak{G}$ be an element which is mapped onto a generator of $\mathfrak{G}/\mathfrak{G}' = \mathfrak{Z}$. Assume that $t^{-1}\mathfrak{A}_r t = \mathfrak{A}_{r+1}$; hence, $t^{-1}\mathfrak{H}_r t = \mathfrak{H}_{r+1}$.

Consider $z \in \mathfrak{C}$, $1 \neq z$. Then $z = ut^m$ where $u \in \mathfrak{G}'$. By 4.9, $m \neq 0$; without loss of generality: $m > 0$. Choose s such that $u \in \mathfrak{H}_s$. Then

$$\mathfrak{H}_s = z^{-1}\mathfrak{H}_s z \quad \text{since } z \in \mathfrak{C}, \quad \text{and}$$
$$z^{-1}\mathfrak{H}_s z = t^{-m}u^{-1}\mathfrak{H}_s u t^m = t^{-m}\mathfrak{H}_s t^m = \mathfrak{H}_{s+m}.$$

This implies $\mathfrak{H}_s = \mathfrak{H}_{s+m}$, contradicting (1).

(b) By (a) a non-trivial centre $\mathfrak{C}$ contains an element $t^n \cdot u$, $n > 0$, $u \in \mathfrak{G}'$ and n minimal. By 4.9,

$$\mathfrak{C}\mathfrak{G}' \cong n\mathfrak{Z} \times \mathfrak{G}',$$
$$\mathfrak{C}\mathfrak{G}'/\mathfrak{G}' \cong \mathfrak{C}/\mathfrak{C} \cap \mathfrak{G}' \cong \mathfrak{C} \cong n\mathfrak{Z}.$$

If $n = 1$ then $\mathfrak{G} = \mathfrak{C} \times \mathfrak{G}'$ which contradicts the fact that $\mathfrak{G}$ collapses if the relator $t = 1$ is introduced. □

Since the group of a torus knot has non-trivial centre we have proved the first statement of the following Theorem:

4.11 Corollary (genus of torus knots). *(a) The group $\mathfrak{G}_{a,b} = \langle x, y | x^a y^{-b} \rangle$ of the torus knot $\mathfrak{t}(a, b)$ $(a, b \in \mathbb{N}, (a, b) = 1)$ has a finitely generated commutator subgroup. It is, following 4.6 (a), a free group of rank 2g where g is the genus of $\mathfrak{t}(a, b)$.*

(b) $\quad g = \dfrac{(a-1) \cdot (b-1)}{2}.$

Proof. It remains to prove (b). Consider the commutative diagram

$$\begin{array}{ccc} \mathfrak{G}_{a,b} & \xrightarrow{\ \varphi\ } & \langle t \mid \rangle \\ \Big\downarrow \lambda & & \Big\downarrow \kappa \\ \mathfrak{Z}_a * \mathfrak{Z}_b & \xrightarrow{\ \psi\ } & \langle t \mid t^{ab} \rangle \end{array} \qquad t = \varphi(x^r y^s),\ as + br = 1$$

where φ, ψ are the abelianizing homomorphisms, λ and κ the natural projections. The centre $\mathfrak{C}$ of $\mathfrak{G}_{a,b}$ is generated by $x^a = y^b$, and it is $\mathfrak{C} = \ker \lambda$. Now

$$\begin{array}{l} \ker(\psi\lambda) = \lambda^{-1}(\ker\psi) \cong \mathfrak{C} \times \ker\psi \\ \quad \| \\ \ker(\kappa\varphi) = \varphi^{-1}(\langle t^{ab} \rangle) \cong \mathfrak{C} \times \ker\varphi ; \end{array}$$

the last isomorphism is a consequence of

$$t^{ab} = \varphi((x^r y^s)^{ab}) = \varphi(x^{rab} \cdot x^{a^2 s}) = \varphi(x^a).$$

Hence, $\ker\varphi \cong \ker\psi$.

We prove next that $(\mathfrak{Z}_a * \mathfrak{Z}_b)' = \ker\psi \cong \mathfrak{F}_{(a-1)(b-1)}$. Consider the 2-complex C^2 consisting of one vertex, two edges ξ, η and two disks δ_1, δ_2 with the boundaries ξ^a and η^b, respectively. Then $\pi_1 C^2 \cong \mathfrak{Z}_a * \mathfrak{Z}_b$. Let $\tilde{C}^2$ be the covering space of C^2 with fundamental group the commutator subgroup of $\mathfrak{Z}_a * \mathfrak{Z}_b$. Each edge of $\tilde{C}^2$ over η (or ξ) belongs to the boundaries of exactly b (resp. a) disks of $\tilde{C}^2$ which have the same boundary. It suffices to choose one to get a system of defining relations of $\pi_1 \tilde{C}^2 \cong (\mathfrak{Z}_a * \mathfrak{Z}_b)'$. Then there are $\frac{ab}{b}$ disks over δ_2 and $\frac{ab}{a}$ disks over δ_1. The new complex $\hat{C}^2$ contains

$$ab \text{ vertices},\ 2ab \text{ edges},\ a+b \text{ disks},$$

and each edge is in the boundary of exactly one disk of $\hat{C}^2$. Thus $\pi_1 \hat{C}^2$ is a free group of rank

$$2ab - (ab-1) - (a+b) = (a-1)(b-1).$$

Theorem 4.6 implies that the genus of $\mathfrak{t}(a,b)$ is $\frac{1}{2}(a-1)(b-1)$. □

The isomorphism $(\mathfrak{Z}_a * \mathfrak{Z}_b)' \cong \mathfrak{F}_{(a-1)(b-1)}$ can also be proved using the (modified) Reidemeister-Schreier method, see [ZVC 1980, 2.2.8]; in the proof above the geometric background of the algebraic method has directly been used.

E Commutator Subgroups of Satellites

According to 3.11, the groups of a satellite $\mathfrak{k}$, its companion $\hat{\mathfrak{k}}$ and the pattern $\tilde{\mathfrak{k}} \subset \tilde{V}$ are related by $\mathfrak{G} = \hat{\mathfrak{G}} *_{\mathfrak{A}} \pi_1(\hat{V} - \mathfrak{k}) \cong \hat{\mathfrak{G}} *_{\mathfrak{A}} \pi_1(\tilde{V} - \tilde{\mathfrak{k}}) = \hat{\mathfrak{G}} *_{\mathfrak{A}} \mathfrak{H}$, where $\mathfrak{A}$

$= \pi_1(\partial \hat{V}) \cong \mathbb{Z}^2$ and $\mathfrak{H} = \pi_1(\tilde{V} - \tilde{\mathfrak{k}})$. For the calculation of $\mathfrak{G}'$ we need a refined presentation, which we will also use in Chapter 9 for the calculation of Alexander polynomials of satellites.

4.12 Presentation of the commutator subgroup of a satellite. Let $\tilde{m}$ and $\tilde{\ell}$ be meridian and longitude of $\tilde{V}$ where $\tilde{\ell}$ is a meridian of $\overline{S^3 - \tilde{V}}$. Starting with a Wirtinger presentation for the link $\tilde{\mathfrak{k}} \cup \tilde{m}$ and after replacing all meridional generators of $\tilde{\mathfrak{k}}$ except t by elements of $\mathfrak{H}'$ one obtains a presentation

$$(1) \qquad \mathfrak{H} = \pi_1(\tilde{V} - \tilde{\mathfrak{k}}) = \langle t, \tilde{u}_i, \hat{\lambda} \mid \tilde{R}_j(\tilde{u}_i^{t^\nu}, \hat{\lambda}) \rangle$$
$$= \langle t, \hat{t}, \tilde{u}_i, \hat{\lambda} \mid \tilde{R}_j(\tilde{u}_i^{t^\nu}, \hat{\lambda}), \hat{t}^{-1} \cdot t^n \tilde{v}(\tilde{u}_i^{t^\nu}, \hat{\lambda}), [\hat{t}, \hat{\lambda}] \rangle$$

where $\tilde{u}_i \in \mathfrak{H}'$, $\tilde{u}_i^{t^\nu} = t^\nu \tilde{u}_i t^{-\nu}$, $\nu \in \mathbb{Z}$, $i \in I$, $j \in J$; I, J finite sets. $\hat{t}$ represents a meridian of $\hat{V}$ on $\partial \hat{V}$, $\hat{t} = t^n \cdot \tilde{v}(\tilde{u}_i^{t^\nu}, \hat{\lambda})$ with $\tilde{v}(\tilde{u}_i^{t^\nu}, \hat{\lambda}) \in \mathfrak{G}'$ and $n = lk(\hat{t}, \tilde{\mathfrak{k}})$. The generator $\hat{\lambda}$ represents the longitude $\hat{\ell}$, hence $\hat{\lambda} \in \mathfrak{G}''$. The relation $[\hat{t}, \hat{\lambda}]$ is a consequence of the remaining relations. The group of the knot $\tilde{\mathfrak{k}}$ is:

$$(2) \qquad \tilde{\mathfrak{G}} = \pi_1(\tilde{S}^3 - \tilde{\mathfrak{k}}) = \langle t, \tilde{u}_i \mid \tilde{R}_j(\tilde{u}_i^{t^\nu}, 1) \rangle$$
$$= \langle t, \tilde{u}_i, \hat{\lambda} \mid R_j(\tilde{u}_i^{t^\nu}, \hat{\lambda}), \hat{\lambda} \rangle .$$

The group of the companion has a presentation

$$(3) \qquad \hat{\mathfrak{G}} = \pi_1(S^3 - \hat{\mathfrak{k}}) = \langle \hat{t}, \hat{u}_k, \hat{\lambda} \mid \hat{R}_l(\hat{u}_k^{\hat{t}^\nu}), \hat{\lambda}^{-1} \cdot \hat{w}(\hat{u}_k^{\hat{t}^\nu}), [\hat{t}, \hat{\lambda}] \rangle$$

for $\hat{u}_k \in \hat{\mathfrak{G}}'$ and some $\hat{w}$. By assumption $\hat{t}, \hat{\lambda}$ generate a subgroup isomorphic to $\mathbb{Z} \oplus \mathbb{Z}$ in $\mathfrak{H}$ as well as in $\hat{\mathfrak{G}}$ since $\hat{\mathfrak{k}}$ is not trivial. By the Seifert-van Kampen theorem

$$(4) \qquad \mathfrak{G} = \pi_1(S^3 - \mathfrak{k}) = \hat{\mathfrak{G}} *_{\pi_1(\partial \hat{V})} \pi_1(\hat{V} - \mathfrak{k}) = \hat{\mathfrak{G}} *_{\langle \hat{t}, \hat{\lambda} \rangle} \mathfrak{H}$$
$$\cong \langle t, \tilde{u}_i, \hat{t}, \hat{u}_k, \hat{\lambda} \mid \tilde{R}_j(\tilde{u}_i^{t^\nu}, \hat{\lambda}), \hat{t}^{-1} \cdot t^n \tilde{v}(\tilde{u}_i^{t^\nu}, \hat{\lambda}), \hat{R}_l(\hat{u}_k^{\hat{t}^\nu}),$$
$$\hat{\lambda}^{-1} \cdot \hat{w}(\hat{u}_k^{\hat{t}^\nu}), [\hat{t}, \hat{\lambda}] \rangle ,$$

a result already obtained in 3.11.

To determine $\mathfrak{G}'$ we drop the generator $\hat{t}$ using the relation $\hat{t} = t^n \tilde{v}(\tilde{u}_i^{t^\nu}, \hat{\lambda})$; however, we will still write $\hat{t}$ for the expression on the right side. Now

$$\mathfrak{G}' = \langle \tilde{u}_i^{t^\varrho}, \hat{u}_k^{t^\varrho}, \hat{\lambda}^{t^\varrho} \mid \tilde{R}_j^{t^\varrho}(\tilde{u}_i^{t^\nu}. \hat{\lambda}), \hat{R}_l^{t^\varrho}(\hat{u}_k^{\hat{t}^\nu}),$$
$$(\hat{\lambda}^{t^\varrho})^{-1} \cdot \hat{w}^{t^\varrho}(\hat{u}_k^{\hat{t}^\nu}), [\hat{t}^{t^\varrho}, \hat{\lambda}^{t^\varrho}] \rangle$$

where ϱ ranges over $\mathbb{Z}$, $\tilde{u}_i^{t^\varrho} = t^\varrho \tilde{u}_i t^{-\varrho}$, $\tilde{R}_j^{t^\varrho}(\tilde{u}_i^{t^\nu}, \hat{\lambda}) = t^\varrho \tilde{R}_j(\tilde{u}_i^{t^\nu}, \hat{\lambda}) t^{-\varrho}$ etc. For $n > 0$ write

$$\varrho = \mu + \sigma \cdot n \quad \text{with} \quad 0 \leqq \mu < n \quad \text{and}$$
$$t^\varrho = t^{\sigma n} t^\mu = \tilde{v}_\sigma(\tilde{u}_i^{t^\nu}, \hat{\lambda}) \hat{t}^\sigma t^\mu .$$

Define $\hat{u}_{\mu,k} = t^\mu \hat{u}_k t^{-\mu}$, $\hat{\lambda}_\mu = t^\mu \hat{\lambda} t^{-\mu}$. Now

(5) $\quad \mathfrak{G}' = \langle \tilde{u}_i^{t\varrho}, \hat{u}_{\mu,k}^{\hat{t}\sigma}, \hat{\lambda}_\mu^{\hat{t}\sigma} | \tilde{R}_j^{t\varrho}(\tilde{u}_i^{t\nu}, \hat{\lambda}), \hat{R}_l^{\hat{t}\sigma}(\hat{u}_{\mu,k}^{\hat{t}\nu}), (\hat{\lambda}_\mu^{\hat{t}\sigma})^{-1} \hat{w}^{\hat{t}\sigma}(\hat{u}_{\mu,k}^{\hat{t}\nu}), \hat{t}^\sigma [\hat{t}^{t\mu}, \hat{\lambda}_\mu] \hat{t}^{-\sigma} \rangle;$

here $\sigma \in \mathbb{Z}$ and $0 \leqq \mu < n$.

On the other hand,

$$(6) \quad \hat{\mathfrak{G}}' = \langle \hat{u}_k^{\hat{t}\sigma}, \hat{\lambda}^{\hat{t}\sigma} | \hat{R}_l^{\hat{t}\sigma}(\hat{u}_k^{\hat{t}\nu}), (\hat{\lambda}^{\hat{t}\sigma})^{-1} \cdot \hat{w}^{\hat{t}\sigma}(\hat{u}_k^{\hat{t}\nu}), [\hat{t}, \hat{\lambda}^{\hat{t}\sigma}] \rangle$$
$$= \langle \hat{u}_k^{\hat{t}\sigma}, \hat{\lambda} | \hat{R}_l^{\hat{t}\sigma}(\hat{u}_k^{\hat{t}\nu}), (\hat{\lambda}^{\hat{t}\sigma})^{-1} \cdot \hat{w}^{\hat{t}\sigma}(\hat{u}_k^{\hat{t}\nu}) \rangle$$

since the relation $[\hat{t}, \hat{\lambda}^{\hat{t}\sigma}]$ implies that $\hat{\lambda}^{\hat{t}\sigma} = \hat{\lambda}^{\hat{t}\sigma+1}$. By conjugation with t^μ we obtain

$$(6\mu) \quad \hat{\mathfrak{G}}'^{t\mu} = t^\mu \hat{\mathfrak{G}}' t^{-\mu} = \langle \hat{u}_{\mu,k}^{\hat{t}\sigma}, \hat{\lambda}_\mu | \hat{R}_l^{\hat{t}\sigma}(\hat{u}_{\mu,k}^{\hat{t}\nu}), (\hat{\lambda}_\mu^{\hat{t}\sigma})^{-1} \cdot \hat{w}^{\hat{t}\sigma}(\hat{u}_{\mu,k}^{\hat{t}\nu}) \rangle.$$

Define

$$(7) \quad \mathfrak{R} = \langle \tilde{u}_i^{t\varrho}, \hat{\lambda}^{t\mu} | \tilde{R}_j^{t\varrho}(\tilde{u}_i^{t\nu}, \hat{\lambda}) \rangle$$
$$= \langle \tilde{u}_i^{t\varrho}, \hat{\lambda}_\mu | \tilde{R}_j^{t\varrho}(\tilde{u}_i^{t\nu}, \hat{\lambda}_\mu) \rangle.$$

Since the presentations of $\hat{\mathfrak{G}}', \hat{\mathfrak{G}}'^t, \ldots, \hat{\mathfrak{G}}'^{t^{n-1}}$ have disjoint sets of generators, it follows from (6) that

$$(8) \quad \langle \hat{u}_k^{t\sigma}, \hat{\lambda}_\mu | \hat{R}_l^{\hat{t}\sigma}(\hat{u}_{\mu,k}^{\hat{t}\nu}), (\hat{\lambda}_\mu^{\hat{t}\sigma})^{-1} \cdot \hat{w}^{\hat{t}\sigma}(\hat{u}_{\mu,k}^{\hat{t}\nu}) \rangle$$
$$= \hat{\mathfrak{G}}' * \hat{\mathfrak{G}}'^t * \ldots * \hat{\mathfrak{G}}'^{t^{n-1}}$$

and that $\hat{\lambda}_0, \ldots, \hat{\lambda}_{n-1}$ generate a free group of rank n. Moreover,

$$(9) \quad \langle \hat{\lambda}^{t\varrho} | \varrho \in \mathbb{Z} \rangle = \langle \hat{\lambda}_0, \ldots, \hat{\lambda}_{n-1} \rangle,$$

as follows from the commutator relations $[\hat{t}, \hat{\lambda}]^{t\varrho}$. If $n = 0$ then $\langle \hat{\lambda}^{t\varrho} \rangle$ is of infinite rank. Now (5), (7) and (8) imply that

$$(10) \quad \mathfrak{G}' = \mathfrak{R} *_{\langle \hat{\lambda}^{t\varrho} \rangle} (\hat{\mathfrak{G}}' * \hat{\mathfrak{G}}'^t * \ldots * \hat{\mathfrak{G}}'^{t^{n-1}}).$$

4.13 Lemma. *For $n \neq 0$, $\mathfrak{G}'$ is finitely generated if and only if $\mathfrak{R}$ and $\hat{\mathfrak{G}}'$ are finitely generated.*

Proof. This is a consequence of

$$\operatorname{rank}(\hat{\mathfrak{G}}' * \ldots * \hat{\mathfrak{G}}'^{t^{n-1}}) = n \cdot \operatorname{rank} \hat{\mathfrak{G}}'$$

and the following Lemma 4.14. □

4.14 Lemma. *Let $\mathfrak{G} = \mathfrak{G}_1 *_{\mathfrak{S}} \mathfrak{G}_2$ where $\mathfrak{S}$ is finitely generated. Then $\mathfrak{G}$ is finitely generated if and only if $\mathfrak{G}_1$ and $\mathfrak{G}_2$ are finitely generated.*

Proof. (R. Bieri). When $\mathfrak{G}$ is finitely generated there are finite subsets $X_i \subset \mathfrak{G}_i$ $(i = 1, 2)$ with $\langle X_1, X_2 \rangle = \mathfrak{G}$. Since $\mathfrak{S}$ is finitely generated we may assume that both X_1 and X_2 contain generators for $\mathfrak{S}$. Let $\mathfrak{H}_i = \langle X_i \rangle \subset \mathfrak{G}_i$. Then

$\mathfrak{S} = \mathfrak{G}_1 \cap \mathfrak{G}_2 \supset \mathfrak{H}_1 \cap \mathfrak{H}_2$, but on the other hand $\mathfrak{H}_1 \cap \mathfrak{H}_2 \supset \mathfrak{S}$, so that $\mathfrak{S} = \mathfrak{G}_1 \cap \mathfrak{G}_2 = \mathfrak{H}_1 \cap \mathfrak{H}_2$. It follows that the map $\mathfrak{H}_1 *_{\mathfrak{S}} \mathfrak{H}_2 \to \mathfrak{G}_1 *_{\mathfrak{S}} \mathfrak{G}_2$ induced by the embeddings $\mathfrak{H}_i \to \mathfrak{G}_i$ is an isomorphism. Now the solution of the word problem implies that $\mathfrak{H}_i = \mathfrak{G}_i$. □

Next we will prove that $\mathfrak{K}$ is finitely generated if and only if $\tilde{\mathfrak{G}}'$ is. To do this we start with a Wirtinger presentation of $\tilde{\mathfrak{k}} \cup \tilde{\ell}$ and get

$$\mathfrak{H} = \langle t, \tilde{u}_i, \hat{\lambda} \mid \tilde{Q}_r(\tilde{u}_i^{t^\nu}), [\hat{\lambda}, \tilde{v}_s(\tilde{u}_i^{t^\nu})] \rangle .$$

The augmentation $\varphi\colon \mathfrak{G} \to \mathbb{Z}$ induces a homomorphism

$$\begin{aligned} &\varphi_0\colon \mathfrak{H} \to \mathbb{Z} \quad \text{with} \quad t \mapsto 1, \tilde{u}_i, \hat{\lambda} \mapsto 0 \quad \text{and} \\ &\ker \varphi_0 = \langle \tilde{u}_i^{t^e}, \hat{\lambda}^{t^e} \mid \tilde{Q}_r^{t^e}(\tilde{u}_i^{t^\nu}), [\hat{\lambda}, \tilde{v}_s(\tilde{u}_i^{t^\nu})]^{t^e} \rangle = \mathfrak{K}. \end{aligned}$$

Moreover,

$$\begin{aligned} \tilde{\mathfrak{G}} &= \langle t, \tilde{u}_i, \hat{\lambda} \mid \tilde{Q}_r(\tilde{u}_i^{t^\nu}), \hat{\lambda} \rangle \quad \text{and} \\ \tilde{\mathfrak{G}}' &= \langle \tilde{u}_i^{t^e}, \hat{\lambda}^{t^e} \mid \tilde{Q}_r^{t^e}(\tilde{u}_i^{t^\nu}), \hat{\lambda}^{t^e} \rangle . \end{aligned}$$

Consider the canonical homomorphism $\psi\colon \mathfrak{H} \to \tilde{\mathfrak{G}}$ with $\ker \psi$ the normal closure of $\hat{\lambda}$ in $\mathfrak{H}$. One has $\ker \psi \subset \mathfrak{K}$, and

$$1 \to \ker \psi \to \mathfrak{K} \to \tilde{\mathfrak{G}}' \to 1$$

is exact. For $n \neq 0$, $\ker \psi$ is generated by $\hat{\lambda}, \hat{\lambda}^t, \ldots \hat{\lambda}^{t^{n-1}}$. *Thus $\mathfrak{K}$ is finitely generated if and only if $\tilde{\mathfrak{G}}'$ is.*

4.15 Proposition (commutator subgroup of a satellite). *The commutator subgroup $\mathfrak{G}'$ of a satellite $\mathfrak{k}$ is finitely generated if and only if $n \neq 0$ and the commutator subgroups of the companion $\hat{\mathfrak{k}}$ and the knot $\tilde{\mathfrak{k}}$ are finitely generated.*

Proof. It remains to prove that $n \neq 0$ is a necessary condition. If $n = 0$ the group $\mathfrak{G}'$ contains the subgroup $\langle \hat{t}, \hat{\lambda} \rangle \cong \mathbb{Z} \oplus \mathbb{Z}$; hence $\mathfrak{G}'$ is not free and, by 4.6(a), cannot be finitely generated. □

F History and Sources

The study of the commutator subgroup $\mathfrak{G}'$ concentrated on $\mathfrak{G}'/\mathfrak{G}''$ in the early years of knot theory. This will be the object of Chapters 8, 9. In [Reidemeister 1932, § 6] there is a group presentation of $\mathfrak{G}'$. But the structure of $\mathfrak{G}'$ eluded the purely algebraic approach.

Neuwirth made the first important step by investigating the infinite cyclic covering space C_∞, $\pi_1 C_\infty = \mathfrak{G}'$, using the then (relatively) new tools *Dehn's*

Lemma and *Loop Theorem* [Neuwirth 1960]: Lemma 4.5. The analysis of $\mathfrak{G}'$ resulted in splitting off a special class of knots, whose commutator subgroups are finitely generated. In this case $\mathfrak{G}'$ proves to be a free group of rank $2g$, g the genus of the knot. These knots will be treated separately in the next Chapter. There remained two different possible types of infinitely generated commutator groups in Neuwirth's analysis, and it took some years till one of them could be excluded [Brown-Crowell 1965]: Lemma 4.7. The remaining one, an infinite free product with amalgamations does occur. This group is rather complicated and its structure surely could do with some further investigation.

G Exercises

E 4.1 Describe the process of cutting along a one-sided surface.

E 4.2 Prove that the commutator subgroup of the group of the trefoil is free of rank 2.

E 4.3 Prove that the commutator subgroup of the group of the knot 6_1 cannot be finitely generated.

If the bands of a Seifert surface spanning $\mathfrak{k}$ form a plat (Fig. 4.8), we call $\mathfrak{k}$ a *braid-like* knot (Compare 8.2.).

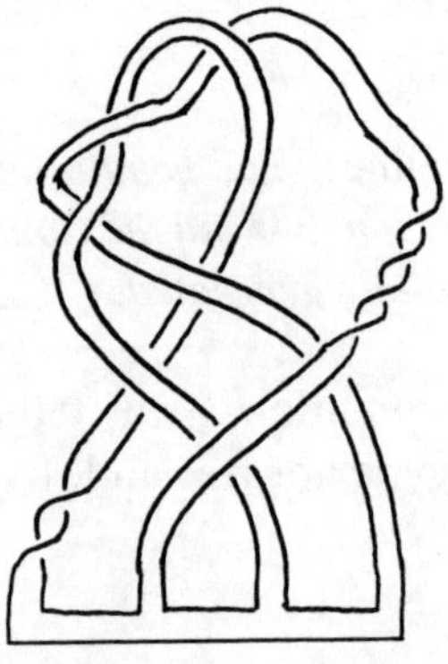

Fig. 4.8

E 4.4 Show that for a braid-like knot the group $\mathfrak{A} = \pi_1 C^*$ is always free. (For the notation see 4.4–6.)

E 4.5 Doubled knots are not braid-like. (See 2.9.)

E 4.6 If $\mathfrak{k}$ is braid-like with respect to a Seifert surface of minimal genus, then there is an algorithm by which one can decide whether $\mathfrak{G}'$ is finitely generated or not. Apply this to E 4.2.

E 4.7 Let $\mathfrak{Z}_a$ and $\mathfrak{Z}_b$ be cyclic groups of order a resp. b. Use the Reidemeister–

Schreier method to prove that the commutator subgroup $(\mathfrak{Z}_a * \mathfrak{Z}_b)'$ of the free product is a free group of rank $(a-1)(b-1)$.

E 4.8 Let C^* be the space obtained by cutting a knot complement along a Seifert surface of minimal genus. Prove that in the case of a trefoil or 4-knot C^* is a handlebody of genus two.

E 4.9 If $\mathfrak{G}$ is the group of a link of multiplicity μ,

$$\mathfrak{G} \underset{\kappa}{\rightarrow} \mathfrak{G}/\mathfrak{G}' \cong \mathfrak{Z}^{\mu} \underset{\Delta}{\rightarrow} \mathfrak{Z}.$$

Generalize the construction of C_∞ to links by replacing $\mathfrak{G}'$ by $\ker(\Delta \circ \kappa)$. ($\Delta$ is the diagonal map.)

E 4.10 Let $\mathfrak{p}(2p+1, 2q+1, 2r+1) = \mathfrak{k}$ be a pretzel-knot, $p, q, r \in \mathbb{Z}$, Figure 8.9. Compute $i_{\#}^{\pm}: \pi_1 S \rightarrow \pi_1 C^*$ and $i_*^{\pm}: H_1(S) \rightarrow H_1(C^*)$ for a Seifert surface S of minimal genus spanning $\mathfrak{k}$ and decide which of these knots have a finitely generated commutator subgroup.

E 4.11 Consider the (generalized) pretzel-knot $\mathfrak{p}(3, 1, 3, -1, -3)$, and show that it spans a Seifert surface F which is not of minimal genus such that the inclusions $i^{\pm}: F \rightarrow C^*$ induce injections $i_{\#}^{\pm}$. (The homomorphisms $i_*^{\pm}$ are necessarily not injective, compare E 8.1.)

Chapter 5: Fibred Knots

By the theorem of Brown, Crowell and Neuwirth, knots fall into two different classes according to the structure of their commutator subgroups. The first of them comprises the knots whose commutator subgroups are finitely generated, and hence free, the second one those whose commutator subgroups cannot be finitely generated. We have seen that all torus-knots belong to the first category and we have given an example – the 2-bridge knot $\mathfrak{b}(7, 3)$ – of the second variety. The aim of this chapter is to demonstrate that the algebraic distinction of the two classes reflects an essential difference in the geometric structure of the knot complements.

A Fibration Theorem

5.1 Theorem (Stallings). *The complement $C = \overline{S^3 - V(\mathfrak{k})}$ of a knot $\mathfrak{k}$ fibres locally trivially over S^1 with Seifert surfaces of genus g as fibres if the commutator subgroup $\mathfrak{G}'$ of the knot group is finitely generated, $\mathfrak{G}' \cong \mathfrak{F}_{2g}$.*

Theorem 5.1 is a special version of the more general Theorem 5.6 of [Stallings 1961]. The following proof of 5.1 is based on Stalling's original argument but takes advantage of the special situation, thus reducing its length and difficulty.

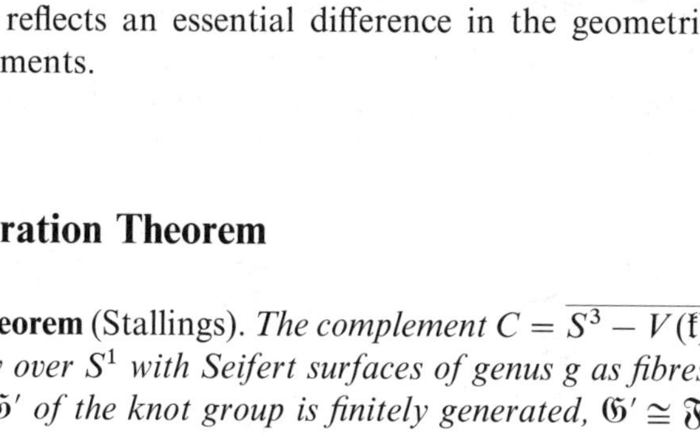

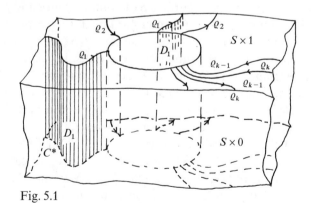

Fig. 5.1

5.2 To prepare the setting imagine C fibred as described in 5.1. Cut along a Seifert surface S of $\mathfrak{k}$. The resulting space C^* is a fibre space with base-space the interval I, hence $C^* \cong S \times I$. The space C is reobtained from C^* by an identification of $S \times 0$ and $S \times 1$: $(x, 0) = (h(x), 1)$, $x \in S$, where $h\colon S \to S$ is an orientation preserving homeomorphism. We write in short:

$$C = S \times I/h.$$

Choose a base point P on ∂S and let $\sigma = P \times I$ denote the path leading from $(P, 1)$ to $(P, 0)$. For $w^0 = (w, 0)$, $w^1 = (w, 1)$ and $w \in \pi_1(S, P)$ there is an equation

$$w^1 = \sigma w^0 \sigma^{-1} \text{ in } \pi_1(C^*, (P, 1)).$$

Let $\kappa_1, \ldots, \kappa_{2g}$ be simple closed curves representing canonical generators of S. Then obviously

$$\sigma \kappa_i^0 \sigma^{-1} (\kappa_i^1)^{-1} = \varrho_i' \simeq 0 \text{ in } C^*.$$

The curves $\{\varrho_i' | 1 \leqq i \leqq 2g\}$ coincide in σ; they can be replaced by a system of simple closed curves $\{\varrho_i\}$ on ∂C^* which are pairwise disjoint, where each ϱ_i is obtained from ϱ_i' by an isotopic deformation near σ, see Figure 5.1. There are disks D_i embedded in C^*, such that $\partial D_i = \varrho_i$. Cut C^* along the disks D_i to obtain a 3-ball C^{**} (Fig. 5.2).

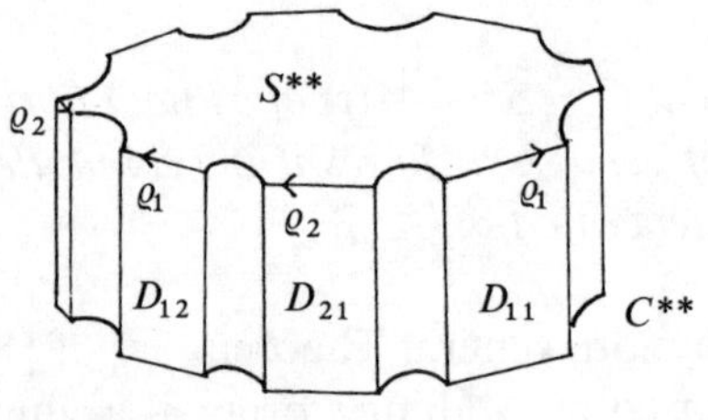

Fig. 5.2

5.3 *Proof of 5.1.* We cut C along a Seifert surface S of minimal genus and get C^* with $S^\pm = S \times 1{,}0$ in its boundary as in Chapter 4. Our aim is to produce a 3-ball C^{**} by cutting C^* along disks. The inclusions $i^+\colon S^+ \to C^*$ and $i^-\colon S^- \to C^*$ induce isomorphisms $i_\#^\pm$ of the fundamental groups. Let $m \subset \partial C$ be a meridian through the base point P on ∂S. Then by the cutting process $C \to C^*$ m will become a path σ leading from $P^+ = (P, 1)$ to $P^- = (P, 0)$. Assign to $\sigma w^- \sigma^{-1}$ for $w^- \in \pi_1(S^-, P^-)$ the element $w^+ \in \pi_1(S^+, P^+)$, $w^+ = \sigma w^- \sigma^{-1}$ in $\pi_1(C^*, P^+)$. We know the map $f_\#(w^-) = w^+$ to be an isomorphism $f_\#\colon \pi_1(S^-, P^-) \to \pi_1(S^+, P^+)$. So by Nielsen's theorem [Nielsen 1927], [ZVC 1980, 5.7] there is a homeomorphism $f\colon S^- \to S^+$ inducing $f_\#$. There are canonical curves κ_i^+, κ_i^- on S^+ and S^- with $f(\kappa_i^-) = \kappa_i^+$ and $\sigma \kappa_i^- \sigma^{-1} \simeq \kappa_i^+$ in C^*. Again the system $\{\sigma \kappa_i^- \sigma^{-1} (\kappa_i^+)^{-1} | 0 \leqq i \leqq 2g\}$ is replaced by an isotopic system $\{\varrho_i | 1 \leqq i \leqq 2g\}$ of disjoint simple curves, which by Dehn's Lemma [Papakyriakopoulos 1957] (see Appendix B4) span non-singular disks D_i, $\partial D_i = \varrho_i = D \cap \partial C^*$ which can be chosen disjoint.

Cut C^* along the D_i. The resulting space C^{**} is a 3-ball (Fig. 5.2) by Alexander's Theorem (see [Graeub 1950]), because its boundary is a 2-sphere in S^3 composed of an annulus $\partial S \times I$ and two 2-cells $(S^+)^*$ and $(S^-)^*$ where S^*, $(S^+)^*$ and $(S^-)^*$ are, respectively, obtained from S, S^+, S^- by the cutting of C^*. So C^{**} can be fibred over I, $C^{**} = S^* \times I$, $(S^*)^+ = S^* \times 1$, $(S^*)^- = S^* \times 0$. It remains to show that the identification $C^{**} \to C^*$ inverse to the cutting-process can be changed by an isotopy such as to be compatible with the fibration. Let g_i' be the identifying homeomorphism, $g_i'(D_{i1}) = D_{i2} = D_i$, $i = 1, 2, \ldots, 2g$. The fibration of C^{**} induces a fibration on D_{ij}, the fibres being parallel to $D_{ij} \cap (S^*)^{\pm}$. There are fibre preserving homeomorphism g_i: $D_{i1} \to D_{i2}$ which coincide with g_i' on the top $(S^*)^+$ and the bottom $(S^*)^-$. Since the D_{i1}, D_{i2} are 2-cells, the g_i are isotopic to the g_i'; hence, $C^* \cong S \times I$ and $C = S \times I/h$ (compare Lemma 5.7). □

5.4 Corollary. *The complement C of a* fibred *knot of genus g is obtained from $S \times I$, S a compact surface of genus g with a connected nonempty boundary, by identification*

$$(x, 0) = (h(x), 1),\ x \in S,$$

where h: $S \to S$ is an orientation preserving homeomorphism:

$$C = S \times I/h.$$

$\mathfrak{G} = \pi_1 C$ is a semidirect product $\mathfrak{G} = \mathfrak{Z} \ltimes_\alpha \mathfrak{G}'$, where $\mathfrak{G}' = \pi_1 S \cong \mathfrak{F}_{2g}$. The automorphism $\alpha(t)$: $\mathfrak{G}' \to \mathfrak{G}'$, $a \mapsto t^{-1} a t$, and $h_\#$ or $h_\#^{-1}$ belong to the same class of automorphisms, in other words, $\alpha(t) \cdot h_\#^{-1}$ or $\alpha(t) \cdot h_\#$ is an inner automorphism of $\mathfrak{G}'$.

The *proof* follows from the construction used in proving 5.1. □

Observe that σ after identification by h becomes a generator of $\mathfrak{Z}$. If t is replaced by another coset representative t^* mod $\mathfrak{G}'$, $\alpha(t^*)$ and $\alpha(t)$ will be in the same class of automorphisms. Furthermore $\alpha(t^{-1}) = \alpha^{-1}(t)$. The ambiguity $h_\#^{\pm 1}$ can be avoided if σ as well as t are chosen to represent a meridian of $\mathfrak{k}$. ($h_\#$ is called the monodromy map of C.)

There is an addendum to theorem 5.1.

5.5 Proposition. *If the complement C of a knot $\mathfrak{k}$ of genus g fibres locally trivially over S^1 then the fibre is a compact orientable surface S of genus g with one boundary component, and $\mathfrak{G}' = \pi_1 S \cong \mathfrak{F}_{2g}$.*

Proof. Since the fibration $C \to S^1$ is locally trivial the fibre is a compact 2-manifold S. There is an induced fibration $\partial C \to S^1$ with fibre ∂S. Consider the exact fibre sequences

$$\begin{array}{ccccccccc}
1 \to \pi_1(\partial S) & \to & \pi_1(\partial C) & \to & \pi_1 S^1 & \to & \pi_0(\partial S) & \to & 1 \\
\downarrow & & \downarrow & & \| & & \downarrow & & \\
1 \to \pi_1 S & \to & \pi_1 C & \to & \pi_1 S^1 & \to & \pi_0 S & \to & 1.
\end{array}$$

The diagram commutes, and $\pi_1(\partial C) \to \pi_1 S^1$ is surjective. Hence $\pi_1 C \to \pi_1 S^1$ is surjective and $\pi_0(\partial S) = \pi_0 S = 1$, that is, S and ∂S are connected. (See E 5.1.)

Now the second sequence pins down $\pi_1 S$ as $(\pi_1 C)'$. □

We conclude this paragraph by stating the general theorem of Stallings without proof:

5.6 Theorem (Stallings). *Let M be a compact irreducible 3-manifold (this means that in M every 2-sphere bounds a 3-ball). Assume that $\varphi\colon \pi_1 M \to \mathbb{Z}$ is an epimorphism with a finitely generated kernel. Then:*

(a) $\ker \varphi$ *is isomorphic to the fundamental group of a compact surface S.*

(b) M can be fibred locally trivially over S^1 with fibre S if $\ker \varphi \ncong \mathbb{Z}_2$. □

B Fibred Knots

The knots of the first class whose commutator subgroups are finitely generated – in fact are free groups of rank $2g$ – are called *fibred knots* by virtue of Theorem 5.1. The fibration of their complements affords additional mathematical tools for the treatment of these knots. They are in a way the simpler knots and in their case the original 3-dimensional problem can to some extent be played down to two dimensions. This is a phenomenon also known in the theory of braids (see Chapter 10) or Seifert fibre spaces.

We shall study the question: How much information on the fibred knot $\mathfrak{k}$ do we get by looking at $h\colon S \to S$ in the formula $S \times I/h = \overline{S^3 - V(\mathfrak{k})}$?

5.7 Lemma (Neuwirth). *If $h_0, h_1\colon S \to S$ are isotopic homeomorphisms then there is a fibre preserving homeomorphism*

$$H\colon S \times I/h_0 \to S \times I/h_1 .$$

Proof. Let h_t be the isotopy connecting h_0 and h_1. Put $g_t = h_t h_0^{-1}$ and define a homeomorphism

$$H'\colon S \times I \to S \times I$$

by $H'(x, t) = (g_t(x), t)$, $x \in S$, $t \in I$. Since $H'(x, 0) = (x, 0)$ and

$$H'(h_0(x), 1) = (g_1 h_0(x), 1) = (h_1(x), 1),$$

H' induces a homeomorphism H as desired. □

5.8 Lemma. *Let $f\colon S \to S$ be a homeomorphism. Then there is a fibre preserving homeomorphism $F\colon S \times I/h \to S \times I/fhf^{-1}$. If f is orientation preserving then there is a homeomorphism F which also preserves the orientation.*

Proof. Take $F(x, t) = (f(x), t)$. □

5.9 Definition (similarity). Two homeomorphisms $h_1\colon S_1 \to S_1$, $h_2\colon S_2 \to S_2$ of homeomorphic oriented compact surfaces S_1 and S_2 are called *similar*, if there is a homeomorphism $f\colon S_1 \to S_2$ respecting orientations, such that fh_1f^{-1} and h_2 are isotopic.

The notion of similarity enables us to characterize homeomorphic complements C_1 and C_2 of fibred knots $\mathfrak{k}_1$ and $\mathfrak{k}_2$ of equal genus g by properties of the gluing homeomorphisms.

5.10 Proposition. *Let $\mathfrak{k}_1$, $\mathfrak{k}_2$ be two (oriented) fibred knots of genus g with (oriented) complements C_1 and C_2. There is an orientation preserving homeomorphism $H\colon C_1 = S_1 \times I/h_1 \to C_2 = S_2 \times I/h_2$, $\lambda_1 = \partial S_1 \simeq \mathfrak{k}_1$, $H(\partial S_1) = \partial S_2 = \lambda_2 \simeq \mathfrak{k}_2$, if and only if there is a homeomorphism $h\colon S_1 \to S_2$, respecting orientations, $h(\lambda_1) = \lambda_2$, such that hh_1h^{-1} and h_2 are isotopic, that is, h_1 and h_2 are similar.*

Proof. If h exists and hh_1h^{-1} and h_2 are isotopic then by Lemma 5.7 there is a homeomorphism which preserves orientation and fibration:

$$F\colon S_2 \times I/hh_1h^{-1} \to S_2 \times I/h_2.$$

Now $F'\colon S_1 \times I/h_1 \to S_2 \times I/hh_1h^{-1}$, $(x, t) \mapsto (h(x), t)$, gives $H = FF'$ as desired.

To show the converse let $H\colon C_1 = S_1 \times I/h_1 \to S_2 \times I/h_2 = C_2$ be an orientation preserving homeomorphism, $H(\lambda_1) = \lambda_2$. There is an isomorphism

$$H_\#\colon \pi_1 C_1 = \mathfrak{G}_1 \to \mathfrak{G}_2 = \pi_1 C_2 \text{ which induces an isomorphism}$$
$$h_\#\colon \pi_1 S_1 = \mathfrak{G}_1' \to \mathfrak{G}_2' = \pi_1 S_2.$$

By Nielsen ([ZVC 1970, Satz V. 9], [ZVC 1980, 5.7.2]) there is a homeomorphism $h\colon S_1 \to S_2$ respecting the orientations induced on ∂S_1 and ∂S_2. We can choose representatives m_1 and m_2 of meridians of $\mathfrak{k}_1$, $\mathfrak{k}_2$, such that

$$h_{i\#}\colon \pi_1 S_i \to \pi_1 S_i,\ x \mapsto m_i^{-1} x m_i, \quad i = 1, 2.$$

Since H preserves the orientation, $H_\#(m_1) = \ell_2^q m_2 \ell_2^{-q}$ where ℓ_i is represented by λ_i, $i = 1, 2$. Now

$$\begin{aligned} h_\# h_{1\#}(x) &= h_\#(m_1^{-1} x m_1) = H_\#(m_1^{-1}) h_\#(x) (H_\#(m_1)) \\ &= \ell_2^q m_2^{-1} \ell_2^{-q} h_\#(x) \ell_2^q m_2 \ell_2^{-q} = a(h_{2\#} h_\#(x)) a^{-1}, \end{aligned}$$

where

$$a = \ell_2^q m_2^{-1} \ell_2^{-q} m_2 \in \pi_1 S_2.$$

By Baer's Theorem ([ZVC 1970, Satz V. 15], [ZVC 1980, 13.1]) hh_1 and $h_2 h$ are isotopic, hence h_1 and h_2 are similar. □

Proposition 5.10 shows that the classification of fibred knot complements can be formulated in terms of the fibring surfaces and maps of such surfaces. The proof also shows that if fibred complements are homeomorphic then there is a fibre preserving homeomorphism. This means: different fibrations of a complement C admit a fibre preserving autohomeomorphism. Indeed, by [Waldhausen 1968] there is even an isotopy connecting both fibrations.

In the case of fibred knots invertibility and amphicheirality can be excluded by properties of surface mappings.

5.11 Proposition. *Let $C = S \times I/h$ be the complement of a fibred knot $\mathfrak{k}$.*

(a) $\mathfrak{k}$ is amphicheiral only if h and h^{-1} are similar.

(b) $\mathfrak{k}$ is invertible only if there is a homeomorphism $f\colon S \to S$, reversing orientation, such that h and fhf^{-1} are similar.

Proof [Burde-Zieschang 1967]. (a) The map $(x, t) \mapsto (x, 1-t)$, $x \in S$, $t \in I$ induces a mapping

$$C = S \times I/h \to S \times I/h^{-1} = C'$$

onto the mirror image C' of C satisfying the conditions of Proposition 5.10.

(b) If $f\colon S \to S$ is any homeomorphism inverting the orientation of S, then $(x, t) \mapsto (f(x), 1-t)$ induces a homeomorphism

$$C = S \times I/h \to S \times I/fh^{-1}f^{-1} = \tilde{C}$$

which maps ∂S onto its inverse. Again apply Proposition 5.10. □

C Applications and Examples

The fibration of a non-trivial knot complement is not easily visualized, even in the simplest cases. (If $\mathfrak{k}$ is trivial, C is a solid torus, hence trivially fibred by disks D^2, $C = S^1 \times D^2$.)

5.12 Fibring the complement of the trefoil. Let C be the complement of a trefoil $\mathfrak{k}$ sitting symmetrically on the boundary of an unknotted solid torus $T_1 \subset S^3$ (Fig. 5.3). $T_2 = \overline{S^3 - T_1}$ is another unknotted solid torus in S^3. A Seifert surface

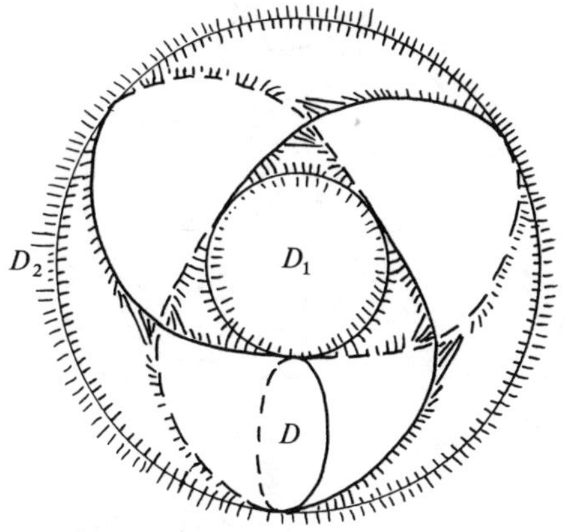

Fig. 5.3

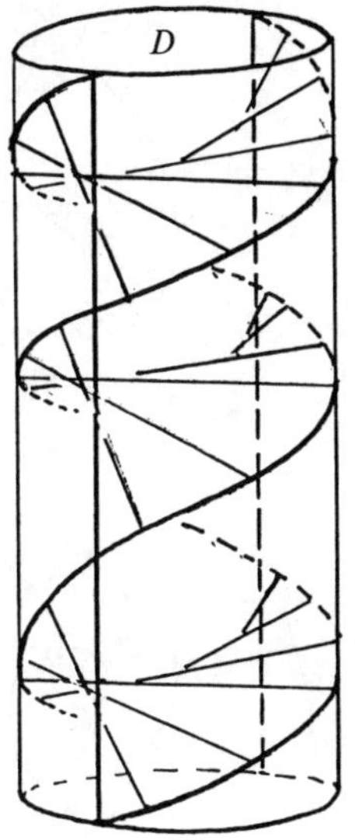

Fig. 5.4

S (hatched regions in Fig. 5.3) is composed of two disks D_1 and D_2 in T_2 and three twisted 2-cells in T_1. (Fig. 5.4 shows T_1 and the twisted 2-cells in a straightened position.) A rotation about the core of T_1 through φ and, at the same time, a rotation about the core of T_2 through $2\varphi/3$ combine to a mapping f_φ: $S^3 \to S^3$. Now C is fibred by $\{f_\varphi(S) | 0 \leqq \varphi \leqq \pi\}$ (see [Rolfson 1976, p. 329]).

5.13 Fibring the complement of the four-knot. The above construction of a fibration takes advantage of the symmetries of the trefoil as a torus knot. It is not so easy to convince oneself of the existence of a fibration of the complement of the figure-eight knot $\mathfrak{k}$ by geometric arguments. The following sequence of figures (5.5a–g) tries to do it: a) depicts a Seifert surface S spanning the four-knot in a tolerably symmetric fashion. b) shows S thickened up to a handlebody V of genus 2. The knot $\mathfrak{k}$ is a curve on its boundary. c) presents $V' = \overline{S^3 - V}$. In order to find $\mathfrak{k}$ on $\partial V'$ express $\mathfrak{k}$ on ∂V by canonical generators α, β, γ, δ of $\pi_1(\partial V)$, $\mathfrak{k} = \beta\alpha^{-1}\gamma^{-1}\delta^{-1}\alpha\beta^{-1}\gamma\delta$. Replace every generator by its inverse to get $\mathfrak{k} = \beta^{-1}\alpha\gamma\delta\alpha^{-1}\beta\gamma^{-1}\delta^{-1}$ on $\partial V'$. The knot $\mathfrak{k}$ divides $\partial V'$ into two surfaces S^+ and S^- of genus one, Figure d). e) just simplifies d); the knot is pushed on the outline of the figure as far as possible. By way of f) we finally reach g), where the fibres of $V' - \mathfrak{k}$ are Seifert surfaces parallel to S^+ and S^-. The fibration extends to $V - \mathfrak{k}$ by the definition of V.

The following proposition shows that the trefoil and the four-knot are not only the two knots with the fewest crossings but constitute a class that can be algebraically characterized.

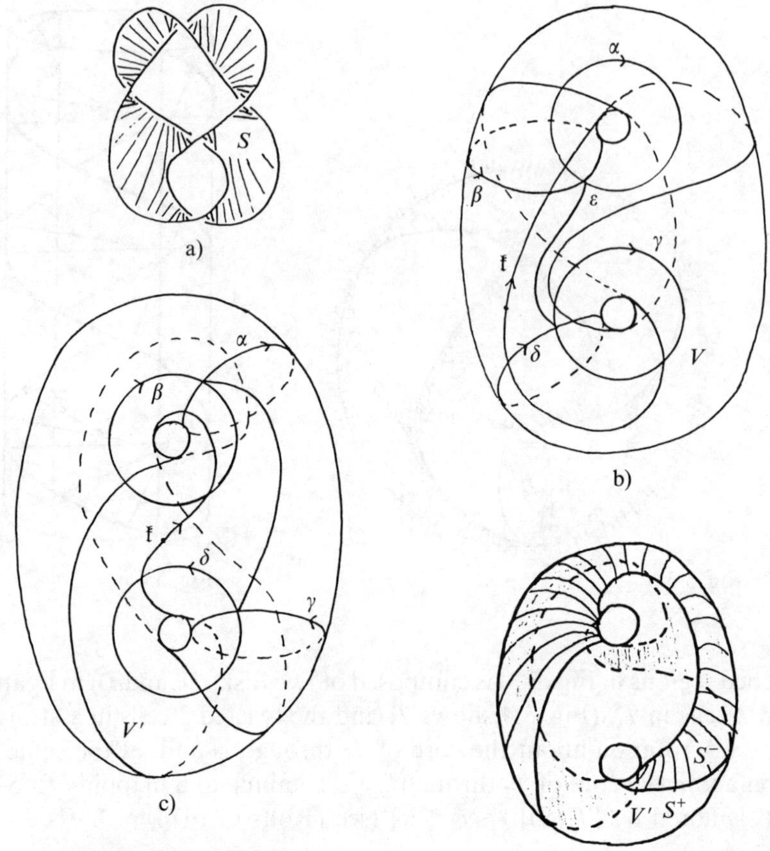

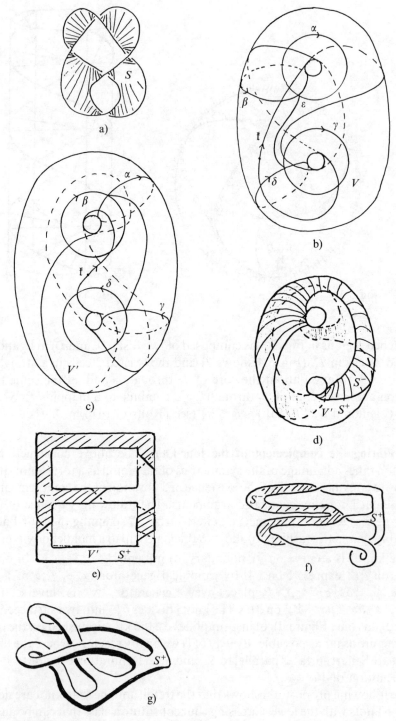

Fig. 5.5

5.14 Proposition. *The trefoil knot and the four-knot are the only fibred knots of genus one.*

At this stage we only prove a weaker result: *A fibred knot of genus one has the same complement as the trefoil or the four-knot.*

Proof (see [Burde-Zieschang 1967]). Let $C = S \times I/h$ be the complement of a knot $\mathfrak{k}$ and assume that S is a torus with one boundary component. Then h induces automorphisms $h_{\#}\colon \pi_1 S \to \pi_1 S$ and $h_*\colon H_1(S) \to H_1(S) \cong \mathbb{Z}^2$. Let A denote the 2×2-matrix corresponding to h_* (after the choice of a basis).

(1) $\det A = 1\,,$

since h preserves the orientation. The automorphism $h_{\#}$ describes the effect of the conjugation with a meridian of $\mathfrak{k}$ and it follows that $\pi_1 S$ becomes trivial by introducing the relations $h_{\#}(x) = x$, $x \in \pi_1 S$. This implies:

(2) $\det\left(A - \begin{pmatrix} 1 & 0 \\ 0 & 1 \end{pmatrix}\right) = \pm 1\,.$

From (1) and (2) it follows that

(3) $\operatorname{trace} A \in \{1, 3\}\,.$

A matrix of trace $+1$ is conjugate in $SL(2, \mathbb{Z})$ to $\begin{pmatrix} 1 & -1 \\ 1 & 0 \end{pmatrix}$ or $\begin{pmatrix} 1 & 1 \\ -1 & 0 \end{pmatrix}$ and a matrix with trace 3 is conjugate to $\begin{pmatrix} 0 & -1 \\ 1 & 3 \end{pmatrix}$, [Zieschang 1981, 21.15]. Two automorphisms of $\mathfrak{F}_2$ which induce the same automorphism on $\mathbb{Z} \oplus \mathbb{Z}$ differ by an inner automorphism ([Nielsen 1918], [Lyndon-Schupp 1977, I.4.5]). The Baer Theorem now implies that the gluing mappings are determined up to isotopy; hence, by Lemma 5.7, the complement of the knot is determined up to homeomorphism by the matrix above. The matrices $\begin{pmatrix} 1 & -1 \\ 1 & 0 \end{pmatrix}$ and $\begin{pmatrix} 1 & 1 \\ -1 & 0 \end{pmatrix}$ are obtained when the complements of the trefoil knots are fibred, see 5.13. The matrix $\begin{pmatrix} 0 & -1 \\ 1 & 3 \end{pmatrix}$ results in the case of the figure-eight knot as follows from the fact that in 3.8 the conjugation by s induces on $\mathfrak{G}'$ the mapping $x_0 \mapsto x_1$, $x_1 \mapsto x_1 x_0^{-1} x_1^2$.

Thus we have proved that the complement of a fibred knot $\mathfrak{k}$ of genus 1 is homeomorphic to the complement of a trefoil knot or the figure-eight knot. Later we shall show that $\mathfrak{k}$ is indeed a trefoil knot (Theorem 6.1) or a four-knot (Theorem 15.8). □

5.15. We conclude this section with an application of Proposition 5.11 and reprove the fact (see 3.29 (b)) that the trefoil knot is not amphicheiral. This was first proved by M. Dehn [1914].

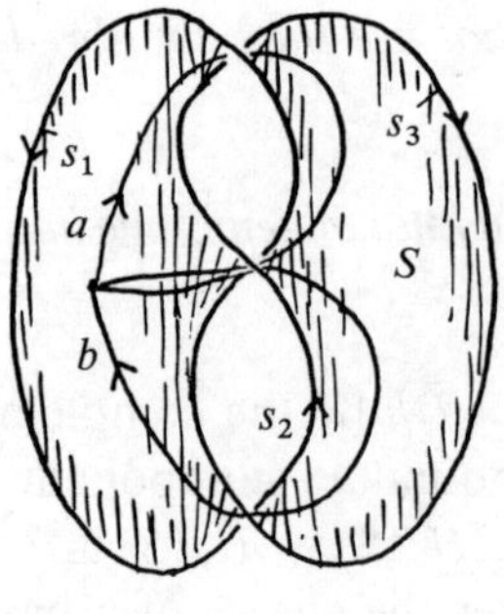

Fig. 5.6

Figure 5.6 shows a trefoil bounding a Seifert surface S of genus one. The Wirtinger presentation of the knot group $\mathfrak{G}$ is

$$\mathfrak{G} = \langle s_1, s_2, s_3 \,|\, s_3 s_1 s_3^{-1} s_2^{-1},\ s_1 s_2 s_1^{-1} s_3^{-1},\ s_2 s_3 s_2^{-1} s_1^{-1} \rangle .$$

The curves a and b in Figure 5.6 are free generators of

$$\pi_1 S = \mathfrak{F}_2 = \langle a, b \rangle .$$

They can be expressed by the Wirtinger generators s_i (see 3.7):

$$a = s_1^{-1} s_2, \quad b = s_2^{-1} s_3 .$$

Using the relations we get:

$$t^{-1} a t = s_1^{-1} s_1^{-1} s_2 s_1 = s_1^{-1} s_2 s_3^{-1} s_1 = s_1^{-1} s_2 s_3^{-1} s_2 s_2^{-1} s_1 = a b^{-1} a^{-1},$$
$$t^{-1} b t = s_1^{-1} s_2^{-1} s_3 s_1 = s_1^{-1} s_2^{-1} s_2 s_3 = s_1^{-1} s_2 \cdot s_2^{-1} s_3 = ab .$$

Let $C = S \times I/h$ be the complement of the trefoil. Relative to the basis $\{a, b\}$ of $H_1(S) = \mathbb{Z} \oplus \mathbb{Z}$

$$h_*\colon H_1(S) \to H_1(S)$$

is given by the matrix $\begin{pmatrix} 0 & -1 \\ 1 & 1 \end{pmatrix}$. (See Corollary 5.4). If the trefoil were amphicheiral, then by Proposition 5.11 there would be a unimodular matrix

$$\begin{pmatrix} \alpha & \beta \\ \gamma & \delta \end{pmatrix}, \ 1 = \alpha\delta - \beta\gamma,$$

such that

$$\begin{pmatrix} \alpha & \beta \\ \gamma & \delta \end{pmatrix} \begin{pmatrix} 1 & 1 \\ -1 & 0 \end{pmatrix} = \begin{pmatrix} 0 & -1 \\ 1 & 1 \end{pmatrix} \begin{pmatrix} \alpha & \beta \\ \gamma & \delta \end{pmatrix},$$

$$\begin{pmatrix} \alpha - \beta & \alpha \\ \gamma - \delta & \gamma \end{pmatrix} = \begin{pmatrix} -\gamma & -\delta \\ \alpha + \gamma & \beta + \delta \end{pmatrix}.$$

This means: $\delta = -\alpha$, $\gamma = \beta - \alpha$. However, $1 = \alpha\delta - \beta\gamma = -\alpha^2 - \beta(\beta - \alpha) = -(\alpha^2 - \alpha\beta + \beta^2)$ has no integral solution.

D History and Sources

The material of this chapter is for the larger part based on J. Stallings' theorem on fibring 3-manifolds [Stallings 1962]. The fibred complement $C = S \times I/f$ of a "fibred knot" was further investigated in [Neuwirth 1961′] and [Burde-Zieschang 1967]. In the first paper the complement was shown to be determined by the peripheral system of the knot group while in the second one C was characterized by properties of the identifying surface map f.

Neuwirth's result is a special case of the general theorems of Waldhausen [1968]. In this fundamental paper manifolds with a Stallings fibration play an important role.

E Exercises

E 5.1 Construct a fibration of a compact orientable 3-manifold M over S^1 such that $\pi_1 M \to \pi_1 S^1$ is not surjective. Observe that the fibre is not connected in this case.

E 5.2 Find a 2×2-matrix A representing f_*: $H_1(S) \to H_1(S)$ in the case of the complement $C = S \times I/f$ of the four-knot. Show that A and A^{-1} are conjugate.

E 5.3 Compute the powers of the automorphism $f_\#$: $\pi_1 S \to \pi_1 S$

$$f_\#(a) = t^{-1}at = b^{-1}$$
$$f_\#(b) = t^{-1}at = ba$$

induced by the identifying map of the trefoil (see 5.15). Describe the manifolds $S \times I/f^i$, $i \in \mathbb{Z}$.

E 5.4 Show that the knot 5_2 can be spanned by a Seifert surface S of minimal genus such that the knot complement C cut along S is a handlebody C^*. Apply the method used in 5.13 to show that nevertheless 5_2 is not fibred!

E 5.5 Show that the knot 8_{20} is fibred.

Chapter 6: A Characterization of Torus Knots

Torus knots have been repeatedly considered as examples in the preceding chapters. If knots are placed on the boundaries of handlebodies as in Chapter 3, the least possible genus of a handlebody carrying a knot defines a hierarchy for knots where the torus knots form the simplest class excepting the trivial knot. Torus knots admit a simple algebraic characterization; see Theorem 6.1.

A Results and Sources

6.1 Theorem (Burde-Zieschang). *A non-trivial knot whose group* $\mathfrak{G}$ *has a non-trivial centre is a torus knot.*

The theorem was first proved in [Burde-Zieschang 1966], and had been proved for alternating knots in [Murasugi 1961] and [Neuwirth 1961]. Since torus knots have Property P (Chapter 15), Theorem 6.1 together with Theorem 3.29 shows: Any knot group with a non-trivial centre determines its complement, and the complement in turn admits just one torus knot $\mathfrak{t}(a, b)$ and its mirror image $\mathfrak{t}(a, -b)$.

F. Waldhausen later proved a more general theorem which includes Theorem 6.1 by way of Seifert's theory of fibred 3-manifolds, see [Waldhausen 1967]:

6.2 Theorem (Waldhausen). *Let M be an orientable compact irreducible 3-manifold. If either $H_1(M)$ is infinite or $\pi_1 M$ a non-trivial free product with amalgamation, and if $\pi_1 M$ has a non-trivial centre, then M is homeomorphic to a Seifert fibred manifold with orientable orbit-manifold (Zerlegungsfläche).* □

The theorem obviously applies to knot complements $C = M$. A closer inspection of the Seifert fibration of C shows that it can be extended to S^3 in such a way that the knot becomes a normal fibre. Theorem 6.1 now follows from a result of [Seifert 1933] which contains a complete description of all fibrations of S^3.

6.3 Theorem (Seifert). *A fibre of a Seifert fibration of S^3 is a torus knot or the trivial knot. Exceptional fibres are always unknotted.* □

We propose to give now a proof of Theorem 6.1 which makes use of a theorem by Nielsen [1942] on mappings of surfaces. (This theorem is also used in

Waldhausen's proof.) We do not presuppose Waldhausen's theory or Seifert's work on fibred manifolds, though Seifert's ideas are applied to the special case in hand. The proof is also different from that given in the original paper [Burde-Zieschang 1966].

Proof of Theorem 6.1. Let $\mathfrak{k}$ be a non-trivial knot whose group $\mathfrak{G}$ has a centre $\mathfrak{C} \neq 1$. Then by 4.10(a) its commutator subgroup $\mathfrak{G}'$ is finitely generated, and hence by 5.1 the complement C is a fibre space over S^1 with a Seifert surface S of minimal genus g as a fibre. Thus $C = S \times I/h$ as defined in 5.2. Let t and $r = \partial(S \times 0)$ represent a meridian and a longitude on ∂C, and choose their point of intersection P as a base point for $\pi_1(C) = \mathfrak{G}$. The homeomorphism $h\colon S \to S$ induces the automorphism:

$$h_\#\colon \mathfrak{G}' \to \mathfrak{G}' = \pi_1(S \times 0),\ x \mapsto t^{-1}xt,$$

since by 5.7 we may assume that $h(P) = P$. Again by 4.10, $\mathfrak{C} \cong \mathbb{Z}$.

6.4 Proposition. *Let $z = t^n u$, $n > 1$, be a generator of the centre $\mathfrak{C}$ of $\mathfrak{G}$. Then u is a power of the longitude r, $u = r^{-m}$, $m \neq 0$, and $h_\#^n$ is the inner automorphism $h_\#^n(x) = r^m x r^{-m}$. The exponent n is the smallest one with this property. The powers of r are the only fixed elements of $h_\#^i$, $i \neq 0$.*

Proof. By assumption $t^{-n}xt^n = uxu^{-1}$ for all $x \in \mathfrak{G}'$. From $h_\#(r) = t^{-1}rt = r$ it follows that u commutes with r. The longitude r is a product of commutators of free generators of $\mathfrak{G}' \cong \mathfrak{F}_{2g}$ and it is easily verified that r is not a proper power of any other element of $\mathfrak{G}'$; hence, $u = r^{-m}$, $m \in \mathbb{Z}$ (see [ZVC 1980, E 1.5]). We shall see $gcd(n, m) = 1$ in 6.8 (2). Fixed elements of $h_\#^i$, $i \neq 0$, are also fixed elements of $h_\#^{in}$, hence they commute with r; they are therefore powers of r.

Now assume that $t^{-k}xt^k = vxv^{-1}$ for all $x \in \mathfrak{G}'$ and some $k \neq 0$ and $v \in \mathfrak{G}'$. Then $t^k v \in \mathfrak{C}$, thus $t^k v = (t^n u)^l = t^{nl} u^l$. This proves that n is the smallest positive exponent such that $h_\#^n$ is an inner automorphism of $\mathfrak{G}'$. □

We now state without proof two theorems on periodic mappings of surfaces due to [Nielsen 1942, 1937]. A proof of a generalization of the first one can be found in [Zieschang 1981]; it is a deep result which requires a considerable amount of technicalities in its proof. A different approach was used by [Fenchel 1948, 1950], a combinatorial proof of his theorem was given by [Zimmermann 1977], for a more general result see also [Kerckhoff 1980, 1983].

6.5 Theorem (Nielsen). *Let S be a compact surface different from the sphere with less than three boundary components. If $h\colon S \to S$ is a homeomorphism such that h^n is isotopic to the identity, then there is a periodic homeomorphism f of order n isotopic to h.* □

We need another theorem which provides additional geometric information on periodic surface mappings:

6.6 Theorem (Nielsen). *Let $f: S \to S$ be an orientation preserving periodic homeomorphism of order n, $f^n = id$, of a compact orientable surface S. Let $q \in S$ be some point with $f^k(q) = q$, $0 < k < n$, and let k be minimal with this property. Then there is a neighbourhood $U(q)$ of q in S, homeomorphic to an open 2-cell, such that $f^l(U(q)) \cap U(q) = \emptyset$ for $0 < l < k$. Furthermore $f^k | U(q)$ is a topological rotation of order $\frac{n}{k}$ with fixed point q.* □

For a proof of Theorem 6.6 see [Nielsen 1937] or [Nielsen 1984]. Points q of S for which such a k exists are called *exceptional* points.

6.7 Corollary (Nielsen). *A periodic mapping $f: S \to S$ as in Theorem 6.6 has at most finitely many exceptional points, none of them on $r = \partial S$.* □

At this point the reader may take the short cut via Seifert manifolds to Theorem 6.1: By Lemma 5.7

$$C = S \times I/h \cong S \times I/f.$$

The trivial fibration of $S \times I$ with fibre I defines a Seifert fibration of C. Exceptional points in S correspond to exceptional fibres by Theorem 6.6. Since a fibre on ∂C is not isotopic to a meridian, the Seifert fibration of C can be extended to give a Seifert fibration of S^3, where $\mathfrak{k}$ is a fibre, normal or exceptional. By Theorem 6.3 normal fibres of Seifert fibrations of S^3 are torus knots or trivial knots, while exceptional fibres are always unknotted. So $\mathfrak{k}$ has to be a normal fibre i.e. a torus knot.

B Proof of the Main Theorem

We shall now give a proof of 6.1 by making use only of the theory of regular coverings.

6.8. The orbit of an exceptional point of S relative to the cyclic group $\mathfrak{Z}_n$ generated by f consists of k_j points, $1 \leqq k_j \leqq n$, $k_j | n$. We denote exceptional points accordingly by $Q_{j\nu}$, $1 \leqq j \leqq s$, $0 \leqq \nu \leqq k_j - 1$, where $Q_{j,\nu+1} = f(Q_{j\nu})$, $\nu \bmod k_j$. By deleting the neighbourhoods $U(Q_{j\nu})$ of 6.6 we obtain $S_0 = S - \cup U(Q_{j\nu})$, which is a compact surface of genus g with $1 + \sum_{j=1}^{s} k_j$ boundary components, on which $\mathfrak{Z}_n = \langle f \rangle$ operates freely. So there is a regular cyclic n-fold covering

$p_0\colon S_0 \to S_0^*$ with $\langle f\rangle$ as its group of covering transformations. We define a covering

$$p\colon C_0 = S_0 \times I/f \to S_0^* \times I/id \cong S_0^* \times S^1$$

by

$$p(u, v) = (p_0(u), v),\ u \in S_0,\ v \in I.$$

This covering is also cyclic of order n, and $f \times id$ generates its group of covering transformations. Let $r_{j\nu}$ represent the boundary of $U(Q_{j\nu})$ in $\pi_1(S_0)$ in such a way that

$$\partial S = r = \prod_{i=1}^{g} [a_i, b_i] \cdot \prod_{j=1}^{s} \prod_{\nu=0}^{k_j-1} r_{j\nu}.$$

The induced homomorphism $p_\#\colon \pi_1(C_0) \to \pi_1(C_0^*)$ then gives

(1) $\quad p_\#(r) = r^{*n},\ p_\#(r_{j\nu}) = (r_j^*)^{m_j},\ m_j k_j = n,$

where r^* and r_j^* represent the boundaries of S_0^* in $\pi_1(S_0^*)$ such that

$$r^* = \prod_{i=1}^{g} [a_i^*, b_i^*] \cdot \prod_{j=1}^{s} r_j^*.$$

Let z^* be a simple closed curve on $r^* \times S^1$ representing a generator of $\pi_1(S^1)$, such that $p_\#^{-1}(z^{*n}) = t^n v,\ v \in \pi_1(S_0)$. Then $t^n v$ is a simple closed curve on the torus $r \times I/f$ and it is central in $\pi_1(C_0)$, since z^* is central in $\pi_1(C_0^*)$. Therefore $t^n v$ is central in $\pi_1(C) \cong \mathfrak{G}$, too; hence, $p_\#^{-1}(z^{*n}) = z = t^n \cdot r^{-m}$, see 6.4. Since $t^n v = t^n r^{-m}$ represents a simple closed curve on the torus $r \times I/f$ it follows that

(2) $\quad gcd(m, n) = 1.$

Furthermore, $z^{*n} = p_\#(z) = (p_\#(t))^n \cdot r^{*-mn}$. Putting $p_\#(t) = t^*$, we obtain

(3) $\quad z^* = t^* r^{*-m}.$

For $\alpha, \beta \in \mathbb{Z}$, satisfying

(4) $\quad \alpha m + \beta n = 1,$

(5) $\quad q = t^\alpha r^\beta$ and $p_\#(q) = q^* = t^{*\alpha} r^{*n\beta}$

are simple closed curves on ∂C and $r^* \times S^1$, respectively. From these formulas we derive:

(6) $\quad t^* = z^{*n\beta} \cdot q^{*m},$

(7) $\quad r^* = z^{*-\alpha} \cdot q^*.$

Since $f|r$ is a rotation of order n (see 6.6), the powers $\{r^{*\mu} | 0 \leqq \mu \leqq n-1\}$ are coset representatives in $\pi_1(C_0^*) \bmod p_\# \pi_1(C_0)$. From (3) it follows that $\{z^{*\mu}\}$ also represent these cosets. By (7),

(8) $\quad z^{*\alpha} r^* = q^* \in p_\# \pi_1(C_0)$.

We shall show that there are similar formulas for the boundaries r_j^*.

6.9 Lemma. *There are* $\alpha_j \in \mathbb{Z}$, $gcd(\alpha_j, m_j) = 1$ *such that*

$$z^{*\alpha_j k_j} r_j^* = q_j^* \in p_\# \pi_1(C_0).$$

The α_j *are determined* mod m_j.

Proof. For some $v \in \mathbb{Z}$: $z^{*v} r_j^* \in p_\# \pi_1(C_0)$. Now $q_j^* = z^{*v} r_j^*$ and z^* generate $\pi_1(r_j^* \times S^1)$, $q_j = p_\#^{-1}(q_j^*)$ and $z = p_\#^{-1}(z^{*n})$ are generators of $\pi_1(p^{-1}(r_j^* \times S^1))$. Hence,

$$r_{j0} = z^{-\alpha_j} q_j^{\beta_j},\ (\alpha_j, \beta_j) = 1 \quad \text{and}$$
$$z^{*-n\alpha_j} q_j^{*\beta_j} = p_\#(r_{j0}) = (r_j^*)^{m_j} = z^{*-vm_j} q_j^{*m_j}, \text{ thus } k_j \alpha_j = v,\ m_j = \beta_j.$$

(Remember that $m_j k_j = n$, see 6.8 (1).) □

6.10 Now let $\hat{C}_0^* = \hat{S}_0^* \times \hat{S}^1$ be a homeomorphic copy of $C_0^* = S_0^* \times S^1$ with $\hat{z}^*$ generating $\pi_1(\hat{S}^1)$ and $\hat{a}_i^*, \hat{b}_i^*, \hat{r}^*, \hat{r}_j^*$ representing canonical generators of $\pi_1(\hat{S}_0^*)$, and $\hat{r}^* = \prod_{i=1}^{g^*} [\hat{a}_i^*, \hat{b}_i^*] \cdot \prod_{j=1}^{s} \hat{r}_j^*$. Define an isomorphism

$$\kappa_\#^*: \pi_1(C_0^*) \to \pi_1(\hat{C}_0^*)$$

by

$$\kappa_\#^*(z^*) = \hat{z}^*,$$
$$\kappa_\#^*(r_j^*) = \hat{z}^{*-\alpha_j k_j} \cdot \hat{r}_j^*,$$
$$\kappa_\#^*(a_i^*) = \hat{z}^{*-\varrho_i} \cdot \hat{a}_i^*,$$
$$\kappa_\#^*(b_i^*) = \hat{z}^{*-\sigma_i} \cdot \hat{b}_i^*,$$

where ϱ_i, σ_i are chosen in such a way that $z^{*\varrho_i} a_i^*, z^{*\sigma_i} b_i^* \in \pi_1(S_0^*)$. (The ϱ_i, σ_i will play no role in the following.)

6.11 Lemma. $\kappa_\#^* p_\# \pi_1(C_0) = \pi_1(\hat{S}_0^*) \times \langle z^{*n} \rangle$.

Proof. By construction $\kappa_\#^{*-1}(\hat{a}_i^*) = z^{*\varrho_i} a_i^* \in p_\# \pi_1(C_0)$, likewise $\kappa_\#^{*-1}(\hat{b}_i^*)$, $\kappa_\#^{*-1}(\hat{r}_j^*) \in p_\# \pi_1(C_0)$. Since $\kappa_\#^*$ is an isomorphism, $\kappa_\#^* p_\# \pi_1(C_0)$ is a normal subgroup of index n in $\pi_1(\hat{S}_0^*) \times \langle \hat{z}^* \rangle$, which contains $\pi_1(\hat{S}_0^*)$, because it contains its generators. This proves Lemma 6.11. □

We shall now see that $\kappa_\#^*$ can be realized by a homeomorphism κ^*: $S_0^* \times S^1 \to \hat{S}_0^* \times \hat{S}^1$, and that there is a homeomorphism κ: $C_0 \to \hat{C}_0 = \hat{S}_0 \times \hat{\hat{S}}^1$ covering κ^* such that the following diagram is commutative

(9)
$$\begin{array}{ccc} C_0 = S_0 \times I/f & \xrightarrow{\kappa} & \hat{S}_0 \times \hat{\hat{S}}^1 = \hat{C}_0 \\ \downarrow p & & \downarrow \hat{p} \\ S_0^* \times S^1 & \xrightarrow{\kappa^*} & \hat{S}_0^* \times \hat{S}^1. \end{array}$$

Here $\hat{p}$ is the n-fold cyclic covering defined by $\hat{p}(x, \zeta) = (x, \zeta^n)$, if the 1-spheres $\hat{S}^1$, $\hat{\hat{S}}^1$ are described by complex numbers ζ of absolute value one.

6.12 Lemma. *There is a homeomorphism κ^*: $S_0^* \times S^1 \to \hat{S}_0^* \times \hat{S}^1$ inducing $\kappa_\#^*$: $\pi_1(S_0^* \times S^1) \to \pi_1(\hat{S}_0^* \times \hat{S}^1)$, and a homeomorphism κ: $C_0 \to \hat{C}_0$ covering κ^*.*

Proof. First observe that S_0^* is not a disk because in this case the Seifert surface S would be a covering space of S_0^* and therefore a disk. The $2g^* + s$ simple closed curves $\{a_i^*, b_i^*, r_j^* | 1 \leqq i \leqq g^*, 1 \leqq j \leqq s\}$ joined at the base point $P^* = p(P)$ represent a deformation retract R^* of S_0 as well as the respective generators $\{\hat{a}_i^*, \hat{b}_i^*, \hat{r}_j^*\} = \hat{R}^*$ in $\hat{S}_0^*$. It is now easy to see that there is a homeomorphism

$$\kappa^*|: R^* \times S^1 \to \hat{R}^* \times \hat{S}^1$$

inducing $\kappa_\#^*$ (Fig. 6.1), because the homeomorphism obviously exists on each of the tori $a_i^* \times S^1$, $b_i^* \times S^1$ and $r_j^* \times S^1$. The extension of $\kappa^* | R^*$ to

$$\kappa^*: S_0^* \times S^1 \to \hat{S}_0^* \times \hat{S}^1$$

presents no difficulty. Lemma 6.11 ensures the existence of a covering homeomorphism κ. □

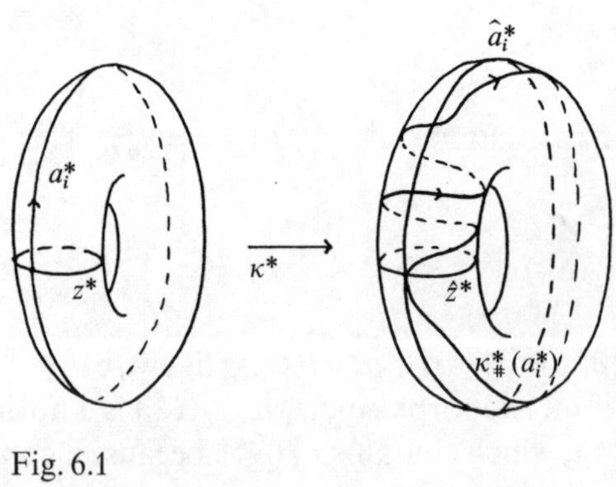

Fig. 6.1

We obtain by $\kappa_\#$: $\pi_1(C_0) \to \pi_1(\hat{C}_0)$ a new presentation of $\pi_1(C_0) \cong \pi_1(\hat{C}_0) = \langle \{\hat{r}_j, \hat{a}_i, \hat{b}_i | 1 \leqq i \leqq g^*, 1 \leqq j \leqq s\} | \rangle \times \langle \hat{z} \rangle$, where

(10) $\quad \hat{p}_\#(\hat{r}_j) = \hat{r}_j^*, \hat{p}_\#(\hat{a}_i) = \hat{a}_i^*, \hat{p}_\#(\hat{b}_i) = \hat{b}_i^*, \hat{p}_\#(\hat{z}) = \hat{z}^{*n}.$

From this presentation we can derive a presentation of $\mathfrak{G} \cong \pi_1(C)$ by introducing the defining relators $\kappa_{\#}(r_{j\nu}) = 1$. It suffices to choose $\nu = 0$ for all $j = 1, \ldots, s$.

We get from 6.8 (1), 6.10, (9):

$$(11) \qquad \kappa_{\#}(r_{j0}) = \hat{p}_{\#}^{-1}\kappa_{\#}^{*}(r_j^{*m_j}) = \hat{z}^{-\alpha_j}\hat{r}_j^{m_j}.$$

Furthermore (see 6.8 (1), 6.10):

$$\kappa_{\#}^{*}(r^{*}) = \hat{z}^{*\,-\sum_{j=1}^{s} k_j\alpha_j} \cdot \hat{r}^{*}.$$

(8) and 6.10 imply

$$\kappa_{\#}^{*}(r^{*}) = \hat{z}^{*\,-\alpha}\kappa_{\#}^{*}(q^{*}).$$

By (5) and (9), $\kappa_{\#}^{*}(q^{*}) \in \hat{p}_{\#}\,\pi_1(\hat{C}_0)$, and by (1) and (10) $\hat{r}^{*} \in \hat{p}_{\#}\,\pi_1(\hat{C}_0)$.

Now the definition of $\hat{p}_{\#}$ (see (9)) yields

$$\alpha \equiv \sum_{j=1}^{s} k_j\alpha_j \bmod n.$$

By 6.9 we may replace α_1 by an element of the same coset mod m_1, such that the equation

$$(12) \qquad \alpha = \sum_{j=1}^{s} k_j\alpha_j$$

is satisfied. Then $\kappa_{\#}^{*}(q^{*}) = \hat{r}^{*}$, and, since $p_{\#}(t) = t^{*}$, it follows from (6) that

$$(13) \qquad \kappa_{\#}(t) = \hat{z}^{\beta} \cdot \hat{r}^{m}.$$

6.13 Lemma. *S_0^{*} is a sphere with two boundary components: $g^{*} = 0$, $s = 2$. Moreover $m_1 \cdot m_2 = n$, $\gcd(m_1, m_2) = 1$. It is possible to choose $m = 1$, $\alpha = 1$, $\beta = 0$.*

There is a presentation

$$\mathfrak{G} = \langle \hat{z}, \hat{r}_1, \hat{r}_2 \mid \hat{z}^{-\alpha_1}\hat{r}_1^{m_1}, \hat{z}^{-\alpha_2}\hat{r}_2^{m_2}, [\hat{z}, \hat{r}_1], [\hat{z}, \hat{r}_2] \rangle$$

of the knot group $\mathfrak{G}$.

Proof. We have to introduce the relators $\hat{z}^{-\alpha_j}\hat{r}_j^{m_j}$ (see (11)) in

$$\pi_1(\hat{C}_0) = \langle \{\hat{r}_j, \hat{a}_i, \hat{b}_i \mid 1 \leqq i \leqq g^{*}, 1 \leqq j \leqq s\} \mid \rangle \times \langle \hat{z} \rangle.$$

The additional relator $\kappa_{\#}(t) = \hat{z}^{\beta} \cdot \hat{r}^{m} = 1$ must trivialize the group. This remains true, if we put $\hat{z} = 1$.

Now $g^{*} = 0$ follows. For $s \geqq 3$ the resulting groups

$$(14) \qquad \langle \{\hat{r}, \hat{r}_j \mid 1 \leqq j \leqq s\} \mid \hat{r}^{-m}, \hat{r}_j^{m_j}, \hat{r}^{-1}\prod_{j=1}^{s} \hat{r}_j \rangle$$

are known to be non-trivial [ZVC 1980, 4.16.4] since by definition $m_j > 1$. For $s = 2$ by the same argument (14) describes the trivial group only if $m = \pm 1$. The cases $s < 2$ cannot occur as $\mathfrak{k}$ was assumed to be non-trivial. By a suitable choice of the orientation of $r = \partial S$ we get $m = 1$. Thus by $\alpha = 1$, $\beta = 0$ equation (4) is satisfied. Now (12) takes the form

$$(15) \qquad \alpha_1 k_1 + \alpha_2 k_2 = 1 .$$

It follows that

$$\langle \hat{z}, \hat{r}_1, \hat{r}_2 | \hat{z}^{-\alpha_1} \hat{r}_1^{m_1}, \hat{z}^{-\alpha_2} \hat{r}_2^{m_2}, \hat{r}_1 \hat{r}_2, [\hat{z}, \hat{r}_1], [\hat{z}, \hat{r}_2] \rangle = 1$$

is a presentation of the trivialized knot group. By abelianizing this presentation yields

$$(16) \qquad \alpha_1 m_2 + \alpha_2 m_1 = \pm 1 .$$

The equations (15) and (16) are proportional since $m_2 k_2 - m_1 k_1 = n - n = 0$. As $m_j, k_j > 0$, they are indeed identical, $m_2 = k_1$, $m_1 = k_2$. □

It is a consequence of Lemma 6.13 that C_0 is obtained from a 3-sphere S^3 by removing three disjoint solid tori. Equation (13) together with $m = 1$, $\beta = 0$ shows $\kappa_\# (t) = \hat{r}$. We use this equation to extend $\kappa\colon C_0 \to \hat{C}_0$ to a homeomorphism $\hat{\kappa}$ defined on $C_0 \cup V(\mathfrak{k})$, obtained from C_0 by replacing the tubular neighbourhood $V(\mathfrak{k})$ of $\mathfrak{k}$. We get

$$\hat{\kappa}\colon C_0 \cup V(\mathfrak{k}) \to B \times \hat{\hat{S}}^1$$

where B is a ribbon with boundary $\partial B = \hat{r}_1 \cup \hat{r}_2$. The fundamental group $\pi_1(B \times \hat{\hat{S}}^1)$ is a free abelian group generated by $\hat{z}$ and $\hat{r}_1 = \hat{r}_2^{-1}$. Define $\hat{q}_1$ and $\hat{q}_2$ by

$$(17) \qquad \begin{aligned} &\hat{\kappa}_\# (r_{10}) = \hat{z}^{-\alpha_1} \hat{r}_1^{m_1} = \hat{q}_1^{-1}, \\ &\hat{\kappa}_\# (r_{20}) = \hat{z}^{-\alpha_2} \hat{r}_1^{m_2} = \hat{q}_2^{-1}, \alpha_1 m_2 + \alpha_2 m_1 = 1 . \end{aligned}$$

(For the notation compare 6.8.) Now we glue two solid tori to $B \times \hat{\hat{S}}^1$ such that their meridians are identified with $\hat{q}_1, \hat{q}_2$, respectively, and obtain a closed manifold $\hat{\hat{S}}^3$. Thus $\hat{\kappa}$ can be extended to a homeomorphism $\hat{\hat{\kappa}}\colon S^3 \to \hat{\hat{S}}^3$. From (17) we see that $\hat{q}_1$ and $\hat{q}_2$ are a pair of generators of $\pi_1(\hat{r}_1 \times \hat{\hat{S}}^1)$. Therefore the torus $\hat{r}_1 \times \hat{\hat{S}}^1$ defines a Heegaard-splitting of $\hat{\hat{S}}^3$ which is the same as the standard Heegaard-splitting of genus one of the 3-sphere. The knot $\mathfrak{k}$ is isotopic (in S^3) to $z \subset \partial C_0$. Its image $\hat{\mathfrak{k}} = \hat{\kappa}(\mathfrak{k})$ can be represented by any curve $(Q \times \hat{\hat{S}}^1) \subset \hat{S}_0^* \times \hat{\hat{S}}^1$, where Q is a point of $\hat{S}_0^*$. Take $Q \in \hat{r}_1$ then $\hat{\mathfrak{k}}$ is represented by a simple closed curve on the unknotted torus $\hat{r}_1 \times \hat{\hat{S}}^1$ in $\hat{\hat{S}}^3$. This finishes the proof of Theorem 6.1. □

C Remarks on the Proof

In Lemma 6.13 we have obtained a presentation of the group of the torus knot which differs from the usual one (see Proposition 3.28). The following substitution connects both presentations:

$$u = \hat{r}_1^{m_2} \cdot \hat{z}^{\alpha_2}$$
$$v = \hat{r}_2^{m_1} \cdot \hat{z}^{\alpha_1}.$$

First observe that $\hat{r}_1$ and $\hat{r}_2$ generate $\mathfrak{G}$:

$$\hat{r}_1^n \cdot \hat{r}_2^n = \hat{r}_1^{m_1 k_1} \cdot \hat{r}_2^{m_2 k_2} = \hat{z}^{\alpha_1 k_1 + \alpha_2 k_2} = \hat{z}.$$

It follows that u and v are also generators:

$$u^{\alpha_1} = \hat{r}_1^{\alpha_1 m_2} \cdot \hat{z}^{\alpha_1 \alpha_2} = \hat{r}_1 \cdot \hat{r}_1^{-\alpha_2 m_1} \cdot \hat{z}^{\alpha_1 \alpha_2} = \hat{r}_1,$$

and similarily, $v^{\alpha_2} = \hat{r}_2$. The relation $u^{m_1} = v^{m_2}$ is easily verified:

$$u^{m_1} = \hat{r}_1^{m_1 m_2} \hat{z}^{\alpha_2 m_1} = \hat{z}^{\alpha_1 m_2 + \alpha_2 m_1} = \hat{z} = v^{m_2}.$$

Starting with the presentation

$$\mathfrak{G} = \langle u, v \mid u^a = v^b \rangle, \; a = m_1, b = m_2,$$

one can re-obtain the presentation of 6.13 by introducing

$$\hat{z} = u^a = v^b \quad \text{and} \quad \hat{r}_1 = u^{\alpha_1}, \hat{r}_2 = v^{\alpha_2}.$$

The argument also identifies the $\mathfrak{k}$ of 6.1 as the torus knot $\mathfrak{t}(m_1, m_2)$; for the definition of m_1, m_2 see 6.8 (1).

6.14. The construction used in the proof gives some additional information. The Hurwitz-formula [ZVC 1980, 4.14.23] of the covering $p_0\colon S_0 \to S_0^*$ gives

$$2g + \sum_{j=1}^{s} k_j = n(2g^* + s - 1) + 1.$$

Since $g^* = 0$, $s = 2$, $k_1 = b$, $k_2 = a$, $ab = n$ it follows that $2g + a + b = ab + 1$, hence

$$g = \frac{(a-1)(b-1)}{2}, \text{ see 4.11}.$$

6.15. On cyclic coverings of torus knots. The q-fold cyclic coverings $C_{a,b}^q$ of the complement $C_{a,b}$ of the knot $\mathfrak{t}(a, b)$ obviously have a period $n = ab$:

$$C_{a,b}^q \cong C_{a,b}^{q+kn}.$$

This is a consequence of the realization of $C_{a,b} \cong S \times I/f$ by a mapping f of period n. The covering transformation of $C_{a,b}^q \to C_{a,b}$ can be interpreted geometrically as a shift along the fibre $z = t^{ab} \cdot r^{-1} \simeq \mathfrak{t}(a, b)$ such that a move from one sheet of the covering to the adjoining one shifts $\mathfrak{t}(a, b)$ through $\frac{1}{ab}$ of its "length". There is an $(ab+1)$-fold cyclic covering of $C_{a,b}$ onto itself:

$$C_{a,b} \cong C_{a,b}^{ab+1} \to C_{a,b}.$$

All its covering transformations $\neq id$ map $\mathfrak{t}(a, b)$ onto itself but no point of $\mathfrak{t}(a, b)$ is left fixed. There is no extension of the covering transformation to the $(ab+1)$-fold cyclic covering $\bar{p}$: $S^3 \to S^3$ branched along $\mathfrak{t}(a, b)$, in accordance with Smith's Theorem [Smith 1934], see also Appendix B8, [Zieschang 1981, 36.4]. The covering transformations can indeed only by extended to a manifold $\hat{C}_{a,b}$ which results from glueing to $C_{a,b}$ a solid torus whose meridian is tr^{-1} instead of t. The manifold $\hat{C}_{a,b}$ is always different from S^3 as long as $\mathfrak{t}(a, b)$ is a non-trivial torus knot. In fact, one can easily compute

$$\pi_1(\hat{C}_{a,b}) = \langle \hat{z}, \hat{r}_1, \hat{r}_2, \hat{r} \mid \hat{r}\hat{r}_1\hat{r}_2, \hat{r}^{ab+1}, \hat{r}_1^a, \hat{r}_2^b, [\hat{z}, \hat{r}_1], [\hat{z}, \hat{r}_2] \rangle$$

by using again the generators $\hat{r}_1, \hat{r}_2$ and $\hat{z}$. The group $\pi_1(\hat{C}_{a,b})$ is infinite since $|a| > 1$, $|b| > 1$, $|ab+1| > 6$, see [ZVC 1980, 6.4.7].

In the case of the trefoil $\mathfrak{t}(3, 2)$ the curves, surfaces and mappings constructed in the proof can be made visible with the help of Figure 5.3. The mapping f of order $6 = 3 \cdot 2$, $a = m_1 = 3$, $b = m_2 = 2$ is the one given by f_φ (at the end of Chapter 5) for $\varphi = \pi$. Its exceptional points Q_{10}, Q_{11} are the centres of the disks D_1 and D_2 (Fig. 5.3 and 6.2) while Q_{20}, Q_{21}, Q_{22} are the points in which the core of T_1 meets the Seifert surface S.

Figure 6.2 shows a fundamental domain of S relative to $\mathfrak{Z}_6 = \langle f \rangle$. If its edges are identified as indicated in Figure 6.2, one obtaines a 2-sphere, the orbit manifold (Zerlegungsfläche), or a 2-sphere twice punctured: S_0^*, if exceptional points are removed.

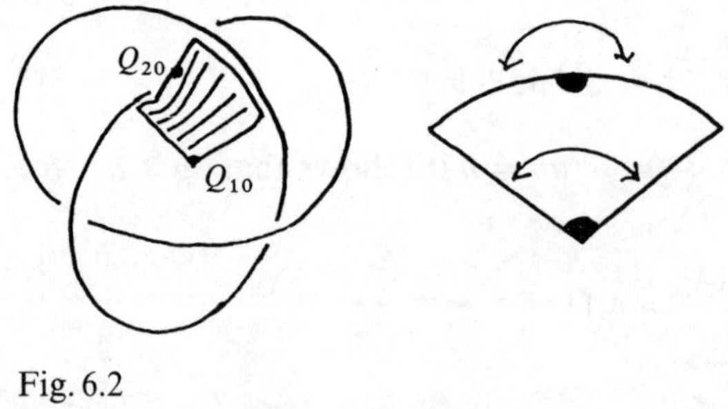

Fig. 6.2

Figure 6.3 finally represents the ribbon B embedded in S^3. One of its boundaries is placed on ∂T_1. The ribbon B represents the orbitmanifold minus two disks. The orbit manifold itself can, of course, not be embedded in S^3, since there is no 2-sphere in S^3 which intersects a fibre z in just one point. The impossibility of such embeddings is also evident because B is twisted by 2π.

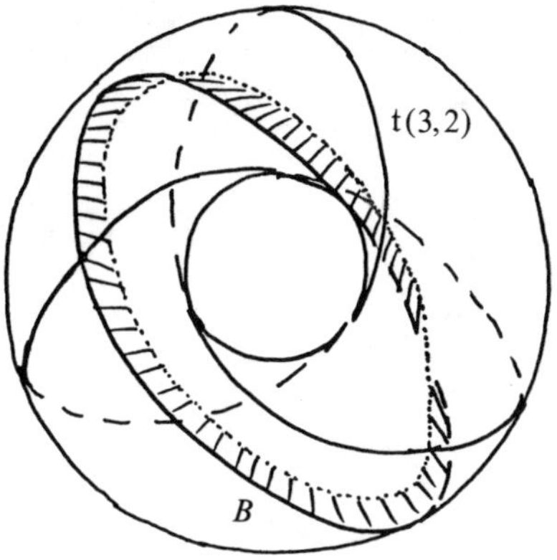

Fig. 6.3

D History and Sources

Torus knots and their groups have beend studied in [Dehn 1914] and [Schreier 1924]. The question of whether torus knots are determined by their groups was treated in [Murasugi 1961] and [Neuwirth 1961], and answered in the affirmative for alternating torus knots. This was proved in the general case in [Burde-Zieschang 1967], where torus knots were shown to be the only knots the groups of which have a non-trivial centre. A generalization of this theorem to 3-manifolds with non-trivial centre is due to Waldhausen [1967], and, as an application of it, the case of link groups with a centre $\neq 1$ was investigated in [Burde-Murasugi 1970].

E Exercises

E 6.1 Let a lens space $L(p, q)$ be given by a Heegaard splitting of genus one, $L(p, q) = V_1 \cup V_2$. Define a torus knot in $L(p, q)$ by a simple closed curve on $\partial V_1 = \partial V_2$. Determine the links in the universal covering S^3 of $L(p, q)$ which cover a torus knot in $L(p, q)$. (Remark: The links that occur in this way classify the genus one Heegaard-splittings of lens spaces.)

E 6.2 Show that the q-fold cyclic covering $C^q_{a,b}$ of a torus knot $\mathfrak{t}(a, b)$ is a Seifert fibre space, and that the fibration can be extended to the branched covering $\hat{C}^q_{a,b}$ without adding another exceptional fibre. Compute Seifert's invariants of fibre spaces for $\hat{C}^q_{a,b}$. (Remark: The 3-fold cyclic branched covering of a trefoil is a Seifert fibre space with three exceptional fibres of order two.)

Chapter 7: Factorization of Knots

In Chapter 2 we have defined a composition of knots. The main result of this chapter states that each tame knot is composed of finitely many indecomposable (prime) knots and that these factors are uniquely determined.

A Composition of Knots

In the following we often consider parts of knots, arcs, embedded in balls, and it is convenient to have the concept of knotted arcs:

7.1 Definition. Let $B \subset S^3$ be a closed ball carrying the orientation induced by the standard orientation of S^3. A simple path $\alpha\colon I \to B$ with $\alpha(\dot{I}) \subset \partial B$ and $\alpha(\mathring{I}) \subset \mathring{B}$ is called a *knotted arc*. Two knotted arcs $\alpha \subset B_1$, $\beta \subset B_2$ are called *equivalent* if there exists an orientation preserving homeomorphism $f\colon B_1 \to B_2$ such that $\beta = f\alpha$.

If α is a knotted arc in B and γ some simple curve on ∂B which connects the endpoints of α then $\alpha\gamma$ – with the orientation induced by α – represents the *knot corresponding to* α. This knot does not depend on the choice of γ and it follows easily that equivalent knotted arcs correspond to equivalent knots.

By a slight alteration of the definition of the composition of knots we get the following two alternative versions of its description. Figures 7.1-2 show that the different definitions are equivalent.

Fig. 7.1

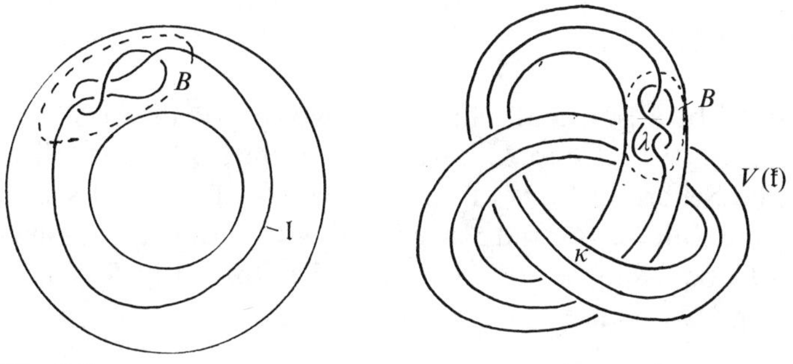

Fig. 7.2

7.2 (a) Figure 7.1 describes the composition $\mathfrak{k} \# \mathfrak{l}$ of the knots $\mathfrak{k}$ and $\mathfrak{l}$ by joining representing arcs.

(b) Let $V(\mathfrak{k})$ be the tubular neighbourhood of the knot $\mathfrak{k}$, and $B \subset V(\mathfrak{k})$ some ball such that $\kappa' = \mathfrak{k} \cap B$ is a trivial arc in B, $\kappa = \mathfrak{k} - \kappa'$. If κ' is replaced by a knotted arc λ defining the knot $\mathfrak{l}$, then $\kappa \cup \lambda$ represents the product $\mathfrak{k} \# \mathfrak{l} = \kappa \cup \lambda$.

The following lemma is a direct consequence of the construction in 7.2 and is proved by Figures 7.3-4.

7.3 Lemma. *(a)* $\mathfrak{l} \# \mathfrak{k} = \mathfrak{k} \# \mathfrak{l}$.
(b) $\mathfrak{k}_1 \# (\mathfrak{k}_2 \# \mathfrak{k}_3) = (\mathfrak{k}_1 \# \mathfrak{k}_2) \# \mathfrak{k}_3$.
(c) If $\mathfrak{i}$ *denotes the trivial knot the* $\mathfrak{k} \# \mathfrak{i} = \mathfrak{k}$.

Proof. (a) Figure 7.3. (b) Figure 7.4. □

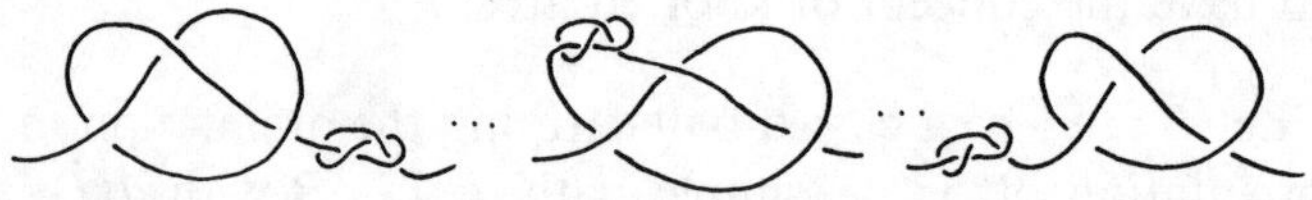

Fig. 7.3

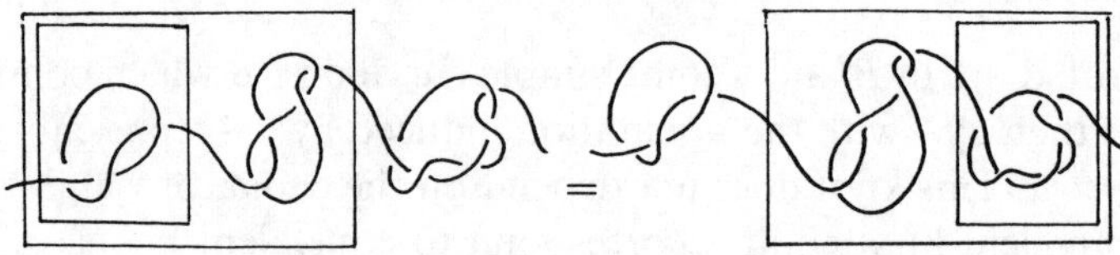

Fig. 7.4

Associativity now permits us to define $\mathfrak{k}_1 \# \ldots \# \mathfrak{k}_n$ for an arbitrary $n \in \mathbb{N}$ without using brackets.

7.4 Proposition (genus of knot compositions). *Let* $\mathfrak{k}, \mathfrak{l}$ *be knots and let* $g(\mathfrak{x})$ *denote the genus of the knot* $\mathfrak{x}$. *Then*

$$g(\mathfrak{k} \# \mathfrak{l}) = g(\mathfrak{k}) + g(\mathfrak{l}).$$

Proof. Let $B \subset S^3$ be a (p.l.-)ball. Since any two (p.l.-)balls in S^3 are ambient isotopic, see [Moise 1977, Chap. 17], we can describe $\mathfrak{k} \# \mathfrak{l}$ in the following way. Let $S_\mathfrak{k}$ and $S_\mathfrak{l}$ be Seifert surfaces of minimal genus of $\mathfrak{k}$ resp. $\mathfrak{l}$ such that $S_\mathfrak{k}$ is contained in some ball $B \subset S^3$, and $S_\mathfrak{l}$ in $S^3 - B$. Furthermore we assume $S_\mathfrak{k} \cap \partial B = S_\mathfrak{l} \cap \partial B = \alpha$ to be a simple arc. (See Fig. 7.5.) Obviously $S_\mathfrak{k} \cup S_\mathfrak{l}$ is a Seifert surface spanning $\mathfrak{k} \# \mathfrak{l}$, hence:

(1) $\quad g(\mathfrak{k} \# \mathfrak{l}) \leq g(\mathfrak{k}) + g(\mathfrak{l})$.

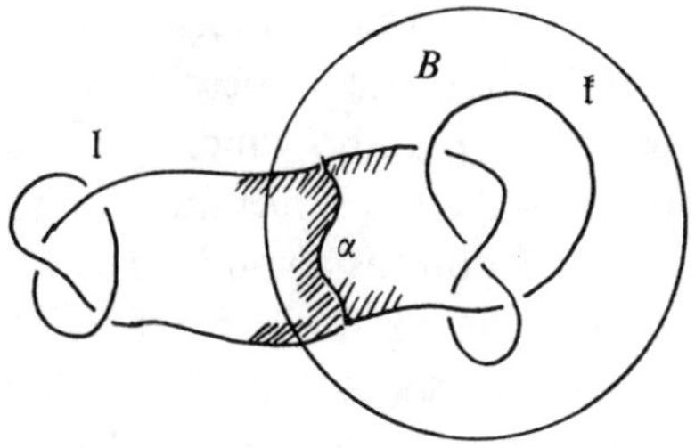

Fig. 7.5

Let S be a Seifert surface of minimal genus spanning $\mathfrak{k} \# \mathfrak{l}$. The 2-sphere $S^2 = \partial B$ is supposed to be in general position with respect to S. Since $\mathfrak{k} \# \mathfrak{l}$ meets ∂B in two points, $\partial B \cap S$ consists of a simple arc α joining these points, and, possibly, a set of pairwise disjoint simple closed curves. An 'innermost' curve σ on ∂B bounds a disk $\delta \subset \partial B$ such that $\delta \cap S = \sigma$. Let us assume that σ does not bound a disk on S. In the case where σ separates S replace the component not containing $\mathfrak{k} \# \mathfrak{l}$ by δ. If σ does not separate S, cut S along σ, and attach two copies of δ along their boundaries to the cuts. (See proof of Lemma 4.5.) In both cases we obtain a Seifert surface for $\mathfrak{k} \# \mathfrak{l}$ of a genus smaller than that of S, contradicting the assumption of minimality.

Thus σ bounds a disk on S as well as on ∂B, and there is an isotopy of S which removes σ. So we may assume $S \cap \partial B = \alpha$, which means

$$g(\mathfrak{k}) + g(\mathfrak{l}) \leqq g(\mathfrak{k} \# \mathfrak{l}). \quad \square$$

7.5 Corollary. *(a)* $\mathfrak{k} \# \mathfrak{l} = \mathfrak{k}$ *implies that* $\mathfrak{l}$ *is the trivial knot.*
(b) If $\mathfrak{k} \# \mathfrak{l}$ *is the trivial knot then* $\mathfrak{k}$ *and* $\mathfrak{l}$ *are trivial.* □

Corollary 7.5 motivates the following definition.

7.6 Definition (prime knot). A knot $\mathfrak{k}$ which is the composition of two non-trivial knots is called *composite*; a non-trivial knot which is not composite is called a *prime knot*.

7.7 Corollary. *Genus* 1 *knots are prime.* □

7.8 Proposition. *Every* 2-*bridge knot* $\mathfrak{b}$ is prime.

Proof. Let δ_1 and δ_2 be disks spanning the arcs of $\mathfrak{b}$ in the upper half-space, and suppose that the other two arcs λ_i', $i \in \{1, 2\}$, of $\mathfrak{b}$ are contained in E. The four "endpoints" of $E \cap \mathfrak{b}$ are joined pairwise by the simple arcs λ_i' and $\lambda_i = E \cap \delta_i$. We suppose the separating sphere S to be in general position with respect to E and δ_i. The intersections of S with $\mathfrak{b}$ may be pushed into two endpoints. Simple closed curves of $\delta_i \cap S$ and those of $E \cap S$ which do not separate endpoints can be removed by an isotopy of S. The remaining curves in $E \cap S$ must now be parallel, separating the arcs λ_1' and λ_2'. If there are more than one of these curves, there is a pair of neighbouring curves bounding annuli on E and S which together form a torus T. The torus T intersects δ_i in simple closed curves, not null-homotopic on T, bounding disks δ in δ_i with $\delta \cap T = \partial\delta$. So T bounds a solid torus which does not intersect $\mathfrak{b}$. There is an isotopy which removes the pair of neighbouring curves. We may therefore assume that $E \cap S$ consists of one simple closed curve separating λ_1' and λ_2'. The ball B bounded by S in $\mathbb{R}^3$ now intersects $\mathfrak{b}$ in – say – λ_1', and λ_1' is isotopic in $E \cap B$ to an arc of $S \cap E$. Hence this factor is trivial. □

A stronger result was proved in [Schubert 1954, Satz 7]:

7.9 Theorem (Schubert). *The minimal bridge number $b(\mathfrak{k})$ minus 1 is additive with respect to the product of knots:*

$$b(\mathfrak{k}_1 \# \mathfrak{k}_2) = b(\mathfrak{k}_1) + b(\mathfrak{k}_2) - 1. \quad \square$$

7.10 Proposition (group of composite knots). *Let $\mathfrak{k} = \mathfrak{k}_1 \# \mathfrak{k}_2$ and denote by $\mathfrak{G}, \mathfrak{G}_1, \mathfrak{G}_2$ the corresponding knot groups.*

Then $\mathfrak{G} = \mathfrak{G}_1 *_{\mathfrak{Z}} \mathfrak{G}_2$, where $\mathfrak{Z}$ is an infinite cyclic group generated by a meridian of $\mathfrak{k}$, and $\mathfrak{G}' = \mathfrak{G}_1' * \mathfrak{G}_2'$. Here $\mathfrak{G}_i$ and $\mathfrak{G}_i'$ are – in the natural way – considered as subgroups of $\mathfrak{G} = \mathfrak{G}_1 *_{\mathfrak{Z}} \mathfrak{G}_2$, $i = 1, 2$.

Proof. Let S be a 2-sphere that defines the product $\mathfrak{k} = \mathfrak{k}_1 \# \mathfrak{k}_2$. Assume that there is a regular neighbourhood V of $\mathfrak{k}$ such that $S \cap V$ consists of two disks. Then $S \cap C$ is an annulus. The complement $C = \overline{S^3 - V}$ is divided by $S \cap C$ into C_1 and C_2 with $C = C_1 \cup C_2$ and $S \cap C = C_1 \cap C_2$. Since $\pi_1(S \cap C) \cong \mathbb{Z}$ is generated by a meridian it is embedded into $\pi_1(C_i)$ and the Seifert-van Kampen Theorem implies that

$$\pi_1(C) = \pi_1(C_1) *_{\pi_1(C_1 \cap C_2)} \pi_1(C_2) = \mathfrak{G}_1 *_{\mathfrak{Z}} \mathfrak{G}_2.$$

Applying Schreier's normal form $hg_1'g_2' \ldots, h \in \mathfrak{Z}, g_1' \in \mathfrak{G}_1', g_2' \in \mathfrak{G}_2'$, the equation $\mathfrak{G}' = \mathfrak{G}_1' * \mathfrak{G}_2'$ follows from the fact that both groups are characterized by $h = 1$. □

7.11 Corollary. *Torus knots are prime.*

Proof. For this fact we give a geometric and a short algebraic proof.

1. Geometric proof. Let the torus knot $\mathfrak{t}(a, b)$ lie on an unknotted torus $T \subset S^3$ and let the 2-sphere S define a decomposition of $\mathfrak{t}(a, b)$ (By definition, $|a|, |b| \geqq 2$.) We assume that S and T are in general position, that is, $S \cap T$ consists of finitely many disjoint simple closed curves. Such a curve either meets $\mathfrak{t}(a, b)$, is parallel to it or it bounds a disk D on T with $D \cap \mathfrak{t}(a, b) = \emptyset$. Choose γ as an innermost curve of the last kind, i.e., $D \cap S = \partial D = \gamma$. Then γ divides S into two disks D', D'' such that $D \cup D'$ and $D \cup D''$ are spheres, $(D \cup D') \cap (D \cup D'') = D$, and they bound disjoint balls. It follows that one of them does not meet $\mathfrak{t}(a, b)$; hence, D' or D'' can be deformed into D by an isotopy of S^3 which leaves $\mathfrak{t}(a, b)$ fixed. By a further small deformation we get rid of one intersection of S with T.

Consider the curves of $T \cap S$ which intersect $\mathfrak{t}(a, b)$. There are one or two curves of this kind since $\mathfrak{t}(a, b)$ intersects S in two points only. If there is one curve it has intersection numbers $+1$ and -1 with $\mathfrak{t}(a, b)$ and this implies that it is either isotopic to $\mathfrak{t}(a, b)$ or nullhomotopic on T. In the first case $\mathfrak{t}(a, b)$ would be the trivial knot. In the second case it bounds a disk D_0 on T and $D_0 \cap \mathfrak{t}(a, b)$ is a segment. It follows that $D_0 \cap \mathfrak{t}(a, b)$, plus an arc on S, represents one of the factor knots of $\mathfrak{t}(a, b)$; this factor would be trivial, contradicting the hypothesis.

The case remains where $S \cap T$ consists of two simple closed curves intersecting $\mathfrak{t}(a, b)$ exactly once. These curves are parallel and bound disks in one of the solid tori bounded by T. But this contradicts $|a|, |b| \geqq 2$.

2. *Algebraic proof.* Let the torus knot $\mathfrak{t}(a, b)$ be the product of two knots. By 7.10,

$$\mathfrak{G} = \langle u, v \mid u^a v^{-b} \rangle = \mathfrak{G}_1 *_{\mathfrak{Z}} \mathfrak{G}_2,$$

where $\mathfrak{Z}$ is generated by a meridian t. The centre of the free product of groups with amalgamated subgroup is the intersection of the centres of the factors, see [ZVC 1980, 2.3.9]; hence, it is generated by a power of t. Since u^a is the generator of the center of $\mathfrak{G}$ it follows from 3.28 (b) that

$$u^a = (u^c v^d)^m \quad \text{where} \quad \begin{vmatrix} a & -b \\ c & d \end{vmatrix} = 1, \quad m \in \mathbb{Z}.$$

From the solution of the word problem it follows that this equation is impossible. □

Now we formulate the main theorem of this chapter which was first proved in [Schubert 1949].

7.12 Theorem (unique prime decomposition of knots). *Every non-trivial knot $\mathfrak{k}$ is a finite product of prime knots and these factors are uniquely determined. More precisely:*

(a) $\mathfrak{k} = \mathfrak{k}_1 \# \ldots \# \mathfrak{k}_n$ where each $\mathfrak{k}_i$ is a prime knot.

(b) If $\mathfrak{k} = \mathfrak{k}_1 \# \ldots \# \mathfrak{k}_n = \mathfrak{k}'_1 \# \ldots \# \mathfrak{k}'_m$ are two decompositions into prime factors $\mathfrak{k}_i$ or $\mathfrak{k}'_j$, respectively, then $n = m$ and $\mathfrak{k}'_i = \mathfrak{k}_{j(i)}$ for some permutation $\begin{pmatrix} 1 & \ldots & n \\ j(1) & \ldots & j(n) \end{pmatrix}$.

Assertion (a) is a consequence of 7.4; part (b) will be proved in section *B*. The results can be summarized as follows:

7.13 Corollary (semigroup of knots). *The knots in S^3 with the operation # form a commutative semigroup with a unit element such that the law of unique prime decomposition is valid.* □

B Uniqueness of the Decomposition into Prime Knots: Proof

We will first describe a general concept for the construction of prime decompositions of a given knot $\mathfrak{k}$. Then we show that any two decompositions can be connected by a chain of 'elementary processes'.

7.14 Definition (decomposing spheres). Let S_j, $1 \leqq j \leqq m$, be a system of disjoint 2-spheres embedded in S^3, bounding $2m$ balls B_i, $1 \leqq i \leqq 2m$, in S^3, and denote by B_j, $B_{c(j)}$ the two balls bounded by S_j. If B_i contains the s balls $B_{l(1)}, \ldots, B_{l(s)}$ as proper subsets, $R_i = (B_i - \bigcup_{q=1}^{s} \mathring{B}_{l(s)})$ is called the *domain* R_i. The *spheres* S_j are said to be *decomposing* with respect to a knot $\mathfrak{k} \subset S^3$ if the following conditions are fulfilled:

(1) Each sphere S_j meets $\mathfrak{k}$ in two points.

(2) The arc $\kappa_i = \mathfrak{k} \cap R_i$, oriented as $\mathfrak{k}$, and completed by simple arcs on the boundary of R_i to represent a knot $\mathfrak{k}_i \subset R_i \subset B_i$, is prime. $\mathfrak{k}_i$ is called the *factor of* $\mathfrak{k}$ *determined by* B_i. By $\mathfrak{S} = \{(S_j, \mathfrak{k}) | 1 \leqq j \leqq m\}$ we denote a decomposing sphere system with respect to $\mathfrak{k}$; if $\mathfrak{k}$ itself is prime we put $\mathfrak{S} = \emptyset$.

It is immediately clear that $\mathfrak{k}_i$ does not depend on the choice of the arcs on ∂R_i. The following Lemma connects this definition with our definition of the composition of a knot.

7.15 Lemma. *If* $\mathfrak{S} = \{(S_j, \mathfrak{k}) | 1 \leqq j \leqq m\}$ *is a decomposing system of spheres, then there are* $m+1$ *balls* B_i *determining prime knots* $\mathfrak{k}_i$, $1 \leqq i \leqq m+1$, *such that*

$$\mathfrak{k} = \mathfrak{k}_{j(1)} \# \ldots \# \mathfrak{k}_{j(m+1)}, \; i \mapsto j(i) \textit{ a permutation.}$$

Proof by induction on m. For $m = 0$ the assertion is obviously true and for $m = 1$ Definition 7.14 reverts to the original definition of the product of knots. For $m > 1$ let B_l be a ball not containing any other ball B_i and determining the prime knot $\mathfrak{k}_l$. Replacing the knotted arc $\kappa_l = B_l \cap \mathfrak{k}$ in $\mathfrak{k}$ by a simple arc on ∂B_l defines a (non-trivial) knot $\mathfrak{k}' \subset S^3$. The induction hypothesis applied to $\{(S_j, \mathfrak{k}') | 1 \leqq j \leqq m, i \neq j\}$ gives $\mathfrak{k}' = \mathfrak{k}_{j(1)} \# \ldots \# \mathfrak{k}_{j(m)}$. Now $\mathfrak{k} = \mathfrak{k}' \# \mathfrak{k}_l = \mathfrak{k}_{j(1)} \# \ldots \# \mathfrak{k}_{j(m+1)}$, $j(m+1) = l$. □

Figure 7.6 illustrates Definition 7.14 and Lemma 7.15.

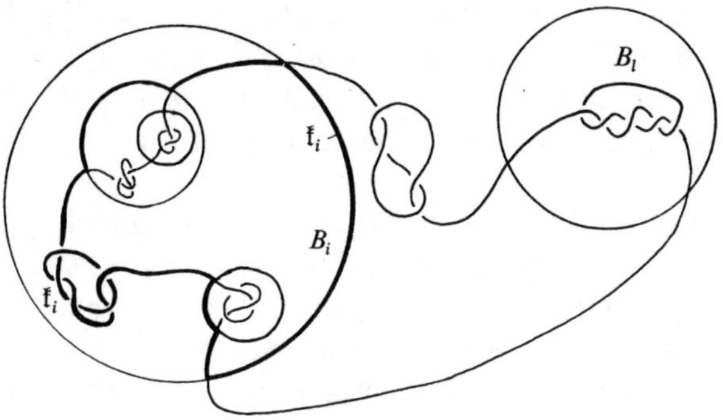

Fig. 7.6

7.16 Definition. Two *decomposing systems of spheres* $\mathfrak{S} = \{S_j, \mathfrak{k}\}$, $\mathfrak{S}' = \{S_j', \mathfrak{k}\}$, $1 \leqq j \leqq m$, are called *equivalent* if they define the same (unordered) $(m+1)$ factor knots $\mathfrak{k}_{l(j)}$.

The following lemma is the crucial tool used in the proof of the Uniqueness Theorem. It describes a process by which one can pass over from a decomposing system to an equivalent one.

7.17 Lemma. *Let $\mathfrak{S} = \{(S_j, \mathfrak{k}) | 1 \leqq j \leqq m\}$ be a decomposing system of spheres, and let S' be another 2-sphere embedded in S^3, disjoint from $\{S_j | 1 \leqq j \leqq m\}$, bounding the balls B' and B'' in S^3. If B_i, $\dot{B}_i = S_i$, is a maximal ball contained in B', that is $B_i \subset B'$ but there is no B_j such that $B_i \subset B_j \subset B'$ for any $j \neq i$, and if B' determines the knot $\mathfrak{k}_i$ relative to the spheres $\{S_j | 1 \leqq j \leqq m, i \neq j\} \cup \{S'\}$, then these spheres define a decomposing system of spheres with respect to $\mathfrak{k}$ equivalent to $\mathfrak{G} = \{(S_j, \mathfrak{k}) | 1 \leqq j \leqq m\}$.*

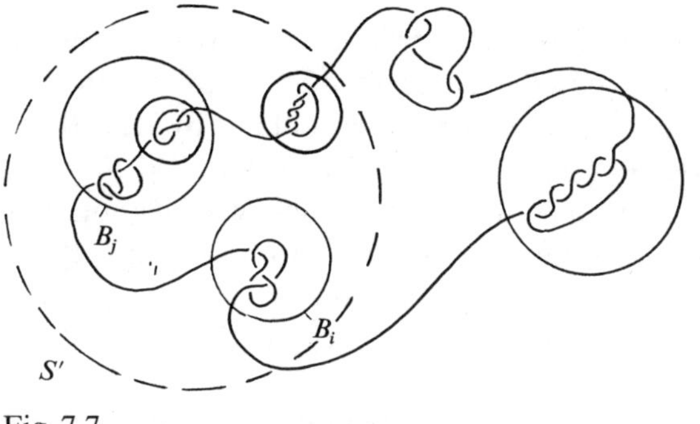

Fig. 7.7

Proof. Denote by $\mathfrak{k}_j$ the knot determined by B_j relative to $\mathfrak{S}$, and assume $B_j \subset B'$. For $i \neq j$, B_j determines the same knot $\mathfrak{k}_j$ relative to $\mathfrak{S}'$ since no inclusion $B_i \subset B_j \subset B'$, $i \neq j$, exists. If there is a ball B_l, $B_j \subset B_l \subset B_i$, then $B_{c(j)}$ determines $\mathfrak{k}_l$

relative to $\mathfrak{S}$ and $\mathfrak{S}'$. If there is no such B_l we have $\mathfrak{k}_{c(i)} = \mathfrak{k}_{c(j)}$ (see Fig. 7.7). Now $B_{c(j)}$ determines $\mathfrak{k}_i$ and B'' the knot $\mathfrak{k}_{c(j)}$. So instead of $\mathfrak{k}_i, \mathfrak{k}_{c(i)}, \mathfrak{k}_j, \mathfrak{k}_{c(j)} = \mathfrak{k}_{c(i)}$ determined by $B_i, B_{c(i)}, B_j, B_{c(j)}$ in $\mathfrak{S}$, we get $\mathfrak{k}_i, \mathfrak{k}_{c(j)}, \mathfrak{k}_j, \mathfrak{k}_i$ determined by $B', B'', B_j, B_{c(j)}$ in $\mathfrak{S}'$. The case $B_j \subset B''$ is dealt with in a similar way. □

7.18 *Proof* of the Uniqueness Theorem 7.12 (b). The proof consists in verifying the assertion that any two decomposing systems $\mathfrak{S} = \{(S_j, \mathfrak{k}) | 1 \leqq j \leqq m\}$, $\mathfrak{S}' = \{(S_j', \mathfrak{k}) | 1 \leqq j \leqq m'\}$ with respect to the same knot $\mathfrak{k}$ are equivalent. We prove this by induction on $m + m'$. For $m + m' = 0$ nothing has to be proved. The spheres S_j and S_j' can be assumed to be in general position relative to each other.

To begin with, suppose there is a ball $B_i \cap \mathfrak{S}' = \emptyset$ not containing any other B_j or B_j'. Then by 7.17 some S_j' can be replaced by S_i and induction can be applied to $\mathfrak{k} \cap B_{c(i)}$.

If there is no such B_i (or B_i'), choose an innermost curve λ' of $S_j' \cap \mathfrak{S}$ bounding a disk $\delta' \subset S_j' = \partial B_j'$ such that B_j' contains no other ball B_k of B_l'. The knot $\mathfrak{k}$ meets δ' in at most two points. The disk δ' divides B_i into two balls B_i^1 and B_i^2, and in the first two cases of Figure 7.8 one of them determines a trivial knot or does not meet $\mathfrak{k}$ at all, and the other one determines the prime knot $\mathfrak{k}_i$ with respect to $\mathfrak{S}$, because otherwise δ' would effect a decomposition of $\mathfrak{k}_i$.

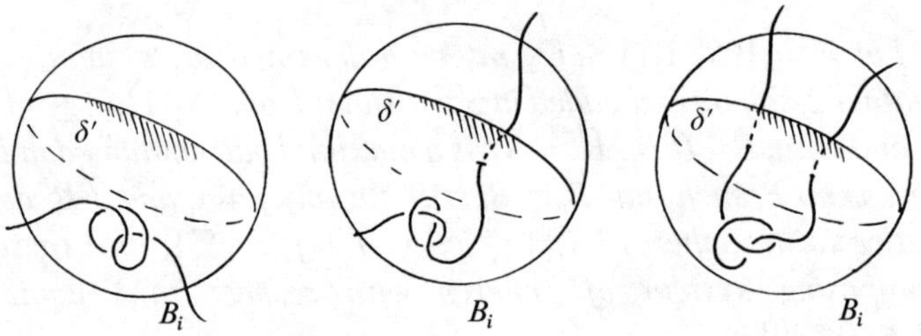

Fig. 7.8

If B_i^1 determines $\mathfrak{k}_i$, replace S_i by ∂B_i^1 or rather by a sphere S' obtained from ∂B_i^1 by a small isotopy such that λ' disappears and general position is restored. The new decomposing system is equivalent to the old one by 7.17. If $\mathfrak{k}$ meets δ' in two points – the third case of Figure 7.8 – one may choose $\delta'' = S_j - \delta'$ instead of δ' if λ' is the only intersection curve on S_j'. If not, there will be another innermost curve $\lambda'' = S_j' \cap S_k$ on S_j' bounding a disk $\delta'' \subset S_j'$. In both events the knot $\mathfrak{k}$ will not meet δ'' and we are back to case one of Figure 7.8. Thus we obtain finally an innermost ball without intersections. This proves the theorem. □

The theorem on the existence and uniqueness of decomposition carries over to the case of links without major difficulties [Hashizume 1958].

C Fibred Knots and Decompositions

It is easily seen that the product of two fibred knots is also fibred. It is also true that factor knots of a fibred knot are fibred. We present two proof of this assertion, an algebraic one which is quite short, and a more complicated geometric one which affords a piece of additional insight.

7.18 Proposition (decomposition of fibred knots). A *composite knot* $\mathfrak{k} = \mathfrak{k}_1 \# \mathfrak{k}_2$ *is a fibred knot if and only if* $\mathfrak{k}_1$ *and* $\mathfrak{k}_2$ *are fibred knots.*

Proof. Let $\mathfrak{G}, \mathfrak{G}_1, \mathfrak{G}_2$ etc. denote the groups of $\mathfrak{k}$, $\mathfrak{k}_1$ and $\mathfrak{k}_2$, respectively. By Proposition 7.10, $\mathfrak{G}' = \mathfrak{G}_1' * \mathfrak{G}_2'$. From the Grushko Theorem, see [ZVC 1980, 2.9.2], it follows that $\mathfrak{G}'$ is finitely generated if and only if $\mathfrak{G}_1'$ and $\mathfrak{G}_2'$ are finitely generated. Now the assertion 7.18 is a consequence of Theorem 5.1. □

7.19 Theorem (decomposition of fibred knots). *Let* $\mathfrak{k}$ *be a fibred knot, V a regular neighbourhood,* $C = \overline{S^3 - V}$ *its complement, and* $p\colon C \to S^1$ *a fibration of C. Let a 2-sphere* $S \subset S^3$ *decompose* $\mathfrak{k}$ *into two non-trivial factors. Then there is an isotopy of* S^3 *deforming S into a sphere S′ with the property that* $S' \cap V$ *consists of two disks and* $S' \cap C$ *intersects each fibre* $p^{-1}(t)$, $t \in S^1$, *in a simple arc. Moreover, the isotopy leaves the points of* $\mathfrak{k}$ *fixed.*

Proof. It follows by standard arguments that there is an isotopy of S^3 that leaves the knot pointwise fixed and maps S into a sphere that intersects V in two disks. Moreover, we may assume that p maps the boundary of each of these disks bijectively onto S^1. Suppose that S already has these properties. Consider the annulus $A = C \cap S$ and the fibre $F = p^{-1}(*)$ where $* \in S^1$. We may assume that S and F are in general position and that $A \cap \partial F$ consists of two points; otherwise S can be deformed by an ambient isotopy to fulfil these conditions.

Now $A \cap F$ is composed of an arc joining the points of $A \cap \partial F$ (which are on different components of ∂A) and, perhaps, further simple closed curves. Each of

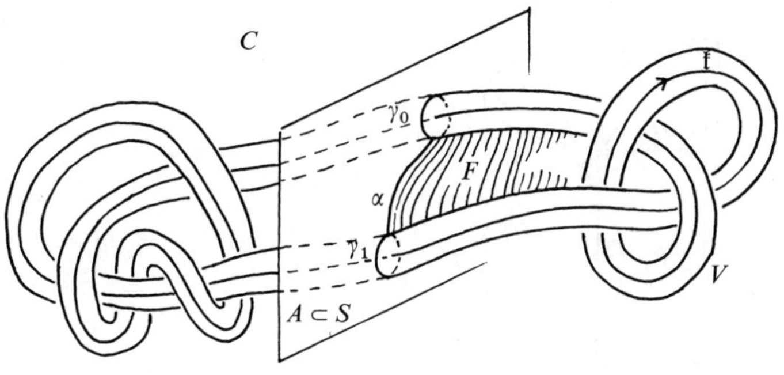

Fig. 7.9

them bounds a disk on A, hence also a disk on F, since $\pi_1(F) \to \pi_1(C)$ is injective. Starting with an innermost disk δ on F we find a 2-sphere $\delta \cup \delta'$ consisting of disks $\delta \subset F$ and $\delta' \subset A$ such that $\delta \cap \delta'$ is the curve $\partial\delta = \partial\delta'$ and $\delta \cap A = \partial\delta$. Now δ' can be deformed to a disk not intersecting A and the number of components of $A \cap F$ becomes smaller. Thus we may assume that $A \cap F$ consists of an arc α joining the boundary components of A, see Figure 7.9.

We cut C along F and obtain a space homeomorphic to $F \times I$. The cut transforms the annulus A into a disk D, $\partial D = \alpha_0 \gamma_0 \alpha_1^{-1} \gamma_1^{-1}$, where the $\alpha_i \subset F \times \{i\}$, $i = 0, 1$, are obtained from α and the γ_i from the meridians $\partial V \cap S$.

Let $q: F \times I \to F$ be the projection. The restriction $q|D$ defines a homotopy $q \circ \alpha_0 \simeq q \circ \alpha_1$. Since $q \circ \alpha_0$ and $q \circ \alpha_1$ are simple arcs with endpoints on ∂F it follows that these arcs are ambient isotopic and the isotopy leaves the endpoints fixed. (This can be proved in the same way as the refined Baer Theorem (see [ZVC 1980, 5.12.1]) which respects the basepoint; it can, in fact, be derived from that theorem by considering ∂F as the boundary of a 'small' disk around the basepoint of a closed surface F' containing F.) Thus there is a homeomorphism

$$H: (I \times I, (\partial I) \times I) \to (F \times I, (\partial F) \times I) \quad \text{with}$$
$$H(t, 0) = \alpha_0(t), H(t, 1) = \alpha_1(t)$$

which is level preserving:

$$H(x, t) = (q(H(x, t)), t) \quad \text{for } (x, t) \in I \times I.$$

Therefore $D' = H(I \times I)$ is a disk and intersects each fibre $F \times \{t\}$ in a simple arc. It is transformed by re-identifying $F \times \{0\}$ and $F \times \{1\}$ into an annulus A' which intersects each fiber $p^{-1}(t)$, $t \in S^1$, in a simple closed curve. In addition $\partial A' = \partial A$.

It remains to prove that A' is ambient isotopic to A. An ambient isotopy takes D into general position with respect to D' while leaving its boundary ∂D fixed. Then $\mathring{D} \cap \mathring{D}'$ consists of simple closed curves. Take an innermost (relative to D') curve β. It bounds disks $\delta \subset D$ and $\delta' \subset D'$. The sphere $\delta \cup \delta' \subset F \times I \subset S^3$ bounds a 3-ball by the Theorem of Alexander. Thus there is an ambient isotopy of $F \times I$ which moves δ to δ' and a bit further to diminish the number of compo-

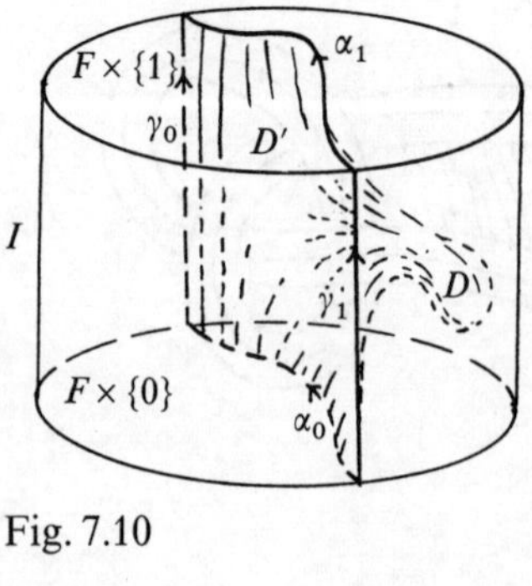

Fig. 7.10

nents in $D \cap D'$; during the deformation the boundary $\partial(F \times I)$ remains fixed. After a finite number of such deformations we may assume that $D \cap D' = \partial D = \partial D'$. Now $D \cup D'$ bounds a ball in $F \times I$ and D can be moved into D' by an isotopy which is the identity on $\partial(F \times I)$. Therefore the isotopy induces an isotopy of C that moves A to A'. (See Fig. 7.10.) □

D History and Sources

The concept and the main theorem concerning products of knots are due to H. Schubert, and they are contained in his thesis [Schubert 1949]. His theorem was shown to be valid for links in [Hashizume 1958] where a new proof was given which in some parts simplified the original one. A further simplification can be derived from Milnor's uniqueness theorem for the factorization of 3-manifolds [Milnor 1962]. The proof given in this chapter takes advantage of it.

Compositions of knots of a more complicated nature have been investigated in [Kinoshita–Terasaka 1957] and [Hashizume–Hosokawa 1958], see E 14.3(b).

Schubert used Haken's theory of incompressible surfaces to give an algorithm which effects the decomposition into prime factors for a given link [Schubert 1961].

In the case of a fibred knot primeness can be characterized algebraically: The subgroup of fixed elements under the automorphism $\alpha(t)$: $\mathfrak{G}' \to \mathfrak{G}'$, $\alpha(x) = t^{-1}xt$, $x \in G'$, t a meridian, consists of an infinite cyclic group generated by a longitude if and only if the knot is prime [Whitten 1972‴].

For higher dimensional knots the factorization is not unique [Kearton 1979′], [Bayer 1980′], see also [Bayer–Hillman–Kearton 1981].

E Exercises

E 7.1 Show that in general the product of two links $\mathfrak{l}_1 \# \mathfrak{l}_2$ (use an analogous definition) will depend on the choice of the components which are joined.

E 7.2 An m-tangle $\mathfrak{t}$ consists of m disjoint simple arcs α_i, $1 \leqq i \leqq m$, in a (closed) 3-ball B, $\partial B \cap \bigcup_{i=1}^{m} \alpha_i = \bigcup_{i=1}^{m} \partial\alpha_i$. An m-tangle $\mathfrak{t}_m$ is called m-rational, if there are disjoint disks $\delta_i \subset B$, $\alpha_i = \overline{\mathring{B} \cap \partial\delta_i}$. Show that $\mathfrak{t}_m$ is m-rational if and only if there is an m-tangle $\mathfrak{t}_m^C$ in the complement $C = \overline{S^3 - B}$ such that $\mathfrak{t}_m \cup \mathfrak{t}_m^C$ is the trivial knot. (Observe that the complementary tangle $\mathfrak{t}_m^C$ is rational.) 2-rational tangles are called just rational.

E 7.3 Let S^3 be composed of two balls B_1, B_2, $S^3 = B_1 \cup B_2$, $B_1 \cap B_2 = S^2 \subset S^3$.

If a knot (or link) $\mathfrak{k}$ intersects the B_i in m-rational tangles $\mathfrak{t}_i = \mathfrak{k} \cap B_i$, $i = 1, 2$, then $\mathfrak{k}$ has a bridge number $\leqq m$.

E 7.4 Prove 7.5(b) using 7.10 and 3.17.

E 7.5 Show that the groups of the product knots $\mathfrak{k}_1 \# \mathfrak{k}_2$ and $\mathfrak{k}_1 \# \mathfrak{k}_2^*$ are isomorphic. The knots are non-equivalent if $\mathfrak{k}_2$ is not amphicheiral.

Chapter 8: Cyclic Coverings and Alexander Invariants

One of the most important invariants of a knot (or link) is known as the Alexander polynomial. Sections A and B introduce the Alexander module, which is closely related to the homomorphic image $\mathfrak{G}/\mathfrak{G}''$ of the knot group modulo its second commutator subgroup $\mathfrak{G}''$. The geometric background is the infinite cyclic covering C_∞ of the knot complement and its homology (Section C). Section D is devoted to the Alexander polynomials themselves. Finite cyclic coverings are investigated in 8 E – they provide further invariants of knots.

Let $\mathfrak{k}$ be a knot, U a regular neighbourhood of $\mathfrak{k}$, $C = \overline{S^3 - U}$ the complement of the knot.

A Alexander Module

We saw in Chapter 3 that the knot group $\mathfrak{G}$ is a powerful invariant of the knot, and the peripheral group system was even shown (3.15) to characterize a knot. Torus knots could be classified by their groups (3.28). In general, however, knot groups are difficult to treat algebraically, and one tries to simplify matters by looking at homomorphic images of knot groups.

The knot group $\mathfrak{G}$ is a semidirect product $\mathfrak{G} = \mathfrak{Z} \ltimes \mathfrak{G}'$, $\mathfrak{Z} \cong \mathfrak{G}/\mathfrak{G}'$, a free cyclic group, and we may choose $t \in \mathfrak{G}$ (representing a meridian of $\mathfrak{k}$) as a representative of a generating coset of $\mathfrak{Z}$. The knot group $\mathfrak{G}$ can be described by $\mathfrak{G}'$ and the operation of $\mathfrak{Z}$ on $\mathfrak{G}'$: $a \mapsto a^t = t^{-1}at$, $a \in \mathfrak{G}'$. In Chapter 4 we studied the group $\mathfrak{G}'$; it is a free group, if finitely generated, but if not, its structure is rather complicated. We propose to study in this chapter the abelianized commutator subgroup $\mathfrak{G}'/\mathfrak{G}''$ together with the operation of $\mathfrak{Z}$ on it. We write $\mathfrak{G}'/\mathfrak{G}''$ additively and the induced operation:

$$a \mapsto ta, \quad a \in \mathfrak{G}'/\mathfrak{G}''.$$

(Note that the induced operation does not depend on the choice of the representative t in the coset $t\mathfrak{G}'$.) The operation $a \mapsto ta$ turns $\mathfrak{G}'/\mathfrak{G}''$ into a module over the group ring $\mathbb{Z}\mathfrak{Z} = \mathbb{Z}(t)$ of $\mathfrak{Z} \cong \langle t \rangle$ by

$$\Big(\sum_{i=-\infty}^{+\infty} n_i t^i\Big)a = \sum_{i=-\infty}^{+\infty} n_i(t^i a), \; a \in \mathfrak{G}'/\mathfrak{G}'', \; n_i \in \mathbb{Z}.$$

8.1 Definition (Alexander module). The $\mathfrak{Z}$-module $\mathfrak{G}'/\mathfrak{G}''$ is called the *Alexander module* $M(t)$ of the knot group where t denotes either a generator of $\mathfrak{Z} = \mathfrak{G}/\mathfrak{G}'$ or a representative of its coset in $\mathfrak{G}$.

$M(t)$ is uniquely determined by $\mathfrak{G}$ except for the change from t to t^{-1}. We shall see, however, that the operations t and t^{-1} are related by a duality in $M(t)$, and that the invariants of $M(t)$ (see Appendix A 6) prove to be symmetric with respect to the substitution $t \mapsto t^{-1}$.

B Infinite Cyclic Covering and Alexander Module

The commutator subgroup $\mathfrak{G}' \lhd \mathfrak{G}$ defines an infinite cyclic covering $p_\infty\colon C_\infty \to C$ of the knot complement, $\mathfrak{G}' \cong \pi_1 C_\infty$. The Alexander module $M(t)$ is the first homology group $H_1(C_\infty) \cong \mathfrak{G}'/\mathfrak{G}''$, and the group of covering transformations which is isomorphic to $\mathfrak{Z} = \mathfrak{G}/\mathfrak{G}'$ induces on $H_1(C_\infty)$ the module operation. Following [Seifert 1934] we investigate $M(t) \cong H_1(C_\infty)$ in a similar way as we did in the case of the fundamental group $\pi_1 C_\infty \cong \mathfrak{G}'$, see 4.4.

Choose a Seifert surface $S \subset S^3$, $\partial S = \mathfrak{k}$ of genus h (not necessarily minimal), and cut C along S to obtain a bounded manifold C^*. Let $\{a_i | 1 \leqq i \leqq 2h\}$ be a canonical system of curves on S which intersect in a basepoint P. We may assume that $a_i \cap \mathfrak{k} = \emptyset$, and that $\sum_{i=1}^{h} [a_{2i-1}, a_{2i}] \simeq \mathfrak{k}$ on S, see 3.12. Retract S onto a regular neighbourhood B of $\{a_i | 1 \leqq i \leqq 2h\}$ consisting of $2h$ bands that start and end in a neighbourhood of P. Figure 8.1 shows two examples.

Choosing a suitable orientation we obtain $\partial B \simeq \prod_{i=1}^{h} [a_{2i-1}, a_{2i}]$ in B, and ∂B represents $\mathfrak{k}$ in S^3. The second assertion is proved as follows: by cutting S along $a_1, \ldots, a_{2h}$ we obtain an annulus with boundaries $\mathfrak{k}$ and $\prod_{i=1}^{h} [a_{2i-1}, a_{2i}]$. This proves the first two parts of the following proposition:

8.2 Proposition (band projection of a knot). *Every knot can be represented as the boundary of an orientable surface S embedded in 3-space with the following properties:*

(a) $S = D^2 \cup B_1 \cup \ldots \cup B_{2h}$ where D^2 and each B_j is a disk.

(b) $B_i \cap B_j = \emptyset$ for $i \neq j$, $\partial B_i = \alpha_i \gamma_i \beta_i \gamma_i'^{-1}$, $D^2 \cap B_i = \alpha_i \cup \beta_i$,
$\partial D^2 = \alpha_1 \delta_1 \beta_2^{-1} \delta_2 \beta_1^{-1} \delta_3 \alpha_2 \delta_4 \ldots \alpha_{2h-1} \delta_{4h-3} \beta_{2h}^{-1} \delta_{4h-2} \beta_{2h-1}^{-1} \delta_{4h-1} \alpha_{2h} \delta_{4h}$.

(c) There is a projection which is locally homeomorphic on S (there are no twists in the bands B_i.)

A projection of this kind is called a band projection of S *or of* $\mathfrak{k}$ *(see Fig. 8.1(b)).*

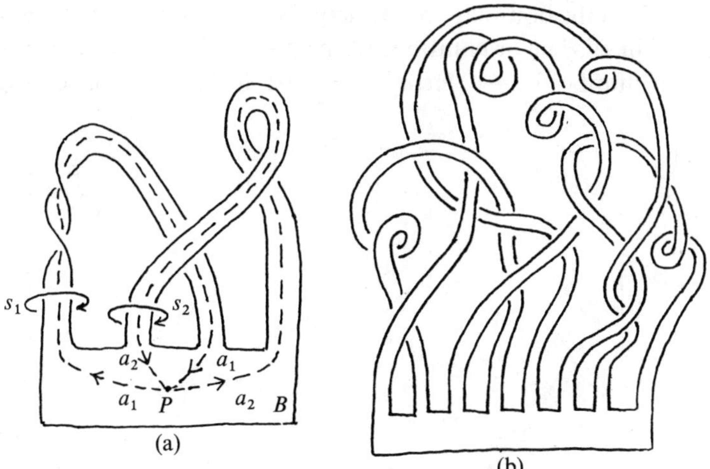

Fig. 8.1

Proof. It remains to verify assertion (c). Since S is orientable every band is twisted through multiples of 2π (full twists). A full twist can be changed into a loop of the band (see Fig. 8.2). □

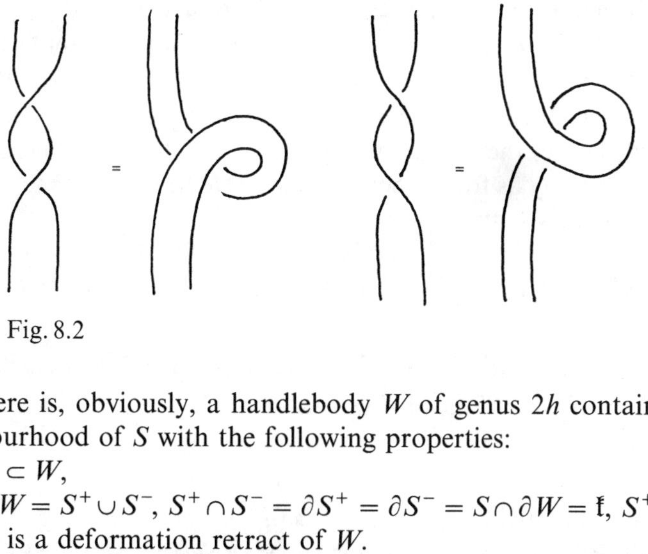

Fig. 8.2

8.3 There is, obviously, a handlebody W of genus $2h$ contained in a regular neighbourhood of S with the following properties:

(a) $S \subset W$,

(b) $\partial W = S^+ \cup S^-$, $S^+ \cap S^- = \partial S^+ = \partial S^- = S \cap \partial W = \mathfrak{k}$, $S^+ \cong S^- \cong S$,

(c) S is a deformation retract of W.

We call S^+ the upside and S^- the downside of W. The curves $a_1, \ldots, a_{2h}$ of S are projected onto curves $a_1^+, \ldots, a_{2h}^+$ on S^+, and $a_1^-, \ldots, a_{2h}^-$ on S^-, respectively. After connecting the basepoints of S^+ and S^- with an arc, they define together a canonical system of curves on the closed orientable surface ∂W of genus $2h$; in particular, they define a basis of $H_1(\partial W) \cong \mathbb{Z}^{4h}$. Clearly

$$a_i^+ \sim a_i^- \text{ in } W.$$

Choose a curve s_i on the boundary of the neighbourhood of the band B_i such that s_i bounds a disk in W. The orientations of the disk and of s_i are chosen such that the intersection number is $+1$, $int(a_i, s_i) = 1$ (right-hand-rule), see Figure 8.3.

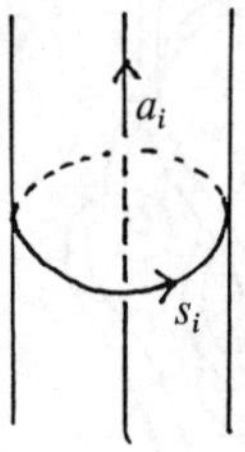

Fig. 8.3

8.4 Lemma. *(a)* $\{a_1^+, \ldots, a_{2h}^+, a_1^-, \ldots, a_{2h}^-\}$ *and* $\{s_1, \ldots, s_{2h}, a_1^\varepsilon, \ldots, a_{2h}^\varepsilon\}$ ($\varepsilon = +$ *or* $\varepsilon = -$) *are bases of* $H_1(\partial W) \cong \mathbb{Z}^{4h}$.

(b) $\{a_1^\varepsilon, \ldots, a_{2h}^\varepsilon\}$ ($\varepsilon \in \{+, -\}$) *is a basis of* $H_1(W)$, *and* $\{s_1, \ldots, s_{2h}\}$ *is a basis of* $H_1(\overline{S^3 - W}) = \mathbb{Z}^{2h}$.

Proof. The first statements in (a) and (b) follow immediately from the definition of W. The second one of (a) is a consequence of the fact that either system of curves $\{s_1, \ldots, s_{2h}, a_1^\varepsilon, \ldots, a_{2h}^\varepsilon\}$, $\varepsilon = +$ or $-$, is canonical on ∂W, that is, cutting ∂W along these curves transformes ∂W into a disk. Finally $\{s_1, \ldots, s_{2h}\}$ is a basis of $H_1(\overline{S^3 - W})$, since W can be retracted to a $2h$-bouquet in S^3. The fundamental group and, hence, the first homology group of its complement can be computed in the same way as for the complement of a knot (3 B). One may also apply the Mayer-Vietoris sequence:

$$0 = H_2(S^3) \to H_1(\partial W) \xrightarrow{\varphi} H_1(W) \oplus H_1(\overline{S^3 - W}) \to H_1(S^3) = 0.$$

Here $\varphi(s_i) = (0, s_i)$. From $H_1(\partial W) \cong \mathbb{Z}^{4h}$ and $H_1(W) \cong \mathbb{Z}^{2h}$ we get $H_1(\overline{S^3 - W}) = \mathbb{Z}^{2h}$. Now it follows from (a) that $\{s_1, \ldots, s_{2h}\}$ is a basis of $H_1(\overline{S^3 - W})$. □

8.5 Definition (Seifert matrix). (a) Let $v_{jk} = lk(a_j^-, a_k)$ be the linking number of a_j^- and a_k. The $2h \times 2h$-matrix $V = (v_{jk})$ is called a *Seifert matrix of* $\mathfrak{k}$.

(b) Define $f_{jk} = lk(a_j^- - a_j^+, a_k)$ and $F = (f_{jk})$.

A Seifert matrix (v_{jk}) can be read off a band projection in the following way: Consider the j-th band B_j endowed with the direction of its core a_j. Denote by l_{jk} (resp. r_{jk}) the number of times where B_j overcrosses B_k from left to right (resp. from right to left), then $v_{jk} = l_{jk} - r_{jk}$.

8.6 Lemma *(a) Let $i^\varepsilon\colon S^\varepsilon \to \overline{S^3 - W}$ denote the inclusion. Then*

$$i_*^+(a_j^+) = \sum_{k=1}^{2h} v_{kj} s_k \quad \text{and} \quad i_*^-(a_j^-) = \sum_{k=1}^{2h} v_{jk} s_k .$$

(b)
$$F = \begin{pmatrix} 0 & 1 & & & & & \\ -1 & 0 & & & & & \\ & & 0 & 1 & & & \\ & & -1 & 0 & & & \\ & & & & \ddots & & \\ & & & & & 0 & 1 \\ & & & & & -1 & 0 \end{pmatrix}.$$

Proof. (a) Let Z_j^- be a projecting cylinder of the curve a_j^-, and close Z_j^- by a point at infinity. $Z_j^- \cap (S^3 - W)$ represents a 2-chain realizing $a_j^- \sim \sum_{k=1}^{2h} v_{jk} s_k$, Figure 8.4. The same construction applied to a_j^+, using a projecting cylinder Z_j^+ directed upward, yields

$$a_j^+ \sim \sum_k v_{kj} s_k .$$

We write these equations frequently in matrix form, $a^- = Vs$, $a^+ = V^T s$, where a^+, a^-, s denote the $2h$-columns of the elements a_j^+, a_j^-, s_j.

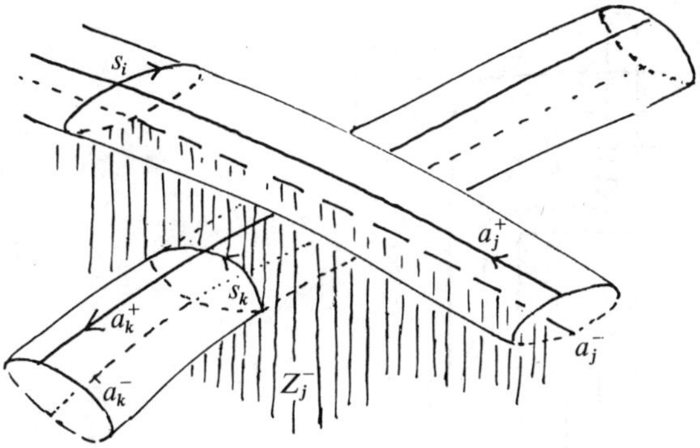

Fig. 8.4

(b) There is an annulus bounded by $a_i^- - a_i^+$. It follows from the definition of the canonical system $\{a_j\}$ that

$$f_{2n-1,2n} = lk(a_{2n-1}^- - a_{2n-1}^+, a_{2n}) = int(a_{2n-1}, a_{2n}) = +1,$$

$$f_{2n,2n-1} = lk(a_{2n}^- - a_{2n}^+, a_{2n-1}) = int(a_{2n}, a_{2n-1}) = -1,$$

$f_{ik} = 0$ otherwise (Fig. 8.5). (A compatible convention concerning the sign of the intersection number is supposed to have been agreed on.) The matrix $F = (f_{jk})$ is the intersection matrix of the canonical curves $\{a_j\}$ (Fig. 8.5). □

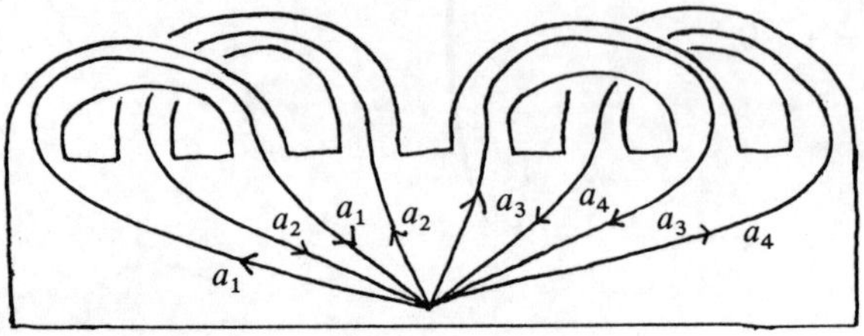

Fig. 8.5

8.5 and 8.6 imply that Seifert matrices have certain properties. The following proposition uses these properties to characterize Seifert matrices:

8.7 Proposition (characterization of Seifert matrices). *A Seifert matrix V of a knot $\mathfrak{k}$ satisfies the equation $V - V^T = F$. (V^T is the transposed matrix of V and F is the intersection matrix defined in 8.6 (b)).*

Every square matrix V of even order satisfying $V - V^T = F$ is a Seifert matrix of a knot.

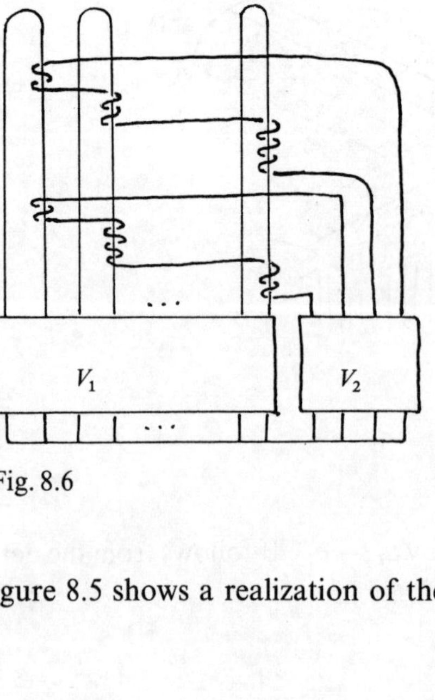

Fig. 8.6

Proof. Figure 8.5 shows a realization of the matrix

$$V_0 = \begin{pmatrix} 0 & 1 & & & & & \\ 0 & 0 & & & & & \\ & & 0 & 1 & & & \\ & & 0 & 0 & & & \\ & & & & \ddots & & \\ & & & & & 0 & 1 \\ & & & & & 0 & 0 \end{pmatrix}.$$

Any $2h \times 2h$ matrix V satisfying $V - V^T = F$ is of the form $V = V_0 + Q, Q = Q^T$. A realization of V is easily obtained by an inductive argument on h as shown in Figure 8.6. (Here a $(2h-2) \times (2h-2)$ matrix V_1 and a 2×2 matrix V_2 are assumed to be already realized; the bands are represented just by lines.) The last two bands can be given arbitrary linking numbers with the first $2h-2$ bands. □

C Homological Properties of C_∞

8.8 Theorem. *Let V be a Seifert matrix of a knot. $A(t) = V^T - tV$ is a presentation matrix of the Alexander module $H_1(C_\infty) = M(t)$. (We call a presentation matrix of the Alexander module an* Alexander matrix.*) More explicitly: $H_1(C_\infty)$ is generated by the elements*

$$t^i s_j,\ i \in \mathbb{Z},\ 1 \leqq j \leqq 2h, \quad and$$

$$t^i a_j^+ = \sum_{j=1}^{2h} t^i v_{kj} s_k = \sum_{j=1}^{2h} t^{i+1} v_{jk} s_k = t^{i+1} a_j^-$$

are defining relations.

Proof. We use the notation of 4.4. By 8.4 (b) the elements $\{t^i s_j \mid 1 \leqq j \leqq 2h\}$ represent a basis of $H_1(C_i^*)$. The defining relations $t^i a_j^+ = t^{i+1} a_j^-$ are obtained from the identification $S_i^+ = S_{i+1}^-$ by abelianizing the Seifert-van Kampen theorem. □

For further use we are interested in the other homology groups of C_∞. (This paragraph may be skipped at first reading.)

8.9 Proposition.

$$\begin{aligned} &H_m(C_\infty) = 0 \qquad \text{for } m > 1, \\ &H_1(C_\infty, \partial C_\infty) \cong H_1(C_\infty), \\ &H_2(C_\infty, \partial C_\infty) \cong \mathbb{Z}, \\ &H_m(C_\infty, \partial C_\infty) = 0 \quad \text{for } m > 2. \end{aligned}$$

Proof. C_∞ is a 3-dimensional non-compact manifold, and ∂C_∞ is an open 2-manifold. Thus: $H_m(C_\infty) = H_m(C_\infty, \partial C_\infty) = 0$ for $m \geqq 3$, and $H_2(\partial C_\infty) = 0$. In 3.1 (a) we showed $H_i(C) = 0$ for $i \geqq 2$. The exact homology sequence of the pair (C, C^*) then gives

$$0 = H_3(C) \to H_3(C, C^*) \to H_2(C^*) \to H_2(C) = 0,$$

or, $H_3(C, C^*) \cong H_2(C^*)$. Now $(C, C^*) \to (W, \partial W)$ is an excision, and $(W, \partial W) \to (S, \partial S)$ a homotopy equivalence. It follows that

$$0 = H_3(S, \partial S) \cong H_2(C^*).$$

We apply the Mayer-Vietoris sequence to the decomposition

$$E_0 \cup E_1 = C_\infty, \quad E_0 = \bigcup_{i \in \mathbb{Z}} C^*_{2i}, \quad E_1 = \bigcup_{i \in \mathbb{Z}} C^*_{2i+1}:$$

$$0 = H_2(E_0) \oplus H_2(E_1) \to H_2(C_\infty) \to H_1(E_0 \cap E_1) \xrightarrow{j_*}$$
$$H_1(E_0) \oplus H_1(E_1) \to H_1(C_\infty) \to H_0(E_0 \cap E_1).$$

(Observe that $E_0 \cap E_1 = \bigcup_{i \in \mathbb{Z}} S_i$.)

Since E_0 and E_1 consist of disjoint copies of C^*, we have $H_2(E_0) = H_2(E_1) = 0$. The homomorphism $H_0(\bigcup_i S_i) \to H_0(E_0) \oplus H_0(E_1)$ is injective, since for $i \neq j$ the surfaces S_i and S_j belong to different components of E_0 or E_1. This implies that

$$0 \to H_2(C_\infty) \to H_1(\bigcup_i S_i) \xrightarrow{j_*} H_1(E_0) \oplus H_1(E_1) \to H_1(C_\infty) \to 0$$
$$\| \qquad\qquad\qquad\qquad \|$$
$$\bigoplus_{i \in \mathbb{Z}} H_1(S_i) \qquad\qquad \bigoplus_{i \in \mathbb{Z}} H_1(C_i)$$

is exact. We prove that j_* is an isomorphism. The inclusion $i: S^+ \cup S^- \to C^*$ induces a homomorphism $i_*: H_1(S^+ \cup S^-) \to H_1(C^*)$ which can be computed by the equations

$$i_*^+(a^+) = V^T s, \; i_*^-(a^-) = Vs$$

of 8.6:

$$i_*(a^-, a^+) = i_*^-(a^-) - i_*^+(a^+) = (V - V^T)s = Fs.$$

If follows that i_*, and hence, j_* is an isomorphism, since det $F = 1$. (The sign in $-i_*^+(a^+)$ is due to the convention that the orientation induced by the orientation of C^* on S^- resp. S^+ coincides with that of S^- but is opposite to that of S^+.)

We conclude: $H_2(C_\infty) = 0$. The homology sequence then yields

$$0 = H_2(C_\infty) \to H_2(C_\infty, \partial C_\infty) \to H_1(\partial C_\infty) \xrightarrow{e_*} H_1(C_\infty) \to H_1(C_\infty, \partial C_\infty) \to 0.$$

∂C_∞ is an annulus: $\partial S_1 \times \mathbb{R}$; this implies that e_* is the null-homomorphism, thus

$$H_2(C_\infty, \partial C_\infty) \cong H_1(\partial C_\infty) \cong \mathbb{Z},$$
$$H_1(C_\infty, \partial C_\infty) \cong H_1(C_\infty). \quad \square$$

D Alexander Polynomials

The Alexander module $M(t)$ of a knot is a finitely presented $\mathfrak{Z}$-module. In the preceding section we have described a method of obtaining a presentation matrix $A(t)$ (an Alexander matrix) of $M(t)$. An algebraic classification of Alexander modules is not known, since the group ring $\mathbb{Z}(t)$ is not a principal ideal domain. But the theory of finitely generated modules over principlal ideal domains can nevertheless be applied to obtain algebraic invariants of $M(t)$.

We call *Alexander matrices $A(t)$, $A'(t)$ equivalent*, $A(t) \sim A'(t)$, if they present isomorphic modules.

Let R be a commutative ring with a unity element 1, and A an $m \times n$-matrix over R. We define *elementary ideals* $E_k(A) \subset R$, for $k \in \mathbb{Z}$

$$E_k(A) = \begin{cases} 0, \text{ if } n-k > m \quad \text{or } k < 0 \\ R, \text{ if } n-k \leqq 0 \\ \text{ideal, generated by the } (n-k) \times (n-k) \text{ minors of } A, \\ \text{if } 0 < n-k \leqq m. \end{cases}$$

It follows from the Laplace expansion theorem that the elementary ideals form an ascending chain

$$0 = E_{-1}(A) \subset E_0(A) \subset E_1(A) \subset \ldots \subset E_n(A) = E_{n+1}(A) = \ldots = R.$$

Given a knot $\mathfrak{k}$, its Alexander module $M(t)$ and an Alexander matrix $A(t)$, we call $E_k(t) = E_{k-1}(A(t))$ the k-th elementary ideal of $\mathfrak{k}$. The proper ideals $E_k(t)$ are invariants of $M(t)$, and hence, of $\mathfrak{k}$. Compare Appendix A 6, [Crowell-Fox 1963, Chapter VII].

8.10 Definition (Alexander polynomials). The greatest common divisor $\Delta_k(t)$ of the elements of $E_k(t)$ is called the *k-th Alexander polynomial of $M(t)$*, resp. of the knot. The first Alexander polynomial $\Delta_1(t)$ is usually called simply the *Alexander polynomial* and is denoted by $\Delta(t)$ (without an index). If there are no proper elementary ideals, we say that the Alexander polynomials are trivial, $\Delta_k(t) = 1$.

Remark: $\mathbb{Z}(t)$ is a unique factorization ring. So $\Delta_k(t)$ exists, and it is determined up to a factor $\pm t^\nu$, a unit of $\mathbb{Z}(t)$. It will be convenient to introduce the following notation:

$$f(t) \doteq g(t) \text{ for } f(t),\ g(t) \in \mathbb{Z}(t), \quad f(t) = \pm t^\nu g(t),\ \nu \in \mathbb{Z}.$$

8.11 Proposition. *The (first) Alexander polynomial $\Delta(t)$ is obtained from the Seifert matrix V of a knot by*

$$|V^T - tV| = \det(V^T - tV) = \Delta(t).$$

The first elementary ideal $E_1(t)$ is a principal ideal.

Proof. $V^T - tV = A(t)$ is a $2h \times 2h$-matrix. $|A(t)|$ generates the elementary ideal $E_0(A(t)) = E_1(t)$. Since $\det(A(1)) = 1$, the ideal does not vanish, $E_1(t) \neq 0$. □

8.12 Proposition. *The Alexander matrix $A(t)$ of a knot $\mathfrak{k}$ satisfies*

(a) $A(t) \sim A^T(t^{-1})$ (duality).

The Alexander polynomials $\Delta_k(t)$ are polynomials of even degree with integral coefficients subject to the following conditions:

(b) $\Delta_k(t) | \Delta_{k-1}(t)$,

(c) $\Delta_k(t) \doteq \Delta_k(t^{-1})$ (symmetry),

(d) $\Delta_k(1) = \pm 1$.

Remark: The symmetry (c) implies, together with $\deg \Delta_k(t) \equiv 0 \bmod 2$, that $\Delta_k(t)$ is a symmetric polynomial:

$$\Delta_k(t) = \sum_{i=0}^{2r} a_i t^i, \; a_{2r-i} = a_i.$$

Proof. Duality follows from the fact that $A(t) = V^T - tV$ is an Alexander matrix by 8.8, $(V^T - t^{-1}V)^T = -t^{-1}(V^T - tV)$. This implies $E_k(t) = E_k(t^{-1})$ and (c). For $t = 1$ we get: $A(1) = F^T$, and since $\det F = 1$, we have $E_k(1) = \mathbb{Z}(1) = \mathbb{Z}$, which proves (d). The fact that $\Delta_k(t)$ is of even degree is a consequence of (c) and (d). Property (b) follows from the definition. □

The symmetry of $\Delta(t)$ suggests a transformation of variables in order to describe the function $\Delta(t)$ by an arbitrary polynomial in $\mathbb{Z}(t)$ of half the degree of $\Delta(t)$. Write

$$\Delta(t) \doteq a_r + a_{r+1}(t + t^{-1}) + \ldots + a_{2r}(t^r + t^{-r}),$$

and note that $t^k + t^{-k}$ is a polynomial in $(t + t^{-1})$ with coefficients in $\mathbb{Z}$. The proof is by induction on k, using the Bernoulli formula. For the sake of normalizing we introduce $u = t + t^{-1} - 2$ as a new variable, and obtain $\Delta(t) \doteq \sum_{i=0}^{r} c_i u^i$, $c_r = 1, c_i \in \mathbb{Z}$. Starting from $\Delta(t) = |V^T - tV|$ we may express the Alexander polynomial as a characteristic polynomial: By $V^T = V - F$ we get $\Delta(t) \doteq |F^T V - \lambda E|$, $\lambda^{-1} = 1 - t$. Now $(\lambda(\lambda - 1))^{-1} = u$, hence,

$$|F^T V - \lambda E| \doteq \sum_{i=0}^{r} c_{r-i}(\lambda(\lambda - 1))^i.$$

8.13 Theorem. *The Alexander polynomial* $\Delta(t) = \sum_{i=0}^{2r} a_i t^i$, $a_{2r-i} = a_i$ *of a knot can be written in the form:*

$$\Delta(t) \doteq \sum_{i=0}^{r} c_i u^i = u^{2r} \sum_{i=0}^{r} c_{r-i}(\lambda(\lambda-1))^i = \pm |F^T V - \lambda E| = \chi(\lambda),$$

with $u = t + t^{-1} - 2$, $\lambda^{-1} = 1 - t$, $c_0 = 1$ *and* $c_i \in \mathbb{Z}$. *Given arbitrary integers* $c_i \in \mathbb{Z}$, $1 \leqq i \leqq r$, *there is a knot* $\mathfrak{k}$ *with Alexander polynomial*

$$\Delta(t) \doteq \sum_{i=0}^{r} c_i u^i, \; c_0 = 1.$$

Proof. The following $(2r \times 2r)$-matrix

$$V = \begin{pmatrix} c_1 & c_1 & 0 & 1 & & & & & & \\ c_1 - 1 & c_1 & 0 & 1 & & & & & & \\ 0 & 0 & c_2 & c_2 & 0 & 1 & & & & \\ 1 & 1 & c_2 - 1 & c_2 - 1 & 0 & 1 & & & & \\ & & 0 & 0 & & & & 0 & 1 & \\ & & 1 & 1 & \ddots & & & 0 & 1 & \\ & & & & & 0 & 0 & c_r & c_r & \\ & & & & & 1 & 1 & c_r - 1 & c_r - 1 & \end{pmatrix}$$

is a Seifert matrix (compare Theorem 8.7). We propose to show:

$$\chi(\lambda) = |F^T V - \lambda E| = \sum_{i=0}^{r-1} c_{r-i}(-1)^{r-i-1} \cdot (\lambda(\lambda-1))^i + (\lambda(\lambda-1))^r.$$

by induction on r.

Denote the determinant consisting of the first $2i$ rows and columns of $(F^T V - \lambda E)$ by D_{2i}, and by D'_{2i} resp. D''_{2i} the determinants that result from D_{2i} when the last column – resp. the last but one – of D_{2i} is replaced by $(0, \ldots, -1, 1)^T$. Then, by expanding D_{2r} by the 2×2-minors of the last two rows, we obtain:

$$D_{2r} = D_{2(r-1)} \cdot \lambda(\lambda-1) - c_r(D'_{2(r-1)} + D''_{2(r-1)}).$$

Again by expanding $D'_{2(r-1)}$ and $D''_{2(r-1)}$ in the same way:

$$D'_{2(r-1)} + D''_{2(r-1)} = -(D'_{2(r-2)} + D''_{2(r-2)}).$$

By induction:

$$D'_{2(r-1)} + D''_{2(r-1)} = (-1)^{r-2}(D'_2 + D''_2) = (-1)^{r-2}.$$

Hence,

$$D_{2r} = D_{2(r-1)}\lambda(\lambda-1) + (-1)^{r-1} \cdot c_r.$$

By induction again:

$$D_{2r} = (\lambda(\lambda-1))^r + \lambda(\lambda-1) \cdot \sum_{i=0}^{r-2} c_{r-1-i}(-1)^{r-2-i} \cdot (\lambda(\lambda-1))^i + (-1)^{r-1} \cdot c_r$$
$$= (\lambda(\lambda-1))^r + \sum_{i=0}^{r-1} c_{r-i}(-1)^{r-i-1}(\lambda(\lambda-1))^i. \quad \square$$

Remark: It is possible to construct a knot with given arbitrary polynomials $\Delta_k(t)$ subject to the conditions (b)–(d) of 8.12 [Levine 1965].

The presentation of the Alexander polynomial in the concise form $\Delta(t) \doteq \sum_{i=0}^{n} c_i u^i$ was first given in [Crowell-Fox 1963, Chapter IX, Exercise 4] and employed later in [Burde 1966] where the coefficients c_i represented twists in a special knot projection. This connection between the algebraic invariant $\Delta(t)$ and the geometry of the knot projection has come to light very clearly through Conway's discovery [Conway 1970]. The Conway polynomial is closely connected to the form $\Sigma c_i u^i$ of the Alexander polynomial. It is, however, necessary to include links in order to get a consistent theory. This will be done in Chapter 13.

8.14 Proposition. *Let $V_{\mathfrak{k}}$ and $V_{\mathfrak{l}}$ be Seifert matrices for the knots $\mathfrak{k}$ and $\mathfrak{l}$, and let $\Delta^{(\mathfrak{k})}(t)$ and $\Delta^{(\mathfrak{l})}(t)$ denote their Alexander polynomials. Then*

$$\begin{pmatrix} V_{\mathfrak{k}} & 0 \\ 0 & V_{\mathfrak{l}} \end{pmatrix} = V$$

is a Seifert matrix of the product knot $\mathfrak{k} \# \mathfrak{l}$, and

$$\Delta^{(\mathfrak{k}\#\mathfrak{l})}(t) = \Delta^{(\mathfrak{k})}(t) \cdot \Delta^{(\mathfrak{l})}(t).$$

Proof. The first assertion is an immediate consequence of the construction of a Seifert surface of $\mathfrak{k} \# \mathfrak{l}$ in 7.4. The second one follows from

$$|V^T - tV| = |V^{(\mathfrak{k})T} - tV^{(\mathfrak{k})}|\,|V^{(\mathfrak{l})T} - tV^{(\mathfrak{l})}|. \quad \square$$

8.15 Examples. (a) The Alexander polynomials of a trivial knot are trivial: $\Delta_k(t) = 1$. (In this case $\mathfrak{G} = \mathfrak{G}/\mathfrak{G}' \cong \mathfrak{Z}$, $\mathfrak{G}' = 1$, $M(t) = (0)$.)

(b) Figure 8.7(a) and (b) show band projections of the trefoil 3_1 and the four-knot 4_1:

The Seifert matrices are:

$$V_{3_1} = \begin{pmatrix} -1 & -1 \\ 0 & -1 \end{pmatrix}, \quad V_{4_1} = \begin{pmatrix} 1 & -1 \\ 0 & -1 \end{pmatrix},$$

$$|V_{3_1}^T - tV_{3_1}| \doteq t^2 - t + 1, \quad |V_{4_1}^T - tV_{4_1}| \doteq t^2 - 3t + 1.$$

(For further examples see E 8.6.)

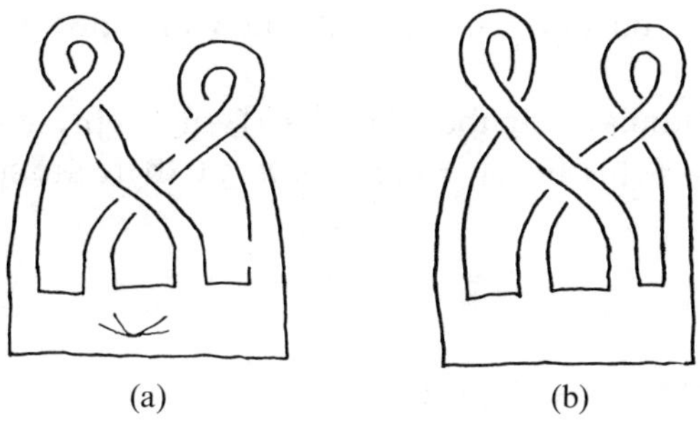

Fig. 8.7

8.16 Proposition (Alexander polynomials of fibred knots). *The Alexander polynomial* $\Delta(t) = \sum_{i=0}^{2g} a_i t^i$ *of a fibred knot* $\mathfrak{k}$ *(see Chapter 5 B) satisfies the conditions*

(a) $\Delta(0) = a_0 = a_{2g} = \pm 1$,
(b) $\deg \Delta(t) = 2g$, *g the genus of* $\mathfrak{k}$.

Proof. If S is a Seifert surface of minimal genus g spanning $\mathfrak{k}$, the inclusion $i^{\pm}$: $S^{\pm} \to C^*$ induces isomorphisms $i^{\pm}_{\#}$: $\pi_1 S^{\pm} \to \pi_1 C^*$ (4.6). Hence, $i^{\pm}_{*}$: $H_1(S^{\pm}) \to H_1(C^*)$ are also isomorphisms. This means (8.6) that the corresponding Seifert matrix V is invertible. By 8.11: $\Delta(t) \doteq |V^T V^{-1} - tE|$, $\Delta(t)$ is the characteristic polynomial of a $2g \times 2g$ regular matrix $V^T V^{-1}$. □

Conditions (a) and (b) of 8.16 characterize Alexander polynomials of fibred knots: There is a fibred knot with Alexander polynomial $\Delta(t)$, if $\Delta(t)$ is any polynomial satisfying (a) and (b), [Burde 1966], [Quach 1981]. Moreover, it was proved in [Burde-Zieschang 1967], [Bing-Martin 1971] that the trefoil and the four-knot are the only fibred knots of genus one. The conjecture that fibred knots are classified by their Alexander polynomials has proved to be false in the case of genus $g > 1$ [Morton 1978]. There are infinitely many different fibred knots to each Alexander polynomial of degree >2 satisfying 8.16(a) [Morton 1983′]. The methods used in Morton's paper are beyond the scope of this book; results of [Johannson 1979], [Jaco-Shalen 1979] and Thurston are employed.

It has been checked that the knots up to ten crossings are fibred if (and only if) $\Delta(0) = \pm 1$ [Kanenobu 1979].

E Finite Cyclic Coverings

Beyond the infinite cyclic covering C_∞ of the knot complement $C = \overline{S^3 - V(\mathfrak{k})}$ the finite cyclic coverings of C are of considerable interest in knot theory. The topological invariants of these covering spaces yield new and powerful knot invariants.

Let $\mathfrak{m}$ be a meridian of a tubular neighbourhood $V(\mathfrak{k})$ of $\mathfrak{k}$ representing the element t of the knot group $\mathfrak{G} = \mathfrak{Z} \ltimes \mathfrak{G}'$, $\mathfrak{Z} = \langle t \rangle$. For $n \geqq 0$ there are surjective homomorphisms:

$$\psi_n \colon \mathfrak{G} \to \mathfrak{Z}_n, \ (\mathfrak{Z}_0 = \mathfrak{Z}).$$

8.17 Proposition. $\ker \psi_n = n\mathfrak{Z} \ltimes \mathfrak{G}' = \mathfrak{G}_n$, $n\mathfrak{Z} = \langle t^n \rangle$.

If $\varphi_n \colon \mathfrak{G} \to \mathfrak{Z}_n \cong \mathfrak{Z}/n\mathfrak{Z}$ *is a surjective homomorphism, then* $\ker \varphi_n = \ker \psi_n$.

Proof. Since $\mathfrak{Z}_n$ is abelian, every homomorphism $\varphi_n \colon \mathfrak{G} \to \mathfrak{Z}_n$ can be factorized, $\varphi_n = j_n \kappa$, $\ker \kappa = \mathfrak{G}'$:

$$\begin{array}{ccc} \mathfrak{G} & \xrightarrow{\varphi_n} & \mathfrak{Z}_n \\ & \kappa \searrow \quad \nearrow j_n & \\ & \mathfrak{G}/\mathfrak{G}' = \mathfrak{Z}. & \end{array}$$

One has $\langle \kappa(t) \rangle = \mathfrak{G}/\mathfrak{G}'$, $\ker j_n = \langle n \cdot \kappa(t) \rangle$, and

$$\ker \psi_n = \ker \varphi_n = n\mathfrak{Z} \ltimes \mathfrak{G}' = \mathfrak{G}_n. \quad \square$$

It follows that for each $n \geqq 0$ there is a (uniquely defined) regular covering space C_n, $(C_0 = C_\infty)$, with $\pi_1 C_n = \mathfrak{G}_n$, and a group of covering transformations isomorphic to $\mathfrak{Z}_n$.

8.18 Branched coverings $\hat{C}_n$. In C_n the n-th ($n > 0$) power $\mathfrak{m}^n$ of the meridian is a simple closed curve on the torus ∂C_n. By attaching a solid torus T_n to C_n, $h \colon \partial T_n \to \partial C_n$, such that the meridian of T_n is mapped onto $\mathfrak{m}^n$, we obtain a closed manifold $\hat{C}_n = C_n \cup_h T_n$ which is called the *n-fold branched covering of* $\mathfrak{k}$. Obviously $p_n \colon C_n \to C$ can be extended to a continuous surjective map $\hat{p}_n \colon \hat{C}_n \to S^3$ that fails to be locally homeomorphic (that is, to be a covering map) only in the points of the core $\hat{p}^{-1}(\mathfrak{k}) = \hat{\mathfrak{k}}$ of T_n. The restriction $p| \colon \hat{\mathfrak{k}} \to \mathfrak{k}$ is a homeomorphism. $\mathfrak{k}$ resp. $\hat{\mathfrak{k}}$ is called the branching set of S^3 resp. $\hat{C}_n$, and $\hat{\mathfrak{k}}$ is said to have *branch index* n. As $\hat{C}_n$ also is uniquely determined by $\mathfrak{k}$, the spaces $\hat{C}_n$ as well as C_n are knot invariants; we shall be concerned especially with their homology groups $H_1(\hat{C}_n)$.

8.19 Proposition. *(a)* $\mathfrak{G}_n \cong \pi_1 C_n \cong (n\mathfrak{Z}) \ltimes \mathfrak{G}'$ *with* $n\mathfrak{Z} = \langle t^n \rangle$.

(b) $H_1(C_n) \cong (n\mathfrak{Z}) \oplus (\mathfrak{G}'/\mathfrak{G}_n')$.

(c) $H_1(\hat{C}_n) \cong \mathfrak{G}'/\mathfrak{G}_n'$.

(d) $H_1(C_n) \cong (n\mathfrak{Z}) \oplus H_1(\hat{C}_n)$.

Proof. (a) by definition, (b) follows since $\mathfrak{G}_n' \lhd \mathfrak{G}'$. Assertion (c) is a consequence of the Seifert-van Kampen theorem applied to $\hat{C}_n = C_n \cup_h T_n$. □

8.20 Proposition (homology of branched cyclic coverings $\hat{C}_n$). *Let V be a* $2h \times 2h$ *Seifert matrix of a knot* $\mathfrak{k}$, $V - V^T = F$, $G = F^T V$, and $\mathfrak{Z}_n = \langle t | t^n \rangle$.

(a) $R_n = (G-E)^n - G^n$ *is a presentation matrix of* $H_1(\hat{C}_n)$ *as an abelian group. In the special case* $n = 2$ *one has* $R_2 \sim V + V^T = A(-1)$.

(b) As a $\mathfrak{Z}_n$*-module* $H_1(\hat{C}_n)$ *is annihilated by* $\varrho_n(t) = 1 + t + \ldots + t^{n-1}$.

(c) $(R_n F)^T = (-1)^n (R_n F)$.

(d) $(V^T - tV)$ *is a presentation matrix of* $H_1(\hat{C}_n)$ *as a* $\mathfrak{Z}_n$*-module.*

Proof. Denote by τ the covering transformation of the covering p_n: $C_n \to C$ corresponding to $\psi_n(t) \in \mathfrak{Z}_n$. Select a sheet C_0^* of the covering, then $\{C_i^* = \tau^i C_0^* | 0 \leqq i \leqq n-1\}$ are the n sheets of C_n (see Fig. 4.2, 8.8). Let s_j, $a_i^{\pm}$ be defined as in 8.3. Apply the Seifert-van Kampen theorem to $X_1 = \mathring{C}_0^* \cup C_1^* \cup \ldots \cup C_{n-2}^* \cup \mathring{C}_{n-1}^*$ and $X_2 = U(S_0^- \cup T_n)$ a tubular neighbourhood of $S_0^- \cup T_n$. As in the proof of 4.6 one gets:

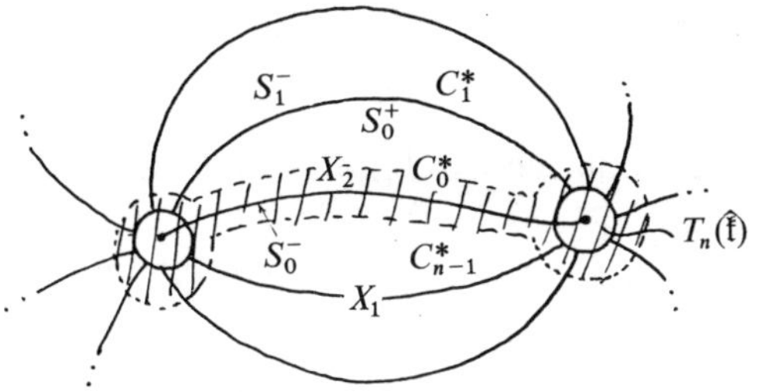

Fig. 8.8

$$\pi_1 X_1 \cong \pi_1 C_0^* *_{\pi_1 S_0^+} \pi_1 C_1^* *_{\pi_1 S_1^+} \cdots *_{\pi_1 S_{n-2}^+} \pi_1 C_{n-1}^*,$$

$$\pi_1 X_2 \cong \pi_1 S_0^-, \ \pi_1(X_1 \cap X_2) \cong \pi_1 S_{n-1}^+ *_{\langle \hat{\ell} \rangle} \pi_1 S_0^-,$$

where $\hat{\ell} = \partial S_0^-$ is a longitude of $\hat{\mathfrak{k}}$ in T_n. It follows by abelianizing $\pi_1(\hat{C}_n) = \pi_1(X_1 \cup X_2)$ that $H_1(\hat{C}_n) \cong \pi_1(\hat{C}_n)/\pi_1'(\hat{C}_n)$ is generated by $\{t^i s_j | 1 \leqq j \leqq 2h, 0 \leqq i \leqq n-1\}$, and its defining relations are $(t^i V^T - t^{i+1} V)s = 0, 0 \leqq i \leqq n-1$, $t^n = 1, s^T = (s_1, s_2, \ldots, s_{2h})$, (see 8.8). (Observe that in $H_1(\hat{C}_n)$ the longitude $\hat{l}$ is 0-homologous.) This proves (d).

Multiply the relations by F^T and introduce the abbreviation $F^T V = G$ (see 8.20). One gets:

(K_i) $\quad Gt^i s - t^i s - Gt^{i+1} s = 0, \ 0 \leqq i \leqq n-1.$

Adding these equations gives

$$(1 + t + \ldots + t^{n-1})s = 0,$$

and proves (b).

Add (K_1) to (K_0) to obtain

(E_1) $\quad (G-E)s - ts - Gt^2 s = 0\,.$

Multiply (E_1) by $G-E$ and add to K_1: The result is

(R_2) $\quad (G-E)^2 s - G^2 t^2 s = 0\,.$

The relations K_0, K_1 can be replaced by the relations (E_1) and (R_2), and (E_1) can be used to eliminate ts. This procedure can be continued. Assume that after $(i-1)$ steps the generators $ts, t^2 s, \dots, t^{i-1} s$ are eliminated, and the equations (K_j), $i \leqq j \leqq n-1$ together with

(R_i) $\quad (G-E)^i s - G^i t^i s = 0$

form a set of defining relations. Now multiply (K_i) by $\sum_{j=0}^{i-1} G^j$ and add to (R_i). One obtains

(E_i) $\quad (G-E)^i s - t^i s - G \sum_{j=0}^{i-1} G^j t^{i+1} s = 0\,.$

Multiply (E_i) by $(G-E)$ and add to (K_i). The result is

(R_{i+1}) $\quad (G-E)^{i+1} s - G^{i+1} t^{i+1} s = 0\,.$

Relations (R_i), (K_i) have thus been replaced by (E_i), (R_{i+1}). Eliminate $t^i s$ by (E_i) and omit (E_i).

The procedure stops when only the generators $s = (s_j)$ are left, and the defining relations

$$G^n s - (G-E)^n s = 0$$

remain. This proves (a).

(c) is easily verified using the definition of R_n and F. □

Remark: It follows from 8.20 (b) for $n=2$ that $1+t$ is the 0-endomorphism of $H_1(\hat{C}_2)$. This means

$$a \mapsto ta = -a \quad \text{for} \quad a \in H_1(\hat{C}_2).$$

8.21 Theorem. *$H_1(\hat{C}_n)$ is finite if and only if no root of the Alexander polynomial $\Delta(t)$ of $\mathfrak{k}$ is an n-th root of unity ζ_i, $1 \leqq i \leqq n$. In this case*

$$|H_1(\hat{C}_n)| = |\prod_{i=1}^{n} \Delta(\zeta_i)|\,.$$

In general, the Betti number of $H_1(\hat{C}_n)$ is even and equals the number of roots of the Alexander polynomial which are also roots of unity; each such root is counted v-times, if it occurs in v different elementary divisors $\varepsilon_k(t) = \Delta_k(t)\Delta_{k+1}^{-1}(t)$, $k = 1, 2, \dots$.

Proof. Since the matrices $G-E$ and G commute,

$$R_n = (G-E)^n - G^n = \prod_{i=1}^{n} [(G-E) - \zeta_i G].$$

By 8.8,

$$(G-E) - tG = F^T(V^T - tV) = F^T A(t)$$

is a presentation matrix of the Alexander module $M(t)$; thus, by 8.11,

$$\det((G-E) - tG) \doteq \Delta(t).$$

This implies that $\det R_n = \prod_{i=1}^{n} \Delta(\zeta_i)$. The order of $H_1(\hat{C}_n)$ is $\det R_n$, if $\det R_n \neq 0$.

In the general case the Betti number of $H_1(\hat{C}_n)$ is equal to $2h - \operatorname{rank} R_n$. To determine the rank of R_n we study the Jordan canonical form $G_0 = L^{-1}GL$ of G, where L is a non-singular matrix with coefficients in $\mathbb{C}$. Then $L^{-1}R_nL = (G_0 - E)^n - G_0^n$. The diagonal elements of G_0 are the roots $\lambda_i = (1-t_i)^{-1}$ of the characteristic polynomial $\chi(\lambda) = \det(G - \lambda E)$, where the t_i are the roots of the Alexander polynomial, see 8.13. The nullity of $L^{-1}R_nL$ equals the number of λ_i which have the property $(\lambda_i - 1)^n - \lambda_i^n = 0 \Leftrightarrow t_i^n = 1,\ t_i \neq 1$, once counted *in* each Jordan block of G_0.

From $\Delta(1) = 1$ and the symmetry of the Alexander polynomial it follows that only non-real roots of unity may be roots of $\chi(\lambda)$ and those occur in pairs. □

The following property of $H_1(\hat{C}_n)$ is a consequence of 8.20(c).

8.22 Proposition ([Plans 1953]). *$H_1(\hat{C}_n) \cong A \oplus A$ if $n \equiv 1 \bmod 2$.*

Proof. $Q = R_nF$ is equivalent to R_n, and hence a presentation matrix of $H_1(\hat{C}_n)$. For odd n the matrix Q is skew symmetric, $Q = -Q^T$. Proposition 8.22 follows from the fact that Q has a canonical form

$$L^TQL = \begin{pmatrix} 0 & a_1 & & & & & & & & \\ -a_1 & 0 & & & & & & & & \\ & & 0 & a_2 & & & & & & \\ & & -a_2 & 0 & & & & & & \\ & & & & \ddots & & & & & \\ & & & & & 0 & a_s & & & \\ & & & & & -a_s & 0 & & & \\ & & & & & & & 0 & & \\ & & & & & & & & 0 & \\ & & & & & & & & & \ddots \\ & & & & & & & & & & 0 \end{pmatrix},$$

where L is unimodular (invertible over $\mathbb{Z}$). A proof is given in Appendix A1. □

8.23 Proposition (Alexander modules of satellites). *Let $\mathfrak{k}$ be a satellite, $\hat{\mathfrak{k}}$ its companion, and $\tilde{\mathfrak{k}}$ the preimage of $\mathfrak{k}$ under the embedding $h\colon \tilde{V} \to \hat{V}$ as defined in 2.8. Denote by $M(t)$, $\hat{M}(t)$, $\tilde{M}(t)$ resp. $\Delta(t)$, $\hat{\Delta}(t)$, $\tilde{\Delta}(t)$ the Alexander modules resp. Alexander polynomials of $\mathfrak{k}$, $\hat{\mathfrak{k}}$ and $\tilde{\mathfrak{k}}$.*

(a) $M(t) = \tilde{M}(t) \oplus [\mathbb{Z}(t) \otimes_{\mathbb{Z}(t^n)} \hat{M}(t^n)]$ *with* $n = lk(\hat{m}, \mathfrak{k})$, $\hat{m}$ *a meridian of* $\hat{\mathfrak{k}}$.

(b) $\Delta(t) = \tilde{\Delta}(t) \cdot \hat{\Delta}(t^n)$.

Proof. The Proposition is a consequence of 4.12, but a direct proof of 8.23 using the trivialization of $\mathfrak{G}''$ in $M(t)$ shows that 8.23 is much simpler than 4.12. Let $\mathfrak{G}$, $\hat{\mathfrak{G}}$, $\tilde{\mathfrak{G}}$ denote the knot groups of $\mathfrak{k}$, $\hat{\mathfrak{k}}$ and $\tilde{\mathfrak{k}}$. There are representations:

$$\hat{\mathfrak{G}} = \langle \hat{t}, \hat{u}_j \mid \hat{R}_k(\hat{u}_j, \hat{t})\rangle, \ \hat{u}_j \in \hat{\mathfrak{G}}',$$

$$\mathfrak{H} = h_{\#}\, \pi_1(\tilde{V} - \tilde{\mathfrak{k}}) = \langle t, \hat{\lambda}, \tilde{u}_j \mid \tilde{R}_l(\tilde{u}_j, \hat{\lambda}, t)\rangle,$$

with $\mathfrak{H}/\langle\hat{\lambda}\rangle \cong \tilde{\mathfrak{G}}$, $\tilde{u}_j \in \tilde{\mathfrak{G}}'$. Here t resp. $\hat{t}$ represent meridians of $\mathfrak{k}$ and $\hat{\mathfrak{k}}$, and $\hat{\lambda}$ a longitude of $\hat{\mathfrak{k}}$. It follows that $\hat{t} \in t^n \mathfrak{G}'$. The Seifert-van Kampen Theorem gives that

$$\mathfrak{G} = \hat{\mathfrak{G}} *_{\langle \hat{t}, \hat{\lambda}\rangle} \mathfrak{H}, \quad \text{where } \langle \hat{t}, \hat{\lambda}\rangle = \pi_1(\partial \hat{V})$$

is a free abelian group of rank 2. (The Definition 2.8 of a companion knot ensures that $\langle \hat{t}, \hat{\lambda}\rangle$ is embedded in both factors.) We apply the Reidemeister-Schreier method to $\mathfrak{G}$, $\hat{\mathfrak{G}}$, $\mathfrak{H}$ with respect the commutator subgroups $\mathfrak{G}'$, $\hat{\mathfrak{G}}'$, $\mathfrak{H}'$ and representatives t^ν, $\hat{t}^\mu$. One obtains generators $\tilde{u}_i^{t^\nu}$, $\hat{u}_j^{\hat{t}^\mu}$, ν, $\mu \in \mathbb{Z}$, and presentations:

$$\hat{\mathfrak{G}}'/\hat{\mathfrak{G}}'' = \langle \hat{u}_j^{\hat{t}^\mu} \mid \hat{R}_k(\hat{u}_j^{\hat{t}^\mu})\rangle, \quad \text{and} \quad \tilde{\mathfrak{G}}'/\tilde{\mathfrak{G}}'' \cong \langle \tilde{u}_i^{t^\nu} \mid \tilde{R}_l(\tilde{u}_i^{t^\nu}, 1)\rangle.$$

Since $\mathfrak{G}' \supset \hat{\mathfrak{G}}', \mathfrak{G}'' \supset \hat{\mathfrak{G}}'' \ni \hat{\lambda}, \mathfrak{G}' \supset \tilde{\mathfrak{G}}'$,

$$\mathfrak{G}'/\mathfrak{G}'' = \langle \hat{u}_j^{\hat{t}^\mu}, \tilde{u}_i^{t^\nu} \mid \hat{R}_k(\hat{u}_j^{\hat{t}^\mu}), \tilde{R}_l(\tilde{u}_i^{t^\nu}, 1)\rangle \cong \hat{\mathfrak{G}}'/\hat{\mathfrak{G}}'' \oplus \tilde{\mathfrak{G}}'/\tilde{\mathfrak{G}}'',$$

where the amalgamation is reduced to the fact that the operations $\hat{t}$ resp. t on the first resp. the second summand are connected by $\hat{t} = t^n$. □

F History and Sources

J.W. Alexander [1928] first introduced Alexander polynomials. H. Seifert [1934] investigated the matter from the geometric point of view and was able to prove the characterizing properties of the Alexander polynomial (Proposition 8.11, 8.12). The presentation of the homology of the finite cyclic coverings in Proposition 8.20 is also due to him [Seifert 1934].

G Exercises

E 8.1 Prove: $\deg \Delta(t) \leqq 2g$, where g is the genus of a knot, and $\Delta(t)$ its Alexander polynomial. (For knots up to ten crossings equality holds.)

E 8.2 Write $\Delta(t) = t^4 - 2t^3 + t^2 - 2t + 1$ in the reduced form $\sum_{i=0}^{2} c_i u^i$ (Proposition 8.13). Construct a knot with $\Delta(t)$ as its Alexander polynomial. Construct a fibred knot with $\Delta(t)$ as its Alexander polynomial. (Hint: use braid-like knots as defined in E 4.4.)

E 8.3 Show that $H_1(C_\infty) = 0$ if and only if $\Delta(t) = 1$. Prove that $\pi_1 C_\infty$ is of finite rank, if it is free.

E 8.4 Prove: $H_1(\hat{C}_n) = 0$ for $n \geqq 2$ if and only if $H_1(C_\infty) = 0$.

E 8.5 Show $|H_1(\hat{C}_2)| \equiv 1 \mod 2$; further, for a knot of genus one with $|H_1(\hat{C}_2)| = 4a \pm 1$, that $H_1(\hat{C}_3) \cong \mathbb{Z}_{3a\pm1} \oplus \mathbb{Z}_{3a\pm1}$, $a \in \mathbb{N}$.

E 8.6 By $\mathfrak{p}(p, q, r)$, p, q, r odd integers, we denote a pretzel knot (Fig. 8.9). (The sign of the integers defines the direction of the twist.) Construct a band projection of $\mathfrak{p}(p, q, r)$, and compute its Seifert matrix V, and its Alexander polynomial. (Fig. 8.10 shows how a band projection may be obtained.)

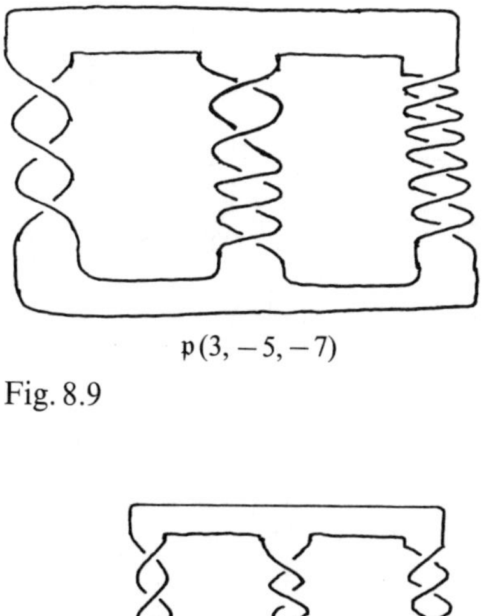

$\mathfrak{p}(3, -5, -7)$

Fig. 8.9

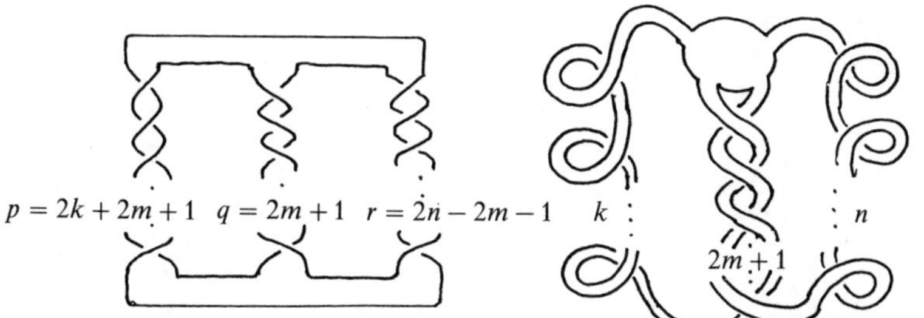

Fig. 8.10

E 8.7 Let $\mathfrak{k}$ be a link of $\mu > 1$ components. Show that there is a homomorphism φ of its group $\mathfrak{G} = \pi_1(S^3 - \mathfrak{k})$ onto a free cyclic group $\mathfrak{Z} = \langle t \rangle$ which maps every Wirtinger generator of $\mathfrak{G}$ onto t. Construct an infinite cyclic covering C_∞ of the link complement using a Seifert surface S of $\mathfrak{k}$, compute its Seifert matrix and define its Alexander polynomial following the lines developed in this chapter in the case of a knot. (See also E 9.5)

E 8.8 Let $\hat{C}_3$ be the 3-fold cyclic branched covering of a knot. If $H_1(\hat{C}_3) \cong \mathbb{Z}_p \oplus \mathbb{Z}_p$ for some prime p, then there are generators a, b of $\mathbb{Z}_p \oplus \mathbb{Z}_p$ such that $t: H_1(\hat{C}_3) \to H_1(\hat{C}_3)$ is given by $ta = b, tb = -a - b$. For all knots one has $p \neq 3$.

E 8.9 Construct a knot of genus one with the Alexander polynomials of the trefoil but not fibred – and hence different from the trefoil.

E 8.10 Show that $\Delta_1(t)\Delta_2^{-1}(t)$ annihilates the Alexander module $M(t)$ of a knot [Crowell 1964].

E 8.11 Let $\mathfrak{k}$ be a fibred knot of genus g, and let $F \times I/h$ denote its complement. Describe $h_*: H_1(F, \mathbb{Q}) \to H_1(F, \mathbb{Q})$ by a matrix $A = \oplus A_i$ where A_i is a companion matrix determined by the Alexander polynomials of $\mathfrak{k}$. (For the notion of a companion matrix see, e.g. [v.d. Waerden 1955, § 117].)

E 8.12 Prove that a satellite is never trivial. Show, that doubled knots (see 2.9) have trivial Alexander module, and therefore trivial Alexander polynomials.

Chapter 9: Free Differential Calculus and Alexander Matrices

In Chapter 8 we studied the homology of the cyclic coverings of the knot complement. Alexander polynomials were defined, and a general method of computing these invariants via a band projection of the knot was developed. Everyone who actually wants to carry out this task will soon find out that the calculations involved increase rapidly with the genus of the knot. There are, however, knots of arbitrary genus with groups of a relatively simple structure (for instance: torus knots). We shall present in this chapter another method of computing Alexander's knot invariants which will prove to be considerably simpler in this case – and in many other cases. The method is based on the theory of Fox derivations in the group ring of a free group. There is a geometric background to the Fox calculus with which we intend to start. It is the *theory of homotopy chains* [Reidemeister 1935′], or, to use the modern terminology, *equivariant homology*.

A Regular Coverings and Homotopy Chains

The one-to-one correspondence between finitely presented groups and fundamental groups of 2-complexes, and between (normal) subgroups and (regular) coverings of such complexes has been exploited in combinatorial group theory to prove group theoretical theorems (as for instance the Reidemeister-Schreier method or the Kurosh subgroup theorem [ZVC 1980, 2.6]) by topological methods. In the case of homology these relationships are less transparent, but some can be retained for the first homology groups.

9.1 On the homology of a covering space. Let $p\colon \tilde{X} \to X$ be a regular covering of a connected 2-complex. We assume X to be a finite CW-complex with one 0-cell P. Then a presentation

$$\mathfrak{G} = \pi_1(X, P) = \langle s_1, \ldots, s_n \mid R_1, \ldots, R_m \rangle$$

of the fundamental group of X is obtained by assigning a generator s_i to each (oriented) 1-cell (also denoted by s_i), and a defining relation to (the boundary of) each 2-cell e_j of X. Choose a base point $\tilde{P} \subset \tilde{X}$ over P, $p_\#(\pi_1(\tilde{X}, \tilde{P})) = \mathfrak{N} \lhd \mathfrak{G}$, and let $\mathfrak{D} \cong \mathfrak{G}/\mathfrak{N}$ denote the group of covering transformations.

Let $\varphi\colon \mathfrak{G} \to \mathfrak{D}$, $w \mapsto w^\varphi$ be the canonical homomorphism. The linear extension to the group ring is also denoted by $\varphi\colon \mathbb{Z}\mathfrak{G} \to \mathbb{Z}\mathfrak{D}$. Observe: $(w_1 w_2)^\varphi = w_2^\varphi w_1^\varphi$.

Our aim is to present $H_1(\tilde{X}, \tilde{X}^0)$ as a $\mathbb{Z}\mathfrak{D}$-module. (We follow a common convention by writing merely $\mathfrak{D}$-module instead of $\mathbb{Z}\mathfrak{D}$-module. $\tilde{X}^0$ denotes the 0-skeleton of $\tilde{X}$.)

The (oriented) edges s_i lift to edges $\tilde{s}_i$ with initial point $\tilde{P}$. By w we denote a closed path in the 1-skeleton X^1 of X, and, at the same time, the element it represents in the free group $\mathfrak{F} = \pi_1(X^1, P) = \langle s_1, \ldots, s_n | - \rangle$. There is a unique lift $\tilde{w}$ of w starting at $\tilde{P}$. Clearly $\tilde{w}$ is a special element of the relative cycles $Z_1(\tilde{X}, \tilde{X}^0)$ which are called *homotopy 1-chains*. Every 1-chain can be written in the form $\sum_{i=1}^{n} \xi_j \tilde{s}_j$, $\xi_j \in \mathbb{Z}\mathfrak{D}$.

There is a rule

(1) $\quad \widetilde{w_1 w_2} = \tilde{w}_1 + w_1^\varphi \cdot \tilde{w}_2$.

To understand it, first lift w_1 to $\tilde{w}_1$. Its endpoint is $w_1^\varphi \cdot \tilde{P}$. The covering transformation w_1^φ maps $\tilde{w}_2$ onto a chain $w_1^\varphi \tilde{w}_2$ over w_2 which starts at $w_1^\varphi \tilde{P}$. If $\tilde{w}_k = \sum_{j=1}^{n} \xi_{kj} \tilde{s}_j$ with $\xi_{kj} \in \mathbb{Z}\mathfrak{D}$, $k = 1, 2$, then $\widetilde{w_1 w_2} = \sum_{j=1}^{n} \xi_j \tilde{s}_j$ with

(2) $\quad \xi_j = \xi_{1j} + w_1^\varphi \cdot \xi_{2j} \quad (1 \leq j \leq n)$.

(The coefficient ξ_{kj} is the algebraic intersection number of the path $\tilde{w}_k$ with the covers of s_j.) This defines mappings

(3) $$\left(\frac{\partial}{\partial s_j}\right)^\varphi : \mathfrak{G} = \pi_1(X, P) \to \mathbb{Z}\mathfrak{D},\ w \mapsto \xi_j, \text{ with } \tilde{w} = \sum_{j=1}^{n} \xi_j \tilde{s}_j,$$

satisfying the rule

(4) $$\left(\frac{\partial}{\partial s_j}(w_1 w_2)\right)^\varphi = \left(\frac{\partial}{\partial s_j} w_1\right)^\varphi + w_1^\varphi \cdot \left(\frac{\partial}{\partial s_j} w_2\right)^\varphi.$$

There is a linear extension to the group ring $\mathbb{Z}\mathfrak{G}$:

(5) $$\left(\frac{\partial}{\partial s_j}(\eta + \zeta)\right)^\varphi = \left(\frac{\partial}{\partial s_j}\eta\right)^\varphi + \left(\frac{\partial}{\partial s_j}\zeta\right)^\varphi \quad \text{for } \eta, \zeta \in \mathbb{Z}\mathfrak{G}.$$

From the definition it follows immediately that

(6) $$\left(\frac{\partial}{\partial s_j} s_k\right)^\varphi = \delta_{jk}, \quad \tilde{w} = \sum \left(\frac{\partial w}{\partial \tilde{s}_j}\right)^\varphi \tilde{s}_j, \quad \delta_{jk} = \begin{cases} 1 & j = k \\ 0 & j \neq k \end{cases}.$$

We may now use this terminology to present $H_1(\tilde{X}, \tilde{X}^0)$ as a $\mathfrak{D}$-module: The 1-chains $\tilde{s}_i$, $1 \leq i \leq n$, are generators, and $\tilde{R}_j$, the lifts of the boundaries $R_j = \partial e_j$ are defining relations. (The boundary of an arbitrary 2-cell of $\tilde{X}$ is of the form $\delta(\tilde{R}_j)$,

$\delta \in \mathfrak{D}$. Hence, in a presentation of $H_1(\tilde{X}, \tilde{X}^0)$ as a $\mathfrak{D}$-module it suffices to include the $\tilde{R}_j$, $1 \leqq j \leqq m$, as defining relations.)

9.2 Proposition. *$H_1(\tilde{X}, \tilde{X}^0) = \langle \tilde{s}_1, \ldots, \tilde{s}_n | \tilde{R}_1, \ldots, \tilde{R}_m \rangle$, $0 = \tilde{R}_j = \sum \left(\frac{\partial R_j}{\partial s_i}\right)^{\varphi} \tilde{s}_i$, $1 \leqq i \leqq m$, is a presentation of $H_1(\tilde{X}, \tilde{X}^0)$ as a $\mathfrak{D}$-module.* □

B Fox Differential Calculus

In this section we describe a purely algebraic approach to the mapping $\left(\frac{\partial}{\partial s_j}\right)^{\varphi}$ [Fox 1953, 1954, 1956]. Let $\mathfrak{G}$ be a group and $\mathbb{Z}\mathfrak{G}$ its group ring (with integral coefficients); $\mathbb{Z}$ is identified with the multiples of the unit element 1 of $\mathfrak{G}$.

9.3 Definition (derivation). (a) There is a homomorphism ε: $\mathbb{Z}\mathfrak{G} \to \mathbb{Z}$, $\tau = \sum n_i g_i \mapsto \sum n_i = \tau^{\varepsilon}$. We call ε the *augmentation homomorphism*, and its kernel $I\mathfrak{G} = \varepsilon^{-1}(0)$, the *augmentation ideal.*

(b) A mapping Δ: $\mathbb{Z}\mathfrak{G} \to \mathbb{Z}\mathfrak{G}$ is called a *derivation* (of $\mathbb{Z}\mathfrak{G}$) if

$$\Delta(\xi + \eta) = \Delta(\xi) + \Delta(\eta) \qquad \textit{(linearity)},$$

and

$$\Delta(\xi \cdot \eta) = \Delta(\xi) \cdot \eta^{\varepsilon} + \xi \cdot \Delta(\eta) \qquad \textit{(product rule)},$$

for $\xi, \eta \in \mathbb{Z}\mathfrak{G}$.

From the definition it follows by simple calculations:

9.4 Lemma. *(a) The derivations of $\mathbb{Z}\mathfrak{G}$ form a (right) $\mathfrak{G}$-module under the operations defined by:*

$$(\Delta_1 + \Delta_2)(\tau) = \Delta_1(\tau) + \Delta_2(\tau),$$
$$(\Delta\gamma)(\tau) = \Delta(\tau) \cdot \gamma.$$

(b) Let Δ be a derivation. Then:

$$\Delta(m) = 0 \textit{ for } m \in \mathbb{Z},$$
$$\Delta(g^{-1}) = -g^{-1} \cdot \Delta(g),$$
$$\Delta(g^n) = (1 + g + \ldots + g^{n-1}) \cdot \Delta(g),$$
$$\Delta(g^{-n}) = -(g^{-1} + g^{-2} + \ldots + g^{-n}) \cdot \Delta(g) \quad \textit{for } n \geqq 1.$$ □

9.5 Examples. (a) Δ_{ε}: $\mathbb{Z}\mathfrak{G} \to \mathbb{Z}\mathfrak{G}$, $\tau \mapsto \tau - \tau^{\varepsilon}$, is a derivation.

(b) If $a, b \in \mathfrak{G}$ commute, $ab = ba$, then $(a-1)\Delta b = (b-1)\Delta a$. (We write Δa instead of $\Delta(a)$ when no confusion can arise.) It follows that a derivation

$\Delta: \mathbb{Z}\mathfrak{Z}^n \to \mathbb{Z}\mathfrak{Z}^n$ of the group ring of a free abelian group $\mathfrak{Z}^n = \langle S_1 \rangle \times \ldots \times \langle S_n \rangle$, $n \geqq 2$, with $\Delta S_i \neq 0$, $1 \leqq i \leqq n$, is a multiple of Δ_ε in the module of derivations.

Contrary to the situation in group rings of abelian groups the group ring of a free group admits a great many derivations.

9.6 Proposition. *Let $\mathfrak{F} = \langle \{S_i \mid i \in J\} \rangle$ be a free group. There is a uniquely determined derivation Δ: $\mathbb{Z}\mathfrak{F} \to \mathbb{Z}\mathfrak{F}$, with $\Delta S_i = w_i$, for arbitrary elements $w_i \in \mathbb{Z}\mathfrak{F}$.*

Proof. $\Delta(S_i^{-1}) = -S_i^{-1} w_i$ follows from $\Delta(1) = 0$ and the product rule. Linearity and product rule imply uniqueness. Define $\Delta(S_{i_1}^{\eta_1} \ldots S_{i_k}^{\eta_k})$ using the product rule:

$$\Delta(S_{i_1}^{\eta_1} \ldots S_{i_k}^{\eta_k}) = \Delta S_{i_1}^{\eta_1} + S_{i_1} \Delta S_{i2}^{\eta_2} + \ldots + S_{i_1}^{\eta_1} \ldots S_{i_{k-1}}^{\eta_{k-1}} \Delta S_{i_k}^{\eta_k}.$$

The product rule then follows for combined words $w = uv$, $\Delta w = \Delta u + u \Delta v$. The equation

$$\begin{aligned} \Delta(u S_i^\eta S_i^{-\eta} v) &= \Delta u + u \Delta S_i^\eta + u S_i^\eta \Delta S_i^{-\eta} + u \Delta v = \Delta u + u \Delta v \\ &= \Delta(uv), \ \eta = \pm 1, \end{aligned}$$

shows that Δ is well defined on $\mathfrak{F}$. □

9.7 Definition (partial derivations). The derivations

$$\frac{\partial}{\partial S_i}: \mathbb{Z}\mathfrak{F} \to \mathbb{Z}\mathfrak{F}, \ S_j \mapsto \begin{cases} 1 & \textit{for } i = j \\ 0 & \textit{for } i \neq j, \end{cases}$$

of the group ring of a free group $\mathfrak{F} = \langle S_i \rangle$ are called *partial derivations.*

The partial derivations form a basis of the module of derivations:

9.8 Proposition. *(a) $\Delta = \sum_{i \in J} \frac{\partial}{\partial S_i} \cdot \Delta(S_i)$ for every derivation Δ: $\mathbb{Z}\mathfrak{F} \to \mathbb{Z}\mathfrak{F}$. (The sum in (a) may be infinite, however, for any $\tau \in \mathbb{Z}\mathfrak{F}$ there are only finitely many $\frac{\partial \tau}{\partial S_i} \neq 0$.)*

(b) $\sum_{i \in J} \frac{\partial}{\partial S_i} \cdot \tau_i = 0 \Leftrightarrow \tau_i = 0, \ i \in J.$

(c) $\Delta_\varepsilon(\tau) = \tau - \tau^\varepsilon = \sum_{i \in J} \frac{\partial \tau}{\partial S_i} (S_i - 1)$ (fundamental formula)

(d) $\tau - \tau^\varepsilon = \sum_{i \in J} v_i (S_i - 1) \Leftrightarrow v_i = \frac{\partial \tau}{\partial S_i}, \ i \in J.$

Proof. $(\Sigma \frac{\partial}{\partial S_i} \Delta S_i) S_j = \Sigma \frac{\partial S_j}{\partial S_i} \Delta S_i = \Delta S_j$ proves (a) by 9.6. For $\Delta =$ 0-map, and $\Delta = \Delta_\varepsilon$ one gets (b) and (c). To prove (d) apply $\frac{\partial}{\partial S_j}$ to the equation. □

The theory of derivations in $\mathbb{Z}\mathfrak{F}$ (free derivations) has been successfully used to study $\mathbb{Z}\mathfrak{F}$ and $\mathfrak{F}$ itself [Zieschang 1962]. There are remarkable parallels to the usual derivations used in analysis. For instance the fundamental formula resembles a Taylor expansion. If $(S_1, \ldots, S_n)$, $(S'_1, \ldots, S'_n)$, $(S''_1, \ldots, S''_n)$ are bases of a free group $\mathfrak{F}_n$, there is a chain rule for the Jacobian matrices:

$$\frac{\partial S''_k}{\partial S_i} = \sum_{j=1}^{n} \frac{\partial S''_k}{\partial S'_k} \cdot \frac{\partial S'_j}{\partial S_i}.$$

(Apply 9.8(a) in the form $\Delta = \sum_{j=1}^{n} \frac{\partial}{\partial S'_j} \Delta S'_j$ for $\Delta = \frac{\partial}{\partial S_i}$ to S''_k.)

J. Birman [1973′] proved that $(S'_1, \ldots, S'_m)$ is a basis of $\mathfrak{F} = \langle S_1, \ldots, S_n \rangle$ if and only if the Jacobian $\left(\frac{\partial S'_j}{\partial S_i}\right)$ is invertible over $\mathbb{Z}\mathfrak{F}$.

For further properties of derivations see E 9.7, 8.

C Calculation of Alexander Polynomials

We return to the regular covering $p\colon \tilde{X} \to X$ of 9.1. Let $\psi\colon \mathfrak{F} = \langle S_1, \ldots, S_n | - \rangle \to \langle S_1, \ldots, S_n | R_1, \ldots, R_m \rangle = \mathfrak{G}$ denote the canonical homomorphism of the groups and, at the same time, its extension to the group rings:

$$\psi\colon \mathbb{Z}\mathfrak{F} \to \mathbb{Z}\mathfrak{G},\ (\Sigma n_i f_i)^{\psi} = \Sigma n_i f_i^{\psi}, \quad \text{for } f_i \in \mathfrak{F},\ n_i \in \mathbb{Z}.$$

Combining ψ with the map $\varphi\colon \mathbb{Z}\mathfrak{G} \to \mathbb{Z}\mathfrak{D}$ of 9.1 (we use the notation $(\xi)^{\varphi\psi} = (\xi^{\psi})^{\varphi}$, $\xi \in \mathbb{Z}\mathfrak{F}$), we may state Proposition 9.2 in terms of the differential calculus.

9.9 Proposition. $\left(\left(\frac{\partial R_k}{\partial S_j}\right)^{\varphi\psi}\right)$, $1 \leqq k \leqq m$, $1 \leqq j \leqq n$, *is a presentation matrix of* $H_1(\tilde{X}, \tilde{X}^0)$ *as a* $\mathfrak{D}$*-module.* (k = *row index*, j = *column index*.)

Proof. Comparing the linearity and the product rule of the Fox derivations 9.3 with (4) and (5) of 9.1, we deduce from 9.6 that the mappings $\left(\frac{\partial}{\partial s_i}\right)^{\varphi}$ in (5) coincide with those defined by $\left(\frac{\partial}{\partial S_i}\right)^{\varphi\psi}$ in 9.7. □

Remark: The fact that the partial derivation of (5) and 9.3 are the same lends a geometric interpretation also to the fundamental formula: For $w \in \mathfrak{G}$ and $\tilde{w}$ its lift,

$$\partial\tilde{w} = (w^{\varphi\psi} - 1)\tilde{P} = \Sigma\left(\frac{\partial w}{\partial S_i}\right)^{\varphi\psi}(S_i^{\varphi\psi} - 1)\tilde{P} = \Sigma\left(\frac{\partial w}{\partial S_i}\right)^{\varphi\psi}\partial\tilde{s}_i.$$

To obtain information about $H_1(\tilde{X})$ we consider the exact homology sequence

$$(8) \qquad 0 = H_1(\tilde{X}^0) \to H_1(\tilde{X}) \to H_1(\tilde{X}, \tilde{X}^0) \xrightarrow{\partial} \underset{\mathbb{Z}\mathfrak{D}}{\underset{\wr\|}{H_0(\tilde{X}^0)}} \xrightarrow{i_*} \underset{\mathbb{Z}}{\underset{\wr\|}{H_0(\tilde{X})}} \to 0.$$

$H_0(\tilde{X}^0)$ is generated by $\{w^{\varphi\psi} \cdot \tilde{P} \mid w \in \mathfrak{F}\}$ as an abelian group. The kernel of i_* is the image $(I\mathfrak{G})^{\varphi\psi}$ of the augmentation ideal $I\mathfrak{G} \subset \mathbb{Z}\mathfrak{F}$ (see 9.3). The fundamental formula shows that $\ker i_*$ is generated by $\{(S_j^{\varphi\psi} - 1)\tilde{P} \mid 1 \leqq j \leqq n\}$ as a $\mathfrak{D}$-module.

Thus we obtain from (8) a short exact sequence:

$$(9) \qquad 0 \to H_1(\tilde{X}) \to H_1(\tilde{X}, \tilde{X}^0) \xrightarrow{\partial} \ker i_* \to 0.$$

In the case of a knot group $\mathfrak{G}$, and its infinite cyclic covering C_∞ ($\mathfrak{N} = \mathfrak{G}'$) the group of covering transformations is cyclic, $\mathfrak{D} = \mathfrak{Z} = \langle t \rangle$, and $\ker i_*$ is a free $\mathfrak{Z}$-module generated by $(t-1)\tilde{P}$. The sequence (9) splits, and

$$(10) \qquad H_1(\tilde{X}, \tilde{X}^0) \cong H_1(\tilde{X}) \oplus \sigma(\mathbb{Z}\mathfrak{Z} \cdot (t-1)\tilde{P}),$$

where σ is a homomorphism σ: $\ker i_* \to H_1(\tilde{X}, \tilde{X}^0)$, $\partial\sigma = id$. This yields the following

9.10 Theorem. *For* $\mathfrak{G} = \langle S_1, \ldots, S_n \mid R_1, \ldots, R_n \rangle$ *and* $\left(\left(\frac{\partial R_j}{\partial S_i}\right)^{\varphi\psi}\right)$, *its* Jacobian, *$\varphi$: $\mathfrak{G} \to \mathfrak{G}/\mathfrak{G}' = \mathfrak{D} = \langle t \rangle$, a presentation matrix (Alexander matrix) of $H_1(\tilde{X}) \cong \mathrm{H}_1(C_\infty)$ as a $\mathfrak{D}$-module is obtained from the Jacobian by omitting its i-th column, if $S_i^{\varphi\psi} = t^{\pm 1}$. (In the case of a Jacobian derived from a Wirtinger presentation any column may be omitted.)*

Proof. It remains to show that the homomorphism σ: $\ker i_* \to H_1(\tilde{X}, \tilde{X}^0)$ can be chosen in such a way that $\sigma(\ker i_*) = \mathbb{Z}\mathfrak{D}\tilde{s}_i$. Put $\sigma(t-1)\tilde{P} = \pm t^\mu \tilde{s}_i$, $S_i^{\varphi\psi} = t^\nu$, $\partial\sigma = id$. Then $(t-1)\tilde{P} = \partial\sigma(t-1)\tilde{P} = \partial(\pm t^\mu \tilde{s}_i) = \pm t^\mu (S_i^{\varphi\psi} - 1)\tilde{P} = \pm t^\mu (t^\nu - 1)\tilde{P}$, that is, $(t-1) = \pm t^\mu (t^\nu - 1)$. It follows $\nu = \pm 1$, and in these cases σ can be chosen as desired. □

If $\mathfrak{D}$ is not free cyclic, the sequence (9) does not necessarily split, and $H_1(\tilde{X})$ can not be identified as a direct summand of $H_1(\tilde{X}, \tilde{X}^0)$. We shall treat the cases $\mathfrak{D} \cong \mathbb{Z}_n$ and $\mathfrak{D} \cong \mathbb{Z}^\mu$ in Section *D*.

There is a useful corollary to Theorem 9.10:

9.11 Corollary. *Every $(n-1) \times (n-1)$ minor Δ_{ij} of the $n \times n$ Jacobian of a Wirtinger presentation $\langle S_i \mid R_j \rangle = \mathfrak{G}$ of a knot group $\mathfrak{G}$ is a presentation matrix of $H_1(C_\infty)$. Furthermore,* $\det \Delta_{ij} \doteq \Delta(t)$. *The elementary ideals of the Jacobian are the elementary ideals of the knot.*

Proof. Every Wirtinger relator R_k is a consequence of remaining ones (Corollary 3.6). Thus, by 9.10, a presentation matrix of $H_1(C_\infty) = M(t)$ is obtained from the Jacobian by leaving out an arbitrary row and arbitrary column. □

Corollary 9.11 shows that a Jacobian of a Wirtinger presentation has nullity one. The following lemma explicitely describes the linear dependence of the rows and columns of the Jacobian of a Wirtinger presentation:

9.12 Lemma. *(a)* $\sum_{i=1}^{n} \left(\frac{\partial R_j}{\partial S_i}\right)^{\varphi\psi} = 0\,.$

(b) $\sum_{j=1}^{n} \eta_j \left(\frac{\partial R_j}{\partial S_i}\right)^{\varphi\psi} = 0, \eta_j = t^{\nu_j}$ *for suitable* $\nu_j \in \mathbb{Z}$ *for a Wirtinger presentation* $\langle S_1, \ldots, S_n | R_1, \ldots, R_n \rangle$ *of a knot group.*

Proof. Equation (a) follows from the fundamental formula 9.8 (c) applied to R_j:

$$0 = (R_j - 1)^{\varphi\psi} = \left[\sum_{i=1}^{n} \left(\frac{\partial R_j}{\partial S_i}\right)(S_i - 1)\right]^{\varphi\psi} = \sum_{i=1}^{n} \left(\frac{\partial R_j}{\partial S_i}\right)^{\varphi\psi} (t-1)\,.$$

Since $\mathbb{Z}\mathfrak{Z}$ has no divisors of zero (E 9.1) equation (a) is proved. To prove (b) we use the identity of Corollary 3.6 which expresses the dependence of Wirtinger relators by the equation $\prod_{j=1}^{n} L_j R_j L_j^{-1} = 1$ in the free group $\langle S_1, \ldots, S_n | - \rangle$. Now

$$\left(\frac{\partial}{\partial S_i} L_j R_j L_j^{-1}\right)^{\varphi\psi} = \left(\frac{\partial L_j}{\partial S_i}\right)^{\varphi\psi} + L_j^{\varphi\psi}\left(\frac{\partial R_j}{\partial S_i}\right)^{\varphi\psi} - (L_j R_j L_j^{-1})^{\varphi\psi}\left(\frac{\partial L_j}{\partial S_i}\right)^{\varphi\psi}$$

$$= L_j^{\varphi\psi}\left(\frac{\partial R_j}{\partial S_i}\right)^{\varphi\psi}, \quad \text{as } (L_j R_j L_j^{-1})^{\varphi\psi} = 1\,.$$

By the product rule:

$$0 = \frac{\partial}{\partial S_i}\left(\prod_{j=1}^{n} L_j R_j L_j^{-1}\right)^{\varphi\psi} = \sum_{j=1}^{n}\left(\prod_{k=1}^{j-1} (L_k R_k L_k^{-1})\right)^{\varphi\psi} L_j^{\varphi\psi}\left(\frac{\partial R_j}{\partial S_i}\right)^{\varphi\psi}$$

$$= \sum_{j=1}^{n} L_j^{\varphi\psi}\left(\frac{\partial R_j}{\partial S_i}\right)^{\varphi\psi},$$

which proves (b) with $L_j^{\varphi\psi} = t^{\nu_j} = \eta_j$. □

9.13 Example. A Wirtinger presentation of the group of the trefoil is:

$$\langle S_1, S_2, S_3 | S_1 S_2 S_3^{-1} S_2^{-1},\ S_2 S_3 S_1^{-1} S_3^{-1},\ S_3 S_1 S_2^{-1} S_1^{-1} \rangle,$$

(see 3.7). If $R = S_1 S_2 S_3^{-1} S_2^{-1}$ then

$$\frac{\partial R}{\partial S_1} = 1, \frac{\partial R}{\partial S_2} = S_1 - S_1 S_2 S_3^{-1} S_2^{-1}, \frac{\partial R}{\partial S_3} = - S_1 S_2 S_3^{-1} \quad \text{and}$$

$$\left(\frac{\partial R}{\partial S_1}\right)^{\varphi\psi} = 1, \left(\frac{\partial R}{\partial S_2}\right)^{\varphi\psi} = t - 1, \left(\frac{\partial R}{\partial S_3}\right)^{\varphi\psi} = - t.$$

By similar calculations we obtain the matrix of derivatives and apply $\varphi\psi$ to get

$$\begin{pmatrix} 1 & t-1 & -t \\ -t & 1 & t-1 \\ t-1 & -t & 1 \end{pmatrix}.$$

It is easy to verify 9.11 (a) and (b). The 2×2 minor $\Delta_{11} = \begin{pmatrix} 1 & t-1 \\ -1 & 1 \end{pmatrix}$, for instance, is a presentation matrix. $|\Delta_{11}| = 1 - t + t^2 = \Delta(t)$, $E_1(t) = (1 - t + t^2)$. For $k > 1$: $E_k(t) = (1) = \mathbb{Z}(t)$, $\Delta_k(t) = 1$.

9.14 Proposition. *Let $\langle S_1, \ldots, S_n | R_1, \ldots, R_m \rangle = \mathfrak{G} = \langle S'_1, \ldots, S'_{n'} | R'_1, \ldots, R'_{m'} \rangle$ be two finite presentations of a knot group. The elementary ideals of the respective Jacobians $\left(\left(\frac{\partial R_j}{\partial S_i}\right)^{\varphi\psi}\right)$ and $\left(\left(\frac{\partial R'_j}{\partial S'_i}\right)^{\varphi\psi}\right)$ coincide, and are those of the knot.*

Proof. This follows from 9.11, and from the fact (Appendix A 6) that the elementary ideals are invariant under Tietze processes. □

9.15 Example (torus knots). $\mathfrak{G} = \langle x, y | x^a y^{-b} \rangle$, $a > 0$, $b > 0$, $gcd(a, b) = 1$, is a presentation of the group of the knot $\mathfrak{t}(a, b)$ (see 3.28). The projection homomorphism $\varphi: \mathfrak{G} \to \mathfrak{G}/\mathfrak{G}' = \mathfrak{Z} = \langle t \rangle$ is defined by: $x^\varphi = t^b$, $y^\varphi = t^a$, (Exercise E 9.3). The Jacobian of the presentation is:

$$\left(\frac{\partial (x^a y^{-b})}{\partial x}, \frac{\partial (x^a y^{-b})}{\partial y}\right)^{\varphi\psi} = \left(\frac{t^{ab} - 1}{t^b - 1}, - \frac{t^{ab} - 1}{t^a - 1}\right).$$

The greatest common divisor

$$gcd\left(\frac{t^{ab} - 1}{t^b - 1}, \frac{t^{ab} - 1}{t^a - 1}\right) = \frac{(t^{ab} - 1)(t - 1)}{(t^a - 1)(t^b - 1)} = \Delta_{a,b}(t)$$

is the Alexander polynomial of $\mathfrak{t}(a, b)$, $\deg \Delta_{a,b}(t) = (a - 1)(b - 1)$. One may even prove something more: *The Alexander module $M_{a,b}(t)$ of a torus knot $\mathfrak{t}(a, b)$ is cyclic: $M_{a,b}(t) \cong \mathbb{Z}(t)/(\Delta_{a,b}(t))$.*

Proof. There are elements $\alpha(t)$, $\beta(t) \in \mathbb{Z}(t)$ such that

(11) $\alpha(t)(t^{a-1} + t^{a-2} + \ldots + t + 1) + \beta(t)(t^{b-1} + t^{b-2} + \ldots + t + 1) = 1.$

This is easily verified by applying the Euclidean algorithm. It follows that

$$\alpha(t)\frac{t^{ab}-1}{t^b-1}+\beta(t)\frac{t^{ab}-1}{t^a-1}=\Delta_{a,b}(t).$$

Hence, the Jacobian can be replaced by an equivalent one:

$$\left(\frac{t^{ab}-1}{t^b-1},\ -\frac{t^{ab}-1}{t^a-1}\right)\begin{pmatrix}\alpha(t) & t^{b-1}+\dots+1\\ -\beta(t) & t^{a-1}+\dots+1\end{pmatrix}=(\Delta_{a,b}(t),0).$$

We may interpret by 9.9 the Jacobian as a presentation matrix of $H_1(\tilde{X},\tilde{X}^0)$:

$$\left(\frac{t^{ab}-1}{t^b-1},\ -\frac{t^{ab}-1}{t^a-1}\right)\begin{pmatrix}\tilde{x}\\ \tilde{y}\end{pmatrix}=0,$$

where $\tilde{x}, \tilde{y}$ are the 1-chains that correspond to the generators x, y (see 9.1).

The transformation of the Jacobian implies a contragredient (dual) transformation of the generating 1-chains:

$$\tilde{u}=(t^{a-1}+\dots+1)\tilde{x}-(t^{b-1}+\dots+1)\tilde{y},$$
$$\tilde{v}=\beta(t)\tilde{x}+\alpha(t)\tilde{y}.$$

The 1-chains form a new basis with:

$$(\Delta_{a,b}(t),0)\begin{pmatrix}\tilde{u}\\ \tilde{v}\end{pmatrix}=0.$$

Since $\partial\tilde{x}=(t^b-1)\tilde{P}$, $\partial\tilde{y}=(t^a-1)\tilde{P}$, one has $\partial\tilde{u}=0$ and $\partial\tilde{v}=(\beta(t)(t^b-1)+\alpha(t^a-1))\tilde{P}=(t-1)\tilde{P}$ by (11). Thus $\tilde{v}$ generates a free summand σ (ker i_*) (see (10)), and $\tilde{u}$ generates $M(t)$, subject to the relation $\Delta_{a,b}(t)\tilde{u}=0$. □

Torus knots are fibred knots, by 4.10 and 5.1. We proved in 4.11 that the commutator subgroup $\mathfrak{G}'$ of a torus knot $\mathfrak{t}(a,b)$ is free of rank $(a-1)(b-1)$. By Theorem 4.6 the genus of $\mathfrak{t}(a,b)$ is $g=\dfrac{(a-1)(b-1)}{2}$, a fact which is reproved by 8.16 and $\deg\Delta_{a,b}(t)=(a-1)(b-1)$.

D Alexander Polynomials of Links

Let $\mathfrak{k}$ be a link of $\mu>1$ components, and $\mathfrak{G}=\pi_1(\overline{S^3-V(\mathfrak{k})})$ its group. $\varphi\colon\mathfrak{G}\to\mathfrak{G}/\mathfrak{G}'=\mathfrak{Z}^\mu=\langle t_1\rangle\times\cdots\times\langle t_\mu\rangle$ maps $\mathfrak{G}$ onto a free abelian group of rank μ. We assume, as in the case of a knot, that t_i, $1\leqq i\leqq\mu$, denotes at the same time a free generator of $\mathfrak{Z}^\mu$ or a representative in $\mathfrak{G}$ mod $\mathfrak{G}'$, representing a meridian of the i-th component $\mathfrak{k}_i$ of $\mathfrak{k}$ with $\varphi(t_i)=t_i$. We may consider $\mathfrak{G}'/\mathfrak{G}''$ as module over the group ring $\mathbb{Z}\mathfrak{Z}^\mu$ using the operation $a\mapsto t_i^{-1}at_i$, $a\in\mathfrak{G}'$, to define the operation of $\mathbb{Z}\mathfrak{Z}^\mu$ on $\mathfrak{G}'/\mathfrak{G}''$. Proposition 9.2 applies to the situation with $\mathfrak{N} = \mathfrak{G}'$, $\mathfrak{D} \cong \mathfrak{Z}^{\mu}$. Denote by ψ the canonical homomorphism

$$\psi: \mathfrak{F} = \langle S_1, \ldots, S_n | - \rangle \to \langle S_1, \ldots, S_n | R_1, \ldots, R_n \rangle = \mathfrak{G}$$

onto the link group $\mathfrak{G}$, described by a Wirtinger presentation. The Jacobian $\left(\left(\frac{\partial R_j}{\partial S_i}\right)^{\varphi\psi}\right)$, then is a presentation matrix of $H_1(\tilde{X}, \tilde{X}^0)$. The exact sequence (9) does not split, so that a submodule isomorphic to $H_1(\tilde{X}) \cong H_1(C_\infty)$ cannot easily be identified. Following [Fox 1954] we call $H_1(\tilde{X}, \tilde{X}^0)$ the *Alexander module of* $\mathfrak{k}$ and denote it by $M(t_1, \ldots, t_\mu)$.

9.16 Proposition. *The first elementary ideal* $E_1(t_1, \ldots, t_\mu)$ *of the Alexander module* $M(t_1, \ldots, t_\mu)$ *of a* μ*-component link* $\mathfrak{k}$ *is of the form:*

$$E_1(t_1, \ldots, t_\mu) = J_0 \cdot (\Delta(t_1, \ldots, t_\mu))$$

where J_0 *is the augmentation ideal of* $\mathbb{Z}\mathfrak{Z}^{\mu}$, *and the second factor is a principal ideal generated by the greatest common divisor of* $E_1(t_1, \ldots, t_\mu)$; *it is called the* Alexander polynomial $\Delta(t_1, \ldots, t_\mu)$ of $\mathfrak{k}$, *and it is an invariant of* $\mathfrak{k}$ – *up to multiplication by a unit of* $\mathbb{Z}\mathfrak{Z}^{\mu}$.

Proof. Corollary 3.6 is valid in the case of a link. The $(n-1) \times n$-matrix $\mathfrak{R}$ resulting from the Jacobian $\left(\left(\frac{\partial R_j}{\partial S_i}\right)^{\varphi\psi}\right)$ by omitting its last row is, therefore, a presentation matrix of $H_1(\tilde{X}, \tilde{X}^0)$, and defines its elementary ideals. Let $\Delta_i' = \det(\mathfrak{a}_1, \ldots, \mathfrak{a}_{i-1}, \mathfrak{a}_{i+1}, \ldots, \mathfrak{a}_n)$ be the determinant formed by the column-vectors $\mathfrak{a}_j$, $i \neq j$, of $\mathfrak{R}$. The fundamental formula $R_k - 1 = \sum_{j=1}^{n} \frac{\partial R_k}{\partial S_j}(S_j - 1)$ yields $\sum_{j=1}^{n} \mathfrak{a}_j(S_j^{\varphi\psi} - 1) = 0$. Hence,

$$\begin{aligned}
\Delta_j'(S_i^{\varphi\psi} - 1) &= \det(\mathfrak{a}_1, \ldots, \mathfrak{a}_i(S_i^{\varphi\psi} - 1), \ldots \mathfrak{a}_{j-1}, \mathfrak{a}_{j+1}, \ldots) \\
&= \det(\mathfrak{a}_1, \ldots, -\sum_{k \neq i} \mathfrak{a}_k(S_k^{\varphi\psi} - 1), \ldots \mathfrak{a}_{j-1}, \mathfrak{a}_{j+1}, \ldots) \\
&= \det(\mathfrak{a}_1, \ldots, -\mathfrak{a}_j(S_j^{\varphi\psi} - 1), \ldots, \mathfrak{a}_{j-1}, \mathfrak{a}_{j+1}, \ldots) \\
&= \pm \Delta_i'(S_j^{\varphi\psi} - 1), \quad \text{thus}
\end{aligned}$$

$$(12) \qquad \Delta_j'(S_i^{\varphi\psi} - 1) = \pm \Delta_i'(S_j^{\varphi\psi} - 1).$$

The $S_i^{\varphi\psi}$, $1 \leqq i \leqq n$ assume all t_k, $1 \leqq k \leqq \mu$. It follows that $(S_i^{\varphi\psi} - 1) | \Delta_i'$. Define $(S_i^{\varphi\psi} - 1)\Delta_i = \Delta_i'$. Since $\mathbb{Z}\mathfrak{Z}^{\mu}$ is a unique factorization ring, (12) implies that $\Delta_i = \pm \Delta$ for $1 \leqq i \leqq n$. The first elementary ideal, therefore, is a product $J_0 \cdot (\Delta)$, where J_0 is generated by the elements $(t_k - 1)$, $1 \leqq k \leqq \mu$. It is easy to prove (E 9.1) that J_0 is the augmentation ideal $I\mathfrak{Z}^{\mu}$ of $\mathbb{Z}\mathfrak{Z}^{\mu}$.

The elementary ideal E_1 is an invariant of $\mathfrak{G}$ (Appendix A 6), hence, its greatest common divisor is an invariant of $\mathfrak{G}$ – up to multiplication by a unit $\pm t_1^{r_1} \ldots t_\mu^{r_\mu}$ of

$\mathbb{Z}\mathfrak{Z}^{\mu}$. The polynomial $\Delta(t_1, \ldots, t_\mu) = \Delta$, though, depends on the choice of a basis of $\mathfrak{Z}^{\mu}$. But it is possible to distinguish a basis of $\mathfrak{Z}^{\mu} \cong H_1(S^3 - \mathring{V}(\mathfrak{k}))$ geometrically by choosing a meridian for each component $\mathfrak{k}_i$ to represent t_i. □

For more information on Alexander modules of links see [Crowell-Strauss 1969], [Hillman 1981′], [Levine 1975].

A *link* $\mathfrak{k}$ is called *splittable*, if it can be separated by a 2-sphere embedded in S^3.

9.17 Corollary. *The Alexander polynomial of a splittable link of multiplicity* $\mu \geq 2$ *vanishes, i.e.* $\Delta(t_1, \ldots, t_\mu) = 0$.

Proof. A splittable link $\mathfrak{k}$ allows a Wirtinger presentation of the following form: There are two disjoint finite sets of Wirtinger generators, $\{S_i | i \in I\}$, $\{T_j | j \in J\}$, and correspondingly, two sets of relators $\{R_k(S_i)\}$, $\{N_l(T_j)\}$. For $i \in I$, $j \in J$ consider

$$\Delta_i'(T_j^{\varphi\psi} - 1) = \pm \Delta_j'(S_i^{\varphi\psi} - 1).$$

The column $\mathfrak{a}_i(S_i^{\varphi\psi} - 1)$ in $\pm \Delta_j'(S_i^{\varphi\psi} - 1)$ is by $\sum_{k \in I} (S_k^{\varphi\psi} - 1)\mathfrak{a}_k = 0$ a linear combination of other columns. It follows that $\Delta_i'(T_j^{\varphi\psi} - 1) = 0$, i.e. $\Delta_i' = 0$. □

Alexander polynomials of links retain some properties of knot polynomials. In [Torres-Fox 1954] they are shown to be symmetric. The conditions (Torres-conditions) do not characterize Alexander polynomials of links ($\mu \geqq 2$), as J.A. Hillman [1981, VII, Theorem 5] showed.

9.18 There is a simplified version of the Alexander polynomial of a link. Consider the homomorphism $\chi: \mathfrak{Z}^{\mu} \to \mathfrak{Z} = \langle t \rangle, t_i \mapsto t$. Put $\mathfrak{N} = \ker \chi\varphi$. The sequence (9) now splits, and, as in the case of a knot, any $(n-1) \times (n-1)$ minor of the Jacobian $\left(\left(\frac{\partial R_j}{\partial S_i}\right)^{\chi\varphi\psi}\right)$ is a presentation matrix of $H_1(\tilde{X}) \cong H_1(C_\infty)$, where C_∞ is the infinite cyclic covering of the complement of the link which corresponds to the normal subgroup $\mathfrak{N} = \ker \chi\varphi \lhd \mathfrak{G}$. The first elementary ideal is generated by $(t-1) \cdot \Delta(t, \ldots, t)$ (see 9.16) where $\Delta(t_1, \ldots, t_\mu)$ is the Alexander polynomial of the link. The polynomial $\Delta(t, \ldots, t)$ (reduced Alexander polynomial) is of the form $\Delta(t, \ldots, t) = (t-1)^{\mu-2} \cdot \nabla(t)$, and $\nabla(t)$ is called the *Hosokawa polynomial of the link* (E 9.5). In [Hosokawa 1958] it was shown that $\nabla(t)$ is of even degree and symmetric. Furthermore, any such polynomial $f(t) \in \mathbb{Z}\mathfrak{Z}$ is the Hosokawa polynomial of a link for any $\mu > 1$.

9.19 Examples.

(a)

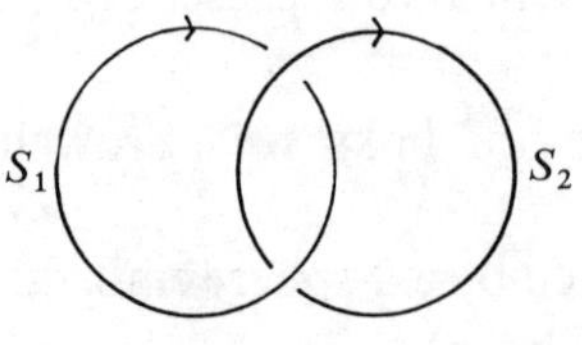

$$\mathfrak{G} = \langle S_1, S_2 | S_1 S_2 S_1^{-1} S_2^{-1} \rangle.$$

Fig. 9.1

$$\mathfrak{R} = ((1 - S_1 S_2 S_1^{-1})^{\varphi\psi}, (S_1 - S_1 S_2 S_1^{-1} S_2^{-1})^{\varphi\psi}) = (1 - t_2, t_1 - 1) \text{ and } \Delta = 1.$$

(b) *Borromean links* (Fig. 9.2)

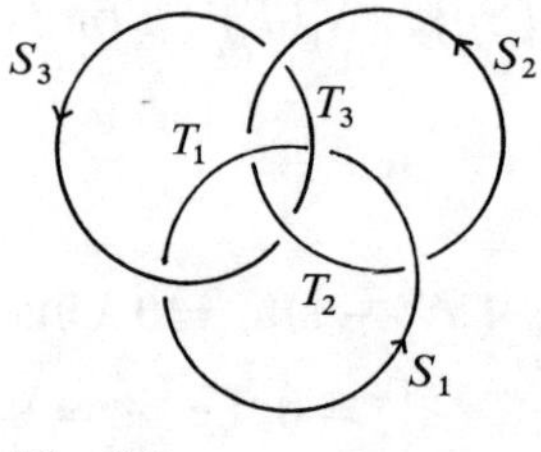

Generators: $S_1, S_2, S_3, T_1, T_2, T_3$

Relators: $T_1^{-1} S_2^{-1} T_1 T_2,\ T_2^{-1} S_3 T_2 T_3,\ S_2^{-1} S_3 S_2 T_3^{-1},\ S_1^{-1} S_3 T_1 S_3^{-1},\ S_1^{-1} S_2 S_1 T_2^{-1}.$

Fig. 9.2

Eliminate $T_1 = S_3^{-1} S_1 S_3$, $T_2 = S_1^{-1} S_2 S_1$ and $T_3 = S_2^{-1} S_3 S_2$, and obtain the presentation

$$\mathfrak{G} = \langle S_1 S_2 S_3 | S_3^{-1} S_1^{-1} S_3 S_2^{-1} S_3^{-1} S_1 S_3 S_1^{-1}, S_1^{-1} S_2^{-1} S_1 S_3 S_1^{-1} S_2 S_1 S_2^{-1} S_3^{-1} S_2 \rangle.$$

From this we get

$$\mathfrak{R} = \begin{pmatrix} -t_1^{-1} t_3^{-1} + t_1^{-1} t_2^{-1} t_3^{-1} - t_1^{-1} t_2^{-1} + t_1^{-1}, 0, -t_3^{-1} + t_1^{-1} t_3^{-1} - t_1^{-1} t_2^{-1} t_3^{-1} + t_2^{-1} t_3^{-1} \\ -t_1^{-1} + t_1^{-1} t_2^{-1} - t_1^{-1} t_2^{-1} t_3 + t_1^{-1} t_3, -t_1^{-1} t_2^{-1} + t_1^{-1} t_2^{-1} t_3 - t_2^{-1} t_3 + t_2^{-1}, 0 \end{pmatrix}$$

$$= \begin{pmatrix} -t_1^{-1} t_2^{-1} t_3^{-1} (t_2 - 1)(t_3 - 1) & 0 & -t_1^{-1} t_2^{-1} t_3^{-1} (t_1 - 1)(t_2 - 1) \\ t_1^{-1} t_2^{-1} (t_2 - 1)(t_3 - 1) & -t_1^{-1} t_2^{-1} (t_1 - 1)(t_3 - 1) & 0 \end{pmatrix}$$

Therefore

$$\Delta_1' = -t_1^{-2} t_2^{-2} t_3^{-1} (t_1 - 1)(t_2 - 1)(t_3 - 1)(t_1 - 1) \doteq -\Delta \cdot (t_1 - 1)$$
$$\Delta_2' = t_1^{-2} t_2^{-2} t_3^{-1} (t_1 - 1)(t_2 - 1)(t_3 - 1)(t_2 - 1) \doteq \Delta \cdot (t_2 - 1)$$
$$\Delta_3' = t_1^{-2} t_2^{-2} t_3^{-1} (t_1 - 1)(t_2 - 1)(t_3 - 1)(t_3 - 1) \doteq \Delta \cdot (t_3 - 1),$$

where $\Delta = \Delta(t_1, t_2, t_3) = (t_1 - 1)(t_2 - 1)(t_3 - 1)$.

E Finite Cyclic Coverings Again

The theory of Fox derivations may also be utilized to compute the homology of finite branched cyclic coverings of knots. (For notations and results compare 8.17–22, 9.1.)

Let C_N, $0 < N \in \mathbb{Z}$, be the N-fold cyclic (unbranched) covering of the complement C. We know (8.20(d)) that $(V^T - tV)s = 0$ are defining relations of $H_1(\hat{C}_N)$ as a $\mathfrak{Z}_N$-module, $\mathfrak{Z}_N = \langle t \,|\, t^N \rangle$.

9.20 Proposition. *(a) Any Alexander matrix $A(t)$ (presentation matrix of $H_1(C_\infty)$ as a $\mathfrak{Z}$-module, $\mathfrak{Z} = \langle t \rangle$) is a presentation matrix of $H_1(\hat{C}_N)$ as a $\mathfrak{Z}_N$-module, $\mathfrak{Z}_N = \langle t, | t^N \rangle$.*

(b) The matrix

$$\begin{pmatrix} & A(t) & \\ \varrho_N & & 0 \\ \vdots & \varrho_N & \vdots \\ & & \ddots \\ 0 & & \varrho_N \end{pmatrix} = B_N(t), \qquad \varrho_N = 1 + t + \ldots + t^{N-1},$$

is a presentation matrix of $H_1(\hat{C}_N)$ as a $\mathfrak{Z}$-module.

Proof. The first assertion follows from the fact that, if two presentation matrices $A(t)$ and $A'(t)$ are equivalent over $\mathbb{Z}\mathfrak{Z}$, they are equivalent over $\mathbb{Z}\mathfrak{Z}_N$. The second version is a consequence of 8.20(b). Observe that $(t^N - 1) = \varrho_N(t)(t-1)$. □

9.21 Corollary. *The homology groups $H_1(\hat{C}_N)$ of the N-fold cyclic branched coverings of a torus knot $\mathfrak{t}(a,b)$ are periodic with the period ab:*

$$H_1(\hat{C}_{N+kab}) \cong \mathrm{H}_1(\hat{C}_N), \quad k \in \mathbb{N}.$$

Moreover

$$H_1(\hat{C}_N) \cong H_1(\hat{C}_{N'}) \quad \textit{if } N' \equiv -N \bmod ab.$$

Proof. By 9.20(b), $B_N(t) = \begin{pmatrix} \Delta(t) \\ \varrho_N(t) \end{pmatrix}$ is a presentation matrix for the $\mathbb{Z}(t)$-module $H_1(\hat{C}_N)$. Since $\Delta(t) | \varrho_{ab}(t)$ and $\varrho_{N+kab} = \varrho_N + t^N \cdot \varrho_k(t^{ab}) \cdot \varrho_{ab}$, the presentation matrices $B_N(t)$ and $B_{N+kab}(t)$ are equivalent. The second assertion is a consequence of

$$\varrho_{ab} - \varrho_N = t^N \cdot \varrho_{ab-N} \quad \text{for } 0 < N < ab. \quad \square$$

9.22 Example. *For the trefoil $\mathfrak{t}(3,2)$ the homology groups of the cyclic branched coverings are:*

$$H_1(\hat{C}_N) \cong \begin{cases} \mathbb{Z} \oplus \mathbb{Z} & \text{for } N \equiv 0 \bmod 6 \\ 0 & \text{for } N \equiv \pm 1 \bmod 6 \\ \mathbb{Z}_3 & \text{for } N \equiv \pm 2 \bmod 6 \\ \mathbb{Z}_2 \oplus \mathbb{Z}_2 & \text{for } N \equiv 3 \bmod 6. \end{cases}$$

Proof.

$N \equiv 0 \bmod 6$: $\begin{pmatrix} 1-t+t^2 \\ 0 \end{pmatrix} \sim (1-t+t^2)$.

$N \equiv 1 \bmod 6$: $\begin{pmatrix} 1-t+t^2 \\ 1 \end{pmatrix} \sim (1)$.

$N \equiv 2 \bmod 6$: $\begin{pmatrix} 1-t+t^2 \\ 1+t \end{pmatrix} \sim \begin{pmatrix} 3 \\ 1+t \end{pmatrix}$.

$N \equiv 3 \bmod 6$: $\begin{pmatrix} 1-t+t^2 \\ 1+t+t^2 \end{pmatrix} \sim \begin{pmatrix} 2 \\ 1+t+t^2 \end{pmatrix}$.

$N \equiv 0$: Let s denote the generator, then

$H_1(\hat{C}_N) \cong \langle s \rangle \oplus \langle ts \rangle$.

$N \equiv 1$: $H_1(\hat{C}_N) = 0$.

$N \equiv 2$: $H_1(\hat{C}_N) \cong \langle s \mid 3s \rangle$.

$N \equiv 3$: $H_1(\hat{C}_N) \cong \langle s \mid 2s \rangle \oplus \langle ts \mid 2ts \rangle$. □

9.23 Remark. In the case of a two-fold covering $\hat{C}_2$ we get a result obtained already in 8.20(a):

$$B_2(t) = \begin{pmatrix} & & A(t) & \\ 1+t & & & \\ & 1+t & & \\ & & \ddots & \\ & & & 1+t \end{pmatrix} \sim A(-1).$$

Proposition 8.20 gives a presentation matrix for $H_1(\hat{C}_N)$ as an abelian group (8.20(a)) derived from the presentation matrix $A(t) = (V^T - tV)$ for $H_1(\hat{C}_N)$ as a $\mathfrak{Z}_N$-module. This can also be achieved by the following trick: Blow up $A(t)$ by replacing every matrix element $r_{ik}(t) = \Sigma\, c_{ik}^{(j)} t^i$ by an $N \times N$-matrix $R_{ik} = \Sigma\, c_{ik}^{(j)} \mathfrak{T}_N^j$,

$$\mathfrak{T}_N = \begin{pmatrix} 0 & 1 & 0 & \dots & 0 \\ 0 & 0 & 1 & & \\ & & & \ddots & \\ & & & & 1 \\ 1 & & & \dots & 0 \end{pmatrix}.$$

This means introducing N generators $s_i, ts_i, \ldots, t^{N-1}s_i$ for each generator s_i, observing $t(t^\nu s_i) = t^{\nu+1}s_i$, $t^N = 1$. The blown up matrix is a presentation matrix of $H_1(\hat{C}_N)$ as an abelian group. For practical calculations of $H_1(\hat{C}_N)$ this procedure is not very useful, because of the high order of the matrices. It may be used, though, to give an alternative proof of 8.21, see [Neuwirth 1965, 5.3.1].

F History and Sources

Homotopy chains were first introduced by Reidemeister [1934], and they were used to classify lens spaces [Reidemeister 1935], [Franz 1935]. R.H. Fox gave an algebraic foundation and generalization of the theory in his free differential calculus [Fox 1953, 1954, 1956], and introduced it to knot theory. Most of the material of this Chapter is connected with the work of R.H. Fox. In connection with the Alexander polynomials of links the contribution of [Crowell-Strauss 1969] and [Hillman 1981′] should be mentioned.

G Exercises

E 9.1 Show (a) that the augmentation ideal $I\mathfrak{Z}^\mu$ of $\mathbb{Z}\mathfrak{Z}^\mu$ is generated by the elements $(t_i - 1)$, $1 \leq i \leq \mu$,
(b) $\mathbb{Z}\mathfrak{Z}^\mu$ is a unique factorization ring with no divisors of zero,
(c) the units of $\mathbb{Z}\mathfrak{Z}$ are $\pm g$, $g \in \mathfrak{Z}^\mu$.

E 9.2 The Alexander module of a 2-bridge knot $\mathfrak{b}(a, b)$ is cyclic. Deduce from this that $\Delta_k(t) = 1$ for $k > 1$.

E 9.3 Let $\varphi\colon \mathfrak{G} \to \mathfrak{G}/\mathfrak{G}' = \langle t \rangle$ be the abelianizing homomorphism of the group $\mathfrak{G} = \langle x, y \mid x^a y^{-b} \rangle$ of a torus knot $\mathfrak{t}(a, b)$. Show that $x^\varphi = t^b$, $y^\varphi = t^a$.

E 9.4 Compute the Alexander polynomial $\Delta(t_1, t_2)$ of the two component link $\mathfrak{k}_1 \cup \mathfrak{k}_2$, where $\mathfrak{k}_1$ is a torus knot, $\mathfrak{k}_1 = \mathfrak{t}(a, b)$, and $\mathfrak{k}_2$ the core of the solid torus T on whose boundary $\mathfrak{t}(a, b)$ lies. Hint: Prove that $\langle x, y, z \mid [x, z], x^a y^{-b} z^b \rangle$ is a presentation of the group of $\mathfrak{k}_1 \cup \mathfrak{k}_2$.

Result: $\Delta(t_1, t_2) = \dfrac{(t_1^a t_2)^b - 1}{t_1^a t_2 - 1}$.

E 9.5 Let C_∞ be the infinite cyclic covering of a link $\mathfrak{k}$ of μ components (see 9 D). Show that $H_1(C_\infty)$ has a presentation matrix of the form $(V^T - tV)$ with

$$V - V^T = F' = \begin{pmatrix} F & 0 \\ 0 & 0 \end{pmatrix}, \quad F = \begin{pmatrix} 0 & 1 & & & \\ -1 & 0 & & & \\ & & \ddots & & \\ & & & 0 & 1 \\ & & & -1 & 0 \end{pmatrix}.$$

F is a $2g \times 2g$ matrix (g the genus of $\mathfrak{k}$), and the order of F' is $2g + \mu - 1$. Deduce from this that the reduced Alexander polynomial of $\mathfrak{k}$ is divisible by $(t-1)^{\mu-2}$ (compare 9.18), and from this: $H_1(\hat{C}_2; \mathbb{Z}_2) = \bigoplus_{i=1}^{\mu-1} \mathbb{Z}_2$. Prove that $|\nabla(1)|$ equals the absolute value of a $(\mu-1) \times (\mu-1)$ principal minor of the linking matrix $(lk(\mathfrak{k}_i, \mathfrak{k}_j))$, $1 \leqq i, j \leqq \mu$. Show that $\nabla(t)$ is symmetric.

E 9.6 Compute the Alexander polynomial of the doubled knot with m half-twists (Fig. 9.3). (Result: $\Delta(t) = kt^2 - (2k+1)t + k$ for $m = 2k$, $\Delta(t) = kt^2 - (2k-1)t + k$ for $m = 2k-1$, $k = 1, 2, \ldots$.)

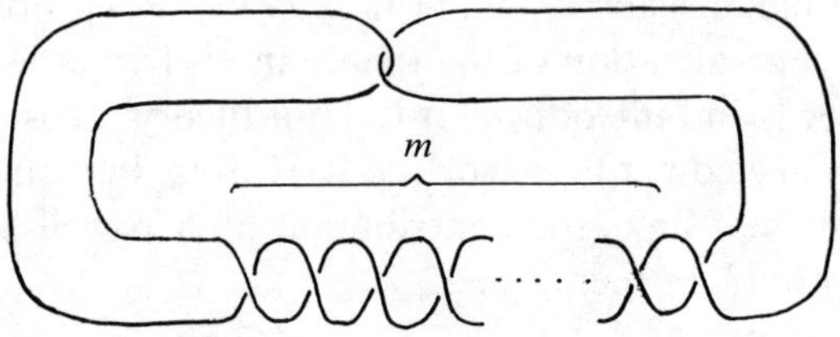

Fig. 9.3

E 9.7 For $\mathfrak{F} = \langle \{s_i | i \in I\} | \rangle$ let l denote the usual length of words with respect to the free generators $\{s_i | i \in I\}$. Extend it to $\mathbb{Z}\mathfrak{F}$ by $l(n_1 x_1 + \ldots + n_k x_k) = \max\{l(x_j) | 1 \leqq j \leqq k, n_j \neq 0\}$; here $n_j \in \mathbb{Z}$ and $x_j \in \mathfrak{F}$ with $x_j \neq x_i$ for $i \neq j$. Introduce the following derivations:

$$\frac{\partial}{\partial s_i^{-1}}: \mathbb{Z}\mathfrak{F} \to \mathbb{Z}\mathfrak{F},\ s_j \mapsto \begin{cases} -s_i & \text{for } j = i \\ 0 & \text{for } j = i. \end{cases}$$

Prove:

(a) $\dfrac{\partial}{\partial s_i^{-1}}(s_i^{-1}) = 1, \quad \dfrac{\partial}{\partial s_i^{-1}} = -\dfrac{\partial}{\partial s_i} \cdot s_i.$

(b) $l\left(\dfrac{\partial \tau}{\partial s_i}\right) \leqq l(\tau), \quad l\left(\dfrac{\partial \tau}{\partial s_i^{-1}}\right) \leqq l(\tau)$ for all $i \in I, \tau \in \mathbb{Z}\mathfrak{F}$.

(c) $l\left(\dfrac{\partial}{\partial s_i^{-1}} \dfrac{\partial}{\partial s_i}(\tau)\right) < l(\tau), \quad l\left(\dfrac{\partial}{\partial s_i} \dfrac{\partial}{\partial s_i^{-1}}(\tau)\right) < l(\tau).$

(d) $\dfrac{\partial}{\partial s_i} = \left(\dfrac{\partial}{\partial s_i^{-1}} \dfrac{\partial}{\partial s_i}\right) \cdot s_i^{-1} - \dfrac{\partial}{\partial s_i} \dfrac{\partial}{\partial s_i^{-1}}.$

E 9.8 (a) Let $\tau, \gamma \in \mathbb{Z}\mathfrak{F}$, $\gamma \neq 0$ and $l(\tau\gamma) \leqq l(\tau)$. Then either $\gamma \in \mathbb{Z}$ or there is a s_i^δ, $i \in I$, $\delta \in \{1, -1\}$ such that $l(\tau s_i^\delta) \leqq l(\tau)$. All elements $f \in \mathfrak{F}$ with $l(f) = l(\tau)$ that have a non-trivial coefficient in τ end with $s_i^{-\delta}$.

(b) If $l(\tau\gamma) < l(\tau)$ and $\gamma \neq 0$ then there is a s_i^δ, $i \in I$, $\delta \in \{1, -1\}$ such that $l(\tau s_i^\delta) < l(\tau)$.

(c) If $\tau\varrho \in \mathbb{Z}$ then either τ or ϱ is 0 or τ and ϱ have the form af with $f \in \mathfrak{F}$, $a \in \mathbb{Z}$.

Chapter 10: Braids

In this Chapter we will present the basic theorems of the theory of braids including their classification or, equivalently, the solution of the word problem for braid groups, but excluding a proof of the conjugation problem (see Garside [1967], Birman [1974]). In Section C we shall consider the Fadell-Neuwirth configuration spaces which present a different aspect of the matter. Geometric reasoning will prevail, as seems appropriate in a subject of such simple beauty.

A The Classification of Braids

Braids were already defined in Chapter 2, Section C. We start by defining an isotopy relation for braids, using combinatorial equivalence. We apply Δ- and Δ^{-1}-moves to the strings f_i, $1 \leqq i \leqq n$, of the braid (see Definition 1.6) assuming that each process preserves the braid properties and keeps fixed the points P_i, Q_i, $1 \leqq i \leqq n$. (See Fig. 10.1)

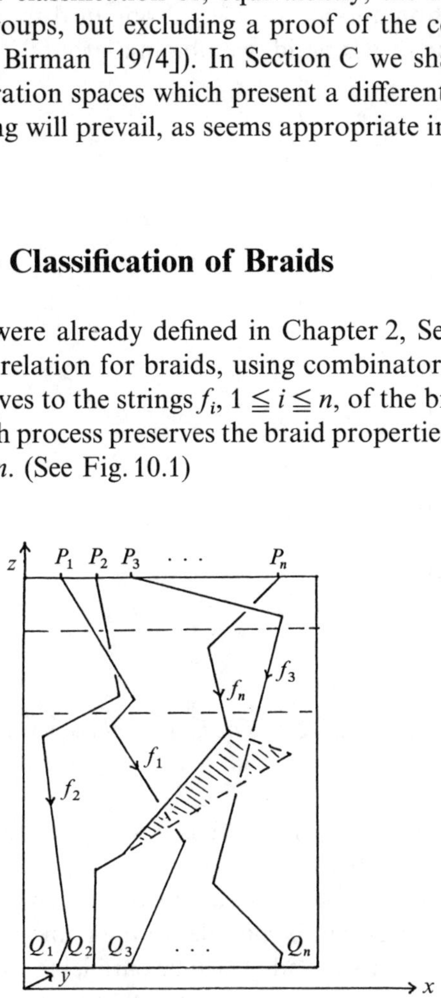

Fig. 10.1

10.1 Definition (isotopy of braids). Two braids $\mathfrak{z}$ and $\mathfrak{z}'$ are called *isotopic* or *equivalent*, if they can be transformed into each other by a finite sequence of $\Delta^{\pm 1}$-processes.

It is obvious that a theorem similar to Proposition 1.10 can be proved. Various notions of isotopy have been introduced [Artin 1947] and shown to be equivalent. As in the case of knots we shall use the term braid and the notation $\mathfrak{z}$ also for a class of equivalent braids. All braids in this section are supposed to be n-braids for some fixed $n > 1$.

There is an obvious composition of two braids $\mathfrak{z}$ and $\mathfrak{z}'$ by identifying the endpoints Q_i of $\mathfrak{z}$ with the initial points P_i' of $\mathfrak{z}'$ (Fig. 10.2). The composition of representatives defines a composition of equivalence classes. Since there is also a unit with respect to this composition and an inverse $\mathfrak{z}^{-1}$ obtained from $\mathfrak{z}$ by a reflection in a plane perpendicular to the braid, we obtain a group:

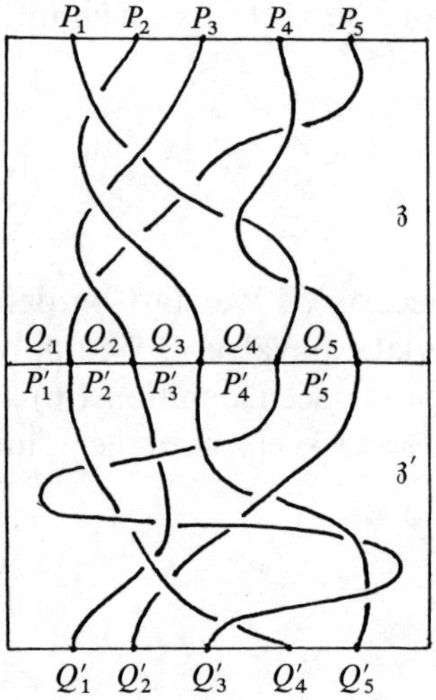

Fig. 10.2

10.2 Proposition and Definition (braid group $\mathfrak{B}_n$). *The isotopy classes $\mathfrak{z}$ of n-braids form a group called the braid group $\mathfrak{B}_n$.* □

We now undertake to find a presentation of $\mathfrak{B}_n$. It is easy to see that $\mathfrak{B}_n$ is generated by $n-1$ generators σ_i (Fig. 10.3).

For easier reference let us introduce cartesian coordinates (x, y, z) with respect to the frames of the braids. The frames will be parallel to the plane $y = 0$ and those of their sides which carry the points P_i and Q_i will be parallel to the x-axis. Now every class of braids contains a representative such that its y-projection (onto the plane $y = 0$) has finitely many double points, all of them with different z-coordinates. Choose planes $z = \text{const}$ which bound slices of $\mathbb{R}^3$ containing parts of $\mathfrak{z}$ with just one double point in their y-projection. If the intersection points of $\mathfrak{z}$ with each of those planes $z = \text{const}$ are moved into equidistant positions on the line in which the frame meets $z = c$ (without introducing new

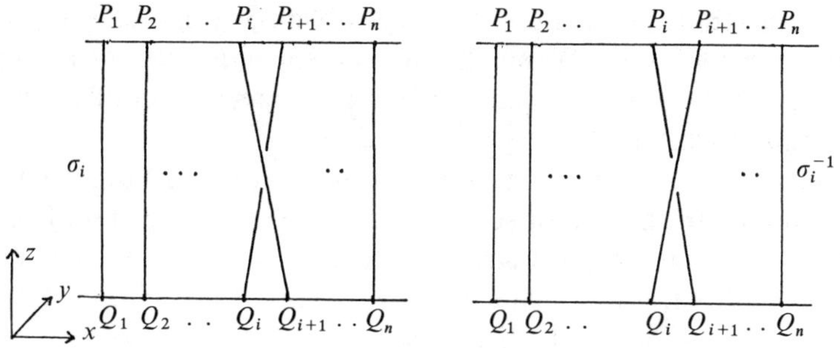

Fig. 10.3

double points in the y-projection) the braid $\mathfrak{z}$ appears as a product of the *elementary braids* σ_i, σ_i^{-1}.

To obtain defining relations for $\mathfrak{B}_n$ we proceed as we did in Chapter 3, Section B, in the case of a knot group. Let $\mathfrak{z} = \sigma_{i_1}^{\varepsilon_1} \dots \sigma_{i_r}^{\varepsilon_r}$, $\varepsilon_i = \pm 1$, be a braid and consider its y-projection. We investigate how a Δ-process will effect the word $\sigma_{i_1}^{\varepsilon_1} \dots \sigma_{i_r}^{\varepsilon_r}$ representing $\mathfrak{z}$. We may assume that the y-projection of the generating triangle of the Δ-process contains one double point or no double points in its interior; in the second case one can assume that the projection of at most one string intersects the interior. Figure 10.4 demonstrates the possible configurations; in the first two positions it is possible to choose the triangle in a slice which contains one (Fig. 10.4(a)), or no double point (Fig. 10.4(b)) in the y-projection.

In Figure (a), σ_{i+1} is replaced by $\sigma_i \sigma_{i+1} \sigma_i \sigma_{i+1}^{-1} \sigma_i^{-1}$; (b) describes an elementary expansion, and in (c) a double point is moved along a string which may lead to a commutator relation $\sigma_i \sigma_k = \sigma_k \sigma_i$ for $|i-k| \geqq 2$. It is easy to verify that any process of type (a) with differently chosen over- and undercrossings leads to the same relation $\sigma_i \sigma_{i+1} \sigma_i \sigma_{i+1}^{-1} \sigma_i^{-1} \sigma_{i+1}^{-1} = 1$; (a) describes, in fact, an Ω_3-process (see 1.13), and one can always think of the uppermost string as the one being moved.

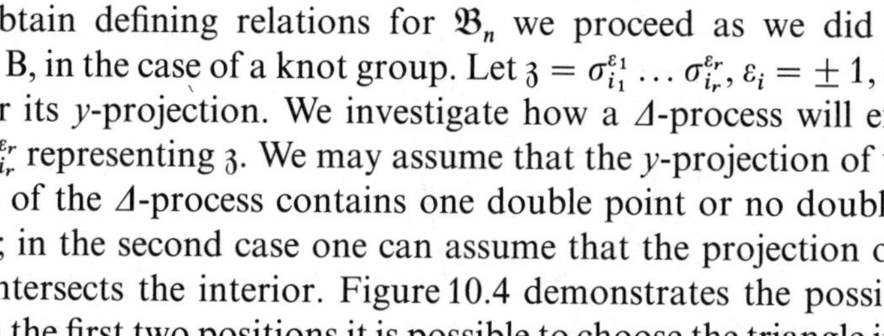

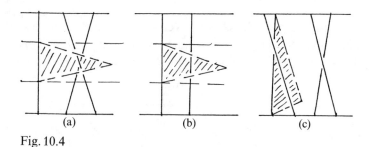

Fig. 10.4

10.3 Proposition (Presentation of the *braid group*). *The braid group* $\mathfrak{B}_n$ *can be presented as follows:*

$$\mathfrak{B}_n = \langle \sigma_1, \dots, \sigma_{n-1} \mid \sigma_j \sigma_{j+1} \sigma_j \sigma_{j+1}^{-1} \sigma_j^{-1} \sigma_{j+1}^{-1} \ (1 \leqq j \leqq n-2), \\ [\sigma_j, \sigma_k] \ (1 \leqq j < k-1 \leqq n-2) \rangle. \quad \square$$

In the light of this theorem the classification problem of braids can be understood as the word problem for $\mathfrak{B}_n$. We shall, however, solve the classification problem by a direct geometric approach and thereby reach a solution of the word problem, rather than vice versa.

As before, let (x, y, z) be the cartesian coordinates of a point in Euclidean 3-space. We modify the geometric setting by placing the frame of the braid askew in a cuboid Q. The edges of Q are supposed to be parallel to the coordinate axes; the upper side of the frame which carries the points P_i coincides with an upper edge of Q parallel to the x-axis, the opposite side which contains the Q_i is assumed to bisect the base-face of Q (see Fig. 10.5).

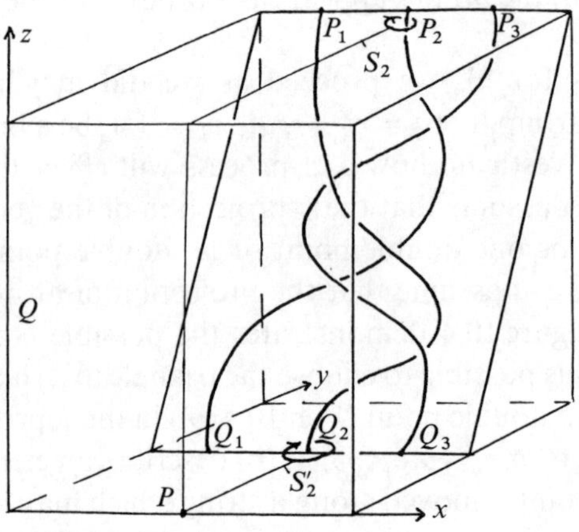

Fig. 10.5

10.4 Lemma. *Every class of braids contains a respresentative the z-projection of which is simple (without double points).*

Proof. The representative $\mathfrak{z}$ of a class of braids can be chosen in such a way that its y-projection and z-projection yield the same word $\sigma_{i_1}^{\varepsilon_1}\sigma_{i_2}^{\varepsilon_2}\ldots\sigma_{i_r}^{\varepsilon_r}$. This can be achieved by placing the strings in a neighbourhood of the frame, compare 2.12.

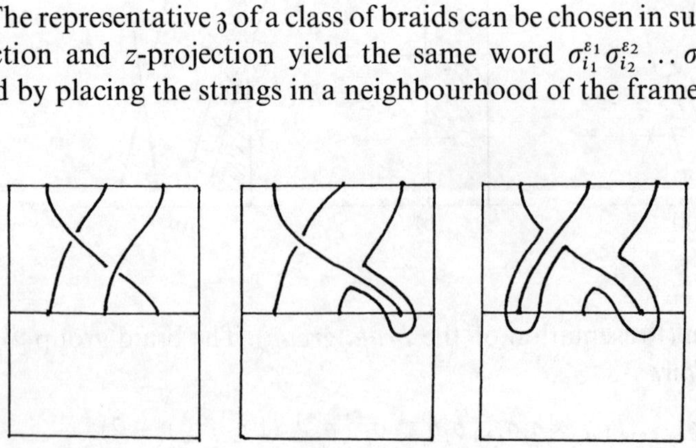

Fig. 10.6

Consider the double point in $z = 0$ corresponding to $\sigma_{i_r}^{\varepsilon_r}$, push the overcrossing along the undercrossing string over its endpoint Q_j (Fig. 10.6) while preserving the z-level. Obviously this process is an isotopy of $\mathfrak{z}$ which can be carried out without disturbing the upper part of the braid which is projected onto $\sigma_{i_1}^{\varepsilon_1} \dots \sigma_{i_{r-1}}^{\varepsilon_{r-1}}$. Proceed by removing the double point in $z = 0$ corresponding to $\sigma_{i_{r-1}}^{\varepsilon_{r-1}}$. The procedure eventually leads to a braid with a simple z-projection as claimed in the Lemma. □

Remark: Every 2m-plat has an m-bridge presentation.

Let us denote the base-face of Q by D, and the z-projections of f_i, P_i by f_i', P_i'. The simple projection of a braid then consists of a set of simple and pairwise disjoint arcs f_i' leading from P'_i to $Q'_{\pi(i)}$, $1 \leqq i \leqq n$, where π is the permutation associated with the braid $\mathfrak{z}$ (see 2.12). We call $\{f_i' | 1 \leqq i \leqq n\}$ a *normal dissection* of the punctured rectangle $D - \bigcup_{j=1}^{n} Q_j = D_n$. By Lemma 10.4 every braid can be represented by a set of strings which projects onto a normal dissection of D_n, and obviously every normal dissection of D_n is a z-projection of some braid in Q. Two normal dissections are called isotopic if they can be transformed into each other by a sequence of $\Delta^{\pm 1}$-processes in D_n. The defining triangle of such a Δ-process intersects $\{f_i'\}$ in one of its sides, a line segment of some f_k'. Any two braids projecting onto isotopic normal dissections evidently are isotopic. The groups $\pi_1(Q - \mathfrak{z})$ as well as $\pi_1 D_n$ are free of rank n. This is clear from the fact that the projecting cylinders of a braid with a simple z-projection dissect $Q - \mathfrak{z}$ into a 3-cell. Every braid $\mathfrak{z}$ in Q defines two sets of free generators $\{S_i\}$, $\{S_i'\}$, $1 \leqq i \leqq n$, of $\pi_1(Q - \mathfrak{z})$: Choose a basepoint P on the x-axis and let S_i be represented by a loop on ∂Q consisting of a small circle around P_i and a (shortest) arc connecting it to P. Similarly define S_i' by encircling Q_i instead of P_i (Fig. 10.5).

Since every isotopy $\mathfrak{z} \mapsto \mathfrak{z}'$ can be extended to an ambient isotopy in Q leaving ∂Q pointwise fixed (Proposition 1.10), a class of braids defines an *associated braid automorphism of* $\mathfrak{F}_n \cong \pi_1(Q - \mathfrak{z})$, $\zeta\colon \mathfrak{F}_n \to \mathfrak{F}_n$, $S_i \mapsto S_i'$. All information on ζ can be obtained by looking at the normal dissection of D_n associated to $\mathfrak{z}$. Every normal dissection defines a set of free generators of $\pi_1 D_n$. A loop in D_n which intersects $\{f_i'\}$ once positively in f_k' represents a free generator $S_k \in \pi_1 D_n$ which is mapped onto $S_k \in \pi_1(Q - \mathfrak{z})$ by the isomorphism induced by the inclusion. Hence $S_i'(S_j)$ as a word in the S_j is easily read off the normal dissection:

(1) $$S_i' = L_i S_{\pi^{-1}(i)} L_i^{-1}.$$

To determine the word $L_i(S_j)$, run through a straight line from P to Q_i, noting down S_k or S_k^{-1} if the line is crossed by f_k' from left to right or otherwise.

The braid automorphism (1) can also be interpreted as an automorphism of $\pi_1 D_n$ with $\{S_i\}$ associated to the normal dissection $\{f_i'\}$, and $\{S_i'\}$ associated to the standard normal dissection consisting of the straight segments from P_i' to Q_i.

The solution of the classification problem of n-braids is contained in the following

10.5 Proposition (E. Artin). *Two n-braids are isotopic if and only if they define the same braid automorphism.*

Proof. Assigning a braid automorphism ζ to a braid $\mathfrak{z}$ defines a homomorphism

$$\mathfrak{B}_n \to \operatorname{Aut} \mathfrak{F}_n, \quad \mathfrak{z} \mapsto \zeta.$$

To prove Proposition 10.5 we must show that this homomorphism is injective. This can be done with the help of

10.6 Lemma. *Two normal dissections define the same braid automorphism if and only if they are isotopic.*

Proof. A Δ-process does not change the $S_i' = L_i S_{\pi^{-1}(i)} L_i^{-1}$ as elements in the free group. This follows also from the fact that isotopic normal dissections are $\mathfrak{z}$-projections of isotopic braids, and the braid automorphism is assigned to the braid class. Now let $\{f_i'\}$ be some normal dissection of D_n and $S_i' = L_i S_{\pi^{-1}(i)} L_i^{-1}$ read off it as described before. If $L(S_i)$ contains a part of the form $S_j^{\varepsilon} S_j^{-\varepsilon}$, the two points on f_j' corresponding to S_j^{ε} and $S_j^{-\varepsilon}$ are connected by two simple arcs on f_j' and the loop in D_n representing S_i'. These arcs bound a 2-cell in D which contains no point Q_k, because otherwise $f_{\pi^{-1}(k)}'$ would have to meet one of the arcs which is impossible. Hence the two arcs bound a 2-cell in D_n, and there is an isotopy moving f_j' across it causing the elementary contraction in L_i which deletes $S_j^{\varepsilon} S_j^{-\varepsilon}$. Thus we can replace the normal dissection by an isotopic one such that the corresponding words $L_i(S_j)$ are reduced. Similarly we can assume $L_i S_{\pi^{-1}(i)} L_i^{-1}$ to be reduced. If the last symbol of $L_i(S_j)$ is $S_{\pi^{-1}(i)}^{\varepsilon}$, there is an isotopy of f_i' which deletes $S_{\pi^{-1}(i)}^{\varepsilon}$ in $L_i(S_j)$ (Fig. 10.7).

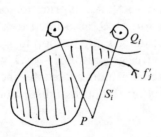

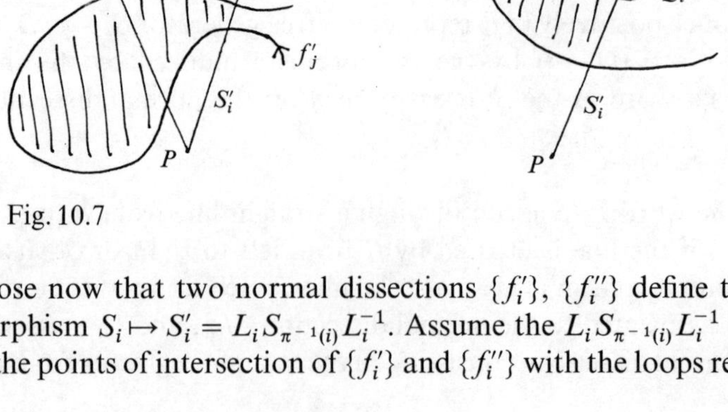

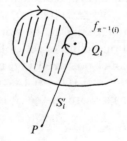

Fig. 10.7

Suppose now that two normal dissections $\{f_i'\}$, $\{f_i''\}$ define the same braid automorphism $S_i \mapsto S_i' = L_i S_{\pi^{-1}(i)} L_i^{-1}$. Assume the $L_i S_{\pi^{-1}(i)} L_i^{-1}$ to be reduced, and let the points of intersection of $\{f_i'\}$ and $\{f_i''\}$ with the loops representing the

S'_j coincide. It follows that two successive intersection points on some f'_k are also successive on f''_k, and, hence, the two connecting arcs on f'_k resp. f''_k can be deformed into each other by an isotopy of $\{f'_i\}$. This is clear if $\{f'_i\}$ is the standard normal dissection and this suffices to prove 10.6. □

We return to the proof of Proposition 10.5. Let $\mathfrak{z}$ and $\mathfrak{z}'$ be n-braids inducing the same braid automorphism. By Lemma 10.4 we may assume that their z-projections are simple. Lemma 10.6 ensures that the z-projections are isotopic; hence $\mathfrak{z}$ and $\mathfrak{z}'$ are isotopic. □

Proposition 10.5 solves, of course, the word problem of the braid group $\mathfrak{B}_n$: *Two braids $\mathfrak{z}$, $\mathfrak{z}'$ are isotopic if and only if their automorphisms coincide* – a matter which can be checked easily, since $\mathfrak{F}_n$ is free.

Propositions 10.5 and 10.6 moreover imply that there is a one-to-one correspondence between braids, braid automorphisms and isotopy classes of normal dissections. These classes represent elements of *the mapping class group of D_n*; its elements are homeomorphisms of D_n which keep ∂D_n pointwise fixed, modulo deformations of D_n.

The injective image of $\mathfrak{B}_n$ in the group Aut $\mathfrak{F}_n$ of automorphisms of the free group of rank n is called the group of braid automorphisms. We shall also denote it by $\mathfrak{B}_n$. The injection $\mathfrak{B}_n \to \text{Aut}\, \mathfrak{F}_n$ depends on a set of distinguished free generators S_i of $\mathfrak{F}_n$. It is common use to stick to these distinguished generators or rather their class modulo braid automorphisms, and braid automorphisms will always be understood in this way. We propose to study these braid automorphisms more closely.

Figure 10.8 illustrates the computations of the braid automorphisms corresponding to the elementary braids $\sigma_i^{\pm 1}$ – we denote the automorphisms by the same symbols:

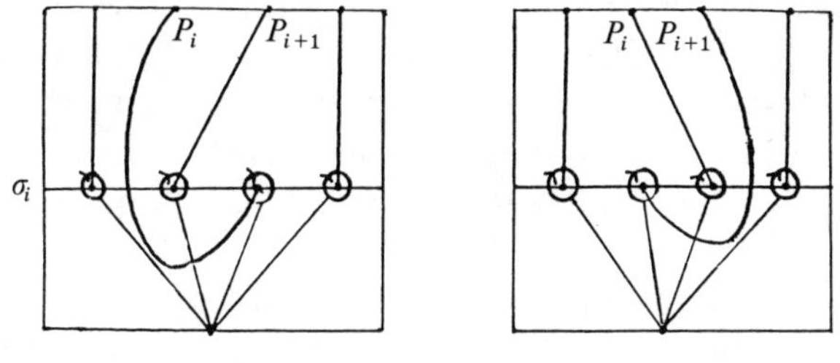

Fig. 10.8

$$(2) \qquad \sigma_i(S_j) = S'_j \quad = \begin{cases} S_i S_{i+1} S_i^{-1}, & j = i \\ S_i, & j = i+1 \\ S_j, & j \neq i,\, i+1 \end{cases}$$

$$(2) \qquad \sigma_i^{-1}(S_j) = S'_j = \begin{cases} S_{i+1}, & j = i \\ S_{i+1}^{-1} S_i S_{i+1}, & j = i+1 \\ S_j, & j \neq i, i+1. \end{cases}$$

From these formulas the identity in $\mathfrak{F}_n$

$$(3) \qquad \prod_{i=1}^{n} S'_i = \prod_{i=1}^{n} S_i$$

follows for any braid automorphism $\zeta \colon S_i \to S'_i$, and,

$$(1) \qquad S'_i = L_i S_{\pi^{-1}(i)} L_i^{-1}.$$

This is also geometrically evident, since ΠS_i as well as $\Pi S'_i$ is represented by a loop which girds the whole braid.

At this point it seems necessary to say a few words about the correct interpretation of the symbols σ_i. If $\mathfrak{z} = \sigma_{i_1}^{\varepsilon_1} \dots \sigma_{i_r}^{\varepsilon_r}$ is understood as braid, the composition is defined from left to right. Denote by $\mathfrak{z}_k = \sigma_{i_1}^{\varepsilon_1} \dots \sigma_{i_k}^{\varepsilon_k}$, $0 \leqq k \leqq r$, the k-th *initial section* of $\mathfrak{z}$ and by ζ_k the braid automorphism associated to $\mathfrak{z}_k$ (operating on the original generators S_i). The injective homomorphism $\mathfrak{B}_n \to \mathrm{Aut}\, \mathfrak{F}_n$ then maps a factor $\sigma_{i_j}^{\varepsilon_j}$ of $\mathfrak{z}$ onto an automorphism of $\mathfrak{F}_n$ defined by (2) where $\zeta_{j-1}(S_i)$ takes the place of S_i.

There is an identity in the free group generated by the $\{\sigma_i\}$:

$$\mathfrak{z} = \prod_{k=1}^{r} \sigma_{i_k}^{\varepsilon_k} = \prod_{k=1}^{r} \mathfrak{z}_{r-k} \sigma_{r-k+1}^{\varepsilon_{r-k+1}} \mathfrak{z}_{r-k}^{-1}, \quad \mathfrak{z}_0 = 1.$$

The automorphism $\zeta_{r-k} \sigma_{r-k+1}^{\varepsilon_{r-k+1}} \zeta_{r-k}^{-1}$ (carried out from right to left!) is the automorphism $\sigma_{r-k+1}^{\varepsilon_{r-k+1}}$ defined by (2) on the original generators S_i (from the top of the braid). We may therefore understand $\mathfrak{z} = \sigma_{i_1}^{\varepsilon_1} \dots \sigma_{i_r}^{\varepsilon_r}$ either as a product (from right to left) of automorphisms $\sigma_{i_j}^{\varepsilon_j}$ in the usual sense, or, performed from left to right, as a successive application of a rule for a substitution according to (2) with varying arguments. The last one was originally employed by Artin, and it makes the mapping $\mathfrak{B}_n \to \mathrm{Aut}\, \mathfrak{F}_n$ a homomorphism rather than an anti-homomorphism. The two interpretations are dual descriptions of the same automorphism.

Braid automorphisms of $\mathfrak{F}_n(S_i)$ can be characterized by (1) and (3). Artin [1925] even proved a slightly stronger theorem where he does not presuppose that the given substitution is an automorphism:

10.7 Proposition. *Let $\mathfrak{F}_n(S_j)$ be a free group on a given set $\{S_j \mid 1 \leqq j \leqq n\}$ of free generators, and let π be a permutation on $\{1, 2, \dots, n\}$. Any set of words $S'_i(S_j)$, $1 \leqq i \leqq n$, subject to the following conditions*

(1) $S'_i = L_i S_{\pi(i)} L_i^{-1}$,

(3) $\prod_{i=1}^{n} S'_i = \prod_{i=1}^{n} S_i$,

generates $\mathfrak{F}_n$; the homomorphism defined by $S_i \mapsto S'_i$ is a braid automorphism.

Proof. Assume S'_i to be reduced and call $\lambda(\zeta) = \sum_{i=1}^{n} l(L_i)$ the length of the substitution $\zeta: S_i \to S'_i$, where $l(L_i)$ denotes the length of L_i. If $\lambda = 0$, it follows from (3) that ζ is the identity. We proceed by induction on λ. For $\lambda > 0$ there will be reductions in

$$\prod_{i=1}^{n} S_i = L_i S_{\pi(1)} L_1^{-1} \dots L_n S_{\pi(n)} L_n^{-1}$$

such that some $S_{\pi(i)}$ is cancelled by $S_{\pi(i)}^{-1}$ contained in L_{i-1}^{-1} or L_{i+1} (If all L_i cancel out, they have to be all equal, and hence empty, since L_1 and L_n have to be empty). Suppose L_{i+1} cancels $S_{\pi(i)}$, then

$$l(L_i S_{\pi(i)} L_i^{-1} L_{i+1}) < l(L_{i+1}).$$

Apply σ_i to S'_j, $\sigma_i(S'_j) = S''_j$, to obtain $\lambda(\zeta\sigma_i) < \lambda(\zeta)$ while $\zeta\sigma_i$ still fulfils conditions (1) and (3). Thus, by induction, $\zeta\sigma_i$ is a braid automorphism and so is ζ. (If $S_{\pi(i)}$ is cancelled by L_{i-1}^{-1}, one has to use σ_{i-1}^{-1} instead of σ_i.) □

B Normal Form and Group Structure

We have derived a presentation of the braid group $\mathfrak{B}_n$, and solved the word problem by embedding $\mathfrak{B}_n$ into the group of automorphisms of the free group of rank n. For some additional information on the group structure of $\mathfrak{B}_n$ first consider the surjective homomorphism

$$\mathfrak{B}_n \to \mathfrak{S}_n, \quad \mathfrak{z} \mapsto \pi,$$

which assigns to each braid $\mathfrak{z}$ its permutation π. We propose to study the kernel $\mathfrak{I}_n \lhd \mathfrak{B}_n$ of this homomorphism.

10.8 Definition (pure braids). A braid of $\mathfrak{I}_n$ is called a *pure i-braid* if there is a representative with the strings f_j, $j \neq i$, constant (straight lines), and if its y-projection only contains double points concerning f_i and f_j, $j < i$, see Figure 10.9.

10.9 Proposition. *The pure i-braids of $\mathfrak{I}_n$ form a free subgroup $\mathfrak{F}^{(i)}$ of $\mathfrak{I}_n$ of rank $i-1$.*

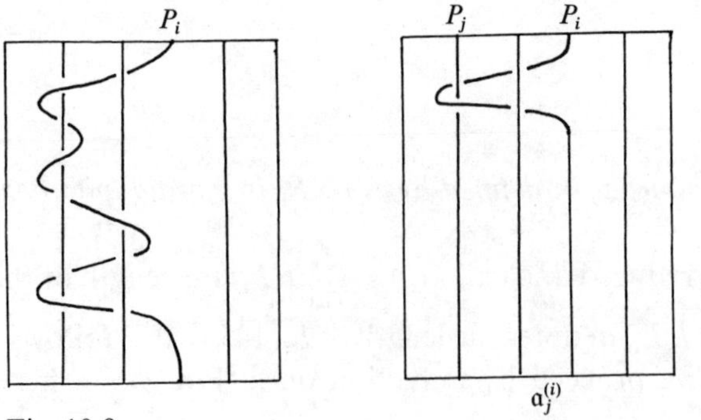

Fig. 10.9

Proof. It is evident that $\mathfrak{F}^{(i)}$ is a subgroup of $\mathfrak{I}_n$. Furthermore $\mathfrak{F}^{(i)}$ is obviously generated by the braids $\mathfrak{a}_j^{(i)}$, $1 \leqq j < i$, as defined in Figure 10.9. Let $\mathfrak{z}^{(i)} \in \mathfrak{F}^{(i)}$ be an arbitrary pure i-braid. Note down $(\mathfrak{a}_{j_k}^{(i)})^{\varepsilon_k}$ as you traverse f_i at every double point in the y-projection where f_i overcrosses f_{j_k}, while choosing $\varepsilon_k = +1$ resp. $\varepsilon_k = -1$ according to the characteristic of the crossing. Then $\mathfrak{z}^{(i)} = \mathfrak{a}_{j_1}^{(i)\varepsilon_1} \mathfrak{a}_{j_2}^{(i)\varepsilon_2} \ldots \mathfrak{a}_{j_r}^{(i)\varepsilon_r}$.

It is easy to see that the $\mathfrak{a}_j^{(i)}$ are free generators. It follows from the fact that the loops formed by the strings f_i of $\mathfrak{a}_j^{(i)}$ combined with an arc on ∂Q can be considered as free generators of $\pi_1(Q - \bigcup_{j=1}^{i-1} f_j) \cong \mathfrak{F}^{(i-1)}$. □

10.10 Proposition. *The subgroup* $\mathfrak{B}_{i-1} \subset \mathfrak{B}_n$ *generated by* $\{\sigma_r | 1 \leqq r \leqq i-2\}$ *operates on* $\mathfrak{F}^{(i)}$ *by conjugation:*

$$\sigma_r^{-1} \mathfrak{a}_j^{(i)} \sigma_r = \begin{cases} \mathfrak{a}_j^{(i)}, & j \neq r,\, r+1 \\ \mathfrak{a}_r^{(i)} \mathfrak{a}_{r+1}^{(i)} \mathfrak{a}_r^{(i)-1}, & j = r \\ \mathfrak{a}_r^{(i)}, & j = r+1 . \end{cases}$$

The *proof* is given in Figure 10.10. □

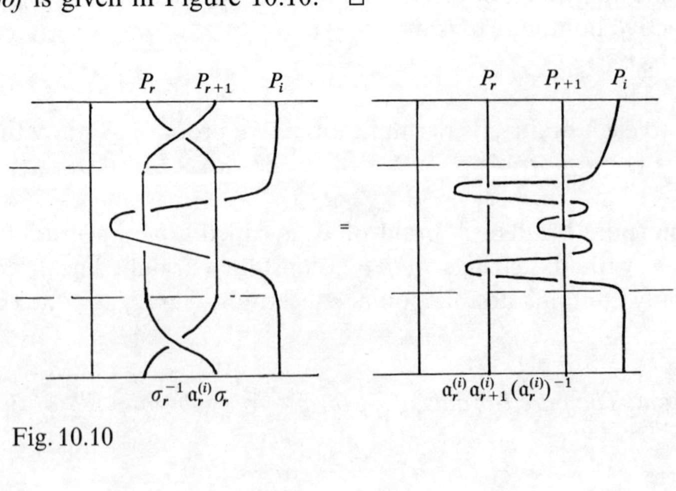

Fig. 10.10

It is remarkable that σ_r induces on $\mathfrak{F}^{(i)}$ the braid automorphism σ_r with respect to the free generators $\mathfrak{a}_j^{(i)}$.

The following theorem describes the group structure of $\mathfrak{Z}_n$ to a certain extent:

10.11 Proposition. *The braids* $\mathfrak{z}$ *of* $\mathfrak{Z}^{(n)}$ *admit a unique decomposition:*

$$\mathfrak{z} = \mathfrak{z}_2 \cdots \mathfrak{z}_n, \quad \mathfrak{z}_i \in \mathfrak{F}^{(i)}, \quad \mathfrak{F}^{(1)} = 1.$$

This decomposition is called the normal form of $\mathfrak{z}$. *There is a product rule for normal forms:*

$$\left(\prod_{i=2}^{n} \mathfrak{x}_i\right)\left(\prod_{i=2}^{n} \mathfrak{y}_i\right) = (\mathfrak{x}_2\mathfrak{y}_2)(\mathfrak{x}_3^{\eta_2}\mathfrak{y}_3)\dots(\mathfrak{x}_n^{\eta_{n-1}\dots\eta_3\eta_2}\mathfrak{y}_n),$$

where η_i *denotes the braid automorphism associated to the braid* $\mathfrak{y}_i \in \mathfrak{F}^{(i)}$.

Proof. The existence of a normal form for $\mathfrak{z} \in \mathfrak{Z}_n$ is an immediate consequence of Lemma 10.4. One has to realize $\mathfrak{z} \in \mathfrak{Z}_n$ from a simple z-projection by letting first f_n ascend over its z-projection while representing the f_j, $j < n$, by straight lines over the endpoints Q_j. This defines the factor $\mathfrak{z}_n$. The remaining part of f_n is projected onto P_n' and therefore has no effect on the rest of the braid. Thus the existence of the normal form follows by induction on n, Figure 10.11.

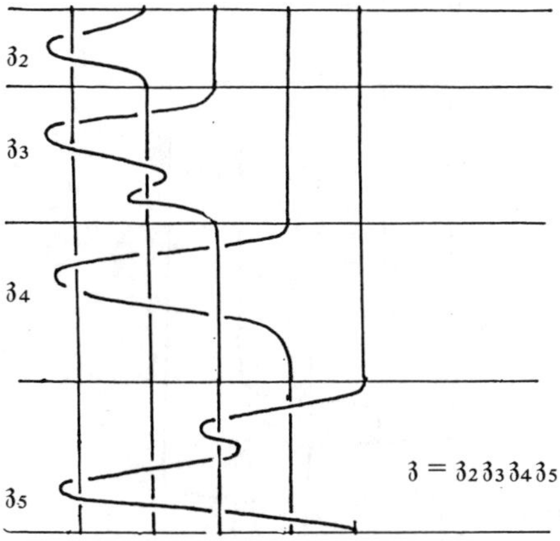

Fig. 10.11

The product rule is a consequence of Proposition 10.10. Uniqueness follows from the fact that, if $\mathfrak{x}_2 \dots \mathfrak{x}_n \cdot \mathfrak{y}_n^{-1} \dots \mathfrak{y}_2^{-1} = 1$, then $(\mathfrak{x}_n \cdot \mathfrak{y}_n^{-1})^{\eta_2^{-1}\dots\eta_{n-1}^{-1}}$ is its component in $\mathfrak{F}^{(n)}$. Its string f_n is homotopic to some arc on ∂Q in $Q - \bigcup_{j=1}^{n-1} f_j$, hence $(\mathfrak{x}_n \cdot \mathfrak{y}_n^{-1})^{\eta_2^{-1}\dots\eta_{n-1}^{-1}} = 1$, $\mathfrak{x}_n = \mathfrak{y}_n$. The rest follows by induction. □

The normal form affords some insight into the structure of $\mathfrak{Z}_n$. By definition $\mathfrak{F}^{(1)} = 1$; the group $\mathfrak{Z}_n$ is a repeated semidirect product of free groups with braid automorphisms operating according to Proposition 10.10:

$$\mathfrak{J}_n = \mathfrak{F}^{(1)} \ltimes (\mathfrak{F}^{(2)} \ltimes (\dots (\mathfrak{F}^{n-1} \ltimes \mathfrak{F}^{(n)})).$$

There is some more information contained in the normal form:

10.12 Proposition. *$\mathfrak{J}_n$ contains no elements $\neq 1$ of finite order. The centre of $\mathfrak{J}_n$ and of $\mathfrak{B}_n$ is an infinite cyclic group generated by*

$$(\sigma_1 \sigma_2 \dots \sigma_{n-1})^n \quad \text{for } n > 2.$$

Proof. Suppose

$$(\mathfrak{x}_2 \dots \mathfrak{x}_n)^m = \mathfrak{y}_2 \dots \mathfrak{y}_n = 1,\ m > 1.$$

By 10.11, $\mathfrak{y}_2 = (\mathfrak{x}_2)^m = 1$. Now $\mathfrak{x}_2 = 1$ follows from Proposition 10.9. In the same way we get $\mathfrak{x}_i = 1$ successively for $i = 3, 4, \dots, n$. This proves the first assertion.

The braid $\mathfrak{z}^0 = (\sigma_1 \sigma_2 \dots \sigma_{n-1})^n$ of Fig. 10.12 obviously is an element of the centre $Z(\mathfrak{B}_n)$. It is obtained from the trivial braid by a full twist of the lower side of the frame while keeping the upper one fixed. The normal form of $\mathfrak{z}^0$ is given on the right of Figure 10.12:

$$\mathfrak{z}^0 = \mathfrak{z}_2^0 \dots \mathfrak{z}_n^0, \quad \mathfrak{z}_i^0 = \mathfrak{a}_1^{(i)} \dots \mathfrak{a}_{i-1}^{(i)}.$$

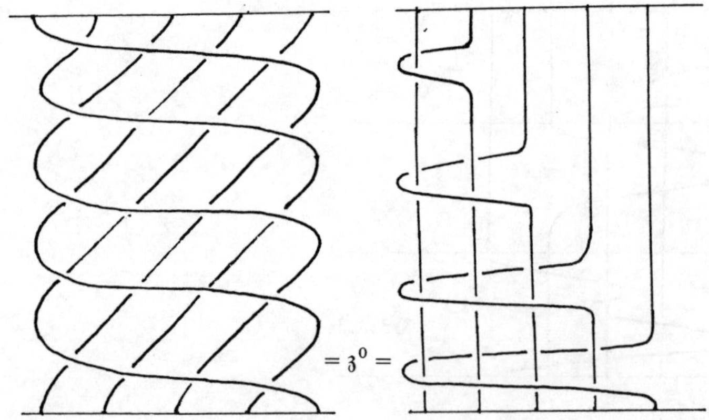

Fig. 10.12

(For the definition of $\mathfrak{a}_j^{(i)}$ see Fig. 10.9.)

It is easily verified that $\mathfrak{z}^0$ determines the braid automorphism

$$\zeta^0\colon S_i \mapsto \left(\prod_{j=1}^{n} S_j\right) S_i \left(\prod_{j=1}^{n} S_j\right)^{-1},$$

and that by (3) $\mathfrak{B}_n \cap \mathfrak{I}_n = \langle \zeta^0 \rangle \cong \mathfrak{Z}$, $\mathfrak{I}_n$ the inner automorphisms of $\mathfrak{F}_n$.

Note that Proposition 10.10 yields, for $1 \leqq i \leqq r < n$:

$$(4)\qquad (\sigma_1 \ldots \sigma_{r-1})^{-r} \mathfrak{a}_i^{(r+1)} (\sigma_1 \ldots \sigma_{r-1})^r = (\mathfrak{a}_i^{(r+1)})^{(\sigma_1 \ldots \sigma_{r-1})^r} =$$
$$= (\mathfrak{a}_1^{(r+1)} \ldots \mathfrak{a}_r^{(r+1)})\, \mathfrak{a}_i^{(r+1)} (\mathfrak{a}_1^{(r+1)} \ldots \mathfrak{a}_r^{(r+1)})^{-1}.$$

For $n > 2$ the symmetric group $\mathfrak{S}_n$ has a trivial centre – this implies that the centres $Z(\mathfrak{B}_n)$ and $Z(\mathfrak{J}_n)$ of $\mathfrak{B}_n$ and $\mathfrak{J}_n$ coincide, $Z(\mathfrak{B}_n) = Z(\mathfrak{J}_n)$. We may therefore write an arbitrary $\mathfrak{z} \in Z(\mathfrak{J}_n)$ in normal form, $\mathfrak{z} = \mathfrak{z}_2 \ldots \mathfrak{z}_n$, $\mathfrak{z}_i \in \mathfrak{F}^{(i)}$. (We denote by ζ_i, ξ_i, η_i the braid automorphisms associated to the braids $\mathfrak{z}_i$, $\mathfrak{x}_i$, $\mathfrak{y}_i$.)

For every $\mathfrak{x}_3 \in \mathfrak{F}^{(3)}$:

$$\mathfrak{z}_2 \mathfrak{x}_3^{\zeta_2} \mathfrak{z}_3 \cdot\cdot \mathfrak{z}_n = \mathfrak{x}_3 \mathfrak{z}_2 \cdots \mathfrak{z}_n = \mathfrak{z}_2 \cdots \mathfrak{z}_n \mathfrak{x}_3 = \mathfrak{z}_2 \mathfrak{z}_3 \mathfrak{x}_3 \mathfrak{z}_4^{\xi_3} \cdots \mathfrak{z}_n^{\xi_3}.$$

It follows that $\mathfrak{x}_3^{\zeta_2} \mathfrak{z}_3 = \mathfrak{z}_3 \mathfrak{x}_3$, or $\mathfrak{x}_3^{\zeta_2} = \mathfrak{z}_3 \mathfrak{x}_3 \mathfrak{z}_3^{-1}$. Now $\mathfrak{z}_2 = (\mathfrak{a}_1^{(2)})^k$ for some $k \in \mathbb{Z}$. Apply (4) for $r = 2$, $\zeta_2 = \sigma_1^{2k}$: $(\mathfrak{a}_i^{(3)})^{\sigma_1^{2k}} = (\mathfrak{a}_1^{(3)} \mathfrak{a}_2^{(3)})^k\, \mathfrak{a}_i^{(3)} (\mathfrak{a}_1^{(3)} \mathfrak{a}_2^{(3)})^{-k}$.
Hence, for $\mathfrak{x}_3 \in \mathfrak{F}^{(3)}$:

$$\mathfrak{z}_3 \mathfrak{x}_3 \mathfrak{z}_3^{-1} = \mathfrak{x}_3^{\sigma_1^{2k}} = (\mathfrak{a}_1^{(3)} \mathfrak{a}_2^{(3)})^k\, \mathfrak{x}_3 (\mathfrak{a}_1^{(3)} \mathfrak{a}_2^{(3)})^{-k}.$$

Since $\mathfrak{F}^{(3)}$ is free, we get $\mathfrak{z}_3 = (\mathfrak{a}_1^{(3)} \mathfrak{a}_2^{(3)})^k$.

The next step determines $\mathfrak{z}_4$ by the following property: For $\mathfrak{x}_4 \in \mathfrak{F}^{(4)}$:

$$\mathfrak{x}_4 \mathfrak{z}_2 \cdots \mathfrak{z}_n = \mathfrak{z}_2 \mathfrak{z}_3 \mathfrak{x}_4^{\zeta_3 \zeta_2} \mathfrak{z}_4 \cdots \mathfrak{z}_n =$$
$$= \mathfrak{z}_2 \cdots \mathfrak{z}_n \mathfrak{x}_4 = \mathfrak{z}_2 \mathfrak{z}_3 \mathfrak{z}_4 \mathfrak{x}_4 \mathfrak{z}_5^{\xi_4} \cdots \mathfrak{z}_n^{\xi_4}.$$

The uniqueness of the normal form gives:

$$\mathfrak{x}_4^{\zeta_3 \zeta_2} = \mathfrak{z}_4 \mathfrak{x}_4 \mathfrak{z}_4^{-1}.$$

The braids $\mathfrak{z}_2$ and $\mathfrak{z}_3$ commute – draw a figure – and so do the corresponding automorphisms: $\zeta_2 \zeta_3 = \zeta_3 \zeta_2$.

We already know $\mathfrak{z}_2 \mathfrak{z}_3 = (\mathfrak{a}_1^{(2)})^k (\mathfrak{a}_1^{(3)} \mathfrak{a}_2^{(3)})^k$, $\zeta_2 \zeta_3 = (\sigma_1 \sigma_2)^{3k}$. By (4) we get $\mathfrak{z}_4 = (\mathfrak{a}_1^{(4)} \mathfrak{a}_2^{(4)} \mathfrak{a}_3^{(4)})^k$. The procedure yields $\mathfrak{z}_i = (\mathfrak{z}_i^0)^k$, $\mathfrak{z} = (\mathfrak{z}^0)^k$. □

The braid group $\mathfrak{B}_n$ itself is also torsion free. This was first proved in [Fadell-Neuwirth 1962]. A different proof is contained in [Murasugi 1982]. We discuss these proofs in Section C.

C Configuration Spaces and Braid Groups

In [Fadell-Neuwirth 1962] and [Fox-Neuwirth 1962] a different approach to braids was developed. We shall prove some results of it here. For details the reader is referred to the papers metioned above.

A braid $\mathfrak{z}$ meets a plane $z = c$ in n points $(p_1, p_2, \ldots, p_n)$ if $0 \leqq c \leqq 1$, and $z = 1$ $(z = 0)$ contains the initial points P_i (endpoints Q_i) of the strings f_i. One may therefore think of $\mathfrak{z}$ as a simultaneous motion of n points in a plane E^2, $\{(p_1(t), \ldots, p_n(t)) | 0 \leqq t \leqq 1\}$. We shall construct a $2n$-dimensional manifold where $(p_1, \ldots, p_n)$ represents a point and $(p_1(t), \ldots, p_n(t))$ a loop such that the braid group $\mathfrak{B}_n$ becomes its fundamental group.

Every n-tuple $(p_1, \ldots, p_n)$ represents a point $P = (x_1, y_1, x_2, y_2, \ldots, x_n, y_n)$ in Euclidean $2n$-space E^{2n}, where (x_i, y_i) are the coordinates of $p_i \in E^2$. Let $i \prec j$ stand for the inequality $x_i < x_j$, $i \triangleq j$ for $x_i = x_j$, $y_i < y_j$, and $i = j$ for $x_i = x_j$, $y_i = y_j$. Any distribution of these symbols in a sequence, e.g. $\pi(1) = \pi(2) \triangleq \pi(3) \prec \pi(4) \ldots \pi(n)$, $\pi \in \mathfrak{S}_n$, then describes a set of linear inequalities and, hence, a convex subset of E^{2n}. Obviously these cells form a cell division of E^{2n}. There are $n!$ cells of dimension $2n$, defined by $(\pi(1) \prec \pi(2) \prec \ldots \prec \pi(n))$.

The dimension of a cell defined by some sequence is easily calculated from the number of times the different signs $\prec, \triangleq, =$ are employed in the sequence. The permutations $\pi \in \mathfrak{S}_n$ under $\pi(p_1, \ldots, p_n) = (p_{\pi(1)}, \ldots, p_{\pi(n)})$ form a group of cellular operations on E^{2n}. The quotient space $\hat{E}^{2n} = E^{2n}/\mathfrak{S}_n$ inherits the cell decomposition. The following example shows how we denote the projected cells:

$$(\pi(1) \prec \pi(2) \triangleq \pi(3) \ldots = \pi(n)) \mapsto (\prec \triangleq \ldots =).$$

(Just omit the numbers $\pi(i)$.) $\mathfrak{S}_n$ operates freely on $E^{2n} - \Lambda$, where Λ is the $(2n - 2)$-dimensional subcomplex consisting of cells defined by sequences in which the sign $=$ occurs at least once. The projection q: $E^{2n} \to \hat{E}^{2n}$ then maps Λ onto a $(2n-2)$-subcomplex $\hat{\Lambda}$ of $\hat{E}^{2n}$, and q: $E^{2n} - \Lambda \to \hat{E}^{2n} - \hat{\Lambda}$ describes a regular covering of an open $2n$-dimensional manifold with $\mathfrak{S}_n$ as its group of covering transformations. $\hat{E}^{2n}$ is called a *configurationspace*.

10.13 Proposition. $\pi_1(\hat{E}^{2n} - \hat{\Lambda}) \cong \mathfrak{B}_n$, $\pi_1(E^{2n} - \Lambda) \cong \mathfrak{J}_n$.

Proof. Choose a base point $\hat{P}$ in the (one) $2n$-cell of $\hat{E}^{2n} - \hat{\Lambda}$ and some P, $q(P) = \hat{P}$. A braid $\mathfrak{z} \in \mathfrak{B}_n$ then defines a loop in $\hat{E}^{2n} - \hat{\Lambda}$, with base point $\hat{P} = q(P_1, \ldots, P_n) = q(Q_1, \ldots, Q_n)$. Two such loops $\mathfrak{z}_t = q(p_1(t), \ldots, p_n(t))$, $\mathfrak{z}'_t = q(p'_1(t), \ldots, p'_n(t))$, $0 \leqq t \leqq 1$, are homotopic relative to $\hat{P}$, if there is a continuous family $\mathfrak{z}_t(s)$, $0 \leqq s \leqq 1$, with $\mathfrak{z}_t(0) = \mathfrak{z}_t$, $\mathfrak{z}_t(1) = \mathfrak{z}'_t$, $\mathfrak{z}_0(s) = \mathfrak{z}_1(s) = \hat{P}$. This homotopy relation $\mathfrak{z}_t \sim \mathfrak{z}'_t$ coincides with Artin's definition of s-isotopy for braids $\mathfrak{z}_t$, $\mathfrak{z}'_t$ [Artin 1947].

It can be shown by using simplicial approximation arguments that s-isotopy is equivalent to the notion of isotopy as defined in Definition 10.1, which would prove 10.13. We shall omit the proof; instead we show that $\pi_1(\hat{E}^{2n} - \hat{\Lambda})$ can be computed directly from its cell decomposition (see [Fox-Neuwirth 1962]).

We already chose a base point $\hat{P}$ in the interior of the only $2n$-cell $\hat{\lambda} = (\prec \ldots \prec)$. There are $n-1$ cells $\hat{\lambda}_i$ of dimension $2n-1$ corresponding to sequences where the sign $\triangleq$ occurs once $(\prec \ldots \triangleq \ldots \prec)$ at the i-th position.

Think of $\hat{P}$ as a 0-cell dual to $\hat{\lambda}$, and denote by σ_i, $1 \leqq i \leqq n-1$, the 1-cells dual to $\hat{\lambda}_i$. By a suitable choice of orientation σ_i will represent the elementary braid. Figure 10.13 describes a loop σ_i which intersects $\hat{\lambda}_i$ at $t = \frac{1}{2}$.

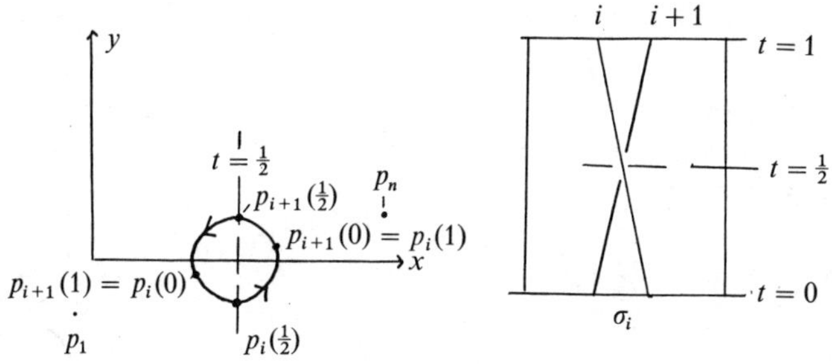

Fig. 10.13

It follows that the σ_i are generators of $\pi_1(\hat{E}^{2n} - \hat{\Lambda})$. Defining relators are obtained by looking at the 2-cells $\hat{r}_{ik}$ dual to the $(2n-2)$-cells $\hat{\lambda}_{ik}$ of $\hat{E}^{2n} - \hat{\Lambda}$ which are characterized by sequences in which two signs $\triangleq$ occur: $\hat{\lambda}_{ik} = (\prec \ldots \prec \triangleq \prec \ldots \prec \triangleq \prec \ldots)$ at position i and k, $1 \leqq i < k \leqq n-1$. The geometric situation will be quite different in the two cases $k = i+1$ and $k > i+1$.

Consider a plane γ transversal to $\hat{\lambda}_{i,i+1}$ in $\hat{E}^{2n} - \hat{\Lambda}$. One may describe it as the plane defined by the equations $x_i + x_{i+1} + x_{i+2} = 0$, $x_j = 0$, $j \neq i, i+1, i+2$. Figure 10.14 shows γ as an (x_i, x_{i+1})-plane with lines defined by $x_i = x_{i+1}$, $x_i = x_{i+2}$, $x_{i+1} = x_{i+2}$.

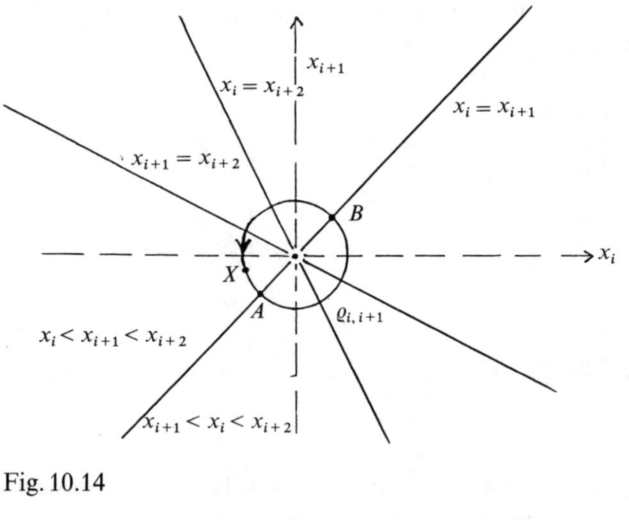

Fig. 10.14

The origin of the (x_i, x_{i+1})-plane is $\gamma \cap \hat{\lambda}_{i,i+1}$ and the half rays of the lines are $\gamma \cap \hat{\lambda}_j$, $i \leqq j \leqq i+2$. We represent the points of $\gamma \cap \hat{\lambda}$ by ordered triples. We choose some point X in $x_i < x_{i+1} < x_{i+2}$ to begin with, and let it run along a simple closed curve $\varrho_{i,i+1}$ around the origin (Fig. 10.14). Traversing $x_i = x_{i+1}$ corresponds to a generator $\sigma_i = (\ldots \triangleq \prec \ldots)$, the point on $\varrho_{i,i+1}$ enters the $2n$-cell $x_{i+1} < x_i < x_{i+2}$ after that. The following diagram describes the whole curcuit $\varrho_{i,i+1}$:

$x_i < x_{i+1} < x_{i+2}$

$(.. \triangleq \prec ..) \Leftrightarrow \sigma_i$

$x_{i+1} < x_i < x_{i+2}$

$(.. \prec \triangleq ..) \Leftrightarrow \sigma_{i+1}$

$x_{i+1} < x_{i+2} < x_i$

$(.. \triangleq \prec ..) \Leftrightarrow \sigma_i$

$x_{i+2} < x_{i+1} < x_i$

$(.. \prec \triangleq ..) \Leftrightarrow \sigma_{i+1}^{-1}$

$x_{i+2} < x_i < x_{i+1}$

$(.. \triangleq \prec ..) \Leftrightarrow \sigma_i^{-1}$

$x_i < x_{i+2} < x_{i+1}$

$(.. \prec \triangleq ..) \Leftrightarrow \sigma_{i+1}^{-1}$

$x_i < x_{i+1} < x_{i+2}$

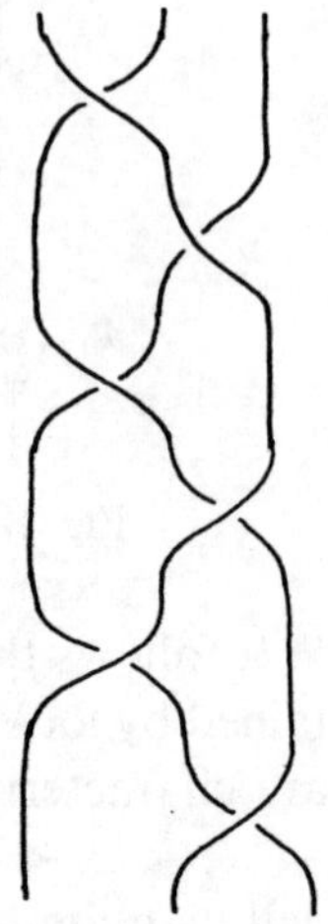

Fig. 10.15

Thus we get: $\varrho_{i,i+1} = \sigma_i \sigma_{i+1} \sigma_i \sigma_{i+1}^{-1} \sigma_i^{-1} \sigma_{i+1}^{-1}$. Whether to use σ_i or σ_i^{-1} can be decided in the following way. In the cross-section γ coordinates x_j, y_j different from x_i, x_{i+1}, x_{i+2} are kept fixed. Thus we have always $y_i < y_{i+1} < y_{i+2}$. Now Figure 10.16 shows the movement of the points $p_i, p_{i+1}, p_{i+2} \in E^2$ at the points A and B of Figure 10.14.

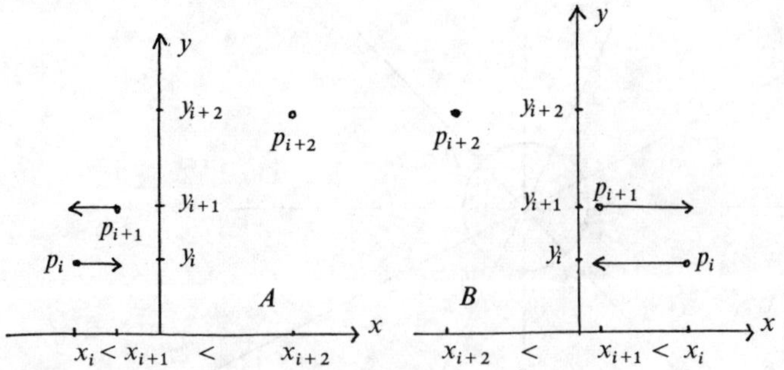

Fig. 10.16

The same procedure applies to the case $k > i + 1$. Here the cross-section to $\hat{\lambda}_{i,k}$ can be described by the solutions of the equations $x_i + x_{i+1} = x_k + x_{k+1} = 0$. We use an (x_i, x_k)-plane and again $\gamma \cap \hat{\lambda}_{i,k}$ is the origin and the coordinate half-rays represent $\gamma \cap \hat{\lambda}_i$, $\gamma \cap \hat{\lambda}_k$ (Fig. 10.17).

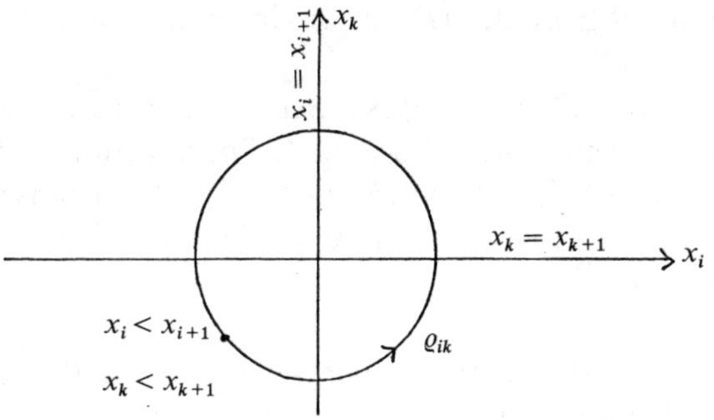

Fig. 10.17

It is left to the reader to verify for $i+1 < k$ that

$$\varrho_{ik} = \sigma_i \sigma_k \sigma_i^{-1} \sigma_k^{-1}.$$

The boundaries $\partial \hat{r}_{ik}$ are homotopic to ϱ_{ik}, thus we have again obtained the standard presentation of the braid group (see 10.3), $\mathfrak{B}_n = \langle \sigma_1, \ldots, \sigma_{n-1} | \varrho_{ik} \ (1 \leqq i < k \leqq n-1) \rangle$. By definition $\pi_1(E^{2n} - \Lambda) \cong \mathfrak{J}_n$. □

A presentation of $\mathfrak{J}_n$ might be obtained in the same way by studying the cell-complex $E^{2n} - \Lambda$, but it is more easily derived from the normal form (Proposition 10.11).

Fadell and Neuwirth [1962] have shown that $\hat{E}^{2n} - \hat{\Lambda}$ is aspherical; in fact, $\hat{E}^{2n} - \hat{\Lambda}$ is a $2n$-dimensional open manifold and a $K(\mathfrak{B}_n, 1)$ space. From this it follows by the argument used in 3.27 that $\mathfrak{B}_n$ has no elements $\neq 1$ of finite order.

10.14 Proposition. *The braid group $\mathfrak{B}_n$ is torsion free.*

We give a proof of this theorem using a result of Waldhausen [1967].

Proof. Let V be a solid torus with meridian m and longitude ℓ and $\hat{\mathfrak{z}} \subset V$ a closed braid derived from an n-braid $\mathfrak{z}$ of finite order k, $\mathfrak{z}^k = 1$. The embedding $\hat{\mathfrak{z}} \subset V$ is chosen in such a way that $\hat{\mathfrak{z}}$ meets each meridional disk D in exactly n points. For some open tubular neighbourhood $U(\hat{\mathfrak{z}})$ then $\pi_1(V - U(\hat{\mathfrak{z}})) \cong \mathfrak{Z} \ltimes \pi_1 D_n$, $D_n = D \cap (V - U(\hat{\mathfrak{z}}))$, where $\mathfrak{Z} (= \langle t \rangle)$ resp. $\pi_1 D_n (= \mathfrak{N})$ are free groups of rank 1 resp. n. The generator t can be represented by the longitude ℓ (compare Corollary 5.4). There is a k-fold cyclic covering

$$p: (\hat{V} - \hat{U}(\hat{\mathfrak{z}}^k)) \to (V - U(\hat{\mathfrak{z}}))$$

corresponding to the normal subgroup $(t^k) \ltimes \mathfrak{N} \lhd (t) \ltimes \mathfrak{N}$. Now $(t^k) \ltimes \mathfrak{N} = (t^k) \times \mathfrak{N}$ since $\mathfrak{z}^k$ is the trivial braid. From this it follows that $\pi_1(V - U(\hat{\mathfrak{z}}))$ has a non-trivial centre containing the infinite cyclic subgroup $\langle t^k \rangle$ generated by t^k

which is not contained in $\mathfrak{N} \cong \pi_1 D_n$. ($D_n$ is an incompressible surface in $V - U(\hat{\mathfrak{z}})$.)

By [Waldhausen 1967, Satz 4.1] $V - U(\hat{\mathfrak{z}})$ is a Seifert fibre space, $\langle t^k \rangle$ is the centre of $\pi_1(V - U(\hat{\mathfrak{z}}))$ and t^k represents a fibre $\simeq \ell^k$. The fibration of $V - U(\hat{\mathfrak{z}})$ can be extended to a fibration of V [Burde-Murasugi 1970]. This means that $\hat{\mathfrak{z}}$ is a torus link $\mathrm{t}(a, b) = \hat{\mathfrak{z}}$. It follows that $\hat{\mathfrak{z}}^k = \mathrm{t}(a, kb)$. Since $\mathfrak{z}^k$ is trivial, we get $kb = 0$, $b = 0$, and $\mathfrak{z} = 1$. □

The proof given above is a special version of an argument used in the proof of a more general theorem in [Murasugi 1982].

D Braids and Links

In Chapter 2, Section D we have described the procedure of *closing* a braid $\mathfrak{z}$ (see Fig. 2.10). The closed braid obtained from $\mathfrak{z}$ is denoted by $\hat{\mathfrak{z}}$ and its axis by b.

10.15 Definition. Two *closed braids* $\hat{\mathfrak{z}}, \hat{\mathfrak{z}}'$ in $\mathbb{R}^3$ are called *equivalent*, if they possess a common axis b, and if there is an orientation preserving homeomorphism $f: \mathbb{R}^3 \to \mathbb{R}^3$, $f(\hat{\mathfrak{z}}) = \hat{\mathfrak{z}}'$, which keeps the axis b pointwise fixed.

Of course, $\mathbb{R}^3$ may again be replaced by S^3 and the axis by a trivial knot. Artin [1925] already noticed the following:

10.16 Proposition. *Two closed braids $\hat{\mathfrak{z}}, \hat{\mathfrak{z}}'$ are equivalent if and only if $\mathfrak{z}$ and $\mathfrak{z}'$ are conjugate in $\mathfrak{B}_n$.*

Proof. If $\mathfrak{z}$ and $\mathfrak{z}'$ are conjugate, the equivalence of $\hat{\mathfrak{z}}$ and $\hat{\mathfrak{z}}'$ is evident. Observe that a closed braid $\hat{\mathfrak{z}}$ can be obtained from several braids which differ by a cyclic permutation of their words in the generators σ_i, and hence are conjugate.

If $\hat{\mathfrak{z}}$ and $\hat{\mathfrak{z}}'$ are equivalent, we may assume that the homeomorphism $f: \mathbb{R}^3 \to \mathbb{R}^3, f(\hat{\mathfrak{z}}) = \hat{\mathfrak{z}}'$, is constant outside a sufficiently large cube containing $\hat{\mathfrak{z}}$ and $\hat{\mathfrak{z}}'$. Since b is also kept fixed, we may choose an unknotted solid torus V containing $\hat{\mathfrak{z}}, \hat{\mathfrak{z}}'$ and restrict f to $f: V \to V$ with $f(x) = x$ for $x \in \partial V$. (We already used this construction at the end of the preceding section.) Let t again be a longitude of ∂V, and $\mathfrak{F}_n \cong \pi_1 D_n$ the free group of rank n. There is a homeomorphism $z: D_n \to D_n$, $z | \partial D_n = id$, inducing the braid automorphism ζ of $\mathfrak{z}$, and $V - U(\hat{\mathfrak{z}}) = (D_n \times I)/z$, $\pi_1(V - U(\hat{\mathfrak{z}})) \cong \langle t \rangle \ltimes \mathfrak{F}_n$, compare 5.2, 10.5, 10.6. For the presentation

$$\pi_1(V - U(\hat{\mathfrak{z}})) = \langle t, u_i \mid t u_i t^{-1} = \zeta(u_i) \rangle, \quad 1 \leqq i \leqq n,$$

choose a base point on $\partial V \cap D_n$ and define the generators $\{u_i\}$ of $\pi_1 D_n$ by a normal dissection of D_n (see 10.4).

The automorphism ζ is then defined with respect to these geometrically distinguished generators $\{u_i\}$ up to conjugation in the group of braid-automorphisms. The class of braid automorphisms conjugate to ζ is then invariant under the mapping

$$f\colon (V - U(\hat{\mathfrak{z}})) \to (V - U(\hat{\mathfrak{z}}')).$$

and, hence, the defining braids $\mathfrak{z}$, $\mathfrak{z}'$ must be conjugate. □

The conjugacy problem in $\mathfrak{B}_n$ is thus equivalent to the problem of classifying closed braids. There have been, therefore, many attempts since Artin's paper in 1925 to solve it, and some partial solutions had been attained [Fröhlich 1936], until in [Makanin 1968], [Garside 1969] the problem was solved completely. Garside invented an ingenious though rather complicated algorithm by which he can decide whether two braids are conjugate or not. This solution implies a new solution of the word problem by way of a new normal form. We do not intend to copy his proof which does not seem to allow any essential simplification (see also [Birman 1974]).

Alexander's theorem (Proposition 2.9) can be combined with Artin's characterization of braid automorphisms (Proposition 10.7) to give a characterization of link groups in terms of special presentations.

10.17 Proposition. *A group $\mathfrak{G}$ is the fundamental group $\pi_1(S^3 - \mathfrak{l})$ for some link $\mathfrak{l}$ (a link group) if and only if there is a presentation of the form*

$$\mathfrak{G} = \langle S_i \mid S_i^{-1} L_i S_{\pi(i)} L_i^{-1} \rangle, \quad 1 \leqq i \leqq n,$$

with π a permutation and $\prod_{i=1}^{n} S_i = \prod_{i=1}^{n} L_i S_{\pi(i)} L_i^{-1}$ in the free group generated by $\{S_i \mid 1 \leqq i \leqq n\}$. □

A group theoretical characterization of knot groups $\pi_1(S^n - S^{n-2})$ has been given by Kervaire [1965] for $n \geqq 5$ only. Kervaire's characterization includes $H_1(S^n - S^{n-2}) \cong \mathbb{Z}$, $H_2(\pi_1(S^n - S^{n-2})) = 0$, and that $\pi_1(S^n - S^{n-2})$ is finitely generated and the normal closure of one element. All these conditions are fulfilled in dimensions 3 and 4 too. For $n = 4$ the characterization is correct modulo a Poincaré conjecture, but for $n = 3$ it is definitely not sufficient. There is an example $G = \langle x, y \mid x^2yx^{-1}y^{-1} \rangle$ given in [Rolfson 1976] which satisfies all conditions, but its Jacobian (see Proposition 9.10)

$$\left(\left(\frac{\partial x^2yx^{-1}y^{-1}}{\partial x} \right)^{\varphi\psi}, \left(\frac{\partial x^2yx^{-1}y^{-1}}{\partial y} \right)^{\varphi\psi} \right) = (2 - t, 0),$$

$x^{\varphi\psi} = 1$, $y^{\varphi\psi} = t$, lacks symmetry. It seems to be a natural requirement to include a symmetry condition in a characterization of classical knot groups $\pi_1(S^3 - S^1)$.

We conclude this chapter by some remarks on closed braids and links defined by them. For a thorough, more complete treatment of the subject see [Birman 1974].

It is evident that two non-equivalent closed braids $\hat{\mathfrak{z}}$, $\hat{\mathfrak{z}}'$ may represent equivalent knots (or links) if the axis of the closed braids is disregarded. For instance $\hat{\sigma}_1$, $\hat{\sigma}_1^{-1}$ both represent an unknotted circle, but σ_1 and σ_1^{-1} are not conjugate in $\mathfrak{B}_2$.

Before presenting more sophisticated examples of this kind we want to mention a positive result. By Alexander's theorem (Proposition 2.9) we know that every link can be presented as a closed braid. Unfortunately this can be done in many ways, but A. A. Markov [1936, 1945] proved a theorem of the following form: Two closed braids $\hat{\mathfrak{z}}$, $\hat{\mathfrak{z}}'$ are equivalent as links if and only if they are connected by a finite sequence of certain elementary moves which Markov specifies. These moves, of course, will in some instances make the link cut through the axis. Moreover the number of strings of the braids may be changed. A proof of the theorem is given in J. Birman's book [Birman 1974].

We return to the braid group $\mathfrak{B}_n$. Let the braid automorphisms operate on the free group $\mathfrak{F}_n$ of rank n with free generators $\{S_i\}$, $\{S_i'\}$, $S_i' = \zeta(S_i)$ such that (1) and (3) in 10.7 are valid. There is a ring homomorphism

$$\varphi\colon \mathbb{Z}\mathfrak{F}_n \to \mathbb{Z}\mathfrak{Z}, \quad \mathfrak{Z} = \langle t \rangle,$$

defined by: $\varphi(S_i) = t$, mapping the group ring $\mathbb{Z}\mathfrak{F}_n$ onto the group ring $\mathbb{Z}\mathfrak{Z}$ of an infinite cyclic group $\mathfrak{Z}$ generated by t.

10.18 Proposition ([Burau 1936]). *The mapping $\beta\colon \mathfrak{B}_n \to GL(n, \mathbb{Z}\mathfrak{Z})$ defined by $\zeta \mapsto \left(\left(\frac{\partial \zeta(S_j)}{\partial S_i}\right)^{\varphi}\right)$ is a homomorphism of the braid group $\mathfrak{B}_n$ into the group of $n \times n$-matrices over $\mathbb{Z}\mathfrak{Z}$.*

$$\beta(\sigma_i) = \begin{array}{c} \begin{array}{cccc} & i & i+1 & \end{array} \\ \left(\begin{array}{cccc} E & & & \\ & 1-t & t & \\ & 1 & 0 & \\ & & & E \end{array}\right) \end{array} \begin{array}{l} \\ \\ i \\ i+1 \\ \\ \end{array}, \quad 1 \leqq i \leqq n.$$

β is called the Burau representation.

The *proof* of 10.18 is a simple consequence of the chain rule for Jacobians:

$$\zeta(S_i) = S_i', \quad \zeta'(S_k') = S_k'',$$

$$\frac{\partial S_k''}{\partial S_i} = \sum_{j=1}^{n} \frac{\partial S_k''}{\partial S_j'} \frac{\partial S_j'}{\partial S_i}.$$

The calculation of $\beta(\sigma_i)$ (and $\beta(\sigma_i^{-1})$) is left to the reader. □

The Burau-matrices $\beta(\zeta)$ have some interesting properties:

10.19 Proposition. $\sum_{j=1}^{n}\left(\frac{\partial\zeta(S_i)}{\partial S_j}\right)^{\varphi}=1,\quad \sum_{i=1}^{n} t^{i-1}\cdot\left(\frac{\partial\zeta(S_i)}{\partial S_j}\right)^{\varphi}=t^{j-1}.$

Again the *proof* becomes trivial by using the Fox calculus. The fundamental formula yields

$$(\zeta(S_i)-1)^{\varphi}=t-1=\sum_{j=1}^{n}\left(\frac{\partial\zeta(S_i)}{\partial S_j}\right)^{\varphi}(t-1).$$

For the second equation we exploit $\prod_{i=1}^{n}\zeta(S_i)=\prod_{i=1}^{n}S_i$ in $\mathfrak{F}_n$:

$$\left(\frac{\partial}{\partial S_j}\prod_{i=1}^{n}\zeta(S_i)\right)^{\varphi}=\sum_{i=1}^{n}t^{i-1}\left(\frac{\partial\zeta(S_i)}{\partial S_j}\right)^{\varphi}=\left(\frac{\partial}{\partial S_j}\prod_{i=1}^{n}S_i\right)^{\varphi}=t^{j-1}.\quad\square$$

The equations of 10.19 express a linear dependence between the rows and columns of the representing matrices. This makes it possible to reduce the degree n of the representation by one. If $C(t)$ is a representing matrix, we get:

(5) $$S^{-1}C(t)S=\begin{pmatrix} & & 0\\ & & 0\\ B(t) & & \\ & & 0\\ **\ldots* & & 1\end{pmatrix},$$

$$S=\begin{pmatrix}1 & 1 & \ldots & 1\\ & 1 & \ldots & 1\\ & & & \\ 0 & & \ldots & 1\end{pmatrix},\quad S^{-1}=\begin{pmatrix}1 & -1 & \ldots & & 0\\ \vdots & 1 & -1 & & \vdots\\ \vdots & & & & \vdots\\ \vdots & & & 1 & -1\\ 0 & \ldots & & \ldots & 1\end{pmatrix}.$$

This is easily verified and it follows that by setting

$$\hat{\beta}(\zeta)=B(t)$$

we obtain a representation of $\mathfrak{B}_n$ in $GL(n-1,\mathbb{Z}\mathfrak{Z})$ which is called the *reduced Burau representation*. Note that

$$\hat{\beta}(\sigma_1)=\left(\begin{array}{cc|c}-t & 0 & \\ 1 & 1 & \\ \hline & & E\end{array}\right),$$

$$\hat\beta(\sigma_i) = \begin{pmatrix} E & & \overset{i}{} & & \\ & 1 & t & 0 & \\ & 0 & -t & 0 & \\ & 0 & 1 & 1 & \\ & & & & E \end{pmatrix}, \qquad 1 < i < n-1,$$

$$\hat\beta(\sigma_{n-1}) = \left(\begin{array}{c|cc} E & & \\ \hline & 1 & t \\ & 0 & -t \end{array}\right)$$

($\hat\beta(\sigma_1) = (t)$ for $n = 2$).

In addition to the advantage of reducing the degree from n to $n-1$, the reduced representation $\hat\beta$ has the property of mapping the centre of $\mathfrak{B}_n$ into the centre of $GL(n-1, \mathbb{Z}\mathfrak{Z})$

$$\hat\beta(\sigma_1 \ldots \sigma_{n-1})^n = \begin{pmatrix} t^n & & 0 \\ & t^n & \\ 0 & & \ddots \; t^n \end{pmatrix}.$$

The original β maps the centre on non-diagonal matrices.

The algebraic level of these representations is clearly that of the Alexander module (Chapter 8 A). There should be a connection.

10.20 Proposition. *For* $\mathfrak{z} \in \mathfrak{B}_n$, $\beta(\mathfrak{z}) = C(t)$, *the matrix* $(C(t) - E)$ *is a Jacobian* (*see* 9.10) *of the link* $\hat{\mathfrak{z}}$. *Furthermore:*

$$\det(B(t) - E) \doteq \nabla(t)\,(1 + t + \ldots + t^{n-1})\,(1-t)^{\mu-1},$$

where $\nabla(t)$ *is the Hosokawa-polynomial of* $\hat{\mathfrak{z}}$ (*see* 9.18), *and* μ *the multiplicity of* $\hat{\mathfrak{z}}$.

Proof. The first assertion is an immediate consequence of 10.17. The second part is a bit harder. (It was first proved in [Burau 1936].)

The matrix $(C(t) - E)S$ (see (5)) is a matrix with the n-th column consisting of zeroes – this is a consequence of the first identity in 10.19. If the vector $\mathfrak{a}_i$ denotes the i-th row of $(C(t) - E)$, the second identity can be expressed by $\sum_{i=1}^{n} t^{i-1}\mathfrak{a}_i = 0$-vector. Hence

$$(6) \qquad \sum_{i=1}^{n} t^{i-1}\mathfrak{d}_i = 0,$$

where $\mathfrak{d}_i$ denotes the vector composed of the first $n-1$ components of $\mathfrak{a}_i S$.

Now $\det(B(t) - E) = \det(\mathfrak{d}_1 - \mathfrak{d}_2, \mathfrak{d}_2 - \mathfrak{d}_3, \ldots, \mathfrak{d}_{n-1} - \mathfrak{d}_n)$ (compare (5)). From this we get that

$$\pm\det(B(t)-E) = \det(\mathfrak{d}_2-\mathfrak{d}_1, \mathfrak{d}_3-\mathfrak{d}_1, \ldots, \mathfrak{d}_n-\mathfrak{d}_1) =$$
$$= \det(\mathfrak{d}_2, \mathfrak{d}_3, \ldots, \mathfrak{d}_n) + \sum_{i=1}^{n-1} \det(\mathfrak{d}_2, \ldots, \mathfrak{d}_i, (-\mathfrak{d}_1), \ldots, \mathfrak{d}_n) =$$
$$= \det(\mathfrak{d}_2, \ldots, \mathfrak{d}_n) + \sum_{i=1}^{n-1} \det(\mathfrak{d}_2, \ldots, t^i\mathfrak{d}_{i+1}, \ldots, \mathfrak{d}_n) =$$
$$= (1 + \mathrm{t} + \ldots + \mathrm{t}^{n-1})\nabla(t)(t-1)^{\mu-1}.$$

The last equation follows from 9.18 since $\det(\mathfrak{d}_2, \ldots, \mathfrak{d}_n)$ by (6) generates the first elementary ideal of $\hat{\mathfrak{z}}$. □

The pairs of non-conjugate closed braids defining the same links or knots are numerous. J. Birman [1969″] gave the following class of examples. Let $\mathfrak{z}^{(n-1)} \in \mathfrak{B}_{n-1} \subset \mathfrak{B}_n$ be any braid, then $\mathfrak{z}^{(n-1)}\sigma_{n-1}$ and $\mathfrak{z}^{(n-1)}\sigma_{n-1}^{-1}$ define equivalent links (Fig. 10.18). The determinant of $B(t) = \hat{\beta}(\mathfrak{z})$ is invariant under conjugation of $\mathfrak{z}$, but $\det\hat{\beta}(\mathfrak{z}^{(n-1)}\sigma_{n-1}) = t^2 \cdot \det\hat{\beta}(\mathfrak{z}^{(n-1)}\sigma_{n-1}^{-1})$.

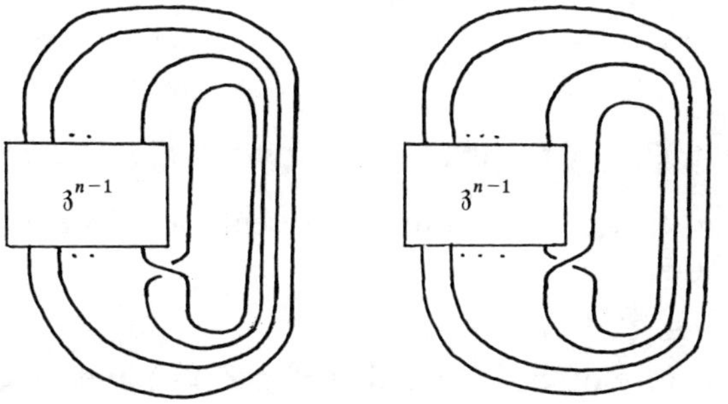

Fig. 10.18

This construction can, of course, be iterated [Birman 1969″].

The determinant det $B(t)$ is one of the coefficients of the characteristic polynomial of $B(t)$ which are all invariants of the conjugacy class. They do not suffice to distinguish conjugacy classes, as the braids $\sigma_1^{-1}\sigma_2^2\sigma_1^{-2}\sigma_2$, $\sigma_2\sigma_1^{-2}\sigma_2^2\sigma_1^{-1}$ show [Murasugi-Thomas 1972].

E History and Sources

There are few theories in mathematics the origin and author of which can be named so definitely as in the case of braids: Emil Artin invented them in his famous paper "Theorie der Zöpfe" in 1925. (O. Schreier, who was helpful with some proofs, should, nevertheless be mentioned.) This paper already contains the fundamental isomorphism between braids and braid automorphisms by which braids are classified. The proof, though, is not satisfying. Artin published a new paper on braids in 1947 with rigorous definitions and proofs including the normal form of a braid. The remaining problem was the conjugacy problem.

The importance of the braid group in other fields became evident in Magnus' paper on the mapping class groups of surfaces [Magnus 1934]. Further contributions in that direction were made by J. Birman and H. Hilden. There have been continual contributions to braid theory by several authors. For a bibliography see [Birman 1974]. The outstanding work was doubtless Makanin's and Garside's solution of the conjugacy problem [Makanin 1968], [Garside 1969].

Braid theory from the point of view of configuration spaces [Fadell-Neuwirth 1962] assigns braid groups to manifolds – the original braid group then is the braid group of the plane $\mathbb{R}^2$. This approach has been successfully applied [Arnol'd 1969] to determine the homology and cohomology groups of braid groups.

F Exercises

E 10.1 (Artin) Prove that $\mathfrak{B}_n = \langle \sigma, \tau \mid \sigma^n (\sigma\tau)^{n-1}, [\sigma^i \tau \sigma^{-i}, \tau] \rangle$, $2 \leqq i \leqq \frac{n}{2}$, $\sigma = \sigma_1 \sigma_2 \dots \sigma_{n-1}$, $\tau = \sigma_1$. Derive from this presentation a presentation of the symmetric groups $\mathfrak{S}_n$.

E 10.2 $\mathfrak{B}_n/\mathfrak{B}'_n \cong \mathfrak{Z}$, $\mathfrak{I}_n/\mathfrak{I}'_n \cong \mathfrak{Z}^{\binom{n}{2}}$

E 10.3 Let $Z(\mathfrak{B}_n)$ be the centre of $\mathfrak{B}_n$. Prove that $\mathfrak{z}^m \in Z(\mathfrak{B}_n)$ and $\mathfrak{z} \in \mathfrak{I}_n$ imply $\mathfrak{z} \in Z(\mathfrak{B}_n)$.

E 10.4 Interpret $\mathfrak{I}_n$ as a group of automorphisms of $\mathfrak{F}_n$ and denote by $\mathfrak{T}_n$ the inner automorphisms of $\mathfrak{F}_n$. Show that

$$\mathfrak{T}_n \mathfrak{I}_n / \mathfrak{T}_n = \mathfrak{T}_{n-1} \mathfrak{I}_{n-1}, \quad \mathfrak{T}_n \cap \mathfrak{I}_n = Z(\mathfrak{I}_n) = \text{centre of } \mathfrak{I}_n.$$

Derive from this that $\mathfrak{T}_n \mathfrak{I}_n$ has no elements of finite order $\neq 1$.

E 10.5 (Garside) Show that every braid $\mathfrak{z}$ can be written in the form

$$\sigma = \sigma_{i_1}^{a_1} \dots \sigma_{i_r}^{a_r} \Delta^k, \; a_i \geqq 1, \text{ with } \Delta = (\sigma_1 \dots \sigma_{n-1})(\sigma_1 \dots \sigma_{n-2}) \dots (\sigma_2 \sigma_1) \sigma_1$$

the *fundamental braid*, k an integer.

E 10.6 Show that the Burau representation β and its reduced version $\hat{\beta}$ are equivalent under $\beta(\mathfrak{z}) \mapsto \hat{\beta}(\mathfrak{z})$. The representations are faithful for $n \leqq 3$.

E 10.7 Show that the notion of isotopy of braids as defined in 10.1 is equivalent to s-isotopy of braids as used in the proof of 10.13.

Chapter 11: Manifolds as Branched Coverings

The first section contains a treatment of Alexander's theorem [Alexander 1920] (Theorem 11.1). It makes use of the theory of braids and plats. The second part of this chapter is devoted to the Hilden-Montesinos theorem (Theorem 11.11) which improves Alexander's result in the case of 3-manifolds. We give a proof following H. Hilden [1976], but prefer to think of the links as plats. This affords a more transparent description of the geometric relations between the branch sets and the Heegaard splittings of the covering manifolds. The Dehn-Lickorish theorem (Theorem 11.7) is used but not proved here.

A Alexander's Theorem

11.1 Theorem (Alexander [1920]). *Every orientable closed 3-manifold is a branched covering of S^3, branched along a link with branching indices $\leqq 2$. (Compare 8.18.)*

Proof. Let M^3 be an arbitrary closed oriented manifold with a finite simplicial structure. Define a map p on its vertices $\hat{P}_i$, $1 \leqq i \leqq N$, $p(\hat{P}_i) = P_i \in S^3$, such that the P_i are in general position in S^3. After choosing an orientation for S^3 we extend p to a map $p\colon M^3 \to S^3$ by the following rule. For any positively oriented 3-simplex $[\hat{P}_{i_1}, \hat{P}_{i_2}, \hat{P}_{i_3}, \hat{P}_{i_4}]$ of M^3 we define p as the affine mapping

$$p\colon [\hat{P}_{i_1}, \hat{P}_{i_2}, \hat{P}_{i_3}, \hat{P}_{i_4}] \to [P_{i_1}, P_{i_2}, P_{i_3}, P_{i_4}],$$

if $[P_{i_1}, P_{i_2}, P_{i_3}, P_{i_4}]$ is positively oriented in S^3; if not, we choose the complement $C[P_{i_1}, P_{i_2}, P_{i_3}, P_{i_4}]$ as image,

$$p\colon [\hat{P}_{i_1}, \hat{P}_{i_2}, \hat{P}_{i_3}, \hat{P}_{i_4}] \to C[P_{i_1}, P_{i_2}, P_{i_3}, P_{i_4}].$$

We will show that p is a branched covering, the 1-skeleton M^1 of M^3 being mapped by p onto the branching set $p(M^1) = T \subset S^3$. For every point $P \in S^3 - p(M^2)$, M^2 the 2-skeleton of M^3, there is a neighbourhood $U \subset S^3 - p(M^2)$ containing P such that $p^{-1}(U(P))$ consists of n disjoint neighbourhoods $\hat{U}_j$ of the points $p^{-1}(P)$. Suppose $\hat{P}$ is contained in the interior of the 2-simplex $[\hat{P}_1, \hat{P}_2, \hat{P}_3]$, in the boundary of $[\hat{P}_0, \hat{P}_1, \hat{P}_2, \hat{P}_3]$ and $[\hat{P}_1, \hat{P}_2, \hat{P}_3, \hat{P}_4]$. Let $[P_0, P_1, P_2, P_3]$ be positively oriented in S^3. If P_0 and P_4 are separated by the plane defined by $[P_1, P_2, P_3]$, we get that

$$p[\hat{P}_0, \hat{P}_1, \hat{P}_2, \hat{P}_3] = [P_0, P_1, P_2, P_3],$$
$$p[\hat{P}_1, \hat{P}_2, \hat{P}_3, \hat{P}_4] = [P_1, P_2, P_3, P_4];$$

if not

$$p[\hat{P}_0, \hat{P}_1, \hat{P}_2, \hat{P}_3] = [P_0, P_1, P_2, P_3],$$
$$p[\hat{P}_1, \hat{P}_2, \hat{P}_3, \hat{P}_4] = C[P_1, P_2, P_3, P_4].$$

In both cases there is a neighbourhood $\hat{U}$ of $\hat{P}$ which is mapped onto a neighbourhood U of $P = p(\hat{P})$, see Figure 11.1.

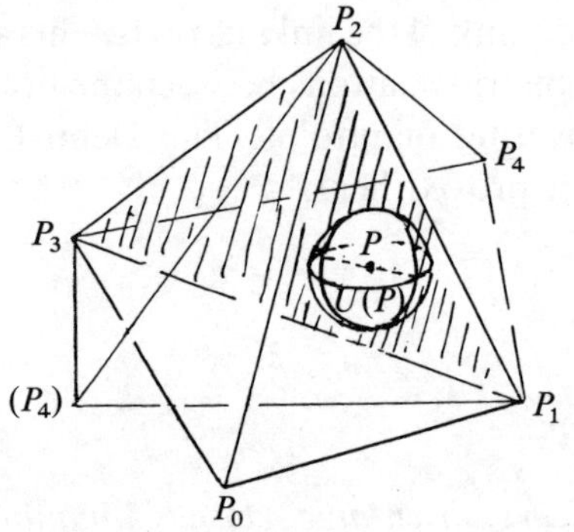

Fig. 11.1

As a consequence p: $M^3 \to S^3$ is surjective; otherwise the compact polyhedron $p(M^3) \subset S^3$ would have boundary points on $p(M^2) - p(M^1)$. It follows from the construction that $p|M^2 \to S^3$ is injective. The preimage $p^{-1}(P_i)$ of a vertex P_i consists of $\hat{P}_i$ and may-be several other points with branching index one. The same holds for the images $[P_i, P_j] = p[\hat{P}_i, \hat{P}_j]$ of edges. It remains to show that p can be modified in such a way that the branching set $T = p(M^1)$ is transformed into a link (without changing M^3).

By $U(T)$ we denote a tubular neighbourhood of $T \subset S^3$, consisting of (closed) balls B_i with centres P_i and cylindrical segments Z_{ij} with axis on $[P_i, P_j]$, and $Z_{ij} \cap B_k$ a disk δ_k for $k = i, j$ and empty otherwise. With $I = [0, 1]$, $Z_{ij} = I \times \delta$, and for $Y \in I$ the disk $Y \times \delta$ is covered by a collection of disjoint disks in M^3, of which at most one may contain a branching point $\hat{Y} \in M^1$ of index $r > 1$. The branched covering $p|$: $\hat{Y} \times \hat{\delta} \to Y \times \delta$ (for short: p: $\hat{\delta} \to \delta$) is cyclic (Fig. 11.2).

A cycle of length r may be written as a product of $r-1$ transpositions, $(12 \ldots r) = (1, 2)(2, 3) \ldots (r-1, r)$. Correspondingly there is a branched covering p': $\hat{\delta}' \to \delta$ with $r-1$ branchpoints $\hat{Y}_i$, $1 \leqq i \leqq r-1$, of index two. $\hat{\delta}'$ is a disk, and $p'|\partial\hat{\delta}' = p|\partial\hat{\delta}$. We substitute p' for p on all cylindrical segments $\hat{Z}_{ij} \subset p^{-1} Z_{ij}$ and obtain a new branched covering

$$p'\colon \overline{M^3 - \cup p^{-1}(B_i)} \to \overline{S^3 - \cup B_i}.$$

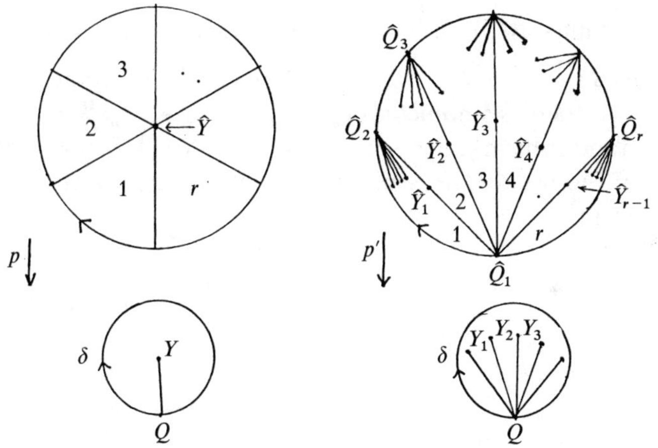

Fig. 11.2

We denote by $\hat{B}_i$ the component of $p^{-1}(B_i)$ which contains $\hat{P}_i$. The branching set consists of lines in the cylindrical segments parallel to the axis of the cylinder. $p'|\partial\hat{B}_i = \hat{S}^2 \to S^2 = \partial B_i$ is a branched covering with branching points Q_j, $1 \leqq j \leqq q$, of index two where the sphere S^2 meets the branching lines contained in the adjoining cylinders. To describe this covering we use a normal dissection of $S^2 - \bigcup_{j=1}^{q} Q_j = \Sigma_q$ joining the Q_j by simple arcs s_j to some $Q \in \Sigma_q$. (The arcs are required to be disjoint save for their common endpoint Q, Fig. 11.3)

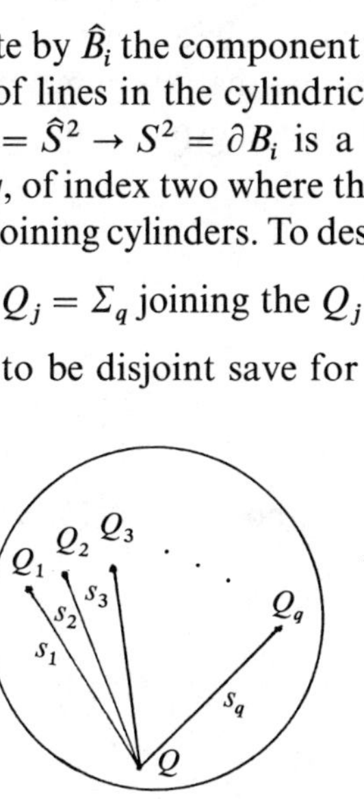

Fig. 11.3

We assign to each s_j a transposition $\tau_j \in \mathfrak{S}_n$, where n is the number of sheets of the covering p': $\hat{S}^2 \to S^2$, and $\mathfrak{S}_n$ is the symmetric group of order n. Crossing an arc of $p^{-1}(s_j)$ in $\hat{S}^2$ means changing from the k-th sheet to the $\tau_j(k)$-th sheet of the covering. Since Q is not a branch point, $\prod_{j=1}^{q} \tau_j = id$, $q = 2m$. Computing $\chi(\hat{S}^2) = 2$ gives $(n-1) = m$. On the other hand, any set of transpositions $\{\tau_j | 1 \leqq j \leqq 2m\}$ which generate a transitive subgroup of $\mathfrak{S}_n$, $n = m+1$, defines a covering p': $\hat{S}^2 \to S^2$, if $\prod_{j=1}^{2m} \tau_j = id$. We may assign generators $S_j \in \pi_1(\Sigma_{2m})$ to the arcs s_j

(see the text preceding 10.5), $\prod_{j=1}^{2m} S_j = 1$, and there is a homomorphism $\varphi\colon \pi_1 \Sigma_{2m} \to \mathfrak{S}_n$, $\varphi(S_j) = \tau_j$. Given two normal dissections $\{s_i\}$ and $\{s'_j\}$ of Σ_{2m} with respect to Q_i, Q, there is a homeomorphism $h\colon \Sigma_{2m} \to \Sigma_{2m}$, $h(s_i) = s'_j$ which induces a braid automorphism $\zeta\colon S_j \mapsto \zeta(S_j) = S'_j = L_j S_i L_j^{-1}$, $\pi(i) = j$, where π is the permutation of the braid. The generator S'_j corresponds to the arc s'_j. The commutative diagram

$$\begin{array}{ccc} \pi_1 \Sigma_{2m} & \xrightarrow{\ \zeta\ } & \pi_1 \Sigma_{2m} \\ \varphi \big\downarrow & & \big\downarrow \varphi' \\ \mathfrak{S}_n & \xrightarrow{\ \zeta^*\ } & \mathfrak{S}_n \end{array}$$

defines a mapping ζ^* called the *induced braid substitution in* $\mathfrak{S}_n$. This can be used to compute the transpositions $\tau'_j = \zeta^*(\tau_j)$ which have to be assigned to the arcs s'_j in order to define the covering $p'\colon \hat{S}^2 \to S^2$. It follows that the homeomorphism $h\colon \Sigma_{2m} \to \Sigma_{2m}$ can be extended and lifted to a homeomorphism $\hat{h}$:

$$\begin{array}{ccc} \hat{S}^2 & \xrightarrow{\ \hat{h}\ } & \hat{S}^2 \\ p' \big\downarrow & & \big\downarrow p' \\ S^2 & \xrightarrow{\ h\ } & S^2 \end{array}$$

We interrupt our proof to show that there are homeomorphisms h, $\hat{h}$ such that the τ_j are replaced by τ'_j with a special property.

11.2 Lemma. *If* $2m$ *transpositions* $\tau_i \in \mathfrak{S}_n$, $1 \leqq i \leqq 2m$, *satisfy* $\prod_{i=1}^{2m} \tau_i = id$, *then there is a braid substitution* $\zeta^*\colon \tau_i \mapsto \tau'_i$, *such that*

$$\tau'_{2j-1} = \tau'_{2j}, \quad 1 \leqq j \leqq m.$$

Proof. Denote by $\sigma_k^{*\pm 1}$ the braid substitutions in $\mathfrak{S}_n$ induced by the elementary braids $\sigma_k^{\pm 1}$ (Chapter 10 B, (2)). If $\tau_k = (ab)$, $\tau_{k+1} = (cd)$, a, b, c, d all different, the effect of $\sigma_k^{*\pm 1}$ is to interchange the transpositions: $\tau'_k = \sigma_k^{*\pm 1}(\tau_k) = \tau_{k+1}$, $\tau'_{k+1} = \sigma_k^{*\pm 1}(\tau_{k+1}) = \tau_k$. If $\tau_k = (ab)$, $\tau_{k+1} = (bc)$ then $\sigma_k^*(\tau_k) = (ac)$, $\sigma_k^*(\tau_{k+1}) = (ab)$ and $\sigma_k^{*-1}(\tau_k) = (bc)$, $\sigma_k^{*-1}(\tau_{k+1}) = (ac)$. Assume $\tau_1 = (12)$. Let $\tau_j = (1a)$ be the transposition containing the figure 1, with minimal $j > 1$. (There is such a τ_j because $\Pi \tau_i = id$.) If $j > 2$, $\tau_{j-1} = (bc)$, $b, c \neq 1$, the braid substitution $\sigma_{j-1}^{*\pm 1}$ will interchange τ_{j-1} and τ_j, if a, b, c are different. A pair $(ab) = \tau_{j-1}$, $(1a) = \tau_j$ is replaced by $(1b)$, (ab) if σ_{j-1}^* is applied, and by $(1a)$, $(1b)$, if σ_{j-1}^{*-1} is used.

Thus the sequence $\tau_1, \tau_2, \ldots, \tau_{2m}$ can be transformed by a braid substitution into (12), $(1\,i_2) \ldots (1\,i_v)$, $\tau''_{v+1}, \ldots, \tau''_{2m}$, where the τ''_j, $j > v$, do not contain the Figure 1. There is an $i_j = 2$, $2 \leqq j \leqq v$. If $j = 2$, the lemma is proved by induction. Otherwise we may replace $(1\,i_{j-1})$, (12) by (12), $(2\,i_{j-1})$ using σ^{*-1}_{j-1}. □

We are now in a position to extend the covering p': $(M^3 - \bigcup p^{-1}(\mathring{\hat{B}}_i)) \to (S^3 - \bigcup \mathring{B}_i)$ to a covering $\tilde{p}$: $M^3 \to S^3$ and complete the proof of Theorem 11.1.

We choose a homeomorphism

$$h\colon \Sigma_{2m} \to \Sigma_{2m}$$

which induces a braid automorphism $\zeta\colon \pi_1 \Sigma_{2m} \to \pi_1 \Sigma_{2m}$ satisfying Lemma 11.2: $\zeta^*(\tau_k) = \tau'_k$, $\tau'_{2j-1} = \tau'_{2j}$, $1 \leqq j \leqq m$. The homeomorphism $h\colon S^2 \to S^2$ is orientation preserving and hence there is an isotopy

$$H\colon S^2 \times I \to S^2,\ H(x,0) = x,\ H(x,1) = h(x).$$

Lift H to an isotopy

$$\hat{H}\colon \hat{S}^2 \times I \to \hat{S}^2,\ \hat{H}(x,0) = x,\ \hat{H}(x,1) = \hat{h}(x).$$

Now identify $S^2 \times 0$ and $\hat{S}^2 \times 0$ with ∂B_i and $\partial \hat{B}_i$ and extend p' to $\hat{S}^2 \times I$ by setting $p'(x,t) = (p'(x), t)$.

It is now easy to extend p' to a pair of balls $\hat{B}'_i$, B'_i with $\partial \hat{B}'_i = \hat{S}^2 \times 1$, $\partial B'_i = S^2 \times 1$. We replace the normal dissection $\{s'_j\}$ of $(S^2 \times 1) - U\{Q'_j\}$, $h(Q_j) = Q'_{\pi^{-1}(j)}$, by disjoint arcs t_j, $1 \leqq j \leqq m$, which connect Q'_{2j-1} and Q'_{2j} (Fig. 11.4.)

There is a branched covering p'': $\hat{B}'_i \to B'_i$ with a branching set consisting of m simple disjoint unknotted arcs t'_j, $t'_j \cap \partial B'_j = Q'_{2j-1} \cup Q'_{2j}$, and m disjoint disks $\delta_j \subset B'_j$ with $\partial \delta_j = t_j \cup t'_j$ (Fig. 11.4).

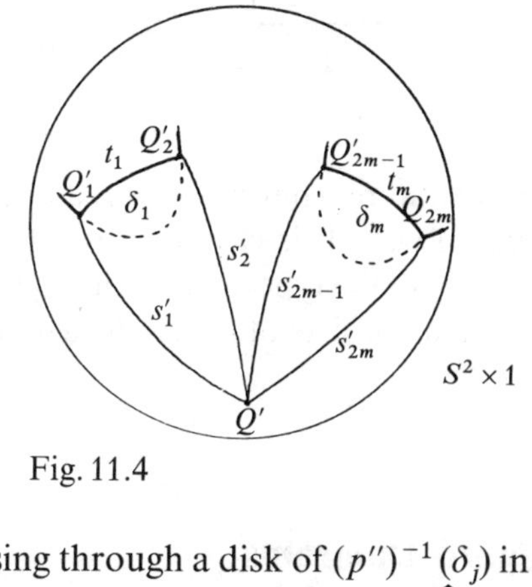

Fig. 11.4

Passing through a disk of $(p'')^{-1}(\delta_j)$ in $\hat{B}'_i$ means changing from sheet number k to sheet number $\tau'_j(k)$. Since $p'' | \partial \hat{B}'_i = p'$ we may thus extend p' to a covering $\tilde{p}$: $M^3 \to S^3$. (There is no problem in extending p' to the balls of $p^{-1}(B_i)$ different from $\hat{B}_i$, since the covering is not branched in these.) □

The branching set of $\tilde{p}$ in $B_i' \cup (S^2 \times I)$ is described in Figure 11.5: The orbits $(Q_i \times t) \in (S^2 \times I)$ form a braid to which in B_i' the arcs $\partial\delta_i - t_i$ are added as in the case of a plat.

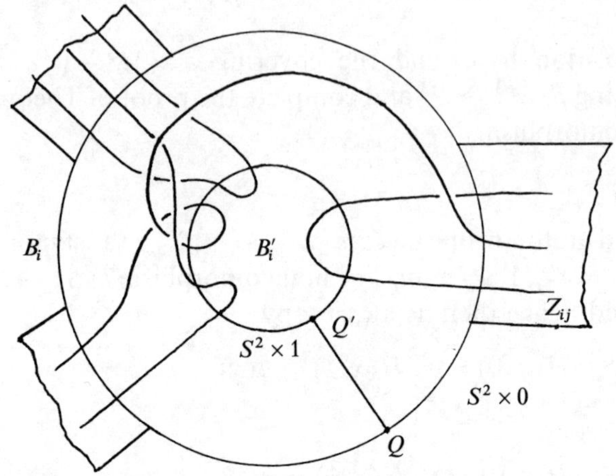

Fig. 11.5

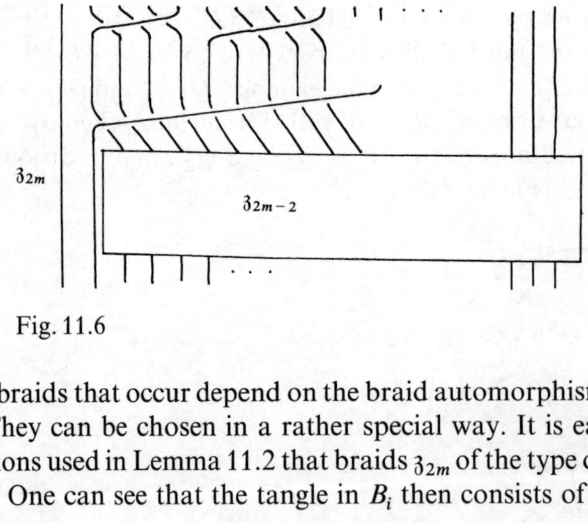

Fig. 11.6

The braids that occur depend on the braid automorphisms required in Lemma 11.2. They can be chosen in a rather special way. It is easy to verify from the operations used in Lemma 11.2 that braids $\mathfrak{z}_{2m}$ of the type depicted in Figure 11.6 suffice. One can see that the tangle in B_i then consists of m unknotted and unlinked arcs.

B Branched Coverings and Heegaard Diagrams

By Alexander's theorem every closed oriented 3-manifold is an n-fold branched covering p: $M^3 \to S^3$ of the sphere. Suppose the branching set $\mathfrak{k}$ is a link of multiplicity μ, $\mathfrak{k} = \bigcup_{i=1}^{\mu} \mathfrak{k}_i$, and it is presented as a $2m$-plat (see Chapter 2D), where m is the bridge number of $\mathfrak{k}$. A component $\mathfrak{k}_i$ is then presented as a $2\lambda_i$-plat, $\sum_{i=1}^{\mu} \lambda_i = m$. Think of S^3 as the union of two disjoint closed balls B_0, B_1, and $I \times S^2$, $\{j\} \times S^2 = \partial B_j = S_j^2$, $j = 0, 1$. Let the plat $\mathfrak{k}$ intersect $\mathring{B}_0$ and $\mathring{B}_1$ in m unknotted arcs each of which span disjoint disks δ_i^j, $1 \leqq i \leqq m$, in B_j, $j = 0, 1$, and denote by $\mathfrak{z} = \mathfrak{k} \cap (I \times S^2)$ the braid part of $\mathfrak{k}$ (Fig. 11.7). Every point of $\mathfrak{k}_i \cap (S_0^2 \cup S_1^2)$ is covered by the same number $\mu_i \leqq n$ of points in M^3.

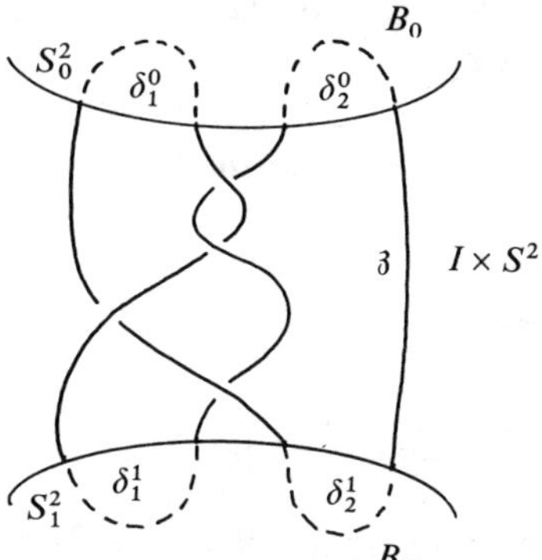

Fig. 11.7

11.3 Proposition. *A manifold M^3 which is an n-fold branched covering of S^3 branched along the plat $\mathfrak{k}$ possesses a Heegaard splitting of genus*

$$g = m \cdot n - n + 1 - \sum_{i=1}^{\mu} \lambda_i \mu_i .$$

Proof. The 2-spheres S_j^2 are covered by orientable closed surfaces $\hat{F}_j = p^{-1}(S_j^2)$, $j = 0, 1$. The group $\pi_1(S^3 - \mathfrak{k})$ can be generated by m Wirtinger generators s_i, $1 \leqq i \leqq m$, encircling the arcs $\mathfrak{k} \cap B_0$. Similarly one may choose generators s_i' assigned to $\mathfrak{k} \cap B_1$; the s_i can be represented by curves in S_0^2, the s_i' by curves in S_1^2. It follows that $\hat{F}_0$ and $\hat{F}_1$ are connected. $p|: \hat{F}_j \to S_j^2$, $j = 0, 1$, are branched coverings with $2m$ branchpoints $\mathfrak{k} \cap S_j^2$ each. The genus g of $\hat{F}_0$ and $\hat{F}_1$ can easily be calculated via the Euler characteristic as follows: $p^{-1}(S_j^2 \cap \mathfrak{k}_i)$ consists of $2\lambda_i \mu_i$ points. Hence, $\chi(\hat{F}_0) = \chi(\hat{F}_1) = n + 2 \cdot \sum_{i=1}^{\mu} \lambda_i \mu_i - 2m \cdot n + n = 2 - 2g$. The balls B_j are covered by handlebodies $p^{-1}(B_j) = \hat{B}_j$ of genus g. This is easily seen by cutting the B_j along the disk δ_i^j and piecing copies of the resulting space together to obtain $\hat{B}_j$. The manifold M^3 is homeomorphic to the Heegaard splitting $\hat{B}_0 \cup_{\hat{h}} \hat{B}_1$. □

The homeomorphism $\hat{h}: \hat{F}_0 \to \hat{F}_1$ can be described in the following way. The braid $\mathfrak{z}$ determines a braid automorphism ζ which is induced by a homeomorphism

$h\colon [S_0^2 - (\mathfrak{k} \cap S_0^2)] \to [S_1^2 - (\mathfrak{k} \cap S_1^2)]$. One may extend h to a homeomorphism $h\colon S_0^2 \to S_1^2$ and lift it to obtain $\hat{h}$:

$$\begin{array}{ccc} \hat{F}_0 & \xrightarrow{\hat{h}} & \hat{F}_1 \\ p \downarrow & & p \downarrow \\ S_0^2 & \xrightarrow{h} & S_1^2 . \end{array}$$

Proposition 11.3 gives an upper bound for the *Heegaard genus* (g minimal) of a manifold M^3 obtained as a branched covering.

11.4 Proposition. *The Heegaard genus g^* of an n-fold branched covering of S^3 along the 2m-plat $\mathfrak{k}$ satisfies the inequality*

$$g^* \leqq m \cdot n - n + 1 - \sum_{i=1}^{\mu} \lambda_i \mu_i \leqq (m-1)(n-1).$$

Proof. The second part of the inequality is obtained by putting $\mu_i = 1$. □

The 2-fold covering of knots or links with two bridges ($n = m = 2$) have Heegaard genus one – a well known fact. (See Chapter 12, [Schubert 1956]). Of special interest are coverings with $g = 0$. In this case the covering space M^3 is a 3-sphere. There are many solutions of the equation $0 = mn - n + 1 - \sum_{i=1}^{\mu} \lambda_i \mu_i$; for instance, the 3-sheeted irregular coverings of 2-bridge knots, $m = 2$, $n = 3$, $\mu_i = 2$, [Fox 1962′], [Burde 1971]. The braid $\mathfrak{z}$ of the plat then lifts to the braid $\hat{\mathfrak{z}}$ of the plat $\hat{\mathfrak{k}}$. Since $\hat{\mathfrak{z}}$ can be determined via the lifted braid automorphism ζ, $p\zeta = \zeta p$, one can actually find $\hat{\mathfrak{k}}$. This was done for the trefoil [Kinoshita 1967] and the four-knot [Burde 1971].

A simple calculation shows that our construction never yields genus zero for regular coverings – except in the trivial cases $n = 1$ or $m = 1$.

For fixed m and n the Heegaard genus of the covering space M^3 is minimized by choosing $\mu_i = n - 1$, $g = m + 1 - n$. These coverings are of the type used in our version of Alexander's Theorem 11.1. From this we get

11.5 Proposition. *An orientable closed 3-manifold M^3 of Heegaard genus g^* is an n-fold branched covering with branching set a link $\mathfrak{k}$ with at least $g^* + n - 1$ bridges.* □

We propose to investigate the relation between the Heegaard splitting and the branched-covering description of a manifold M^3 in the special case of a 2-fold covering, $n = 2$. Genus and bridge-number are then related by $m = g + 1$.

The covering $p|\colon \hat{F}_0 \to S_0^2$ is described in Figure 11.8.

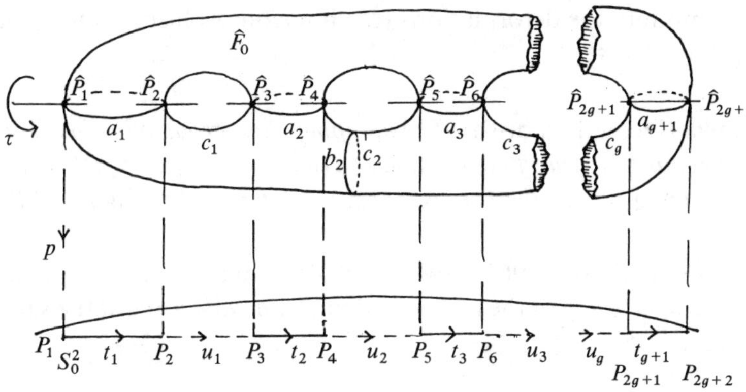

Fig. 11.8

Connect P_{2j} and P_{2j+1}, $1 \leqq j \leqq g$, by simple arcs u_j, such that $t_1 u_1 t_2 u_2 \ldots u_g t_{g+1}$ is a simple arc, $t_i = S_0^2 \cap \delta_i^0$. A rotation through π about an axis which pierces $\hat{F}_0$ in the branch points $\hat{P}_j = p^{-1}(P_j)$, $1 \leqq j \leqq 2g+2$ is easily seen to be the covering transformation. The preimages $a_i = p^{-1}(t_i)$, $c_j = p^{-1}(u_j)$, $1 \leqq i \leqq g+1$, $1 \leqq j \leqq g$ are simple closed curves on $\hat{F}_0$. We consider homeomorphisms of the punctured sphere $S_0^2 - \bigcup_{j=1}^{2g+2} P_j$ which induce braid automorphisms, especially the homeomorphisms that induce the elementary braid automorphisms σ_k, $1 \leqq k \leqq 2g+1$. We extend them to S_0^2 and still denote them by σ_k. We are going to show that $\sigma_k\colon S_0^2 \to S_0^2$ lifts to a homeomorphism of $\hat{F}_0$, a so-called Dehn-twist.

11.6 Definition (Dehn twist). Let a be a simple closed (unoriented) curve on a closed oriented surface F, and $U(a)$ a closed tubular neighbourhood of a in F. A right-handed 2π-twist of $U(a)$ (Fig. 11.9), extended by the identity map to F is called a *Dehn twist* α about a.

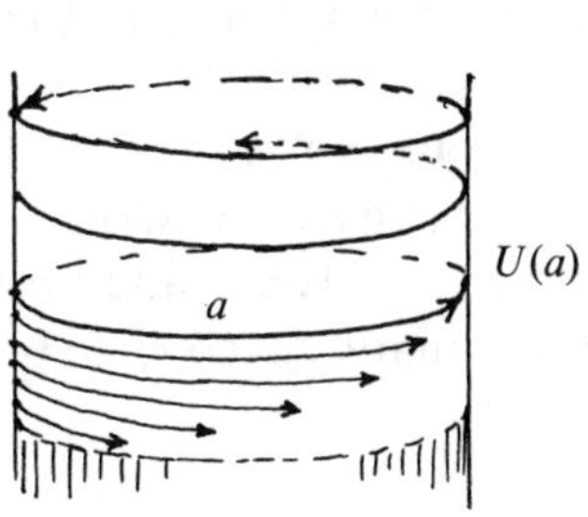

Fig. 11.9

Up to isotopy a Dehn twist is well defined by the simple closed curve a and a given orientation of F. Dehn twists are important because a certain finite set of Dehn twists generates the mapping class group of F – the group of autohomeomorphisms of F modulo the deformations (the homeomorphisms homotopic to the identity) [Dehn 1938].

11.7 Theorem (Dehn, Lickorish). *The mapping class group of a closed orientable surface F of genus g is generated by the Dehn twists α_i, β_k, γ_j, $1 \leqq i \leqq g+1$, $2 \leqq k \leqq g-1$, $1 \leqq j \leqq g$, about the curves a_i, b_k, c_j as depicted in Figure 11.8.*

For a *proof* see [Lickorish 1962, 1964, 1966]. We remark that a left-handed twist about a is the inverse α^{-1} of the right-handed Dehn twist α about the same simple closed curve a. □

11.8 Lemma. *The homeomorphisms σ_{2i-1}, $1 \leqq i \leqq g+1$ lift to Dehn twists α_i about $a_i = p^{-1}(t_i)$ and the homeomorphisms σ_{2j}, $1 \leqq j \leqq g$, lift to Dehn twists γ_j about $c_j = p^{-1}(u_j)$.*

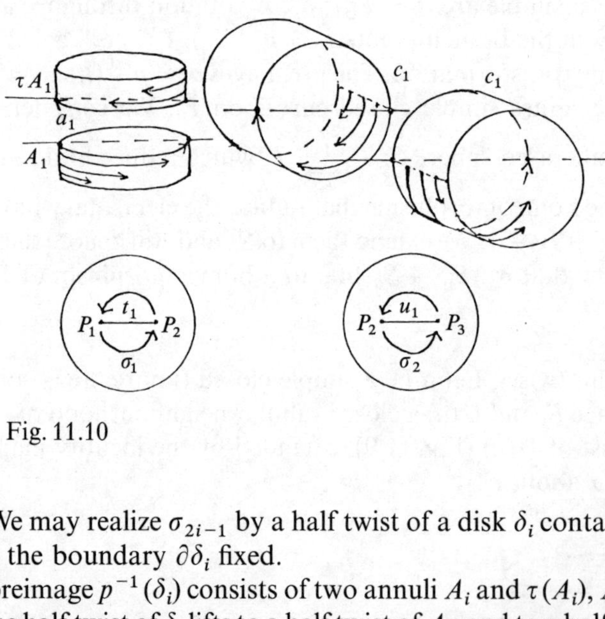

Fig. 11.10

Proof. We may realize σ_{2i-1} by a half twist of a disk δ_i containing t_i (Fig. 11.10), keeping the boundary $\partial\delta_i$ fixed.

The preimage $p^{-1}(\delta_i)$ consists of two annuli A_i and $\tau(A_i)$, $A_i \cap \tau(A_i) = p^{-1}(t_i) = a_i$. The half twist of δ_i lifts to a half twist of A_i, and to a half twist of $\tau(A_i)$ in the opposite direction. Since $A_i \cap \tau(A_i) = a_i$, these two half twists add up to a full Dehn twist α_i along a_i. A similar construction shows that σ_{2j} is covered by a Dehn twist γ_j along $c_j = p^{-1}(u_j)$. □

There is an immediate corollary to 11.5, 11.7 and 11.8.

11.9 Corollary. *A closed oriented 3-manifold M^3 of Heegaard genus $g \leqq 2$ is a two-fold branched covering of S^3 with branching set a link $\mathfrak{k} \subset S^3$ with $g+1$ bridges.* □

There are, of course, closed oriented 3-manifolds which are not 2-fold coverings, if their Heegaard genus is at least three. $S^1 \times S^1 \times S^1$ is a well known example [Fox 1972].

11.10 Proposition (R.H. Fox). *The manifold $S^1 \times S^1 \times S^1$ is not a two-fold branched covering of S^3; its Heegaard genus is three.*

Proof. We have seen earlier that for any n-fold branched cyclic covering $\hat{C}_n$ of a knot the endomorphism $1 + t + \ldots + t^{n-1}$ annihilates $H_1(\hat{C}_n)$ (Proposition 8.20(b)). This holds equally for the second homology group, even if the branching set is merely a 1-complex. (It is even true for higher dimensions, see [Fox 1972].) Let M^3 be a closed oriented manifold which is an n-fold cyclic branched covering of S^3. Let $\hat{c}_q = \sum_{i=0}^{n-1} \sum_k n_{ik} t^{\nu_{ik}} \hat{c}_k^q$, $\partial \hat{c}_q = 0$, be a q-cycle of $H_q(M^3)$, $q \in \{1, 2\}$, with $\hat{c}_k^q$ a simplex over c_k^q, $p\hat{c}_k^q = c_k^q$, $\langle t \rangle$ the covering transformations.

$$
\begin{aligned}
(\sum_{j=0}^{n-1} t^j)\hat{c}_q &= \sum_{i,j,k} n_{ik} t^{\nu_{ik}+j} \hat{c}_k^q = \sum_{i,k} n_{ik} \hat{c}_k^q \sum_j t^{\nu_{ik}+j} \\
&= (\sum_j t^j)(\sum_{i,k} n_{ik} \hat{c}_k^q) = p^{-1}(\sum n_{ik} c_k^q) = p^{-1}\partial c^{q+1} \\
&= \partial p^{-1} c^{q+1} \sim 0 .
\end{aligned}
$$

Suppose $M = S_1^1 \times S_2^1 \times S_3^1$ is a 2-fold covering of S^3. One has

$$
\pi_1(S_1^1 \times S_2^1 \times S_3^1) \cong H_1(S_1^1 \times S_2^1 \times S_3^1) = \mathbb{Z} \oplus \mathbb{Z} \oplus \mathbb{Z},
$$

and t can be described by the 3×3-matrix $-E$ with respect to the basis represented by the three factors. As $S_1^1 \times S_2^1 \times S_3^1$ is aspherical the covering transformation τ which induces t in the homology is homotopic to a map which inverts each of the 1-spheres S_i^1 [Spanier 1966, Chapter 8, Theorem 11]. Poincaré duality assigns to each S_i^1 a torus $S_j^1 \times S_k^1$, i, j, k all different, which represents a free generator of $H_2(S_1^1 \times S_2^1 \times S_3^1)$. Thus t operates on $H_2(S_1^1 \times S_2^1 \times S_3^1)$ as the identity which contradicts $1 + t = 0$.

It is easy to see that $S^1 \times S^1 \times S^1$ can be presented by a Heegaard splitting of genus three – identify opposite faces of a cube K (Fig. 11.11). After two pairs are identified one gets a thickened torus. Identifying its two boundary tori obviously gives $S^1 \times S^1 \times S^1$. On the other hand H_1 and $H_2 = \overline{K - H_1}$ become handlebodies of genus three under the identifying map. □

The method developed in this section can be used to study knots with two bridges by looking at their 2-fold branched covering spaces – a tool already used by H. Seifert [Schubert 1956]. It was further developed by Montesinos who was able to classify a set of knots comprising knots with two bridges and bretzel knots by similar means. We shall take up the matter in Chapter 12.

We conclude this section by proving the following

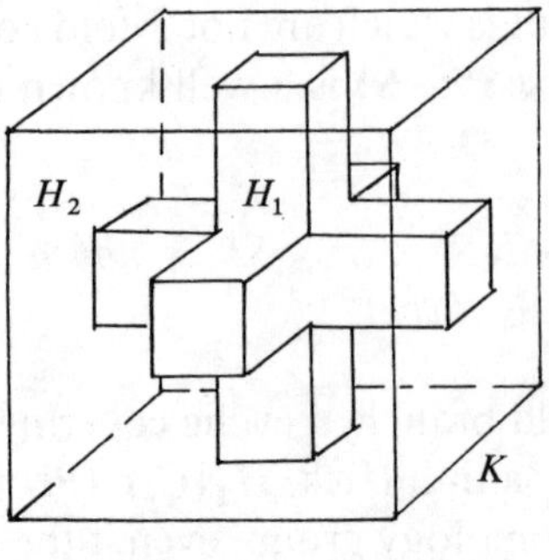

Fig. 11.11

11.11 Theorem (Hilden-Montesinos). *Every closed orientable 3-manifold M is an irregular 3-fold branched covering of S^3. The branching set $\mathfrak{k}$ can be chosen in different ways, for instance as a knot or a link with unknotted components. If g is the Heegaard genus of M, it suffices to use a $(g+2)$-bridged branching set $\mathfrak{k}$.*

Before starting on the actual proof in 11.14 we study irregular 3-fold branched coverings $p\colon \hat{F} \to S^2$ of S^2 with branch indices $\leqq 2$. If $\hat{F}$ is an orientable closed surface of genus g, a calculation of $\chi(\hat{F})$ shows that the branching set in S^2 consists of $2(g+2)$ points P_i, $1 \leqq i \leqq 2(g+2)$. Let us denote by ϱ, σ, τ the transpositions (1 2), (2 3), (1 3). Then by choosing $g+2$ disjoint simple arcs t_i, $1 \leqq i \leqq g+2$ in S^2, t_i connecting P_{2i-1} and P_{2i} (Fig. 11.12), and assigning to each t_i one of the transpositions ϱ, σ, τ, we may construct a 3-fold branched covering $p\colon\ \hat{F} \to S^2$ (see Fig. 11.12). The sheets $\hat{F}^{(j)}$, $1 \leqq j \leqq 3$, of the covering are homeomorphic to a 2-sphere with $g+2$ boundary components obtained from S^2

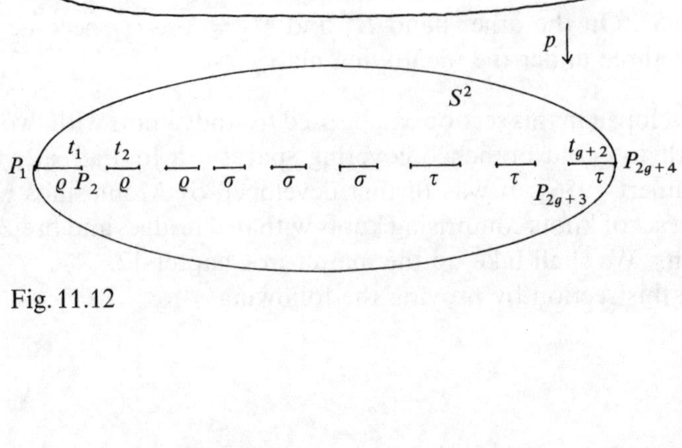

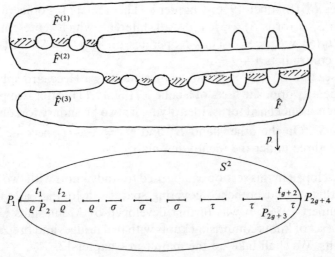

Fig. 11.12

by cutting along the t_i, $1 \leqq i \leqq g+2$. Traversing an arc of $p^{-1}(t_i)$ in $\hat{F}$ means changing from $\hat{F}^{(j)}$ to $\hat{F}^{(\sigma(j))}$, if σ is assigned to t_i. (For $\hat{F}$ to be connected it is necessary and sufficient that at least two of the three transpositions are used in the construction.)

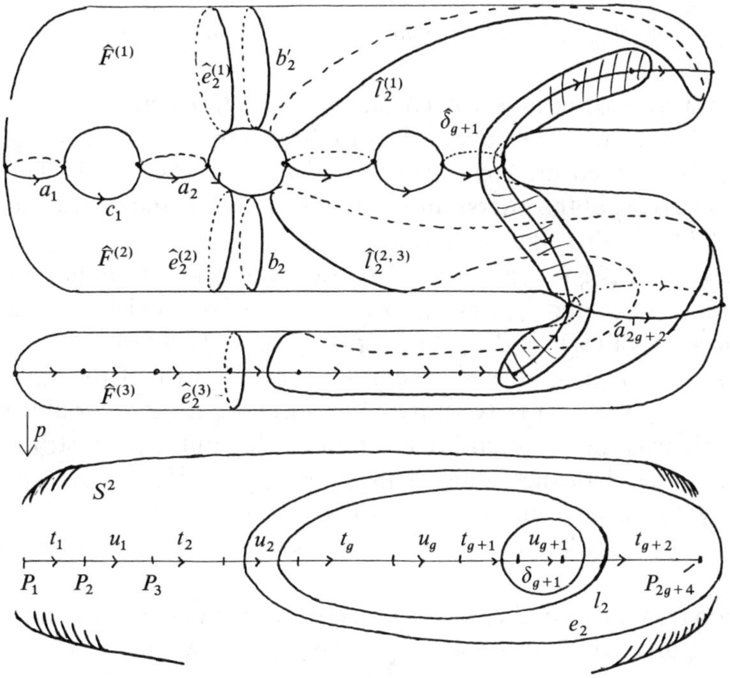

Fig. 11.13

It will be convenient to use a very special version of such a covering. We assign ϱ to t_i, $1 \leqq i \leqq g+1$, and σ to t_{g+2} (Fig. 11.13).

As in Figure 11.8 we introduce arcs u_j, $1 \leqq j \leqq g+1$, connecting P_{2j} and P_{2j+1}. We direct the t_i, u_j coherently (Fig. 11.13) and lift these orientations. $p^{-1}(t_i)$, $1 \leqq i \leqq g+2$, consists of a closed curve a_i which will be regarded as unoriented, since its two parts carry opposite orientations, and an arc in $\hat{F}_3$ for $1 \leqq i \leqq g+1$, resp. in $\hat{F}_1$ for $i = g+2$. By the Dehn-Lickorish Theorem 11.7 the mapping class group of $\hat{F}$ is generated by the Dehn twists α_i, β_k, γ_j, $1 \leqq i \leqq g+1$, $2 \leqq k \leqq g-1$, $1 \leqq j \leqq g$ about the curves a_i, b_k, c_j. Lemma 11.8. can be applied to the situation in hand: σ_{2i-1} in S^2 lifts to α_i, $1 \leqq i \leqq g+1$ and σ_{2j} lifts to γ_j, $1 \leqq j \leqq 2g$, because the effect of the lifting in $\hat{F}_3$ is isotopic to the identity. (Observe that σ_{2g+3} lifts to a deformation.) The only difficulty to overcome is to find homeomorphisms of $S^2 - \bigcup_{i=1}^{2g+4} P_i$ that lift to homeomorphisms of $\hat{F}$ isotopic to the Dehn twists β_k, $2 \leqq k \leqq g-1$. These are provided by the following

11.12 Lemma. *Let $p\colon \hat{F} \to S^2$ be the 3-fold branched covering described in Figure 11.13.*

(a) σ_{2i-1} lifts to α_i, $1 \leqq i \leqq g+1$; σ_{2j} lifts to γ_j, $1 \leqq j \leqq g$.

(b) $\omega_k = (\sigma_{2g+2}\sigma_{2g+1} \ldots \sigma_{2k+2}\sigma_{2k+1}^2\sigma_{2k+2} \ldots \sigma_{2g+2})^2$ lifts to β_k for $2 \leqq k \leqq g-1$.

(c) The lifts of ω_1 resp. ω_g are isotopic to α_1 resp. α_{g+1}.

(d) σ_{2g+2}^3 and σ_{2g+3} lift to mappings isotopic to the identity.

Proof. (a) was proved in 11.8. (b): consider simple closed curves e_i, l_i, $1 \leqq i \leqq g+1$, in S^2 (Fig. 11.13). The curve e_i lifts to three simple closed curves $\hat{e}_i^{(j)} \in \hat{F}^{(j)}$, $1 \leqq j \leqq 3$, while l_i^2 is covered by two curves $(\hat{l}_i^{(1)})^2, \hat{l}_i^{(2,3)}$ (Fig. 11.13). This is easily checked by looking at the intersections of e_i and l_i with t_i and u_i, resp. at those of $\hat{e}_i^{(j)}$ and $\hat{l}_i^{(1)}, \hat{l}_i^{(2,3)}$ with a_i and c_i. Since $\hat{e}_k^{(1)} \simeq b'_k \simeq \hat{l}_k^{(1)}$, $\hat{e}_k^{(2)} \simeq b_k$ for $2 \leqq k \leqq g-1$, and $\hat{e}_i^{(3)} \simeq 1$, $1 \leqq i \leqq g+1$, a Dehn twist ε_k in S^2 along e_k lifts to the composition of the Dehn twists β_k and β'_k, while the square of the Dehn twist λ_k along l_k lifts to the composition of $(\beta'_k)^2$ and β_k. Thus $\varepsilon_k^2\lambda_k^{-2}$ lifts to $\beta_k^2\beta_k'^2(\beta'_k)^{-2}\beta_k^{-1} = \beta_k$. We may think of ε_k as a braid which represents a full twist of the strings f_{2k+1}, $f_{2k+2}, \ldots, f_{2g+4}$ (Fig. 11.13). (Compare Fig. 10.11). ε_k^2 is then a double twist and λ_k^{-2} a double twist in the opposite direction leaving out the last string f_{2g+4}. It follows that $\varepsilon_k^2\lambda_k^{-2}$ defines a braid $(\sigma_{2g+3}\sigma_{2g+2} \ldots \sigma_{2k+1}^2\sigma_{2k+2} \ldots \sigma_{2g+3})^2$ in which only the last string f_{2g+4} is not constant, encircling its neighbours $f_{2k+1}, \ldots, f_{2g+3}$ to the left, twice. Since obviously σ_{2g+3} lifts to a deformation, (b) is proved.

Assertion (c) follows in the same way as (b). To prove (d) consider a disk δ_{g+1} which is a regular neighbourhood of u_{g+1}. The third power $(\partial\delta_{g+1})^3$ of its boundary lifts to a simple closed curve in $\hat{F}$ bounding a disk $\hat{\delta}_{g+1} = p^{-1}(\delta_{g+1})$. The deformation σ_{2g+2}^3 in S^3 lifts to a "half-twist" of $\hat{\delta}_{g+1}$, a deformation of $\hat{F}$ which leaves the boundary $\partial\hat{\delta}_{g+1}$ pointwise fixed, and thus is isotopic to the identity. □

An easy consequence of Lemma 11.12 is the following

11.13 Corollary. *For a given permutation $\pi \in \mathfrak{S}_{2g+4}$ there is a braid automorphism $\sigma \in \mathfrak{B}_{2g+4}$ with permutation π induced by a homeomorphism of $S^2 - \bigcup_{i=1}^{2g+4} P_i$ which lifts to a deformation of $\hat{F}$.*

Proof. Together with σ_{2g+2}^3 the conjugates

$$\sigma_i\sigma_{i+1} \ldots \sigma_{2g+1}\sigma_{2g+2}^3\sigma_{2g+1}^{-1} \ldots \sigma_i^{-1},\ 1 \leqq i \leqq 2g+1,$$

lift to deformations. Hence, the transpositions $(i, 2g+3) \in \mathfrak{S}_{2g+4}$ can be realized by deformations. Since σ_{2g+3} also lifts to a deformation, the lemma is proved. □

11.14 *Proof of Theorem 11.11.* Let $M = \hat{B}_0 \cup_{\hat{h}} \hat{B}_1$ be a Heegaard splitting of genus g, and $p_j\colon \hat{F}_j \to S_j$, $j \in \{0, 1\}$, be 3-fold branched coverings of the type described in Figure 11.13, $\partial \hat{B}_j = \hat{F}_j$. Extend p_j to a covering $p_j\colon \hat{B}_j \to B_j$, $\partial B_j = S_j^3$, B_j a ball, in the same way as in the proof of Theorem 11.1. (Compare Fig. 11.4). The branching set of p_j consists in B_j of $g + 2$ disjoint unknotted arcs, each joining a pair P_{2i-1}, P_{2i} of branch points.

By Lemma 11.8, 11.12 there is a braid $\mathfrak{z}$ with given permutation π defining a homeomorphism $h\colon S_0^2 \to S_1^2$ which lifts to a homeomorphism isotopic to $\hat{h}\colon \hat{F}_0 \to \hat{F}_1$. The plat $\mathfrak{k}$ defined by $\mathfrak{z}$ is the branching set of a 3-fold irregular covering $p\colon M \to S^3$, and if π is suitably chosen, $\mathfrak{k}$ is a knot. In the case $\pi = id$ the branching set $\mathfrak{k}$ consists of $g + 2$ trivial components. □

There are, of course, many plats $\mathfrak{k}$ defined by braids $\mathfrak{z} \in \mathfrak{B}_{2g+4}$ which by this construction lead to equivalent Heegaard diagrams and, hence, to homeomorphic manifolds. Replace $\mathfrak{k}$ by $\mathfrak{k}'$ with a defining braid $\mathfrak{z}' = \mathfrak{z}_1 \mathfrak{z} \mathfrak{z}_0$ such that $\mathfrak{z}_i \subset B_i$, and $\mathfrak{k}' \cap B_i$ is a trivial half-plat (E 11.3). $\mathfrak{z}'$ then lifts to a map $\hat{h}' = \hat{h}_1 \hat{h} \hat{h}_0\colon \hat{F}_0 \to \hat{F}_1$, and there are homeomorphisms $\hat{H}_i\colon \hat{B}_i \to \hat{B}_i$ extending the homeomorphisms $\hat{h}_i\colon \hat{F}_i \to \hat{F}_i = \partial \hat{B}_i$, $i \in \{0, 1\}$. Obviously $\hat{B}_0 \cup_{\hat{h}} \hat{B}_1$ and $\hat{B}_0 \cup_{\hat{h}'} \hat{B}_1$ are homeomorphic. The braids $\mathfrak{z}_i$ of this type form a finitely generated subgroup in $\mathfrak{B}_{2g+4}$ (Exercise E 11.3).

Lemmata 11.8 and 11.12 can be exploited to give some information on the mapping class group $M(g)$ of an orientable closed surface of genus g. The group $M(1)$ is well known [Goeritz 1932], and will play an important role in Chapter 12. $M(2)$ is by Lemma 11.8 and Corollary 11.9 a homomorphic image of the braid group $\mathfrak{B}_6$. A presentation is known [Birman 1974]. Since one string of braids of $\mathfrak{B}_6$ can be kept constant, $M(2)$ is even a homomorph of $\mathfrak{B}_5$. For $g > 2$

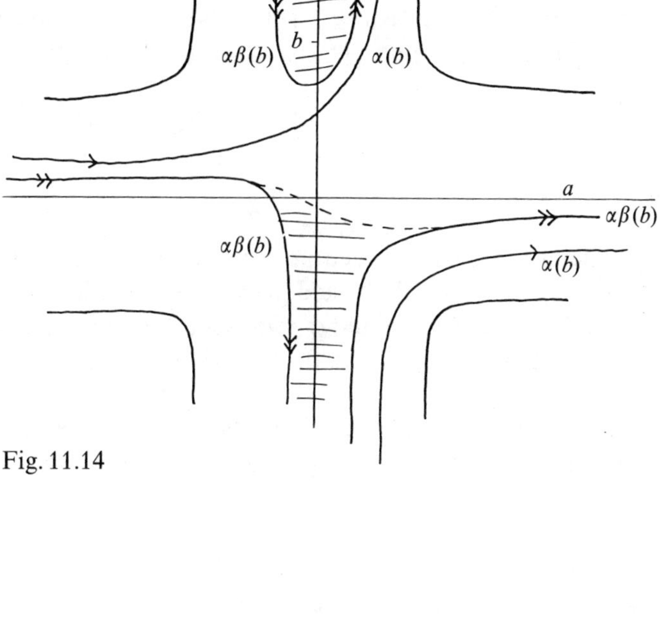

Fig. 11.14

the group $M(g)$ is a homomorphic image of the subgroup $\mathfrak{Z}^*_{2g+3}$ of $\mathfrak{Z}_{2g+3}$ generated by $\mathfrak{Z}_{2g+2} \subset \mathfrak{Z}_{2g+3}$ and the pure $2g+3$-braids ω_k, $2 \leqq k \leqq g-1$, of Lemma 11.12(b). There will, however, be a kernel $\neq 1$. It is an easy exercise to prove that Dehn twists α, β about simple closed curves a, b (on a closed orientable surface) which intersect in one point satisfy a relation $\alpha^{-1}\beta^{-1}\alpha^{-1}\beta\alpha\beta = id$. This follows from the fact that $\alpha\beta$ maps b onto $\alpha\beta(b) \simeq a$ (the product $\alpha\beta$ is to be applied from left to right) which can be verified with the help of Figure 11.14.

The braids $\varrho_i = \omega_i\sigma_{2i}\omega_i\sigma_{2i}^{-1}\omega_i^{-1}\sigma_{2i}^{-1}$, $1 \leqq i \leqq g$, lift to $\beta_i\gamma_i\beta_i\gamma_i^{-1}\beta_i^{-1}\gamma_i^{-1} \simeq id$, and the braids

$$v_j = (\sigma_j\sigma_{j+1} \dots \sigma_{2g+1})\sigma^3_{2g+2}(\sigma_j\sigma_{j+1} \dots \sigma_{2g+1})^{-1}$$

also lift to deformations. The permutation of ϱ_i is the transposition $(2i, 2i+1)$, and the permutation of v_j is $(j, 2g+3)$. Hence, $v_{2i}v_{2i+1}v_{2i}\varrho_i^{-1} \in \mathfrak{Z}^*_{2g+3}$, is in the kernel of the map $\mathfrak{Z}^*_{2g+3} \to M(g)$. One can verify easily that these elements are not trivial in $\mathfrak{Z}^*_{2g+3}$. Presentations of $M(g)$ are known, see [McCool 1975], [Hatcher-Thurston 1980], [Wajnryb 1983].

C History and Sources

J.W. Alexander [1920] proved that every closed oriented n-manifold M is a branched covering of the n-sphere. The branching set is a $(n-2)$-subcomplex. Alexander claims in his paper (without giving a proof) that for $n = 3$ the branching set can be assumed to be a closed submanifold – a link in S^3. J.S. Birman and H.M. Hilden [1975] gave a proof, and, at the same time, obtained some information on the relations between the Heegaard genus of M, the number of sheets of the covering and the bridge number of the link. Finally Hilden [1976] and Montesinos [1976′] independently showed that every orientable closed 3-manifold is a 3-fold irregular covering of S^3 over a link $\mathfrak{k}$. It suffices to confine oneself to rather special types of branching sets $\mathfrak{k}$ [Hilden-Montesinos-Thickstun 1976].

D Exercises

E 11.1 Show that a Dehn-twist α of an orientable surface F along a simple closed (unoriented) curve a in F is well defined (up to a deformation) by a and an orientation of F. Dehn-twists α and α' represent the same element of the mapping class group ($\alpha' = \delta\alpha$, δ a deformation) if the corresponding curves are isotopic.

E 11.2 Apply the method of Lemma 11.2 to the following situation: Let $p: S^3 \to S^3$ be the cyclic 3-fold covering branched along the triangle A, B, C

(Fig. 11.15). Replace the branch set outside the balls around the vertices of the triangle as was done in the proof of Theorem 11.1. It follows that the 3-fold irregular covering along a trefoil is also a 3-sphere.

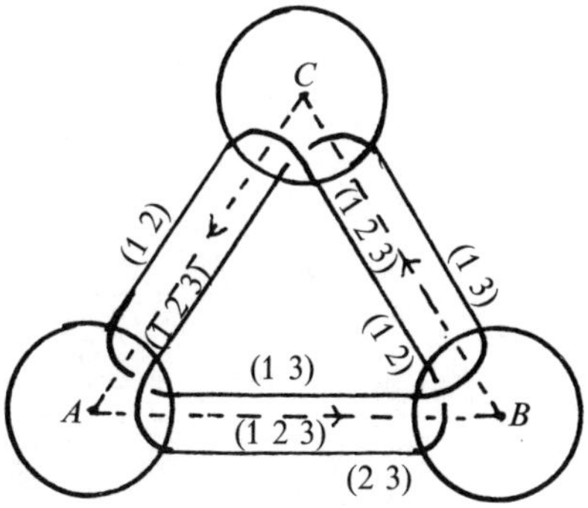

Fig. 11.15

E 11.3 Let $\mathfrak{k}$ be a $2m$-plat in 3-space $\mathbb{R}^3$ and (x, y, z) cartesian coordinates of $\mathbb{R}^3$. Suppose $x = 0$ meets $\mathfrak{k}$ transversally in the $2m$ points $P_i = (i, 0, 0)$, $1 \leqq i \leqq 2m$. We call the intersection of $\mathfrak{k}$ with the upper half-space $\mathbb{R}^3_0 = \{(x, y, z | x \geqq 0\}$ a *half-plat* $\mathfrak{k}_0$, and denote its defining braid by $\mathfrak{z}_0 \in \mathfrak{B}_{2m}$. *The half-plat* $\mathfrak{k}_0$ *is trivial* if it consists of m arcs α_j, $1 \leqq j \leqq m$.

Show that the braids $\mathfrak{z}_0 \in \mathfrak{B}_{2m}$ which define trivial half-plats form a subgroup of $\mathfrak{B}_{2m}$ generated by the braids σ_{2i-1}, $1 \leqq i \leqq m$, $\varrho_k = \sigma_{2k}\sigma_{2k-1}\sigma_{2k+1}\sigma_{2k}$, $\tau_k = \sigma_{2k}\sigma_{2k-1}\sigma_{2k+1}^{-1}\sigma_{2k}^{-1}$, $1 \leqq k \leqq m-1$.

E 11.4 Construct $S^1 \times S^1 \times S^1$ as a 3-fold irregular covering of S^3 along a 5-bridged knot.

Chapter 12: Montesinos Links

This chapter contains a study of a special class of knots. Section A deals with the 2-bridge knots which are classified by their twofold branched coverings – a method due to H. Seifert.

Section B looks at 2-bridge knots as 4-plats (Viergeflechte). This yields interesting geometric properties and new normal forms [Siebenmann 1975]. They are used in section *C* to derive some properties concering the genus and the possibility of fibring the complement, [Funcke 1978], [Hartley 1979′].

Section D is devoted to the classification of the Montesinos links which generalize knots and links with two bridges with respect to the property that their twofold branched coverings are Seifert fibre spaces. These knots have been introduced by Montesinos [1973, 1979], and the classification, conjectured by him, was given in [Bonahon 1979]. The last part gives a report of a recent result of Bonahon-Siebenmann and Boileau from 1979 on the symmetries of Montesinos links. The proof of Bonahon-Siebenmann will appear in the book [Bonahon-Siebenmann 1984]; we follow the proof of [Boileau-Zimmermann 1984].

Montesinos knots include also the so-called pretzel knots which furnished the first examples of non-invertible knots [Trotter 1964].

A Schubert's Normal Form of Knots and Links with Two Bridges

H. Schubert [1956] classified knots and links with two bridges. His proof is a thorough and quite involved geometric analysis of the problem, his result a complete classification of these oriented knots and links. Each knot is presented in a normal form – a distinguished projection.

If one considers these knots as unoriented, their classification can be shown to rest on the classification of 3-dimensional lens spaces. This was already noticed by Seifert [Schubert 1956].

12.1 We start with some geometric properties of a 2-bridge knot, using Schubert's terminology. The knot $\mathfrak{k}$ meets a projection plane $\mathbb{R}^2 \subset \mathbb{R}^3$ in four points: A, B, C, D. The plane $\mathbb{R}^2$ defines an upper and a lower halfspace, and each of them intersects $\mathfrak{k}$ in two arcs. Each pair of arcs can be projected onto $\mathbb{R}^2$ without double points (see 2.13). We may assume that one pair of arcs is projected onto straight segments $w_1 = AB$, $w_2 = CD$ (Fig. 12.1); the other pair is projected onto two disjoint simple curves v_1 (from B to C) and v_2 (from D to A). The

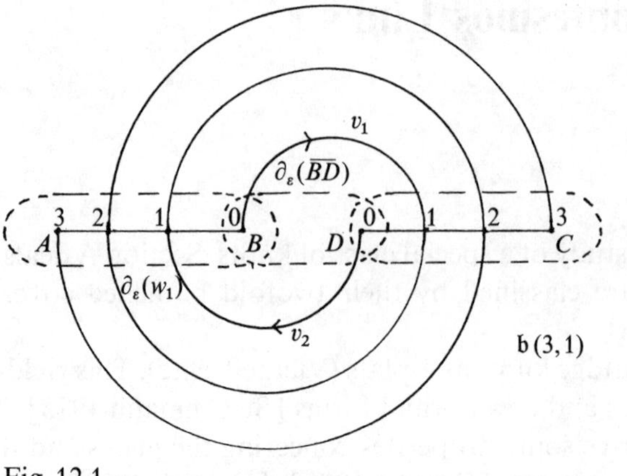

Fig. 12.1

diagram can be reduced in the following way: v_1 first meets w_2. A first double point on w_1 can be removed by an isotopy. In the same way one can arrange for each arc v_i to meet the w_j alternately, and for each w_j to meet the v_i alternately. The number of double points, hence, is even in a reduced diagram with $\alpha - 1$ ($\alpha \in \mathbb{N}$) double points on w_1 and on w_2. We attach numbers to these double points, counting against the orientation of w_1 and w_2 (Fig. 12.1). Observe that for a knot α is odd; α even and $\partial v_1 = \{A, B\}$, $\partial v_2 = \{C, D\}$ yields a link.

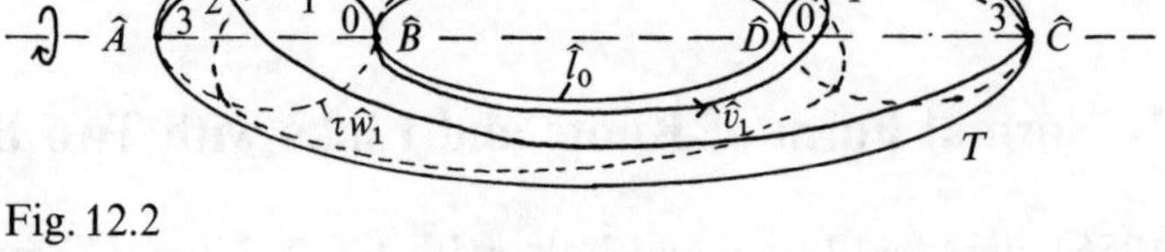

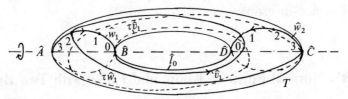

Fig. 12.2

12.2 We now add a point ∞ at infinity, $S^3 = \mathbb{R}^3 \cup \{\infty\}$, $S^2 = \mathbb{R}^2 \cup \{\infty\}$, and consider the two-fold branched covering T of S^2 with the branch set $\{A, B, C, D\}$, $\hat{p}$: $T \to S^2$, see Figure 12.2. The covering transformation τ: $T \to T$ is a rotation through π about an axis which pierces T in the points $\hat{A} = \hat{p}^{-1}(A)$, $\hat{B} = \hat{p}^{-1}(B)$, $\hat{C} = \hat{p}^{-1}C)$, $\hat{D} = \hat{p}^{-1}(D)$.

w_1 and w_2 lift to $\{\hat{w}_1, \tau\hat{w}_1\}$, $\{\hat{w}_2, \tau\hat{w}_2\}$ and in the notation of homotopy chains, see 9.1, $(1-\tau)\hat{w}_1$ and $(1-\tau)\hat{w}_2$ are isotopic simple closed curves on T. Likewise, $(1-\tau)\hat{v}_1$, $(1-\tau)\hat{v}_2$ are two simple closed curves on T, each mapped onto its inverse by τ. They intersect with the $(1-\tau)\hat{w}_i$ alternately: $int((1-\tau)\hat{v}_i, (1-\tau)\hat{w}_j) = \alpha$. Denote by $\partial_\varepsilon(c)$ the boundary of a small tubular neighbourhood of an arc c in $\mathbb{R}^2$. We choose an orientation on $\mathbb{R}^2$, and let $\partial_\varepsilon(c)$ have the induced orientation. The curve $\partial_\varepsilon(w_i)$ lifts to two curves isotopic to $\pm(1-\tau)\hat{w}_i$, $1 \leqq i \leqq 2$. The preimage $p^{-1}(\partial_\varepsilon(\overline{BD})$ consists of two curves; one of them, $\hat{\ell}_0$ together with

$\hat{m}_0 = (1-\tau)\hat{w}_1$ can be chosen as canonical generators of $H_1(T)$ – we call $\hat{m}_0$ a meridian, and $\hat{\ell}_0$ a longitude. Equally $p^{-1}(\partial_\varepsilon(v_i))$ consists of two curves isotopic to $\pm(1-\tau)\hat{v}_i$.

We assume for the moment $\alpha > 1$. (This excludes the trivial knot and a splittable link with two trivial components.) Then $(1-\tau)\hat{v}_i = \beta\hat{m}_0 + \alpha\hat{\ell}_0$ where $\beta \in \mathbb{Z}$ is positive, if at the first double point of v_1 the arc w_2 crosses from left to right in the double point $|\beta|$, and negative otherwise. From the construction it follows that $|\beta| < \alpha$ and that $gcd(\alpha, \beta) = 1$.

12.3 Proposition. *For any pair* α, β *of integers subject to the conditions:*

(1) $\alpha > 0,\ -\alpha < \beta < +\alpha,\ gcd(\alpha, \beta) = 1,\ \beta$ *odd*,

there is a knot or link with two bridges $\mathfrak{k} = \mathfrak{b}(\alpha, \beta)$ *with a reduced diagram with numbers* α, β. *We call* α *the* torsion, *and* β *the* crossing number *of* $\mathfrak{b}(\alpha, \beta)$. *The number of components of* $\mathfrak{b}(\alpha, \beta)$ *is* $\mu \equiv \alpha \bmod 2, 1 \leqq \mu \leqq 2$.
The 2-fold covering of S^3 *branched along* $\mathfrak{b}(\alpha, \beta)$ *is the lens space* $L(\alpha, \beta)$.

Proof. We first prove the last assertion. Suppose $\mathfrak{k} = \mathfrak{b}(\alpha, \beta)$ is a knot with two bridges whose reduced diagram determines the numbers α and β. We try to extend the covering $p\colon T \to S^2$ to a covering of S^3 branched along $\mathfrak{b}(\alpha, \beta)$. Denote by B_0, B_1 the two balls bounded by S^2 in S^3 with $\mathfrak{k} \cap B_0 = w_1 \cup w_2$. The 2-fold covering $\hat{B}_i$ of B_i branched along $B_i \cap \mathfrak{k}$ can be constructed by cutting B_i along two disjoint disks δ_1^i, δ_2^i spanning the arcs $B_i \cap \mathfrak{k}$, $i = 0,1$.

This defines a sheet of the covering, and $\hat{B}_i$ itself is obtained by identifying corresponding cuts of two such sheets. $\hat{B}_i$, $0 \leqq i \leqq 1$, is a solid torus, and $(1-\tau)\hat{w}_1 = \hat{m}_0$ represents a meridian of $\hat{B}_0$ while $\hat{m}_1 = (1-\tau)\hat{v}_1$ represents a

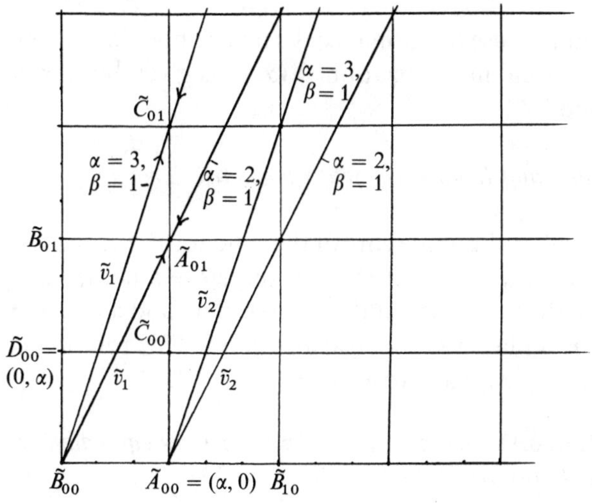

Fig. 12.3

meridian of $\hat{B}_1$. This follows from the definition of the curves $\partial_\varepsilon(v_i)$, $\partial_\varepsilon(w_i)$. Since

(2) $\hat{m}_1 = (1-\tau)\hat{v}_1 \simeq \beta\hat{m}_0 + \alpha\hat{\ell}_0$,

the covering $\hat{B}_0 \cup_T \hat{B}_1$ is the Heegaard splitting of the lens space $L(\alpha, \beta)$.

Further information is obtained by looking at the universal covering $\tilde{T} \cong \mathbb{R}^2$ of T. The curve $\hat{v}_1$ is covered by $\tilde{v}_1$ which may be drawn as a straight line through a lattice point over $\hat{B}$ and another over $\hat{C}$ (resp. $\hat{A}$) for α odd (resp. α even). If cartesian coordinates are introduced with $\tilde{B}_{00}$ as the origin and $\tilde{D}_{00} = (0, \alpha)$, $\tilde{A}_{00} = (\alpha, 0)$, see Figure 12.3, $\tilde{v}_1$ is a straight line through $(0, 0)$ and (β, α), and $\tilde{v}_2$ is a parallel through $(\alpha, 0)$ and $(\alpha + \beta, \alpha)$. The $2\alpha \times 2\alpha$ square is a fundamental domain of the covering $\tilde{p}$: $\tilde{T} \to T$. Any pair of coprime integers (α, β) defines such curves which are projected onto simple closed curves of the form $(1-\tau)\hat{v}_i$ on T, and, by $\hat{p}$: $T \to S^2$, onto a reduced diagram. □

One may choose $\alpha > 0$. If $\tilde{v}_1$ starts in $\tilde{B}_{00}$, it ends in $(\beta\alpha, \alpha^2)$. Thus $\beta \equiv 1 \bmod 2$, since v_1 ends in C or A.

We attached numbers γ to the double points of the reduced projection of $\mathfrak{b}(\alpha, \beta)$ (Fig. 12.1). To take into account also the characteristic of the double point we assign a residue class modulo 2α to it, represented by γ (resp. $-\gamma$) if w_i crosses v_j from left to right (resp. from right to left). Running along v_i one obtains the sequence:

(3) $0, \beta, 2\beta, \ldots, (\alpha - 1)\beta$ modulo 2α.

This follows immediately by looking at the universal covering $\tilde{T}$ (Fig. 12.3). Note that $\tilde{v}_i$ is crossed from right to left in the strips where the attached numbers run from right to left, and that $-(\alpha - \delta) \equiv \alpha + \delta$ modulo 2α.

12.4 Remark. It is common use to normalize the invariants α, β of a lens space in a different way. In this usual normalization, $L(\alpha, \beta)$ is given by $L(\alpha, \beta^*)$ where $0 < \beta^* < \alpha$, $\beta^* \equiv \beta \bmod \alpha$.

12.5 Proposition. *Knots and links with two bridges are invertible.*

Proof. A rotation through π about the core of the solid torus $\hat{B}_0$ (or $\hat{B}_1$) commutes with the covering transformation τ. It induces therefore a homeomorphism of $S^2 = p(T)$ – a rotation through π about the centres of w_1 and w_2 (resp. v_1 and v_2) if the reduced diagram is placed symmetrically on S^2. This rotation can be extended to an isotopy of S^3 which carries $\mathfrak{k}$ onto $-\mathfrak{k}$. □

12.6 Theorem (H. Schubert). *(a)* $\mathfrak{b}(\alpha, \beta)$ *and* $\mathfrak{b}(\alpha', \beta')$ *are equivalent as oriented knots (or links), if and only if:*

$$\alpha = \alpha', \quad \beta^{\pm 1} \equiv \beta' \bmod 2\alpha.$$

(b) $\mathfrak{b}(\alpha, \beta)$ *and* $\mathfrak{b}(\alpha', \beta')$ *are equivalent as unoriented knots (or links), if and only if:*

$$\alpha = \alpha', \quad \beta^{\pm 1} \equiv \beta' \bmod \alpha.$$

For the *proof* of (a) we refer to [Schubert 1956]. The weaker proposition (b) follows from the classification of lens spaces [Reidemeister 1935], [Brody 1960]. □

12.7 Remark. In the case of knots (α odd) propositions (a) and (b) are equivalent – this follows also from 12.5. For links Schubert gave examples which show that *one can obtain non-equivalent links (with linking number zero) by reversing the orientation of one component.* (A link $\mathfrak{b}(\alpha, \beta)$ is transformed into $\mathfrak{b}(\alpha, \beta')$, $\beta' \equiv \alpha + \beta \bmod 2\alpha$, if one component is reoriented). The link $\mathfrak{b}(32, 7)$ is an example. The sequence (3) can be used to compute the linking number $lk(\mathfrak{b}(\alpha, \beta))$ of the link:

$$lk(\mathfrak{b}(\alpha, \beta)) = \sum_{v=1}^{\frac{\alpha}{2}} \varepsilon_v, \quad \varepsilon_v = (-1)^{\left[\frac{(2v-1)\beta}{\alpha}\right]}.$$

($[a]$ denotes the integral part of a.) One obtains for $\alpha = 32$, $\beta = 7$:

$$\sum_{v=1}^{16} \varepsilon_v = 1+1-1-1-1+1+1-1-1+1+1-1-1-1+1+1=0.$$

12.8 Lastly, our construction has been unsymmetric with respect to B_0 and B_1. If the balls are exchanged, $(\hat{m}_0, \hat{\ell}_0)$ and $(\hat{m}_1, \hat{\ell}_1)$ have to change places, where $\hat{m}_1$ is defined by (2) and forms a canonical basis together with $\hat{\ell}_1$:

$$\begin{aligned} \hat{m}_1 &= \beta \hat{m}_0 + \alpha \hat{\ell}_0 \\ \hat{\ell}_1 &= \alpha' \hat{m}_0 + \beta' \hat{\ell}_0 \end{aligned}, \quad \begin{vmatrix} \beta & \alpha \\ \alpha' & \beta' \end{vmatrix} = 1.$$

It follows $\hat{m}_0 = \beta' \hat{m}_1 - \alpha \hat{\ell}_1$. Since B_0 and B_1 induce on their common boundary opposite orientations, we may choose $(\hat{m}_1, -\hat{\ell}_1)$ as canonical curves on T. Thus $\mathfrak{b}(\alpha, \beta) = \mathfrak{b}(\alpha, \beta')$, $\beta\beta' - \alpha\alpha' = 1$ i.e. $\beta\beta' \equiv 1 \bmod \alpha$.

A reflection in a plane perpendicular to the projection plane and containing the straight segments w_i transforms a normal form $\mathfrak{b}(\alpha, \beta)$ into $\mathfrak{b}(\alpha, -\beta)$. Therefore: $\mathfrak{b}^*(\alpha, \beta) = \mathfrak{b}(\alpha, -\beta)$.

B Viergeflechte (4-Plats)

Knots with two bridges were first studied in the form of 4-plats (see Chapter 2D), [Bankwitz-Schumann 1934], and certain advantages of this point of view will become apparent in the following. We return to the situation described in 11B (Fig. 11.7).

12.9 S^3 now is composed of two balls B_0, B_1 and $I \times S^2$ in between, containing a 4-braid $\mathfrak{z}$ which defines a 2-bridge knot $\mathfrak{b}(\alpha, \beta)$. The 2-fold branched covering M^3 is by 12.3 a lens space $L(\alpha, \beta)$. (In this section we always choose $0 < \beta < \alpha$, β odd or even.) Lemma 11.8 shows that the braid operations σ_1, σ_2 lift to Dehn twists δ_1, δ_2 such that

$$\delta_1(\hat{m}_0) = \hat{m}_0, \qquad \delta_2(\hat{m}_0) = \hat{m}_0 + \hat{\ell}_0$$
$$\delta_1(\hat{\ell}_0) = \hat{m}_0 - \hat{\ell}_0, \quad \delta_2(\hat{\ell}_0) = \hat{\ell}_0.$$

Thus we may assign to σ_1, σ_2 matrices

$$\sigma_1 \mapsto A_1 = \begin{pmatrix} 1 & -1 \\ 0 & 1 \end{pmatrix}, \quad \sigma_2 \mapsto A_2 = \begin{pmatrix} 1 & 0 \\ 1 & 1 \end{pmatrix}$$

which describe the linear mappings induced on $H_1(\hat{F}_0)$ by δ_1, δ_2 with respect to the basis $\hat{m}_0, \hat{\ell}_0$. A braid $\zeta = \sigma_2^{a_1}\sigma_1^{-a_2}\sigma_2^{a_3} \dots \sigma_2^{a_m}$ induces the transformation

(1) $$A = \begin{pmatrix} 1 & 0 \\ a_1 & 1 \end{pmatrix} \begin{pmatrix} 1 & a_2 \\ 0 & 1 \end{pmatrix} \cdots \begin{pmatrix} 1 & a_{m-1} \\ 0 & 1 \end{pmatrix} \begin{pmatrix} 1 & 0 \\ a_m & 1 \end{pmatrix}.$$

Suppose the 2-fold covering M^3 of a 4-plat as in Fig. 11.7 is given by a Heegaard splitting $M^3 = T_0 \cup_{\hat{h}} T_1$, $\partial T_j = \hat{F}_j$. Relative to bases $(\hat{m}_0, \hat{\ell}_0)$, $(\hat{m}_1, \hat{\ell}_1)$ of $H_1(\hat{F}_0)$, $H_1(\hat{F}_1)$, the isomorphism $\hat{h}_*\colon H_1(\hat{F}_0) \to H_1(\hat{F}_1)$ is represented by a unimodular matrix:

$$A = \begin{pmatrix} \beta & \alpha' \\ \alpha & \beta' \end{pmatrix}; \quad \alpha, \alpha', \beta, \beta' \in \mathbb{Z}; \ \beta\beta' - \alpha\alpha' = 1.$$

The integers α' and β' are determined up to a change $\alpha' \mapsto \alpha' + c\beta$, $\beta' \mapsto \beta' + c\alpha$ which can be achieved by

$$\begin{pmatrix} \beta & \alpha' \\ \alpha & \beta' \end{pmatrix} \begin{pmatrix} 1 & c \\ 0 & 1 \end{pmatrix} = \begin{pmatrix} \beta & \alpha' + c\beta \\ \alpha & \beta' + c\alpha \end{pmatrix}.$$

This corresponds to a substitution $\zeta \mapsto \zeta\sigma_1^c$ which does not alter the plat. The product (1) defines a sequence of equations ($r_0 = \alpha$, $r_1 = \beta$):

(2) $$\begin{aligned} r_0 &= a_1 r_1 + r_2 \\ r_1 &= a_2 r_2 + r_3 \\ &\vdots \\ r_{m-1} &= a_m r_m + 0, \quad |r_m| = 1, \end{aligned}$$

following from:

$$\begin{pmatrix} 1 & 0 \\ -a_i & 1 \end{pmatrix} \begin{pmatrix} r_i & * \\ r_{i-1} & * \end{pmatrix} = \begin{pmatrix} r_i & * \\ r_{i-1} - a_i r_i & * \end{pmatrix} = \begin{pmatrix} r_i & * \\ r_{i+1} & * \end{pmatrix},$$

$$\begin{pmatrix} 1 & -a_{i+1} \\ 0 & 1 \end{pmatrix} \begin{pmatrix} r_i & * \\ r_{i+1} & * \end{pmatrix} = \begin{pmatrix} r_i - a_{i+1} r_{i+1} & * \\ r_{i+1} & * \end{pmatrix} = \begin{pmatrix} r_{i+2} & * \\ r_{i+1} & * \end{pmatrix}.$$

If we postulate $0 \leqq r_i < r_{i-1}$, the equations (2) describe a euclidean algorithm which is uniquely defined by $\alpha = r_0$ and $\beta = r_1$.

12.10 Definition. We call a system of equations (2) with $r_i, a_j \in \mathbb{Z}$, a *generalized euclidean algorithm of length m*, if $0 < |r_i| < |r_{i-1}|$, $1 \leqq i \leqq m$, and $r_0 \geqq 0$.
Such an algorithm can also be expressed by a continued fraction:

$$\frac{\beta}{\alpha} = \frac{r_1}{r_0} = \cfrac{1}{a_1 + \cfrac{1}{a_2 + \cfrac{1}{a_3 + \cdots \cdots + a_{m-1} + \cfrac{1}{a_m}}}} = [a_1, a_2, \ldots, a_m].$$

The integers a_i are called the *quotients of the continued fraction.* From $0 < |r_m| < |r_{m-1}|$ it follows that $|a_m| \geqq 2$. We allow the augmentation

$$(3) \qquad [a_1, a_2, \ldots, (a_m \pm 1), \mp 1] = [a_1, a_2, \ldots, a_m],$$

since

$$a_m \pm 1 + \frac{1}{\mp 1} = a_m.$$

Thus, by allowing $|r_{m-1}| = |r_m| = 1$, we may assume m to be odd.

12.11 To return to the 2-bridge knot $\mathfrak{b}(\alpha, \beta)$ we assume $\alpha > 0$ and $0 \leqq \beta < \alpha$, $gcd(\alpha, \beta) = 1$. For any integral solution of (2) with $r_0 = \alpha$, $r_1 = \beta$, one obtains a matrix equation:

$$(4) \qquad \begin{pmatrix} \beta & \alpha' \\ \alpha & \beta' \end{pmatrix} = \begin{pmatrix} 1 & 0 \\ a_1 & 1 \end{pmatrix} \begin{pmatrix} 1 & a_2 \\ 0 & 1 \end{pmatrix} \cdots \begin{pmatrix} 1 & 0 \\ a_m & 1 \end{pmatrix} \begin{pmatrix} \pm 1 & * \\ 0 & \pm 1 \end{pmatrix}, \ m \text{ odd},$$

$$(5) \qquad \begin{pmatrix} \beta & \alpha' \\ \alpha & \beta' \end{pmatrix} = \begin{pmatrix} 1 & 0 \\ a_1 & 1 \end{pmatrix} \begin{pmatrix} 1 & a_2 \\ 0 & 1 \end{pmatrix} \cdots \begin{pmatrix} 1 & a_m \\ 0 & 1 \end{pmatrix} \begin{pmatrix} 0 & \pm 1 \\ \pm 1 & * \end{pmatrix}, \ m \text{ even}.$$

The first equation (m odd) shows that a 4-plat defined by the braid $\mathfrak{z} = \sigma_2^{a_1} \sigma_1^{-a_2} \sigma_2^{a_3} \ldots \sigma_2^{a_m}$ is the knot $\mathfrak{b}(\alpha, \beta)$, since its 2-fold branched covering is the (oriented) lens space $L(\alpha, \beta)$. The last factor on the right represents a power of σ_1 which does not change the knot, and which induces a homeomorphism of $\hat{B}_1$. In the case when m is even, observe that

$$\begin{pmatrix} 0 & -1 \\ 1 & b \end{pmatrix} = \begin{pmatrix} 1 & 0 \\ -b & 1 \end{pmatrix} \begin{pmatrix} 0 & -1 \\ 1 & 0 \end{pmatrix}.$$

From this it follows (Fig. 12.4) that $\mathfrak{b}(\alpha, \beta)$ is defined by $\mathfrak{z} = \sigma_2^{a_1} \sigma_1^{-a_2} \ldots \sigma_2^{-a_m}$ but

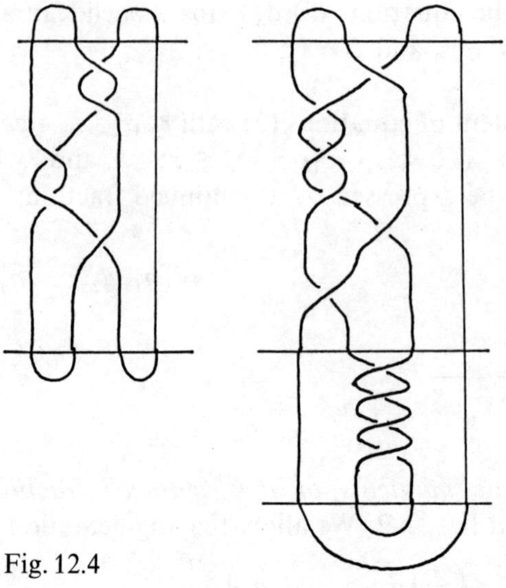

Fig. 12.4

that the plat has to be closed at the lower end in a different way, switching meridian $\hat{m}_1$ and longitude $\hat{\ell}_1$ corresponding to the matrix

$$\begin{pmatrix} 0 & -1 \\ 1 & 0 \end{pmatrix}.$$

12.12 Remark. The case $\alpha = 1$, $\beta = 0$, is described by the matrix

$$\begin{pmatrix} 0 & -1 \\ 1 & 0 \end{pmatrix} = \begin{pmatrix} \beta & \alpha' \\ \alpha & \beta' \end{pmatrix}.$$

The corresponding plat (Fig. 12.5) is a trivial knot. The matrix

$$\begin{pmatrix} 1 & 0 \\ 0 & 1 \end{pmatrix} = \begin{pmatrix} \beta & \alpha' \\ \alpha & \beta' \end{pmatrix}$$

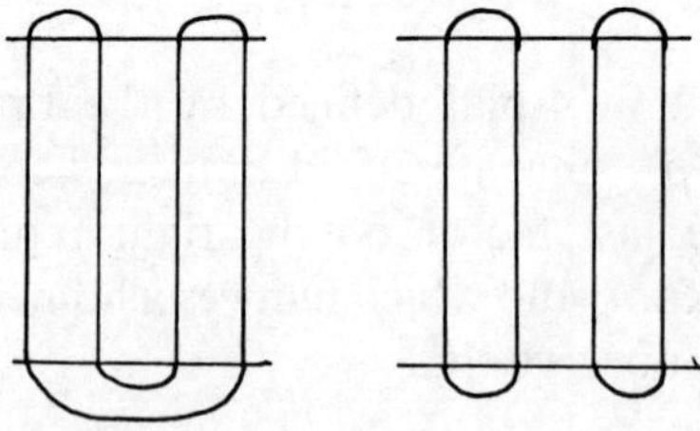

Fig. 12.5

is characterized by the pair $(0, 1) = (\alpha, \beta)$ (Fig. 12.5). It is therefore reasonable to denote by $\mathfrak{b}(1, 0)$ resp. $\mathfrak{b}(0, 1)$ the unknot resp. two split unknotted components, and to put: $L(1,0) = S^3$, $L(0,1) = S^1 \times S^2$. Using the connection between the numbers a_i and the quotient $\beta\alpha^{-1}$ one may invent many different normal forms of (unoriented) knots with two bridges as 4-plats. All it requires is to make the algorithm (2) unique and to take into account that the balls B_0 and B_1 are exchangeable.

12.13 Proposition. *The (unoriented) knot (or link)* $\mathfrak{b}(\alpha, \beta)$, $0 < \beta < \alpha$, *has a presentation as a 4-plat with a defining braid* $\mathfrak{z} = \sigma_2^{a_1}\sigma_1^{-a_2} \ldots \sigma_2^{a_m}$, $a_i > 0$, *m odd, where the* a_i *are the quotients of the continued fraction* $[a_1, \ldots, a_m] = \beta\alpha^{-1}$. *Sequences* $(a_1, \ldots, a_m)$ *and* $(a'_1, \ldots, a'_{m'})$ *define the same knot or link if and only if* $m = m'$, *and* $a_i = a'_i$ *or* $a_i = a'_{m-i}$, $1 \leqq i \leqq m$.

Proof. The algorithm (2) is unique, since $a_i > 0$ implies that $r_i > 0$ for $m \geqq i \geqq 1$. The expansion of $\beta\alpha^{-1}$ as a continued fraction of odd length m is unique [Perron 1954]. A rotation through π about an axis in the projection plane containing $\overline{AB}$ and $\overline{CD}$ finally exchanges B_0 and B_1; its lift exchanges $\hat{B}_0$ and $\hat{B}_1$. □

Remark: It is an easy exercise in continued fractions (E 12.3) to prove $\beta'\alpha^{-1} = [a_m, \ldots, a_1]$ if $\beta\alpha^{-1} = [a_1, \ldots, a_m]$, and $\beta\beta' \equiv 1 \bmod \alpha$.

Note that the normal form of 4-plats described in 12.13 represents alternating plats, hence:

12.14 Proposition (Bankwitz-Schumann). *Knots and links with two bridges are alternating.* □

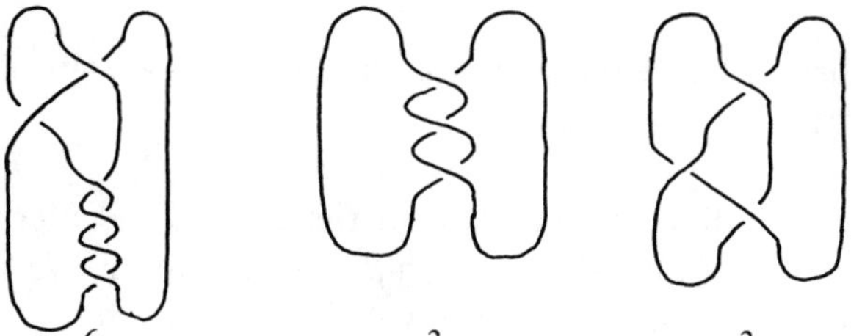

6_1 3_1 3_1

Fig. 12.6

12.15 Examples. Consider $\mathfrak{b}(9,5) = 6_1$ as an example: $5/9 = [1,1,4]$. The corresponding plat is defined by $\sigma_2\sigma_1^{-1}\sigma_2^4$ (Fig. 12.6). (Verify: $2/9 = [4,1,1]$, $2 \cdot 5 \equiv 1 \bmod 9$.) Figure 12.6 also shows the normal forms of the two trefoils: $\mathfrak{z} = \sigma_2^3$ resp. $\mathfrak{z}' = \sigma_2\sigma_1^{-1}\sigma_2$, according to $1/3 = [3]$, $2/3 = [1,1,1]$.

A generalized euclidean algorithm is, of course, not unique. One may impose various conditions on it to make it so, for instance, the quotients a_i, $1 \leqq i < m$, can obviously be chosen either even or odd. Combining such conditions for the quotients with $r_j > 0$ for some j gives multifarious possibilities for normal forms of 4-plats.

We choose from each pair of mirror images the one with $\beta > 0$, β odd.

12.16 Proposition. *There is a unique generalized euclidean algorithm*

$$r_{i-1} = c_i r_i + r_{i+1}$$

of length m with:

$$r_0 = \alpha > 0,\ r_1 = \beta > 0,\ gcd(\alpha, \beta) = 1,\ \beta \text{ odd},$$
$$r_{2j} > 0,\ c_{2j} = 2b_j,\ 1 \leqq 2j \leqq m,$$
$$|r_{i-1}| > |r_i| \quad \text{for } 0 \leqq i < m,\ |r_{m-1}| \geqq |r_m|.$$
$$\text{If } |r_{m-1}| = |r_m|, \text{ then } c_{m-1} c_m > 0.$$

The length m of the algorithm is odd ($r_{m+1} = 0$), $r_{2j-1} \equiv 1 \bmod 2$, *and* $a_j b_j > 0$ *for* $a_j = c_{2j-1}$, $1 \leqq j \leqq \dfrac{m+1}{2}$.

Proof. The algorithm is easily seen to be unique, and $r_{2j-1} \equiv m \equiv 1 \bmod 2$ is an immediate consequence. From

$$r_{2j-2} = a_j r_{2j-1} + r_{2j},$$
$$r_{2j-1} = 2b_j r_{2j} + r_{2j+1}$$

one derives

$$(r_{2j-1} - r_{2j+1}) a_j = 2a_j b_j r_{2j}$$

and that the sign of the left hand expression is the same as the sign of $r_{2j-1} a_j = r_{2j-2} - r_{2j} > 0$, since $|r_{2j-1}| > |r_{2j+1}|$. □

12.17 Remark. The quotients a_i obtained from the generalized algorithm of 12.16 may change if $r_1 = \beta$ is replaced by β' with $\beta\beta' \equiv \pm 1 \bmod \alpha$. We are, however, only interested in the fact that there is always a presentation according to 12.16 of any knot $\mathrm{b}(\alpha, \beta)$ or $\mathrm{b}^*(\alpha, \beta) = \mathrm{b}(\alpha, -\beta)$, and we shall exploit this to get information about the Alexander polynomial and the genus of $\mathrm{b}(\alpha, \beta)$.

C Alexander Polynomial and Genus of a Knot with Two Bridges

We have shown in 8.13 that the Alexander polynomial $\Delta(t)$ of a knot may be written as a polynomial with integral coefficients in $u = t + t^{-1} - 2$, $\Delta(t) = f(u)$. Hence, $\Delta(t^2)$ is a polynomial in $z = (t - t^{-1})$. (It is even a polynomial in z^2.)

J.H. Conway [1970] defined a polynomial $\nabla_{\mathfrak{k}}(z)$ with integral coefficients for (oriented) links which can be inductively computed from a regular projection of a link $\mathfrak{k}$ in the following way:

12.18 (Conway potential function). (1) $\nabla_{\mathfrak{k}}(z) = 1$, if $\mathfrak{k}$ is trivial.

(2) $\nabla_{\mathfrak{k}}(z) = 0$, if $\mathfrak{k}$ is a split link.

(3) $\nabla_{\mathfrak{k}_+} - \nabla_{\mathfrak{k}_-} = z \cdot \nabla_{\mathfrak{k}_0}$, if $\mathfrak{k}_+$, $\mathfrak{k}_-$, and $\mathfrak{k}_0$ differ by a local operation of the kind depicted in Figure 12.7.

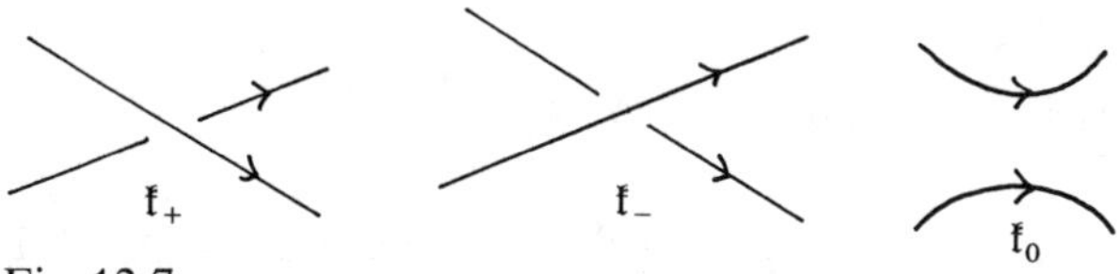

Fig. 12.7

Changing overcrossings into undercrossings eventually transforms any regular projection into that of a trivial knot or splittable link, compare 2.2. Equation (3) may therefore be used as an algorithm (*Conway algorithm*) to compute $\nabla_{\mathfrak{k}}(z)$ with initial conditions (1) and (2). Thus, if there is a function $\nabla_{\mathfrak{k}}(z)$ satisfying conditions (1), (2), (3) which is an invariant of the link, it must be unique.

12.19 Proposition. *(a) There is a unique integral polynomial $\nabla_{\mathfrak{k}}(z)$ satisfying (1), (2), (3); it is called the* Conway potential function *and is an invariant of the link.*

(b) $\nabla_{\mathfrak{k}}(t - t^{-1}) \doteq \Delta(t^2)$ *for* $\mu = 1$,

$\nabla_{\mathfrak{k}}(t - t^{-1}) \doteq (t^2 - 1)^{\mu - 1} \nabla(t^2)$ *for* $\mu > 1$.

(Here $\Delta(t)$ denotes the Alexander polynomial, and $\nabla(t)$ the Hosokawa polynomial of $\mathfrak{k}$, see 9.18.)

We shall prove 12.19 in 13.35 by defining an invariant function $\nabla_{\mathfrak{k}}(t)$. Observe that the equations that relate $\nabla_{\mathfrak{k}}(t - t^{-1})$ with the Alexander polynomial and the Hosokawa polynomial suffice to show the invariance of $\nabla_{\mathfrak{k}}(z)$ in the case of knots, whereas for $\mu > 1$ there remains the ambiguity of the sign.

12.20 Definition. The polynomials $f_n(z)$, $n \in \mathbb{Z}$, defined by:

$$f_{n+1}(z) = z f_n(z) + f_{n-1}(z),$$
$$f_0(z) = 0, f_1(z) = 1,$$
$$f_{-n}(z) = (-1)^{n+1} f_n(z) \quad \text{for } n \geqq 0$$

are called *Fibonacci polynomials*.

12.21 Lemma. *The Fibonacci polynomials are of the form:*

$$f_{2n-1} = 1 + a_1 z^2 + a_2 z^4 + \dots + a_{n-1} z^{2(n-1)}$$
$$f_{2n} = z(b_0 + b_1 z^2 + b_2 z^4 + \dots + b_{n-1} z^{2(n-1)}),$$
$$a_i,\ b_i \in \mathbb{Z}, \quad n \geqq 0,\ a_{n-1} = b_{n-1} = 1\,.$$

Consequence: $\deg f_n = \deg f_{-n} = n-1$.

Proof. An easy exercise E 12.6. □

Let $\mathfrak{b}(\alpha, \beta)$, $\alpha > \beta > 0$, $\alpha \equiv \beta \equiv 1 \bmod 2$, be represented by the 4-plat defined by the braid

$$\mathfrak{z} = \sigma_2^{a_1} \sigma_1^{-2b_1} \sigma_2^{a_2} \sigma_1^{-2b_2} \dots \sigma_1^{-2b_{k-1}} \sigma_2^{a_k},\ k = \frac{m+1}{2},$$

with $\beta/\alpha = [a_1, 2b_1, a_2, 2b_2, \dots, a_k]$ according to the algorithm of 12.16. We know $a_j b_j > 0$, but $b_j a_{j+1}$ may be positive or negative. Assign a sequence $(i_1, i_2, \dots, i_r)$ to the sequence of quotients noting down i_j, if $b_{i_j} a_{i_j+1} < 0$.

12.22 Proposition. *Let* $\mathfrak{b}(\alpha, \beta)$ *be defined as a 4-plat by the braid*

$$\mathfrak{z} = \sigma_2^{a_1} \sigma_1^{-2b_1} \dots \sigma_1^{-2b_{k-1}} \sigma_2^{a_k}, \quad m = 2k-1,$$

and let $i_1, i_2, \dots, i_r$ *denote the sequence of indices where a change of sign occurs in the sequence of quotients.*

(a) $\deg \nabla_{\mathfrak{b}}(z) = (\sum_{j=1}^{k} |a_j|) - 1$

where $\nabla_{\mathfrak{b}}(z)$ *is the Conway polynomial of* $\mathfrak{b}(\alpha, \beta) = \mathfrak{b}$.

(b) The absolute value of the leading coefficient $C(\nabla_{\mathfrak{b}})$ *of* $\nabla_{\mathfrak{b}}(z)$ *is*

$$\prod_{j=1}^{k-1} (|b_j| + 1 - \eta_j) = |\,C(\nabla_{\mathfrak{b}})|,\ \eta_j = \begin{cases} 1, j \in \{i_1, \dots, i_r\} \\ 0 \ \ \textit{otherwise} \end{cases}.$$

Proof. Orient the 4-plat defined by $\mathfrak{z}$ as in Fig. 12.8 – the fourth string downward. By applying the Conway algorithm it is easy to compute the Conway polynomial $\nabla_a(z)$ of the 4-plat defined by $\mathfrak{z} = \sigma_2^a$, $a > 0$: $\nabla_a = (-1)^{a+1} f_a$, f_a the a-th Fibonacci polynomial. Equally $\nabla_{-a} = (-1)^{a+1} \nabla_a$. Now assume $a > 0, b > 0, \mathfrak{z} = \sigma_2^a \sigma_1^{-2b} \sigma_2^c$ (The conditions of 12.16 exclude $c = -1$.) The Conway polynomial of the 4-plat defined by $\mathfrak{z}$ is denoted by ∇_{abc}. Apply again the Conway algorithm to the double points of σ_2^a, working downward from the top of the braid:

$$\begin{aligned} \nabla_{abc} &= (-1)^a f_{a-1} \nabla_c + (-1)^{a+1} f_a \nabla_{c+1} - b(-1)^{a+1} z \cdot f_a \nabla_c \\ &= ((-1)^a f_{a-1} + (-1)^a b \cdot z f_a)(-1)^{c+1} f_c + (-1)^{a+1+c} f_a f_{c+1} \\ &= \nabla_{a-1} \nabla_c + \nabla_a \nabla_{c+1} - bz \nabla_a \nabla_c . \end{aligned}$$

Using 12.21 one obtains

$$c > 0:\ \deg \nabla_{abc} = a + c - 1,$$
$$|C(\nabla_{abc})| = |b + 1|.$$
$$c < 0:\ \deg \nabla_{abc} = 1 + a - 1 - c - 1 = a - c - 1,$$
$$|C(\nabla_{abc})| = |b|.$$

In the same way the case $a < 0$, $b < 0$, $c \neq 1$ can be treated:

$$\nabla_{abc} = \nabla_{a+1}\nabla_c + \nabla_a \nabla_{c-1} - bz\nabla_a \nabla_c.$$

Again

$$\deg \nabla_{abc} = |a| + |c| - 1,$$
$$C(\nabla_{abc}) = |b| + 1 - \eta, \quad \eta = \begin{cases} 1, & c > 0 \\ 0, & c < 0 \end{cases}.$$

Now suppose $\mathfrak{z} = \sigma_2^{a_1}\sigma_1^{-2b_1} \cdot \mathfrak{z}'$, $\mathfrak{z}' = \sigma_2^{a_2} \cdot \sigma_1^{-2b_2} \ldots$, $a_1 > 0$, $a_2 > 0$. One has

$$\nabla_{\mathfrak{z}} = \nabla_{a_1}\nabla_{\sigma_2\mathfrak{z}'} + \nabla_{a_1-1}\nabla_{\mathfrak{z}'} - b_1 z\nabla_{a_1}\nabla_{\mathfrak{z}'},$$
$$\deg \nabla_{\mathfrak{z}} = \deg \nabla_{a_1}\nabla_{\sigma_2\mathfrak{z}'}.$$

($\nabla_{\mathfrak{z}}$ is the polynomial of the 4-plat defined by $\mathfrak{z}$.)
It follows by induction that

$$\deg \nabla_{\mathfrak{z}} = |a_1| - 1 + \sum_{j>1} |a_j| = \Big(\sum_{j=1}^{k} |a_j|\Big) - 1,$$

and

$$|C(\nabla_{\mathfrak{z}})| = \prod_{j=1}^{k-1} (|b_j| + 1 - \eta_j).$$

Similarly, for $a_1 > 0$, $a_2 < 0$

$$\deg \nabla_{\mathfrak{z}} = \deg \nabla_{a_1}\nabla_{\mathfrak{z}'} + 1$$
$$= (|a_1| - 1) + \Big[\Big(\sum_{j>1}^{k} |a_j|\Big) - 1\Big] + 1$$
$$= \Big(\sum_{j=1}^{k} |a_j|\Big) - 1. \quad \square$$

Since 2-bridge knots are alternating, $\deg \nabla_{\mathfrak{b}}(z) = 2g + \mu - 1$ where g is the genus of $\mathfrak{b}(\alpha, \beta)$ [Crowell 1959]. Moreover, $|C(\nabla_{\mathfrak{b}}(z))| = |C(\Delta(t))| = 1$ characterizes fibred knots [Murasugi 1960, 1963]. A proof of both results is given in 13.26. From this follows

12.23 Proposition. *The genus of a 2-bridge knot* $\mathfrak{b}(\alpha, \beta)$ *is* $g(\alpha, \beta) = \frac{1}{2}\big[\big(\sum_{j=1}^{k} |a_j|\big) - \mu\big]$. *The knot* $\mathfrak{b}(\alpha, \beta)$ *is fibred if and only if its defining braid is of the form*

$$\mathfrak{z} = \sigma_2^{a_1}\sigma_1^{-2}\sigma_2^{-a_2}\sigma_1^{2}\sigma_2^{a_3}\sigma_1^{-2} \ldots \sigma_2^{\pm a_k},\ a_j > 0,\ k > 0.$$

(The quotients a_j, b_j of $\beta\alpha^{-1}$ are determined by the algorithm of 12.16.)

Proof. It remains to prove the second assertion. It follows from 12.22 that $|b_j| = 1$, $\eta_j = 1$ for $1 \leqq j < k$. Since $b_1 = 1$, one has $b_j = (-1)^{j-1}$. □

12.24 Corollary. *There are infinitely many knots* $\mathfrak{b}(a, \beta)$ *of genus* $g > 0$*, and infinitely many fibred knots with two bridges. However, for any given genus there are only finitely many knots with two bridges which are fibred.* □

12.25 Proposition. *A knot with two bridges of genus one or its mirror image is of the form* $\mathfrak{b}(\alpha, \beta)$ *with:*

$$\beta = 2c, \quad \alpha = 2b\beta \pm 1, \quad c, b \in \mathbb{N}.$$

The trefoil and the four knot are the only fibred 2-bridge knots of genus one.

Proof. This is a special case of 12.23 and the proof involves only straight forward computations. By 12.23, $k < 4$.

For $k = 1$ one obtains the sequence [3] which defines the trefoil (see Fig. 12.6).

For $k = 2$ there are two types of sequences, see 12.23 and 12.16:

$$[2, 2b, 1], [1, 2b, \pm 2], \quad b \in \mathbb{N}.$$

The sequence $[1, 2, -2]$ defines a fibred knot – the four knot.

$k = 3$: The sequences are then of the form:

$[1, 2b, 1, 2c, 1]$ or $[1, 2b, -1, -2c, -1]$, $b, c \in \mathbb{N}$. This leads to

$$\alpha = 4(b+1)(c+1) - 1, \quad \beta = 2(c+1)(2b+1) - 1, \quad \textit{resp.}$$
$$\alpha = 4b(c+1) + 1, \quad \beta = 2(c+1)(2b-1) + 1.$$

The formulae become simpler if β is replaced by $\alpha - \beta$. □

12.26 Remark. If $\mathfrak{b}(\alpha, \beta)$ is given in a normal form according to 12.16 the band marked as a hatched region in Figure 12.8 is an orientable surface of minimal genus spanning $\mathfrak{b}(\alpha, \beta)$.

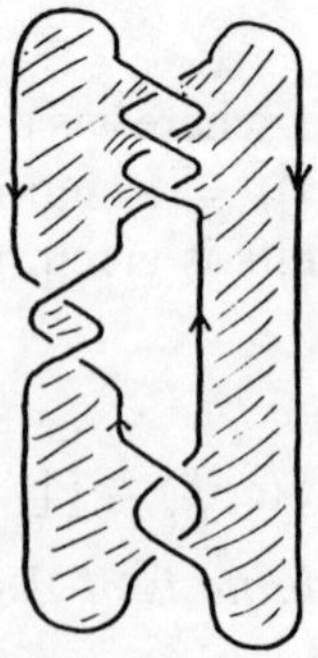

Fig. 12.8

Proposition 12.23 is a version of a theorem proved first in [Funcke 1978] and [Hartley 1979]. R. Hartley also proves in this paper a monotony property of the coefficients of the Alexander polynomial of $\mathfrak{b}(\alpha, \beta)$. See also [Burde 1984, 1985].

D Classification of Montesinos Links

The classification of knots and links with two bridges was achieved by classifying their twofold branched coverings – the lens spaces. It is natural to use this tool in the case of a larger class of manifolds which can be classified. Montesinos [1973, 1979] defined a set of links whose twofold branched covering spaces are Seifert fibre spaces. Their classification is a straight forward generalization of Seifert's idea in the case of 2-bridge knots.

We start with a definition of Montesinos links, and formulate the classification theorem of [Bonahon 1979]. Then we show that the twofold branched covering is a Seifert fibre space. Those Seifert fibre spaces are classified by their fundamental groups. By repeating the arguments for the classification of those groups we classify the Seifert fibre space together with the covering transformation. This then gives the classification of Montesinos links.

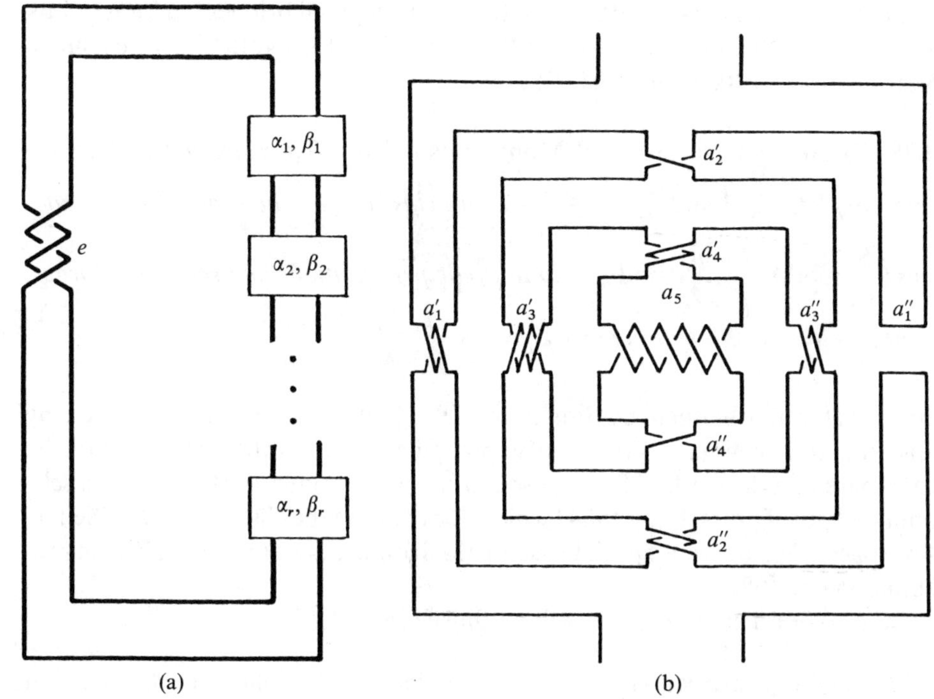

Fig. 12.9

12.27 Definition (Montesinos link). A *Montesinos link* (or *knot*) has a projection as shown in Figure 12.9. The numbers e, a_i', a_i'' denote numbers of half twists. A box $\boxed{\alpha, \beta}$ stands for a so-called *rational tangle* as illustrated in Fig. 12.9(b), and α, β are defined by the continued fraction $\frac{\beta}{\alpha} = [a_1, -a_2, a_3, \ldots, \pm a_m]$, $a_j = a_j' + a_j''$ together with the conditions that α and β are relatively prime and $\alpha > 0$. A further assumption is that $\frac{\beta}{\alpha}$ is not an integer, that is $\boxed{\alpha, \beta}$ is not 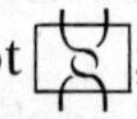; in this case the knot has a simpler projection. The above Montesinos link is denoted by $\mathfrak{m}(e; \alpha_1/\beta_1, \ldots, \alpha_r/\beta_r)$. (In Fig. 12.9(a): $e = 3$; in Fig. 12.9(b): $n = 5$, $a_1' = 2$, $a_1'' = 0 \Rightarrow a_1 = 2$; $a_2' = -1$, $a_2'' = -2 \Rightarrow a_2 = -3$; $a_3 = -1$, $a_4 = 3$, $a_5 = 5$ and $\beta/\alpha = 43/105$.)

As before in the case of 2-bridge knots we think of $\mathfrak{m}$ as unoriented. It follows from Section B that *the continued fractions* $\frac{\beta}{\alpha} = [a_1, \ldots, \pm a_m]$ *(including 1/0* $= \infty$*) classify the rational tangles up to isotopies which leave the boundary of the box pointwise fixed.*

It is easily seen that a rational tangle (α, β) is the intersection of the box with a 4-plat: there is an isotopy which reduces all twists a_j'' to 0-twists. A tangle in this position may gradually be deformed into a 4-plat working from the outside towards the inside. A rational tangle closed by two trivial bridges is a knot or link $\mathfrak{b}(\alpha, \beta)$, see the definition in 12.1 and Proposition 12.13. (Note that we excluded the trivial cases $\mathfrak{b}(0, 1)$ and $\mathfrak{b}(1, 0)$.)

12.28 Theorem (classification of Montesinos links). *Montesinos links with r rational tangles,* $r \geqq 3$ *and* $\sum_{j=1}^{r} \frac{1}{\alpha_j} \leqq r - 2$, *are classified by the ordered set of fractions* $\left(\frac{\beta_1}{\alpha_1} \bmod 1, \ldots, \frac{\beta_r}{\alpha_r} \bmod 1\right)$, *up to cyclic permutations and reversal of order, together with the rational number* $e_0 = e + \sum_{j=1}^{r} \frac{\beta_j}{\alpha_j}$.

This result was obtained by Bonahon [1979]. Another proof was given by Boileau and Siebenmann [1980]. The proof here follows the arguments of the latter, based on the method Seifert used to classify 2-bridge knots. We give a self-contained proof [Zieschang 1984] which does not use the classification of Seifert fibre spaces. We prove a special case of the Isomorphiesatz 3.7 in [Zieschang-Zimmermann 1982].

The *proof* of Theorem 12.28 will be finished in 12.37.

12.29 Another construction of Montesinos links. For the following construction we use Proposition 12.3. From S^3 we remove $r + 1$ disjoint balls $B_0, B_1, \ldots, B_r$

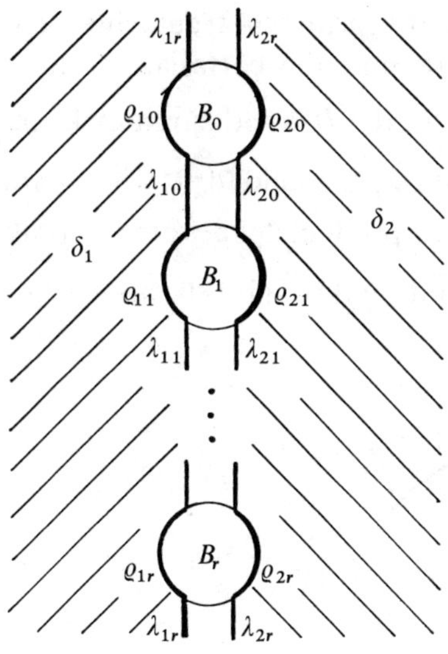

Fig. 12.10

and consider two disjoint disks δ_1 and δ_2 in $\overline{S^3 - \bigcup_{i=0}^{r} B_i} = W$ where the boundary $\partial\delta_j$ intersects B_i in an arc $\varrho_{ji} = \partial B_i \cap \delta_j = B_i \cap \delta_j$. Assume that $\partial\delta_j = \varrho_{j0}\lambda_{j0}\varrho_{j1}\lambda_{j1}\dots\varrho_{jr}\lambda_{jr}$. In B_i let κ_{1i} and κ_{2i} define a tangle of type (α_i, β_i). We assume that in B_0 there is only an e-twist, that is $\alpha_0 = 1$, $\beta_0 = e$. *Then* $\bigcup(\lambda_{ji} \cup \kappa_{ji})$ $(j = 1, 2;\ i = 0, \dots, r)$ *is the Montesinos link* $\mathfrak{m}(e; (\alpha_1, \beta_1), \dots, (\alpha_r, \beta_r))$, see Figure 12.10 and Proposition 12.13.

12.30 Proposition. *(a) The twofold branched covering $\hat{C}_2$ of S^3 branched over the Montesinos link $\mathfrak{m}(e; \alpha_1/\beta_1, \dots, \alpha_r/\beta_r)$ is a Seifert fibre space with the fundamental group*

12.31 $\pi_1 \hat{C}_2 = \langle h, s_1, \dots, s_r \mid s_i^{\alpha_i} h^{\beta_i}, [s_i, h]\ (1 \leqq i \leqq r), s_1 \dots s_r h^{-e} \rangle.$

(b) The covering transformation Φ of the twofold covering induces the automorphism

12.32 $\varphi\colon \pi_1 \hat{C}_2 \to \pi_1 \hat{C}_2, h \mapsto h^{-1}, s_i \mapsto s_1 \dots s_{i-1} s_i^{-1} s_{i-1}^{-1} \dots s_1^{-1}\ (1 \leqq i \leqq r).$

(c) The covering transformations of the universal cover of $\hat{C}_2$ together with the lift of Φ form a group $\mathfrak{H}$ with the following presentations:

12.33
$$\begin{aligned}\mathfrak{H} &= \langle h, s_1, \dots, s_r, c \mid chc^{-1}h, cs_ic^{-1} \cdot (s_1 \dots s_{i-1} s_i s_{i-1}^{-1} \dots s_1^{-1}),\\ &\qquad [s_i, h], s_i^{\alpha_i} h^{\beta_i}\ (1 \leqq i \leqq r), s_1 \dots s_r h^{-e}, c^2 \rangle\\ &= \langle h, c_0, \dots, c_r \mid c_i^2, c_i h c_i^{-1} h\ (0 \leqq i \leqq r), (c_{i-1}c_i)^{\alpha_i} h^{\beta_i}\ (1 \leqq i \leqq r), c_0^{-1} c_r h^{-e} \rangle.\end{aligned}$$

Proof. We use the notation of 12.29 and repeat the arguments of the proof 12.3. Cutting along δ_1 and δ_2 turns W into the cartesian product $\overline{(D^2 - \bigcup_{i=1}^{r} D_i)} \times I$ where D^2 is a 2-disk and the D_i are disjoint disks in D^2. The twofold covering T_r of W branched over the λ_{ji} is a solid torus with r parallel solid tori removed: $T_r = \overline{(D^2 - \bigcup_{i=1}^{r} D_i)} \times S^1$. The product defines an S^1-fibration of T_r. The covering transformation Φ is the rotation through 180° about the axis containing the arcs λ_{ji}, comp. Figure 12.11.

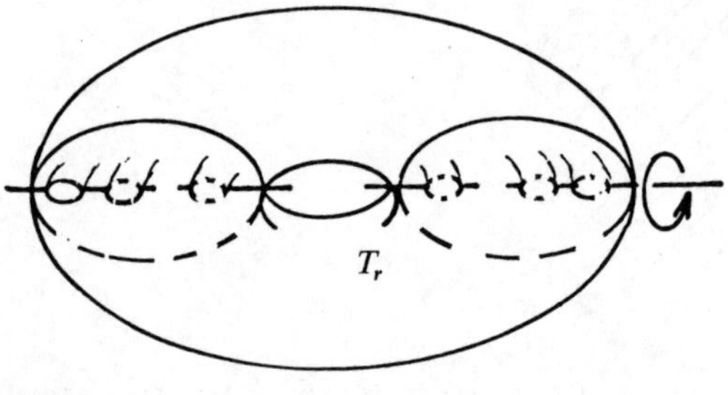

Fig. 12.11

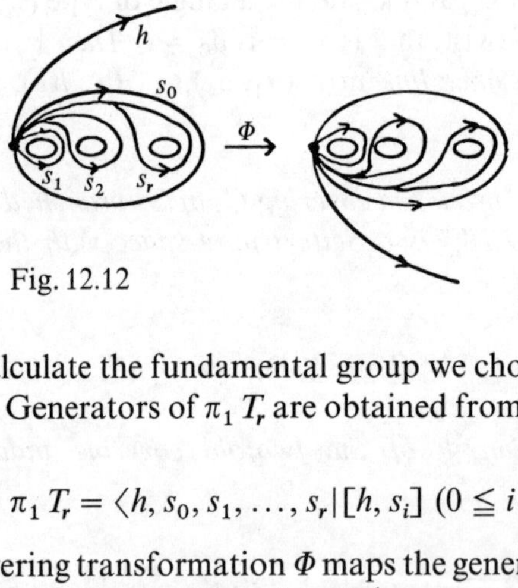

Fig. 12.12

To calculate the fundamental group we choose the base point on the axis and on ∂B_0. Generators of $\pi_1 T_r$ are obtained from the curves shown in Figure 12.12, and

$$\pi_1 T_r = \langle h, s_0, s_1, \ldots, s_r \mid [h, s_i] \ (0 \leqq i \leqq r), s_0 s_1 \ldots s_r \rangle .$$

The covering transformation Φ maps the generators as described in Figure 12.12; hence Φ_*: $\pi_1 T_r \to \pi_1 T_r$, $h \mapsto h^{-1}$, $s_0 \mapsto s_0^{-1}$, $s_1 \mapsto s_1^{-1}$, $s_2 \mapsto s_1 s_2^{-1} s_1^{-1}, \ldots,$ $s_r \mapsto s_1 \ldots s_{r-1} s_r^{-1} s_{r-1}^{-1} \ldots s_1^{-1}$. The twofold covering of $B_i (0 \leqq i \leqq r)$, branched over the arcs κ_{ji}, is a solid torus $\hat{V}_i$, see 12.3. Thus the twofold covering $\hat{C}_2$ of S^3 branched over m is $T_r \cup \bigcup_{i=0}^{r} \hat{V}_i = \hat{C}_2$ with corresponding boundaries identified. The fibration of T_r can be extended to the solid tori $\hat{V}_i$ as we have excluded the case $(\alpha_i, \beta_i) = (0, 1)$, and $\hat{C}_2$ obtains a Seifert fibration. Adding the solid tori $\hat{V}_i$ introduces the relations $s_i^{\alpha_i} h^{\beta_i}$ for $1 \leqq i \leqq r$ and $s_0 h^e$. This finishes the proof of (a).

The proof of (b) follows from the effect of Φ on $\pi_1 T_r$. The first presentation of 12.33 follows from 12.31 and 12.32 by interpreting $\pi_1 \hat{C}_2$ as the group of covering transformations of the universal covering of $\hat{C}_2$. It remains to show $c^2 = 1$. This follows from the fact that Φ has order 2 and has the base point as a fixed point.

Define $c_i = cs_1 \dots s_i$ $(1 \leqq i \leqq r)$ and $c_0 = c$. Then $s_i = c_{i-1}^{-1} c_i$ $(1 \leqq i \leqq r)$ and

$$\begin{aligned}\mathfrak{H} &= \langle h, c_0, \dots, c_r \,|\, c_0 h c_0^{-1} h,\ c_0 (c_{i-1}^{-1} c_i) c_0^{-1} \cdot c_0^{-1} (c_i c_{i-1}^{-1}) c_0, \\ &\qquad [c_{i-1}^{-1} c_i, h],\ (c_{i-1}^{-1} c_i)^{\alpha_i} h^{\beta_i}\ (1 \leqq i \leqq r),\ c_0^{-1} c_r h^{-e},\ c_0^2 \rangle \\ &= \langle h, c_0, \dots, c_r \,|\, c_i h c_i^{-1} h,\ c_i^2\ (0 \leqq i \leqq r), \\ &\qquad (c_{i-1} c_i)^{\alpha_i} h^{\beta_i}\ (1 \leqq i \leqq r),\ c_0^{-1} c_r h^{-e} \rangle. \quad \square\end{aligned}$$

12.34 Remark. For later use we note a geometric property of the twofold branched covering: The branch set $\hat{\mathfrak{m}}$ in $\hat{C}_2$ is the preimage of the Montesinos link $\mathfrak{m}$. From the construction of $\hat{C}_2$ it follows that $\hat{\mathfrak{m}}$ intersects each exceptional fibre exactly twice, in the "centres" of the pair of disks in Figure 12.11 belonging to one $\hat{V}_i$.

12.35 Lemma. *For* $\sum_{i=1}^{r} \frac{1}{\alpha_i} \leqq r - 2$ *the element h in the presentation 12.31 of* $\pi_1 \hat{C}_2$ *generates an infinite cyclic group* $\langle h \rangle$, *the centre of* $\pi_1 \hat{C}_2$.

Proof. $\pi_1 \hat{C}_2 / \langle h \rangle$ is a discontinuous group with compact fundamental domain of motions of the euclidean plane, if equality holds in the hypothesis, otherwise of the non-euclidean plane, and all transformations preserve orientation; see [ZVC 1980, 4.5.6, 4.8.2]. In both cases the group is generated by rotations and there are r rotation centres which are pairwise non-equivalent under the action of $\pi_1 \hat{C}_2$. A consequence is that the centre of $\pi_1 \hat{C}_2 / \langle h \rangle$ is trivial, see [ZVC 1980, 4.8.1c)]; hence, $\langle h \rangle$ is the centre of $\pi_1 \hat{C}_2$.

The proof that h has infinite order is more complicated. It is simple for $r > 3$. Then

$$\begin{aligned}\pi_1 \hat{C}_2 = \langle h, s_1, s_2 \,|\, s_i^{\alpha_i} h^{\beta_i}, [h, s_i]\ (1 \leqq i \leqq 2) \rangle *_{\mathbb{Z}^2} \\ \langle h, s_3, \dots, s_r \,|\, s_i^{\alpha_i} h^{\beta_i}, [h, s_i]\ (3 \leqq i \leqq r) \rangle\end{aligned}$$

where $\mathbb{Z}^2 \cong \langle h, s_1 s_2 \rangle \cong \langle h, (s_3 \dots s_r)^{-1} \rangle$. (It easily follows by arguments on free products that the above subgroups are isomorphic to $\mathbb{Z}^2$.) In particular, $\langle h \rangle \cong \mathbb{Z}$.

To show the lemma for $r = 3$ we prove the following Theorem 12.36 by repeating the arguments of the proof of Theorem 3.30.

12.36 Theorem. *Let M be an orientable 3-manifold with no sphere in its boundary. If* $\pi_1 M$ *is infinite, non-cyclic, and not a free product then M is aspherical and* $\pi_1 M$ *is torsion-free.*

Proof. If $\pi_2 M \neq 0$ there is, by the sphere theorem [Papakyriakopoulos 1957'], Appendix B6, [Hempel 1976, 4.3], an S^2, embedded in M, which is not null-homotopic in M. If S^2 does not seperate M then there is a simple closed curve λ that properly intersects S^2 in exactly one point. The regular neighbourhood U of $S^2 \cup \lambda$ is bounded by a separating 2-sphere. One has

$$\pi_1 M = \pi_1 U * \pi_1 \overline{(N-U)} \cong \mathbb{Z} * \pi_1 \overline{(N-U)}$$

contradicting the assumptions that $\pi_1 M$ is neither cyclic nor a free product. Thus S^2 separates M into two manifolds M', M''. Since $\pi_1 M$ is not a free product we may assume that $\pi_1 M' = 1$. It follows that $\partial M' = S^2$, since by assumption every other boundary component is a surface of genus $\geqq 1$ and, therefore, $H_1(M') \neq 0$, see [Seifert-Threfall 1934, p. 223 Satz IV], contradicting $\pi_1 M' = 1$. This proves that S^2 is null-homologous in M'. Since $\pi_1 M' = 1$, it follows by the Hurewicz theorem, see [Spanier 1966, 7.5.2], that S^2 is nullhomotopic – a contradiction. This proves $\pi_2 M = 0$.

Now consider the universal cover $\tilde{M}$ of M. Since $|\pi_1 M| = \infty$, $\tilde{M}$ is not compact and this implies that $H_3(\tilde{M}) = 0$. Moreover

$$1 = \pi_1 \tilde{M},\ H_2(\tilde{M}) = \pi_2 \tilde{M} = \pi_2 M = 0 .$$

By the Hurewicz theorem, $\pi_3 \tilde{M} \cong H_3(\tilde{M}) = 0$, and by induction $\pi_j \tilde{M} \cong \mathrm{H}_j(\tilde{M}) = 0$ for $j \geqq 3$. Since $\pi_j M \cong \pi_j \tilde{M}$, M is aspherical and therefore a $K(\pi_1 M, 1)$-space.

Assume that $\pi_1 M$ contains an element of finite order r. Then there is a cover M^+ of M with $\pi_1 M^+ \cong \mathbb{Z}_r$. Since $[\pi_1 M \colon \pi_1 M^+] = \infty$ we can apply the same argument as above to prove that M^+ is a $K(\mathbb{Z}_r, 1)$-space. This implies that $H_j(\mathbb{Z}_r) = H_j(M^+)$ for all $j \in \mathbb{N}$. Since the sequence of homology groups of a cyclic group has period 2, there are non-trivial homology groups in arbitrary high dimensions. (These results can be found in [Spanier 1966, 9.5].) This contradicts the fact that $H_j(M^+) = 0$ for $j \geqq 3$. □

To complete the proof of Lemma 12.35 it remains to show that $\pi_1 \hat{C}_2$ is not a free product. Otherwise it cannot have a non-trivial centre, that is, in that case $h = 1$, $\pi_1 \hat{C}_2 = \langle s_1, s_2 \,|\, s_1^{\alpha_1}, s_2^{\alpha_2}, (s_1 s_2)^{\alpha_3} \rangle$. By the Grushko Theorem [ZVC 1980, 2.9.2, E 4.10] both factors of the free product have rank $\leqq 1$, and $\pi_1 \hat{C}_2$ is one of the groups $\mathbb{Z}_n * \mathbb{Z}_m$, $\mathbb{Z}_n * \mathbb{Z}$ or $\mathbb{Z} * \mathbb{Z}$. But in the group $\langle s_1, s_2 \,|\, s_1^{\alpha_1}, s_2^{\alpha_2}, (s_1 s_2)^{\alpha_3} \rangle$ there are three non-conjugate maximal finite subgroups, namely those generated by s_1, s_2 and $s_1 s_2$, respectively, (for a proof see [ZVC 1980, 4.8.1]), while there are at most 2 in the above free products of cyclic groups. This proves also that h is non-trivial; hence, by Theorem 12.36, h has infinite order. □

12.37 *Proof of the Classification Theorem 12.28*. Let $\mathfrak{H}'$ and $\mathfrak{H}$ be groups presented in the form of 12.33, and let $\psi\colon \mathfrak{H}' \to \mathfrak{H}$ be an isomorphism. By Lemma 12.35,

$\psi(h') = h^\varepsilon$, $\varepsilon \in \{1, -1\}$, and ψ induces an isomorphism

$$\bar{\psi}\colon \mathfrak{C}' = \mathfrak{H}'/\langle h'\rangle \to \mathfrak{H}/\langle h\rangle = \mathfrak{C}.$$

The groups $\mathfrak{C}'$ and $\mathfrak{C}$ are crystallographic groups of the euclidean or non-euclidean plane E with compact fundamental region. Hence, $\bar{\psi}$ is induced by a homeomorphism $\chi\colon E/\mathfrak{C}' \to E/\mathfrak{C}$, see [ZVC 1980, 6.6.11]. Both surfaces $E/\mathfrak{C}'$ and $E/\mathfrak{C}$ are compact and have one boundary component, on which the images of the centres of the rotations $\bar{c}'_1\bar{c}'_2, \bar{c}'_2\bar{c}'_3, \ldots, \bar{c}'_{r'}\bar{c}'_1$ and $\bar{c}_1\bar{c}_2, \bar{c}_2\bar{c}_3, \ldots, \bar{c}_r\bar{c}_1$, respectively, follow in this order, see [ZVC 1980, 4.6.3, 4]. (The induced mappings on the surfaces are denoted by a $^-$.) Now χ preserves or reverses this order up to a cyclic permutation, and it follows that $(\alpha'_1, \ldots, \alpha'_{r'})$ differs from $(\alpha_1, \ldots, \alpha_r)$ or $(\alpha_r, \ldots, \alpha_1)$ only by a cyclic permutation. In the first case χ preserves the direction of the rotations, in the second case it reverses it, and we obtain the following equations:

$$\bar{\psi}(\bar{s}'_i) = \bar{x}_i \bar{s}^\eta_{j(i)} \bar{x}_i^{-1} \;(\eta \in \{1, -1\}, \begin{pmatrix} 1 & \ldots & r \\ j(1) & \ldots & j(r)\end{pmatrix} \text{ a permutation with } \alpha'_i = \alpha_{j(i)}).$$

Moreover,

$$\bar{x}_1 \bar{s}^\eta_{j(1)} \bar{x}_1^{-1} \ldots \bar{x}_r \bar{s}^\eta_{j(r)} \bar{x}_r^{-1} = \bar{x}(\bar{s}_1 \ldots \bar{s}_r)^\eta \bar{x}^{-1}$$

in the free group generated by the $\bar{s}_i$, see [ZVC 1980, 5.8.2]. Hence, ψ is of the following form:

$$\psi(h') = h^\varepsilon, \; \psi(s'_i) = x_i s^\eta_{j(i)} x_i^{-1} h^{\lambda_i}, \quad \lambda_i \in \mathbb{Z},$$

where the x_i are the same words in the s_i as the $\bar{x}_i$ in the $\bar{s}_i$.

The orientation of S^3 determines orientations on the twofold branched covering spaces $\hat{C}'_2$ and $\hat{C}_2$. When the links $\mathfrak{m}'$ and $\mathfrak{m}$ are isotopic then there is an orientation preserving homeomorphism from $\hat{C}'_2$ to $\hat{C}_2$. This implies that $\varepsilon\eta = 1$, since the orientations of $\hat{C}'_2$ and $\hat{C}_2$ are defined by the orientations of the fibres and the bases and $\varepsilon = -1$ corresponds to a change of the orientation in the fibres while $\eta = -1$ corresponds to a change of the bases. Therefore,

$$\begin{aligned} h^{\varepsilon\beta'_i} &= \psi(h'^{\beta'_i}) = \psi(s_i'^{-\alpha'_i}) = x_i (s^\varepsilon_{j(i)} h^{\lambda_i})^{-\alpha'_i} x_i^{-1} = \\ &= x_i s_{j(i)}^{-\varepsilon\alpha_{j(i)}} x_i^{-1} h^{-\alpha_{j(i)}\lambda_i} = h^{\varepsilon\beta_{j(i)} - \alpha_{j(i)}\lambda_i}, \end{aligned}$$

that is,

$$\beta'_i = \beta_{j(i)} - \varepsilon\alpha_{j(i)}\lambda_i \quad \text{for } 1 \leqq i \leqq r.$$

This proves the invariance of the β_i/α_i and their ordering.

From the last relation we obtain:

$$\begin{aligned} h^{\varepsilon e'} &= \psi(h'^{e'}) = \psi(s'_1 \ldots s'_r) = x_1 s^\varepsilon_{j(1)} x_1^{-1} h^{\lambda_1} \ldots x_r s^\varepsilon_{j(r)} x_r^{-1} h^{\lambda_r} \\ &= h^{\lambda_1 + \ldots + \lambda_r} x(s_1 \ldots s_r)^\varepsilon x^{-1} = h^{\lambda_1 + \ldots + \lambda_r + \varepsilon e}; \end{aligned}$$

hence,

$$e' = e + \varepsilon(\lambda_1 + \ldots + \lambda_r).$$

Now,

$$e' + \sum_{i=1}^{r} \frac{\beta'_i}{\alpha'_i} = e + \varepsilon(\lambda_1 + \ldots + \lambda_r) + \sum_{i=1}^{r} \frac{\beta_{j(i)} - \varepsilon\alpha_{j(i)}\lambda_i}{\alpha_{j(i)}}$$

$$= e + \sum_{j=1}^{r} \frac{\beta_j}{\alpha_j}. \quad \square$$

12.38 Remark. The "orbifold" $E/\mathfrak{C}$ of fibres is a disk with r marked vertices on the boundary. A consequence of 12.34 is that the image of $\hat{\mathfrak{m}}$ consists of the edges of the boundary of $E/\mathfrak{C}$. In other words, the fundamental domain of $\mathfrak{C}$ is an r-gon, the edges of which are the images of $\hat{\mathfrak{m}}$. Each component $\hat{\mathfrak{k}}$ of $\hat{\mathfrak{m}}$ determines an element of $\mathfrak{C}$ which is fixed when conjugated with a suitable reflection of $\mathfrak{C}$. The reflections of $\mathfrak{C}$ are conjugate to the reflections in the (euclidean or non-euclidean) lines containing the edges of the fundamental domain. From geometry we know that the reflection $\bar{c}$ with axis l fixes under conjugation the following orientation preserving mappings of E:

i) the rotations of order 2 with centres on l,

ii) the hyperbolic transformations with axis l.

Since the image of $\hat{\mathfrak{k}}$ contains the centres of different non-conjugate rotations of $\mathfrak{C}$ it follows that $\hat{\mathfrak{k}}$ determines, up to conjugacy, a hyperbolic transformation in $\mathfrak{C}$.

Improving slightly the proof of the Classification Theorem one obtains

12.39 Corollary. *If* $\sum_{i=1}^{r} \frac{1}{\alpha_i} < r - 2$, *that is,* $\mathfrak{L} = \mathfrak{H}/\langle h \rangle$ *is a non-euclidean crystallographic group, each automorphism of* $\mathfrak{H}$ *is induced by a homeomorphism of* $E \times \mathbb{R}$.

Proofs can be found in [Conner-Raymond 1970, 1977], [Kamishima-Lee-Raymond 1983], [Lee-Raymond 1984], [Zieschang-Zimmermann 1982, 2.10]. □

Moreover, the outer automorphism group of $\mathfrak{H}$ can be realized by a group of homeomorphisms. This can be seen directly by looking at the corresponding extensions of $\mathfrak{H}$ and realizing them by groups of mappings of $E \times \mathbb{R}$, see the papers mentioned above.

E Symmetries of Montesinos Links

Using the Classification Theorem 12.28 and 12.39 we can easily decide about amphicheirality and invertibility of Montesinos links.

12.40 Proposition (amphicheiral Montesinos links). *(a) The Montesinos link* $\mathfrak{m}(e_0; \beta_1/\alpha_1, \ldots, \beta_r/\alpha_r)$, $r \geq 3$, *is amphicheiral if and only if*

1. $e_0 = 0$ *and*

2. there is a permutation π *– an r-cycle or a reversal of the ordering – such that*

$$\beta_{\pi(i)}/\alpha_{\pi(i)} \equiv -\beta_i/\alpha_i \bmod 1 \quad \text{for } 1 \leqq i \leqq r.$$

(b) For $r \geqq 3$, *r odd, Montesinos knots are never amphicheiral.*

Proof. The reflection in the plane maps $\mathfrak{m}$ to the Montesinos link $\mathfrak{m}(-e_0; -\beta_1/\alpha_1, \ldots, -\beta_r/\alpha_r)$; hence, (a) is a consequence of the Classification Theorem 12.28. Proof of (b) as exercise E 12.7. □

A *link* $\mathfrak{l}$ is called *invertible*, see [Whitten 1969, 1969′], if there exists a homeomorphism f of S^3 which maps each component of $\mathfrak{l}$ into itself reversing the orientation. Let us use this term also for the case where f maps each component of $\mathfrak{l}$ into itself and reverses the orientation of at least one of them. In the following proof we will see that both concepts coincide for Montesinos links.

12.41 Theorem (invertible Montesinos links). *The Montesinos link* $\mathfrak{m} = \mathfrak{m}(e_0; \beta_1/\alpha_1, \ldots, \beta_r/\alpha_r)$, $r \geqq 3$, *is invertible if and only if, with an appropriate enumeration,*

(a) one of the α_i, $1 \leqq i \leqq r$, *is even, or*

(b) $\mathfrak{m} = \mathfrak{m}(e_0; \beta_1/\alpha_1, \ldots, \beta_p/\alpha_p, \beta_p/\alpha_p, \ldots, \beta_1/\alpha_1)$ *when* $r = 2p$,
$\mathfrak{m} = \mathfrak{m}(e_0; \beta_1/\alpha_1, \ldots, \beta_p/\alpha_p, \beta_{p+1}/\alpha_{p+1}, \beta_p/\alpha_p, \ldots, \beta_1/\alpha_1)$ *when* $r = 2p+1$.

Proof. That the conditions (a) or (b) are sufficient follows easily from 12.39 (and the corresponding result for the euclidean cases) or from Figure 12.13.

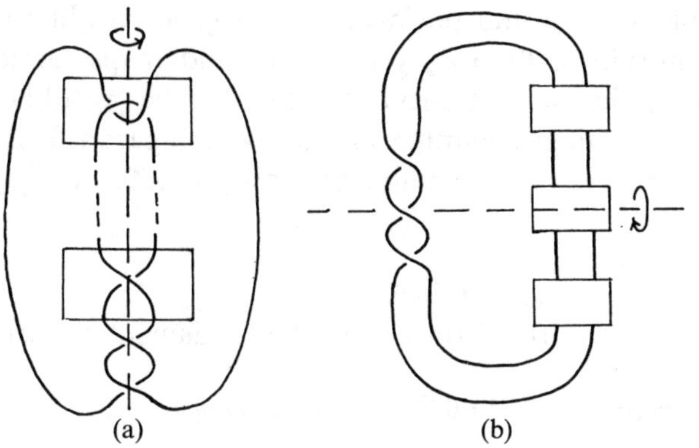

Fig. 12.13

For case (a), the rotation through 180° about the dotted line maps the Montesinos link onto an equivalent one. If α_i is even, a component of $\mathfrak{m}$ enters the i-th box from above and leaves it in the same direction. The rotation inverts the components. In case (b) the rotation through 180° shown in Figure 12.13(b) gives the required symmetry.

For the proof that the conditions are necessary we may restrict ourselves to the case where $\mathfrak{C}$ operates on the hyperbolic plane $\mathbb{H}$, since in the euclidean cases either an exponent 2 occurs or all α_i are equal to 3 and the links are invertible. Let $f: S^3 \to S^3$ be an orientation preserving homeomorphism that maps $\mathfrak{m}$ onto $\mathfrak{m}$ and maps one component $\mathfrak{k}$ of $\mathfrak{m}$ onto itself, but reverses the orientation on $\mathfrak{k}$. Then, after a suitable choice of the base point, f induces an automorphism φ of $\mathfrak{C}$ that maps the element $k \in \mathfrak{C}$ defined by $\mathfrak{k}$ into its inverse. By 12.38, k is a hyperbolic transformation.

If φ is the inner automorphism $x \mapsto g^{-1}xg$ of $\mathfrak{C}$ then g has a fixed point on the axis A of k. Hence, g is either a rotation of order 2 with centre on A or g is the reflection with an axis perpendicular to A. In both cases $\mathfrak{C}$ contains an element of even order, i.e. one of the α_i is even.

If φ is not an inner automorphism then φ corresponds to a rotation or a reflection of the disk $\mathbb{H}/\mathfrak{C}$ that preserves the fractions β_i/α_i. It must reverse the orientation since the direction of one of the edges of $\mathbb{H}/\mathfrak{C}$ is reversed. Therefore φ corresponds to a reflection of the disk and this implies (b). □

Next we study the isotopy classes of symmetries of a Montesinos link $\mathfrak{m}$ with $r \geqq 3$ tangles, in other words, we study the group $\mathfrak{M}(S^3, \mathfrak{m})$ of mapping classes of the pair $(S^3, \mathfrak{m})$. This group can be described as follows: using the compact-open topology on the set of homeomorphisms or diffeomorphisms of $(S^3, \mathfrak{m})$ we obtain topological spaces Homeo$(S^3, \mathfrak{m})$ and Diff$(S^3, \mathfrak{m})$, respectively. Now $\mathfrak{M}(S^3, \mathfrak{m})$ equals the set of path-components of the above spaces:

12.42 $\mathfrak{M}(S^3, \mathfrak{m}) \cong \pi_0 \mathrm{Homeo}(S^3, \mathfrak{m}) \cong \pi_0 \mathrm{Diff}(S^3, \mathfrak{m})$.

Each symmetry induces an automorphism of the knot group $\mathfrak{G}$ which maps the kernel of the homomorphism $\mathfrak{G} \to \mathbb{Z}_2$ onto itself, and maps meridians to meridians; hence, symmetries and isotopies can be lifted to the twofold branched covering $\hat{C}_2$ such that the liftings commute with the covering transformation of $\hat{C}_2 \to S^3$. Lifting a symmetry to the universal cover $\mathbb{H} \times \mathbb{R}$ of $\hat{C}_2$ yields a homeomorphism

12.43 $\gamma: \mathfrak{M}(S^3, \mathfrak{m}) \to \mathrm{Out}\, \mathfrak{H} = \mathrm{Aut}\, \mathfrak{G}/\mathrm{In}\, \mathfrak{G}$.
where $\mathfrak{H}$ has a presentation of the form 12.33. The fundamental assertion is:

12.44 Proposition. $\gamma: \mathfrak{M}(S^3, \mathfrak{m}) \to \mathrm{Out}\, \mathfrak{H}$ *is an isomorphism.*

Unfortunately, we cannot give a self-contained proof here, but have to use results of Thurston and others which are not common knowledge. But this proof shows the influence of these theorems on knot theory. An explicit and simple description of Out $\mathfrak{H}$ is given afterwards in 12.46.

Proof ([Boileau-Zimmermann 1984]). Consider first the case $\sum_{i=1}^{r} \frac{1}{\alpha_i} < r-2$. From 12.39 it follows that γ is surjective and it remains to show that γ is injective. By [Bonahon-Siebenmann 1984] $\mathfrak{m}$ is a simple knot, that means, $\mathfrak{m}$ does not have a companion. By [Thurston 1984] $S^3 - \mathfrak{m}$ has a complete hyperbolic structure with finite volume. Mostow's rigidity theorem [Mostow 1968] implies that $\mathfrak{M}(S^3, \mathfrak{m})$ is finite and that every element of $\mathfrak{M}(S^3, \mathfrak{m})$ can be represented by an isometry of the same order as its homotopy class. Now we represent a non-trivial element of the kernel of γ by a homeomorphism f with the above properties. Let $\bar{f}$ be the lift of f to $\mathbb{H} \times \mathbb{R}$; then $\bar{f}^m \in \mathfrak{H}$ for a suitable $m > 0$. Since the class of f is in the kernel of γ we may assume that the conjugation by $\bar{f}$ yields the identity in $\mathfrak{H}$. As the centre of $\mathfrak{H}$ is trivial it follows that $\bar{f}^m = id_{\mathbb{H}\times\mathbb{R}}$ and, thus, that $\bar{f}$ is a periodic diffeomorphism commuting with the operation of $\pi_1 \hat{C}_2$. Therefore $\bar{f}$ is a rotation of the hyperbolic 3-space and its fixed point set is a line. The elements of $\pi_1 \hat{C}_2$ commute with $\bar{f}$; hence, they map the axis of $\bar{f}$ onto itself and it follows from the discontinuity that $\pi_1 \hat{C}_2$ is infinite cyclic or dihedral. This is a contradiction. Therefore γ is injective.

The euclidean cases ($\sum_{i=1}^{r} \frac{1}{\alpha_i} = r-2$) are left. There are four cases: (3,3,3), (2,3,6), (2,4,4) and (2,2,2,2). They can be handled using [Bonahon-Siebenmann 1984] and [Zimmermann 1982]. The last paper depends strongly on Thurston's paper [1984] which we used above, and, furthermore, on [Jaco-Shalen 1979], [Johannson 1979]. □

Next we determine Out $\mathfrak{H}$ for the knot $\mathfrak{m}(e; (\alpha_1, \beta_1), \ldots, (\alpha_r, \beta_r))$. We assume $0 < \beta_j < \alpha_j$, $1 \leqq j \leqq r$, for the sake of simplicity.

12.45 Definition. Let $\mathbb{D}_r$ denote the dihedral group of order 2r, realized as a group of rotations and reflections of a regular polygon with vertices $(1, 2, \ldots, r)$. Define

$$\tilde{\mathbb{D}}_r = \{\varrho \in \mathbb{D}_r \mid \alpha_{\varrho(i)} = \alpha_i \quad \text{for } 1 \leqq i \leqq r\}.$$

Let $\tilde{\tilde{\mathbb{D}}}_r \subset \tilde{\mathbb{D}}_r$ consist of

(i) the rotations ϱ with $\alpha_{\varrho(i)} = \alpha_i$ and $\beta_{\varrho(i)} = \beta_i$ and the reflections ϱ with $\alpha_{\varrho(i)} = \alpha_i$ and $\beta_{\varrho(i)} = \alpha_i - \beta_i$ if $e_0 \neq 0$,

(ii) the rotations ϱ with $(\alpha_{\varrho(i)}, \beta_{\varrho(i)}) = (\alpha_i, \alpha_i - \beta_i)$ and the reflections ϱ with $(\alpha_{\varrho(i)}, \beta_{\varrho(i)}) = (\alpha_i, \beta_i)$ if $e_0 = 0$.

12.46 Proposition. Out $\mathfrak{H}$ *is an extension of* $\mathbb{Z}_2$ *or* $\mathbb{Z}_2 \oplus \mathbb{Z}_2$ *by the finite dihedral or cyclic group* $\tilde{\tilde{\mathbb{D}}}_r$.

Proposition 12.46 is a direct consequence of the following Lemmas 12.47 and 12.49.

Since $\langle h \rangle$ is the centre of $\mathfrak{H}$ the projection $\mathfrak{H} \to \mathfrak{H}/\langle h \rangle = \mathfrak{C}$ is compatible with every automorphism of $\mathfrak{H}$ and we obtain a homomorphism χ: Out $\mathfrak{H} \to$ Out $\mathfrak{C} \cong \tilde{\mathbb{D}}_r$. It is easy to determine the image of χ; thus the main problem is to calculate the kernel.

Consider an automorphism ψ of $\mathfrak{H}$ which induces the identity on $\mathfrak{C}$. Then $\psi(c_j) = c_j h^{m_j}$, $\psi(h) = h^{\varepsilon}$ where $\varepsilon \in \{1, -1\}$, and

$$(1) \qquad h^{\varepsilon\beta_1} = \psi(h^{\beta_1}) = \psi((c_0 c_1)^{-\alpha_1}) = (c_0 h^{m_0} c_1 h^{m_1})^{-\alpha_1} = (c_0 c_1)^{-\alpha_1} h^{-\alpha_1(m_1 - m_0)} = h^{\beta_1 - \alpha_1(m_1 - m_0)}.$$

1. Case $\varepsilon = 1$. Since h has infinite order it follows that $m_1 = m_0$ and, by copying this argument, $m_0 = m_1 = \ldots = m_r = 2l + \eta$ with $\eta \in \{0, 1\}$. Now multiply ψ by the inner automorphism $x \mapsto h^l x h^{-l}$:

$$c_j \mapsto h^l c_j h^{-l} \mapsto h^l c_j h^{m_0} h^{-l} = c_j h^{\eta};$$

hence, these automorphisms define a subgroup of ker χ isomorphic to $\mathbb{Z}_2$.

2. Case $\varepsilon = -1$. Now $2\beta_1 = -\alpha_1(m_0 - m_1)$ by (1). Since α_1 and β_1 are relatively prime and $0 < \beta_1 < \alpha_1$ it follows that $\alpha_1 = 2$, $\beta_1 = 1$ and $m_0 = m_1 - 1$. By induction: $\alpha_1 = \ldots = \alpha_r = 2$, $\beta_1 = \ldots = \beta_r = 1$, $m_j = m_0 + j$ for $1 \leqq j \leqq r$. Now

$$h^{-e} = \psi(h^e) = \psi(c_0^{-1} c_r) = h^{-m_0} c_0^{-1} c_r h^{m_r} = h^{e + m_r - m_0} = h^{e+r}.$$

It follows that $e = -\dfrac{r}{2}$ and that the Euler number e_0 vanishes:

$$e_0 = e + \sum_{j=1}^{r} \frac{\beta_j}{\alpha_j} = 0.$$

Thus we have proved

12.47 Lemma. ker $\chi \cong \mathbb{Z}_2$ *is generated by* ψ_0: $\mathfrak{H} \to \mathfrak{H}$, $c_j \mapsto c_j h$, $h \mapsto h$, *except in the case where* $(\alpha_j, \beta_j) = (2, 1)$ *for* $1 \leqq j \leqq r$ *and* $e_0 = 0$; *then* ker $\chi \cong \mathbb{Z}_2 \oplus \mathbb{Z}_2$, *generated by* ψ_0 *and* ψ_1: $\mathfrak{H} \to \mathfrak{H}$, $h \mapsto h^{-1}$, $c_j \mapsto c_j h^{r-j}$. □

Using the generalized Nielsen theorem, see [ZVC 1980, 5.8.3, 6.6.9], Out $\mathfrak{C}$ is easily calculated:

12.48 Lemma. *(a) An automorphism* φ: $\mathfrak{C} \to \mathfrak{C}$ *mapping each conjugacy class of elliptic subgroups* $\langle (c_j c_{j+1}) \rangle$ *onto itself is an inner automorphism of* $\mathfrak{C}$.

(b) The canonical mapping $\tilde{\mathbb{D}}_r \to$ Out $\mathfrak{C}$ *is an isomorphism.*

Proof. By the generalized Nielsen theorem, see [ZVC 1980, 6.6.11], φ is induced by a homeomorphism f of $\mathbb{H}/\mathfrak{C} \cong D^2$ onto itself which fixes the rotation centres lying on ∂D^2. Now the Alexander trick [Alexander 1923] can be used to isotope f into the identity. This implies that φ is an inner automorphism. □

12.49 Lemma. *The image of* Out $\mathfrak{H}$ *in* Out $\mathfrak{C}$ *is the subgroup* $\tilde{\tilde{\mathbb{D}}}_r$ *of* $\tilde{\mathbb{D}}_r$.

Proof. Let φ be an automorphism of $\mathfrak{H}$. By 12.48 (b), φ induces a 'dihedral' permutation π of the cyclic set $\bar{c}_1, \dots, \bar{c}_{r-1}, \bar{c}_r = \bar{c}_0$. We discuss the cases with $\varphi(h) = h$.

1. π is a rotation. Then

$$\begin{aligned} h^{\beta_1} &= \varphi(h^{\beta_1}) = \varphi((c_0 c_1)^{-\alpha_1}) = (c_{i-1} h^{m_0} c_i h^{m_1})^{-\alpha_1} \\ &= h^{\beta_i - \alpha_1(m_1 - m_0)} \end{aligned}$$

and $\alpha_i = \alpha_1$. Since, by assumption, $0 < \beta_i < \alpha_i$, it follows that $m_1 = m_0$ and $\beta_1 = \beta_i$. Therefore φ preserves the pairs (α_j, β_j) and maps c_j to $c_j h^m$ for a fixed m. By multiplication with an inner automorphism and, if necessary, with ψ_1 from 12.47 we obtain $m = 0$. The image of φ in Out $\mathfrak{C}$ is in $\tilde{\tilde{\mathbb{D}}}_r$, and each rotation $\pi \in \tilde{\tilde{\mathbb{D}}}_r$ is obtained from a $\varphi \in$ Out $\mathfrak{H}$.

2. π is a reflection. Then

$$\begin{aligned} h^{\beta_1} &= \varphi(h^{\beta_1}) = \varphi((c_0 c_1)^{-\alpha_1}) = (c_i h^{m_0} c_{i-1} h^{m_1})^{-\alpha_1} \\ &= h^{-\beta_i - \alpha_1(m_1 - m_0)} \end{aligned}$$

and $\alpha_1 = \alpha_i$. Therefore $m_1 - m_0 = -1$, $\beta_i + \beta_1 = \alpha_1$, and φ assigns to a pair (α_k, β_k) a pair $(\alpha_j, \beta_j) = (\alpha_k, \alpha_k - \beta_k)$. The generators c_i are mapped as follows:

$$\begin{array}{ccccccc} c_0, & c_1, & \dots, & c_i, & c_{i+1}, & \dots, & c_r \\ \downarrow & \downarrow & & \downarrow & \downarrow & & \downarrow \\ c_i h^m, & c_{i-1} h^{m-1}, & \dots, & c_0 h^{m-i}, & c_{r-1} h^{-e+m-i-1}, & \dots, & c_i h^{-e+m-r}, \\ & & & \| & & & \\ & & & c_r h^{-e+m+i} & & & \end{array}$$

and

$$c_i h^{-e+m-r} = \varphi(c_r) = \varphi(c_0 h^e) = c_i h^{m+e}.$$

This implies $e = -\dfrac{r}{2}$ and

$$e_0 = e + \sum_{j=1}^{r} \frac{\beta_j}{\alpha_j} = e + \frac{1}{2} \sum_{j=1}^{r} \left[\frac{\beta_j}{\alpha_j} + \frac{\alpha_{i-j} - \beta_{i-j}}{\alpha_j} \right] = 0;$$

here $i - j$ is considered mod r. By normalizing as before we obtain $m = 0$.

The cases for $\varphi(h) = h^{-1}$ can be handled the same way; proof as E 12.8. □

Lemmas 12.47 and 12.49 imply Proposition 12.46. As a corollary of Proposition 12.44 and 12.46 we obtain the results of [Bonahon-Siebenmann 1984] (for $r \geqq 4$) and [Boileau 1982] (for $r = 3$).

12.50 Corollary. *The symmetry group* $\mathfrak{M}(S^3, \mathfrak{m})$ *is an extension of* $\mathbb{Z}_2$ *or* $\mathbb{Z}_2 \oplus \mathbb{Z}_2$ *by the finite dihedral or cyclic group* $\tilde{\tilde{\mathbb{D}}}_r$. □

F History and Sources

4-plats (Viergeflechte) were first investigated in [Bankwitz-Schumann 1934] where they were shown to be alternating and invertible. They were classified by H. Schubert [1956] as knots and links with two bridges. A different proof using linking numbers of covering spaces was given in [Burde 1975]. Special properties of 2-bridge knots (genus, Alexander polynomial, fibring, group structure) were studied in [Funcke 1975, 1978], [Hartley 1979′], [Mayland 1976].

J. Montesinos then introduced a more general class of knots and links which could nevertheless be classified by essentially the same trick that H. Seifert had used to classify (unoriented) knots with two bridges: Montesinos links are links with 2-fold branched covering spaces which are Seifert fibre spaces, see [Montesinos 1973, 1979], [Boileau-Siebenmann 1980]. In recent papers on Montesinos links their group of symmetries was determined in most cases [Bonahon-Siebenmann 1984], [Boileau 1982], [Boileau-Zimmermann 1984].

G Exercises

E 12.1 Show that a reduced diagram of $\mathfrak{b}(\alpha, \beta)$ leads to the following Wirtinger presentations:

$$\mathfrak{G}(\alpha, \beta) = \langle S_1, S_2 \mid S_2^{-1} L_1^{-1} S_1 L_1 \rangle,$$
$$L_1 = S_2^{\varepsilon_1} S_1^{\varepsilon_2} \dots S_2^{\varepsilon_{\alpha-2}} S_1^{\varepsilon_{\alpha-1}}, \ \alpha \equiv 1 \bmod 2,$$
$$\mathfrak{G}(\alpha, \beta) = \langle S_1, S_2 \mid S_1^{-1} L_1^{-1} S_1 L_1 \rangle,$$
$$L_1 = S_2^{\varepsilon_1} S_1^{\varepsilon_2} \dots S_1^{\varepsilon_{\alpha-2}} S_2^{\varepsilon_{\alpha-1}}, \ \alpha \equiv 0 \bmod 2,$$
$$\varepsilon_i = (-1)^{\left[\frac{i\beta}{\alpha}\right]}, \ [a] = \text{integral part of } a.$$

E 12.2 The matrices

$$A_1 = \begin{pmatrix} 1 & -1 \\ 0 & 1 \end{pmatrix}, A_2 = \begin{pmatrix} 1 & 0 \\ 1 & 1 \end{pmatrix}$$

generate the mapping class group of the torus (Section B).
Show that $\langle A_1, A_2 \mid A_1 A_2 A_1 = A_2 A_1 A_2, (\mathrm{A}_1 \mathrm{A}_2)^6 \rangle$ is a presentation of the group $SL(2, \mathbb{Z})$ and connect it with the classical presentation

$$SL(2, \mathbb{Z}) = \langle S, T, Z \mid S^2 = T^3 = Z, Z^2 = 1 \rangle.$$

E 12.3 Let α, β, β' be positive integers, $gcd(\alpha, \beta) = gcd(\alpha, \beta') = 1$ and $\beta\beta' \equiv 1 \bmod \alpha$. If $\beta \cdot \alpha^{-1} = [a_1, \dots, a_m]$, are the quotients of the continued fraction $\beta \cdot \alpha^{-1}$ of odd length m, then $\beta' \cdot \alpha^{-1} = [a_m, \dots, a_1]$. (Find an algebraic proof.).

E 12.4 Let α, β, β' (α odd) be integers as in E 12.3, and let $\beta \cdot \alpha^{-1} = [a_1, \dots, a_k]$ be the quotients obtained from the generalized algorithm 12.16. Prove: If $\mathfrak{b}(\alpha, \beta)$ is a fibred knot, then for $\varepsilon = (-1)^{k+1}$:

$\beta' \alpha^{-1} = [\varepsilon a_k - 1, \varepsilon a_{k-1}, \dots, \varepsilon a_2, \varepsilon a_1 + 1]$.

E 12.5 Compute a Seifert matrix $V(\alpha, \beta)$ for $\mathfrak{b}(\alpha, \beta)$ using a Seifert surface as described in 12.26. Prove

$$\text{(a)}\ |\det V(\alpha, \beta)| = \prod_{i=1}^{k-1} \left[b_i + \frac{1}{2}\left(\frac{a_i}{|a_i|} + \frac{a_{i+1}}{|a_{i+1}|} \right) \right],$$

$$\text{(b)}\ \sigma[V(\alpha, \beta) + V^T(\alpha, \beta)] = (\sum_{i=1}^{k} a_i) - \frac{a_k}{|a_k|}.$$

(σ denotes the signature of a matrix, see Appendic A 2.) Deduce 12.23 from (a).

E 12.6 Prove 12.21.

E 12.7 Prove 12.40(b).

E 12.8 Finish the proof of 12.49 for the cases $\varphi(h) = h^{-1}$.

E 12.9 Prove that Montesinos knots are prime. (Use the Smith conjecture for involutions.)

Chapter 13: Quadratic Form of a Knot

In this chapter we propose to reinvestigate the infinite cyclic covering C_∞ of a knot and to extract another knot invariant from it: the quadratic form of the knot. The first section gives a cohomological definition of the quadratic form $q(x)$ of a knot. The main properties of $q(x)$ and its signature are derived. The second part is devoted to the description of a method of computation of $q(x)$ from a special knot projection. Part C then compares the different quadratic forms of Goeritz [1933], Trotter [1962], Murasugi [1965], and Milnor-Erle [1969]. Some examples are discussed.

A The Quadratic Form of a Knot

In Proposition 8.9 we have determined the integral homology groups $H_i(C_\infty)$, $H_i(C_\infty, \partial C_\infty)$ of the infinite cyclic covering C_∞ of a knot $\mathfrak{k}$. It will become necessary to consider these homology groups with more general coefficients. Let A be an integral domain with identity. Then:

$$H_i(X, Y; A) = H_i(X, Y) \otimes_{\mathbb{Z}} A$$

for a pair $Y \subset X$. So we have:

13.1 Proposition. *Let A be an integral domain with identity and C_∞ the infinite cyclic covering of a knot $\mathfrak{k}$. Then*

$$H_1(C_\infty; A) \cong H_1(C_\infty, \partial C_\infty; A),$$
$$H_2(C_\infty, \partial C_\infty; A) \cong A. \quad \square$$

As we use throughout this chapter homology (and cohomology) with coefficients in A, this will be omitted in our notation.

Again, as in Chapter 8, we start by cutting the knot complement C along a Seifert surface S. Let $\{a_i | 1 \leqq i \leqq 2g\}$ (see Chapter 8B) be a canonical set of generators of $H_1(S)$, where g denotes the genus of S. The cutting produces the surfaces S^+ and S^- contained in ∂C^*. We assume S^3, and hence, C and C^* oriented; the induced orientation on S^- is supposed to induce on ∂S^- an orientation which coincides with that of $\mathfrak{k}$. The orientation of S^+ then induces the orientation of $-\mathfrak{k}$. The canonical curves $\{a_i\}$ become canonical curves $\{a_i^+\}$, $\{a_i^-\}$

on S^+, S^-. The space C^* is the complement of a handlebody of genus $2g$ in S^3 and there are $2g$ free generators $\{s_k\}$ of $H_1(C^*)$ associated to $\{a_i\}$ by linking numbers in S^3:

$$lk(a_i, s_k) = \delta_{ik}, \quad i, k = 1, \ldots, 2g.$$

One sees easily that the s_k are determined by the a_i, if the above condition is imposed on their linking matrix: For $s'_j = \sum_k \alpha_{kj} s_k$ and $\delta_{ij} = lk(a_i, s'_j)$, we get $\delta_{ij} = lk(a_i, \sum_k \alpha_{kj} s_k) = \sum_k \alpha_{kj} \delta_{ik} = \alpha_{ij}$.

We are now going to free ourselves from the geometrically defined canonical bases $\{a_i\}$ of S and introduce a more general concept of a Seifert matrix $V = (v_{ik})$ (see Chapter 8).

13.2 Definition. Let $\{a_i | 1 \leqq i \leqq 2g\}$ be a basis of $H_1(S)$. A basis $\{s_i | 1 \leqq i \leqq 2g\}$ of $H_1(C^*)$ is called an *associated basis* with respect to $\{a_i\}$, if $lk(a_i, s_k) = \delta_{ik}$. The matrix $V = (v_{ik})$ defined by the inclusion

$$i^-: S^- \to C^*, \; i^-_*(a^-_i) = \sum v_{ik} s_k$$

is called a *Seifert matrix.*

To abbreviate notations we use vectors $s = (s_k)$, $a = (a_i)$, $a^\pm = (a^\pm_i)$ etc. In Chapter 8 we have used special associated bases a and s derived from a band projection. For these we deduced $i^-_*(a^-) = Vs$ from $i^+_*(a^+) = Vs$. Moreover, in this case $V - V^T = F$ represents the intersection matrix of the canonical basis $\{a_i\}$, if a suitable convention concerning the sign of the intersection numbers is agreed upon. The following proposition shows that these assertions remain true in the general case.

13.3 Proposition. *Let a, s be associated bases of $H_1(S)$, $H_1(C^*)$, respectively. If $i^-_*(a^-) = Vs$ then $i^+_*(a^+) = V^T s$. Moreover $V - V^T$ is the intersection matrix of the basis $a = (a_i)$.*

Proof. We have to investigate how a change from one pair a, s of associated bases to another one $\tilde{a}$, $\tilde{s}$ affects the Seifert matrix. If C, D are unimodular $2g \times 2g$ matrices over A, then $\tilde{a} = Ca$, $\tilde{s} = Ds$. Now $lk(a_i, s_k) = lk(\tilde{a}_i, \tilde{s}_k) = \delta_{ik}$ gives $C^T D = E$. From this we get $\tilde{V} = CVC^T$ for $\tilde{a}^+ = \tilde{V}\tilde{s}$. Now $\tilde{V}^T = CV^T C^T$ and $\tilde{a}^- = \tilde{V}^T s$ follows. Lastly, $C(V - V^T) C^T = \tilde{V} - \tilde{V}^T$. If a, s are the special bases of a band projection, $V - V^T = F$ is the intersection matrix of a. A change of bases $\tilde{a} = Ca$ transforms an intersection matrix by the rule $(V - V^T) \to C(V - V^T) C^T$, because intersections are bilinear. This proves that $\tilde{V} - \tilde{V}^T$ is the intersection matrix relative to $\tilde{a}$. □

We shall use the following

13.4 Definition. Two symmetric $n \times n$-matrices M, M' over A are called *A-equivalent* if there is an A-unimodular matrix P – *a* matrix over A with $\det P$ a unit of A – with $M' = PMP^T$.

We use the term equivalent instead of $\mathbb{Z}$-equivalent.

13.5 Lemma (Trotter, Erle). *Let A be an integral domain with identity in which $\Delta(0)$ is a unity. ($\Delta(t)$ denotes the Alexander polynomial of a knot $\mathfrak{k}$). Every Seifert matrix V is A-equivalent to a matrix*

$$\begin{pmatrix} U & 0 \\ 0 & W \end{pmatrix}$$

where W is a $2m \times 2m$ integral matrix, $|W| = \det W \neq 0$, and U is of the form:

$$U = \begin{pmatrix} 0 & \cdots & & & & & 0 \\ -1 & 0 & & & & & \vdots \\ 0 & * & 0 & & & & \vdots \\ \vdots & \vdots & -1 & 0 & & & \vdots \\ \vdots & \vdots & 0 & * & & & \vdots \\ \vdots & \vdots & & & & 0 & \vdots \\ 0 & * & 0 & * & & -1 & 0 \end{pmatrix}.$$

(W is called a "reduced" Seifert matrix *and may be empty.)*

Proof. If $|V| \neq 0$, V itself is reduced and nothing has to be proved. Let us assume $|V| = 0$. There are unimodular matrices Q and R such that QVR will have a first row of zeroes. The same holds for $QVQ^T = QVRR^{-1}Q^T$. Since $F = V - V^T$ is unimodular and skew-symmetric, so is $QVQ^T - (QVQ^T)^T = QFQ^T$. Therefore its first column has a zero at the top and the remaining entries are relatively prime. But the first column of QFQ^T coincides with that of QVQ^T, because $(QVQ^T)^T$ has zero entries in its first column. So there is a unimodular R such that

$$RQVQ^T = \begin{pmatrix} 0 & 0 & \cdots & 0 \\ -1 & * & \cdots & * \\ 0 & \vdots & & \vdots \\ \vdots & \vdots & & \vdots \\ 0 & * & \cdots & * \end{pmatrix}, \quad R = \begin{pmatrix} 1 & 0 & \cdots & 0 \\ 0 & * & & * \\ \vdots & \vdots & & \vdots \\ \vdots & \vdots & & \vdots \\ 0 & * & \cdots & * \end{pmatrix}.$$

To find R look for the element of smallest absolute value in the first column of QVQ^T. Subtract its row from other rows until a smaller element turns up in the first column. Since the elements of the first column are relatively prime one ends up with an element ± 1; the desired form is then easily reached. The operations on the rows can be realized by premultiplication by R. The matrix $RQVQ^T R^T$ has the same first row and column as $RQVQ^T$.

Similarly, for a suitable unimodular $\tilde{R}$,

$$RQVQ^T R^T \tilde{R}^T = \begin{pmatrix} 0 & 0 & 0 & \dots & 0 \\ -1 & 0 & 0 & \dots & 0 \\ 0 & * & * & \dots & * \\ \vdots & \vdots & \vdots & & \vdots \\ 0 & * & * & \dots & * \end{pmatrix}, \quad \tilde{R}^T = \begin{pmatrix} 1 & * & \dots & * \\ & 1 & & \vdots \\ & & \ddots & * \\ & & & 1 \end{pmatrix}$$

and $\tilde{R}RQVQ^T R^T \tilde{R}^T$ is of the same form.

By repeating this process we obtain a matrix

$$\tilde{V} = \begin{pmatrix} 0 & 0 & \vdots & \vdots & \vdots & \vdots & 0 \\ -1 & 0 & \cdot & \cdot & \cdot & \cdot & 0 \\ 0 & * & 0 & 0 & \cdot & \cdot & 0 \\ \vdots & \vdots & -1 & 0 & \cdot & \cdot & 0 \\ \cdot & \cdot & \cdot & * & \cdot & \cdot & \\ \cdot & \cdot & \cdot & \cdot & & \cdot & \\ 0 & * & 0 & * & & \multicolumn{2}{|c}{W} \end{pmatrix}$$

equivalent to V (over $\mathbb{Z}$), $|W| \neq 0$. For further simplification of $\tilde{V}$ we now make use of the assumption that $\Delta(0)$ is in A a unit. $|V^T - tV| = \Delta(t)$, $|\tilde{V}^T - t\tilde{V}|$ and $|W^T - tW|$ all represent the Alexander polynomial up to a factor $\pm t^\nu$. So $|W| = \Delta(0)$ is a unit of A. There is a unimodular P_1 over A with

$$\tilde{V}P_1 = \left(\begin{array}{|ccc} \hline & 0 & \\ -1 & 0 & \\ 0 & 0 & \\ \hline \vdots & \vdots & \multicolumn{1}{|c}{W} \\ 0 & 0 & \multicolumn{1}{|c}{} \end{array}\right), \quad P_1 = \left(\begin{array}{ccc|ccc} 1 & \ddots & & & & \\ & & 1 & & & \\ \hline & & * & 1 & & \\ & & \vdots & & \ddots & \\ & & * & & & 1 \end{array}\right)$$

where the column adjoining W has been replaced by zeroes, because it is a linear combination of the columns of W. Now

$$P_1^T \tilde{V} P_1 = \left(\begin{array}{|cc|cccc} \hline 0 & 0 & 0 & \dots & \dots & 0 \\ -1 & 0 & * & \dots & \dots & * \\ \hline 0 & 0 & & & & \\ \vdots & \vdots & & W & & \\ 0 & 0 & & & & \end{array}\right).$$

Since the row over W contains -1, there is a unimodular P_2 with

$$P_1^T \tilde{V} P_1 P_2 = \left(\begin{array}{cc|cccc} 0 & 0 & 0 & \dots & 0 \\ -1 & 0 & 0 & \dots & 0 \\ \hline 0 & 0 & & & \\ \vdots & \vdots & & W & \\ 0 & 0 & & & \end{array}\right),$$

and $P_2^T P_1^T \tilde{V} P_1 P_2$ is of the same type. The process can be repeated until the desired form is reached. □

There is a

13.6 Corollary. *If A is an integral domain in which $\Delta(0)$ is a unit, then $(W^T - tW)$ is a presentation matrix of $H_1(C_\infty)$ as an $A(t)$-module, and $|W^T - tW| = \Delta(t)$. The A-module $H_1(C_\infty)$ is finitely generated and free and there is an A-basis of $H_1(C_\infty)$ such that the generating covering transformation $t = h_{j+1} h_j^{-1}$ (see 4.4) induces an isomorphism $t_*: H_1(C_\infty) \to H_1(C_\infty)$ which is represented by the matrix $W^{-1} W^T$.*

Proof. We may assume that as an $A(t)$-module $H_1(C_\infty)$ has a presentation matrix $(V^T - tV)$ where V is of the special form which can be achieved according to Lemma 13.5:

(1) $$V^T - tV = \left(\begin{array}{c|c} U^T - tU & \\ \hline & W^T - tW \end{array}\right),$$

$$U^T - tU = \begin{pmatrix} 0 & -1 & 0 & \cdot & \cdot & \cdot & \cdot & 0 \\ t & 0 & 0 & * & \cdot & \cdot & \cdot & * \\ 0 & * & 0 & -1 & 0 & \cdot & \cdot & 0 \\ \cdot & \cdot & t & 0 & 0 & * & \cdot & \\ \cdot & \cdot & 0 & * & & & & \\ 0 & * & \cdot & \cdot & & & & \end{pmatrix}.$$

There is an equivalent presentation matrix in whose second column all entries but the first are zero, the first remaining -1. So the first row and second column can be omitted. In the remaining matrix the first row and the first column again may be omitted. This procedure can be continued until the presentation matrix takes the form $(W^T - tW)$, or, $(W^T W^{-1} - tE)$, since $|W| = \Delta(0)$ is a unit of A. This means that defining relations of $H_1(C_\infty)$ as an $A(t)$-module take the form: $W^T W^{-1} s = ts$, where $s = (s_i)$ are generators of $H_1(C_\infty)$. This proves the corollary. □

There is a distinguished generator $z \in H_2(S, \partial S) \cong \mathbb{Z}$ represented by an orientation of S which induces on ∂S the orientation of $\mathfrak{k}$. We shall now make use of cohomology to define a bilinear form. Since all homology groups $H_i(C_\infty)$, $H_i(C_\infty, \partial C_\infty)$, are torsion free, we have

$$H^i \cong \mathrm{Hom}_A(H_i, A) \cong H_i$$

for these spaces ([Franz 1965, Satz 17.6], [Spanier 1966, 5.5.3]). For every free basis $\{b_j\}$ of a group H_i there is a dual free basis $\{b^k\}$ of H^i defined by $\langle b^k, b_j\rangle = \delta_{kj}$, where the brackets denote the Kronecker product, that is $\langle b^k, b_j\rangle = b^k(b_j) \in A$ for $b^k \in \mathrm{Hom}_A(H_i, A)$. We use the cup-product [Hilton-Wylie 1960], [Stöcker-Zieschang 1985] to define

$$(2) \qquad \beta\colon H^1(C_\infty, \partial C_\infty) \times H^1(C_\infty, \partial C_\infty) \to A, \quad (x, y) \mapsto \langle x \cup y, j_*(z)\rangle,$$

where $j\colon S \to C_\infty$ is the inclusion. (Here we write S instead of $S_0 \subset p^{-1}(S)$.) Now let $\{a_j | 1 \leqq j \leqq 2g\}$ and $\{s_i | 1 \leqq i \leqq 2g\}$ denote associated bases of $H_1(S)$ and $H_1(C_\infty, \partial C_\infty)$, respectively, $lk(a_j, s_i) = \delta_{ji}$, such that j_* according to these bases is represented by a Seifert matrix

$$V = \left(\begin{array}{c|c} W & 0 \\ \hline 0 & U \end{array}\right), \quad W = (w_{ji})$$

where the reduced Seifert matrix W is $2m \times 2m$, $m \leqq g$. (See Lemma 13.5; observe that U and W are interchanged for technical reasons.) From Corollary 13.6 it follows that $H_1(C_\infty, \partial C_\infty) \cong H_1(C_\infty)$ is already generated by $\{s_i | 1 \leqq i \leqq 2m\}$. It therefore suffices to consider the matrix

$$\begin{pmatrix} W \\ 0 \end{pmatrix}$$

to describe the homomorphism $j_*\colon H_1(S) \to H_1(C_\infty, \partial C_\infty)$ with respect to the bases $\{a_j | 1 \leqq j \leqq 2g\}$ and $\{s_i | 1 \leqq i \leqq 2m\}$. The transpose

$$(w_{ij}) = (W^T\ 0)$$

then describes the homomorphism

$$j^*\colon H^1(C_\infty, \partial C_\infty) \to H^1(S)$$

for dual bases $\{s^j\}$, $\{a^i\}$, and we get from (2)

$$(3) \qquad B = (\beta(s^i, s^k)) = (\langle s^i \cup s^k, j_*(z)\rangle) = (\langle j^*(s^i) \cup j^*(s^k), z\rangle).$$

We define another free basis $\{b^i | 1 \leqq i \leqq 2g\}$ of $H^1(S)$ by the Lefschetz-duality-isomorphism:

$$H^1(S) \xrightarrow{\ \cap z\ } H_1(S, \partial S), \qquad b^i \mapsto b^i \cap z = a_i.$$

The b^i connect z with the intersection matrix

$$V - V^T = (int(a_i, a_k)) = (\langle b^i \cup b^k, z\rangle) = \Sigma.$$

On the other hand:

$$\langle a^i \cup b^k, z\rangle = \langle a^i, b^k \cap z\rangle = \langle a^i, a_k\rangle = \delta_{ik}.$$

(See [Hilton-Wylie 1960, Theorem 4.4.13], [Stöcker-Zieschang 1985].)

The matrix L effecting the transformation $(a^i) = L(b^i)$ is $(\langle a^i \cup a^k, z\rangle) = L \cdot (\langle a^i \cup b^k, z\rangle) = L \cdot E = L$. Now $L = L\Sigma L^T$ or $(\Sigma^T)^{-1} = L$, and, by (1),

$$(W^T\ 0)\, L \begin{pmatrix} W \\ 0 \end{pmatrix} = (W^T\ 0)\, (\Sigma^T)^{-1} \begin{pmatrix} W \\ 0 \end{pmatrix}.$$

From

$$\Sigma = \left(\begin{array}{c|c} W - W^T & 0 \\ \hline 0 & U - U^T \end{array}\right)$$

and (3) it follows that

(4) $$B = -\, W^T (W - W^T)^{-1} W.$$

13.7 Proposition. *The bilinear form* β: $H^1(C_\infty, \partial C_\infty) \times H^1(C_\infty, \partial C_\infty) \to A$, $(x, y) \mapsto \langle x \cup y, j_*(z)\rangle$ *can be represented by the matrix*

$$-(W - W^T)^{-1},$$

W is a reduced Seifert matrix, and β is non-degenerate.

Proof. It remains to show that β is non-degenerate. But $|V - V^T| = 1$, and $|U - U^T| = 1$, see Lemma 13.5 and (1); hence $|W - W^T| = 1$. □

We are now in a position to define an invariant quadratic form associated to a knot $\mathfrak{k}$. Let t: $C_\infty \to C_\infty$ denote the generator of the group of covering transformations which corresponds to a meridian linking the knot positively in the oriented S^3.

13.8 Proposition. *The bilinear form*

$$q\colon H^1(C_\infty, \partial C_\infty) \times H^1(C_\infty, \partial C_\infty) \to A,\ q(x, y) = \langle x \cup t^* y + y \cup t^* x, j_*(z)\rangle$$

defines a quadratic form $q(x, x)$, which can be represented by the matrix $W + W^T$, where W, see 13.5, is a reduced Seifert matrix of $\mathfrak{k}$. The quadratic form is non-degenerate. $\Delta(0)$ is required to be a unit in A.

Proof. Remember that t_* is represented by $W^{-1} W^T$ with respect to the basis $\{s_i\}$, so t^* will be represented by $W(W^T)^{-1}$ relative to the dual basis $\{s^i\}$.

To calculate the matrix

$$Q = (q(s^i, s^k)) = (\langle j^*(s^i) \cup j^* t^*(s^k) + j^*(s^k) \cup j^* t^*(s^i), z\rangle)$$

we use $B = (\langle j^*(s^i) \cup j^*(s^k), z\rangle) = -\, W^T (W - W^T)^{-1} W$, see (3) and (4). We obtain

$$Q = BW^{-1}W^T + W(W^T)^{-1}B^T = \\ - W^T(W-W^T)^{-1}W^T + W((W-W^T)^{-1})^T W.$$

Since $|W-W^T| = 1$, the matrices $(W-W^T)^{-1}$ and $W-W^T$ are equivalent, because there is only one skew symmetric form over $\mathbb{Z}$ with determinant $+1$ – its normal form is F. (See Appendix A1.) Let M be unimodular over $\mathbb{Z}$ with

$$(5)\quad \begin{aligned} &(W-W^T)^{-1} = M(W-W^T)M^T, \quad \text{or} \\ &(W-W^T)M(W-W^T)M^T = E. \end{aligned}$$

Now, $Q = -W^T M(W-W^T)M^T W^T + WM(W-W^T)M^T W$.

Using (5), we get

$$Q = (E - WM(W-W^T)M^T)W^T + (WM(W-W^T)M^T W = \\ = W^T + WM(W-W^T)M^T(W-W^T) = W^T + W.$$

The quadratic form is non-degenerate, since $|W+W^T| \equiv |W-W^T| \equiv 1 \bmod 2$. □

Let us summarize the results of this section: Given a knot, we have proved, that $H_1(C_\infty, \partial C_\infty)$ is a free A-module, if $\Delta(0)$ is invertible in the integral domain A. By using the cup product, we defined a quadratic form on $H^1(C_\infty, \partial C_\infty) \cong H_1(C_\infty, \partial C_\infty)$, invariantly associated to the knot. The form can be computed from a Seifert matrix. q is known as Trotter's *quadratic form*.

In the course of our argument we used both, an orientation of S^3 and of the knot. Nevertheless, the quadratic form proves to be independent of the orientation of $\mathfrak{k}$. Clearly $j_*(z) = t_* j_*(z)$ in $H_1(C_\infty, \partial C_\infty)$, by the construction of C_∞, so that $q(x, y) = \langle x \cup (t^* - t^{*-1})y, j_*(z)\rangle$ is an equivalent definition of $q(x, y)$. Replacing z by $-z$ and t by t^{-1} does not change $q(x, y)$ (see Proposition 3.15). A reflection σ of S^3 which carries $\mathfrak{k}$ into its mirror image $\mathfrak{k}^*$ induces an isomorphism $\sigma^*: H^1(C_\infty, \partial C_\infty) \to H^1(C_\infty, \partial C_\infty)$. If $q_\mathfrak{k}$ and $q_{\mathfrak{k}^*}$ are the quadratic forms of $\mathfrak{k}$ and $\mathfrak{k}^*$, respectively, then $q_{\mathfrak{k}^*} = -q_\mathfrak{k}$, because $\sigma^* t^* = t^{*-1}\sigma^*$.

13.9 Proposition. *The quadratic form of a knot is the same as that of its inverse. The quadratic forms of $\mathfrak{k}$ and its mirror image $\mathfrak{k}^*$ are related by $q_{\mathfrak{k}^*} = -q_\mathfrak{k}$.* □

The quadratic form is easily seen to behave naturally with respect to the composition of knots (Chapter 7). Let us assume that in A the leading coefficients of the Alexander polynomials of $\mathfrak{k}_1$ and $\mathfrak{k}_2$ are invertible such that $q_{\mathfrak{k}_1}$ and $q_{\mathfrak{k}_2}$ are defined.

13.10 Proposition. $q_{(\mathfrak{k}_1 \# \mathfrak{k}_2)} = q_{\mathfrak{k}_1} \oplus q_{\mathfrak{k}_2}$

Proof. Obviously the Seifert matrix of $\mathfrak{k}_1 \# \mathfrak{k}_2$ has the form

$$V = \left(\begin{array}{c|c} V_1 & 0 \\ \hline 0 & V_2 \end{array}\right)$$

with V_i Seifert matrix of $\mathfrak{k}_i$, $i = 1, 2$. The same holds for the reduced Seifert matrices. □

Invariants of the quadratic form are, of course, invariants of the knot.

13.11 Definition (signature). The *signature* σ of the quadratic form of a knot $\mathfrak{k}$ is called the signature $\sigma(\mathfrak{k})$ of $\mathfrak{k}$.

The signature of the quadratic form – the number of its positive eigenvalues minus the number of its negative eigenvalues – can be computed without much difficulty [Jones 1950, Theorem 4], see Appendix A 2. Obviously the signature of a quadratic form is an additive function with respect to the direct sum. Moreover the signature of $\begin{pmatrix} 0 & 1 \\ 1 & 0 \end{pmatrix}$ is zero.

13.12 Proposition. *(a) For any Seifert matrix V for $\mathfrak{k}$, $\sigma(\mathfrak{k}) = \sigma(V + V^T)$.*
(b) $\sigma(\mathfrak{k}_1 \# \mathfrak{k}_2) = \sigma(\mathfrak{k}_1) + \sigma(\mathfrak{k}_2)$
(c) If $\mathfrak{k}$ is amphicheiral, $\sigma(\mathfrak{k}) = 0$.

Proof. We can replace V by an equivalent matrix of the form as obtained in Lemma 13.5. Then

$$V + V^T \sim \left(\begin{array}{cc|c|c} 0 & -1 & & * \quad * \\ -1 & 0 & & 0 \ldots 0 \\ \hline & & \ddots & \\ \hline * & 0 & & W + W^T \\ * & 0 & & \end{array}\right) \sim \left(\begin{array}{cc|c|c} 0 & -1 & & \\ -1 & 0 & & 0 \\ \hline & & \ddots & \\ \hline & 0 & & W + W^T \\ & & & \end{array}\right).$$

□

B Computation of the Quadratic Form of a Knot

The computation of the quadratic form q of a given knot $\mathfrak{k}$ was based in the last paragraph on a Seifert matrix V which in turn relied on Seifert's band projection (see 8.2). Such a projection might not be easily obtainable from some given regular knot projection. Murasugi [1965] defined a knot matrix M over $\mathbb{Z}$, which can be read off any regular projection of a link. A link defines a class of *s-equivalent* matrices $\{M\}$ (see 13.34), and, by symmetrizing, a class of *S-equivalent* matrices $\{M + M^T\}$ is obtained which can be described in the following way:

13.13 Definition. Two symmetric integral matrices M and M' are called *S-equivalent*, if there is a matrix

$$\begin{pmatrix} \begin{matrix} 0 & 1 \\ 1 & 0 \end{matrix} & & & 0 \\ & \ddots & & \\ & & \begin{matrix} 0 & 1 \\ 1 & 0 \end{matrix} & \\ 0 & & & M \end{pmatrix}$$

A-equivalent (see 13.4) to M'. (Or, vice versa, exchanging M and M'.)

Murasugi [1965] proves that the class $\{M + M^T\}$ of S-equivalent symmetrized knot matrices is an invariant of the knot (or link). He thereby attaches a class of quadratic forms to a link.

Obviously, S-equivalent matrices have the same signature (see proof of 13.12), so the signature $\sigma\{M + M^T\}$ is defined and is a knot invariant. We shall prove: *If W is a reduced Seifert matrix of $\mathfrak{k}$, then $W + W^T \in \{M + M^T\}$*. This means that the quadratic form $q_\mathfrak{k}$ as defined in the first section of this chapter is a member of the class of quadratic forms represented by $M + M^T$. Since the rule given by Murasugi to read off M from an arbitrary regular projection is rather complicated, we shall confine ourselves to so-called special projections, which hold a position between arbitrary projections and band projections. Any projection can be converted into a special one without much difficulty.

13.14 Definition (special projection). Let $p(\mathfrak{k})$ be a regular projection of a knot $\mathfrak{k}$ on $\mathbb{R}^2$. Choose a chessboard colouring (colours α and β) of the regions of $\mathbb{R}^2$ defined by $p(\mathfrak{k})$ such that the infinite region is an α-region (see Chapter 2). $p(\mathfrak{k})$ is called a *special projection* or *special diagram*, if the union of the β-regions is the image of a Seifert surface of $\mathfrak{k}$ under the projection p.

13.15 Proposition. *Every knot $\mathfrak{k}$ possesses a special projection.*

Proof. Starting from an arbitrary regular projection of $\mathfrak{k}$ we use Seifert's procedure (see 2.4) to construct an orientable surface S spanning $\mathfrak{k}$. We obtain S as a union of several disks spanning the Seifert circuits, and a couple of bands twisted by π, joining the disks, which may occur in layers over each other. There is an isotopy which places the disks separately into the projection plane $\mathbb{R}^2$, so that they do not meet each other or any bands, save those which are attached to them (Fig. 13.1a). By giving the overcrossing section at a band crossing a half-twist (Fig. 13.1b) it can be arranged, that only the type of crossing as shown in Figure 13.1b occurs.

Now apply again Seifert's method. All Seifert circuits bound disjoint regions (β-regions) in $\mathbb{R}^2$. So they define a Seifert surface which – except in the neighbourhood of double points – consists of β-regions. □

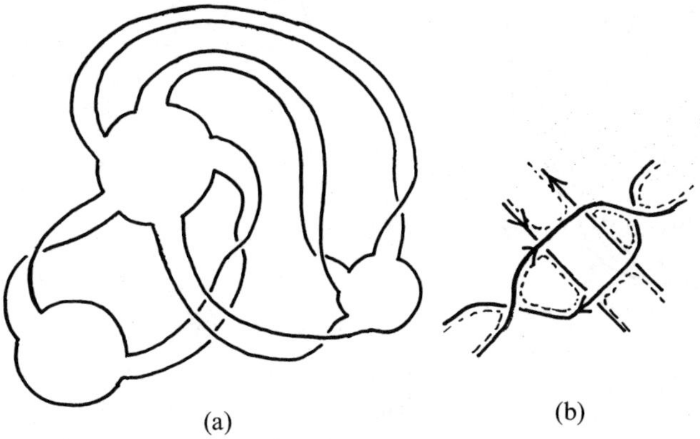

Fig. 13.1

It follows that the number of edges (arcs of $p(\mathfrak{k})$ joinig double points) of every α-region in a special projection must be even. This also suffices to characterize a special projection, if the boundaries of β-regions are simple closed curves, that is, if at double points always different β-regions meet. It is easy to arrange that the boundaries of β- and α-regions are simple: in case they are not, a twist through π removes the double point which occurs twice in the boundary (Fig. 13.2).

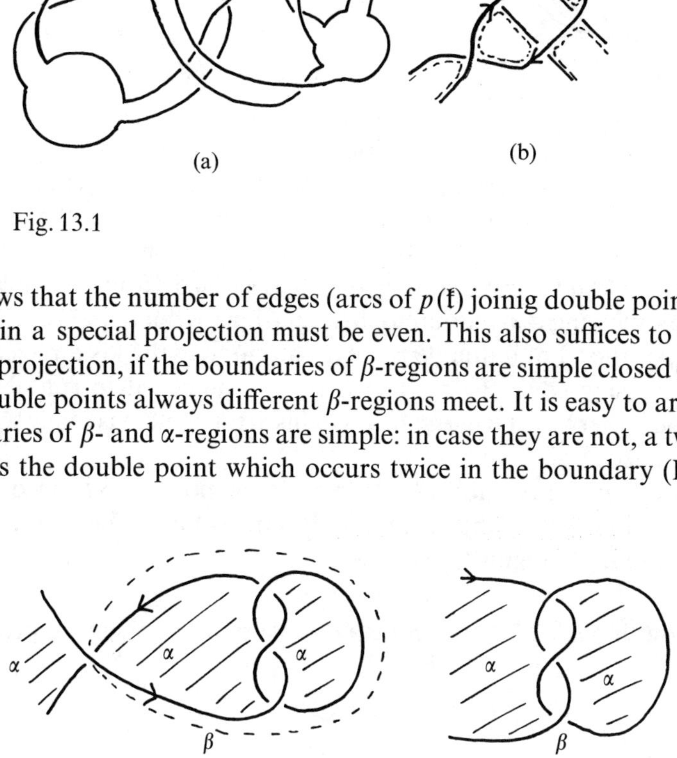

Fig. 13.2

We now use a special projection to define associated bases $\{a_i\}$, $\{s_k\}$ of $H_1(S)$ and $H_1(C^*)$, respectively, and compute their Seifert matrix V. (It turns out that V is Murasugi's knot matrix M of the special diagram; see [Murasugi 1965, 3.3].) Let S be the Seifert surface of $\mathfrak{k}$ which projects onto the β-regions $\{\beta_j\}$ of a special projection. The special projection suggests a geometric free basis of $H_1(S)$. Choose simple closed curves a_i on S whose projections are the boundaries $\partial\alpha_i$ of the finite α-regions $\{\alpha_i | 1 \leqq i \leqq 2h\}$, oriented counterclockwise in the projection plane. (See Fig. 13.3.) The number of finite α-regions is $2h$, where h is the genus of S. (We denote the infinite α-region by α_0.)

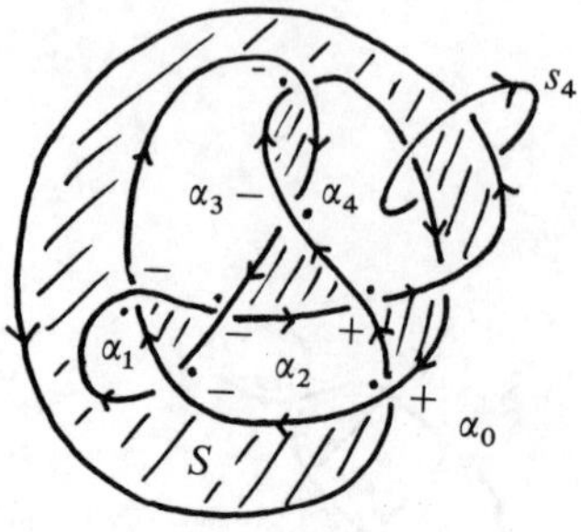

Fig. 13.3

Now cut the knot complement C along S to obtain C^*. There is again a geometrically defined free basis $\{s_k | 1 \leqq k \leqq 2h\}$ of $H_1(C^*)$ associated to $\{a_i\}$ by linking numbers: $lk(a_i, s_k) = \delta_{ik}$. The curve representing s_k pierces the projection plane once (from below) in a point belonging to α_k and once in α_0.

a_i splits up into a_i^+ and a_i^-. We move $i_*^+(a_i^+)$ by a small deformation away from S^+ and use the following convention to distinguish between $i_*^+(a_i^+)$ and $i_*^-(a_i^-)$. If in the neighbourhood of a double point P the curve $i_*^+(a_i^+)$ is directed as the parallel undercrossing edge of $\partial\alpha_i$, then $i_*^+(a_i^+)$ is supposed to run above the projection plane; otherwise it will run below. This arrangement is easily seen to be consistent in a special diagram.

We have defined in 2.3 the index $\theta(P)$ of a double point P. We need another function which takes care of the geometric situation at a double point with respect to the adjoining α-regions.

13.16 Definition (index $\varepsilon_i(P)$). Let P be a double point in a special projection, $P \in \partial\alpha_i$. Then

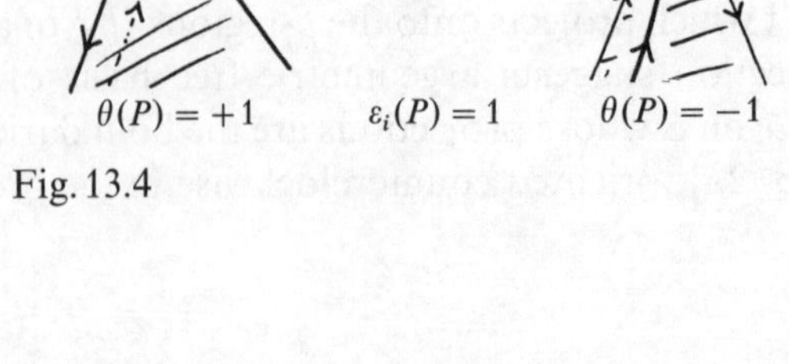

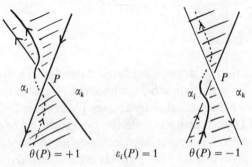

Fig. 13.4

$$\varepsilon_i(P) = \begin{cases} 1 & \text{if } \alpha_i \text{ is on the left of the underpassing arc at } P, \\ 0 & \text{if } \alpha_i \text{ is on the right,} \end{cases}$$

is called *ε-index of P*. (See Fig. 13.4.)

From this definition it follows that $\varepsilon_i(P) + \varepsilon_k(P) = 1$ for $P \in \partial\alpha_i \cap \partial\alpha_k$. Because of this symmetry it suffices to consider the two cases described in Figure 13.4.

We compute the Seifert matrix $V = (v_{ik})$, $i^+(a_i^+) = \Sigma\, v_{ik} s_k$:

$$(6) \qquad \begin{cases} v_{ii} = \sum\limits_{P \in \partial\alpha_i} \theta(P)\, \varepsilon_i(P) \\ v_{ik} = \sum\limits_{P \in \partial\alpha_i \cap \partial\alpha_k} \theta(P)\, \varepsilon_k(P) \end{cases}$$

This can be verified from our geometric construction using Fig. 13.4. The formulas (6) coincide with Murasugi's definition of his knot matrix M [Murasugi 1965, Definition 3.3] in the case of a special projection. (A difference in sign is due to another choice of $\theta(P)$.)

The formulas (6) may be regarded as the definition of M; we do not give a definition of Murasugi's knot matrix for arbitrary projections because it is rather intricate. The result of the consideration above can be formulated in the following way.

13.17 Proposition. *Let $p(\mathfrak{k})$ be a special diagram of $\mathfrak{k}$ with α-regions α_i, index functions $\theta(P)$ and $\varepsilon_i(P)$ according to 2.3 and 13.16. Then a Seifert matrix (v_{ik}) of $\mathfrak{k}$ is defined by* (6). *(The Seifert matrix coincides with Murasugi's knot matrix of $p(\mathfrak{k})$.)* □

13.18 Proposition. *If W is a reduced Seifert matrix then $(W + W^T)$ is contained in the class $\{M + M^T\}$ of S-equivalent matrices. The signature $\sigma_{\mathfrak{k}}$ coincides with the signature $\sigma(M + M^T)$ of* [Murasugi 1965].

Proof. If S is a Seifert surface which admits a special diagram as a projection the assertion follows from 13.13 and 13.17. Any Seifert surface S allows a band projection. By twists through π it can be arranged that the bands only cross as shown in Figure 13.1b. At each crossing we change S, as we did in the proof of 13.17, in order to get a spanning surface S' which projects onto the β-regions of a special diagramme. We then compare the band projections of S and S' and their Seifert matrices V and V'. It suffices to consider the case shown in Figure 13.5a.

It is not difficult to perform the local isotopy which carries Figure 13.5c over to Figure 13.5d. The genus of the new surface is $g(S') = g(S) + 2$. Let $\{a_k\}$, $\{s_l\}$ be associated bases of $H_1(S)$, (see 13.2) and $H_1(C^*)$, and let V be their Seifert matrix. Substitute $\tilde{a}$, a_j', a_j'' for $a_j \in \{a_k\}$ and $\tilde{s}$, s_j', s_j'' for $s_j \in \{s_l\}$ to obtain associated bases relative to S'. The corresponding Seifert matrix V' is of the form

$$\begin{array}{c} \\ \tilde{a} \\ a_j' \\ a_j'' \\ \\ \end{array} \begin{array}{c} \tilde{s} \quad s_j' \quad s_j'' \\ \begin{pmatrix} 0 & 1 & -1 & 0\ldots \\ 0 & * & * & \ldots \\ 0 & * & * & \ldots \\ 0 & \vdots & \vdots & (v_{kl}) \end{pmatrix} \end{array} .$$

Adding the s_j'-column to the s_j''-column and then the a_j'-row to the a_j''-row we get

$$\begin{array}{r} \\ \tilde{a} \\ a_j' \\ a_j = a_j' + a_j'' \\ \\ \\ \end{array} \begin{array}{c} \tilde{s} \quad s_j' - s_j'' \quad s_j'' \\ \begin{pmatrix} 0 & 1 & 0 & 0 & \ldots \\ 0 & * & * & * & \ldots \\ 0 & * & & & \\ 0 & * & & V & \\ \vdots & \vdots & & & \end{pmatrix} \end{array} .$$

This follows from Figure 13.5d, because the overcrossings of s_j' and s_j'' add up to those of s_j, and $a_j = a_j' + a_j''$. Evidently, by adding multiples of the first row to the

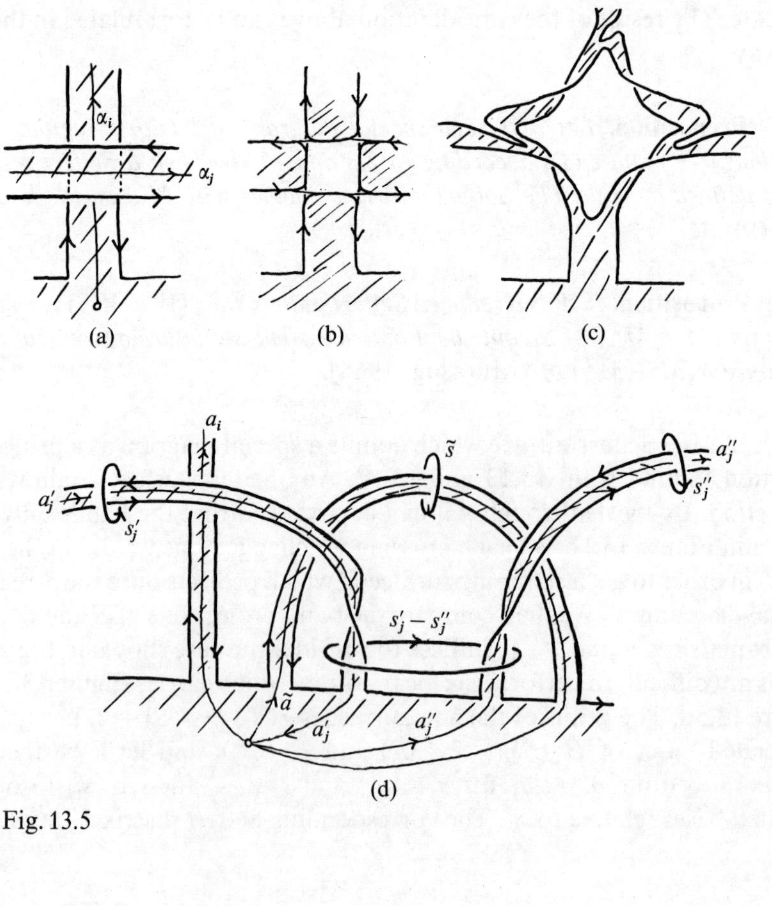

Fig. 13.5

other rows the second column can be replaced by zeroes excepting the 1 on top. After these changes the bases remain associated. We have proved: $(V' + V'^T)$ and $(V + V^T)$ are S-equivalent (see Definition 13.13). The procedure can be repeated until a Seifert surface is reached which allows a special projection. (Observe: Twists in the bands do not hamper the process.) □

C Alternating Knots and Links

The concepts which have been developed in the preceding section provide a means to obtain certain results on alternating knots and links first proved in [Crowell 1959], [Murasugi 1958, 1958′, 1960, 1963]. R.H. Crowell's paper rests on a striking application of a graph theoretical result, the Bott-Mayberry matrix tree theorem [Bott-Mayberry 1954].

In 2.3 we defined the graph of a regular projection $p(\mathfrak{k})$ of a knot (or link) by assigning a vertex P_i to each α-region α_i; we call this graph the α-graph of $p(\mathfrak{k})$ and denote it by Γ_α. Its dual Γ_β is obtained by considering β-regions instead of α-regions.

We always assume the infinite region to be the α-region α_0. The following definition endows Γ_α and Γ_β with orientations and valuations.

13.19 Definition. Let Γ_α be the α-graph of $p(\mathfrak{k})$. Call P_i the *initial* point of the edge u_{ik}^λ joining $P_i \in \alpha_i$ and $P_k \in \alpha_k$, if $\varepsilon_k(P) = 1$, where P is the double point of $p(\mathfrak{k})$ assigned to u_{ik}^λ. (Loops ($P_i = P_k$) are oriented arbitrarily.) The oriented edge u_{ik}^λ obtains the *valuation* $f(u_{ik}^\lambda) = \theta(P)$. The edges of the dual graph Γ_β are oriented in such a way that $int(u_{ik}^\lambda, v_{jl}^\mu) = +1$ for every pair of dual edges with respect to a fixed orientation of the plane containing $p(\mathfrak{k})$. Now the valuation of Γ_β is defined by $f(v_{jl}^\mu) = -f(u_{ik}^\lambda)$. Denote the graphs with orientation and valuation by Γ_α^*, Γ_β^* respectively.

13.20 A Seifert matrix of a Seifert surface of $\mathfrak{k}$ which is composed of the β-regions of a special projection may now be interpreted in terms of Γ_α^*. Define a square matrix $H(\Gamma_\alpha^*) = (h_{ik})$ by

$$(7) \qquad \begin{cases} h_{ii} = \sum\limits_{j,\lambda} f(u_{ji}^\lambda), \\ h_{ik} = -\sum\limits_{\lambda} f(u_{ik}^\lambda), \quad i \neq k. \end{cases}$$

Denote by H_{ii} the submatrix of H obtained by omitting the i-th row and column of H. From equations (6) and (7) we obtain

13.21 Proposition. *Let $p(\mathfrak{k})$ be a special projection of a knot or link, Γ_α^* its α-graph, and H the graph matrix of Γ_α^*. Then H_{00} is a Seifert matrix of $\mathfrak{k}$ with respect to a Seifert surface which is projected onto the β-regions of $p(\mathfrak{k})$.* □

There is a theorem in [Bott-Mayberry 1954] connecting the principal minors $\det(H_{ii})$ of a graph matrix with the number of *rooted trees* in a graph Γ; for definitions and the proof see Appendix A 3–5.

13.22 Theorem (matrix tree theorem of Bott-Mayberry). *Let Γ_α^* be an oriented graph with vertices P_i and edges u_{ik}^λ, and a valuation $f\colon \{u_{ik}^\lambda\} \mapsto \{1, -1\}$. Then*

(8) $$\det(H_{ii}) = \sum f(Tr(i)),$$

where the sum is taken over the rooted trees $Tr(i) \subset \Gamma_\alpha^*$ with root P_i, and $f(Tr(i)) = \prod f(u_{jk}^\lambda)$, the product taken over all $u_{jk}^\lambda \in Tr(i)$. □

13.23 Proposition. *The graphs Γ_α^* and Γ_β^* of a special alternating projection have the following properties (see Fig. 13.6).*

(a) Every region of Γ_α^* can be oriented such that the induced orientation on every edge in its boundary coincides with the orientation of the edge.

(b) No vertex of Γ_β^* is at the same time initial point and endpoint.

(c) The valuation is constant (we always choose $f(u_{ik}^\lambda) = +1$).

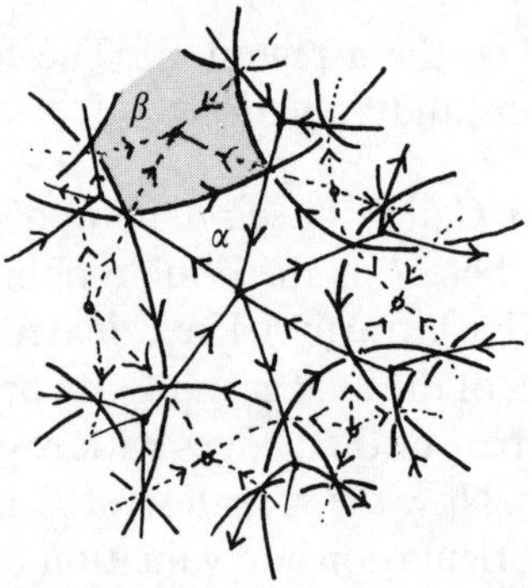

Fig. 13.6

The *proof* of the assertion is left to the reader. It relies on geometric properties of special projections, see Figure 13.6, and the definitions 2.3 and 13.19. Note that the edges of Γ_α^* with P_i in their boundary, cyclically ordered, have P_i alternatingly as initial point and endpoint, and that the edges in the boundary of a region of Γ_β^* also alternate with respect to their orientation. □

13.24 Proposition. *Let S be the Seifert surface determined by the β-regions of a special alternating projection $p(\mathfrak{k})$, and V a Seifert matrix of S. Then* $\det V \neq 0$ *and S is of minimal genus. Furthermore,* $\det V = \pm 1$, *if and only if* $\deg P_i = \sum_k |h_{ik}| = 2$ *for $i \neq 0$.*

Proof. It follows from 13.23 (a) that every two vertices of Γ_α^* can be joined by a path in Γ_α^*. So there is at least one rooted tree for any root P_i. Since $f(u_{ik}^\lambda) = +1$

the number of P_i-rooted trees is by 13.22 equal to $\det(H_{ii}) > 0$. If $V = H_{00}$ is a $m \times m$ matrix then $\deg \Delta(t) = m$ in the case of a knot, and $\deg \nabla(t) = m - \mu + 1$ in the case of a μ-component link. It follows that $2h = m$ where h is the genus of S. Since $\deg \Delta(t) \leqq 2g$ resp. $\deg \nabla(t) + \mu - 1 \leqq 2g$ (g the genus of $\mathfrak{k}$), we get $g = h$, see 8.11, 9.18 and E 9.5.

To prove the last assertion we characterize the graphs Γ_α^* which admit only one P_0-rooted tree. We claim that for $i \neq 0$ one must have $\deg P_i = 2$. Suppose $\deg P_k \geqq 4$ for some $k \neq 0$, with $u_{ik}^{\lambda} \neq u_{jk}^{\lambda'}$, and u_{ik}^{λ} contained in a P_0-rooted tree T_0. Then $u_{jk}^{\lambda'} \notin T_0$ and there are two simple paths w_i, w_j in T_0 which intersect only in their common initial point P_l with endpoints P_i and P_j respectively, see Figure 13.7. Substitute $u_{jk}^{\lambda'}$ for u_{ik}^{λ} to obtain a different P_0-rooted tree.

Obviously every graph Γ_α^* with $\deg P_i = 2$ for all $i \neq 0$ has exactly one P_0-rooted tree. □

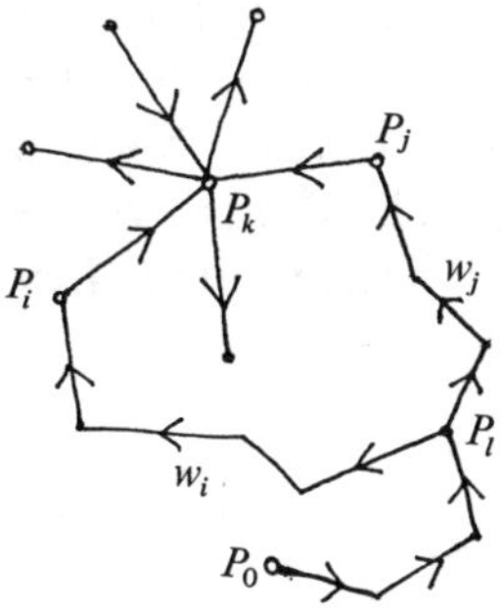

Fig. 13.7

As an easy consequence one gets:

13.25 Proposition. *A knot or link $\mathfrak{k}$ with a special alternating projection is fibred, if and only if it is the product of torus knots or links $\mathfrak{k}_i = \mathfrak{t}(a_i, 2)$, $\mathfrak{k} = \mathfrak{k}_1 \# \ldots \# \mathfrak{k}_r$.*

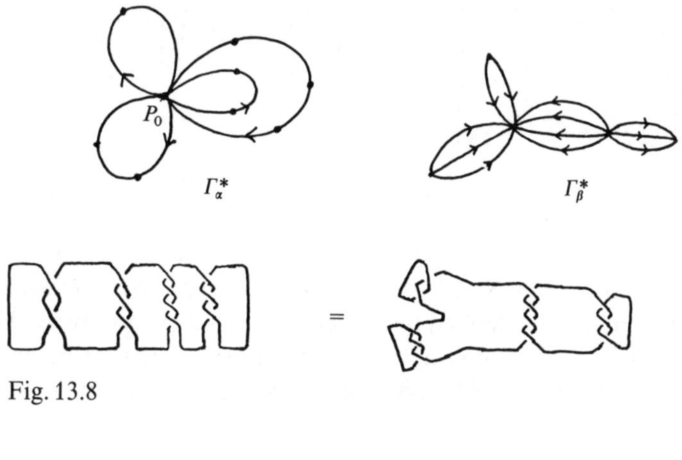

Fig. 13.8

Proof. See Figure 13.8. It follows from 13.24 that $\mathfrak{k}$ is of this form. By 4.11 and 7.18 we know that knots of this type are fibred. □

Proposition 13.25 was first proved in [Murasugi 1960].

13.26 Proposition. *Let $\mathfrak{k}$ be an alternating knot or link of multiplicity μ, and $p(\mathfrak{k})$ an alternating regular projection.*

(a) The genus of the Seifert surface S obtained from the Seifert construction 2.4 is the genus $g(\mathfrak{k})$ of $\mathfrak{k}$ (genus and canonical genus coincide).

(b) $\deg \Delta(t) = 2g$, *resp.* $\deg \nabla(t) = 2g$.

(c) $\mathfrak{k}$ *is fibred if and only if* $|\Delta(0)| = 1$ *resp.* $|\nabla(0)| = 1$.

Proof. Consider the Seifert cycles of the alternating projection $p(\mathfrak{k})$. If a Seifert cycle contains another Seifert cycle in the projection of the disk it spans, it is called a *cycle of the second kind*, otherwise it is *of the first kind* [Murasugi 1960]. If there are no cycles of the second kind, the projection is special, see 2.4 and 13.14. Suppose there are cycles of the second kind; choose a cycle c bounding a disk $D \subset S^3$ such that $p(D)$ contains only cycles of the first kind. Place S in $\mathbb{R}^3$ in such a way that the part of $\mathfrak{k}$ which is projected on $p(D)$ is above a plane $E \supset D$, while the rest of $\mathfrak{k}$ is in the lower halfspace (Fig. 13.9).

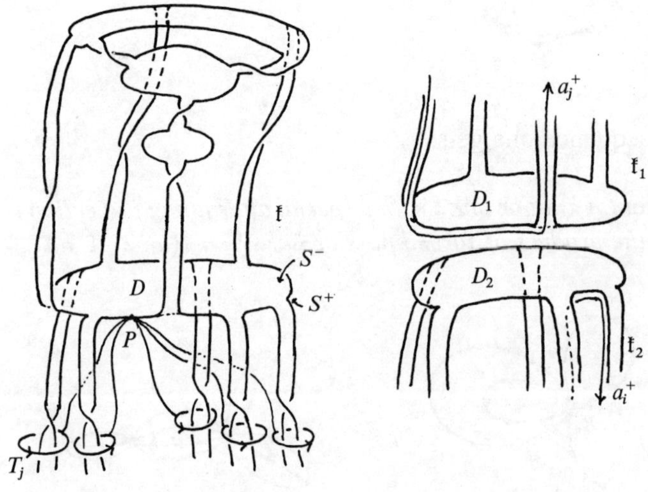

Fig. 13.9

Cut S along D such that S splits into two surfaces S_1, S_2, contained in the upper resp. lower halfspace defined by E such that D is replaced by two disks D_1, D_2. The knots (or links) $\mathfrak{k}_1 = \partial S_1$, $\mathfrak{k}_2 = \partial S_2$ then possess alternating projections $p(\mathfrak{k}_1)$, $p(\mathfrak{k}_2)$, and $p(\mathfrak{k}_1)$ is special. One may obtain S back from S_1 and S_2 by identifying the disks D_1 and D_2. If $\mathfrak{k}$ results in this way from the components $\mathfrak{k}_1$ and $\mathfrak{k}_2$, we write $\mathfrak{k} = \mathfrak{k}_1 * \mathfrak{k}_2$ and call it $*$-product [Murasugi 1960]. (The reader is warned that the $*$-product does not depend merely on its factors $\mathfrak{k}_1$ and $\mathfrak{k}_2$.)

Let C^*, C_i^*, $1 \leqq i \leqq 2$, be obtained from the complements of $\mathfrak{k}$, $\mathfrak{k}_i$ by cutting along S, S_i, see 4.4. Choose a base point P on ∂D (Fig. 13.9), then

$$(9)\quad \begin{aligned} \pi_1 C^* &\cong \pi_1 C_1^* * \pi_1 C_2^*, \\ \pi_1 S &\cong \pi_1 S_1 * \pi_1 S_2, \text{ resp.} \\ H_1(C^*) &\cong H_1(C_1^*) \oplus H_1(C_2^*), \\ H_1(S) &\cong H_1(S_1) \oplus H_1(S_2). \end{aligned}$$

It is evident that every alternating projection may be obtained by forming $*$-products of special alternating projections. We shall prove 13.26 by induction on the number of $*$-products needed to build up a given alternating projection $p(\mathfrak{k})$.

Proposition 13.25 proves the assertion if $p(\mathfrak{k})$ is special alternating. Suppose $\mathfrak{k} = \mathfrak{k}_1 * \mathfrak{k}_2$, $p(\mathfrak{k}_1)$ special alternating.

Let $i_1^{\pm}\colon S_1^{\pm} \to C_1^*$, $i_2^{\pm}\colon S_2^{\pm} \to C_2^*$, $i^{\pm}\colon S \to C^*$ denote the inclusions. If S^+ and S^- are chosen as indicated in Figure 13.9, the Seifert matrix V^+ associated with i_*^+ can be written in the form

$$V^+ = \left(\begin{array}{c|c} V_1^+ & \begin{matrix} * \dots * \\ * \dots * \end{matrix} \\ \hline \begin{matrix} 0 \dots 0 \\ \vdots \quad \vdots \\ 0 \dots 0 \end{matrix} & V_2^+ \end{array}\right)$$

where V_1^+ and V_2^+ are Seifert matrices belonging to i_{1*}^+, i_{2*}^+. Assume (a) for $\mathfrak{k}_2$, S_2 as an induction hypothesis. By $|V^+| = |V_1^+| \cdot |V_2^+|$ property (a) follows for $\mathfrak{k}$, and (b) is a consequence of (a). To prove (c) let

$$w_1^{(1)} w_1^{(2)} w_2^{(1)} w_2^{(2)} \dots w_j^{(1)} w_j^{(2)},$$

$w_j^{(k)} \in \pi_1(C_k^*)$, $1 \leq k \leq 2$, be an element of $\pi_1(C_1^*) * \pi_1(C_2^*) \cong \pi_1(C^*)$. If $\mathfrak{k}_2$ is fibred, $i_{2\#}^+$ is an isomorphism. A closed curve $\omega_j^{(2)}$ in C^* representing $w_j^{(2)}$ is, therefore, homotopic rel P in C^* to a curve on S^+. Since $\mathfrak{k}_1$ is also fibred, a curve $\omega_j^{(1)}$ corresponding to a factor $w_j^{(1)}$ is homotopic to a closed curve composed of factors a_j^+ on S^+ and $T_j^{\pm 1}$, see Figure 13.9. But the T_j can be treated as the curves $\omega_j^{(2)}$ and are homotopic to curves on S^+. Thus $i_\#^+$ is surjective; it is also injective, since S is of minimal genus [Neuwirth 1960]. □

This shows, together with Proposition 13.25, that a fibred alternating knot or link must be a $*$-product composed of factors $\mathfrak{k}_i = \mathfrak{t}(a_1, 2) \# \mathfrak{t}(a_2, 2) \# \dots \# \mathfrak{t}(a_r, 2)$.

There is a

13.27 Corollary. *The commutator subgroup of an alternating knot is either*

$$\mathfrak{G}' = \mathfrak{F}_{2g} \quad or \quad \mathfrak{G}' = \dots * \mathfrak{F}_{2g} *_{\mathfrak{F}_{2g}} \mathfrak{F}_{2g} *_{\mathfrak{F}_{2g}}, \mathfrak{F}_{2g} * \dots$$

where g is the genus of the knot. C^* is a handlebody of genus 2g for a suitable Seifert surface.

Proof. The space C_1^* is a handlebody of genus $2g_1$, g_1 the genus of $\mathfrak{k}_1$. This follows by thickening the β-regions of $p(\mathfrak{k}_1)$. By the same inductive argument used in the proof of 13.26 one can see that C^* is a handlebody of genus $2g$ obtained by identifying two disks D_1 and D_2 on the boundary of the handlebodies C_1^* and C_2^*. □

D Comparison of Different Concepts and Examples

In the Sections A and B we defined the quadratic form of a knot according to Trotter and Erle, and pointed out the connection to Murasugi's class of forms [Murasugi 1965]. Let us add now a few remarks on Goeritz's form. We shall give an example which shows that Goeritz's invariant is weaker than that of Trotter-Murasugi. Nevertheless, Goeritz's form is still of interest because it can be more easily computed than the other ones, and C. McA. Gordon and R. A. Litherland [Gordon-Litherland 1978] have shown that it can be used to compute the Trotter-Murasugi signature.

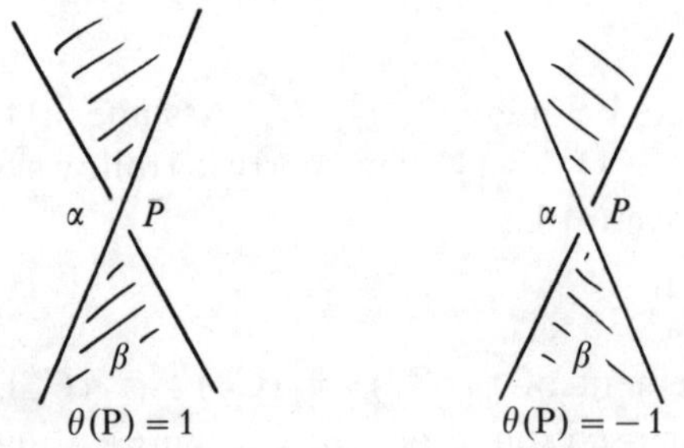

Fig. 13.10

A regular knot projection is coloured as in 13.14. $\theta(P)$ is defined as in 2.3, see Figure 13.10. (Here we may assume again that at no point P the two α-regions coincide; if they do, define $\theta(P) = 0$ for such points.)

$$(10) \quad \begin{cases} g_{ii} = \sum_{P \in \partial \alpha_i} \theta(P) \\ g_{ij} = -\sum_{P \in \partial \alpha_i \cap \partial \alpha_j} \theta(P) \end{cases}$$

then determines a symmetric $n \times n$-matrix $G = (g_{ij})$, where $\{\alpha_i | 1 \leqq i \leqq n\}$ are the finite α-regions. G is called *Goeritz matrix* and the quadratic form, defined by G, is called *Goeritz form*. (Observe that the orientation of the arcs of the projection do not enter into the definition of the index $\theta(P)$, but that G changes its sign if $\mathfrak{k}$ is mirrored.) Transformations $G \mapsto LGL^T$ with unimodular L and the following matrix operation (and its inverse)

$$G \mapsto \left(\begin{array}{c|c} G & \begin{matrix} 0 \\ \vdots \end{matrix} \\ \hline 0 \dots & \pm 1 \end{array}\right)$$

define a class of quadratic forms associated to the knot $\mathfrak{k}$ which Goeritz showed to be a knot invariant [Goeritz 1933]. A Goeritz matrix representing the quadratic form of a knot $\mathfrak{k}$ is denoted by $G(\mathfrak{k})$.

13.28 Proposition. *Let $p(\mathfrak{k})$ be a special diagram and V a Seifert matrix defined by* (6) *(see 13.17). Then $V + V^T = G(\mathfrak{k})$ is the Goeritz matrix of $p(\mathfrak{k})$.*

Proof. This is clear for elements g_{ij}, $i \neq j$, since $\varepsilon_i(P) + \varepsilon_k(P) = 1$ for $P \in \partial\alpha_i \cap \partial\alpha_k$. For $i = j$ it follows from the equality

$$v_{ii} = \sum_{P \in \partial\alpha_i} \theta(P)\varepsilon_i(P) = \sum \theta(P)(1 - \varepsilon_i(P));$$

the first sum describes the linking number of $i_*^+(a_i^+)$ with $\partial\alpha_i$, the second the linking number of $i_*^-(a_i^-)$ with $\partial\alpha_i$, which are the same for geometric reasons. (There is a ribbon $S^1 \times I \subset S^3$, $S^1 \times 0 = a_i^-$, $S^1 \times 1 = a_i^+$, $S^1 \times \frac{1}{2} = \partial\alpha_i$.) □

From this it follows that each Goeritz matrix G can be interpreted as presentation matrix of $H_1(\hat{C}_2)$ (see 8.21). H. Seifert [1936], M. Kneser and D. Puppe [1953] have investigated this connection and were able to show that the Goeritz matrix defines the linking pairing $H_1(\hat{C}_2) \times H_1(\hat{C}_2) \to \mathbb{Z}$.

Figure 13.11a shows the trefoil's usual (minimal) diagram and 13.11b, a special diagram of it. The sign at a crossing point P denotes the sign of $\theta(P)$, a dot at P in an α-region α_i indicates $\varepsilon_i(P) = 1$ for $P \in \partial\alpha$. Thus we get $G_a = (-3)$ from Figure 13.11a and

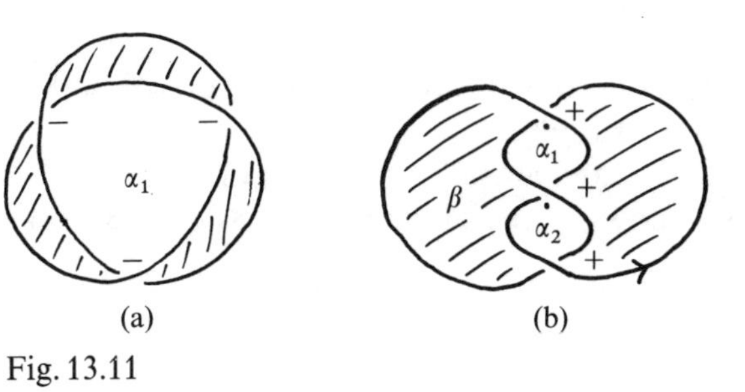

Fig. 13.11

$$M + M^T = G_b = \begin{pmatrix} 2 & -1 \\ -1 & 2 \end{pmatrix}.$$

G_a and G_b can be transformed into each other by Goeritz moves which are described before 13.28. (It is necessary to use an extension by 3×3 matrices.) Figures 13.12a and 13.12b show a minimal and a special projection of the knot 8_{19}. Figure 13.12a yields a Goeritz matrix

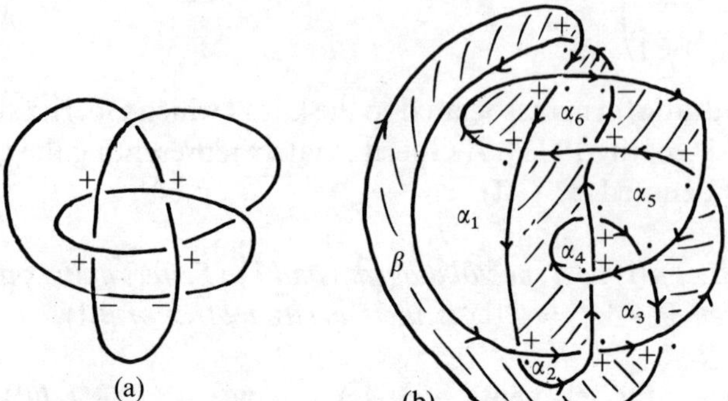

(a) (b)

Fig. 13.12

$$G = \begin{pmatrix} 0 & -1 & -1 & 0 \\ -1 & 1 & 0 & -1 \\ -1 & 0 & 2 & -1 \\ 0 & -1 & -1 & 1 \end{pmatrix} \sim (-3)$$

which is equivalent to that of a trefoil of Figure 13.11a. A Seifert matrix V can be read off Figure 13.12b:

$$V = \begin{pmatrix} 2 & 0 & 0 & 0 & 0 & -1 \\ -1 & 1 & 0 & 0 & 0 & 0 \\ 0 & -1 & 1 & 0 & 0 & 0 \\ 0 & 0 & -1 & 1 & 0 & 0 \\ 0 & 0 & 1 & -1 & 1 & 0 \\ -1 & 0 & 0 & 0 & -1 & 1 \end{pmatrix}$$

Since $|V| = 1$, V is already reduced, so its quadratic form q_t is of rank 6, different to that of a trefoil which is of rank 2.

We finally demonstrate the advantage of using a suitable integral domain A instead of $\mathbb{Z}$. Figure 13.3 shows a special diagram of 8_{20}. Its Seifert matrix is

$$V = \begin{pmatrix} -1 & 0 & 1 & 0 \\ 1 & 0 & 0 & 0 \\ 0 & 1 & -2 & 1 \\ 0 & -1 & 1 & 0 \end{pmatrix}, \quad |V| = 1,$$

$$V + V^T = \begin{pmatrix} -2 & 1 & 1 & 0 \\ 1 & 0 & 1 & -1 \\ 1 & 1 & -4 & 2 \\ 0 & -1 & 2 & 0 \end{pmatrix} \sim \left(\begin{array}{cc|cc} 0 & 1 & \multicolumn{2}{c}{0} \\ 1 & 0 & & \\ \hline & & -2 & 3 \\ \multicolumn{2}{c|}{0} & 3 & 0 \end{array}\right).$$

$V + V^T$ is S-equivalent (see 13.13) to

$$\begin{pmatrix} -2 & 3 \\ 3 & 0 \end{pmatrix} = V' + V'^T, \quad V' = \begin{pmatrix} -1 & 2 \\ 1 & 0 \end{pmatrix}.$$

Using the construction of 8.7 one obtains a knot $\mathfrak{k}'$ with Seifert matrix V'. Thus over $\mathbb{Z}_2$ there are different Trotter forms represented by

$$\begin{pmatrix} -2 & 3 \\ 3 & 0 \end{pmatrix} \text{ resp. } \begin{pmatrix} 0 & 1 & & \\ 1 & 0 & & \\ & & -2 & 3 \\ & & 3 & 0 \end{pmatrix}$$

associated to 8_{20} resp. $\mathfrak{k}'$, while their Murasugi matrices are equivalent. Moreover both knots have zero-signature, but over $\mathbb{Z}_3$ their forms prove that they are not amphicheiral.

13.29 Corollary. *The absolute value of the determinant of the quadratic form is an invariant of the knot. It is called the determinant of the knot. It can be expressed in several forms:*

$$|\det(M + M^T)| = |\det(W + W^T)| = |\det G| = |H_1(\hat{C}_2)| = |\Delta(-1)|.$$

Proof. See 8.11 and 8.20. □

In the case of alternating knots the determinant is a strong invariant; in fact, it can be used to classify alternating knots in a certain sense:

13.30 Proposition ([Bankwitz 1930], [Crowell 1959]). *The order with respect to regular alternating projections of a knot does not exceed its determinant.*

Proof. Let $p(\mathfrak{k})$ be a regular alternating projection of minimal order n. Consider the (unoriented) graph Γ_α of $p(\mathfrak{k})$. Since n is minimal, Γ_α does not contain any loops, and every edge of Γ_α is contained in a circuit, compare Figure 13.2. It follows from the Corollary to the Bott-Mayberry Theorem (Appendix A 4) that the determinant $\det G(\mathfrak{k})$ of $\mathfrak{k}$ is equal to the number of trees of Γ_α. It remains to show that in a planar graph Γ_α with the aforesaid properties the number n of edges never exceeds the number of trees. One may reduce Γ_α by omitting points of order two and loops. If then Γ_α defines more than two regions on S^2 there exists an edge b in the boundary of two regions such that these two regions have no other edge in common. $(\Gamma_\alpha - b)$ then is a connected planar graph with no loops where every edge is in a circuit. Every tree of $(\Gamma_\alpha - b)$ is a tree of Γ_α. There is at least one tree more in Γ_α which contains b. □

The inequality $n \leqq \det G(\mathfrak{k})$ can be improved [Crowell 1959], see E 13.4.

Since there are only finitely many alternating knots with $\Delta(-1) = d$, there are a forteriori only finitely many such knots with the same Alexander polynomial. If $\Delta(-1) = \pm 1$ (in particular, if $\Delta(t) = 1$), the knot is either non-alternating or any alternating projection of it can be trivialized by twists of the type of Figure 13.2. Consider as an example the knot 6_2, see Figure 13.13. The Goeritz matrix is

$$(g_{ij}) = \begin{pmatrix} 5 & -3 & -2 \\ -3 & 4 & -1 \\ -2 & -1 & 3 \end{pmatrix}.$$

One checks easily in Figure 13.13 that the graph has $11 = \Delta(-1) = \begin{vmatrix} 4 & -1 \\ -1 & 3 \end{vmatrix}$ maximal trees.

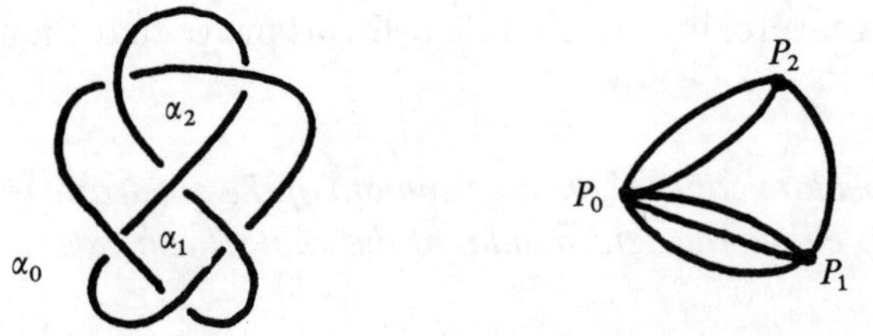

Fig. 13.13

Proposition 13.30 of Bankwitz can also be used to show that certain knots are non-alternating, that is, do not possess an alternating projection. This is true for all non-trivial knots with trivial Alexander polynomial. Crowell was able to prove that most of the knots with less than ten crossings which are depicted in Reidemeister's table as non-alternating, really are non-alternating. If, for instance, 8_{19} were alternating, it would have a projection of order $\Delta(-1) = 3$ or less. But 8_{19} is non-trivial and different from 3_1 by its Alexander polynomial.

We now give a description of a result of Gordon and Litherland. In a special diagram the β-regions are bounded by Seifert circuits. If in a chessboard colouring of an arbitrary projection the Seifert circuits follow the boundaries of α-regions in the neighbourhood of a crossing P we call P exceptional, and by v we denote the number $v = \Sigma\,\theta(P)$, where the sum is taken over the exceptional points of the projection. (The β-regions form an orientable Seifert surface if and only if there are no exceptional points.) Obviously the signature $\sigma(G)$ of a Goeritz matrix is no invariant in the class of equivalent Goeritz matrices. But in [Gordon-Litherland 1978] the following proposition is proved.

13.31 Proposition. $\sigma(q_{\mathfrak{k}}) = \sigma(G) - v$, *where* v *is defined above.* □

The fact that $\sigma(G) - v$ is a knot invariant can be proved by the use of Reidemeister moves Ω_i (Exercise E 13.3).

Since the order of G will in most cases be considerably smaller than that of $M + M^T$, Proposition 13.29 affords a useful practical method for calculating $\sigma(q_{\mathfrak{k}})$. To compute the signature of any symmetric matrix over $\mathbb{Z}$ one can take one's choice from a varied spectrum of methods in numerics. The following proposition was used in [Murasugi 1965] and can be found in [Jones 1950]; we give a proof in Appendix A 2.

13.32 Proposition. *Let Q be a symmetric matrix of rank r over a field. There exists a chain of principal minors D_i, $i = 0, 1, \ldots, r$ such that D_i is principal minor of D_{i+1} and that no two consecutive determinants D_i, D_{i+1} vanish* ($D_0 = 1$). *For any such sequence of minors,* $\sigma(Q) = \sum_{i=0}^{r-1} \operatorname{sign} D_i D_{i+1}$. □

As an application consider the two projections of the trefoil 3_1 in Figure 13.11. The signature of the Goeritz matrix G_a of Figure 13.11 (a) is -1 and $v = 3$. Figure 13.11 (b) yields $\sigma(3_1) = 2$, hence $\sigma(G_a) - v = \sigma(q_{3_1})$.

13.33 *Proof* of Proposition 12.19. Let $\mathfrak{k}$ be a link of multiplicity μ, and S any Seifert surface spanning it. As in the case of a knot one may use S to construct the infinite cyclic covering C_∞ of $\mathfrak{k}$ corresponding to the normal subgroup $\mathfrak{N} = \ker \chi\varphi$ of 9.18. There is a band projection of $\mathfrak{k}$ (see 8.2), and $H_1(C_\infty)$ – as a $Z(t)$-module – is defined by a presentation matrix

$$(V^T - tV)$$

where V is the Seifert matrix of the band projection. We show in 13.35 the result of [Kauffman 1981] that the (unique) Conway potential function $\nabla_{\mathfrak{k}}(t - t^{-1})$ is equal to $\det(tV - t^{-1}V^T)$ for any Seifert matrix V.

To prove that $\det(tV - t^{-1}V^T)$ is a link invariant, we use a result of [Murasugi 1965].

13.34 Definition (s-equivalence). Two square *integral matrices* are *s-equivalent* if they are related by a finite chain of the following operations and their inverses:

$$\Lambda_1\colon V \mapsto L^T V L, \quad L \text{ unimodular},$$

$$\Lambda_2\colon V \mapsto \left(\begin{array}{cc|cc} 0 & 1 & 0 & 0 \\ 0 & 0 & * & * \\ \hline \vdots & \vdots & & \\ & & V & \\ 0 & 0 & & \end{array}\right),$$

$$\Lambda_3\colon V \mapsto \left(\begin{array}{cc|cc} 0 & 0 & \ldots & 0 \\ 1 & 0 & \ldots & 0 \\ \hline 0 & * & & \\ & & V & \\ 0 & * & & \end{array}\right).$$

It is proved in [Murasugi 1965] that any two Murasugi knot matrices of isotopic links are s-equivalent. (This can be done by checking their invariance under Reidemeister moves Ω_i (see 1.13).) We showed in the proof of 13.18 that every Seifert matrix is s-equivalent to a Murasugi knot matrix. Hence, any two Seifert matrices of a link are s-equivalent.

13.35 Proposition. *The function* $\Omega_{\mathfrak{k}}(t) = \det(tV - t^{-1}V^T)$ *is the (unique) Conway potential function for any Seifert matrix* V.

Proof. By 8.11 and E 9.5,

$$\Omega_{\mathfrak{k}}(t) \doteq \Delta(t^2) \quad \text{for a knot,}$$
$$\Omega_{\mathfrak{k}}(t) \doteq (t^2-1)^{\mu-1}\nabla(t^2) \quad \text{for a link.}$$

Moreover $\Omega_{\mathfrak{k}}(1) = |V - V^T| = 1$. This proves 12.18 (1). For a split link $\Delta(t) = 0$ (see 9.17, 9.18). It remains to prove 12.18 (3). If $\mathfrak{k}_+$ is split so is $\mathfrak{k}_-$ and $\mathfrak{k}_0$, and all functions are zero. Figure 13.14 demonstrates the position of the Seifert surfaces S_+, S_-, S_0 in the region where a change occurs. (An orientation of a Seifert surface induces the orientation of the knot).

We may assume that the projection of $\mathfrak{k}_0$ is not split, because otherwise $\Omega_{\mathfrak{k}_0} = 0$, and $\mathfrak{k}_+$, $\mathfrak{k}_-$ are isotopic. If the projection of $\mathfrak{k}_+$, $\mathfrak{k}_-$, $\mathfrak{k}_0$ are all not split, then the change from $\mathfrak{k}_0$ to $\mathfrak{k}_+$ or $\mathfrak{k}_-$ adds a free generator a to $H_1(S_0)$: $H_1(S_+) \cong \langle a\rangle \oplus H_1(S_0) \cong \mathrm{H}_1(S_-)$. Likewise $H_1(S^3 - S_\pm) \cong H_1(S^3 - S_0) \oplus \langle s\rangle$, see Figure 13.14.

We denote by V_+, V_-, V_0 the Seifert matrices of $\mathfrak{k}_+$, $\mathfrak{k}_-$, $\mathfrak{k}_0$, which correspond to connected Seifert surfaces obtained from the projections as described in 2.4. It follows that

$$V_+ = V_- + \begin{pmatrix} 1 & 0 & 0 & \ldots & 0 \\ 0 & & & & \vdots \\ \vdots & & & & \vdots \\ 0 & . & . & \ldots & 0 \end{pmatrix}, \quad V_+ = \left(\begin{array}{c|c} * & * \\ \hline & \\ & V_0 \\ * & \end{array}\right),$$

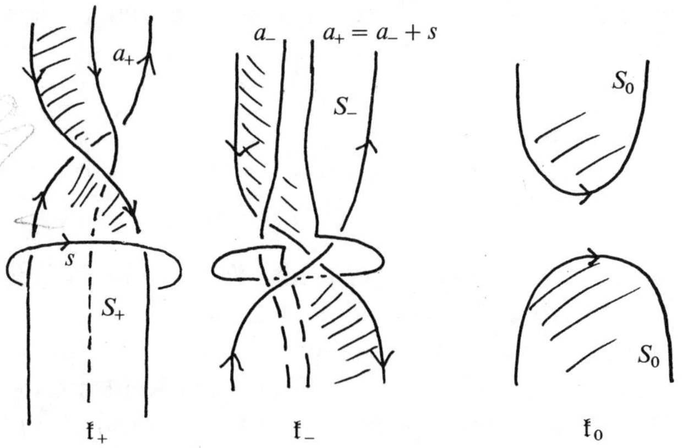

Fig. 13.14

where the first column and first row correspond to the generators s and $a_\pm$. The rest is a simple calculation:

$$\Omega_{\mathfrak{k}_+}(t) - \Omega_{\mathfrak{k}_-}(t) = |tV_+ - t^{-1}V_+^T| - |tV_- - t^{-1}V_-^T|$$

$$= \begin{vmatrix} t - t^{-1} & * & * \\ 0 & & \\ \vdots & \multicolumn{2}{c}{tV_0 - t^{-1}V_0^T} \\ 0 & & \end{vmatrix} = (t - t^{-1})\,\Omega_{\mathfrak{k}_0}(t). \quad \square$$

Remark: It is possible to introduce a Conway potential function in μ variables corresponding to the Alexander polynomials of links rather than to the Hosokawa polynomial [Hartley 1982]. The function is defined as a certain normalized Alexander polynomial $\Delta(t_1^2, \ldots, t_n^2) \cdot t_1^{\mu_1} \ldots t_n^{\mu_n}$ where the μ_i are determined by curvature and linking numbers. Invariance is checked by considering Reidemeister moves.

E History and Sources

An invariant consisting of a class of quadratic forms was first defined by L. Goeritz [1933]. They yielded the Minkowski units, new knot invariants [Reidemeister 1932]. Further contributions were made by H. Seifert [1936], M. Kneser and D. Puppe [1953], K. Murasugi [1965], H.F. Trotter [1962], J. Milnor, D. Erle and others. Our exposition is based on [Erle 1969] and [Murasugi 1965], the quadratic form is that of Trotter [1962].

In [Gordon-Litherland 1978] a new quadratic form was introduced which simultaneously generalized the forms of Trotter and Goeritz. As a by-product a simple way to compute the signature of a knot from a regular projection was obtained.

F Exercises

E 13.1 Compute the quadratic forms of Goeritz and Trotter and the signature of the knot 6_1 and the torus knots or links $\mathfrak{t}(2, b)$.

E 13.2 Characterize the 2×2 matrices which represent quadratic forms of knots.

E 13.3 Prove the invariance of $\sigma(G) - v$ (see 13.31) under Reidemeister moves.

E 13.4 [Crowell 1959] An alternating prime knot $\mathfrak{k}$ has a graph Γ_α with m vertices and k regions in S^2 such that the number of trees $tr(\Gamma_\alpha)$ satisfies the inequality $\det G(\mathfrak{k}) = tr(\Gamma_\alpha) \geqq 1 + (m-1)(k-1)$. Show that 8_{20}, 9_{42}, 9_{43} and 9_{46} are non-alternating knots.

Chapter 14: Representations of Knot Groups

Knot groups as abstract groups are rather complicated. Invariants which can be effectively calculated will, in general, be extracted from homomorphic images of knot groups. We use the term representation in this chapter as a synonym for homomorphism, and we call two representations $\varphi, \psi: \mathfrak{G} \to \mathfrak{H}$ equivalent, if there is an automorphism $\alpha: \mathfrak{H} \to \mathfrak{H}$ with $\psi = \alpha\varphi$. There have been many contributions to the field of representations of knot groups in the past decade, and the material of this chapter comprises a selection from a special point of view – the simpler and more generally applicable types of representations.

The first section deals with metabelian (2-step metabelian) representations, the second with a class of 3-step metabelian representation which means that the third commutator group of the homomorphic image of the knot group vanishes. These representations yield an invariant derived from the peripheral system of the knot which is closely connected to linking numbers in coverings defined by the homomorphisms. These relations are studied in Section C. Section D contains some theorems on periodic knots, and its presence in this chapter is, perhaps, justified by the fact that a special metabelian representation in Section A of a geometric type helps to prove one of the theorems and makes it clearer.

A Metabelian Representations

14.1 Throughout this chapter we consider only knots of multiplicity $\mu = 1$. A knot group $\mathfrak{G}$ may then be written as a semidirect product $\mathfrak{G} = \mathfrak{Z} \ltimes \mathfrak{G}'$, where $\mathfrak{Z}$ is a free cyclic group generated by a distinguished generator t represented by a meridian of the knot $\mathfrak{k}$. An abelian homomorphic image of $\mathfrak{G}$ is always cyclic, and an *abelian representation of* $\mathfrak{G}$ *will*, hence, *be called trivial.* A group $\mathfrak{G}$ is called *k-step metabelian,* if its k-th commutator subgroup $\mathfrak{G}^{(k)}$ vanishes. ($\mathfrak{G}^{(k)}$ is inductively defined by $\mathfrak{G}^{(k)} =$ commutator subgroup of $\mathfrak{G}^{(k-1)}$, $\mathfrak{G} = \mathfrak{G}^{(0)}$.) The 1-step metabelian groups are the abelian groups, and 2-step metabelian groups are also called *metabelian.* It seems reasonable, therefore, to try to find metabelian representations as a first step. They turn out to be plentiful and useful.

Let $\varphi: \mathfrak{G} \to \mathfrak{H}$ be a surjective homomorphism onto a metabelian group $\mathfrak{H}$. Then $\varphi(\mathfrak{G}) = \mathfrak{H} = \varphi(\mathfrak{Z}) \ltimes \varphi(\mathfrak{G}')$ is a semidirect product and can be considered as a $\varphi(\mathfrak{Z})$-module. Since $\mathfrak{G}$ is trivialized by putting $t = 1$, the same holds for $\varphi(\mathfrak{G})$, if the φ-image of t (also denoted by t) is made a relator. For the normal closure $\overline{\langle t\rangle}$ one has $\overline{\langle t\rangle} = \mathfrak{G}$ and $\overline{\langle t\rangle} = \varphi(\mathfrak{Z}) \times \mathfrak{H}'$. We claim $\mathfrak{H}' = (t - id)\mathfrak{H}'$. The inclusion $(t - id)\mathfrak{H}' \subset \mathfrak{H}'$ is trivial; on the other hand $\overline{\langle t\rangle} \cap \mathfrak{H}' = \mathfrak{H}'$ is generated by elements of the form $(t^{\nu} - id)a \in (t - id)\mathfrak{H}'$, $a \in \mathfrak{H}'$. Thus $(t - id)$: $\mathfrak{H}' \to \mathfrak{H}'$ is an isomorphism, since $\mathfrak{H}'$ is a finitely generated $\varphi(\mathfrak{Z})$-module, and as a consequence, $\varphi(\mathfrak{Z})$ operates on $\mathfrak{H}'$ without fixed points $\neq 0$.

14.2 Proposition. *Let φ: $\mathfrak{G} \to \mathfrak{H}$ be any nontrivial surjective metabelian representation of a knot group $\mathfrak{G} = \mathfrak{Z} \ltimes \mathfrak{G}'$, $\mathfrak{Z} = \langle t\rangle$, t a meridian. Then $\mathfrak{H} = \varphi(\mathfrak{Z}) \ltimes \mathfrak{H}'$ and $t - id$: $\mathfrak{G}' \to \mathfrak{G}'$ is an isomorphism.* □

Since $\varphi(\mathfrak{G}') = \mathfrak{H}'$ is abelian the homomorphism φ factors through $\mathfrak{Z} \ltimes \mathfrak{G}'/\mathfrak{G}''$. If $\varphi(\mathfrak{Z}) = \mathfrak{Z}_n$ is finite, it factors through $\mathfrak{Z}_n \ltimes \mathfrak{G}'/\mathfrak{G}'_n$, $\mathfrak{G}_n = n\mathfrak{Z} \rhd \mathfrak{G}'$, compare 8.19. The group $\mathfrak{G}'/\mathfrak{G}''$ is the first homology group of the infinite cyclic covering C_∞ of $\mathfrak{k}$, $\mathfrak{G}'/\mathfrak{G}'' = H_1(C_\infty)$ and may be regarded as a $\mathfrak{Z}$-module (Alexander module) where the operation is defined by that of the semidirect product. Likewise $\mathfrak{G}'/\mathfrak{G}'_n = H_1(\hat{C}_n)$ is the homology group of the n-fold cyclic branched covering of $\mathfrak{k}$, see 8.19(c). The following proposition summarizes our result.

14.3 Proposition. *A metabelian representation of a knot group φ: $\mathfrak{G} \to \mathfrak{Z} \ltimes \mathfrak{A}$, respectively φ_n: $\mathfrak{G} \to \mathfrak{Z}_n \ltimes \mathfrak{A}$, $\mathfrak{A}$ abelian, factors through β: $\mathfrak{G} \to \mathfrak{Z} \ltimes H_1(C_\infty)$, respectively β_n: $\mathfrak{G} \to \mathfrak{Z}_n \ltimes H_1(\hat{C}_n)$, mapping a meridian of $\mathfrak{k}$ onto a generator of $\mathfrak{Z}$ resp. $\mathfrak{Z}_n$. The group $\mathfrak{A}$ may be considered as a $\mathfrak{Z}$-module resp. $\mathfrak{Z}_n$-module. One has* $\ker\beta = \mathfrak{G}''$, $\ker\beta_n = n\mathfrak{Z} \ltimes \mathfrak{G}'_n$. □

We give a simple example with a geometric background.

14.4 The equiform group of the plane (group of similarities). Replacing the Alexander module $H_1(C_\infty) = \mathfrak{G}'/\mathfrak{G}''$ by $H_1(C_\infty) \otimes_{\mathbb{Z}} \mathbb{C}$ suggests a metabelian representation of $\mathfrak{G}$ by linear mappings $\mathbb{C} \to \mathbb{C}$ of the complex plane. Starting from a Wirtinger presentation $\mathfrak{G} = \langle S_1, \ldots, S_n \mid R_1, \ldots, R_n\rangle$, a relation

(1) $\quad S_k^{-1} S_i S_k S_{i+1}^{-1} = 1$

takes the form

(2) $\quad -tu_k + tu_i + u_k - u_{i+1} = 0$

for $u_j = \beta(S_j S_1^{-1})$, $1 \leq j \leq n$. ($u \mapsto tu$, $u \in H_1(C_\infty)$ denotes the operation of a meridian.) The equations (2) form a system of linear equations with coefficients in $\mathbb{Z}(t)$. We may omit one equation (Corollary 3.6) and the variable $u_1 = 0$.

The determinant of the remaining $(n-1) \times (n-1)$ linear system equals the Alexander polynomial $\Delta_1(t)$, see 8.10, 9.11. Thus, by interpreting (2) as linear equations over $\mathbb{C}$, one obtains non-trivial solutions if and only if t takes the value of a root α of $\Delta_1(t)$. For suitable $z_i \in \mathbb{C}$ (z a complex variable)

(3) $\quad S_i \mapsto \delta_\alpha(S_i)$: $z \mapsto \alpha(z - z_i) + z_i$

maps $\mathfrak{G}$ into the group $\mathfrak{C}^+$ of orientation preserving equiform mappings of the plane $\mathbb{C}$, since a Wirtinger relator (1) results in an equation (2) for $t = \alpha$, $u_i = z_i$. The representation δ_α is non-trivial (non-cyclic) if and only if $\Delta_1(\alpha) = 0$; it is metabelian because $\mathfrak{G}'$ is mapped into the group of translations. The class K of elements in $\mathfrak{G}$ conjugate to a meridian (K = *Wirtinger class*) is mapped into the class K_α of conjugate equiform mappings of $\mathfrak{C}^+$ characterized by α. (Note that $\alpha \neq 1$.)

14.5 Proposition. *There exist non-trivial representations* δ_α: $(\mathfrak{G}, K) \to (\mathfrak{C}^+, K_\alpha)$ *if and only if* α *is a root of the Alexander polynomial* $\Delta_1(t)$. *When* α *and* α' *are roots of an (over* $\mathbb{Z}$*) irreducible factor of* $\Delta_1(t)$ *which does not occur in* $\Delta_2(t)$, *then any two representations* δ_α, $\delta'_{\alpha'}$, *are equivalent. In particular, any two such maps* δ_α, δ'_α *differ by an inner automorphism of* $\mathfrak{C}^+$.

Proof. The first assertion has been proved above. For α satisfying $\Delta_1(\alpha) = 0$, $\Delta_2(\alpha) \neq 0$ there are indices i and k such that there is a unique non-trivial representation δ_α of the form (3) for any choice of a pair (z_i, z_k) of distinct complex numbers. Since $\mathfrak{C}^+$ is 2-transitive on $\mathbb{C}$ it follows that δ_α and δ'_α differ by an inner automorphism of $\mathfrak{C}^+$. Finally there is a Galois automorphism τ: $\mathbb{Q}(\alpha) \to \mathbb{Q}(\alpha')$, if α and α' are roots of an irreducible factor of $\Delta_1(t)$. Put $\delta_{\alpha'}(S_i)$: $z \mapsto \alpha'(z - \tau(z_i)) + \tau(z_i)$ to obtain a representation equivalent to $\delta_\alpha(S_i)$: $z \mapsto \alpha(z - z_i) + z_i$. (In the special case $\alpha' = \bar{\alpha}$ a reflection may be used.) □

Remark: The complex numbers α for which there are non-trivial representations

$$\delta_\alpha: (\mathfrak{G}, K) \to (\mathfrak{C}^+, K_\alpha)$$

are invariants of $\mathfrak{G}$ in their own right. The Alexander polynomial $\Delta_1(t)$, though, is a stronger invariant, because it includes also the powers of its prime factors. This is, of course, exactly what is lost when the operation of t is replaced by complex multiplication by α: $(p(\alpha))^\nu \cdot a = 0$, $a \neq 0$ implies $p(\alpha) \cdot a = 0$, but $(p(t))^\nu \cdot a = 0$ does not imply $(p(t))^{\nu-1} \cdot a = 0$. (Compare [Burde 1967].)

Example: Figure 14.1 shows a class of knots (compare Fig. 9.3, E 9.6) with Alexander polynomials of degree two. They necessarily have trivial second Alexander polynomials. Figure 14.2 shows the configuration of the fixed points z_i of $\delta_\alpha(S_i)$ for $m = 5$, $k = 3$. The $\delta_\alpha(S_i)$ are rotations through α, $\cos\alpha = \dfrac{2k-1}{2k} = \dfrac{5}{6}$.

14.6 Metacyclic representations. A *representation* β^* of $\mathfrak{G}$ is called *metacyclic*, if $\beta^*(\mathfrak{G}') = \mathfrak{H}'$ is a cyclic group $\langle a \rangle \neq 1$:

$$\beta^*(\mathfrak{G}) = \langle t \rangle \ltimes \langle a \rangle.$$

The operation of t is denoted by $a \mapsto ta$. Putting

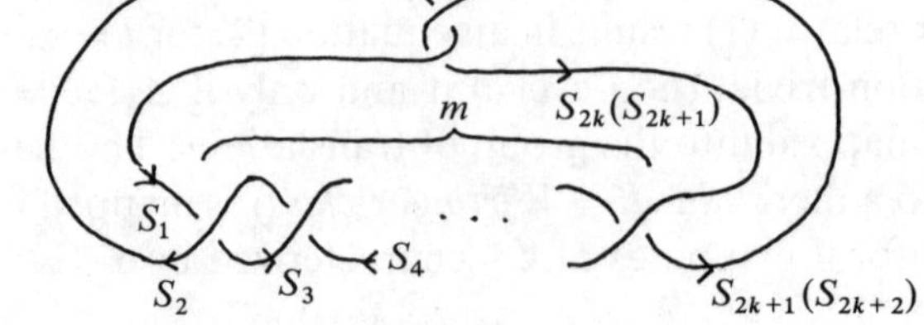

Fig. 14.1

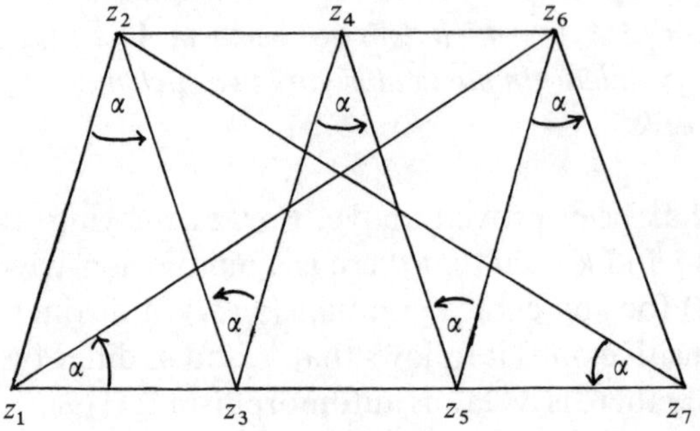

Fig. 14.2

$$\beta^*(S_i) = (t, v_i a), \quad v_i \in \mathbb{Z},$$

transforms a set of Wirtinger relators (1) into a system of n equations in n variables v_j:

(4) $$-v_{i+1} + tv_i + (1-t)v_k = 0.$$

These equations are to be understood over $\mathbb{Z}$ if $\langle a \rangle$ is infinite, and as congruences modulo m if $\langle a \rangle \cong \mathfrak{Z}_m$. In the first case β^* is trivial when $t = 1$. If $t = -1$, β^* must also be trivial, because the rank of (4) is $n-1$: Every $(n-1) \times (n-1)$ minor of its matrix is $\pm \Delta_1(-1) = \pm |H_1(\hat{C}_2)|$ which is an odd integer by 8.21, 13.19.

We may, therefore, confine ourselves to the finite case $\langle a \rangle = \mathfrak{Z}_m$.

14.7 Proposition (Fox). *A non-trivial metacyclic representation of a knot group is of the form*

$$\beta_m^*\colon \mathfrak{G} \to \mathfrak{Z} \ltimes \mathfrak{Z}_m, \quad m > 1,$$

mapping a meridian onto a generator t of the cyclic group $\mathfrak{Z}$. The existence of a surjective homomorphism β_m^* implies $m \mid \Delta_1(k)$ with $ka = ta$, $a \in \mathfrak{Z}_m$.

For a prime p, $p \mid \Delta_1(k)$, $gcd(k, p) = 1$, there exists a surjective representation β_p^*. If the rank of the system (4) *of congruences modulo p is $n-2$, all representations β_p^* are equivalent.*

Proof. If a surjective representation β_m^* exists, the system (4) admits a solution with $v_1 = 0, gcd(v_2, \dots, v_n) = 1$. Let $Ax \equiv 0$ denote the system of congruences in matrix form obtained from (4) by omitting one equation and putting $v_1 = 0$. By multiplying Ax with the adjoint matrix A^* one obtains $A^* A = (\det A) \cdot E \cdot x \equiv 0 \bmod m$. This means $m | \Delta_1(k)$.

The rest of Proposition 14.7 follows from standard arguments of linear algebra, since (4) is a system of linear equations over a field $\mathbb{Z}_p$ if $m = p$. □

Remark: If m is not a prime, the existence of a surjective representation β_m^* does not follow from $m | \Delta_1(k)$. We shall give a counterexample in the case of a dihedral representation. By a chinese remainder argument, however, one can construct β_m^* for composite m, if m is square-free. One may obtain from β_m^* a homomorphism onto a finite group by mapping $\mathfrak{Z}$ onto $\mathfrak{Z}_r$, where r is a multiple of the order of the automorphism $t: a \mapsto ka$. As a special case we note

14.8 Dihedral representations. *There is a surjective homomorphism*

$$\gamma_p^*: \mathfrak{G} \to \mathfrak{Z}_2 \ltimes \mathfrak{Z}_p$$

onto the dihedral group $\mathfrak{Z}_2 \ltimes \mathfrak{Z}_p$ *if and only if the prime p divides the order of* $H_1(\hat{C}_2)$. *If p does not divide the second torsion coefficient of* $H_1(\hat{C}_2)$, *then all representations* γ_p^* *are equivalent. (See Appendix A6.)* □

Since any such homomorphism γ_p^* must factor through $\mathfrak{Z}_2 \ltimes H_1(\hat{C}_2)$, see 14.3, the existence of dihedral representations $\mathfrak{G} \to \mathfrak{Z}_2 \ltimes \mathfrak{Z}_m$, $m \| H_1(\hat{C}_2)|$, depends on the cyclic factors of $H_1(\hat{C}_2)$. If $H_1(\hat{C}_2)$ is not cyclic – for instance $H_1(\hat{C}_2) \cong \mathbb{Z}_{15} \oplus \mathbb{Z}_3$ for 8_{18} – there is no homomorphism onto $\mathfrak{Z}_2 \ltimes \mathfrak{Z}_{45}$, though $45 | \Delta_1(-1)$.

The group $\gamma_p^*(\mathfrak{G})$ can be interpreted as the symmetry group of a regular p-gon in the euclidean plane. A meridian of the knot is mapped onto a reflection.

14.9 Example. Consider a Wirtinger presentation of the four-knot:

$$\mathfrak{G} = \langle S_1, S_2, S_3, S_4 | S_3 S_1 S_3^{-1} S_2^{-1}, S_4^{-1} S_2 S_4 S_3^{-1}, S_1 S_3 S_1^{-1} S_4^{-1}, S_2^{-1} S_4 S_2 S_1^{-1} \rangle,$$

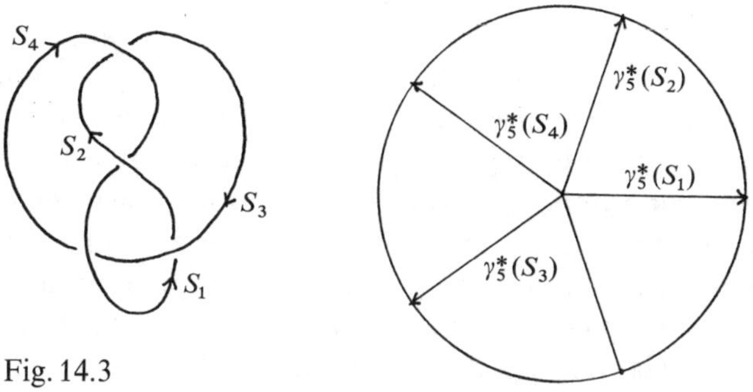

Fig. 14.3

see Figure 14.3. One has $\Delta_1(-1) = 5 = p$. The system (4) of congruences mod p takes the form

$$\left.\begin{array}{rl} -v_1 - v_2 + 2v_3 & \equiv 0 \\ -v_2 - v_3 + 2v_4 & \equiv 0 \\ +2v_1 - v_3 - v_4 & \equiv 0 \\ -v_1 + 2v_2 - v_4 & \equiv 0 \end{array}\right\} \bmod 5$$

Putting $v_1 \equiv 0$, $v_2 \equiv 1$, one obtains $v_3 \equiv 3$, $v_4 \equiv 2 \bmod 5$. The relations of $\mathfrak{G}$ are easily verified in Figure 14.3.

Remark: Since $\Delta_1(-1)$ is always odd, only odd primes p occur.

B A Class of Homomorphisms of $\mathfrak{G}$ into the Group of Motions of the Euclidean Plane

We have interpreted the dihedral representations γ_p^* as homomorphisms of $\mathfrak{G}$ into the group $\mathfrak{B}$ of motions of E^2, and we studied a class of maps δ_α: $\mathfrak{G} \to \mathfrak{C}$ into the 2-dimensional equiform group $\mathfrak{C}$. It seems rather obvious to choose any other suitable conjugacy class in one of these well-known geometric groups as a candidate to map a Wirtinger class K onto. It would be especially interesting to obtain new non-metabelian representations, because metabelian representations necessarily map a longitude, see 3.12, onto units, and are, therefore, not adequate to exploit the peripheral system of the knot. We propose to "lift" the representation γ_p^* to a homomorphism γ_p: $\mathfrak{G} \to \mathfrak{B}$ which maps the Wirtinger class K into a class of glide-reflections. The representation γ_p will not be metabelian and will yield a useful tool in proving non-amphicheirality of knots. As above, *p is a prime*.

Let γ_p^* be a homomorphism of the knot group $\mathfrak{G}$ onto the dihedral group $\mathfrak{Z}_2 \ltimes \mathfrak{Z}_p$. There is a regular covering q: $R_p \to C$ corresponding to the normal subgroup $\ker \gamma_p^*$. One has $2\mathfrak{Z} \ltimes \mathfrak{G}' = \mathfrak{G}_2 \supset \ker \gamma_p^* \supset \mathfrak{G}''$ and $\mathfrak{G}_2/\ker \gamma_p^* \cong \mathfrak{Z}_p$. The space R_p is a p-fold cyclic covering of the 2-fold covering C_2 of C. For a meridian m and longitude ℓ of the knot $\mathfrak{k}$ we have: $m^2 \in \ker \gamma_p^*$, $\ell \in \mathfrak{G}'' \subset \ker \gamma_p^*$. The torus ∂C is covered by p tori T_i, $0 \leqq i \leqq p-1$, in R_p. There are distinguished canonical curves $\hat{m}_i$, $\hat{\ell}_i$ on T_i with $q(\hat{m}_i) = m^2$, $q(\hat{\ell}_i) = \ell$. By a theorem of H. Seifert the set $\{\hat{m}_i, \hat{\ell}_i\}$ of $2p$ curves contains a subset of $p(>2)$ linearly independent representatives of the Betti group of $H_1(R_p)$ [Seifert 1932]. From this it follows that the cyclic subgroup $\mathfrak{Z}_p \lhd \mathfrak{Z}_2 \ltimes \mathfrak{Z}_p$ of covering transformations operates non-trivially on the Betti group of $H_1(R_p)$. Now abelianize $\ker \beta_p^*$ and trivialize the torsion subgroup of $H_1(R_p) = \ker \gamma_p^*/(\ker \gamma_p^*)'$ to obtain a homomorphism of the knot group $\mathfrak{G}$ onto an extension $[\mathfrak{D}_p, \mathbb{Z}^q]$ of the Betti group $\mathbb{Z}^q$ of $H_1(R_p)$, $q \geqq p$, with factor group $\mathfrak{D}_p = \mathfrak{Z}_2 \ltimes \mathfrak{Z}_p$. The operation of $\mathfrak{D}_p$ on $\mathbb{Z}^q$ is the one induced by the covering transformations. We embed $\mathbb{Z}^q$ in a vector space $\mathbb{C}^q$ over the complex numbers and use a result of the theory of representations of finite groups: The dihedral group $\mathfrak{D}_p$ admits only irreducible representations of degree 1 and degree 2 over $\mathbb{C}$.

This follows from Burnside's formula and the fact that the degree must divide the order $2p$ of $\mathfrak{D}_p$. (See [Serre 1967].) Since $\mathfrak{Z}_p \lhd \mathfrak{D}_p$ operates non-trivially on $\mathbb{Z}^q$, the operation of $\mathfrak{D}_p$ on $\mathbb{C}^q$ contains at least one summand of degree 2. Such a representation has the form

$$(5)\qquad \begin{aligned} &\tau \mapsto \begin{pmatrix} 0 & 1 \\ 1 & 0 \end{pmatrix}, \\ &a \mapsto \begin{pmatrix} \zeta & 0 \\ 0 & \zeta^{-1} \end{pmatrix} \end{aligned}$$

with $\mathfrak{Z}_2 = \langle \tau \rangle$, $\mathfrak{Z}_p = \langle a \rangle$ and ζ a primitive p-th root of unity. (The representation is faithful, hence irreducible.)

This representation is equivalent to the following when $\mathbb{C}^2$ is replaced by $\mathbb{R}^4$:

$$\tau \mapsto \begin{pmatrix} 1 & 0 & 0 & 0 \\ 0 & -1 & 0 & 0 \\ 0 & 0 & 1 & 0 \\ 0 & 0 & 0 & -1 \end{pmatrix},$$

$$a \mapsto \begin{pmatrix} \xi & -\eta & 0 & 0 \\ \eta & \xi & 0 & 0 \\ 0 & 0 & \xi & -\eta \\ 0 & 0 & \eta & \xi \end{pmatrix}, \qquad \zeta = \xi + i\eta.$$

It splits into two identical summands. Introduce again a complex structure on each of the invariant subspaces $\mathbb{R}^2$; the operation of $\mathfrak{D}_p$ on each of them may then be described by:

$$(6)\qquad \begin{aligned} \tau(z) &= \bar{z}, \\ a(z) &= \zeta z. \end{aligned}$$

By this construction the knot group $\mathfrak{G}$ is mapped onto an extension of a finitely generated (additive) subgroup $\mathfrak{T} \subset \mathbb{C}$, $\mathfrak{T} \neq 0$, with factor group $\mathfrak{D}_p$ operating on $\mathfrak{T}$ according to (6). First consider the extension $[\mathfrak{Z}_p, \mathfrak{T}]$ and denote its elements by pairs (a^ν, z).

One has

$$(a, 0)\,((a^{p-1}, 0)\,(a, 0)) = (a, 0)\,(1, w) = (a, w), \quad \text{for } w = a^P \in \mathfrak{T},$$

and

$$((a, 0)\,(a^{p-1}, 0))\,(a, 0) = (1, w)\,(a, 0) = (a, \zeta w).$$

It follows that $w = \zeta w, \zeta \neq 1$, hence, $w = 0$, and $[\mathfrak{Z}_p, \mathfrak{T}] = \mathfrak{Z}_p \ltimes \mathfrak{T}$. Similarly one may denote the elements of $[\mathfrak{D}_p, \mathfrak{T}] = [\mathfrak{Z}_2, \mathfrak{Z}_p \ltimes \mathfrak{T}]$ by triples (τ^ν, a^μ, z). Put $(\tau, 1, 0)^2 = (1, 1, v)$, $v \in \mathbb{C}$. Then

$$(\tau, 1, 0)^2 (\tau, 1, 0) = (\tau, 1, 2\bar{v}) = (\tau, 1, 0)(\tau, 1, 0)^2 = (\tau, 1, 2v).$$

This proves $v = \bar{v} \in \mathbb{R}$.

As a consequence $\gamma_p(\mathfrak{G})$ may be embedded in the group $\mathfrak{B}$ of motions of the complex plane $\mathbb{C}$. Put

$$(7) \quad \begin{aligned} &(1, a, b)\colon z \mapsto \zeta z + b, \zeta \text{ a primitive } p\text{-th root of unity,} \\ &(\tau, 1, 0)\colon z \mapsto \bar{z} + v. \end{aligned}$$

There are two distinct cases: $v \neq 0$ and $v = 0$. In the first case a Wirtinger generator is mapped onto a glide reflection whereas in the second case its image is a reflection. We may in the first case choose $v = 1$ by replacing a representation by an equivalent one.

14.10 Proposition. *For any dihedral representation $\gamma_p^*\colon \mathfrak{G} \to \mathfrak{Z}_2 \ltimes \mathfrak{Z}_p \subset \mathfrak{B}$ of a knot group $\mathfrak{G}$ into the group $\mathfrak{B}$ of motions of the plane there is a lifted representation $\gamma_p\colon \mathfrak{G} \to \mathfrak{B}$ such that $\gamma_p^* = \kappa \cdot \gamma_p$, $\kappa\colon \gamma_p(\mathfrak{G}) \to \gamma_p(\mathfrak{G})/\mathfrak{T}$, where $\mathfrak{T} \neq 0$ is the subgroup of translations in $\gamma_p(\mathfrak{G}) \subset \mathfrak{B}$ (p is a prime).*

An element of the Wirtinger class K is either mapped onto a glide reflection ($v = 1$) or a reflection ($v = 0$).

If γ_p^* is unique up to equivalence, that is, if p divides the first but not the second torsion coefficient of $H_1(\hat{C}_2)$, see 14.8, the first case takes place and γ_p is determined up to equivalence.

Proof. The existence of a lifted mapping γ_p has already been proved. We proof uniqueness by describing γ_p with the help of a system of linear equations which at the same time serves to carry out an effective calculation of the representation. Denote by $\mathbb{Q}(\zeta)$ the cyclotomic field over the rationals and by ζ_j a p-th root of unity. Put

$$(8) \qquad \gamma_p^*(S_j)\colon z \mapsto \zeta_j^2 \bar{z}$$

$$(9) \qquad \gamma_p(S_j)\colon z \mapsto \zeta_j^2 \bar{z} + b_j$$

for Wirtinger generators S_j of $\mathfrak{G} = \langle S_1, \dots S_n | R_1, \dots, R_n \rangle$. Equation (9) describes a reflection followed by the translation through

$$(10) \qquad 2\zeta_j v = \zeta_j^2 \bar{b}'_j + b'_j$$

in the direction of the fixed line. The two cases are characterized by $v = 1$ resp. $v = 0$. We prove that $v = 0$ cannot occur if the dihedral representation γ_p^* is unique. A Wirtinger relator

$$(11) \qquad R_j = S_j S_i^{-\eta_j} S_k^{-1} S_i^{\eta_j}, \quad \eta_j = \pm 1,$$

yields

(12) $\zeta_i^2 = \zeta_j \zeta_k$

under (8), and

(13) $-\bar{\zeta}_k b'_k - \bar{\zeta}_j b'_j + (\bar{\zeta}_k \zeta_i + \bar{\zeta}_j \zeta_i) \bar{\zeta}_i b'_i = 0$

under (9), if $v = 0$. Here we introduce the convention that on the right hand side of $\gamma_p(W_1 W_2) = \gamma_p(W_1)\gamma_p(W_2)$, $W_1, W_2 \in \mathfrak{G}$, the combination is carried out from right to left, as is usual in a group of motions, whereas in the fundamental group the combination $W_1 W_2$ is understood from left to right.

The linear equations (13) form a system over $\mathbb{Q}(\zeta)$ with real variables $x_j = \bar{\zeta}_j b'_j$ (use (10)). The rank of (13) is at least $n-2$, because the homomorphism ψ: $\mathbb{Q}(\zeta) \to \mathbb{Z}_p$, defined by $\psi(\zeta) = 1$, transforms (13) into the system of congruences mod p:

(14) $-v_k - v_j + 2v_i \equiv 0 \bmod p$

which has rank $= n-2$ as γ_p^* is unique. (Compare 14.7 and (4).) If there is a proper lift γ_p – that is $\mathfrak{T} \neq 0$ – the fixed lines g_i of $\gamma_p(S_i)$ cannot pass through one point or be parallel. But then there is a 3-dimensional manifold of such representations, obtained by conjugation with $\mathfrak{C}^+$, the orientation preserving equiform group. This contradicts rank $\geqq n-2$.

Remark: The non-existence of γ_p under the assumption we made is a property of the Euclidean plane. In a hyperbolic plane where there are no similarities, and lifts γ_p may exist.

We may assume that there is a lift γ_p of γ_p^* which maps Wirtinger generators on glide reflections with $v = 1$. Substitute

(15) $b'_j = \zeta_j b_j + \zeta_j$.

Instead of (13) we get the following system of inhomogeneous linear equations

(16) $-b_k - b_j + (\bar{\zeta}_j \zeta_i + \bar{\zeta}_i \zeta_j) b_j = \eta_j (\bar{\zeta}_j \zeta_i - \bar{\zeta}_i \zeta_j)$.

(Observe that the equations (12) are valid.) We may again employ the homomorphism ψ: $\mathbb{Q}(\zeta) \to \mathbb{Z}_p$ to see that the rank of the homogeneous part of (16) is $n-2$. Since conjugation by translations gives a 2-dimensional manifold of solutions, the rank of (16) is exactly equal to $n-2$. □

For a given primitive p-th root of unity ζ and a suitable enumeration of the Wirtinger generators we may assume

$$\gamma_p(S_1)\colon z \mapsto \bar{z} + 1,$$
$$\gamma_p(S_2)\colon z \mapsto \zeta^2 \bar{z} + \zeta.$$

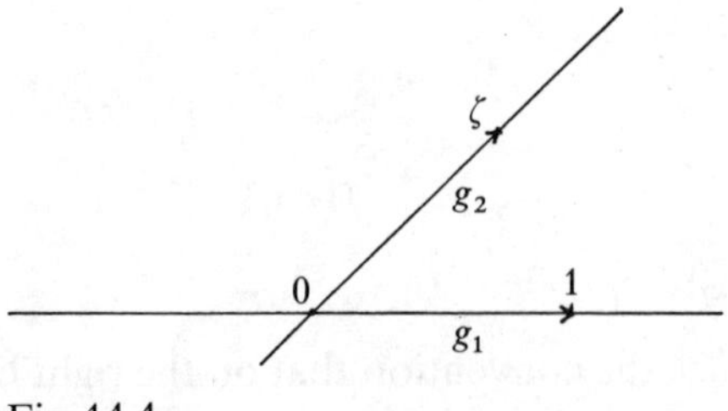

Fig. 14.4

This corresponds to putting $b_1 = b_2 = 0$. The fixed lines g_1 and g_2 of $\gamma_p(S_1)$ and $\gamma_p(S_2)$ meet in the origin and pass through 1 and ζ (Fig. 14.4). A representation normalized in this way is completely determined up to the choice of ζ.

The main application of Proposition 14.10 is the exploitation of the peripheral system $(\mathfrak{G}, m, \ell)$ by a normalized representation γ_p. Let m be represented by S_1, then γ_p *maps the longitude* ℓ *onto a translation by* $\lambda(\zeta)$:

$$\gamma_p(\ell)\colon z \mapsto z + \lambda(\zeta),$$

since $\ell \in \mathfrak{G}'' \subset \ker \gamma_p^*$. The solutions b_j of (16) are elements of $\mathbb{Q}(\zeta)$. From $m \cdot \ell = \ell \cdot m$ it follows that $\lambda(\zeta) \in \mathbb{Q}(\zeta) \cap \mathbb{R}$.

14.11 Definition and Proposition. *The set* $[\lambda(\zeta)] = \{\lambda(\tau(\zeta)) \mid \tau \in \mathfrak{G}(\mathbb{Q}(\zeta) \mid \mathbb{Q})\}$ *where* $\mathfrak{G}(\mathbb{Q}(\zeta) \mid \mathbb{Q})$ *is the Galois group of the extension* $\mathbb{Q}(\zeta) \supset \mathbb{Q}$ *is called the* longitudinal invariant with respect to γ_p. *It is an invariant of the knot.* □

14.12 Example. We want to lift the homomorphism γ_5^* of the group of the four knot which we computed in 14.9. We had obtained $\zeta_1 = 1$, $\zeta_2 = \zeta$, $\zeta_3 = \zeta^3$, $\zeta_4 = \zeta^2$ for $\gamma_5^*(S_j) = \zeta_j$, and we may put $\zeta = e^{\frac{2\pi i}{5}}$. The equations (16) are then:

$$\begin{aligned}
-b_2 - b_1 + (\zeta^3 + \zeta^2) b_3 &= \zeta^3 - \zeta^2\\
-b_3 - b_2 + (\zeta + \zeta^4) b_4 &= -(\zeta - \zeta^4)\\
-b_4 - b_3 + (\zeta^2 + \zeta^3) b_1 &= (\zeta^2 - \zeta^3)\\
-b_1 - b_4 + (\zeta^4 + \zeta) b_2 &= -(\zeta^4 - \zeta).
\end{aligned}$$

Putting $b_1 = b_2 = 0$ yields

$$b_3 = 1 + 2\zeta + 2\zeta^3,\ b_4 = \zeta^4 - \zeta$$

and, using (15),

$$b_1' = 1,\ b_2' = \zeta,\ b_3' = -2(1 + \zeta^2),\ b_4' = \zeta + \zeta^2 - \zeta^3;$$

$$\begin{aligned}
\gamma_5(S_1)&\colon z \mapsto \bar{z} + 1\\
\gamma_5(S_2)&\colon z \mapsto \zeta^2 \bar{z} + \zeta\\
\gamma_5(S_3)&\colon z \mapsto \zeta \bar{z} - 2 - 2\zeta^2\\
\gamma_5(S_4)&\colon z \mapsto \zeta^4 \bar{z} + \zeta + \zeta^2 - \zeta^3.
\end{aligned}$$

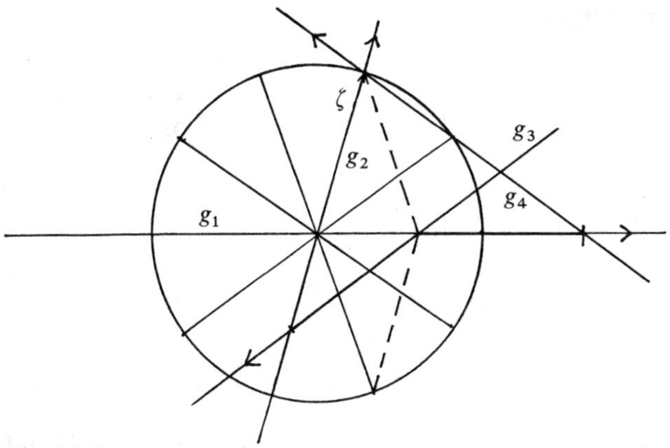

Fig. 14.5

Figure 14.5 shows the configuration of the fixed lines g_j of the glide reflections $\gamma_5(S_j)$. One may verify the Wirtinger relations by wellknown geometric properties of the regular pentagon. The longitude ℓ of $(\mathfrak{G}, m, \ell)$ with $m = S_1$ may be read off the projection drawn in Figure 14.3:

$$\ell = S_3^{-1} S_4 S_1^{-1} S_2 .$$

One obtains

$$\gamma_5(\ell)\colon z \mapsto z + \lambda(\zeta), \quad \lambda(\zeta) = 2(\zeta + \zeta^{-1} - (\zeta^2 + \zeta^{-2})).$$

The class $[\lambda(\zeta)]$ contains only two different elements, $\lambda(\zeta)$ and $-\lambda(\zeta)$ which reflects the amphicheirality of the four-knot.

14.13 Proposition. *The invariant class* $[\lambda(\zeta)]$ *of an amphicheiral knot always contains* $-\lambda(\zeta)$ *if it contains* $\lambda(\zeta)$.

Proof. A conjugation by a rotation through π maps $(\gamma_p(m), \gamma_p(\ell))$ onto $(-\gamma_p(m), -\gamma_p(\ell))$. Hence, 3.19 implies that the group of an amphicheiral knot admits normalized representations γ_p and γ'_p with $\gamma_p(\ell^{-1}) = -\gamma_p(\ell) = \gamma'_p(\ell)$. □

Remark: The argument shows at the same time that the invariant $[\lambda(\zeta)]$ is no good at detecting that a knot is non-invertible. Similarly, γ_p is not strong enough to prove that a knot has Property P: a relation $\gamma_p(\ell^a) = \gamma_p(m)$, $a \neq 0$, would abelianize $\gamma_p(\mathfrak{G})$, and, hence, trivialize it.

The invariant has been computed and a table is contained in Appendix C, Table III.

Representations of the type γ_p have been defined for links [Hafer 1974], [Henninger 1978]. In [Hartley-Murasugi 1977] linking numbers in covering spaces were investigated in a more general setting which yielded the invariant $[\lambda(\zeta)]$ as a special case.

C Linkage in Coverings

The covering $q: R_p \to C$ of the complement C of a knot $\mathfrak{k}$ defined by $\ker \gamma_p^* \cong \pi_1 R_p$ is an invariant of $\mathfrak{k}$ as long as there is only one class of equivalent dihedral representations

$$\gamma_p^*: \pi_1(C) = \mathfrak{G} \to \mathfrak{D}_p = \mathfrak{Z}_2 \ltimes \mathfrak{Z}_p.$$

The same holds for the branched covering $\hat{q}: \hat{R}_p \to S^3$, obtained from R_p, with branching set $\mathfrak{k}$. *In the following p is a prime.*

The *linking numbers* $lk(\hat{\mathfrak{k}}_i, \hat{\mathfrak{k}}_j)$ of the link $\hat{\mathfrak{k}} = \bigcup_{i=0}^{p-1} \hat{\mathfrak{k}}_i = \hat{q}^{-1}(\mathfrak{k})$ have been used since the beginning of knot theory to distinguish knots which could not be distinguished by their Alexander polynomials. $\ker \gamma_p^*$ is of the form $\langle t^2 \rangle \ltimes \mathfrak{K}$, t a meridian, and is contained in the subgroup $\langle t \rangle \ltimes \mathfrak{K} = \mathfrak{U} \subset \mathfrak{G}$ with $[\mathfrak{G}: \mathfrak{U}] = p$. The subgroup $\mathfrak{U}$ defines an irregular covering I_p, $\pi_1(I_p) \cong \mathfrak{U}$, and an associated branched covering $\hat{I}_p$ which was, in fact, used in [Reidemeister 1929, 1932] to study linking numbers. The regular covering $\hat{R}_p$ is a two-fold branched covering of $\hat{I}_p$, and its linking numbers $lk(\hat{\mathfrak{k}}_i, \hat{\mathfrak{k}}_j)$ determine those in $\hat{I}_p$ [Hartley 1979]. We shall, therefore, confine ourselves mainly to $\hat{R}_p$.

Linking numbers exist for pairs of disjoint closed curves in $\hat{R}_p$ which represent elements of finite order in $H_1(\hat{R}_p)$ [Seifert-Threlfall 1934], [Stöcker-Zieschang 1985, 16.6].

In the preceding section we made use of a theorem in [Seifert 1932] which guaranteed that there are at least p linearly independent free elements of $H_1(R_p)$ represented in the set $\{\hat{m}_0, \ldots, \hat{m}_{p-1}, \hat{\ell}_0, \ldots, \hat{\ell}_{p-1}\}$. To obtain more precise information, one has to employ a certain amount of algebraic topology [Hartley-Murasugi 1977]. Consider a section of the exact homology sequence $\to H_2(\hat{R}_p, V; \mathbb{Q}) \xrightarrow{\partial_*} H_1(V; \mathbb{Q}) \xrightarrow{i_*} H_1(\hat{R}_p; \mathbb{Q}) \to$ of the pair $(\hat{R}_p, V)$, where V is the union $V = \bigcup_{i=0}^{p-1} V_i$, $\partial V_i = T_i$, of the tubular neighbourhoods V_i of $\hat{\mathfrak{k}}_i$ in $\hat{R}_p$. As indicated, we use rational coefficients. The Lefschetz Duality Theorem and excision yield isomorphisms

$$H^1(R_p; \mathbb{Q}) \cong H_2(R_p, \partial R_p; \mathbb{Q}) \cong H_2(\hat{R}_p, V; \mathbb{Q}).$$

One has [Stöcker-Zieschang 1985]

$$\Delta^*: H^1(R_p; \mathbb{Q}) \to H_2(\hat{R}_p, V; \mathbb{Q}),$$
$$\langle z^1, z_1 \rangle = int(z_2, z_1), \quad z_2 = \Delta^*(z^1), z^1 \in H^1(R_p; \mathbb{Q})$$

where $<, >$ denotes the Kronecker product.

We claim that the surjective homomorphism

$$\partial_* \Delta^*: H^1(R_p; \mathbb{Q}) \to \ker i_*$$

is described by

$$(1) \qquad z^1 \mapsto \sum_{i=0}^{p-1} \langle z^1, \hat{m}_i \rangle \hat{\ell}_i .$$

To prove (1) put

$$\partial_* \Delta^* z^1 = \partial_* z_2 = \sum_{j=0}^{p-1} a_j \hat{\ell}_j, \ a_j \in \mathbb{Q} .$$

Let δ_i be a disk in T_i bounded by $\hat{m}_i = \partial \delta_i$. Then

$$\langle z^1, \hat{m}_i \rangle = int\,(z_2, \partial\delta_i) = int\,(\partial_* z_2, \delta_i) = int\,(\sum_{j=0}^{p-1} a_j \hat{\ell}_j, \delta_i) = a_i .$$

Since $j_*\colon H_1(R_p; \mathbb{Q}) \to H_1(\hat{R}_p; \mathbb{Q})$, induced by the inclusion j, is surjective, $j^*\colon H^1(\hat{R}_p; \mathbb{Q}) \to H^1(R_p; \mathbb{Q})$ is injective. $j^*(H^1(\hat{R}_p))$ consists exactly of the homomorphisms $\varphi\colon H_1(R_p) \to \mathbb{Q}$ which factor through $H_1(\hat{R}_p; \mathbb{Q})$. But these constitute $\ker \partial_* \Delta^*$ by (1). Thus, one has

$$\dim \ker \partial_* \Delta^* = \dim H^1(\hat{R}_p) = \dim H_1(\hat{R}_p) \quad \text{and}$$
$$\dim \partial_* \Delta^*(H_1(R_p; \mathbb{Q})) = \dim \ker i_* .$$

14.14 Proposition (Hartley-Murasugi). $\dim H_1(R_p; \mathbb{Q}) = \dim H_1(\hat{R}_p; \mathbb{Q}) + \dim \ker i_*$ *where* $i\colon V \to \hat{R}_p$ *is the inclusion.* □

It is now easy to prove that only two alternatives occur:

14.15 Proposition. *Either (case 1) all longitudes* $\hat{\ell}_i$, $0 \leqq i \leqq p-1$ *represent in* $H_1(\hat{R}_p; \mathbb{Z})$ *elements of finite order (linking numbers are defined) and the meridians* $\hat{m}_i$, $0 \leqq i \leqq p-1$, *generate a free abelian group of rank p in* $H_1(R_p; \mathbb{Z})$, *or (case 2) the longitudes* ℓ_i *generate a free abelian group of rank* $p-1$ *presented by* $\langle \hat{\ell}_0, \ldots, \hat{\ell}_{p-1} | \hat{\ell}_0 + \hat{\ell}_1 + \ldots + \hat{\ell}_{p-1} \rangle$, *and the meridians* $\hat{m}_i$ *generate a free group of rank one in* $H_1(R_p; \mathbb{Z})$; *more precisely,* $\hat{m}_i \sim \hat{m}_j$ *in* $H_1(R_p; \mathbb{Q})$ *for any two meridians.*

Proof. A Seifert surface S of $\mathfrak{k} = \partial S$ lifts to a surface $\hat{S}$ with $\partial \hat{S} = \sum_{i=0}^{p=1} \hat{\ell}_i \sim 0$ in R_p or $\hat{R}_p$: the construction of C_2 (see 4.4) shows that S can be lifted to S_2 in C_2 resp. $\hat{C}_2$. The inclusion $i\colon S_2 \to \hat{C}_2$ induces an epimorphism $i_*\colon H_1(S_2) \to H_1(\hat{C}_2)$. This follows from $(a^- + a^+) = Fs$ (see 8.6) and $a^+ = ta^- = -a^-$ in the case of the twofold covering where $t = -1$ (8.20). Thus S_2 is covered in R_p by a connected surface $\hat{S}$ bounded by the longitudes $\hat{\ell}_i$. If the longitudes $\hat{\ell}_i$ satisfy in $H_1(\hat{R}_p)$ only relations $c \cdot \Sigma \hat{\ell}_i \sim 0$, $c \in \mathbb{Z}$, which are consequences of $\Sigma \hat{\ell}_i \sim 0$, we have $\dim(\ker i_*) = 1$ in Proposition 14.14. It follows that the meridians $\hat{m}_i$ generate a free group of rank one in $H_1(R_p)$. There is a covering transformation of $R_p \to C_2$

which maps $\hat{m}_i$ onto $\hat{m}_j \sim r\hat{m}_i$, $i \neq j$, $r \in \mathbb{Q}$. From this one gets $r^p = 1$, $r = 1$. This disposes of case 2. If the longitudes $\hat{\ell}_i$ are subject to a relation that is not a consequence of $\Sigma\hat{\ell}_i \sim 0$, then one may assume $\Sigma a_i \hat{\ell}_i \sim 0$, $\Sigma a_i \neq 0$. (If necessary, replace a_i by $a_i + 1$). Applying the cyclic group $\mathfrak{Z}_p$ of covering transformation to this relation yields a set of p relations forming a cyclic relation matrix. Such a cyclic determinant is always different from zero [Neiss 1962, § 19.6.]. Hence, the longitudes generate a finite group. In fact, since the $\hat{\ell}_i$ are permuted by the covering transformations their orders coincide; we denote it by $|\ell|$ = order of $\hat{\ell}_i$ in $H_1(\hat{R}_p)$. It follows that dim ker $i_* = p$, and by 14.14 that the meridians $\hat{m}_i$ generate a free group of rank p. □

14.16 Proposition. *If there is exactly one class of equivalent dihedral homomorphisms $\gamma_p^*: \mathfrak{G} \to \mathfrak{D}_p$, ($p$ divides the first torsion coefficient of $H_1(\hat{C}_2)$ but not the second), then the dihedral linking numbers $v_{ij} = lk(\hat{\mathfrak{k}}_i, \hat{\mathfrak{k}}_j)$ are defined (case 1). The invariant $[\lambda(\zeta)]$ (see 14.11) associated to the lift γ_p of γ_p^* (14.10) then takes the form:*

$$(2) \qquad \lambda_j(\zeta) = 2\sum_{i=0}^{p-1} v_{ij}\zeta^i \quad \textit{with } v_{ii} = -\sum_{j \neq i} v_{ij}.$$

(Here we have put $[\lambda(\zeta)] = \{\lambda_j/\zeta), 1 \leqq j < p\}$. Case 1 and case 2 refer to 14.15.)

Proof. The occurence of case 2 implies $\gamma_p(\hat{m}_i) = \gamma_p(\hat{m}_j)$ for all meridians $\hat{m}_i$, $\hat{m}_j$. But in the case of a representation γ_p, mapping Wirtinger generators on glide reflections, $\gamma_p(\hat{m}_i)$ and $\gamma_p(\hat{m}_j)$ will be translations in different directions for some i, j. Thus the Wirtinger class is mapped onto reflections, that is, $\gamma_p(\hat{m}_i) = 0$. This contradicts 14.10.

In case 1 the longitudes $\hat{\ell}_j$ are of finite order in $H_1(\hat{R}_p; \mathbb{Z})$. Since the covering transformations permute the $\hat{\ell}_j$, they all have the same order $|\hat{\ell}_j| = |\ell|$. Consider a section of the Mayer-Vietoris sequence:

$$\to H_1(\partial V) \xrightarrow{\psi_*} H_1(R_p) \oplus H_1(V) \xrightarrow{\varphi_*} H_1(\hat{R}_p) \to .$$

Since $\varphi_*(|\ell|\hat{\ell}_j, 0) = 0$, one has, for suitable b_k, $c_k \in \mathbb{Z}$,

$$(|\ell|\hat{\ell}_j, 0) = \psi_*\Big(\sum_{k=0}^{p-1} b_k \hat{m}_k + \sum_{k=0}^{p-1} c_k \hat{\ell}_k\Big) = (\Sigma b_k \hat{m}_k + \Sigma c_k \hat{\ell}_k, -\Sigma c_k \hat{\ell}_k).$$

This gives

$$|\ell|\hat{\ell}_j = \sum_{k=0}^{p-1} b_k \hat{m}_k, \quad \text{and} \quad |\ell| \cdot lk(\hat{\ell}_i, \hat{\ell}_j) = lk(\hat{\ell}_i, \Sigma b_k \hat{m}_k) = b_i.$$

Since $lk(\hat{\ell}_i, \hat{\ell}_j) = lk(\hat{\mathfrak{k}}_i, \hat{\mathfrak{k}}_j)$, one has

$$(3) \qquad \hat{\ell}_j = \Sigma v_{ij} \hat{m}_i.$$

The relation $\sum_{j=0}^{p-1} \hat{\ell}_j \sim 0$ yields $0 = lk(\hat{\ell}_i, \Sigma\hat{\ell}_j) = \sum_j v_{ij}$. Formula (2) of 14.16 follows from $\gamma_p(\hat{m}_j)$: $z \mapsto z + 2\zeta^j$ for a suitable indexing after the choice of a primitive p-th root of unity ζ. □

Remark: Evidently any term $\sum_{i=0}^{p-1} a_i \zeta^i$, $a_i \in \mathbb{Q}$, can be uniquely normalized such that $\Sigma a_i = 0$ holds. In Table III the invariant $[\lambda(\zeta)]$ is listed, but a different normalization was chosen: $a_0 = 0$. One obtains from a sequence $\{a_1, \ldots, a_{p-1}\}$ in this table a set of linking numbers v_{0j}, $0 < j \leqq p-1$, by the formula

(4) $$2v_{0j} = a_j - \frac{1}{p} \sum_{k=1}^{p-1} a_k .$$

14.17 Linking numbers associated with the dihedral representations $\gamma_\alpha^*\colon \mathfrak{G} \to \mathfrak{Z}_2 \ltimes \mathfrak{Z}_\alpha$ for two bridge knots $\mathfrak{b}(\alpha, \beta)$ have been computed explicitly. In this case a unique lift γ_α always exists even if α is not a prime. The linking matrix is

(5) $$\begin{pmatrix} -\sum_{i=1}^{\alpha-1} \varepsilon_j & \varepsilon_1 & \cdots & \varepsilon_{\alpha-1} \\ \varepsilon_{\alpha-1} & -\sum \varepsilon_j & \cdots & \varepsilon_{\alpha-2} \\ \vdots & \vdots & & \vdots \\ \varepsilon_1 & \varepsilon_2 & \cdots & -\sum \varepsilon_j \end{pmatrix}$$

with $\varepsilon_k = (-1)^{\left[\frac{k\beta}{\alpha}\right]}$, $[x]$ = integral part of x, [Burde 1975].

The property $|\varepsilon_k| = 1$ affords a good test for two-bridged knots. Most of the knots with more than 2 bridges (see Table I) can be detected by this method, (compare [Perko 1976]).

A further property of dihedral linking numbers follows from the fact that $\lambda(\zeta)$ is a real number, $\lambda(\zeta) = \overline{\lambda(\zeta)}$. This gives.

(6) $$v_{i,i-j} = v_{ij},\ i \neq j,$$

where $i - j$ is to be taken mod p. Furthermore,

(7) $$v_{ij} = v_{ji} = v_{i+k,\,j+k} .$$

The first equation expresses a general symmetry of linking numbers, and the second one the cyclic p-symmetry of $\hat{R}_p$.

As mentioned at the beginning of this section, $\hat{R}_p$ is a two-fold branched covering of the irregular covering space $\hat{I}_p$ with one component $\hat{\mathfrak{k}}_j$ of $\hat{\mathfrak{k}} = q^{-1}(\mathfrak{k})$ as branching set in $\hat{R}_p$. (There are, indeed, p equivalent covering spaces $\hat{I}_p$ corresponding to p conjugate subgroups $\mathfrak{U}_j = \langle t_j \rangle \ltimes \mathfrak{K}$, depending on the choice of the meridian t_j resp. the component $\hat{\mathfrak{k}}_j$.) We choose $j = 0$. Let $\bar{q}\colon \hat{R}_p \to \hat{I}_p$ be the covering map. The link $\mathfrak{k}' = \bar{q}(\hat{\mathfrak{k}})$ consists of $\frac{p+1}{2}$ components $\mathfrak{k}'_0 = \bar{q}(\hat{\mathfrak{k}}_0)$, $\mathfrak{k}'_j = \bar{q}(\hat{\mathfrak{k}}_j) = \bar{q}(\hat{\mathfrak{k}}_{-j})$, $0 < j \leqq \frac{p-1}{2}$. (Indices are read mod p.) Going back to the geometric definition of linking numbers by intersection numbers one gets for $\mu_{ij} = lk(\mathfrak{k}'_k, \mathfrak{k}'_j)$,

$$(8) \qquad \mu_{0j} = 2\nu_{0j}, \quad \mu_{ij} = \nu_{ij} + \nu_{i,-j}, \; i \neq j.$$

This yields by (6) and (7) Perko's identities [Perko 1976]:

$$(9) \qquad 2\mu_{ij} = \mu_{0,i-j} + \mu_{0,i+j}, \quad \text{or} \quad \mu_{ij} = \nu_{0,i-j} + \nu_{0,i+j}.$$

As $\nu_{ij} = \pm 1$ for two bridge knots, $\mu_{ij} = \pm 2$ or 0 for these.

It follows from (7), (8) and 14.16 that the linking numbers ν_{ij}, the linking numbers μ_{ij}, and the invariant $[\lambda(\zeta)]$ determine each other. All information is already contained in the ordered set $\left\{\nu_{0j} \mid 1 \leqq j \leqq \frac{p-1}{2}\right\}$. Equation (8) shows that Theorem 6.3 of [Hartley-Murasugi 1977] is a consequence of 14.16.

The theory developed in this section has been generalized in [Hartley 1983]. Many results carry over to metacyclic homomorphisms $\beta^*_{r,p}\colon \mathfrak{G} \to \mathfrak{Z}_r \ltimes \mathfrak{Z}_p$, see 14.7 and [Burde 1970]. The homomorphism $\beta^*_{r,p}$ can be lifted and the invariant $[\lambda(\zeta)]$ can be generalized to the metacyclic case. This invariant has a new quality, in that it can identify non-invertible knots which $[\lambda(\zeta)]$ cannot, as we pointed out at the end of Section B, [Hartley 1983′].

14.18 Examples. (a) The four-knot is a two-bridge knot, $4_1 = \mathfrak{b}(5, 3)$. Thus

$$\nu_{0j} = (-1)^{\left[\frac{3j}{5}\right]}, \; (\nu_{ij}) = \begin{pmatrix} 0 & 1 & -1 & -1 & 1 \\ 1 & 0 & 1 & -1 & -1 \\ -1 & 1 & 0 & 1 & -1 \\ -1 & -1 & 1 & 0 & 1 \\ 1 & -1 & -1 & 1 & 0 \end{pmatrix},$$

and

$$(\mu_{ij}) = \begin{pmatrix} * & 2 & -2 \\ 2 & * & 0 \\ -2 & 0 & * \end{pmatrix}.$$

The link $\mathfrak{k}' = \bar{q}^{-1}(4_1)$ in $\hat{I}_5 \cong S^3$ has been determined (Fig. 14.6) in [Burde 1971]. (For the definition of $\hat{I}_p$ see the beginning of Section C.)

(b) As a second example consider the knot $7_4 = \mathfrak{b}(15, 11)$ and the irregular covering $\hat{I}_{15}$. Its linking matrix (μ_{ij}) is

$$(\mu_{ij}) = \begin{pmatrix} * & 2 & -2 & 2 & 2 & -2 & 2 & -2 \\ 2 & * & 2 & 0 & 0 & 2 & -2 & 0 \\ -2 & 2 & * & 0 & 0 & 0 & 0 & 0 \\ 2 & 0 & 0 & * & 0 & -2 & 2 & 0 \\ 2 & 0 & 0 & 0 & * & 2 & -2 & 2 \\ -2 & 2 & 0 & -2 & 2 & * & 2 & 0 \\ 2 & -2 & 0 & 2 & -2 & 2 & * & 0 \\ -2 & 0 & 0 & 0 & 2 & 0 & 0 & * \end{pmatrix}$$

by (9) and $\nu_{0j} = (-1)^{\left[\frac{11j}{15}\right]}$, $0 < j < 15$.

The numbers $\frac{1}{2} \sum_{j \neq i} |\mu_{ij}| = v_i$, $0 \leqq i \leqq 7$, are 7, 4, 2, 3, 4, 5, 5, 2. (Compare [Reidemeister 1932, p. 69].)

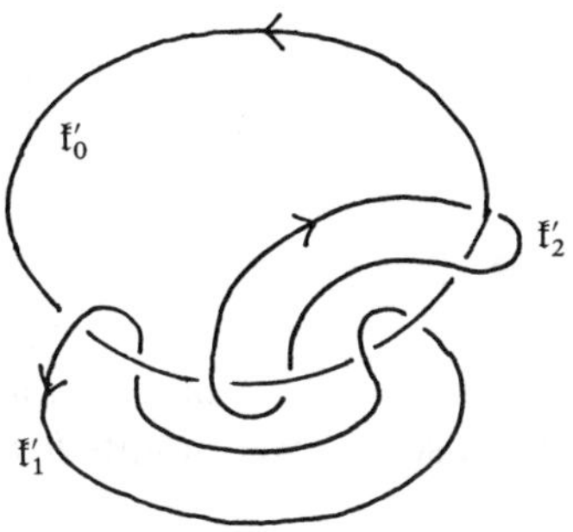

Fig. 14.6

In general an effective computation of linking numbers can be carried out in various ways. One may solve equations (14) and (16) in the proof of 14.10 and thereby determine γ_p^*, γ_p and $[\lambda(\zeta)]$. A more direct way is described in [Hartley-Murasugi 1977] using the Reidemeister-Schreier algorithm. See also [Perko 1974].

D Periodic Knots

Some knots show geometric symmetries – for instance torus knots. The term "geometric" implies "metric", a category into which topologists usually do not enter. Nevertheless, symmetries have been defined and considered in various ways [Fox 1962‴]. We shall, however, occupy ourselves with only one of the different versions of symmetry, the one most frequently investigated. It serves in this chapter as an application of the metabelian representation δ_α of the knot group introduced in 14.5 – in this section $\mathfrak{k}$ will always have one component.

A knot will be said to have period $q > 1$, if it can be represented by a curve in euclidean 3-space E^3 which is mapped onto itself by a rotation r of E^3 of order q. The axis h must not meet the knot. The positive solution of the Smith conjecture (see B8) allows a topological definition of periodicity.

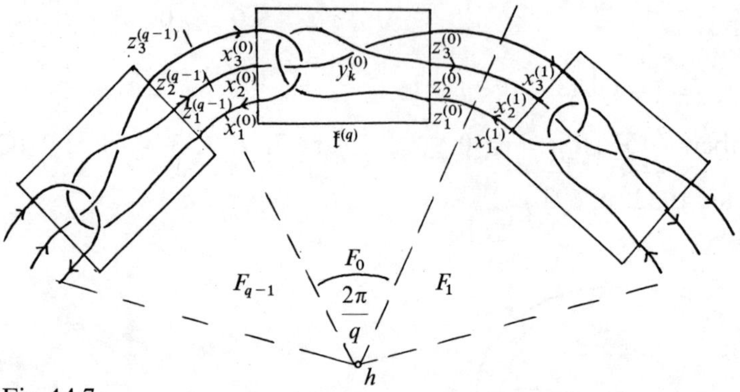

Fig. 14.7

14.19 Definition. A *knot* $\mathfrak{k} \subset S^3$ *has period* $q > 1$, if there is an orientation preserving homeomorphism $S^3 \to S^3$ of order q with a set of fixed points $h \cong S^1$ disjoint from $\mathfrak{k}$ and mapping $\mathfrak{k}$ into itself.

Remark: The orientation of $\mathfrak{k}$ is not essential in this definition. A period of an unoriented knot automatically respects an orientation of the knot (E 14.7).

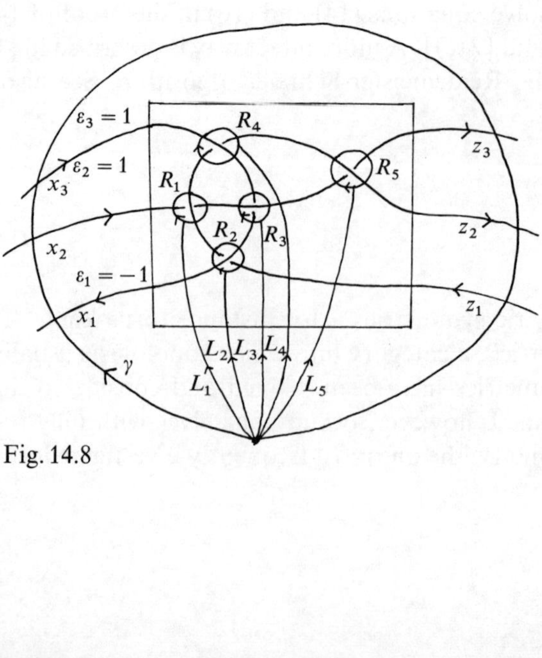

Fig. 14.8

Suppose a knot $\mathfrak{k}$ has period q. We assume that a regular projection of $\mathfrak{k}$ onto a plane perpendicular to the axis of the rotation has period q with respect to a rotation of the plane (Fig. 14.7). Denote by $E_q^3 = E^3/\mathfrak{Z}_q$ the Euclidean 3-space which is the quotient space of E^3 under the action of $\mathfrak{Z}_q = \langle r \rangle$. There is a cyclic branched covering $f^{(q)}\colon E^3 \to E_q^3$ with branching set h in E^3 and $f^{(q)}(\mathfrak{k}) = \mathfrak{k}^{(q)}$ a knot in E_q^3. We call $\mathfrak{k}^{(q)}$ the *factor knot* of $\mathfrak{k}$. It is obtained from $\mathfrak{k}$ in Figure 14.8 by identifying x_i and z_i.

One has $\lambda = lk(\mathfrak{k}, h) = lk(\mathfrak{k}^{(q)}, h^{(q)}) \neq 0$, $h^{(q)} = f^{(q)}(h)$. The equality of the linking numbers follows by looking at the intersections of $\mathfrak{k}$ resp. $\mathfrak{k}^{(q)}$ with half-planes in E^3 resp. E_q^3 spanning h resp. $h^{(q)}$. If $\lambda = lk(\mathfrak{k}^{(q)}, h^{(q)}) = 0$, then $\mathfrak{k}^{(q)} \simeq 1$ in $\pi_1(E_q^3 - h^{(q)})$, and $\mathfrak{k} \subset E^3$ would consist of q components. By choosing a suitable direction of h we may assume $\lambda > 0$. Moreover, $gcd(\lambda, q) = 1$, (E 14.8).

The symmetric projection (Fig. 14.7) yields a symmetric Wirtinger presentation of the knot group of $\mathfrak{k}$ (see 3.4):

$$(1)\qquad \mathfrak{G} = \langle x_i^{(0)}, y_k^{(0)}, z_i^{(0)}, x_i^{(1)}, y_k^{(1)}, z_i^{(1)}, \dots \mid R_j^{(0)}, R_j^{(1)}, \dots, x_i^{(l)} = z_i^{(l-1)}, \dots \rangle,$$
$$1 \leqq i \leqq n, \quad 1 \leqq k \leqq m, \quad 1 \leqq j \leqq m+n.$$

The arcs entering a fundamental domain F_0 of $\mathfrak{Z}_q$, a $2\pi/q$-sector, from the left side, correspond to generators $x_i^{(0)}$ and its images under the rotation r to generators $z_i^{(0)} = r_\#(x_i^{(0)})$. The remaining arcs in F_0 give rise to generators $y_k^{(0)}$. Double points in F_0 define relators R_j. The generators $x_i^{(l)}, y_k^{(l)}, z_i^{(l)}$, $0 \leqq l \leqq q-1$, correspond to the images of the arcs of $x_i^{(0)}, y_k^{(0)}, z_i^{(0)}$ under the rotation through $2\pi\, l/q$, and $R_j^{(l)} = R_j^{(0)}(x_i^{(l)}, y_k^{(l)}, z_i^{(l)})$.

The Jacobian of the Wirtinger presentation

$$\left(\frac{\partial R_j^{(l)}}{\partial(x_i^{(l)}, y_k^{(l)}, z_i^{(l)})}\right)^{\varphi\psi} = A(t),\ \varphi(x_i^{(l)}) = \varphi(y_k^{(l)}) = \varphi(z_i^{(l)}) = t,$$

see 9.9, is of the following form:

$$\left(\begin{array}{c|c|c|c}
-E_n & E_n & & \\
\hline
\multicolumn{2}{c|}{\bar{A}(t)} & & \\
\hline
 & E_n \quad -E_n & & \\
\hline
 & \bar{A}(t) & & \\
\hline
 & & \ddots & \\
\hline
E_n & & & -E_n \\
\hline
 & & & \bar{A}(t)
\end{array}\right) = A(t).$$

Here E_n is an $n \times n$ identity matrix, and $\bar{A}(t)$ is a $(n+m) \times (2n+m)$ matrix over

$\mathbb{Z}(t)$. We rearrange rows and columns of $A(t)$ in such a way that the columns correspond to generators ordered in this way: $x_1^{(0)}, x_1^{(1)}, \ldots, x_1^{(q-1)}, x_2^{(0)}, x_2^{(1)}, \ldots x_n^{(q-1)}, y_1^{(0)}, \ldots y_m^{(q-1)}, z_1^{(0)} \ldots$ The relators and rows have the following order:

$$x_1^{(1)}(z_1^{(0)})^{-1}, x_1^{(2)}(z_1^{(1)})^{-1}, \ldots, x_1^{(0)}(z_1^{(q-1)})^{-1}, \ldots, R_1^{(0)}, R_1^{(1)}, \ldots.$$

This gives a matrix

$$A^*(t) = \left(\begin{array}{cccccc} Z_q & & & & -E_q & \\ & Z_q & & & & \ddots \\ & & Z_q & & & \ddots \\ & & & \ddots & & -E_q \\ & & & & Z_q & -E_q \\ \hline & & & \bar{A}^*(t) & & \end{array}\right).$$

Here $\bar{A}^*(t)$ is obtained from $\bar{A}(t)$ by replacing every element $a_{ik}(t)$ of $\bar{A}(t)$ by the $q \times q$ diagonal matrix

$$a_{ik}^{(q)}(t) = \begin{pmatrix} a_{ik}(t) & & & 0 \\ \vdots & a_{ik}(t) & & \vdots \\ \vdots & & \ddots & \vdots \\ 0 & & & a_{ik}(t) \end{pmatrix}.$$

The $q \times q$-matrix

$$Z_q = \begin{pmatrix} 0 & 1 & \ldots & 0 \\ 0 & 0 & 1 & \\ \cdot & & \ddots & \\ \cdot & & & 1 \\ 1 & & & 0 \end{pmatrix}$$

is equivalent to the diagonal matrix

$$Z(\zeta) = WZ_qW^{-1} = \begin{pmatrix} 1 & \cdot & \cdot & \cdot & 0 \\ \cdot & \zeta & & & \cdot \\ \cdot & & \zeta^2 & & \cdot \\ \cdot & & & \ddots & \cdot \\ 0 & \cdot & \cdot & \cdot & \zeta^{q-1} \end{pmatrix}$$

over $\mathbb{C}$ where ζ is a primitive q-th root of unity (Exercise E 14.9). The matrix $\tilde{W}A^*(t)\tilde{W}^{-1}$ with

$$\tilde{W} = \left(\begin{array}{c|c|c|c} W & & & \\ \hline & W & & \\ \hline & & \ddots & \\ \hline & & & W \end{array}\right)$$

may be obtained from $A^*(t)$ by replacing the submatrices Z_q by $Z(\zeta)$. Returning to the original ordering of rows and columns as in $A(t)$, the matrix $\tilde{W}A^*(t)\tilde{W}^{-1}$ takes the form

$$(2) \qquad A(t, \zeta) = \left(\begin{array}{c|c|c|c} A^{(q)}(t, 1) & & & \cdots\cdots \ 0 \\ \hline & A^{(q)}(t, \zeta) & & \vdots \\ \hline & & & \\ \hline & & \ddots & \\ \hline 0 \ \ldots & & & A^{(q)}(t, \zeta^{q-1}) \end{array}\right)$$

where

$$A^{(q)}(t, \zeta^\nu) = \left(\begin{array}{ccccc} \zeta^\nu & & & -1 & \\ & \ddots & & & \ddots \\ & & \zeta^\nu & & & -1 \\ \hline & & & \bar{A}(t) & & \end{array}\right).$$

$A(t, \zeta)$ is equivalent to $A(t)$ over $\mathbb{C}$, and $A^{(q)}(t, 1)$ is a Jacobian of the factor knot $\mathfrak{k}^{(q)}$. We replace ζ^ν by a variable τ and prove:

14.20 Proposition. $\det(A^{(q)}(t, \tau)) = (\tau - 1)\, D(t, \tau)$ *with*

$$D(t, 1) \doteq \varrho_\lambda(t)\, \Delta_1^{(q)}(t),$$
$$\varrho_\lambda(t) \ = 1 + t + \ldots + t^{\lambda - 1}, \quad \lambda = lk(h, \mathfrak{k}).$$

$\Delta_1^{(q)}(t)$ is the Alexander polynomial of the factor knot $\mathfrak{k}^{(q)}$.

Proof. Replace the first column of $A^{(q)}(t, \tau)$ by the sum of all columns and expand according to the first column:

$$\det(A^{(q)}(t, \tau)) = (\tau - 1) \cdot \sum_{i=1}^{n} D_i(t, \tau)$$

where $(-1)^{i+1} D_i(t, \tau)$ denotes the minor obtained from $A^{(q)}(t, \tau)$ by omitting the first column and i-th row. This proves the first assertion for $D(t, \tau) = \sum_{i=1}^{n} D_i(t, \tau)$.

To prove the second one we show that the rows $\mathfrak{a}_l$ of the Jacobian

$$A^{(q)}(t,1) = \left(\begin{array}{ccccc} 1 & & -1 & & \\ & & & \ddots & \\ & & 1 & & -1 \\ \hline & & \bar{A}(t) & & \end{array}\right)$$

of $\mathfrak{k}^{(q)}$ satisfies a special linear dependence $\sum_{l=1}^{2n+m} \alpha_l \mathfrak{a}_l = 0$ with $\sum_{l=1}^{n} \alpha_l = \varrho_\lambda(t)$. (Compare 9.12(b).) Denote by $\mathfrak{F}$ the free group generated by $\{X_i, Y_k, Z_i | 1 \leqq i \leqq n, 1 \leqq k \leqq m\}$, $\psi(X_i) = x_i^{(0)}$, $\psi(Y_k) = y_k^{(0)}$, $\psi(Z_i) = z_i^{(0)}$. There is an identity

(3) $$\prod_{i=1}^{n} (X_i^{\varepsilon_i}) (\prod_{i=1}^{n} Z_i^{\varepsilon_i})^{-1} = \prod_{j=1}^{n+m} L_j R_j L_j^{-1}$$

for $L_j \in \mathfrak{F}$, $\varepsilon_i = \pm 1$, and $R_j = R_j^{(0)}(X_i, Y_k, Z_i)$. This follows by the argument used in the proof of 3.6: The closed path γ in Figure 14.8 can be expressed by both sides of equation (3). From this we define:

$$\alpha_l = \frac{\partial}{X_l} (\prod_{i=1}^{n} X_i^{\varepsilon_i})^{\varphi\psi} = \sum_{j=1}^{n+m} (L_j)^{\varphi\psi} \left(\frac{\partial R_j}{\partial X_l}\right)^{\varphi\psi}, \quad \text{hence,}$$

$$-\alpha_l = \sum_{j=1}^{n+m} (L_j)^{\varphi\psi} \left(\frac{\partial R_j}{\partial Z_l}\right)^{\varphi\psi}, \quad 1 \leqq l \leqq n,$$

$$0 = \sum_{j=1}^{n+m} (L_j)^{\varphi\psi} \left(\frac{\partial R_j}{\partial Y_k}\right)^{\varphi\psi}, \quad 1 \leqq k \leqq m.$$

Putting $\alpha_{n+j} = -(\mathrm{L}_j)^{\varphi\psi}$, $1 \leqq j \leqq n+m$, gives $\sum_{i=1}^{2n+m} \alpha_i \mathfrak{a}_i = 0$. The fundamental formula 9.8(c) yields

$$(t-1) \sum_{l=1}^{n} \alpha_l = \sum_{l=1}^{n} \frac{\partial}{\partial X_l} (\prod_{i=1}^{n} X_i^{\varepsilon_i})^{\varphi\psi} (t-1) = (\prod X_i^{\varepsilon_i})^{\varphi\psi} - 1$$

$$= \mathrm{t}^\lambda - 1, \quad \text{hence } \sum_{l=1}^{n} \alpha_l = \varrho_\lambda(t).$$

Now $D_1(t,1) \doteq \Delta_1^{(q)}(t)$, and $\alpha_i D_1(t,1) = D_i(t,1)$. The last equation is a consequence of $\Sigma \alpha_i \mathfrak{a}_i = 0$, compare 10.20. □

14.21 Proposition (Murasugi). *The Alexander polynomial $\Delta_1(t)$ of a knot $\mathfrak{k}$ with period q satisfies the equation*

(4) $$\Delta_1(t) \doteq \Delta_1^{(q)}(t) \cdot \prod_{i=1}^{q-1} D(t, \zeta^i).$$

Here $D(t, \zeta)$ is an integral polynomial in two variables with

$$D(t,1) \doteq \varrho_\lambda(t)\Delta_1^{(q)} t),$$

and ζ is a primitive q-th root of unity. $0 < \lambda = lk(h, \mathfrak{k})$ is the linking number of $\mathfrak{k}$ with the axis h of rotation.

Proof. To determine the first elementary ideal of $A(t, \zeta)$, see (2), it suffices to consider the minors obtained from $A(t, \zeta)$ by omitting an i-th row and a j-th column, $1 \leqq i, j \leqq n$, because $\det(A^{(q)}(t, 1)) = 0$. Proposition 14.21 follows from the fact that $A^{(q)}(t, 1)$ is a Jacobian of $\mathfrak{k}^{(q)}$. □

14.22 Corollary (Murasugi's congruence). $\Delta_1(t) \doteqdot (\Delta_1^{(p^a)}(t))^{p^a} \cdot (\varrho_\lambda(t))^{p^a-1}$ mod p *for $p^a \mid q$, p a prime.*

Proof. A knot $\mathfrak{k}$ with period q also has period $p^a, p^a \mid q$. Let $0(p^a)$ denote the cyclotomic integers in $\mathbb{Q}(\zeta)$, ζ a p^a-th root of unity. There is a homomorphism

$$\Phi_p\colon 0(p^a) \to \mathbb{Z}_p, \quad \sum_{i=1}^{p^a} n_i \zeta^i \mapsto \sum_{i=1}^{p^a} [n_i] \bmod p.$$

Extending Φ_p to the rings of polynomial over $0(p^a)$ resp. $\mathbb{Z}_p$ yields the corollary. □

14.23 Proposition. *Let $\mathfrak{k}$ be a knot of period p^a and $\Delta_1(t) \not\equiv 1$ mod p. Then $D(t, \zeta_i)$ is not a monomial for some p^a-th root of unity $\zeta_i \neq 1$. Any common root of $\Delta_1^{(p^a)}(t)$ and $D(t, \zeta_i)$ is also a root of $\Delta_2(t)$. If all roots of $D(t, \zeta_i)$ are roots of $\Delta_1^{(p^a)}(t)$, then $\lambda \equiv \pm 1$ mod p.*

Proof. If $D(t, \zeta_i)$ is monomial, $1 \leqq i \leqq p^a$, then (4) yields $\Delta_1(t) = \Delta_1^{(p^a)}(t)$. Apply Φ_p to this equation and use 14.22 to obtain $\Delta_1^{(p^a)} \doteqdot 1$ mod p and $\lambda = 1$. From this it follows that $\Delta_1(t) \equiv 1$ mod p.

Suppose now that $D(t, \zeta_i)$ and $\Delta_1^{(p^r)}(t)$ have a common root η. Transform $A(t, \zeta)$ over $\mathbb{Q}(\zeta)[t]$ into a diagonal matrix by replacing each block $A^{(q)}(t, \zeta_i)$, $0 \leqq i \leqq p^a$, see (2), by an equivalent diagonal block. Since $\det(A^q(t, 1)) = 0$, it follows that the second elementary ideal $E_2(t)$ vanishes for $t = \eta$, hence, $\Delta_2(\eta) = 0$.

If all roots of $D(t, \zeta_i)$ are roots of $\Delta_1^{(p^a)}(t)$, every prime factor $f(t)$ of $D(t, \zeta_i)$ is a prime factor of $\Delta_1^{(p^a)}(t)$ in $\mathbb{Q}(\zeta)[t]$.

Since $\Delta_1^{(p^a)}(1) = \pm 1$, it follows that $\Phi_p(f(1)) \equiv \pm 1$ mod p. But $|D(1, 1)| = \lambda$. To prove this consider $A^{(q)}(1, \tau)$. This matrix is associated to the knot projection, but it treats overcrossings in the same way as undercrossings. By a suitable choice of undercrossings and overcrossings one may replace $\mathfrak{k}$ by a simple type of closed braid (Fig. 14.9) while preserving its symmetry. The elimination of variables does not alter $|\det A^{(q)}(1, \tau)|$. Finally $A^{(q)}(1, \tau)$ takes the form:

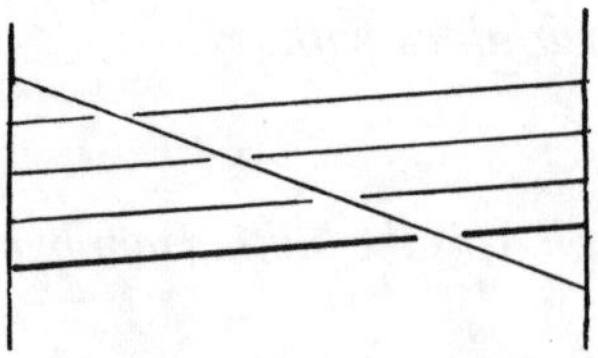

Fig. 14.9

$$\begin{pmatrix} \tau E_\lambda & -E_\lambda \\ -E_\lambda & P_\lambda \end{pmatrix}$$

where E_λ is the $\lambda \times \lambda$-identity matrix and P_λ the representing matrix of a cyclic permutation of order λ. It follows that

$$\det(A^{(q)}(1, \tau)) = \pm \det(E_\lambda - \tau P_\lambda) = \pm(1 - \tau^\lambda),$$

because the characteristic polynomial of P_λ is $\pm(1 - \tau^\lambda)$. Proposition 14.20 then shows

$$D(1, \tau) = \pm(1 + \tau + \ldots + \tau^{\lambda-1}) = \pm \varrho_\lambda(\tau) \quad \text{and}$$
$$|D(1,1)| = \lambda. \quad \square$$

14.24 Proposition. *Let $\mathfrak{k}$ be a knot of period p^a, $a \geqq 1$, p a prime. If $\Delta_1(t) \not\equiv 1 \bmod p$ and $\Delta_2(t) = 1$, the splitting field $\mathbb{Q}(\Delta_1)$ of $\Delta_1(t)$ over the rationals $\mathbb{Q}$ contains the p^a-th roots of unity.*

Proof. By 14.20 and 14.21 (4) there is a root $\alpha \in \mathbb{C}$ of $\Delta_1(t)$ which is not a root of $\Delta_1^{(p^a)}(t)$. Thus, there exists a uniquely determined equivalence class of representations δ_α: $\mathfrak{G} \to \mathfrak{C}^+$ of the knot group $\mathfrak{G}$ of $\mathfrak{k}$ into the equiform group $\mathfrak{C}^+$ of the plane, see 14.5. If $D(\alpha, \zeta_i) = 0$, the fixed points $b_j(S_j)$ of

$$\delta_\alpha(S_j)\colon z \mapsto \alpha(z - b_j) + b_j$$

assigned to Wirtinger generators S_j are solutions of a linear system of equations with coefficient matrix $\bar{A}(\alpha)$, satisfying $b_j(z_j) = \zeta_i b_j(x_j)$. Thus the configuration of fixed points b_j associated to the symmetric projection of Fig. 14.7 also shows a cyclic symmetry; its order is that of ζ_i. All representations are equiformly equivalent, and all configurations of fixed points are, therefore, similar. Since the b_j are solutions of the system of linear equations (2) in 14.4 for $t = \alpha$, $u_j = b_j$, they may be assumed to be elements of $\mathbb{Q}(\alpha)$. It follows that

$$b_j(z_j) b_j^{-1}(x_j) = \zeta_i \in \mathbb{Q}(\alpha).$$

We claim that there exists a representation δ_α such that the automorphism

$$r_*(\alpha)\colon \delta_\alpha(\mathfrak{G}) \to \delta_\alpha(\mathfrak{G})$$

induced by the rotation r has order p^a. If p^b, $b < a$, were the maximal order occuring for any δ_α, all (non-trivial) presentations δ_α would induce non-trivial presentations of the knot group $\mathfrak{G}^{(p^a-b)}$ of the factor knot $\mathfrak{k}^{(p^a-b)}$. Then α would be a root of $\Delta_2(t)$ by 14.23, contradicting $\Delta_2(t) = 1$. □

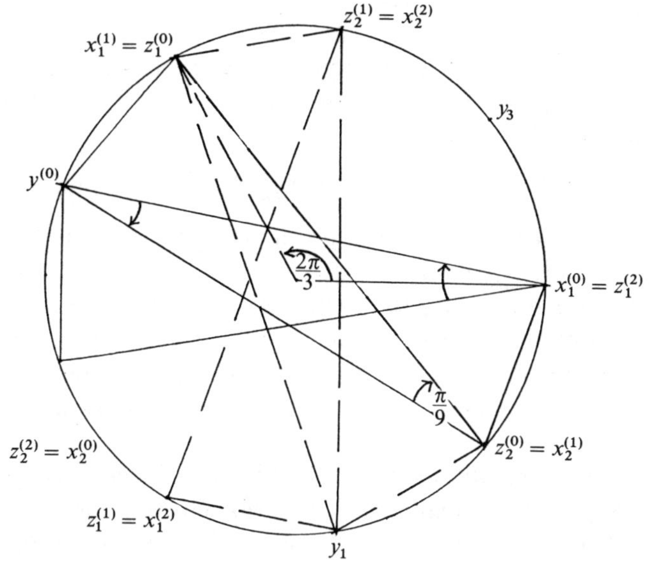

Fig. 14.10

Figure 14.10 shows the fixed point configuration of the knot 9_1 as a knot of period three. One finds: $D(t, \tau) = t^3 + \tau$, $D(t, 1) = \varrho_2(t) \cdot \Delta_1^{(3)}(t)$, $\Delta_1^{(3)} = t^2 - t + 1$. For $\tau = e^{\frac{2\pi i}{3}}$, and $D(\alpha, \tau) = 0$, we get $\alpha = e^{\frac{-\pi i}{9}}$.

14.25 Corollary. *Let $\mathfrak{k}$ be a knot of period $q > 1$ with $\Delta_1(t) \neq 1$, $\Delta_2(t) = 1$. Then the splitting field of $\Delta_1(t)$ contains the q-th roots of unity or $\Delta_1(t) \equiv 1 \bmod p$ for some $p \mid q$.*

If $\mathfrak{k}$ is a non-trivial fibred knot of period q with $\Delta_2(t) = 1$, the splitting field of $\Delta_1(t)$ contains the q-th roots of unity [Trotter 1961]. □

The preceding proof contains additional information in the case of a prime period.

14.26 Corollary. *If $\mathfrak{k}$ is a knot of period p and $\Delta_1(\alpha) = 0$, $\Delta_1^{(p)}(\alpha) \neq 0$, then the p-th roots of unity are contained in $\mathbb{Q}(\alpha)$.*

Proof. There is a non-trivial representation δ_α of the knot group of $\mathfrak{k}$ with $b_j(z_j) = \zeta b_j(x_j)$, ζ a primitive p-th root of unity. □

As an application we prove

14.27 Proposition. *The periods of a torus knot* $\mathfrak{t}(a, b)$ *are the divisors of* a *and* b.

Proof. By 9.15,

$$\Delta_1(t) = \frac{(t^{ab}-1)(t-1)}{(t^a-1)(t^b-1)}, \quad \Delta_2(t) = 1 .$$

From Corollary 14.25 we know that a period q of $\mathfrak{t}(a, b)$ must be a divisor of ab. Suppose $p_1 p_2 | q, p_1 | a, p_2 | b$ for two prime numbers p_1, p_2, then $\mathfrak{t}(a, b)$ has periods p_1, p_2, and Corollary 14.22 gives

$$(t-1)^{\lambda}(t^{a'b}-1)^{p_1^c} \doteq (t^a-1)(t^b-1)\,[\varrho_\lambda(t)\,\Delta_1^{(p_1^c)}(t)]^{p_1^c} \bmod p_1$$

with $a = p_1^c a'$, $gcd(p_1, a') = 1$. Let ζ_0 be a primitive b-th root of unity. We have $gcd(b, p_1) = 1$ and $gcd(\lambda, p_1 p_2) = 1$, hence $p_2 \nmid \lambda$. (*See E.* 14.8.) The root ζ_0 has multiplicity s with $s \equiv 1 \bmod p_1$ on the right-hand side of the congruence, but since ζ_0 is not a λ-th root of unity, its multiplicity on the left-hand side ought to be $s \equiv 0 \bmod p_1$. So there is no period q containing primes from both a and b.

It is evident that the divisors of a and b are actually periods of $\mathfrak{t}(a, b)$. □

There have been further contributions to this topic. In [Lüdicke 1978] the dihedral representations γ_p have been exploited. The periodicity of a knot is reflected in its invariant $[\lambda(\zeta)]$. In [Murasugi 1980] these results were generalized, completed and formulated in terms of linking numbers of coverings. In addition to that, certain conditions involving the Alexander polynomial and the signature of a knot have been proved when a knot is periodic [Gordon-Litherland-Murasugi 1981]. Together all these criteria suffice to determine the periods of knots with less than ten crossings, see Table I. There is a table in [Murasugi 1980] which has been completed by himself leaving open only a possible period 3 of 9_{25}. But this can be ruled out by Lüdicke's method [Lüdicke 1984]. Many results on periodic knots carry over to links [Knigge 1981], [Sakuma 1981′, 1981″].

It follows from Murasugi's congruence in 14.22 that a knot of period p^a either has Alexander polynomial $\Delta_1(t) \equiv 1 \bmod p$ or $\deg \Delta_1(t) \geqq p^a - 1$. Thus a knot with $\Delta_1(t) \not\equiv 1$ can have only finitely many prime periods. No limit could be obtained for periods p^a, if $\Delta_1(t) \equiv 1 \bmod p$. A fibred knot has only finitely many periods, since its Alexander polynomial is of degree $2g$ with a leading coefficient ± 1. It has, though, recently been proved in [Flapan 1983] that only the trivial knot admits infinitely many periods. A new proof of this theorem and a generalization to links was proved in [Hillman 1984]. The generalization reads: A link with infinitely many periods consists of μ trivial components spanned by disjoint disks.

14.28 Knots with deg $\Delta_1(t) = 2$. Murasugi's congruence 14.22 shows that a knot with a quadratic Alexander polynomial can only have period three. Furthermore it follows from 14.22 that

$$\Delta_1(t) \equiv t^2 - t + 1 \bmod 3.$$

Corollary 14.25 yields further information: If $\mathfrak{k}$ has period three, its Alexander polynomial has the form

$$\Delta_1(t) = nt^2 + (1-2n)t + n, \quad n = 3m(m+1)+1,\ m = 0, 1, \ldots,$$

see E 14.11.

There are, in fact, symmetric knots which have these Alexander polynomials, the pretzel knots $\mathfrak{p}(2m+1, 2m+1, 2m+1)$, (Fig. 14.11). Their factor knot $\mathfrak{p}^{(3)}$ is trivial. One obtains

$$D(t,\tau) = (\tau + n(\tau - 1))t + n(1-\tau) + 1,$$
$$D(t,1) = 1 + t,\ D(t,\tau) = 1 + \tau, \quad (\lambda = 2),$$
$$D(t,\zeta)D(t,\zeta^{-1}) = \Delta_1(t),\ \zeta \text{ a primitive third root of unity.}$$

(We omit the calculations.) $\mathfrak{p}(1,1,1)$ is the trefoil, $\mathfrak{p}(3,3,3) = 9_{35}$.

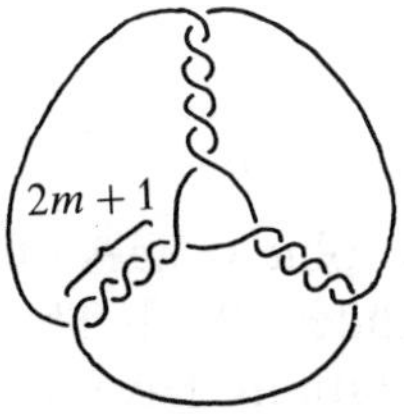

Fig. 14.11

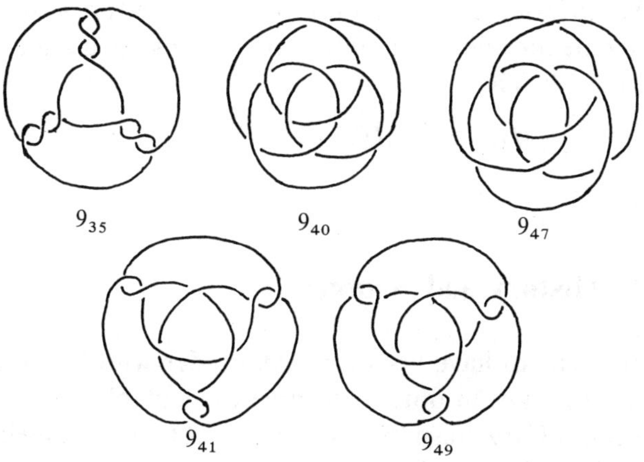

Fig. 14.12

14.29 The different criteria or a combination of them can be applied to exclude periods of given knots. As an example consider $\mathfrak{k} = 8_{11}$. Its polynomials are $\Delta_1(t) = (t^2 - t + 1)(2t^2 - 5t + 2)$, $\Delta_2(t) = 1$. Murasugi's congruence excludes all periods different from three, but $\Delta_1(t) \doteq t^4 + t^3 + t + 1 \equiv (1+t)^4 \bmod 3$, hence, $\lambda = 2$ and $\Delta_1^{(3)} \equiv 1 \bmod 3$ would satisfy the congruence. The splitting field of $\Delta_1(t)$ obviously contains the third roots of unity. The second factor $2t^2 - 5t + 2$, though, has a splitting field contained in $\mathbb{R}$. By 14.25 and 14.26 this excludes a period three, since $2t^2 - 5t + 2 \not\equiv 1 \bmod 3$.

Figure 14.12 shows symmetric versions of the knots of period three with less than ten crossings, $9_{35}, 9_{40}, 9_{41}, 9_{47}, 9_{49}$. (The torus knots are omitted, $\mathfrak{t}(4,3) = 8_{19}$, $\mathfrak{t}(5,3) = 10_{124}$ and $\mathfrak{t}(2m+1, 2)$, $1 \leqq m \leqq 4$.)

We conclude this section by showing that the condition $\Delta_2(t) = 1$ cannot be omitted. The 'rosette'-knot 8_{18} evidently has period four. The Alexander polynomials are $\Delta_1(t) = (1 - t + t^2)^2(1 - 3t + t^2)$, $\Delta_2(t) = (1 - t + t^2)$. One has $D(t, \tau) = \tau t^2 + (\tau^2 - \tau + 1)t + \tau$. It follows that $D(t, 1) = 1 + t + t^2 = \varrho_3(t)$, $\Delta_1^{(4)}(t) = 1$, $D(t, -1) = 1 - 3t + t^2$, $D(t, \pm i) = \pm i(1 - t + t^2)$. The representations δ_α, $D(\alpha, i) = \Delta_2(\alpha) = 0$, are not unique. $1 - 3\beta + \beta^2 = 0$ yields unique representations with period 2. In fact, the splitting field $\mathbb{Q}(\Delta_1(t))$ does not contain i. (See also [Trotter 1961].) Nevertheless, the condition $\Delta_2(t) = 1$ can be replaced by a more general one involving higher Alexander polynomials [Hillman 1983].

Remark: It is not clear whether the second condition $\Delta_1(t) \not\equiv 1 \bmod p$ in 14.23, 14.24 is necessary. The Alexander polynomials of the knots 9_{41} and 9_{49} (which have period three) satisfy $\Delta_1(t) \equiv 1 \bmod 3$, their splitting fields nevertheless contain the third roots of unity.

When looking at the material one may venture a conjecture: Let $M(\mathfrak{k})$ and $M(\mathfrak{k}^{(q)})$ denote the minimal numbers of crossings of a knot $\mathfrak{k}$ of period q and of its factor knot $\mathfrak{k}^{(q)}$. Then

$$M(\mathfrak{k}) \geqq q \cdot M(\mathfrak{k}^{(q)}).$$

E History and Sources

It seems to have been J.W. Alexander who first used homomorphic images of knot groups to obtain effectively calculable invariants, [Alexander 1928]. The groups $\mathfrak{G}/\mathfrak{G}''$ resp. $\mathfrak{G}'/\mathfrak{G}''$, ancestral to all metabelian representations, have remained the most important source of knot invariants.

In [Reidemeister 1932] a representation of the group of alternating pretzel knots onto Fuchsian groups is used to classify these knots. This representation is not metabelian but, of course, is restricted to a rather special class of groups. It was repeatedly employed in the years to follow to produce counterexamples concerning properties which escape Alexander's invariants. By it, in [Seifert 1934], a pretzel knot with the same Alexander invariants as the trivial knot could be proved to be non-trivial – shattering all hopes of classifying knot types by these invariants. Trotter [1964] used it to show that non-invertible knots (pretzel knots) exist. The natural class of knots to which the method developed for pretzel knots can be extended is the class of Montesinos knots (Chapter 12).

R.H. Fox drew the attention to a special case of metabelian representations – the metacyclic ones. Here the image group could be chosen finite. (Compare also [Hartley 1979].) A lifting process of these representations obtained by abelianizing its kernel yielded a further class of non-metabelian representations [Burde 1967, 1970], [Hartley 1983].

A class of representations of fundamental importance in the theory of 3-manifolds was introduced by R. Riley. The image groups are discrete subgroups of $PSL(2, \mathbb{C})$, and they can be understood as groups of orientation preserving motions of hyperbolic 3-space. The theory of these representations (Riley-reps), [Riley 1973, 1975, 1975′] has not been considered in this book – the same holds for homomorphisms onto the finite groups $PSL(2, p)$ over a finite field $\mathbb{Z}_p$, see [Magnus-Peluso 1967], [Riley 1971], [Hartley-Murasugi 1978].

F Exercises

E 14.1 Show that the group of symmetries of a regular a-gon is the image of a dihedral representation γ_a^* of the knot group of the torus knot $\mathfrak{t}(a, 2)$. Give an example of a torus knot that does not allow a dihedral representation.

E 14.2 Let $\delta_\alpha\colon \mathfrak{G} \to \mathfrak{C}^+$ be a representation into the equiform group (14.5) of the group $\mathfrak{G}$ of a knot $\mathfrak{k}$, and $\{b_j\}$ the configuration of fixed points in $\mathbb{C}$ corresponding to Wirtinger generators S_j of a regular projection $p(\mathfrak{k})$. Show that one obtains a representation δ_α^* of $\mathfrak{k}^*$ with a fixed point configuration $\{b_j'\}$ resulting from $\{b_j\}$ by reflection in a line.

E 14.3 (a) Let $\mathfrak{k} = \mathfrak{k}_1 \# \mathfrak{k}_2$ be a product knot and $\Delta_1^{(1)}(t) \neq 1$, $\Delta_1^{(2)}(t) \neq 1$ be the Alexander polynomials of its summands. Show that there are non-equivalent representations δ_α for $\Delta_1^{(1)}(\alpha) = \Delta_1^{(2)}(\alpha) = 0$. Derive from this that $\Delta_2(\alpha) = 0$.

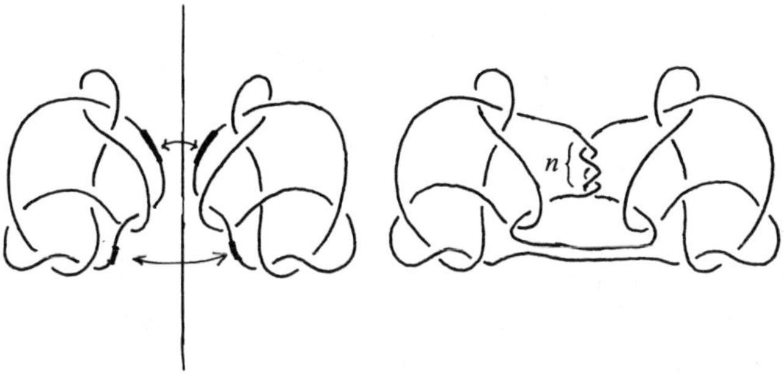

Fig. 14.13

(b) Consider a regular knot projection $p(\mathfrak{k})$ and a second projection $p^*(\mathfrak{k})$ in the same plane E obtained from a mirror image $\mathfrak{k}^*$ reflected in a plane perpendicular to E. Join two corresponding arcs of $p(\mathfrak{k})$ and $p^*(\mathfrak{k})$

as shown in Figure 14.13 one with an n-twist and one without a twist – the resulting projection is that of a *symmetric union* $\mathfrak{k} \cup \mathfrak{k}^*$ of $\mathfrak{k}$ [Kinoshita-Terasaka 1957]. Show that a representation δ_α for $\mathfrak{k}$ can always be extended to a representation δ_α for the symmetric union, hence, that every root of the Alexander polynomial of $\mathfrak{k}$ is a root of that of $\mathfrak{k} \cup \mathfrak{k}^*$. (Use E 14.2.)

E 14.4 Compute the representations γ_a for torus knots $\mathfrak{t}(a,2)$ that lift the dihedral representations γ_a^* of E 14.1, see 14.10. Show that $[\lambda(\zeta)] = \{2a\}$. Derive from this that $\mathfrak{t}(a,2) \# \mathfrak{t}(a,2)$ and $\mathfrak{t}(a,2) \# \mathfrak{t}^*(a,2)$ have non-homeomorphic complements but isomorphic groups.

E 14.5 (Henninger) Let $\gamma_p\colon \mathfrak{G} \to \mathfrak{B}$ be a normalized representation according to 14.10, $\gamma_p(S_1)\colon z \mapsto \bar{z} + 1$, $\gamma_p(S_2)\colon z \mapsto \zeta^2 \bar{z} + \zeta$, with ζ a primitive p-th root of unity. Show that $\gamma_p(\mathfrak{G}) \cong \mathfrak{D}_p \ltimes \mathbb{Z}^{p-1}$. (Hint: use a translation of the plane by $2 \cdot \sum_{j=0}^{\frac{p-3}{2}} \zeta^{2j+1} + \sum_{j=1}^{\frac{p-1}{2}} \zeta^{2j}$.)

E 14.6 Compute the matrix (μ_{ij}) of linking numbers (14.10(b)) of the irregular covering $\hat{I}_{15}$ of 9_2. Compare the invariants $\frac{1}{2} \sum_{j \neq i} |\mu_{ij}| = v_i$, $0 \leq i \leq 7$ with those of 7_4.
(Result: 7, 6, 5, 4, 4, 3, 2, 1, [Reidemeister 1932].)

E 14.7 If a knot has period q as an unoriented knot, it has period q as an oriented knot. Show that the axis of a rotation through π which maps $\mathfrak{k}$ onto $-\mathfrak{k}$ must meet $\mathfrak{k}$.

E 14.8 Let $\mathfrak{k}$ be a knot of period q and h the axis of the rotation. Prove that $gcd(lk(h,\mathfrak{k}), q) = 1$.

E 14.9 Produce a matrix W over $\mathbb{C}$ such that

$$WZ_qW^{-1} = Z(\zeta),\; Z_q = \begin{pmatrix} 0 & 1 & . & \vdots \\ \vdots & 0 & 1 & \vdots \\ \vdots & & & \vdots \\ \vdots & & & 1 \\ 1 & & & 0 \end{pmatrix},\; Z(\zeta) = \begin{pmatrix} 1 & & & \\ & \zeta & & \\ & & \ddots & \\ & & & \zeta^{q-1} \end{pmatrix},$$

ζ a primitive q-th root of unity.

E 14.10 We call an *oriented tangle* $\mathfrak{T}_n$ *circular*, if its arcs have an even number of boundary points $X_1, \dots, X_n, Z_1, \dots, Z_n$ which can be joined pairwise (Fig. 14.14) to give an oriented knot $\mathfrak{k}(\mathfrak{T}_n)$, inducing on $\mathfrak{T}_n$ the original orientation. A q-periodic knot $\mathfrak{k}$ may be obtained by joining q circular tangles $\mathfrak{T}_n$; the knot $\mathfrak{k}(\mathfrak{T}_n)$ is then the factor knot $\mathfrak{k}^{(q)} = \mathfrak{k}(\mathfrak{T}_n)$, see Fig. 14.7. A circular tangle defines a polynomial $D(t,\tau)$, see 14.20.
(a) Show $D(t+\tau) = t + \tau$ for the circular tangle $\mathfrak{T}_2$ with one crossing and compute $\Delta_1(t) = \prod_{i=1}^{q-1} (t + \zeta^i)$, ζ a primitive q-th root of unity, q odd.

$\Delta_1(t)$ is the Alexander polynomial of $\mathfrak{t}(q, 2)$. (b) Find all circular tangles with less than four crossings. Construct knots of period ≤ 4 by them.

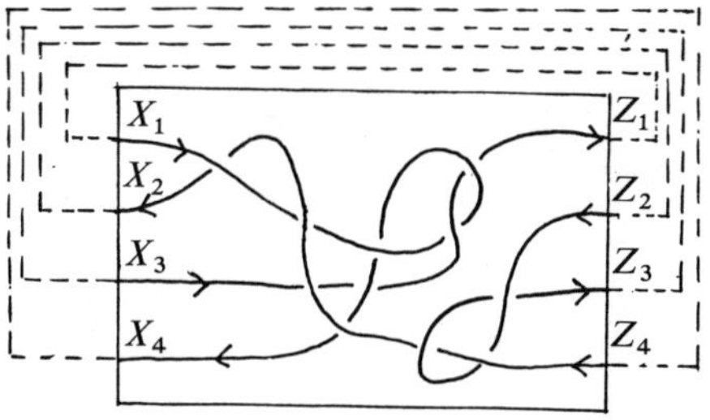

Fig. 14.14

E 14.11 If the Alexander polynomial $\Delta_1(t)$ of a periodic knot of period three is quadratic, it has the form

$$\Delta_1(t) = nt^2 + (1-2n)t + n,\ n = 3m(m+1)+1, \quad m = 0, 1, \ldots .$$

Prove that the pretzel knot $\mathfrak{p}(2m+1, 2m+1, 2m+1)$ has this polynomial as $\Delta_1(t)$. Hint: Compute $D(\tau, t)$.

E 14.12 [Lüdicke 1979]. Let $\mathfrak{k}$ be a knot with prime period q. Suppose there is a unique dihedral presentation $\gamma_p^*\colon \mathfrak{G} \to \mathfrak{Z}_2 \ltimes \mathfrak{Z}_p$ of its group, and $p \nmid \Delta_1^{(q)}(-1)$.
Then either $q = p$ or $q | p-1$.

Chapter 15: Knots, Knot Manifolds, and Knot Groups

How many knots have the same complement or knot group? Of course, a knot $\mathfrak{k}$, the inverse knot $-\mathfrak{k}$, the mirrored knots $\mathfrak{k}^*$ and $-\mathfrak{k}^*$ have homeomorphic complements, but may be different. Are there other possibilities? The corresponding question for links has a positive answer; the problem for knots is still undecided, although large classes of knots are known where the answer is negative.

A consequence of the famous theorem of Waldhausen [1968] (see Appendix B 7) on sufficiently large irreducible 3-manifolds is that the complements of two knots are homeomorphic if there is an isomorphism between the fundamental groups preserving the peripheral group system. We study to what extent the assumption concerning the boundary is necessary.

In Part A we describe examples which show that there are links of two components which do not have Property P, see Definition 3.18, and that there are non-homeomorphic knot complements with isomorphic groups. In Part B we investigate Property P for knots. In Part C we discuss the relation between the complement and its fundamental group for prime knots and in Part D for composite knots.

A Examples

The following example of [Whitehead 1937] shows that, in general, the complement of a link does not characterize the link.

15.1 Proposition (Whitehead). *Let $\mathfrak{l}_n$, $n \in \mathbb{Z}$ denote the link consisting of a trivial knot $\mathfrak{h}$ and the n-twist knot $\mathfrak{d}_n$, see Figure 15.1. Then:*
(a) The links $\mathfrak{l}_{2n}$ and $\mathfrak{l}_{2m}$ are not isotopic if $n \neq m$.
(b) $S^3 - \mathfrak{l}_{2n} \cong S^3 - \mathfrak{l}_0$ for all $n \in \mathbb{Z}$.

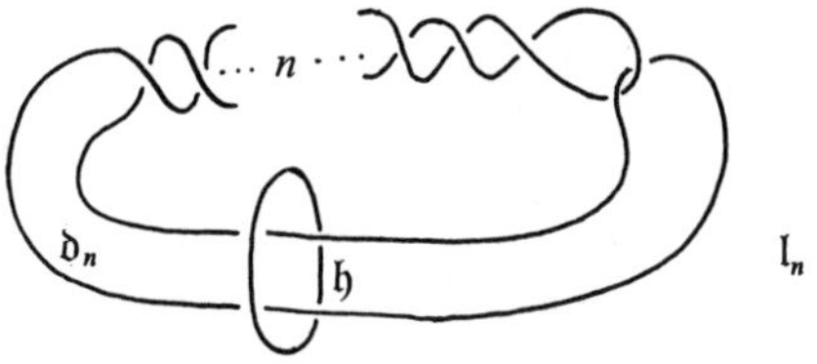

Fig. 15.1

Proof. By E 9.6, the Alexander polynomial of $\mathfrak{d}_{2n}$ is $nt^2 + (1-2n)t + n$; hence, $\mathfrak{d}_{2n} = \mathfrak{d}_{2m}$ only if $n = m$.

To prove (b) take an unknotted solid torus V and the trivial doubled knot $\mathfrak{d}_0 \subset V$ "parallel" to the core of V. $W = \overline{S^3 - V}$ is a solid torus with core $\mathfrak{h}$ and $W - \mathfrak{h} \cong \partial W \times [0,1) = \partial V \times [0,1)$. Consider the following homeomorphism $V \to V$: cut V along a meridional disk, turn it $|n|$ times through 2π in the positive sense if $n > 0$, in the negative sense if $n < 0$ and glue the disks together again. This twist maps $\mathfrak{d}_0$ to $\mathfrak{d}_{2n}$. The map can be extended to $W - \mathfrak{h} \cong \partial V \times [0,1) = \overline{(S^3 - V)} - \mathfrak{h}$ to get the desired homeomorphism. □

For later use we determine from Figure 15.2, 3 the group and peripheral system of the twist knots $\mathfrak{d}_n$, following [Bing-Martin 1971]. (See E 3.5.)

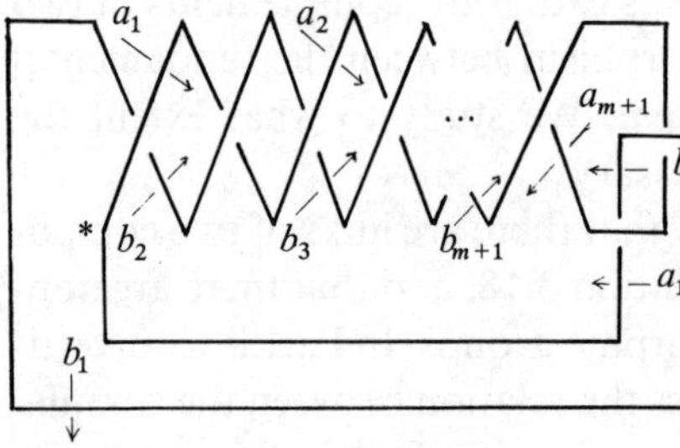

Fig. 15.2

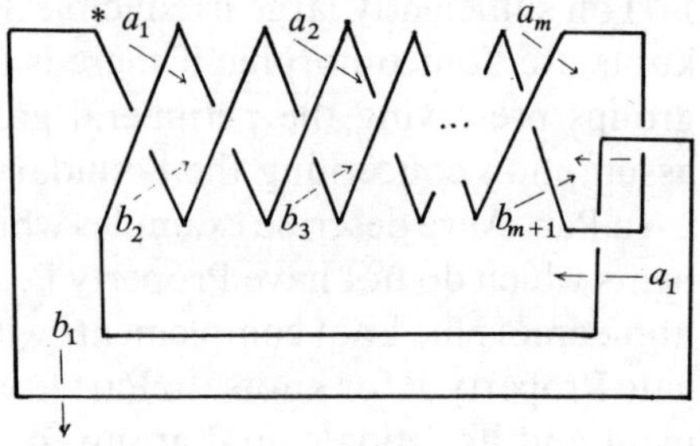

Fig. 15.3

15.2 Lemma. *The twist knot $\mathfrak{d}_n$ has the following group $\mathfrak{T}_n$ and peripheral system.*

15.3 *(a)* $\mathfrak{T}_{2m} = \langle a, b \,|\, b^{-1}(a^{-1}b)^m a (a^{-1}b)^{-m} a (a^{-1}b)^m a^{-1} (a^{-1}b)^{-m} \rangle$
meridian a, longitude $(a^{-1}b)^m a^{-1} (a^{-1}b)^{-m} b^m (a^{-1}b)^{-1-m} a^{-1} (a^{-1}b)^m a^{2-m}$;
(b) $\mathfrak{T}_{2m-1} = \langle a, b \,|\, b^{-1}(a^{-1}b)^m b^{-1} (a^{-1}b)^{-m} a (a^{-1}b)^m b (a^{-1}b)^{-m} \rangle$
meridian b, longitude $(a^{-1}b)^{-m} b (a^{-1}b)^{2m-1} b (a^{-1}b)^{-m} b^{-2}$.

Proof. In Figure 15.2 we have drawn the Wirtinger generators and we obtain the defining relations (here $a = a_1$, $b = b_1$)

$$\begin{aligned}
b_2 &= a_1^{-1} b_1 a_1 = a^{-1}ba \\
a_2 &= b_2 a_1 b_2^{-1} = (a^{-1}b) a (a^{-1}b)^{-1} \\
b_3 &= a_2^{-1} b_2 a_2 = (a^{-1}b)^2 b (a^{-1}b)^{-2} \\
&\vdots \\
b_{m+1} &= a_m^{-1} b_m a_m = (a^{-1}b)^m b (a^{-1}b)^{-m} \\
a_{m+1} &= b_{m+1} a_m b_{m+1}^{-1} = (a^{-1}b)^m a (a^{-1}b)^{-m} \\
b_1 = b &= a_{m+1} a_1 a_{m+1}^{-1} = (a^{-1}b)^m a (a^{-1}b)^{-m} a (a^{-1}b)^m a^{-1} (a^{-1}b)^{-m}
\end{aligned}$$

for $n = 2m$. For $n = 2m - 1$ the last two relations from above must be replaced by one relation

$$b = b_{m+1}^{-1} a b_{m+1} = (a^{-1} b)^m b^{-1} (a^{-1} b)^{-m} a (a^{-1} b)^m b (a^{-1} b)^{-m}$$

(see Fig. 15.3).

For the calculation of the longitude we use the formulas

$$a_1 \dots a_m = b^m (a^{-1} b)^{-m},$$
$$b_m \dots b_2 = (a^{-1} b)^{m-1} a^{m-1}.$$

A longitude of $\mathfrak{d}_{2m}$ associated to the meridian a is given by

$$\begin{aligned} &a_{m+1}^{-1} a_1 a_2 \dots a_m b_1^{-1} b_{m+1} \dots b_2 a^{2-2m} \\ &= (a^{-1} b)^m a^{-1} (a^{-1} b)^{-m} b^m (a^{-1} b)^{-m} b^{-1} (a^{-1} b)^m a^m a^{2-2m} \\ &= a^m (a^{-1} b)^m a^{-1} (a^{-1} b)^{-2m-1} a^{-1} (a^{-1} b)^m a^{2-m}; \end{aligned}$$

for the last step we applied the defining relation from 15.2(a) and replaced b by a conjugate of a. Since the longitude commutes with the meridian a we get the expression in 15.3(a).

For $\mathfrak{d}_{2m-1}$ a longitude is given by

$$\begin{aligned} &a_1 a_2 \dots a_m b_1 b_m b_{m-1} \dots b_2 b_{m+1} b_1^{-1-2m} \\ &= b^m (a^{-1} b)^{-m} b (a^{-1} b)^{m-1} a^{m-1} (a^{-1} b)^m b (a^{-1} b)^{-m} b^{-1-2m} \\ &= b^m (a^{-1} b)^{-m} b (a^{-1} b)^{2m-1} b (a^{-1} b)^{-m} b^{-2-m}; \end{aligned}$$

here we used the relation from 15.3(b). □

As we have pointed out in 3.15, the results of [Waldhausen 1968] imply that the peripheral system determines the knot up to isotopy and the complement up to orientation preserving homeomorphisms. A knot and its mirror image have homeomorphic complements; however, if the knot is not amphicheiral every homeomorphism of S^3 taking the knot onto its mirror image is orientation reversing. Using this, one can construct non-homeomorphic knot complements which have isomorphic groups:

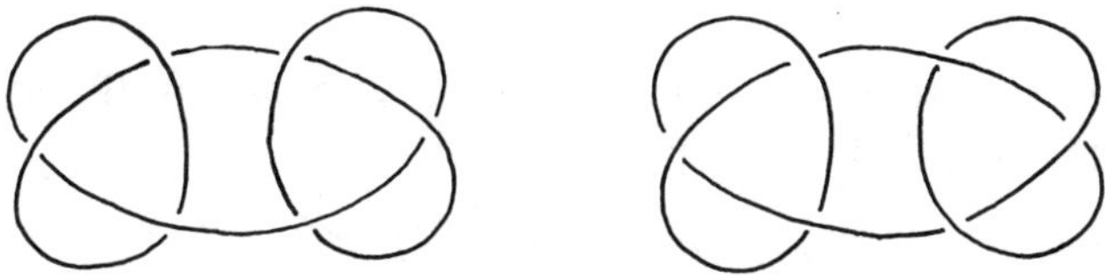

Fig. 15.4

15.4 Example ([Fox 1952]). The knots $\mathfrak{k} \# \mathfrak{k}^*$ and $\mathfrak{k} \# \mathfrak{k}$ where $\mathfrak{k}$ is a trefoil are known as the *square* and the *granny knot* (see Fig. 15.4). They are different knots by Schubert's theorem on the uniqueness of the prime decomposition of knots, see Theorem 7.12, and their complements are not homeomorphic. This is a consequence of Theorem 15.11. The first proof of this fact was given by R.H. Fox [1952] who showed that the peripheral systems of the square and granny knots have different properties. We derive it from E 14.4: the longitudes ℓ and ℓ' are mapped by a normalized presentation $\gamma_p, p = 3$, onto $12 = 6 + 6$ resp. $0 = 6 - 6$, comp. E 14.4 ([Fox 1952]). Their groups, though, are isomorphic by E 7.5.

B Property P for Special Knots

For torus and twist knots suitable presentations of the groups provide a means to prove Property P. This method, however, reflects no geometric background. For product knots and satellite knots a nice geometric approach gives Property P. The results and methods of this section are mainly from [Bing-Martin 1971].

15.5 Definition. (a) The unoriented knots $\mathfrak{k}_1, \mathfrak{k}_2$ are of the *same knot type* if there is a homeomorphism $h\colon S^3 \to S^3$ with $h(\mathfrak{k}_1) = h(\mathfrak{k}_2)$.

(b) Let $\mathfrak{k}$ be a non-trivial knot, V a neighbourhood of $\mathfrak{k}$, $C(\mathfrak{k}) = \overline{S^3 - V}$ the knot complement and m, ℓ meridian and longitude of $\mathfrak{k}$ on $\partial V = \partial C(\mathfrak{k})$. Then $C(\mathfrak{k})$ is called a *knot manifold*. For $gcd(r, n) = 1$ let $M = srg(S^3, \mathfrak{k}, r/n)$ denote the closed 3-manifold $C(\mathfrak{k}) \cup_f V'$ where V' is a solid torus with meridian m' and f an identifying homeomorphism $f\colon \partial V' \to \partial C(\mathfrak{k}), f(m') \sim rm + n\ell$ on $\partial C(\mathfrak{k})$. We say that *M is obtained from S^3 by surgery on $\mathfrak{k}$.*

Thus $H_1(srg(S^3, \mathfrak{k}, r/n)) = \mathbb{Z}_{|r|}$. The knot $\mathfrak{k}$ has Property P, (compare Definition 3.18), if and only if $\pi_1(srg(S^3, \mathfrak{k}, 1/n)) = 1$ implies $n = 0$.

15.6 Proposition. *Torus knots have Property P.*

Proof. By 3.28,

$$\pi_1(srg(S^3, \mathfrak{t}(a, b), 1/n)) = \langle u, v \mid u^a v^{-b}, u^c v^d (u^a (u^c v^d)^{-ab})^n \rangle,$$
$$(|a|, |b| > 1, ad + bc = 1)$$

and we have to show that this group is trivial only for $n = 0$. By adding the relation u^a we obtain the factor group

$$\langle u, v \mid u^a, v^b, (u^c v^d)^{1-nab} \rangle = \langle \tilde{u}, \tilde{v} \mid \tilde{u}^a, \tilde{v}^b, (\tilde{u}\tilde{v})^{1-nab} \rangle$$

with $\tilde{u} = u^c, \tilde{v} = v^d$. For $n \neq 0$ this is a non-trivial triangle group, see [ZVC 1980, pg. 124], since $|1 - nab| > 1$. □

In the proof of Property P for twist knots we construct homeomorphisms onto the so-called *Coxeter groups* and in the next lemma we convince ourselves that the Coxeter groups are non-trivial.

15.7 Lemma ([Coxeter 1962]). *The Coxeter group* $\mathfrak{A} = \langle x, y \mid x^3, y^s, (xy)^3, (x^{-1}y)^r \rangle$ *is not trivial when,* $s, r \geqq 3$.

Proof. We assume that $3 \leqq s \leqq r$; otherwise replace x by x^{-1}. Introducing $t = xy$ and eliminating y gives

$$\mathfrak{A} = \langle t, x \mid x^3, t^3, (x^{-1}t)^s, (xt)^r \rangle .$$

We choose a complex number c such that

$$c\bar{c} = 4\cos^2\frac{\pi}{r} \quad \text{and} \quad c + \bar{c} = 4\cos^2\frac{\pi}{s} - 4\cos^2\frac{\pi}{r} - 1 .$$

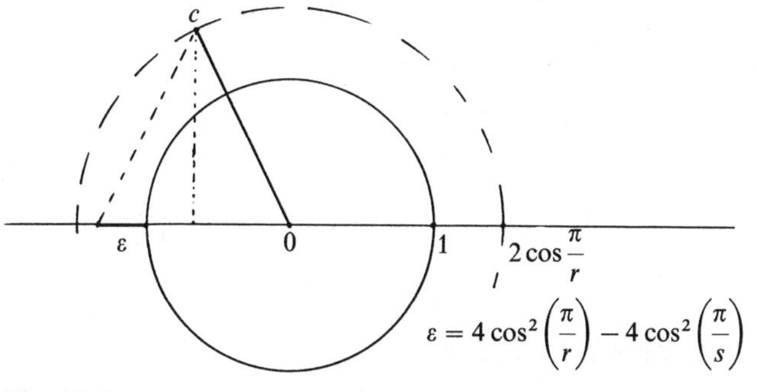

Fig. 15.5

This choice is always possible if $r \geqq s \geqq 3$, see Figure 15.5. Let X, T be the following 3×3 matrices:

$$X = \begin{pmatrix} 1 & c & c+1 \\ 0 & -1 & -1 \\ 0 & 1 & 0 \end{pmatrix}, \quad T = \begin{pmatrix} 0 & 0 & 1 \\ 1+\bar{c} & 1 & 1 \\ -1 & 0 & -1 \end{pmatrix}.$$

Then

$$XT = \begin{pmatrix} c\bar{c}-1 & c & 0 \\ -\bar{c} & -1 & 0 \\ 1+\bar{c} & 1 & 1 \end{pmatrix}, \quad X^{-1}T = \begin{pmatrix} c+\bar{c}+c\bar{c} & c+1 & c+1 \\ -1 & 0 & -1 \\ -\bar{c} & -1 & 0 \end{pmatrix}.$$

The characteristic polynomials are $p_X = 1 - \lambda^3$, $p_T = 1 - \lambda^3$,

$$p_{XT} = 1 - (c\bar{c}-1)\lambda + (c\bar{c}-1)\lambda^2 - \lambda^3 = -(\lambda - 1)(\lambda^2 - 2\lambda\cos\frac{2\pi}{r} + 1),$$

$$\begin{aligned} p_{X^{-1}T} &= 1-(c+\bar{c}+c\bar{c})\lambda+(c+\bar{c}+c\bar{c})\lambda^2-\lambda^3 \\ &= -(\lambda-1)(\lambda^2-2\lambda\cos\frac{2\pi}{s}+1). \end{aligned}$$

The roots of the last two polynomials are 1, $e^{\pm 2\pi i/r}$ and 1, $e^{\pm 2\pi i/s}$, respectively. This proves that $p_{XT}|\lambda^r-1$ and $p_{X^{-1}T}|\lambda^s-1$. Since a matrix annihilates its characteristic polynomial, see [v. d. Waerden 1955, § 118], it follows that X^3, T^3, $(XT)^r$ and $(X^{-1}T)^s$ are unit matrices. So X, T generate a non-trivial homomorphic image of $\mathfrak{A}$. □

15.8 Theorem (Bing-Martin). *The twist knot* $\mathfrak{d}_n$, $n \neq 0, -1$, *has Property P. In particular, the figure-eight knot* $4_1 = \mathfrak{d}_2$ *has Property P.*

Proof. We use the presentation 15.3 (a). Define $w = a^{-1}b$ and replace b by aw. Then

(1) $\quad \mathfrak{T}_{2m} = \langle a, w \,|\, (aw)^{-1} w^m a w^{-m} a w^m a^{-1} w^{-m} \rangle$

and, introducing $k = aw^{-m}$ instead of $a = kw^m$,

(2) $\quad \mathfrak{T}_{2m} = \langle k, w \,|\, w^{-2m-1} k^{-1} w^m k^2 w^m k^{-1} \rangle$.

The longitude is

$$\begin{aligned} \ell &= (a^{-1}b)^m a^{-1} (a^{-1}b)^{-m} b^m (a^{-1}b)^{-1-m} a^{-1} (a^{-1}b)^m a^{2-m} \\ &= w^m a^{-1} w^{-m} (aw)^m w^{-1-m} a^{-1} w^m a^{2-m}. \end{aligned}$$

By the relation in the presentation (1),

$$aw = w^m a w^{-m} \cdot a \cdot (w^m a w^{-m})^{-1};$$

hence, $(aw)^m = w^m a w^{-m} \cdot a^m \cdot w^m a^{-1} w^{-m}$ and

$$\ell = a^m w^m a^{-1} w^{-1-2m} a^{-1} w^m a^{2-m}.$$

Since ℓ commutes with the meridian a, the surgery on $\mathfrak{d}_{2m}$ gives an additional relation

$$(w^m a^{-1} w^{-1-2m} a^{-1} w^m a^2)^n a = 1,$$

or,

$$(k^{-1} w^{-1-3m} k^{-1} w^m k w^m k w^m)^n k w^m = 1.$$

Therefore

(3) $$\begin{aligned} \mathfrak{H}_{2m,n} &= \pi_1(srg(S^3, \mathfrak{d}_{2m}, 1/n)) \\ &= \langle k, w \,|\, kw^{2m+1} k \cdot (w^m k^2 w^m)^{-1}, (k^{-1} w^{-1-3m} k^{-1} w^m k w^m k w^m)^n k w^m \rangle. \end{aligned}$$

We introduce in $\mathfrak{H}_{2m,n}$ the additional relations $w^{3m+1} = 1$, $k^3 = 1$. Then the relations of (3) turn into $(kw^{-m})^3 = 1$, $(kw^m)^{3n+1} = 1$, and the factor group has the presentation

$$\langle u, v \mid u^{3m+1}, v^3, (uv^{-1})^3, (uv)^{3n+1}\rangle.$$

By Lemma 15.7 this Coxeter group is not trivial if $m \neq 0$ and $|3n+1| > 2$. The latter condition is violated only if $n = 0, -1$.

For $n = -1$ the group is

$$\mathfrak{H}_{2m,-1} = \langle k, w \mid kw^{2m+1}k(w^m k^2 w^m)^{-1}, w^{-m}k^{-1}w^{-m}kw^{3m+1}k\rangle.$$

By $w \mapsto y^{-6}$, $k \mapsto yx^{-1}$, we obtain an epimorphism of $\mathfrak{H}_{2m,-1}$ to the triangle group $\langle x, y \mid y^{6m+1}, x^3, (xy)^2\rangle$ since

$$yx^{-1}y^{-12m-6}yx^{-1}y^{6m}xy^{-1}xy^{-1}y^{6m} = yx^{-1}y^{-3}x^{-1}y^{-1}xy^{-1}xy^{-1}y^{-1} =$$
$$= yx^{-1}y^{-2}x^2y^{-1}xy^{-2} = yx^{-1}y^{-1}x^2y^{-2} = yx^{-1}y^{-1}x^{-1}y^{-2} = yy^{-1} = 1,$$

and

$$y^{6m}xy^{-1}y^{6m}yx^{-1}y^{-18m-6}yx^{-1} = y^{-1}xy^{-1}x^{-1}y^{-2}x^{-1} = y^{-1}x^2y^{-1}x^{-1} = 1.$$

The triangle group is not trivial, see [ZVC 1980, p. 124].

Next we consider $\mathfrak{d}_{2m-1}$. To achieve a more convenient presentation we define $w = a^{-1}b$ and replace a by bw^{-1}. Further we substitute $k = bw^{-m}$ and eliminate b by kw^m. Then we obtain from 15.3 (b)

$$\mathfrak{T}_{2m-1} = \langle b, w \mid b^{-1}w^m b^{-1}w^{-m}bw^{-1+m}bw^{-m}\rangle$$
$$= \langle k, w \mid w^{-1}k^{-2}w^{-m}kw^{-1+2m}k\rangle.$$

The longitude is

$$\ell = w^{-m}bw^{2m-1}bw^{-m}b^{-2} = w^{-m}kw^{3m-1}kw^{-m}k^{-1}w^{-m}k^{-1}.$$

Thus

(4) $$\mathfrak{H}_{2m-1,n} = \pi_1(srg(S^3, \mathfrak{d}_{2m-1}, 1/n))$$
$$= \langle k, w \mid w^{-m}k^{-2}w^{-m}kw^{2m-1}k,$$
$$(w^{-m}kw^{3m-1}kw^{-m}k^{-1}w^{-m}k^{-1})^n kw^m\rangle.$$

Adding the relations w^{3m-1}, k^3 we obtain the group

$$\langle k, w \mid k^3, w^{3m-1}, (kw^{-m})^3, (k^{-1}w^{-1})^{3n-1}\rangle$$
$$= \langle x, y \mid x^{3m-1}, y^3, (xy^{-1})^3, (xy)^{3n-1}\rangle$$

with $x = w^{-m}$, $y = k^{-1}$.

By Lemma 15.7 this group is not trivial unless $|3m-1| \leqq 2$ or $|3n-1| \leqq 2$, that is, unless $m, n = 0, 1$. For $m = 0$ we get the trivial knot and this case was excluded. In the case $m = 1$ the knot $\mathfrak{d}_1$ is the trefoil which has Property P by 15.6. So we may assume that $|3m-1| \geqq 3$. For $n = 1$

$$\mathfrak{H}_{2m-1,1} = \langle k, w \mid w^{-m}k^{-2}w^{-m}kw^{2m-1}k, w^{-m}kw^{3m-1}kw^{-m}k^{-1}\rangle.$$

The relations are the equations

$$kw^{2m-1}k = w^m k^2 w^m, \; w^m k w^m = kw^{3m-1}k.$$

We rewrite the first as

$$(w^m k w^m) w^{-2m} (w^m k w^m) = kw^{2m-1}k$$

and substitute the second in this expression to obtain

$$kw^{-2m}k = w^{1-4m}, \; kw^{3m-1}k = w^m k w^m.$$

Put $k = xw^m$. Now the defining equations are

$$xw^{-m}xw^{-m} = w^{1-6m}, \; w^{1-6m} = w^{-m}xw^{-m}x^{-1}w^{-m}xw^{-m}.$$

Substituting the first in the second we obtain

$$w^{1-6m} = (xw^{-m})^2, \; x^3 = (xw^{-m})^2.$$

Hence the non-trivial triangle group $\langle x, w \mid x^3, w^{6m-1}, (xw)^2\rangle$ is a homomorphic image of $\mathfrak{H}_{2m-1,1}$. □

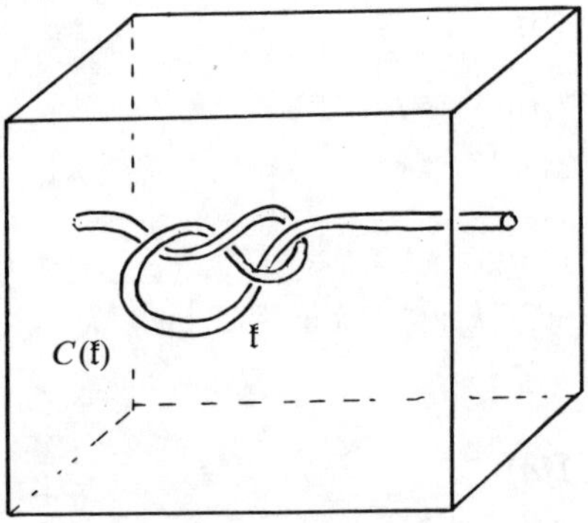

Fig. 15.6

Next we establish Property P for product knots. It is now convenient to use a new view of the knot complement: one looks at the complement $C(\mathfrak{k})$ of a regular neighbourhood of the knot $\mathfrak{k}$ from the centre of a ball in the regular neighbourhood. Now $C(\mathfrak{k})$ looks like a ball with a knotted hole. Following [Bing-Martin 1971] we say that the complement of $\mathfrak{k}$ is a *cube with a* $\mathfrak{k}$*-knotted hole* or, simply, a cube with a (knotted) hole, see Figure 15.6. A cube with an unknotted hole is a solid torus. Suppose that W is a regular neighbourhood of a knot $\mathfrak{h}$ and $C(\mathfrak{k})$ a knotted hole, associated to the knot $\mathfrak{k}$, such that $C(\mathfrak{k}) \subset W$ and $C(\mathfrak{k}) \cap \partial W = \partial C(\mathfrak{k}) \cap \partial W$ is an annulus, then $\overline{(S^3 - W)} \cup C(\mathfrak{k})$ is the complement of $\mathfrak{k} \# \mathfrak{h}$, if the annulus is meridional with respect to $\mathfrak{h}$ and $\mathfrak{k}$, Figure 15.8.

15.9 Lemma. *Let V be a homotopy solid torus, that is a 3-manifold with boundary a torus and infinite cyclic fundamental group. Suppose that K is a cube with a knotted hole in the interior of V. Then there is a homotopy 3-ball $B \subset V$ such that $K \subset B$. (B is a compact 3-manifold bounded by a sphere with trivial fundamental group).*

Proof. $\pi_1 V \cong \mathbb{Z}$ implies, as follows from the loop theorem (Appendix B5), that there is a disk $D \subset V$ with $D \cap \partial V = \partial D$ and ∂D is not null-homologous on ∂V. By general position arguments we may assume that $D \cap \partial K$ consists of mutually disjoint simple closed curves and that, after suitable simplifications, each component of $D \cap \partial K$ is not homotopic to 0 on ∂K. Let γ be an innermost curve of the intersection on D and let D_0 be the subdisk of D bounded by γ. As K is a knotted cube, $\pi_1 \partial K \to \pi_1 K$ is injective; hence, $D_0 \subset \overline{V - K}$. By adding a regular neighbourhood of D_0 to K we obtain $B \supset K$, $\partial B = S^2$. So we may assume $D \cap \partial K = \emptyset$. Let U be a regular neighbourhood of D in V. Now $\overline{V - U}$ is a homotopy 3-ball containing K. □

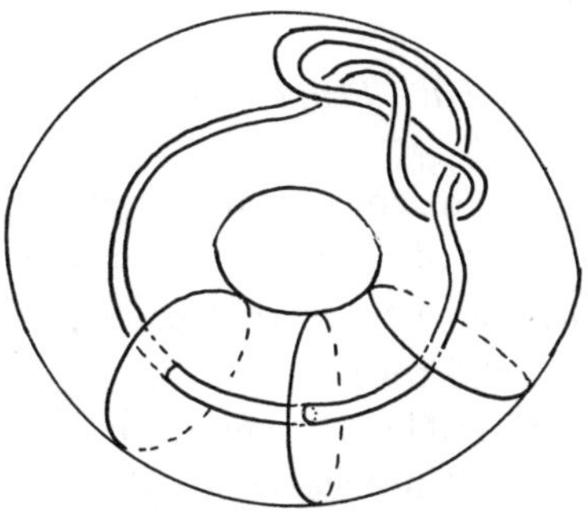

Fig. 15.7

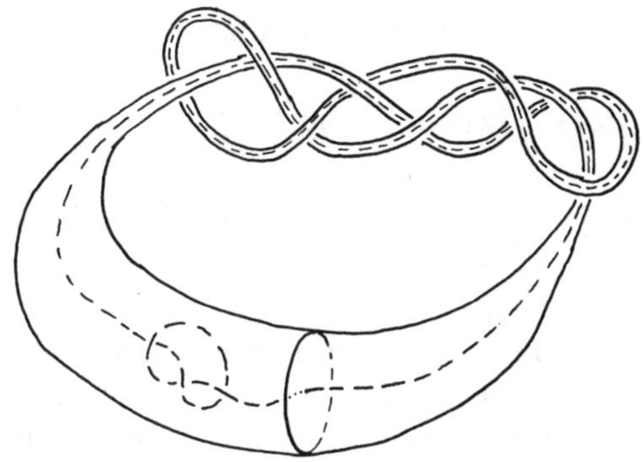

Fig. 15.8

15.10 Lemma. *Let V_1, V_2 be solid tori, $V_2 \subset \mathring{V}_1$ such that*

(a) there is a meridional disk of V_1 whose intersection with V_2 is a meridional disk of V_2 and

(b) V_2 is not parallel to V_1, see Figure 15.7.

Then the result of removing V_2 from V_1 and sewing it back differently is not a homotopy solid torus.

Proof. Let F be a meridional disk of V_1, that is $F \cap \partial V_1 = \partial F \not\simeq 0$ on ∂V_1, which intersects V_2 in a meridional disk of V_2. Let N be a regular neighbourhood of F in V_1. Then $K_1 = \overline{V_1 - (N \cup V_2)}$ is a cube with a knotted hole since V_2 is not parallel to V_1. Now $K_1 \cap \partial V_1$ is an annulus. We push this annulus slightly into the interior of V_1 and call the resulting cube with a knotted hole $\tilde{K}_1$.

Suppose that V_2 is removed from V_1 and a solid torus V_2' is sewn back differently; denote the resulting manifold by V_1'. Assume that V_1' is a homotopy solid torus. Then there is a disk $D \subset V_1'$ such that $D \cap \partial V_1' = D \cap \partial V_1 = \partial D$ and $\partial D \not\simeq 0$ on $\partial V_1'$. Since, by Lemma 15.9, $\tilde{K}_1$ lies in a homotopy 3-ball contained in V_1' we may assume that $D \cap \tilde{K}_1 = \emptyset$ and, hence, that also $D \cap K_1 = \emptyset$. This implies that $D \cap \partial V_1 = D \cap \partial V_1'$ is parallel to $F \cap \partial V_1$. Moreover, suppose that D and $\partial V_2' = \partial V_2$ are in general position so that $D \cap \partial V_2' = D \cap \partial V_2$ is a finite collection of mutually disjoint simple closed curves, none of which is contractible on ∂V_2. Now the complement of K_1 in $\overline{V_1 - V_2}$ is the Cartesian product of an annulus and an interval, and the boundary contains an annulus on ∂V_1 and another on $\partial V_2 = \partial V_2'$. Therefore each curve of $D \cap \partial V_2'$ is homotopic on $\partial V_2'$ to the simple closed curve $F \cap \partial V_2$ which is meridional in V_2. Let γ be an innermost curve of $D \cap \partial V_2'$ and $D_0 \subset D$ the disk bounded by γ, $D_0 \cap \partial V_2' = \gamma$. Since γ is a meridian of V_2 it is not a meridian of V_2'; hence, $D_0 \subset \overline{V_1' - V_2'} = \overline{V_1 - V_2}$, in fact $D_0 \subset \overline{V_1 - (V_2 - K_1)} \cong (S^1 \times I) \times I$ which contradicts the fact that γ represents the generator of the annulus $S^1 \times I$. Consequently, $D \cap \partial V_2 = \emptyset$ and $\partial D \simeq 0$ in $\overline{V_1 - (V_2 \cup K_1)}$, contradicting the fact that ∂D also represents the generator of $\pi_1(S^1 \times I)$. This shows that V_1' is not a homotopy solid torus. □

15.11 Theorem (Bing-Martin, Noga). *Product knots have Property P.*

Proof. Let $\mathfrak{k} = \mathfrak{k}_1 \# \mathfrak{k}_2$ be a product knot in S^3. We use the construction shown in Figure 7.2 and 15.8. Let V be a regular neighbourhood of $\mathfrak{k}_2$. Replace a segment of $\mathfrak{k}_2$ by $\mathfrak{k}_1$ such that $\mathfrak{k}_1 \subset V$, see Figure 15.8. Notice that $\overline{S^3 - V}$ is a cube with a $\mathfrak{k}_2$-knotted hole and, hence, it is not a homotopy solid torus.

Now let N be a regular neighbourhood of $\mathfrak{k}$, $N \subset \mathring{V}$, and let M result from S^3 by removing N and sewing it back differently. Lemma 15.10 implies that ∂V does not bound a homotopy solid torus in M. Thus $\pi_1 M$ is the free product of two groups amalgamated over $\pi_1(\partial V) \cong \mathbb{Z} \oplus \mathbb{Z}$ and therefore $\pi_1 M$ is not trivial. □

15.12 Theorem (Bing-Martin). *Let $\mathfrak{k} \subset S^3$ be a satellite, $\hat{\mathfrak{k}}$ its companion and $(\tilde{V}, \tilde{\mathfrak{k}})$ its pattern. Denote by m, ℓ; $\hat{m}$, $\hat{\ell}$; $\tilde{m}$, $\tilde{\ell}$ the meridian and longitude of $\mathfrak{k}$, $\hat{\mathfrak{k}}$, $\tilde{\mathfrak{k}}$ and by m_V, ℓ_V those of $\tilde{V}$. Then $\mathfrak{k}$ has Property P if*

(a) $\hat{\mathfrak{k}}$ has Property P, or

(b) $\tilde{\mathfrak{k}}$ has Property P and $q = lk(m_V, \tilde{\mathfrak{k}}) \neq 0$.

Proof of 15.12 (a). (The proof for (b) will be given in 15.15.)

There is a homeomorphism $h: \tilde{V} \to \hat{V}$, $h(\tilde{\mathfrak{k}}) = \mathfrak{k}$. Let $\tilde{U}$ be a regular neighbourhood of $\tilde{\mathfrak{k}}$ in $\tilde{V}$. We remove $h(\tilde{U})$ from S^3 and sew it back differently to obtain a manifold M. If $\hat{\mathfrak{k}}$ is the trivial knot then h can be extended to a homeomorphism $S^3 \to S^3$ and it follows from assumption (a) that M is not simply connected.

So we may assume that $\hat{\mathfrak{k}}$ is a non-trivial knot. If the result W of a surgery on $\tilde{\mathfrak{k}}$ in $\tilde{V}$ does not yield a homotopy solid torus, then $h(\partial \tilde{V})$ divides M into two manifolds which are not homotopy solid tori. Since $\hat{\mathfrak{k}}$ is a knot, $\pi_1(h(\partial\tilde{V})) \to \pi_1\overline{(M-W)} = \pi_1\overline{(S^3 - h(\tilde{V}))}$ is injective. When $\pi_1(h(\partial\tilde{V})) \to \pi_1 W$ has non-trivial kernel, there is a disk $D \subset W$, $\partial D \subset \partial W$, $\partial D \not\simeq 0$ in ∂W such that $X = \overline{W - U(D)}$ is bounded by a sphere, $U(D)$ being a regular neighbourhood of D in W. Now X cannot be a homotopy ball because W is not a homotopy solid torus. Therefore $\pi_1 M \neq 1$. If $\pi_1(h(\partial\tilde{V})) \to \pi_1 W$ is injective, $\pi_1 M$ is a free product with an amalgamation over $\pi_1(h(\partial\tilde{V})) \cong \mathbb{Z}^2$, hence non-trivial.

Finally, suppose that $\hat{\mathfrak{k}}$ is non-trivial and the sewing back of $h(\tilde{U})$ in $h(\tilde{V})$ yields a homotopy solid torus W. Then a meridian of W can be presented in the form $ph(m_V) + qh(\ell_V)$ where p, q are relatively prime intergers. From $h(\ell_V) \sim 0$ in $\overline{S^3 - h(\tilde{V})}$ it follows that $H_1(M)$ is isomorphic to $\mathbb{Z}_{|p|}$ or $\mathbb{Z}$ (for $p = 0$). To see that $|p| \neq 1$, we perform the surgery on $\tilde{\mathfrak{k}}$ in $\tilde{V}$ which transforms $\tilde{V}$ into the manifold $\tilde{V}' = h^{-1}(W)$. (The new meridian defining the surgery represents $m_V^p \ell_V^q \in \pi_1(\partial\tilde{V})$.) Now $\tilde{V}' \cup \overline{S^3 - \tilde{V}}$ is obtained from S^3 by surgery on $\tilde{\mathfrak{k}}$. Since $\ell_V \simeq 1$ in $\overline{S^3 - \tilde{V}}$ the relation $m_V^p \ell_V^q \simeq 1$ is equivalent to $m_V^p \simeq 1$, and $|p| = 1$ implies that $\tilde{V}' \cup \overline{S^3 - \tilde{V}}$ is a homotopy sphere. Thus $|p| \neq 1$ because $\tilde{\mathfrak{k}}$ has Property P. □

15.13 Remark. The knot $h(\tilde{\mathfrak{k}})$ is a satellite and $(\tilde{V}, \tilde{\mathfrak{k}})$ is the pattern of $h(\tilde{\mathfrak{k}})$. The condition $h(\ell_V) \sim 0$ in $C(\hat{\mathfrak{k}})$ ensures that the mapping h does not unknot $\tilde{\mathfrak{k}}$; this could be done, for instance, with the twist knots $\mathfrak{d}_n$, $n \neq 0, -1$ when h removes the twists. As an example, using Definition of twisted double knots in E 9.6 and Theorem 15.8, we obtain

15.14 Corollary. *Double knots with q twists, $q \neq 0, -1$ have Property P.* □

15.15 *Proof of 15.12 (b).* We consider surgery along the knot $h(\tilde{\mathfrak{k}})$. Replace a tubular neighbourhood $\tilde{U} \subset \tilde{V}$ of $\tilde{\mathfrak{k}}$ by another solid torus $\tilde{T}$ using a gluing map $f\colon \partial\tilde{T} \to \partial\tilde{U}$. The manifold obtained is

$$M = \overline{(S^3 - \hat{V})} \cup_h (\overline{(\tilde{V} - \tilde{U})} \cup_f \tilde{T}).$$

Define $\hat{C} = C(\hat{\mathfrak{k}}) = \overline{S^3 - \hat{V}}$ and $X = \overline{(\tilde{V} - \tilde{U})} \cup_f \tilde{T}$. Since $\hat{\mathfrak{k}}$ is non-trivial the inclusion $\partial\hat{C} \to \hat{C}$ defines a monomorphism $\pi_1(\partial\hat{C}) \to \pi_1\hat{C}$. If $\partial X \to X$ induces also a monomorphism $\pi_1(\partial X) \to \pi_1 X$, then $\pi_1 M$ is a free product with amalgamated subgroup $\pi_1(\partial\hat{C}) = \pi_1(\partial X) \cong \mathbb{Z}^2$.

Therefore, if M is a homotopy sphere, $\ker(\pi_1(\partial X) \to \pi_1 X) \neq 1$. By the loop theorem (Appendix B 5), there is a simple closed curve $v \subset \partial X$, v not contractible on ∂X, which bounds a disk D in X, $\partial D \cap \partial X = \partial D = v$. Then $v \simeq \hat{m}^a \hat{\ell}^b$ on ∂X with $gcd(a, b) = 1$ and $a \geqq 0$.

If W is a regular neighbourhood of D in X, the boundary of $\overline{X - W}$ is a

2-sphere S^2 and

$$M = (C \cup W) \cup \overline{(X - W)}, \; S^2 = (C \cup W) \cap \overline{(X - W)}.$$

Therefore $\pi_1 M = \pi_1 (C \cup W) * \pi_1 \overline{(X - W)}$. Thus $\pi_1 (C \cup W) = 1$. Since by assumption (b) $\hat{\mathfrak{k}}$ has Property P, it follows that v must be the meridian $\hat{m}$ of $\hat{\mathfrak{k}}$ and $b = 0$ and $a = 1$; moreover, $\hat{m} = h(m_V)$ if m_V in a meridian of $\tilde{V}$.

Let $\tilde{m}$ be a meridian of the tubular neighbourhood $\tilde{U}$ of $\tilde{\mathfrak{k}}$. Then, for the meridian m_V of $\tilde{V}$

(5) $\quad m_V \sim q\tilde{m}$ in $\overline{\tilde{V} - \tilde{U}}$.

Moreover, there is a longitude $\tilde{\ell}$ of $\tilde{U}$ such that

(6) $\quad \tilde{\ell} \sim q\ell_V$ in $\overline{\tilde{V} - \tilde{U}}$.

$\tilde{\ell}$ can be obtained from an arbitrary longitude $\tilde{\ell}_0$ as follows. There is a 2-chain c_2 in $\overline{\tilde{V} - \tilde{U}}$ – the intersection of $\overline{\tilde{V} - \tilde{U}}$ with a projecting cylinder of $\tilde{\ell}_0$ – such that

$$\partial c_2 = \tilde{\ell}_0 + \alpha\tilde{m} + \beta m_V + \gamma\ell_V.$$

Now

$$q = lk(m_V, \tilde{\mathfrak{k}}) = lk(m_V, \tilde{\ell}_0) = lk(m_V, -\alpha\tilde{m} - \beta m_V - \gamma\ell_V) = -\gamma,$$

$$\text{and} \quad \tilde{\ell} = \tilde{\ell}_0 + (\alpha + \beta q)\tilde{m} = \tilde{\ell}_0 + \alpha\tilde{m} + \beta m_V \sim q\ell_V \quad \text{in } \overline{\tilde{V} - \tilde{U}}.$$

(See E 15.1.)

For a meridian m_T of $\tilde{T}$ one has

(7) $\quad m_T \sim \varrho\tilde{m} + \sigma\tilde{\ell}$ on $\partial\tilde{T} = \partial\tilde{U}$, $gcd(\varrho, \sigma) = 1$.

Here $\varrho = \pm 1$ since we assume that the surgery along $\mathfrak{k}$ gives a homotopy sphere. The disk D is bounded by m_V. We assume that D is in general position with respect to $\partial\tilde{T}$ and that $D \cap \partial\tilde{T}$ does not contain curves that are contractible on $\partial\tilde{T}$; otherwise D can be altered to get fewer components of $\partial\tilde{T} \cap D$. This implies that $\partial\tilde{T} \cap D$ is a collection of disjoint meridians of $\tilde{T}$ and that $\partial\tilde{T} \cap D$ consists of parallel meridional disks, and, thus, for a suitable p

(8) $\quad m_V \sim p m_T$ in $\overline{\tilde{V} - \tilde{U}}$.

ℓ_V and $\tilde{m}$ are a basis of $H_1\overline{(\tilde{V} - \tilde{U})} \cong \mathbb{Z}^2$. The formulas (5)–(8) imply

$$q\tilde{m} \sim m_V \sim p m_T \sim p\varrho\tilde{m} + p\sigma\tilde{\ell};$$

thus

$$p\sigma = 0, \; p\varrho = q, \text{ that is, since } q \neq 0, \; \sigma = 0, \; \varrho = \pm 1, \; p = \pm q.$$

So we may assume that $\varrho = 1$ and $p = q$. But then $m_T = \tilde{m}$. □

15.16 Proposition. *(a) (p, q)-cable knots with $2 \leq |p|, |q|$ have Property P.*

(b) Let $\mathfrak{k}$ be a $(\pm 1, q)$-cable knot about the non-trivial knot $\hat{\mathfrak{k}}$. If $|q| \geq 3$ then $\mathfrak{k}$ has Property P. (For the notation see 15.20.)

Proof. The first statement is a consequence of 15.6 and 15.12(a). For the proof of the second assertion, we consider the pattern $(\tilde{V}, \tilde{\mathfrak{k}})$. It can be constructed as follows. Let ϱ denote the rotation of the unit disk $\tilde{B}$ through the angle $2\pi/q$. Choose in $\tilde{B}$ a small disk $\tilde{D}_1$ with centre $\tilde{x}_1$ such that $\tilde{D}_1$ is disjoint to all its images $\varrho^j \tilde{D}_1$, $1 \leqq j \leqq q-1$. Then the pattern consists of the solid torus $\tilde{B} \times I/\varrho$, that is, the points $(\tilde{x}, 1)$ and $(\varrho(\tilde{x}), 0)$ are identified, and the knot $\tilde{\mathfrak{k}}$ consists of the arcs $\varrho^j(\tilde{x}_1) \times I$, $0 \leqq j < q$. A regular neighbourhood $\tilde{U}$ of $\tilde{\mathfrak{k}}$ is $\bigcup_{j=0}^{q-1} (\varrho^j(\tilde{D}_1) \times I)$, see Figure 15.9.

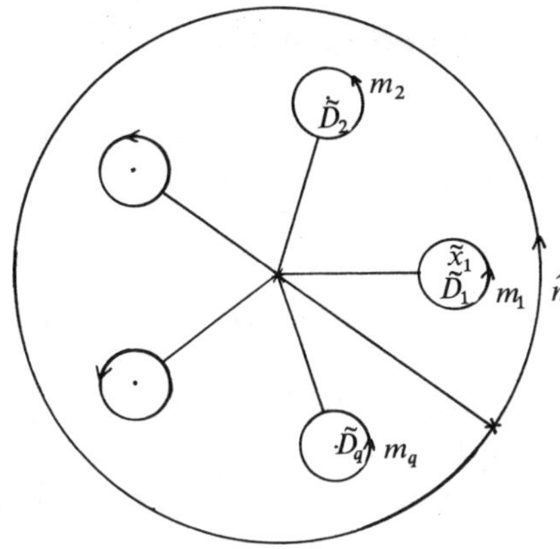

Fig. 15.9

Then $C(\mathfrak{k}) = C(\hat{\mathfrak{k}}) \cup X$, $C(\hat{\mathfrak{k}}) \cap X = \partial C(\mathfrak{k}) \subset \partial X$, where X is homeomorphic to the pattern described above. Let $\hat{m}$ be a meridian of $\hat{\mathfrak{k}}$ ($\hat{m}$ is the image of $\partial \tilde{B}$) and $m_1, \ldots, m_q$ meridians of $\mathfrak{k}$ corresponding to $\partial \tilde{D}_1, \ldots, \partial \tilde{D}_q$. Let $\hat{\ell}$ be the longitude of $\hat{\mathfrak{k}}$. Then

$$\begin{aligned}\pi_1 X &= \langle \hat{m}, m_1, \ldots, m_q, \hat{\ell} \mid \hat{m}^{-1} \cdot m_1 \ldots m_q, [\hat{m}, \hat{\ell}], \\ &\qquad \hat{\ell}^{-1} m_j \hat{\ell} \cdot m_{j+1}^{-1} \ (1 \leqq j < q), \hat{\ell}^{-1} m_q \hat{\ell} \cdot (\hat{m}^{-1} m_1 \hat{m})^{-1} \rangle \\ &= \langle \hat{m}, m_1, \hat{\ell} \mid \hat{m}^{-1}(m_1 \hat{\ell}^{-1})^q \hat{\ell}^q, \hat{\ell}^{-q} m_1 \hat{\ell}^q (\hat{m}^{-1} m_1 \hat{m})^{-1}, [\hat{m}, \hat{\ell}] \rangle \\ &= \langle m_1, \hat{\ell} \mid [m_1, (m_1 \hat{\ell}^{-1})^q], [(m_1 \hat{\ell}^{-1})^q, \hat{\ell}] \rangle .\end{aligned}$$

Note that $m_1^{-q}(m_1 \hat{\ell}^{-1})^q$ is a longitude of $\mathfrak{k}$.

Next we attach a solid torus W to $C(\mathfrak{k})$ such that the result is a homotopy sphere. The meridian of W has the form $m_1^{1-nq}(m_1 \hat{\ell}^{-1})^{nq}$. If we show that $n = 0$ the assertion (b) is proved. We have

$$\pi_1(X \cup W) = \langle m_1, \hat{\ell} \mid [m_1, (m_1 \hat{\ell}^{-1})^q], [(m_1 \hat{\ell}^{-1})^q, \hat{\ell}], m_1^{1-nq}(m_1 \hat{\ell}^{-1})^{nq} \rangle$$

and $\pi_1 M = \pi_1(C(\hat{\mathfrak{k}}) \cup X \cup W)$ is obtained by adding the relation $\hat{m} = (m_1 \hat{\ell}^{-1})^q \hat{\ell}^q = 1$. Put $v = m_1 \hat{\ell}^{-1}$ and replace $\hat{\ell}$ by $v^{-1} m_1$ to get

$$\pi_1 M = \langle m_1, v \mid [m_1, v^q], [v^q, v^{-1} m_1], m_1^{1-nq} v^{nq}, v^q (v^{-1} m_1)^q \rangle.$$

Adding the relator $v^q = 1$ we obtain the group

$$\langle m_1 v \mid m_1^{1-nq}, v^q, (v^{-1} m_1)^q \rangle$$

which must be trivial. Since $|q| \geqq 3$ this implies $1 - nq = \pm 1$, see [ZVC 1980, pg. 122]; hence, $n = 0$. □

C Prime Knots and their Manifolds and Groups

In this section we discuss to what extent the group of a prime knot determines the knot manifold and the knot. For this we need some concepts from 3-dimensional topology.

15.17 Definition. (a) A submanifold $N \subset M$ is *properly embedded* if $\partial N = N \cap \partial M$.

(b) Let A be an annulus and $a \subset A$ a non-separating properly embedded arc, a so-called *spanning arc. A mapping* $f\colon (A, \partial A) \to (M, \partial M)$, M a 3-manifold, is called *essential* if $f_{\#}\colon \pi_1 A \to \pi_1 M$ is injective and if there is no relative homotopy $f_t\colon (A, \partial A) \to (M, \partial M)$ with $f_0 = f, f_1(a) \subset \partial M$. The *annulus* $f(A)$ is also called *essential.*

(c) The properly embedded surface $F \subset M$ is *boundary parallel* if there is an embedding $g\colon F \times I \to M$ such that $g(F \times \{0\}) = F$ and $g((F \times \{1\} \cup (\partial F \times I)) \subset \partial M$.

An annulus A is boundary parallel if and only if there is a solid torus $V \subset M$ such that $A \subset \partial V$, $\partial V - A \subset \partial M$ and the core of A is a longitude of V. (Proof as exercise E 15.2).

To illustrate the notion of an essential annulus we give another characterizing condition and discuss two important examples.

15.18 Lemma. *Let A be a properly embedded incompressible annulus in a knot manifold C. Then A is boundary parallel if and only if the inclusion $i\colon A \to C$ is not essential.*

Proof. Clearly, if A is boundary parallel, then i is homotopic rel ∂A to a map into ∂C, thus not essential. If i is not essential then, since A is incompressible, that is $i_{\#}\colon \pi_1 A \to \pi_1 C$ is injective, a spanning arc a of A is homotopic to an arc $b \subset \partial C$. We may assume that b intersects ∂A transversally, intersects the two components of ∂A alternatingly and is simple; the last assumption is not restrictive since any arc on a torus with different endpoints can be deformed into a simple arc by a homotopy keeping the endpoints fixed. The annulus A decomposes C into two 3-manifolds C_1, C_2: $C = C_1 \cup C_2$, $A = C_1 \cap C_2$, such that $\partial C_j = (\partial C_j \cap \partial C) \cup A$ $(j = 1, 2)$ is a torus. We have

$$\pi_1 C = \pi_1 C_1 *_{\pi_1 A} \pi_1 C_2 .$$

If $b \subset \partial C_j$ for some j then $b \cup a \subset \partial C_j$ is nullhomotopic in C_j, thus bounds a disk in C_j. This implies that C_j is a solid torus and ∂A consists of two longitudes of C_j. By the remark above, A is boundary parallel.

If b intersects ∂A more than twice then $b = b_1 \dots b_n$ where b_j and b_{j+1} are alternately contained in C_1 and C_2. The boundary points of each b_j are on different components of ∂A. By adding segments $c_j \subset A$ we obtain

$$b \simeq (b_1 c_1)(c_1^{-1} b_2 c_2)(c_2^{-1} \dots (c_{n-1}^{-1} b_n)$$

such that $ab_1 c_1, c_1^{-1} b_2 c_2, \dots, c_{n-1}^{-1} b_n$ are closed and are contained in ∂C_1 or ∂C_2. If in some C_j, $ab_1 c_1$ is contractible or homotopic to a power c^p of the core of A we replace b by $b_1 c_1 c^{-p}$ and argue as above. If one of the $c_{k-1}^{-1} b_k c_k$ (c_n is the trivial arc) is contractible or homotopic to a curve in A in some C_j it can be eliminated and we obtain a simpler arc, taking the role of b. Thus we may assume that none of $ab_1 c_1$, $c_1^{-1} b_2 c_2, \dots, c_{n-1}^{-1} b_n$ is homotopic to a curve in A. Then the above product determines a word in $\pi_1 C$ where consecutive factors are alternatingly in $\pi_1 C_1$ and $\pi_1 C_2$ and none is in the amalgamated subgroup; thus the word has length n and represents a non-trivial element of $\pi_1 C$, see [ZVC 1980, 2.3.3], contradicting $ab \simeq 0$ in C. □

15.19 Proposition. *Let $C(\mathfrak{k}) = C(\mathfrak{k}_1) \cup C(\mathfrak{k}_2)$ be the knot manifold of a product* knot $\mathfrak{k} = \mathfrak{k}_1 \# \mathfrak{k}_2$ *with $A = C(\mathfrak{k}_1) \cap C(\mathfrak{k}_2)$ an annulus. If $\mathfrak{k}_1$ and $\mathfrak{k}_2$ are non-trivial, then A is essential in $C(\mathfrak{k})$.*

Proof. Otherwise, by 15.18, A and one of the annuli of $\partial C(\mathfrak{k})$, defined by ∂A bounds a solid torus which must be one of the $C(\mathfrak{k}_j)$. This is impossible since a knot with complement a solid torus is trivial, see 3.17. □

15.20 Example (Cable knots). Let W be a solid torus in S^3 with core $\mathfrak{k}$, m and ℓ meridian and longitude of W where $\ell \sim 0$ in $C(\mathfrak{k}) = \overline{S^3 - W}$. A simple closed curve $\mathfrak{c} \subset \partial W$, $\mathfrak{c} \sim pm + q\ell$ on ∂W, $|q| \geqq 2$ is called a *(p, q)-cable knot with core* $\mathfrak{k}$. (Compare 2.9.) Another description is the following: *Let V be a solid torus with core* $\mathfrak{k}$ in S^3 *and $C(\mathfrak{k}) \cap V = (\partial C(\mathfrak{k})) \cap (\partial V) = A$ an annulus the core of which is of type (p, q) on $\partial C(\mathfrak{k})$. Then $\partial(C(\mathfrak{k}) \cup V)$ is a torus and $U(\mathfrak{c}) = \overline{S^3 - (C(\mathfrak{k}) \cup V)}$ is a solid torus the core of which is a (p, q)-cable knot $\mathfrak{c}$ with core* $\mathfrak{k}$, see Figure 15.10. This follows from the fact that the core of $\overline{S^3 - (C(\mathfrak{k}) \cup V)}$ is isotopic in W to the core of A.

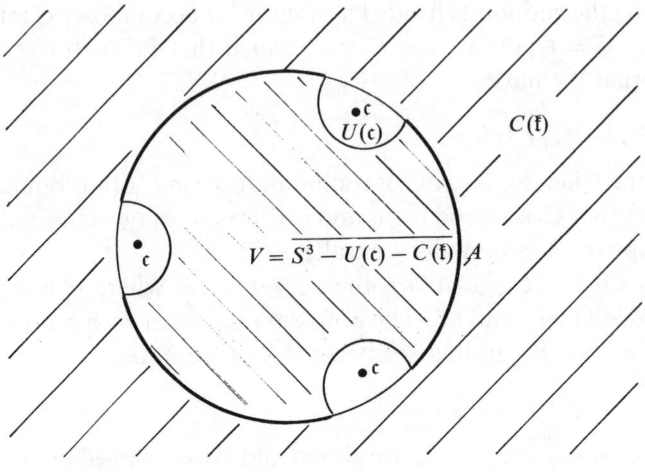

Fig. 15.10

We will see that the annuli of 15.19, 20 are the prototypes of essential annuli in knot manifolds. To see this we need the following consequence of Feustel's Theorem [Feustel 1976, Theorem 10], which we cannot prove here.

15.21 Theorem (Feustel). *Let M and N be compact, connected, irreducible, boundary irreducible 3-manifolds. Suppose that ∂M is a torus and that M does not admit an essential embedding of an annulus. If $\varphi\colon \pi_1 M \to \pi_1 N$ is an isomorphism then there is a homeomorphism $h\colon M \to N$ with $h_\# = \varphi$.* □

We prove in 15.36 the following result of [Simon 1980′], without using Feustel's Theorem 15.21.

15.22 Theorem (Simon). *There are at most two cable knots with the same knot group.*

A consequence of 15.21 and 15.22 is the following

15.23 Corollary ([Simon 1980′]). *The complements of at most two prime knot types can have the same group.*

Proof. Suppose $\mathfrak{k}_0, \mathfrak{k}_1, \mathfrak{k}_2$ are prime knots whose groups are isomorphic to $\pi_1(C(\mathfrak{k}_0))$. If $\mathfrak{k}_j$ is not a cable knot then $C(\mathfrak{k}_j)$ does not contain essential annuli, see 15.26. Now Theorem 15.21 implies that the $C(\mathfrak{k}_j), j = 0, 1\ 2$ are homeomorphic. So we may assume that $\mathfrak{k}_0$, $\mathfrak{k}_1$, $\mathfrak{k}_2$ are cable knots and the assertion follows from Theorem 15.22. □

It remains to prove 15.22 and 15.26.

15.24 Lemma ([Simon 1973, Lemma 2.1]). *Let C, W_0, W_1 be knot manifolds, $C = W_0 \cup (A \times [0,1]) \cup W_1$, $W_0 \cap ((A \times [0,1]) \cup W_1) = A \times \{0\}$, $W_1 \cap (W_0 \cup (A \times [0,1])) = A \times \{1\}$, where A is an annulus, see Figure 15.11. Then either the components of ∂A bound disks in ∂C or the components bound meridional disks in $\overline{S^3 - C}$ and the groups $\pi_1 C$, $\pi_1 W_0$, $\pi_1 W_1$ are the normal closures of the images of $\pi_1 A$.*

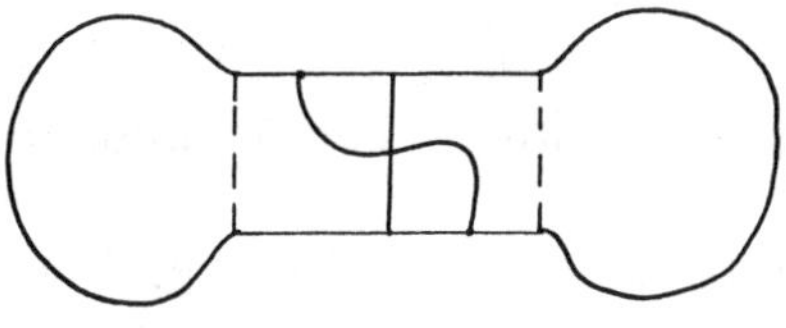

Fig. 15.11

Proof. Since W_0 is a knot manifold, $\overline{S^3 - W_0}$ is a solid torus containing W_1. By Lemma 15.9, there is a 3-ball B such that $W_1 \subset \mathring{B} \subset B \subset S^3 - W_0$; so the 2-sphere $S^2 = \partial B$ separates W_0 and W_1 and therefore must intersect $A \times (0,1)$. We may assume that $S^2 \cap (\partial A \times (0,1))$ consists of a finite number of pairwise disjoint curves $\sigma_1, \ldots, \sigma_r$. If σ_i is innermost in S^2 then σ_i bounds a disk $D \subset S^2$ such that either $D \subset \overline{S^3 - C}$ or $D \subset A \times (0,1)$.

If σ_i also bounds a disk $E \subset \partial A \times (0,1)$ – which it necessarily does in the latter case – then the intersection line σ_i can be removed by an isotopy which replaces S^2 by a sphere S_1^2 still separating W_0 and W_1. It is impossible that all curves σ_j can be eliminated in this way, as $\partial A \times \{0\}$ and $\partial A \times \{1\}$ are separated by S^2. There exists a curve $\gamma \subset S^2 \cap (\partial A \times (0,1))$ bounding a disk in $\overline{S^3 - C}$ which is not trivial on $\partial A \times (0,1)$. So there are non-trivial curves γ_1, γ_2 on each component of $\partial A \times (0,1)$ bounding disks in $\overline{S^3 - C}$. They are isotopic on $\partial A \times [0,1]$ to the components of $\partial A \times \{0\}$, respectively, which, hence bound disks in $\overline{S^3 - C}$. □

15.25 Lemma. *Let C be a knot manifold in S^3, $C = W_0 \cup W_1$, where W_0 is a cube with a hole, W_1 is a solid torus, and $A = W_0 \cap W_1 = \partial W_0 \cap \partial W_1$ is an annulus. Denote by $\mathfrak{k}_C$ the core of the solid torus $\overline{S^3 - C}$. Assume that $\pi_1 A \to \pi_1 W_1$ is not surjective. Then $\mathfrak{k}_C$ is a (p,q)-cable of the core $\mathfrak{k}_0$ of $\overline{S^3 - W_0}$, $|q| \geqq 2$. If W_0 is a solid torus then $\mathfrak{k}_C$ is a torus knot.*

Proof. We may write $C = W_0 \cup_f W_1$ where f is an attaching map on A. This mapping f is uniquely determined up to isotopy by the choice of the core of A on ∂W_1, since $\overline{S^3 - C}$ is a solid torus. Hence, the core $\mathfrak{k}_C$ of $\overline{S^3 - C}$ is by 15.20 the (p,q)-cable of $\mathfrak{k}_0$. When $|q| = 1$ the homomorphism $\pi_1 A \to \pi_1 W_1$ is surjective. If $q = 0$, $\mathfrak{k}_C$ is trivial and C is not a knot manifold. In the special case where W_0 is a solid torus, $\mathfrak{k}_0$ is trivial and $\mathfrak{k}_C$ a torus knot. □

15.26 Lemma. *Let C be a knot manifold in S^3, and let A be an annulus in C, $\partial A \subset \partial C$, with the following properties:*
(a) the components of ∂A do not bound disks in ∂C;
(b) A is not boundary parallel in C.
Then a core of $\overline{S^3 - C}$ is either a product knot or a cable knot isotopic to each of the components of ∂A.

Proof. By (a), the components of ∂A bound annuli in ∂C. Hence, there are submanifolds X_1 and X_2 bounded by tori such that $C = X_1 \cup X_2$, $X_1 \cap X_2 = A$, and, by Alexander's theorem (Appendix B2) X_i is either a knot manifold or a solid torus.

If X_1 and X_2 are both knot manifolds then, by Lemma 15.24, each component of ∂A bounds a meridional disk in $\overline{S^3 - C}$, and a core of $\overline{S^3 - C}$ is, by Definition 2.7, a product knot.

Suppose now that X_2 is a solid torus. There is an annulus $B \subset \partial C$ satisfying $A \cup B = \partial X_2$. If the homomorphism $\pi_1 A \to \pi_1 X_2$, induced by the inclusion, is not surjective, then, by Lemma 15.25, a core of $\overline{S^3 - C}$ is a cable knot. Now assume that $\pi_1 A \to \pi_1 X_2$ is surjective. Then a simple arc $\beta \subset B$ which leads from one component of ∂B to the other can be extended by a simple arc $\alpha \subset A$ to a simple closed curve $\mu \subset \partial X_2$ which is 0-homotopic in the solid torus X_2 and, hence, a meridian of X_2. Since μ intersects each component of ∂A in exactly one point it follows that A is boundary parallel, contradicting hypothesis (b). □

15.27 Lemma. *Let $\mathfrak{k}_1$ and $\mathfrak{k}$ be cable knots with complements $C(\mathfrak{k}_1)$ and $C(\mathfrak{k})$. Assume that $\mathfrak{k}$ is not a torus knot and that*

$$C(\mathfrak{k}) = X \cup V,\ A = X \cap V = \partial X \cap \partial V,$$

where X is a knot manifold, V a solid torus, and A an annulus. Let $\mathfrak{k}$ be a (p, q)-curve on a torus parallel to the boundary of $\overline{S^3 - X}$, $|q| \geqq 2$.

If $\pi_1 C(\mathfrak{k}_1) \cong \pi_1 C(\mathfrak{k})$ then there is a homotopy equivalence $f\colon C(\mathfrak{k}_1) \to C(\mathfrak{k})$ such that $f^{-1}(A)$ is an annulus.

15.28 Remark. We do not use the fact that $\mathfrak{k}_1$ and $\mathfrak{k}$ are cable knots in the first part of the proof including Claim 15.30. By Theorem 6.1 we know that $\mathfrak{k}_1$ is not a torus knot. The proof of Lemma 15.27 is quite long and of a technical nature. However, some of the intermediate steps have already been done in Chapter 5. The proof of Lemma 15.27 will be finished in 15.34.

Proof. Since $C(\mathfrak{k}_1)$ and $C(\mathfrak{k})$ are $K(\pi, 1)$-spaces any isomorphism $\pi_1 C(\mathfrak{k}_1) \xrightarrow{\cong} \pi_1 C(\mathfrak{k})$ is induced by a homotopy equivalence $g\colon C(\mathfrak{k}_1) \to C(\mathfrak{k})$, [Spanier 1966, 7.6.24], [Stöcker-Zieschang 1985]. We may assume that g has the following properties:

(1) g is transversal with respect to A, that is, there is a neighbourhood $g^{-1}(A) \times [-1,1] \subset C(\mathfrak{k}_1)$ of $g^{-1}(A) = g^{-1}(A) \times \{0\}$ and a neighbourhood $A \times [-1,1]$ of A such that $g(x,t) = (g(x),t)$ for $x \in g^{-1}(A)$, $t \in [-1,1]$.

(2) $g^{-1}(A)$ is a compact 2-manifold, properly imbedded and two-sided in $C(\mathfrak{k}_1)$.

(3) If A' is a component of $g^{-1}(A)$ then

$$\ker\left(\pi_j(A') \xrightarrow{g_\#} \pi_j(C(\mathfrak{k}))\right) = 0 \quad \text{for } j = 1, 2.$$

These properties can be obtained by arguments similar to those used in 5.3; see also [Waldhausen 1968, pg. 60].

Choose among all homotopy equivalences g that have the above properties one with minimal number n of components A_i of $g^{-1}(A)$.

15.29 Claim. *Each A_i is an annulus which separates $C(\mathfrak{k}_1)$ into a solid torus V_i and a knot manifold W_i, and $\pi_1 A_i \to \pi_1 V_i$ is not surjective.*

Proof. Since $\pi_2 C(\mathfrak{k}_1) = 0$ it follows from (3) that $\pi_2 A_i = 0$; moreover, since $\pi_1 A_i \to \pi_1 C(\mathfrak{k}_1)$ is injective and $g_\#\colon \pi_1 C(\mathfrak{k}_1) \to \pi_1 C(\mathfrak{k})$ is an isomorphism, $(g\,|\,A_i)_\#\colon \pi_1 A_i \to \pi_1 A$ is injective. This shows that $\pi_1 A_i$ is a subgroup of $\mathbb{Z}$, hence, trivial or isomorphic to $\mathbb{Z}$. Now A_i is an orientable compact connected surface and therefore either a disk, a sphere or an annulus. We will show that A_i is an annulus. $\pi_2 A_i = 0$ excludes spheres. If A_i is a disk then $\partial A_i \subset \partial C(\mathfrak{k}_1)$ is contractible in $C(\mathfrak{k}_1)$. If ∂A_i is not nullhomotopic on $\partial C(\mathfrak{k}_1)$ then $C(\mathfrak{k}_1)$ is a solid torus and $\mathfrak{k}_1$ is the trivial knot. But then $\pi_1 C(\mathfrak{k}_1) \cong \mathbb{Z}$ and this implies that $\mathfrak{k}$ is also unknotted, contradicting the assumption that it is a (p,q)-cable knot. Therefore ∂A_i also bounds a disk $D \subset \partial C(\mathfrak{k}_1)$ and $D \cup A_i$ is a 2-sphere that bounds a ball B in $C(\mathfrak{k}_1)$. Now $Q = \overline{C(\mathfrak{k}_1) - B}$ is homeomorphic to $C(\mathfrak{k}_1)$, $g\,|\,Q\colon Q \to C(\mathfrak{k})$ satisfies the conditions (1)–(3), and $(g\,|\,Q)^{-1}(A)$ has at most $(n-1)$ components. This proves that there is also a mapping $g'\colon C(\mathfrak{k}_1) \to C(\mathfrak{k})$ satisfying (1)–(3) with less components in $g'^{-1}(A)$ than in $g^{-1}(A)$, contradicting the minimality of n.

Thus we have proved that A_i is an annulus. Because of (3), ∂A_i is not nullhomotopic on $\partial C(\mathfrak{k}_1)$ and decomposes $\partial C(\mathfrak{k}_1)$ into two annuli, while A_i decomposes $C(\mathfrak{k}_1)$ into two submanifolds W_i, V_i which are bounded by tori and, thus, are either knot manifolds or solid tori.

If V_i and W_i are knot manifolds then, by 15.24, $\pi_1 C(\mathfrak{k}_1)/\overline{\pi_1 A_i} = 1$, where $\overline{\pi_1 A_i}$ denotes the normal closure of $\pi_1 A_i$ in $\pi_1 C(\mathfrak{k}_1)$, and so, since g is a homotopy equivalence,

$$\pi_1 C(\mathfrak{k})/\overline{\pi_1 A} = 1\,.$$

This implies that each 1-cycle of $C(\mathfrak{k})$ is homologous to a cycle of A, that is $H_1(A) \to H_1(C(\mathfrak{k}))$ is surjective and, hence, an isomorphism. From the exact sequence

$$\begin{array}{ccccc} \dots \to H_1(A) & \to & H_1(C(\mathfrak{k})) & \to & H_1(C(\mathfrak{k}), A) = 0 \\ \wr\| & & \wr\| & & \\ \mathbb{Z} & & \mathbb{Z} & & \\ & t \mapsto \pm pqt & & & \end{array}$$

it follows that $|pq| = 1$, a contradiction. (Prove in exercise E 15.4 that $H_1(A) \to H_1(C(\mathfrak{k}))$ is defined by $t \mapsto \pm pqt$, where t denotes a generator of $\mathbb{Z}$.)

So we may assume that V_i is a solid torus. If $\pi_1 A_i \to \pi_1 V_i$ is surjective, that is $|q| = 1$, then g can be modified homotopically such that A_i disappears, i.e. we can find a neighbourhood U of V_i in $C(\mathfrak{k}_1)$ such that $U \cong A_i \times [-1, 1]$, $A_i \times \{-1\} = V_i \cap \partial C(\mathfrak{k}_1)$, $A_i \times \{0\} = A_i$, $A_i \times [-1, 0] = V_i$, $U \cap g^{-1}(A) = A_i$. Then $Q = \overline{C(\mathfrak{k}_1) - U} \cong C(\mathfrak{k}_1)$ and $g|Q\colon Q \to C(\mathfrak{k})$ is a homotopy equivalence satisfying (1)–(3) and having fewer than n components in $g^{-1}(A)$; this defines a mapping $C(\mathfrak{k}_1) \to C(\mathfrak{k})$ with the same properties, contradicting the choice of g. Therefore $\pi_1 A_i \to \pi_1 V_i$ is not surjective.

W_i is not a solid torus, since $\mathfrak{k}_1$ is not a torus knot. □

15.30 Claim. *$W_1 \subset \dots \subset W_n$, after a suitable enumeration of the annuli A_i.*

Proof. It suffices to show that for any two components A_1, A_2 either $W_1 \subset W_2$ or $W_2 \subset W_1$. Otherwise either (a) $W_2 \subset V_1$ or (b) $V_2 \subset W_1$.

Case (a). By 15.29, W_2 is a knot manifold which can be contracted slightly in order to be contained in the interior of the solid torus V_1. By Lemma 15.9, there is a 3-ball B such that $W_2 \subset \mathring{B} \subset B \subset V_1$; hence $A_2 \subset \partial W_2$ is contractible in $C(\mathfrak{k}_1)$, contradicting (3).

Case (b). Put $Y = W_1 \cap W_2$ and denote by $\mathfrak{k}_{W_i}$ the core of $\overline{S^3 - W_i}$. Since ∂Y consists of the two annuli A_1, A_2 and two parallel annuli on $\partial C(\mathfrak{k}_1)$ and since S^3 does not contain Klein bottles it follows that ∂Y is a torus. $W_2 = Y \cup V_1$, $A_1 = Y \cap V_1 = \partial Y \cap \partial V_1$ and $\pi_1 A_1 \to \pi_1 V_1$ is not surjective. When Y is a solid torus then $\mathfrak{k}_{W_2}$ is a non-trivial torus knot. When Y is a knot manifold then, by Lemma 15.25, $\mathfrak{k}_{W_2}$ is a cable about the core $\mathfrak{k}_Y$ of Y. The knot $\mathfrak{k}_{W_2}$ is non-trivial and parallel to each component of ∂A_1, see Lemma 15.26.

Since $A_2 = V_2 \cap W_2$ and $\pi_1 A_2 \to \pi_1 V_2$ is not surjective, Lemma 15.25 implies also that $C(\mathfrak{k}_1) = V_2 \cup W_2$ is the complement of an (iterated) cable knot of type (p', q') with $|q'| > 1$ about $\mathfrak{k}_{W_2}$. This implies for the genera that

$$g(\mathfrak{k}_1) \geqq \frac{(|q'|-1)(|p'|-1)}{2} + |q'| g(\mathfrak{k}_{W_2}), \tag{4}$$

see 2.10. However, $\mathfrak{k}_1$ is parallel to a component of ∂A_2, by 15.26, which bounds, together with a component of ∂A_1, an annulus; hence, the knots $\mathfrak{k}_1$ and $\mathfrak{k}_{W_2}$ are equivalent, contradicting (4) since $|q'| \geqq 2$. □

15.31 Claim. *$(W_n \cap V_1, A_1, \dots, A_n)$ is homeomorphic to $(A_1 \times [1, n], A_1 \times \{1\}, \dots, A_1 \times \{n\})$.*

Proof. $V_i \cap W_{i+1}$ is bounded by four annuli, hence by a torus. This shows that $V_i \cap W_{i+1}$ is either a knot manifold or a solid torus contained in the solid torus V_i. The first case is impossible by Lemma 15.9, since A_i is incompressible in $C(\mathfrak{k}_1)$. Now

$$V_i = (V_i \cap W_{i+1}) \cup V_{i+1}, \; (V_i \cap W_{i+1}) \cap V_{i+1} = A_{i+1}$$

where V_i, V_{i+1}, $V_i \cap W_{i+1}$ are solid tori and A_{i+1} is incompressible. Therefore

$$\mathfrak{Z} \cong \pi_1 V_i = \pi_1 (V_i \cap W_{i+1}) *_{\pi_1 A_{i+1}} \pi_1 V_{i+1}.$$

Since, by 15.29, $\pi_1 A_{i+1}$ is a proper subgroup of $\pi_1 V_{i+1}$ it follows that $\pi_1 A_{i+1} = \pi_1 (V_i \cap W_{i+1})$. Since ∂A_i is parallel to ∂A_{i+1} which contains the generator of $\pi_1 A_{i+1}$ it follows that $\pi_1 A_i$ also generates $\pi_1 (V_i \cap W_{i+1})$. Moreover, $A_i \cup A_{i+1} \subset \partial (V_i \cap W_{i+1})$ and $A_i \cap A_{i+1} = \emptyset$.

This means that

$$(V_i \cap W_{i+1}, A_i, A_{i+1}) \cong (A_i \times [i, i+1], A_1 \times \{i\}, A_1 \times \{i+1\}). \quad \square$$

15.32 Claim. *$g|A_i$ is homotopic to a homeomorphism.*

Proof. In the following commutative diagram all groups are isomorphic to $\mathbb{Z}$.

$$\begin{array}{ccc} H_1(A_i) & \xrightarrow{j_{i*}} & H_1(C(\mathfrak{k}_1)) \\ {\scriptstyle (g|A_i)_*}\downarrow & & \cong \downarrow {\scriptstyle g_*} \\ H_1(A) & \xrightarrow[j_*]{} & H_1(C(\mathfrak{k})) \end{array}$$

where $j_i: A_i \hookrightarrow C(\mathfrak{k}_1)$ and $j: A \hookrightarrow C(\mathfrak{k})$ are the inclusions. As g is a homotopy equivalence, g_* is an isomorphism.

By Claim 15.29, A_i decomposes $C(\mathfrak{k}_1)$ into a knot manifold W_i and a solid torus V_i: $C(\mathfrak{k}_1) = W_i \cup V_i$, $A_i = W_i \cap V_i$, and by Lemma 15.26 a component b_i of ∂A_i is isotopic to $\mathfrak{k}_1$. The component b_i is, for suitable p', q', $|q'| \geqq 2$, a (p', q')-curve on $\partial\overline{(S^3 - W_i)}$. For generators of the cyclic groups of the above diagram and for some $r \in \mathbb{Z}$ we obtain

$$\begin{array}{ccc} z_i & \xmapsto{j_{i*}} & t'^{\pm|p'q'|} \\ \downarrow & & \downarrow {\scriptstyle g_*} \\ z^r & \longmapsto & t^{\pm r|pq|}; \end{array}$$

here we used the fact that a component of ∂A is a (p, q)-curve on $\partial\overline{(S^3 - X)}$ (for the notations, see 15.27). Since g_* is an isomorphism, $g_*(t') = t$; hence, $|p'q'| = \pm r|pq|$. This implies that pq divides $p'q'$.

By a deep theorem of Schubert [1953, pg. 253, Satz 5], $\mathfrak{k}_1$ determines the core $\mathfrak{k}_{W_i}$ and the numbers p', q'. Hence, since g is a homotopy equivalence, we may apply the above argument with the roles of $\mathfrak{k}_1$ and $\mathfrak{k}$ interchanged and obtain that $p'q'$ divides pq; thus $|r| = 1$.

This implies that $g|A_i: A_i \to A$ can be deformed into a homeomorphism. Since A_i and A are two-sided, g is homotopic to a mapping g' such that $g'|A_i: A_i \to A$ is a homeomorphism and g' coincides with g outside a small regular neigbourhood $U(A_i) \cong A_i \times [0,1]$ of A_i. □

For the following, we assume that g has the property of 15.32 for all A_i.

15.33 Claim. *$g^{-1}(A) \neq \emptyset$. In fact, the number of components of $g^{-1}(A)$ is odd.*

Proof. By 15.31, V_n contains a core v_1 of V_1. Let δ be a path in V_1 from $x_1 \in A_1$ to v_1. Then $\pi_1 W_1$ and $\delta v_1 \delta^{-1}$ generate the group $\pi_1(C(\mathfrak{k}_1)) = \pi_1(W_1, x_1) *_{\pi_1(A_1, x_1)} \pi_1(V_1, x_1)$. Since g is transversal with respect to A, it follows that $\mathring{V}_i \cap \mathring{W}_{i+1}$ and $\mathring{V}_{i+1} \cap \mathring{W}_{i+2}$ are mapped to different sides of A; hence, if the number of components of $g^{-1}(A)$ is even, g maps W_1 and V_n – and hence v_1 – both into X or both into V. Since g is a homotopy equivalence, hence $g_\#$ an isomorphism, it follows that $\pi_1 C(\mathfrak{k})$ is isomorphic to a subgroup of $\pi_1 X$ or $\pi_1 V$, in fact, to $\pi_1 X$ or $\pi_1 V$, respectively. In the latter case $\pi_1 C(\mathfrak{k})$ is cyclic; hence, $\mathfrak{k}$ is the trivial knot, contradicting the assumption that $\mathfrak{k}$ is a cable knot. In the first case $\pi_1 C(\mathfrak{k})/\pi_1 X = 1$. This implies that $H_1(X) \to H_1(C(\mathfrak{k}))$ is isomorphic; hence $H_1(C(\mathfrak{k}), X) = 0$ as follows from the exact sequence

$$\begin{array}{ccccccccc} H_1(X) & \to & H_1(C(\mathfrak{k})) & \to & H_1(C(\mathfrak{k}), X) & \to & H_0(X) & \xrightarrow{\cong} & H_0(C(\mathfrak{k})). \\ & & & \searrow\ 0 \nearrow & & \searrow\ 0 \nearrow & & & \end{array}$$

On the other hand by the excision theorem,

$$H_i(C(\mathfrak{k}), X) \cong H_i(V, A)$$

and

$$\begin{array}{ccccccccccc} H_2(V, A) & \to & H_1(A) & \to & H_1(V) & \to & H_1(V, A) & \to & H_0(A) & \xrightarrow{\cong} & H_0(V); \\ & & & z \mapsto t^{\pm pq} & & & & \searrow\ 0 \nearrow & & & \end{array}$$

this implies $H_1(V, A) \cong \mathbb{Z}_{|pq|} \neq 0$. Thus the assumption that the number of components of $g^{-1}(A)$ is even was wrong. □

15.34 Claim. *The number n of components of $g^{-1}(A)$ is 1. (This finishes the proof of Lemma 15.27.)*

Proof. It will be shown that for $n > 1$ the mapping g can be homotopically deformed to reduce the number of components of $g^{-1}(A)$ by 2, contradicting the minimality of n; thus, by Claim 15.33, $n = 1$. The proof applies a variation of Stallings' technique of *bindung ties* from [Stallings 1962] which was used in the original proof of Theorem 5.1, but in a more general setting.

Choose $x \in A$, $x_i \in A_i$ for $1 \leqq i \leqq n$ such that $g(x_i) = x$. There is a path α in $C(\mathfrak{k}_1)$ from x_1 to x_n with the following properties:

(1) $g(\alpha) \simeq 0$ in $C(\mathfrak{k})$;

(2) i) $\alpha = \alpha_1 \dots \alpha_r$ where

ii) $\mathring{\alpha}_j \subset C(\mathfrak{k}_1) - \bigcup_{i=1}^{n} A_i$, $\partial\alpha_j \in \bigcup_{i=1}^{n} A_i$ and

iii) α_j is either a loop with some x_i as basepoint or a path from x_i to $x_{i\pm 1}$.

A path with these properties can be obtained as follows:
Let β be a path from x_1 to x_n. Then $[g \circ \beta] \in \pi_1(C(\mathfrak{k}), x)$ and, since g_* is an isomorphism, there is a loop $\delta \subset C(\mathfrak{k}_1)$ in the homotopy class $g^{-1}[g \circ \beta] \in \pi_1(C(\mathfrak{k}_1), x_n)$. Then $\alpha = \beta\delta^{-1}$ has property (1). We can choose α transversal to $g^{-1}(A)$ and, since each A_i is connected, intersecting an A_i in x_i.

Assume that α is chosen such that the number r is minimal for all paths with the properties (1, 2). In $\pi_1 C(\mathfrak{k}) = \pi_1 X *_{\pi_1 A} \pi_1 V$,

$$1 = [g \circ \alpha] = [g \circ \alpha_1] \cdots [g \circ \alpha_r].$$

Since $g \circ \alpha_i$ and $g \circ \alpha_{i+1}$ are in different components X, V it follows that there is at least one α_j with $[g \circ \alpha_j] \in \pi_1 A$. A loop α_j from x_i to x_i in $V_i \cap W_{i+1}$ with $[g \circ \alpha_j] \in \pi_1 A$ can be pushed into $V_{i-1} \cap W_i$, contradicting the minimality of r. Therefore α_j connects x_i and x_{i+1}, for a suitable i.

By 15.31, $V_i \cap W_{i+1} \cong A_1 \times [i, i+1]$ and $A_i = A_1 \times \{i\}$, $A_{i+1} = A_1 \times \{i+1\}$, and therefore α_j is homotopic to an arc $\beta \subset \partial(V_i \cap W_{i+1})$ connecting x_i and x_{i+1}. Let γ be an arc in $\partial(V_i \cap W_{i+1})$ such that $\beta \cap \gamma$ is a meridian of the solid torus $V_i \cap W_{i+1}$ and bounds a disk D. We may assume that $\partial D \cap A_i$ and $\partial D \cap A_{i+1}$ are arcs connecting the boundary components, see Figure 15.12.

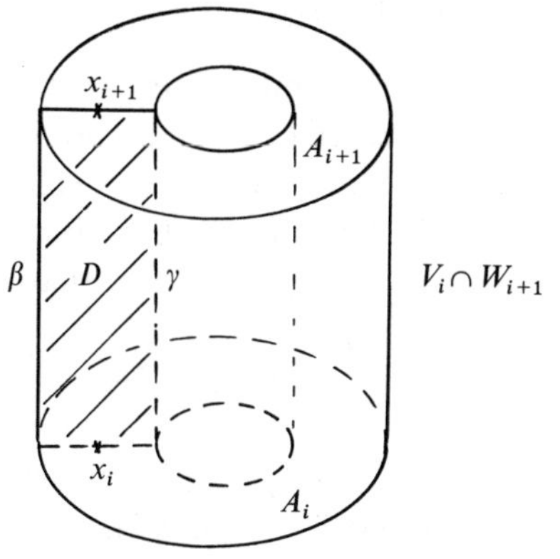

Fig. 15.12

Let B^3 be the closure of the complement of a regular neighbourhood of $A_i \cup D \cup A_{i+1}$ in $V_i \cap W_{i+1}$; then B^3 is a 3-ball.

In the following we keep g fixed outside of a regular neighbourhood of $V_i \cap W_{i+1}$. Since $[g \circ \beta] \in \pi_1 A$ and $g \circ \beta \simeq g \circ \gamma$, g may be deformed such that $g(\beta) \subset A$ and $g(\gamma) \subset A$. Since A is incompressible in $C(\mathfrak{k})$ and $\pi_2 C(\mathfrak{k}) = 0$, g can be altered such that g maps D and also the small neighbourhood into A, that is, $g(V_i \cap W_{i+1} - B^3) \subset A$. Finally since $\pi_3 C(\mathfrak{k}) = 0$, we obtain $g(B^3) \subset A$; thus $g(V_i \cap W_{i+1}) \subset A$, and an additional slight adjustment eliminates both components A_i, A_{i+1} of $g^{-1}(A)$. □

15.35 Lemma. *Let $\mathfrak{k}_1$ and $\mathfrak{k}$ be (p_1, q_1)- and (p, q)-cable knots about the cores $\mathfrak{h}_1$ and $\mathfrak{h}$ where $|q_1|$, $|q| \geqq 2$, and let $C(\mathfrak{k}) = C(\mathfrak{h}) \cup V$, $C(\mathfrak{h}) \cap V = \partial C(\mathfrak{h}) \cap \partial V = A$ an annulus. If $\pi_1 C(\mathfrak{k}_1) \cong \pi_1 C(\mathfrak{k})$ then*

(a) there is a homeomorphism $F\colon C(\mathfrak{h}_1) \to C(\mathfrak{h})$ such that $A_1 = F^{-1}(A)$ defines a cable presentation of $\mathfrak{k}_1$, that is $C(\mathfrak{k}_1) = \overline{C(\mathfrak{k}_1) - C(\mathfrak{h}_1)} \cup C(\mathfrak{h}_1)$, $\overline{C(\mathfrak{k}_1) - C(\mathfrak{h}_1)} \cap C(\mathfrak{h}_1) = \overline{\partial C(\mathfrak{k}_1) - C(\mathfrak{h}_1)} \cap \partial C(\mathfrak{h}_1) = A_1$, and

(b) $|p_1| = |p|$ and $|q_1| = |q|$.

Proof. We may assume that $\mathfrak{h}_1$ and $\mathfrak{h}$ are non-trivial, because otherwise $\mathfrak{k}_1$ and $\mathfrak{k}$ are torus knots and 15.35 follows from 15.5. We have

$$\pi_1 C(\mathfrak{k}) = \pi_1 C(\mathfrak{h}) *_{\pi_1 A} \pi_1 V.$$

Since $\pi_1 A \to \pi_1 V_1$ is not surjective (as $|q| \geqq 2$), the free product with amalgamation is not trivial. By Lemma 15.27, there is a homotopy equivalence $f\colon C(\mathfrak{k}_1) \to C(\mathfrak{k})$ such that $f^{-1}(A) = A_1$ is an annulus. Then A_1 decomposes $C(\mathfrak{k}_1)$ into a knot manifold X_1 and a solid torus V_1:

$$C(\mathfrak{k}_1) = X_1 \cup V_1,\ X_1 \cap V_1 = \partial X_1 \cap \partial V_1 = A_1.$$

For any basepoint $a_1 \in A_1$,

$$\pi_1(C(\mathfrak{k}_1), a_1) = \pi_1(X_1, a_1) *_{\pi_1(A_1, a_1)} \pi_1(V_1, a_1).$$

Since $f^{-1}(A) = A_1$ consists of one component only, one of the groups $f_\#(\pi_1(X_1, a_1))$ and $f_\#(\pi_1(V_1, a_1))$ is contained in $\pi_1(C(\mathfrak{h}), f(a_1))$ and the other in $\pi_1(V, f(a_1))$. By assumption $C(\mathfrak{h})$ and X_1 are knot manifolds, V, V_1 solid tori and $f_\#$ is an isomorphism. From the solution of the word problem in free products with amalgamated subgroups, see [ZVC 1980, 2.3.3], it follows that

$$f_\#(\pi_1(X_1, a_1)) = \pi_1(C(\mathfrak{h}), f(a_1)) \quad \text{and} \quad f_\#(\pi_1(V_1, a_1)) = \pi_1(V, f(a_1)).$$

This implies

(1) $f(X_1) \subset C(\mathfrak{h})$, $f(V_1) \subset V$, and that $(f|X_1)_\#$ and $(f|V_1)_\#$ are isomorphisms and $f|X_1\colon X_1 \to C(\mathfrak{h})$ and $f|V_1\colon V_1 \to V$ are homotopy equivalences because all spaces are $K(\pi, 1)$.

For the proof of (b) we note that $(f|A_1)_\#\colon \pi_1 A_1 \to \pi_1 A$ is also an isomorphism.

Assume that $f|X_1$ is homotopic to a mapping $f_0\colon X_1 \to C(\mathfrak{h})$ such that $f_0(\partial X_1) \subset \partial C(\mathfrak{h})$ and $f_0|\partial A_1 = f|\partial A_1$. Then, by [Waldhausen 1968, Theorem 6.1], see Appendix B7, there is a homotopy $f_t\colon (X_1, \partial X_1) \to (C(\mathfrak{h}), \partial C(\mathfrak{h}))$, $0 \leqq t \leqq 1$ such that f_1 is a homeomorphism; this proves (a).

To prove the above assumption on ∂X_1 we consider $B_1 = \partial X_1 \cap \partial C(\mathfrak{k}_1)$. Now $\partial B_1 = \partial A_1$. We have to show that $f|B_1\colon (B_1, \partial B_1) \to (C(\mathfrak{h}), \partial C(\mathfrak{h}))$ is not essential. Otherwise, by Lemma 15.18 there is a properly imbedded essential annulus $A' \subset C(\mathfrak{h})$ such that $\partial A' = \partial A$. The components of ∂A are (p, q)-curves on $\partial C(\mathfrak{h})$ and $(n, \pm 1)$-curves on $\partial C(\mathrm{k})$ for a suitable n; the last statement is a consequence of the fact that the components of ∂A are isotopic to $\mathfrak{k}$.

Since A' is essential, $C(\mathfrak{h})$ is either the complement of a cable knot or of a product knot, see Lemma 15.26. In the first case the components of $\partial A'$ are isotopic to the knot $\mathfrak{h}$; hence $(n', \pm 1)$-curves on $\partial C(\mathfrak{h})$. In the latter case they are $(\pm 1, 0)$-curves. Both cases contradict the fact $\partial A = \partial A'$ and the assumption $|q| \geqq 2$.

For the proof of (b), let m_1 and m be meridians on the boundaries $\partial V_1, \partial V$ of the regular neighbourhoods V_1, V of $\mathfrak{h}_1, \mathfrak{h}$. In the proof of (a) we saw that there is a homotopy equivalence $f\colon C(\mathfrak{k}_1) \to C(\mathfrak{k})$ with $f(A_1) = A$. Let s_1 be a component of ∂A_1 and $s = f(s_1)$; consider s_1 and s as oriented curves. Then s_1 represents $\pm p_1 m_1$ in $H_1(X_1)$ and s represents $\pm pm$ in $H_1(C(\mathfrak{h}))$. The homotopy equivalence f induces an isomorphism $f_*\colon H_1(X_1) \to H_1(C(\mathfrak{h}))$ and $f_*(p_1 m_1) = pm$; hence, $|p_1| = |p|$.

By (1), $(f|V_1)_\#$ and $(f|A_1)_\#$ are isomorphisms, thus $f_*\colon H_1(V_1, A_1) \to H_1(V, A)$ is an isomorphism. Now $H_1(V_1, A_1) \cong \mathbb{Z}_{|q_1|}$ and $H_1(V, A) \cong \mathbb{Z}_{|q|}$ imply $|q_1| = |q|$. □

15.36 *Proof of Theorem 15.22.* Assume that $\mathfrak{k}_0, \mathfrak{k}_1, \mathfrak{k}_2$ are (p, q)-, (p_1, q_1)-, (p_2, q_2)-cables about $\mathfrak{h}_0, \mathfrak{h}_1, \mathfrak{h}_2$ with the same group. If $\mathfrak{h}_0$ is unknotted then $\mathfrak{k}_0$ is a torus knot and the equivalence of $\mathfrak{k}_0, \mathfrak{k}_1, \mathfrak{k}_2$ is a consequence of 15.5. Now we assume that $\mathfrak{h}_0$, $\mathfrak{h}_1$, $\mathfrak{h}_2$ are knotted. By Lemma 15.35, $C(\mathfrak{h}_i) \cong C(\mathfrak{h}_0)$, $|p_i| = |p|$, $|q_i| = |q|$ for $i = 1, 2$.

Let, for $i = 0, 1, 2$, an essential annulus A_i decompose $C(\mathfrak{k}_i)$ into a knot manifold $C(\mathfrak{h}_i)$ and a solid torus V_i; now the knot $\mathfrak{k}_i$ is parallel to each of the components of ∂A_i. Because of Lemma 15.35 there are homotopy equivalences

$$F_{ij}\colon C(\mathfrak{k}_i) \to C(\mathfrak{k}_j) \quad (i = 0, 1; j = 1, 2)$$

such that

$$\tilde{F}_{ij} = F_{ij}|C(\mathfrak{h}_i)\colon (C(\mathfrak{h}_i), A_i) \to (C(\mathfrak{h}_j), A_j))$$

are homeomorphisms.

It suffices to prove that $\tilde{F}_{01}$, $\tilde{F}_{12}$ or $\tilde{F}_{02} = \tilde{F}_{12} \circ \tilde{F}_{01}$ can be extended to a homeomorphism of S^3, because by [Schubert 1953, pg. 253] cable knots are determined by their cores and winding numbers.

Let (m_i, ℓ_i) be meridian-longitude for $\mathfrak{h}_i$, $i = 0, 1, 2$; assume that they are oriented such that the components of ∂A_i are homologous to $pm_i + q\ell_i$ on $\partial C(\mathfrak{h}_i)$. There are numbers $\alpha, \beta, \gamma, \delta, \varepsilon, \eta \in \{1, -1\}$ and $x, y \in \mathbb{Z}$ such the $\tilde{F}_{ij}|\partial C(\mathfrak{h}_i)$ are given by the following table.

$\tilde{F}_{01}$	$\tilde{F}_{12}$	$\tilde{F}_{02}$
$m_0 \mapsto m_1^{\alpha}\ell_1^{x}$	$m_1 \mapsto m_2^{\gamma}\ell_2^{y}$	$m_0 \mapsto m_2^{\alpha\gamma}\ell_2^{\alpha y+\delta x}$
$\ell_0 \mapsto \ell_1^{\beta}$	$\ell_1 \mapsto \ell_2^{\delta}$	$\ell_0 \mapsto \ell_2^{\beta\delta}$
$m_0^p\ell_0^q \mapsto (m_1^p\ell_1^q)^{\varepsilon}$	$m_1^p\ell_1^q \mapsto (m_2^p\ell_2^q)^{\eta}$	$m_0^p\ell_0^q \mapsto (m_2^p\ell_2^q)^{\varepsilon\eta}$;

the last row is a consequence of the fact that the $\tilde{F}_{ij}$: $A_i \to A_j$ are homeomorphisms.

If some m_i is mapped to $m_j^{\pm 1} = m_j^{\pm 1}\ell^0$ then the homeomorphism $\tilde{F}_{ij}$ can be extended to S^3 and this finishes the proof. Hence, we will show that one of the exponents x, y and $\alpha y + \delta x$ vanishes. Assume that $x \neq 0 \neq y$. Now

$$(m_1^p\ell_1^q)^{\varepsilon} = \tilde{F}_{01}(m_0^p\ell_0^q) = m_1^{\alpha p}\ell_1^{\beta q + xp}$$
$$\Rightarrow \quad \varepsilon p = \alpha p,\ \varepsilon q = \beta q + xp;$$
$$\Rightarrow \quad \varepsilon = \alpha,\ xp = (\alpha - \beta)q.$$

Now $p \neq 0 \neq x$ implies $\alpha \neq \beta$, and $|\alpha| = |\beta| = 1$ gives $\alpha = -\beta$. Therefore $xp = 2\alpha q$ and $x = \dfrac{2\alpha q}{p}$. The same arguments for $\tilde{F}_{12}$ imply that $\delta = -\gamma$ and $y = \dfrac{2\gamma q}{p}$. Therefore

$$\alpha y + \delta x = \alpha\frac{2\gamma q}{p} - \gamma\frac{2\alpha q}{p} = 0. \quad \square$$

D Groups of Product Knots

Next we consider problems similar to those in Part C for product knots. The situation now is in some sense simpler, since product knots have Property P, see 15.11; hence, product knots with homeomorphic complements are of the same type. However, the groups of two product knots of different type may be isomorphic as we have shown in 15.4. We will now prove that there are no other possibilities than those described in Example 15.4.

15.37 Lemma. *Let $\mathfrak{k}_1$ and $\mathfrak{k}_2$ be knots with $\pi_1 C(\mathfrak{k}_1) \cong \pi_1 C(\mathfrak{k}_2)$. Then both knots are prime or both are product knots.*

Proof. Assume that $\mathfrak{k}_2$ is a product knot. Then there is a properly embedded incompressible annulus $A \subset C(\mathfrak{k}_2)$ such that $C(\mathfrak{k}_2) = X' \cup X''$, $A = X' \cap X''$ where X' and X'' are knot manifolds. Since $\pi_n C(\mathfrak{k}_i) = 0$ for $i = 1, 2, n \geqq 2$ there is a homotopy equivalence f: $C(\mathfrak{k}_1) \to C(\mathfrak{k}_2)$. By Claim 15.29, see Remark 15.28, we may assume that the components of $f^{-1}(A)$ are incompressible, properly embedded annuli which are not boundary parallel in $C(\mathfrak{k}_1)$. Now $f^{-1}(A) = \emptyset$ is impossible since, otherwise, $f_\#(\pi_1 C(\mathfrak{k}_1)) \subset \pi_1 X'$ or $f_\#(\pi_1 C(\mathfrak{k}_1)) \subset \pi_1 X''$, contradicting the assumption that $\pi_1 X'$ and $\pi_1 X''$ are proper subgroups of $\pi_1 C(\mathfrak{k}_2)$ and that $f_\#$ is an isomorphism. By Lemma 15.26, $C(\mathfrak{k}_1)$ is the complement of a product knot or a cable knot. In the first case the assertion is proved. In the latter case, $\pi_1 C(\mathfrak{k}_2) = \pi_1 C(\mathfrak{k}_1)$ is the group of a cable knot and, thus, applying the arguments of 15.29 to $C(\mathfrak{k}_2)$ and the inverse homotopy equivalence, it follows that $C(\mathfrak{k}_2)$ is also the complement of a cable knot. Since products knots have Property P (Theorem 15.11), we conclude that $\mathfrak{k}_2$ is a cable knot, contradicting the fact that cable knots are prime, see [Schubert 1953, pg. 250, Satz 4]. □

15.38 Theorem ([Feustel-Whitten 1978]). *Let $\mathfrak{k} = \mathfrak{k}_1 \# \ldots \# \mathfrak{k}_m$ and $\mathfrak{h} = \mathfrak{h}_1 \# \ldots \# \mathfrak{h}_n$ be knots in S^3, where the $\mathfrak{k}_i$ and $\mathfrak{h}_j$ are prime and $n > 1$. If $\pi_1(S^3 - \mathfrak{k}) \cong \pi_1(S^3 - \mathfrak{h})$ then $\mathfrak{k}$ is a product knot, $m = n$ and there is a permutation σ such that $\mathfrak{k}_j$ and $\mathfrak{h}_{\sigma(j)}$ are of the same type.*

Proof. By Lemma 15.37, $\mathfrak{k}$ is also a product knot, i.e. $m > 1$. Let A be a properly embedded annulus in $C(\mathfrak{h}) = X' \cup X''$, $A = X' \cap X''$ where X' and X'' are knot manifolds. As in the proof above we conclude that there is a homotopy equivalence f: $C(\mathfrak{k}) \to C(\mathfrak{h})$ such that $f^{-1}(A)$ consists of disjoint incompressible, properly embedded essential annuli. Let A_1 be a component of $f^{-1}(A)$. In the following commutative diagram all groups are isomorphic to $\mathbb{Z}$.

$$\begin{array}{ccc} H_1(A_1) & \xrightarrow{j_{1*}} & H_1(C(\mathfrak{k}_1)) \\ {\scriptstyle (f|A_1)_*}\downarrow & & \downarrow{\scriptstyle f_*} \\ H_1(A) & \xrightarrow[j_*]{} & H_1(C(\mathfrak{k})); \end{array}$$

where j_1: $A_1 \to C(\mathfrak{k})$, j: $A \to C(\mathfrak{h})$ are the inclusions. As f is a homotypy equivalence, f_* is an isomorphism. Since $C(\mathfrak{k})$ and $C(\mathfrak{h})$ are complements of product knots the components of ∂A_1 and ∂A bound disks in $\overline{S^3 - C(\mathfrak{k})}$ and $\overline{S^3 - C(\mathfrak{h})}$, respectively, see Lemma 15.24. The boundaries of these disks are generators of $H_1(C(\mathfrak{k}))$ and $H_1(C(\mathfrak{h}))$; hence, j_{1*} and j_* are isomorphisms. This proves that

$(f|A_1)_*$ is an isomorphism and, consequently, that $f|A_1\colon A_1 \to A$ is a homotopy equivalence homotopic to a homeomorphism. Since f is tranversal with respect to A, see (1) in the proof of 15.27, there is a neighbourhood $A \times [0, 1) \subset C(\mathfrak{h})$ such that the homotopy $f|A_1$ can be extended to a homotopic deformation of f which is constant outside of $A \times [0, 1)$. By the same arguments as in the proof of 15.34 one concludes that in addition f can be chosen such that $A_1 = f^{-1}(A)$ is connected. The annulus A_1 decomposes $C(\mathfrak{k})$ into two subspaces Y', Y'' of S^3 bounded by tori, which are mapped to X' and X'', respectively: $f(Y') \subset X'$, $f(Y'') \subset X''$. It follows that $(f|Y')_\#$ and $(f|Y'')_\#$ are isomorphisms. This proves that Y' and Y'' are knot manifolds. Therefore $\mathfrak{k} = \mathfrak{k}' \# \mathfrak{k}''$ and $\mathfrak{h} = \mathfrak{h}' \# \mathfrak{h}''$ where $\mathfrak{k}'$ and $\mathfrak{h}'$ have isomorphic groups. This isomorphism maps meridional elements to meridional elements, since they are realized by the components of ∂A_1 and ∂A. The same is true for $\mathfrak{k}''$ and $\mathfrak{h}''$.

Assume that $\mathfrak{h}'$ and, hence, $\mathfrak{k}'$ are prime knots. Then $\partial(C(\mathfrak{k}')) = B_1 \cup A_1$ where B_1 is an annulus. If $f(B_1)$ is essential then there is a properly embedded essential annulus in $C(\mathfrak{k}')$. One has $\partial B_1 = \partial A_1$ and $f(\partial B_1) = \partial A$. Now ∂A bounds meridional disks in $\overline{S^3 - C(\mathfrak{h})}$ and therefore also in $\overline{S^3 - C(\mathfrak{h}')}$; this contradicts the assumption that $\mathfrak{h}'$ is prime. Therefore $f(B_1)$ is not essential and thus $f|B_1$ is homotopic to a mapping with image in $\partial C(\mathfrak{h}')$ – by a homotopy constant on $\partial B_1 = \partial A_1$. This homotopy can be extended to a homotopy of f which is constant on A_1. Finally one obtains a homotopy equivalence $(Y', \partial Y') \to (X', \partial X')$ which preserves meridians. By Corollary 6.5 of [Waldhausen 1968], $Y' \cong X'$, where the homeomorphism maps meridians to meridians and, thus, can be extended to S^3, see 3.15. This proves that $\mathfrak{k}'$ and $\mathfrak{h}'$ are of the same knot type.

Now the theorem follows from the uniqueness of the prime factor decomposition of knots. □

In fact, we have proved more than claimed in Theorem 15.38:

15.39 Proposition. *Under the assumptions of Theorem 15.38, there is a system of pairwise disjoint, properly embedded annuli* $A_1, \ldots, A_{n-1}$ *in* $C(\mathfrak{k})$ *and a homeomorphism* $f\colon C(\mathfrak{k}) \to C(\mathfrak{h})$ *such that* $\{A_1, \ldots, A_{n-1}\}$ *decomposes* $C(\mathfrak{k})$ *into the knot manifolds* $C(\mathfrak{k}_1), \ldots, C(\mathfrak{k}_n)$ *and* $\{f(A_1), \ldots, f(A_{n-1})\}$ *decomposes* $C(\mathfrak{h})$ *into* $C(\mathfrak{h}_{\sigma(1)}), \ldots, C(\mathfrak{h}_{\sigma(n)})$.

Since product knots have Property P, the system of homologous meridians $(\mathfrak{m}(\mathfrak{k}_1), \ldots, \mathfrak{m}(\mathfrak{k}_n))$ *is mapped onto the system of homologous meridians* $(\mathfrak{m}(\mathfrak{h}_{\sigma(1)})^\varepsilon, \ldots, \mathfrak{m}(\mathfrak{h}_{\sigma(n)})^\varepsilon)$, *for a fixed* $\varepsilon \in \{1, -1\}$. □

15.40 Proposition ([Simon 1980′]). *If* $\mathfrak{G}$ *is the group of a knot with n prime factors* $(n \geqq 2)$, *then* $\mathfrak{G}$ *is the group of at most* 2^{n-1} *knots of mutually different knot types. Moreover, when the n prime factors are of mutually different knot types and when each of them is non-invertible and non-amphicheiral, then* $\mathfrak{G}$ *is the group of exactly* 2^{n-1} *knots of mutually different types and of* 2^{n-1} *knot manifolds.*

Proof. By Theorem 3.15, an oriented knot $\mathfrak{k}$ is determined up to isotopy by the peripheral system $(\mathfrak{G}, \mathscr{m}, \ell)$ and we use this system now to denote the knot. Clearly (proof as E 15.5, see also 3.19),

$$-\mathfrak{k} = (\mathfrak{G}, \mathscr{m}, \ell^{-1}),\ \mathfrak{k}^* = (\mathfrak{G}, \mathscr{m}^{-1}, \ell),\ -\mathfrak{k}^* = (\mathfrak{G}, \mathscr{m}^{-1}, \ell^{-1}), \quad \text{and}$$
$$\mathfrak{k}_1 \# \mathfrak{k}_2 = (\mathfrak{G}_1 *_{\mathscr{m}_1 = \mathscr{m}_2} \mathfrak{G}_2, \mathscr{m}_1, \ell_1 \ell_2).$$

Let $\mathfrak{k} = \mathfrak{k}_1 \# \ldots \# \mathfrak{k}_n$, $n \geqq 2$. By 15.11, $\mathfrak{k}$ has Property P; hence, on $\partial C(\mathfrak{k})$ the meridian is uniquely determined up to isotopy and reversing the orientation. It is

$$\begin{aligned}(\mathfrak{G}, \mathscr{m}, \ell) &= (\mathfrak{G}_1, \mathscr{m}_1, \ell_1) \# \ldots \# (\mathfrak{G}_n, \mathscr{m}_n, \ell_n)\\ &= (\mathfrak{G}_1 \underset{\mathscr{m}_1 = \ldots \mathscr{m}_n}{* \ldots *} \mathfrak{G}_n, \mathscr{m}_1, \ell_1 \ell_2 \ldots \ell_n).\end{aligned}$$

Suppose $\mathfrak{h}$ is a knot whose group is isomorphic to $\mathfrak{G}$. Now the above remark and 15.39 imply that

$$\begin{aligned}\mathfrak{h} &= (\mathfrak{G}_1, \mathscr{m}_1^{\varepsilon}, \ell_1^{\delta_1}) \# \ldots \# (\mathfrak{G}_n, \mathscr{m}_n^{\varepsilon}, \ell_n^{\delta_n})\\ &= (\mathfrak{G}_1 \underset{\mathscr{m}_1 = \ldots \mathscr{m}_n}{* \ldots *} \mathfrak{G}_n, \mathscr{m}_1^{\varepsilon}, \ell_1^{\delta_1} \ldots \ell_n^{\delta_n}).\end{aligned}$$

Corresponding to the choices of $\varepsilon, \delta_1, \ldots, \delta_n$ there are 2^{n+1} choices for $\mathfrak{h}$. Therefore $\mathfrak{h}$ represents one of, possible, 2^{n+1} oriented isotopy types and $\frac{1}{4}2^{n+1}$ knot type.

Clearly, this number is attained for knots with the properties mentioned in the second assertion of the proposition. □

If prime knots are indeed determined by their groups, then the hypothesis $n \geqq 2$ in 15.40 is unnecessary.

E History and Sources

The theorem of F. Waldhausen [1967] on sufficiently large irreducible 3-manifolds implies that the peripheral group system determines the knot complement. Then thc question arises to what extent the knot group characterizes the knot type. The difficulty of this problem becomes obvious by the example of J.H.C. Whitehead [1937] of different links with homeomorphic complements (see 15.1). First results were obtain by D. Noga [1967] who proved Property P for product knots and R.H. Bing – J.M. Martin [1971] who showed it for the four-knot, twist knots, product knots again and for some satellites. The Annulus Theorem and the Torus Theorem of C.D. Feustel [1972, 1976], [Cannon-Feustel 1976] gave strong tools to approach the problem of to what extent the group determines the complement, and the complement the knot. The results of

J. Simon [1970, 1973, 1976′, 1980′], W. Whitten [1974] and [Feustel Whitten 1978], K. Johannson [1979] and recent work of Whitten [1985], Culler-Shalen [1985] and C. McA. Gordon-J. Luecke combine to give a positive answer to the question: Is the complement of a prime knot determined by its group?

The status of Property P is according to [Whitten 1985]: At most two knot types have homeomorphic complements. This theorem is based on earlier work of W. P. Thurston, C. McA. Gordon and others mentioned above who showed that at most a finite number of knot types may have the same complements.

F Exercises

E 15.1 Use Lemma 2.11 to prove that $h^{-1}(\ell) = \pm\tilde{\ell}$ satisfies equation (6) in 15.15.

E 15.2 Let M be a 3-manifold, $V \subset M$ a solid torus, $\overline{\partial V \cap \mathring{M}} = A$ an annulus such that the core of A is a longitude of V. Then A is boundary parallel.

E 15.3 Show that both descriptions in 15.20 define the same knot.

E 15.4 Let $\mathfrak{k}$ be a (p, q)-cable knot and let A be an annulus, defining $\mathfrak{k}$ as cable. Then $\mathbb{Z} \cong H_1(A) \to H_1(C(\mathfrak{k})) \cong \mathbb{Z}$ is defined by $t \mapsto \pm pqt$, where t is the generator of $\mathbb{Z}$,

E 15.5 Let $\mathfrak{k} = (\mathfrak{G}, m, \ell)$ and $\mathfrak{k}_i = (\mathfrak{G}_i, m_i, \ell_i)$. Prove that

$-\mathfrak{k} = (\mathfrak{G}, m, \ell^{-1})$, $\mathfrak{k}^* = (\mathfrak{G}, m^{-1}, \ell)$, $-\mathfrak{k}^* = (\mathfrak{G}, m^{-1}, \ell^{-1})$, and

$\mathfrak{k}_1 \# \mathfrak{k}_2 = (\mathfrak{G}_1 *_{m_1 = m_2} \mathfrak{G}_2, m_1, \ell_1\ell_2)$.

Appendix A: Algebraic Theorems

A1 Theorem. *Let Q be a $n \times n$ skew symmetric matrix ($Q = -Q^T$) over the integers $\mathbb{Z}$. Then there is an integral unimodular matrix L such that*

$$L^T Q L = \begin{pmatrix} 0 & a_1 & & & & & & & & \\ -a_1 & 0 & & & & & & & & \\ & & 0 & a_2 & & & & & & \\ & & -a_2 & 0 & & & & & & \\ & & & & \ddots & & & & & \\ & & & & & 0 & a_s & & & \\ & & & & & -a_s & 0 & & & \\ & & & & & & & 0 & & \\ & & & & & & & & \ddots & \\ & & & & & & & & & 0 \end{pmatrix}$$

Proof. Let $\mathfrak{M}$ denote the module of $2n$-columns with integral coefficients: $\mathfrak{M} \cong \mathbb{Z}^{2n}$. Every $\mathfrak{x}_1 \in \mathfrak{M}$ defines a principal ideal

$$\{\mathfrak{x}_1^T Q \mathfrak{y} \mid \mathfrak{y} \in \mathfrak{M}\} = (a_1) \subset \mathbb{Z}.$$

We may choose $a_1 > 0$ if $Q \neq 0$. So there is a vector $\mathfrak{y}_1 \in \mathfrak{M}$ such that $\mathfrak{x}_1^T Q \mathfrak{y}_1 = a_1$, hence, $\mathfrak{y}_1^T Q \mathfrak{x}_1 = -a_1$. It follows that a_1 also generates the ideal defined by $\mathfrak{y}_1$. Let $\mathfrak{x}_1$ be chosen in such a way that $a_1 > 0$ is minimal.

Put

$$\mathfrak{M}_1 = \{\mathfrak{u} \mid \mathfrak{x}_1^T Q \mathfrak{u} = \mathfrak{y}_1^T Q \mathfrak{u} = 0\}.$$

We prove that

$$\mathfrak{M} = \mathbb{Z}\mathfrak{x}_1 \oplus \mathbb{Z}\mathfrak{y}_1 \oplus \mathfrak{M}_1;$$

in particular, $\mathfrak{M}_1 \cong \mathbb{Z}^{2n-2}$.

Consider $\mathfrak{z} \in \mathfrak{M}$ and define $\alpha, \beta \in \mathbb{Z}$ by

$$\mathfrak{x}_1^T Q \mathfrak{z} = \beta a_1, \quad \mathfrak{y}_1^T Q \mathfrak{z} = \alpha a_1.$$

Then

$$\mathfrak{x}_1^T Q (\mathfrak{z} - \beta \mathfrak{y}_1 - \alpha \mathfrak{x}_1) = \beta a_1 - \beta a_1 - 0 = 0$$
$$\mathfrak{y}_1^T Q (\mathfrak{z} - \beta \mathfrak{y}_1 - \alpha \mathfrak{x}_1) = \alpha a_1 - 0 - \alpha a_1 = 0;$$

note that $Q^T = -Q$ implies that $\mathfrak{x}^T Q \mathfrak{x} = 0$. Now $\mathfrak{z} - \beta \mathfrak{y}_1 - \alpha \mathfrak{x}_1 \in \mathfrak{M}_1$ and $\mathfrak{x}_1$ and

$\mathfrak{y}_1$ generate a module isomorphic to $\mathbb{Z}^2$. From

$$\mathfrak{x}_1^T Q(\xi\mathfrak{x}_1 + \eta\mathfrak{y}_1) = \eta a_1, \quad \mathfrak{y}_1^T Q(\xi\mathfrak{x}_1 + \eta\mathfrak{y}_1) = -\xi a_1$$

it follows that $\xi\mathfrak{x}_1 + \eta\mathfrak{y}_1 \in \mathfrak{M}_1$ implies that $\xi = \eta = 0$. Thus $\mathfrak{M} = \mathbb{Z}\mathfrak{x}_1 \oplus \mathbb{Z}\mathfrak{y}_1 \oplus \mathfrak{M}_1$.

The skew-symmetric form Q induces on $\mathfrak{M}_1$ a skew-symmetric form Q'. As an induction hypothesis we may assume that there is a basis $\mathfrak{x}_2, \mathfrak{y}_2, \ldots, \mathfrak{x}_n, \mathfrak{y}_n$ of $\mathfrak{M}_1$ such that Q' is represented by a matrix as desired. □

Moreover, we may assume that $1 \leqq a_1 | a_2 | \ldots | a_s$: Let $1 \leqq a_2 | a_3 | \ldots | a_s$ already be true. Denote the vectors belonging to a_i by $\mathfrak{x}_i, \mathfrak{y}_i$. If $1 \leqq d = gcd(a_1, a_2)$ and $d = ba_1 + ca_2$ then

$$(b\mathfrak{x}_1 + c\mathfrak{x}_2)^T Q(\mathfrak{y}_1 + \mathfrak{y}_2) = ba_1 + ca_2 = d.$$

Hence, by the minimality of a_1: $d = a_1$.

A2 Theorem [Jones 1950]. *Let $Q_n = (q_{ik})$ be a symmetric $n \times n$ matrix over $\mathbb{R}$, and $p(Q_n)$ the number of its positive, $q(Q_n)$ the number of its negative eigenvalues, then $\sigma(Q_n) = p(Q_n) - q(Q_n)$ is called the* signature *of Q_n. There is a sequence of principal minors $D_0 = 1, D_1, D_2, \ldots$ such that D_i is principal minor of D_{i+1} and no two consecutive D_i, D_{i+1} are both singular for $i <$ rank A. For any such (admissible) sequence*

(1) $$\sigma(Q_n) = \sum_{i=0}^{n-1} \operatorname{sign}(D_i D_{i+1}).$$

Proof. The rank r of Q_n is the number of non-vanishing eigenvalues λ_i of Q_n; it is, at the same time, the maximal index i for which a non-singular principal minor exists – this follows from the fact that Q_n is equivalent to a diagonal matrix containing the eigenvalues λ_i in its diagonal. We may, therefore, assume $r = n$ and $D_i = \lambda_1 \ldots \lambda_i$, $D_n \neq 0$.

The proof is by induction on n. Assume first that we have chosen a sequence $D_0, D_1, \ldots$ with a non-singular minor D_{n-1}. (It will be admissible by induction.) We may suppose that $D_{n-1} = \det Q_{n-1}$ where Q_{n-1} is the submatrix of Q_n consisting of its first $n-1$ rows and columns. Now sign $(D_{n-1} D_n) =$ sign λ_n, and (1) follows by induction.

Suppose we choose a sequence with $D_{n-1} = 0$. Then $D_{n-2} \neq 0$, and, since $D_n \neq 0$, we obtain an admissible sequence for Q_n. There is a transformation $B_n^T Q_n B_n = Q_n'$ with

$$B_n = \left(\begin{array}{ccc|c} & & & 0 \\ & & & \vdots \\ & B_{n-1} & & 0 \\ \hline 0 & \ldots & 0 & 1 \end{array}\right), \quad B_{n-1} \in SO(n-1, \mathbb{R})$$

which takes Q_{n-1} into diagonal form

$$Q'_{n-1} = \begin{pmatrix} \lambda_1 & & & \\ & \ddots & & \\ & & \lambda_{n-2} & \\ & & & 0 \end{pmatrix}, \quad \lambda_i \neq 0.$$

By a further transformation

$$C_n^T Q'_n C_n = Q''_n, \quad C_n = \left(\begin{array}{ccc|c} & & & t_1 \\ & E_{n-1} & & \vdots \\ & & & t_{n-2} \\ & & & 0 \\ \hline 0 & \dots & 0 & 1 \end{array}\right), \quad t_i \in \mathbb{R},$$

one can achieve the following form

$$Q''_n = \begin{pmatrix} \lambda_1 & \cdot & \cdot & \cdot & 0 \\ \vdots & \ddots & & & \vdots \\ \vdots & & \lambda_{n-2} & & \vdots \\ \vdots & & & 0 & \alpha \\ 0 & \cdot & \cdot & \alpha & \beta \end{pmatrix}.$$

Now $\sigma\begin{pmatrix} 0 & \alpha \\ \alpha & \beta \end{pmatrix} = 0$, and

$$\sigma(Q_n) = \sigma\begin{pmatrix} \lambda_1 & & 0 \\ & \ddots & \\ 0 & & \lambda_{n-2} \end{pmatrix}.$$

The same result is obtained by (1) if $D_{n-1} = 0$. □

Let Γ be a finite oriented graph with vertices $\{P_i | 1 \leqq i \leqq n\}$ and oriented edges $\{u_{ij}^{\lambda}\}$, such that P_i is the initial point and P_j the terminal point of u_{ij}^{λ}. (For the basic terminology see [Berge 1970]). By a *rooted tree* (root P_1) we mean a subgraph of $n-1$ edges such that every point P_k is terminal point of a path with initial point P_1.

Let a_{ij} denote the number of edges with initial point P_i and terminal point P_j.

A3 Theorem (Bott-Mayberry). *Let Γ be a finite oriented graph without loops ($a_{ii} = 0$). The principal minor H_{ii} of the graph matrix*

$$H(\Gamma) = \begin{pmatrix} (\sum_{k \neq 1} a_{k1}) & -a_{12} & -a_{13} & \dots & -a_{1n} \\ -a_{21} & (\sum_{k \neq 2} a_{2k}) & -a_{23} & \dots & -a_{2n} \\ \vdots & \vdots & & & \vdots \\ -a_{n1} & -a_{n2} & & & (\sum_{k \neq n} a_{kn}) \end{pmatrix}$$

is equal to the number of rooted trees with root P_i.

Proof. The principal minor H_{ii} is the determinant of the submatrix obtained from $H(\Gamma)$ by omitting the i-th row and column. We need a

Lemma. *A graph* C *(without loops) with* n *vertices and* $n-1$ *edges is a rooted tree, root* P_i, *if* $H_{ii}(C) = 1$; *otherwise* $H_{ii}(C) = 0$.

Proof of the Lemma. Suppose C is a rooted tree with root P_1. One has $\sum_{k \neq j} a_{kj} = 1$ for $j \neq 1$, because there is just one edge in C with terminal point P_j. If the indexing of vertices is chosen in such a way that indices increase along any path in C, then H_{11} has the form

$$H_{11} = \begin{vmatrix} 1 & * & & * \\ 0 & 1 & & \\ \vdots & \vdots & & \\ \vdots & \vdots & & * \\ 0 & 0 & & 1 \end{vmatrix} = 1 .$$

To prove the converse it suffices to show that C is connected, if $H_{11} \neq 0$. Assuming this, use the fact that every point $P_j, j \neq 1$, must be a terminal point of C, otherwise the j-th column would consist of zeroes, contradicting $H_{11} \neq 0$. There is, therefore, an unoriented spanning tree in the (unoriented) graph C. The graph C coincides with this tree, since a spanning tree has $n-1$ edges. It must be a tree, rooted in P_1, because every vertex P_j, $j \neq 1$, is a terminal point.

The rest is proved by induction on n. We assume that C is not connected. Then we may arrange the indexing such that H_{11} is of the form:

$$H_{11} = \begin{pmatrix} B' & 0 \\ 0 & B'' \end{pmatrix}, \ \det B' \neq 0, \det B'' \neq 0 .$$

By the induction hypothesis we know that the subgraphs Γ' resp. Γ'' each containing P_1 and the vertices associated with the rows of B' resp. B'' – together with all edges of C joining these points – are P_1-rooted trees. This contradicts the assumption that C is not connected. □

We return to the proof of the main theorem. One may consider H_{11} as a multilinear function in the $n-1$ column vectors $\mathfrak{a}_j, j=2, \ldots, n$ of the matrix $(a_{ij}), i \neq j$. This is true, since the diagonal elements $\sum_{k \neq j} a_{kj}$ are themselves linear functions. Let $\mathfrak{e}_i$ denote a column vector with an i-th coordinate equal to one, and the other coordinates equal to zero. Then

$$(1) \qquad H_{11}(\mathfrak{a}_2, \ldots, \mathfrak{a}_n) = \sum_{1 \leqq k_2, \ldots, k_n \leqq n} a_{k_2 2} \ldots a_{k_n n} H_{11}(\mathfrak{e}_{k_2}, \ldots, \mathfrak{e}_{k_n})$$

with

$$\mathfrak{a}_i = \sum_{k_i=1}^{n} a_{k_i i} \mathfrak{e}_{k_i}.$$

By the Lemma $H_{11}(\mathfrak{e}_{k_2}, \ldots, \mathfrak{e}_{k_n}) = 1$ if and only if the $n-1$ edges $u_{k_2 2}$, $u_{k_3 3}, \ldots, u_{k_n n}$ form a P_1-rooted tree. Any such tree is to be counted $a_{k_2 2} \ldots a_{k_n n}$ times. □

Two corollaries follow easily.

A4 Corollary. *Let Γ be an unoriented finite graph without loops, and let b_{ij} the number of edges joining P_i and P_j. A principal minor H_{ii} of*

$$\begin{pmatrix} \sum_{k \neq 1} b_{k1} & -b_{12} & -b_{13} & \ldots & \\ -b_{21} & \sum_{k \neq 2} b_{k2} & \ldots & & \\ \vdots & & & \vdots & \\ \vdots & & & \sum_{k \neq n} b_{kn} & \end{pmatrix}$$

gives the number of spanning trees of Γ, independent of i.

Proof. Replace every unoriented edge of Γ by a pair of edges with opposite directions, and apply Theorem A3. □

A5 Corollary. *Let Γ be a finite oriented loopless graph with a valuation $f: \{u_{ij}^{\lambda}\} \to \{1, -1\}$ on edges. Then the principal minor H_{ii} of $(f(a_{ij}))$, $f(a_{ij}) = \sum_{\lambda} f(u_{ij}^{\lambda})$, satisfies the following equation:*

$$H_{ii} = \sum f(tr(i))$$

where the sum is to be taken over all P_i-rooted trees $tr(i)$, and where

$$f(tr(i)) = \prod_{u_{kj}^{\lambda} \in tr(i)} f(u_{kj}^{\lambda}).$$

Proof. The proof of Theorem A 3 applies; it is only necessary to replace a_{ij} by $f(a_{ij})$. □

For other proofs and generalizations see [Bott-Mayberry 1954]. We add a well known theorem without giving a proof. For a proof see [Bourbaki, Algèbre Chap. 7].

A 6 Theorem. *Let M be a finitely generated module over a principal ideal domain. Then*

$$M \cong M_{\varepsilon_1} \oplus \ldots \oplus M_{\varepsilon_r} \oplus M_\beta$$

where M_β is a free module of rank β and $M_{\varepsilon_i} = \langle a \mid \varepsilon_i a \rangle$ is a cyclic module generated by an element a and defined by $\varepsilon_i a = 0$, $\varepsilon_i \in R$. The ε_i are not units of R, different from zero, and form a chain of divisors $\varepsilon_i \mid \varepsilon_{i+1}$, $1 \leqq i \leqq r$. They are called the elementary divisors of *M*; *the rank β of the free part of M is called the* Betti number *of M.*

The Betti numbers β and β' of finitely generated modules M and M' coincide and their elementary divisors are pairwise associated, $\varepsilon_i' = \alpha_i \varepsilon_i$, α_i a unit of R, if and only if M and M' are isomorphic. □

Remark: If M is a finitely presented module over an abelian ring A with unit element, the theorem is not true. Nevertheless the elementary ideals of its presentation matrix are invariants of M.

In the special case $R = \mathbb{Z}$ the theorem applies to finitely generated abelian groups. The elementary divisors form a chain $T_1 \mid T_2 \mid \ldots \mid T_r$ of positive integers >1, the orders of the cyclic summands. T_r is called the *first*, T_{r-1} the *second torsion number* etc. of the abelian group.

Appendix B: Theorems of 3-dimensional Topology

This section contains a collection of theorems in the field of 3-dimensional manifolds which have been frequently used in this book. In each case a source is given where a proof may be found.

B1 Theorem (Alexander). *Let S^2 be a semilinearly embedded 2-sphere in S^3. There is a semilinear homeomorphism $h: S^3 \to S^3$ mapping S^2 onto the boundary $\partial[\sigma^3]$ of a 3-simplex σ^3.* □ [Alexander 1924′], [Graeub 1950].

B2 Theorem (Alexander). *Let T be a semilinearly embedded torus in S^3. Then $S^3 - T$ consists of two components X_1 and X_2, $\bar{X}_1 \cup \bar{X}_2 = S^3$, $\bar{X}_1 \cap \bar{X}_2 = T$, and at least one of the subcomplexes $\bar{X}_1, \bar{X}_2$ is a solid torus.* □ [Alexander 1924′], [Schubert 1953].

B3 Theorem (Seifert-van Kampen). *(a) Let X be a connected polyhedron and X_1, X_2 connected subpolyhedra with $X = X_1 \cup X_2$ and $X_1 \cap X_2$ a (non-empty) connected subpolyhedron. Suppose*

$$\pi_1(X_1, P) = \langle S_1, \ldots, S_n \mid R_1, \ldots, R_m \rangle$$
$$\pi_1(X_2, P) = \langle T_1, \ldots, T_k \mid N_1, \ldots, N_l \rangle$$

with respect to a base point $P \in X_1 \cap X_2$. A set $\{v_j \mid 1 \leqq j \leqq r\}$ of generating loops of $\pi_1(X_1 \cap X_2, P)$ determines sets $\{V_{1j}(S_i)\}$ and $\{V_{2j}(T_i)\}$ respectively of elements in $\pi_1(X_1, P)$ or $\pi_1(X_2, P)$ respectively. Then

$$\pi_1(X, P) = \langle S_1, \ldots, S_n, T_1, \ldots, T_k \mid R_1, \ldots, R_m, N_1, \ldots, N_l, V_{11} V_{21}^{-1}, \ldots, V_{1r} V_{2r}^{-1} \rangle.$$

(b) Let X_1, X_2 be disjoint connected homeomorphic subpolyhedra of a connected polyhedron X, and denote by $\bar{X} = X/h$ the polyhedron which results from identifying X_1 and X_2 via the homeomorphism $h: X_1 \to X_2$. For a base point $P \in X_1$ and its image $\bar{P}$ under the identification a presentation of $\pi_1(\bar{X}; \bar{P})$ is obtained from one of $\pi_1(X; P)$ by adding a generator S and the defining relations $ST_iS^{-1} = h_\#(T_i)$, $1 \leqq i \leqq r$ where $\{T_i \mid 1 \leqq i \leqq r\}$ generate $\pi_1(X_1; P)$. □

For a proof see [ZVC 1980, 2.8.2]. A topological version of B3(a) is valid when X, X_1, X_2, $X_1 \cap X_2$, are path-connected and X_1, X_2 are open, [Crowell-Fox 1963], [Massey 1967]. A topological version of B3(b) may be obtained if X, X_1, X_2 are path-connected, X_1, X_2 are closed, and if the identifying homeomorphism can be extended to a collaring.

B4 Theorem (generalized Dehn's lemma). *Let* $h: S(0, r) \to M$ *be a simplicial immersion of an orientable compact surface* $S(0, r)$ *of genus* 0 *with* r *boundary components into the 3-manifold* M *with no singularities on the boundary* $\partial h(S(0, r)) = \{C_1, C_2, \ldots, C_r\}$, C_i *a closed curve. Suppose that the normal closure* $\overline{\langle C_1, \ldots, C_r \rangle}$ *in* $\pi_1(M)$ *is contained in the subgroup* $\hat{\pi}_1(M) \subset \pi_1(M)$ *of orientation preserving paths. Then there is a non-singular disk* $S(0, q)$ *embedded in* M *with* $\partial S(0, q)$ *a non-vacuous subset of* $\{C_1, \ldots, C_r\}$. □ [Papakyriakopoulos 1957], [Shapiro-Whitehead 1958], [Hempel 1976], [Rolfsen 1976], [Jaco 1977].

Remark: Theorem B4 was proved by Shapiro and Whitehead. The original Lemma of Dehn $r = 1\,(= q)$ was formulated by M. Dehn in 1910 but proved only in 1957 by Papakyriakopoulos.

B5 Theorem (generalized loop theorem). *Let* M *be a 3-manifold and let* B *be a component of its boundary. If there are elements in* $\ker(\pi_1 B \to \pi_1 M)$ *which are not contained in a given normal subgroup* $\mathfrak{N}$ *of* $\pi_1(B)$ *then there is a simple loop* C *on* B *such that* C *bounds a non-singular disk in* M *and* $[C] \notin \mathfrak{N}$. □ [Papakyriakopoulos 1957], [Stallings 1959], [Rolfsen 1967], [Hempel 1976], [Jaco 1977].

Remark: The proof is given in the second reference. The original version of the loop theorem ($\mathfrak{N} = 1$) was first formulated and proved by Papakyriakopoulos. Another generalization analogous to the Shapiro-Whitehead version of Dehn's Lemma was proved in [Waldhausen 1967].

B6 Theorem (sphere theorem). *Let* M *be an orientable 3-manifold and* $\mathfrak{N}$ *a* $\pi_1 M$-*invariant subgroup of* $\pi_2 M$. *(*$\mathfrak{N}$ *is* $\pi_1 M$-*invariant if the operation of* $\pi_1 M$ *on* $\pi_2 M$ *maps* $\mathfrak{N}$ *onto itself.) Then there is an embedding* $g: S^2 \to M$ *such that* $[g] \notin \mathfrak{N}$. □ [Papakyriakopoulos 1957], [Hempel 1976], [Jaco 1977].

This triad of Papakyriakopoulos theorems started a new era in 3-dimensional topology. The next impulse came from W. Haken and F. Waldhausen:

A surface F is *properly embedded* in a 3-manifold M if $\partial F = F \cap \partial M$. A 2-sphere ($F = S^2$) is called *incompressible in* M, if it does not bound a 3-ball in M, and $F \neq S^2$ is called *incompresible*, if there is no disk $D \subset M$ with $D \cap F = \partial D$, and ∂D not contractible in F. A manifold is *sufficiently large* when it contains a properly embedded 2-sided incompressible surface.

B7 Theorem (Waldhausen). *Let* M, N *be sufficiently large irreducible 3-manifolds not containing 2-sided projective planes. If there is an isomorphism* $f_\#: (\pi_1 M, \pi_1 \partial M) \to (\pi_1 N, \pi_1 \partial N)$ *between the peripheral group systems, then there is a boundary preserving map* $f: (M, \partial M) \to (N, \partial N)$ *inducing* $f_\#$. *Either* f *is homotopic to a homeomorphism of* M *to* N *or* M *is a twisted I-bundle over a closed surface and* N *is a product bundle over a homeomorphic surface.* □ [Waldhausen 1967], [Hempel 1976].

Remark: The Waldhausen theorem states for a large class of manifolds what has long been known of surfaces: there is a natural isomorphism between the mapping class group of M and the group of automorphisms of $\pi_1(M)$ modulo inner automorphisms.

Evidently Theorem B7 applies to knot complements $C = M$. A Seifert surface of minimal genus is a properly embedded incompressible surface in C.

B8 Theorem (Smith conjecture). *A simplicial orientation preserving map $h: S^3 \to S^3$ of period q is conjugate to a rotation.* □

A conference on the Smith conjecture was held in 1979 at Columbia University in New York, the proceedings of which are recorded in [Morgan-Bass 1984], it contains a proof. The case $q = 2$ is due to Waldhausen, a proof is given in [Waldhausen 1969].

Appendix C: Tables

The following Table I lists certain invariants of knots up to ten crossings. The identification (first column) follows [Rolfsen 1976] but takes into account that there is a duplication ($10_{161} = 10_{162}$) in his table which was detected by Perko. For each crossing number alternating knots are grouped in front, a star indicates the first non-alternating knot in each order.

The first column ($\Delta_1(t), \Delta_2(t)$) contains the Alexander polynomials, factorized into irreducible polynomials. The polynomials $\Delta_k(t)$, $k > 2$, are always trivial. (See Chapter 8.) Alexander polynomials of links or of knots with eleven crossings are to be found in [Rolfsen 1976], [Conway 1970] and [Perko 1980].

The second column (T) gives the torsion numbers of the first homology group $H_1(\bar{C}_2)$ of the two-fold branched covering of the knot. The numbers are $T_r, T_{r-1}, \ldots$ where $T_1 | T_2 | \ldots | T_r$ is the chain of elementary divisors of $H_1(\hat{C}_2)$. (See Chapter 9.) For torsion numbers of cyclic coverings of order $n > 2$, see [Metha 1980]. Torsion numbers for $n = 3$ (knots with less than ten crossings) are listed in [Reidemeister 1932].

The column (σ) records the signature of the knot. (See Chapter 13.)

The column (q) states the periods of the knot; a question-mark indicates that a certain period is possible but has not been verified. (See Chapter 14D.)

The column headed α, β contains Schubert's notation of the knot as a two-bridged knot. (The first number α always coincides with T_r.) Where no entry appears the bridge number is three. (See Chapter 12.)

The column (s) contains complete information about symmetries in Conway's notation. (See Chapter 2.)

	amphicheiral	non-amphicheiral
invertible	f	r
non-invertible	i	n

It has been checked that up to ten crossings the genus of a knot always equals half the degree of its Alexander polynomial.

Acknowledgements: The Alexander polynomials, the signature and most of the periods have been computed by U. Lüdicke. Periods up to nine crossings were taken from [Murasugi 1980]. Symmetries and 2-bridge numbers (α, β) were copied from [Conway 1967] and compared with other results on amphicheirality and invertibility [Hartley 1980].

Table I

$\mathfrak{k}$	$\Delta_1(t)$	$\Delta_2(t)$	T	σ	q	α, β	s
3_1	t^2-t+1		3	2	2,3	3,1	r
4_1	t^2-3t+1		5	0	2	5,2	f
5_1	$t^4-t^3+t^2-t+1$		5	4	2,5	5,1	r
5_2	$2t^2-3t+2$		7	2	2	7,3	r
6_1	$2t^2-5t+2$		9	0	2	9,4	r
6_2	$t^4-3t^3+3t^2-3t+1$		11	2	2	11,4	r
6_3	$t^4-3t^3+5t^2-3t+1$		13	0	2	13,5	f
7_1	$t^6-t^5+t^4-t^3+t^2-t+1$		7	6	2,7	7,1	r
7_2	$3t^2-5t+3$		11	2	2	11,5	r
7_3	$2t^4-3t^3+3t^2-3t+2$		13	4	2	13,4	r
7_4	$4t^2-7t+4$		15	2	2	15,4	r
7_5	$2t^4-4t^3+5t^2-4t+2$		17	4	2	17,7	r
7_6	$t^4-5t^3+7t^2-5t+1$		19	2	2	19,7	r
7_7	$t^4-5t^3+9t^2-5t+1$		21	0	2	21,8	r
8_1	$3t^2-7t+3$		13	0	2	13,6	r
8_2	$t^6-3t^5+3t^4-3t^3+3t^2-3t+1$		17	4	2	17,6	r
8_3	$4t^2-9t+4$		17	0	2	17,4	f
8_4	$2t^4-5t^3+5t^2-5t+2$		19	2	2	19,5	r
8_5	$(t^2-t+1)(-t^4+2t^3-t^2+2t-1)$		21	4	2		r
8_6	$2t^4-6t^3+7t^2-6t+2$		23	2	2	23,10	r
8_7	$t^6-3t^5+5t^4-5t^3+5t^2-3t+1$		23	2	2	23,9	r
8_8	$2t^4-6t^3+9t^2-6t+2$		25	0	2	25,9	r
8_9	$t^6-3t^5+5t^4-7t^3+5t^2-3t+1$		25	0	2	25,7	f
8_{10}	$(t^2-t+1)^3$		27	2			r
8_{11}	$(2t^2-5t+2)(t^2-t+1)$		27	2	2	27,10	r
8_{12}	$t^4-7t^3+13t^2-7t+1$		29	0	2	29,12	f
8_{13}	$2t^4-7t^3+11t^2-7t+2$		29	0	2	29,11	r
8_{14}	$2t^4-8t^3+11t^2-8t+2$		31	2	2	31,12	r
8_{15}	$(t^2-t+1)(3t^2-5t+3)$		33	4	2		r
8_{16}	$t^6-4t^5+8t^4-9t^3+8t^2-4t+1$		35	2			r
8_{17}	$t^6-4t^5+8t^4-11t^3+8t^2-4t+1$		37	0			i
8_{18}	$(t^2-t+1)^2(t^2-3t+1)$,	t^2-t+1	15,3	0	2		f

Table I

$\mathfrak{k}$	$\Delta_1(t)$	$\Delta_2(t)$	T	σ	q	α, β	s
$*8_{19}$	$(t^2-t+1)(t^4-t^2+1)$		3	6	2,3		r
8_{20}	$(t^2-t+1)^2$		9	0			r
8_{21}	$(t^2-t+1)(t^2-3t+1)$		15	2	2		r
9_1	$(t^2-t+1)(t^6-t^3+1)$		9	8	2,3,9	9,1	r
9_2	$4t^2-7t+4$		15	2	2	15,7	r
9_3	$2t^6-3t^5+3t^4-3t^3+3t^2-3t+2$		19	6	2	19,6	r
9_4	$3t^4-5t^3+5t^2-5t+3$		21	4	2	21,5	r
9_5	$6t^2-11t+6$		23	2	2	23,6	r
9_6	$(t^2-t+1)(-2t^4+2t^3-t^2+2t-2)$		27	6	2	27,5	r
9_7	$3t^4-7t^3+9t^2-7t+3$		29	4	2	29,13	r
9_8	$2t^4-8t^3+11t^2-8t+2$		31	2	2	31,11	r
9_9	$2t^6-4t^5+6t^4-7t^3+6t^2-4t+2$		31	6	2	31,9	r
9_{10}	$4t^4-8t^3+9t^2-8t+4$		33	4	2	33,10	r
9_{11}	$t^6-5t^5+7t^4-7t^3+7t^2-5t+1$		33	4	2	33,14	r
9_{12}	$(t^2-3t+1)(2t^2-3t+2)$		35	2	2	35,13	r
9_{13}	$4t^4-9t^3+11t^2-9t+4$		37	4	2	37,10	r
9_{14}	$2t^4-9t^3+15t^2-9t+2$		37	0	2	37,14	r
9_{15}	$2t^4-10t^3+15t^2-10t+2$		39	2	2	39,16	r
9_{16}	$(t^2-t+1)(-2t^4+3t^3-3t^2+3t-2)$		39	6	2		r
9_{17}	$t^6-5t^5+9t^4-9t^3+9t^2-5t+1$		39	2	2	39,14	r
9_{18}	$4t^4-10t^3+13t^2-10t+4$		41	4	2	41,17	r
9_{19}	$2t^4-10t^3+17t^2-10t+2$		41	0	2	41,16	r
9_{20}	$t^6-5t^5+9t^4-11t^3+9t^2-5t+1$		41	4	2	41,15	r
9_{21}	$2t^4-11t^3+17t^2-11t+2$		43	2	2	43,18	r
9_{22}	$t^6-5t^5+10t^4-11t^3+10t^2-5t+1$		43	2			r
9_{23}	$(t^2-t+1)(4t^2-7t+4)$		45	4	2	45,19	r
9_{24}	$(t^2-t+1)^2(t^2-3t+1)$		45	0			r
9_{25}	$3t^4-12t^3+17t^2-12t+3$		47	2			r
9_{26}	$t^6-5t^5+11t^4-13t^3+11t^2-5t+1$		47	2	2	47,18	r
9_{27}	$t^6-5t^5+11t^4-15t^3+11t^2-5t+1$		49	0	2	49,19	r
9_{28}	$(t^2-t+1)(-t^4+4t^3-7t^2+4t-1)$		51	2	2		r
9_{29}	$(t^2-t+1)(-t^4+4t^3-7t^2+4t-1)$		51	2			r

Table I

𝔨	$\Delta_1(t)$	$\Delta_2(t)$	T	σ	q	α, β	s
9_{30}	$t^6-5t^5+12t^4-17t^3+12t^2-5t+1$		53	0			r
9_{31}	$t^6-5t^5+13t^4-17t^3+13t^2-5t+1$		55	2	2	55,21	r
9_{32}	$t^6-6t^5+14t^4-17t^3+14t^2-6t+1$		59	2			n
9_{33}	$t^6-6t^5+14t^4-19t^3+14t^2-6t+1$		61	0			n
9_{34}	$t^6-6t^5+16t^4-23t^3+16t^2-6t+1$		69	0			r
9_{35}	$7t^2-13t+7$		9,3	2	3		r
9_{36}	$t^6-5t^5+8t^4-9t^3+8t^2-5t+1$		37	4			r
9_{37}	$(t^2-3t+1)(2t^2-5t+2)$		15,3	0			r
9_{38}	$(t^2-t+1)(5t^2-9t+5)$		57	4			r
9_{39}	$(t^2-3t+1)(3t^2-5t+3)$		55	2			r
9_{40}	$(t^2-t+1)(t^2-3t+1)^2$,	t^2-3t+1	15,5	2	2,3		r
9_{41}	$3t^4-12t^3+19t^2-12t+3$		7,7	0	3		r
$*9_{42}$	$t^4-2t^3+t^2-2t+1$		7	2			r
9_{43}	$t^6-3t^5+2t^4-t^3+2t^2-3t+1$		13	4			r
9_{44}	$t^4-4t^3+7t^2-4t+1$		17	0			r
9_{45}	$t^4-6t^3+9t^2-6t+1$		23	2			r
9_{46}	$2t^2-5t+2$		3,3	0	2		r
9_{47}	$t^6-4t^5+6t^4-5t^3+6t^2-4t+1$		9,3	2	3		r
9_{48}	$t^4-7t^3+11t^2-7t+1$		9,3	2			r
9_{49}	$3t^4-6t^3+7t^2-6t+3$		5,5	4	3		r
10_1	$4t^2-9t+4$		17	0	2	17,8	r
10_2	$t^8-3t^7+3t^6-3t^5+3t^4-3t^3+3t^2-3t+1$		23	6	2	23,8	r
10_3	$6t^2-13t+6$		25	0	2,3?	25,6	r
10_4	$3t^4-7t^3+7t^2-7t+3$		27	2	2,3	27,7	r
10_5	$(t^2-t+1)(t^6-2t^5+2t^4-t^3+2t^2-2t+1)$		33	4	2	33,13	r
10_6	$2t^6-6t^5+7t^4-7t^3+7t^2-6t+2$		37	4	2	37,16	r
10_7	$3t^4-11t^3+15t^2-11t+3$		43	2	2	43,16	r
10_8	$2t^6-5t^5+5t^4-5t^3+5t^2-5t+2$		29	4	2	29,6	r
10_9	$(t^2-t+1)(t^6-2t^5+2t^4-3t^3+2t^2-2t+1)$		39	2	2	39,11	r
10_{10}	$3t^4-11t^3+17t^2-11t+3$		45	0	2,3?	45,17	r
10_{11}	$4t^4-11t^3+13t^2-11t+4$		43	2	2	43,13	r
10_{12}	$2t^6-6t^5+10t^4-11t^3+10t^2-6t+2$		47	2	2	47,17	r

Table I

$\mathfrak{k}$	$\Delta_1(t)$	$\Delta_2(t)$	T	σ	q	α, β	s
10_{13}	$2t^4-13t^3+23t^2-13t+2$		53	0	2	53,22	r
10_{14}	$2t^6-8t^5+12t^4-13t^3+12t^2-8t+2$		57	4	2,3	57,22	r
10_{15}	$2t^6-6t^5+9t^4-9t^3+9t^2-6t+2$		43	2	2	43,19	r
10_{16}	$4t^4-12t^3+15t^2-12t+4$		47	2	2	47,14	r
10_{17}	$t^8-3t^7+5t^6-7t^5+9t^4-7t^3+5t^2-3t+1$		41	0	2	41,9	f
10_{18}	$4t^4-14t^3+19t^2-14t+4$		55	2	2,5	55,23	r
10_{19}	$2t^6-7t^5+11t^4-11t^3+11t^2-7t+2$		51	2	2	51,14	r
10_{20}	$3t^4-9t^3+11t^2-9t+3$		35	2	2,3?	35,16	r
10_{21}	$(2t^2-5t+2)(-t^4+t^3-t^2+t-1)$		45	4	2	45,16	r
10_{22}	$2t^6-6t^5+10t^4-13t^3+10t^2-6t+2$		49	0	2	49,13	r
10_{23}	$2t^6-7t^5-13t^4-15t^3+13t^2-7t+2$		59	2	2	59,23	r
10_{24}	$4t^4-14t^3+19t^2-14t+4$		55	2	2,5	55,24	r
10_{25}	$2t^6-8t^5+14t^4-17t^3+14t^2-8t+2$		65	4	2	65,24	r
10_{26}	$2t^6-7t^5+13t^4-17t^3+13t^2-7t+2$		61	0	2	61,17	r
10_{27}	$2t^6-8t^5+16t^4-19t^3+16t^2-8t+2$		71	2	2	71,27	r
10_{28}	$4t^4-13t^3+19t^2-13t+4$		53	0	2	53,19	r
10_{29}	$t^6-7t^5+15t^4-17t^3+15t^2-7t+1$		63	2	2,3	63,26	r
10_{30}	$4t^4-17t^3+25t^2-17t+4$		67	2	2	67,26	r
10_{31}	$4t^4-14t^3+21t^2-14t+4$		57	0	2	57,25	r
10_{32}	$(t^2-t+1)(-2t^4+6t^3-7t^2+6t-2)$		69	0	2,3?	69,29	r
10_{33}	$4t^4-16t^3+25t^2-16t+4$		65	0	2	65,18	f
10_{34}	$3t^4-9t^3+13t^2-9t+3$		37	0	2,3	37,13	r
10_{35}	$2t^4-12t^3+21t^2-12t+2$		49	0	2	49,20	r
10_{36}	$3t^4-13t^3+19t^2-13t+3$		51	2	2	51,20	r
10_{37}	$4t^4-13t^3+19t^2-13t+4$		53	0	2	53,23	f
10_{38}	$4t^4-15t^3+21t^2-15t+4$		59	2	2	59,25	r
10_{39}	$2t^6-8t^5+13t^4-15t^3+13t^2-8t+2$		61	4	2	61,22	r
10_{40}	$(t^2-t+1)(-2t^4+6t^3-9t^2+6t-2)$		75	2	2	75,29	r
10_{41}	$t^6-7t^5+17t^4-21t^3+17t^2-7t+1$		71	2	2	71,26	r
10_{42}	$t^6-7t^5+19t^4-27t^3+19t^2-7t+1$		81	0	2	81,31	r
10_{43}	$t^6-7t^5+17t^4-23t^3+17t^2-7t+1$		73	0	2	73,27	f
10_{44}	$t^6-7t^5+19t^4-25t^3+19t^2-7t+1$		79	2	2	79,30	r

Table I

𝔨	$\Delta_1(t)$	$\Delta_2(t)$	T	σ	q	α, β	s
10_{45}	$t^6-7t^5+21t^4-31t^3+21t^2-7t+1$		89	0	2	89,34	f
10_{46}	$t^8-3t^7+4t^6-5t^5+5t^4-5t^3+4t^2-3t+1$		31	6			r
10_{47}	$t^8-3t^7+6t^6-7t^5+7t^4-7t^3+6t^2-3t+1$		41	4			r
10_{48}	$t^8-3t^7+6t^6-9t^5+11t^4-9t^3+6t^2-3t+1$		49	0			r
10_{49}	$3t^6-8t^5+12t^4-13t^3+12t^2-8t+3$		59	6			r
10_{50}	$2t^6-7t^5+11t^4-13t^3+11t^2-7t+2$		53	4	2		r
10_{51}	$2t^6-7t^5+15t^4-19t^3+15t^2-7t+2$		67	2	2		r
10_{52}	$2t^6-7t^5+13t^4-15t^3+13t^2-7t+2$		59	2	2		r
10_{53}	$6t^4-18t^3+25t^2-18t+6$		73	4	2,3		r
10_{54}	$2t^6-6t^5+10t^4-11t^3+10t^2-6t+2$		47	2	2		r
10_{55}	$5t^4-15t^3+21t^2-15t+5$		61	4	2,5		r
10_{56}	$2t^6-8t^5+14t^4-17t^3+14t^2-8t+2$		65	4	2		r
10_{57}	$2t^6-8t^5+18t^4-23t^3+18t^2-8t+2$		79	2	2		r
10_{58}	$(t^2-3t+1)(3t^2-7t+3)$		65	0	2		r
10_{59}	$(t^2-t+1)(t^2-3t+1)^2$		75	2	2,3?		r
10_{60}	$(t^2-3t+1)(-t^4+4t^3-7t^2+4t-1)$		85	0	2		r
10_{61}	$(t^2-t+1)(-2t^4+3t^3-t^2+3t-2)$		33	4	2,3?		r
10_{62}	$(t^2-t+1)^2(t^4-t^3+t^2-t+1)$		45	4	2		r
10_{63}	$(t^2-t+1)(5t^2-9t+5)$		57	4	2		r
10_{64}	$(t^2-t+1)(t^6-2t^5+3t^4-5t^3+3t^2-2t+1)$		51	2	2		r
10_{65}	$(t^2-t+1)^2(-2t^2+3t-2)$		63	2	2		r
10_{66}	$(t^2-t+1)(-3t^4+6t^3-7t^2+6t-3)$		75	6	2,3?		r
10_{67}	$(2t^2-3t+2)(2t^2-5t+2)$		63	2	2		n
10_{68}	$4t^4-14t^3+21t^2-14t+4$		57	0	2		r
10_{69}	$t^6-7t^5+21t^4-29t^3+21t^2-7t+1$		87	2	2,3?		r
10_{70}	$t^6-7t^5+16t^4-19t^3+16t^2-7t+1$		67	2			r
10_{71}	$t^6-7t^5+18t^4-25t^3+18t^2-7t+1$		77	0			r
10_{72}	$2t^6-9t^5+16t^4-19t^3+16t^2-9t+2$		73	4			r
10_{73}	$t^6-7t^5+20t^4-27t^3+20t^2-7t+1$		83	2			r
10_{74}	$(2t^2-3t+2)(2t^2-5t+2)$		21,3	2	2		r
10_{75}	$t^6-7t^5+19t^4-27t^3+19t^2-7t+1$		27,3	0	2		r
10_{76}	$(t^2-t+1)(-2t^4+5t^3-5t^2+5t-2)$		57	4	2		r

Table I

$\mathfrak{k}$	$\Delta_1(t)$	$\Delta_2(t)$	T	σ	q	α, β	s
10_{77}	$(t^2-t+1)^2(-2t^2+3t-2)$		63	2	2		r
10_{78}	$(t^2-t+1)(-t^4+6t^3-9t^2+6t-1)$		69	4	2		r
10_{79}	$t^8-3t^7+7t^6-12t^5+15t^4-12t^3+7t^2-3t+1$		61	0			i
10_{80}	$3t^6-9t^5+15t^4-17t^3+15t^2-9t+3$		71	6	2,3		n
10_{81}	$t^6-8t^5+20t^4-27t^3+20t^2-8t+1$		85	0			i
10_{82}	$(t^2-t+1)^2(t^4-2t^3+t^2-2t+1)$		63	2	2		n
10_{83}	$2t^6-9t^5+19t^4-25t^3+19t^2-9t+2$		83	2	2		n
10_{84}	$(t^2-t+1)(-2t^4+7t^3-11t^2+7t-2)$		87	2	2		n
10_{85}	$(t^2-t+1)(t^6-3t^5+4t^4-3t^3+4t^2-3t+1)$		57	4			n
10_{86}	$2t^6-9t^5+19t^4-23t^3+19t^2-9t+2$		85	0	2		n
10_{87}	$(t^2-t+1)^2(-2t^2+5t-2)$		81	0	2,3		n
10_{88}	$t^6-8t^5+24t^4-35t^3+24t^2-8t+1$		101	0			i
10_{89}	$t^6-8t^5+24t^4-33t^3+24t^2-8t+1$		99	2			r
10_{90}	$2t^6-8t^5+17t^4-23t^3+17t^2-8t+2$		77	0	2		n
10_{91}	$t^8-4t^7+9t^6-14t^5+17t^4-14t^3+9t^2-4t+1$		73	0	3		n
10_{92}	$2t^6-10t^5+20t^4-25\mathrm{t}^3+20t^2-10t+2$		89	4	2		n
10_{93}	$2t^6-8t^5+15t^4-17t^3+15t^2-8t+2$		67	2	2		n
10_{94}	$t^8-4t^7+9t^6-14t^5+15t^4-14t^3+9t^2-4t+1$		71	2			n
10_{95}	$(2t^2-3t+2)(-t^4+3t^3-5t^2+3t-1)$		91	2	2,3?		n
10_{96}	$t^6-7t^5+22t^4-33t^3+22t^2-7t+1$		93	0			r
10_{97}	$5t^4-22t^3+33t^2-22t+5$		87	2			r
10_{98}	$(t^2-t+1)^2(-2t^2+5+5t-2)$,	(t^2-t+1)	27,3	4	2,3		n
10_{99}	$(t^2-t+1)^4$	$(t^2-t+1)^2$	9,9	0	2,3		f
10_{100}	$(t^4-t^3+t^2-t+1)(t^4-3t^3+5t^2-3t+1)$		65	4	2		r
10_{101}	$7t^2-21t^3+29t^2-21t+7$		85	4	2,7?		r
10_{102}	$2t^6-8t^5+16t^4-21t^3+16t^2-8t+2$		73	0	2		n
10_{103}	$(t^2-t+1)(-2t^4+6t^3-9t^2+6t-2)$		15,5	2	2		r
10_{104}	$t^8-4t^7+9t^6-15t^5+19t^4-15t^3+9t^2-4t+1$		77	0			r
10_{105}	$t^6-8t^5+22t^4-29t^3+22t^2-8t+1$		91	2	7?		r
10_{106}	$(t^2-t+1)(t^6-3t^5+5t^4-7t^3+5t^2-3t+1)$		75	2			n
10_{107}	$t^6-8t^5+22t^4-31t^3+22t^2-8t+1$		93	0			n
10_{108}	$2t^6-8t^5+14t^4-15t^3+14t^2-8t+2$		63	2	2		r

Table I

𝔱	$\Delta_1(t)$	$\Delta_2(t)$	T	σ	q	α, β	s
10_{109}	$t^8-4t^7+10t^6-17t^5+21t^4-17t^3+10t^2-4t+1$		85	0			i
10_{110}	$t^6-8t^5+20t^4-25t^3+20t^2-8t+1$		83	2			n
10_{111}	$(2t^2-3t+2)(-t^4+3t^3-3t^2+3t-1)$		77	4	2		r
10_{112}	$(t^2-t+1)(t^6-4t^5+6t^4-7t^3+6t^2-4t+1)$		87	2	2		r
10_{113}	$(t^2-t+1)(-2t^4+9t^3-15t^2+9t-2)$		111	2	2		r
10_{114}	$(t^2-t+1)(-2t^4+8t^3-11t^2+8t-2)$		93	0	2		r
10_{115}	$t^6-9t^5+26t^4-37t^3+26t^2-9t+1$		109	0			i
10_{116}	$t^8-5t^7+12t^6-19t^5+21t^4-19t^3+12t^2-5t+1$		95	2			r
10_{117}	$2t^6-10t^5+24t^4-31t^3+24t^2-10t+2$		103	2	2		n
10_{118}	$t^8-5t^7+12t^6-19t^5+23t^4-19t^3+12t^2-5t+1$		97	0			i
10_{119}	$2t^6-10t^5+23t^4-31t^3+23t^2-10t+2$		101	0	2		n
10_{120}	$(2t^2-3t+2)(4t^2-7t+4)$		105	4	2		r
10_{121}	$2t^6-11t^5+27t^4-35t^3+27t^2-11t+2$		115	2	2		r
10_{122}	$(t^2-t+1)(t^2-3t+1)(-2t^2+3t-2)$		105	0	2,3?		r
10_{123}	$(t^4-3t^3+3t^2-3t+1)^2$,	$t^4-3t^3+3t^2-3t+1$	11,11	0	2,5		f
$*10_{124}$	$t^8-t^7+t^5-t^4+t^3-t+1$			8	3,5		r
10_{125}	$t^6-2t^5+2t^4-t^3+2t^2-2t+1$		11	2			r
10_{126}	$t^6-2t^5+4t^4-5t^3+4t^2-2t+1$		19	2			r
10_{127}	$t^6-4t^5+6t^4-7t^3+6t^2-4t+1$		29	4			r
10_{128}	$2t^6-3t^5+t^4+t^3+t^2-3t+2$		11	6	2		r
10_{129}	$2t^4-6t^3+9t^2-6t+2$		25	0	2		r
10_{130}	$2t^4-4t^3+5t^2-4t+2$		17	0	2		r
10_{131}	$2t^4-8t^3+11t^2-8t+2$		31	2	2		r
10_{132}	$t^4-t^3+t^2-t+1$		5	0	2,5		r
10_{133}	$t^4-5t^3+7t^2-5t+1$		19	2	2		r
10_{134}	$2t^6-4t^5+4t^4-3t^3+4t^2-4t+2$		23	6	2		r
10_{135}	$3t^4-9t^3+13t^2-9t+3$		37	0	2,3		r
10_{136}	$(t^2-t+1)(t^2-3t+1)$		15	2	2		r
10_{137}	$(t^2-3t+1)^2$		25	0	2,5		r
10_{138}	$(t^2-3t+1)(-t^4+2t^3-t^2+2t-1)$		35	2	2		r
10_{139}	$(t^2-t+1)(-t^6+t^4-t^3+t^2-1)$		3	6	2		r
10_{140}	$(t^2-t+1)^2$		9	0	2		r

Table I

𝔨	$\Delta_1(t)$	$\Delta_2(t)$	T	σ	q	α, β	s
10_{141}	$(t^2-t+1)(-t^4+2t^3-t^2+2t-1)$		21	0	2		r
10_{142}	$(t^2-t+1)(-2t^4+t^3+t^2+t-2)$		15	6	2		r
10_{143}	$(t^2-t+1)^3$		27	2	2,3		r
10_{144}	$(t^2-t+1)(3t^2-7t+3)$		39	2	2,3		r
10_{145}	$t^4+t^3-3t^2+t+1$		3	2	2		r
10_{146}	$2t^4-8t^3+13t^2-8t+2$		33	0	2		r
10_{147}	$(t^2-t+1)(2t^2-5t+2)$		27	2	2		n
10_{148}	$t^6-3t^5+7t^4-9t^3+7t^2-3t+1$		31	2	2		n
10_{149}	$t^6-5t^5+9t^4-11t^3+9t^2-5t+1$		41	4	2		n
10_{150}	$t^6-4t^5+6t^4-7t^3+6t^2-4t+1$		29	4			n
10_{151}	$t^6-4t^5+10t^4-13t^3+10t^2-4t+1$		43	2			n
10_{152}	$t^8-t^7-t^6+4t^5-5t^4+4t^3-t^2-t+1$		11	6			r
10_{153}	$t^6-t^5-t^4+3t^3-t^2-t+1$			0	2		n
10_{154}	$t^6-4t^4+7t^3-4t^2+1$		13	4			r
10_{155}	$t^6-3t^5+5t^4-7t^3+5t^2-3t+1$		5,5	0	2		r
10_{156}	$t^6-4t^5+8t^4-9t^3+8t^2-4t+1$		35	2			r
10_{157}	$t^6-6t^5+11t^4-13t^3+11t^2-6t+1$		7,7	4			r
10_{158}	$t^6-4t^5+10t^4-15t^3+10t^2-4t+1$		45	0			r
10_{159}	$(t^2-t+1)(-t^4+3t^3-5t^2+3t-1)$		39	2	3		r
10_{160}	$t^6-4t^5+4t^4-3t^3+4t^2-4t+1$		21	4			r
10_{161}	$t^6-2t^4+3t^3-2t^2+1$		5	4			r
10_{162}	$3t^4-9t^3+11t^2-9t+3$		35	2	2,3?		r
10_{163}	$(t^2-t+1)(-t^4+4t^3-7t^2+4t-1)$		51	2	2?		r
10_{164}	$3t^4-11t^3+17t^2-11t+3$		45	0	2,3?		r
10_{165}	$2t^4-10t^3+15t^2-10t+2$		39	2	2		r

The Table II gives non-singular Seifert matrices of knots up to ten crossings, computed by U. Lüdicke. $2m$ is the number of rows; the entries run through successive rows, $x+y$ resp. $x-y$ means that the entry $+y$ resp. $-y$ has to be repeated x times. As an example

$$\begin{pmatrix} 1 & 0 & -1 & 0 \\ 0 & 1 & 0 & -1 \\ 0 & 0 & 1 & 0 \\ -1 & 0 & 0 & 1 \end{pmatrix}$$

is the Seifert matrix of 5_1 according to the table. (See Chapter 13.)

Table II

3_1	m = 1	1 −1 0 1
4_1	m = 1	−1 0 2+1
5_1	m = 2	1 0 −1 2+0 1 0 −1 2+0 1 0 −1 2+0 1
5_2	m = 1	2 −2 −1 2
6_1	m = 1	−1 0 1 2
6_2	m = 2	1 0 −1 2+0 1 3+0 −1 1 0 −1 0 1 −1
6_3	m = 2	1 −1 3+0 1 2+0 1 2−1 0 −1 2+1 −1
7_1	m = 3	1 2+0 −1 3+0 1 2+0 −1 3+0 1 2+0 −1 3+0 1 2+0 −1 3+0 1 2+0 −1 3+0 1
7_2	m = 1	3 −3 −2 3
7_3	m = 2	−2 0 2+1 0 −1 2+0 2 0 −2 2+0 1 0 −1
7_4	m = 1	−2 0 1 −2
7_5	m = 2	2 0 2−1 0 1 4+0 1 3−1 0 2
7_6	m = 2	1 0 −1 2+0 1 −1 0 −1 0 2 0 1 −1 0 −1
7_7	m = 2	1 3+0 −1 1 2+0 1 2−1 2+0 1 0 −1
8_1	m = 1	−1 0 1 3
8_2	m = 3	1 2+0 −1 3+0 1 2+0 −1 3+0 1 5+0 −1 1 2+0 −1 3+0 1 0 −1 2+0 1 0 −1
8_3	m = 1	−2 0 1 2
8_4	m = 2	1 0 −1 2+0 1 3+0 −1 1 2+0 1 −1 −2
8_5	m = 3	−1 6+0 −1 0 1 4+0 −1 0 1 3+0 1 −1 2+0 1 3+0 −1 0 1 2+0 −1 0 1
8_6	m = 2	2 0 −2 2+0 1 2+0 2−1 2 0 −1 0 1 −1
8_7	m = 3	−1 2+0 1 3+0 −1 4+0 1 0 −1 4+0 1 0 −1 6+0 1 −1 1 0 −1 2+0 1

Table II

8_8	m = 2	1 −1 3+0 1 2+0 −1 1 −2 2+1 −1 2 −2
8_9	m = 3	−1 6+0 −1 1 3+0 1 0 −1 3+0 1 0 −1 1 6+0 1 −1 3+0 −1 0 1
8_{10}	m = 3	1 −1 5+0 1 4+0 −1 0 −1 2+0 1 3+0 −1 4+0 1 0 −1 4+0 1 0 −1
8_{11}	m = 2	2 0 −2 0 −1 1 2+0 −1 0 2 0 1 −1 0 −1
8_{12}	m = 2	−2 1 2+0 1 −1 2+0 1 −1 1 2+0 1 0 1
8_{13}	m = 2	1 −1 3+0 1 4+0 −2 1 −1 0 2 −2
8_{14}	m = 2	−1 3+0 2+1 4+0 1 −1 0 −1 0 2
8_{15}	m = 2	2 2−1 2+0 2 −1 0 −1 0 2 −1 0 −1 0 1
8_{16}	m = 3	−1 1 5+0 −1 4+0 1 −1 1 0 −1 2+0 1 0 1 2+0 −1 3+0 1 −1 3+0 −1 0 1
8_{17}	m = 3	−1 1 5+0 −1 4+0 1 0 −1 3+0 1 −1 0 1 3+0 1 −1 0 1 −1 3+0 −1 0 1
8_{18}	m = 3	1 0 −1 4+0 1 5+0 −1 1 3+0 −1 0 1 −1 3+0 1 −1 1 −1 2+0 −1 2+0 1 −1
8_{19}	m = 3	−1 6+0 −1 1 3+0 1 0 −1 3+0 −1 0 1 −1 0 2+1 −1 2+0 −1 5+0 1 −1
8_{20}	m = 2	1 3+0 1 0 1 0 −1 0 4−1 2+0
8_{21}	m = 2	1 2+0 −1 0 1 −1 0 2−1 1 0 −2 −1 2+0
9_1	m = 4	1 3+0 −1 4+0 1 3+0 −1 4+0 1 3+0 −1 4+0 1 3+0 −1 4+0 1 3+0 −1 4+0 1 3+0 −1 4+0 1 3+0 −1 4+0 1
9_2	m = 1	4 −4 −3 4
9_3	m = 3	−1 3+0 1 2+0 −1 3+0 1 2+0 −1 3+0 1 2+0 −2 3+0 1 2+0 −1 3+0 1 2+0 −1
9_4	m = 2	3 0 −1 −2 0 1 0 −1 2+0 1 0 −3 2+0 3
9_5	m = 1	−2 0 1 −3
9_6	m = 3	1 2+0 −1 3+0 1 2+0 −1 3+0 2 −1 0 −1 2+0 −1 2 2+0 −1 3+0 1 2+0 −1 3+0 1
9_7	m = 2	3 0 −1 −2 0 1 4+0 1 −1 −2 −1 0 3
9_8	m = 2	−2 4+0 2 3−1 0 1 0 1 −1 0 1
9_9	m = 3	2 0 2−1 3+0 1 2+0 −1 0 −1 0 2 2+0 −1 3+0 1 2+0 −1 3+0 1 2+0 −1 3+0 1
9_{10}	m = 2	−2 2+0 2 0 −2 0 2+1 0 −1 0 1 2 0 −3
9_{11}	m = 3	−1 2+0 1 3+0 −1 2+0 1 3+0 −1 3+0 2+1 0 −2 4+0 1 0 −1 0 1 −1 3+0 1
9_{12}	m = 2	2 0 −2 2+0 1 −1 0 −2 0 3 0 1 −1 0 −1

Table II

9_{13}	m = 2	−1 2+0 1 0 −2 0 1 0 1 −2 1 0 1 2 −3
9_{14}	m = 2	1 3+0 −1 1 2+0 1 −1 −2 2+0 1 0 −1
9_{15}	m = 2	−1 3+0 2+1 4+0 −1 2+0 −1 1 −2
9_{16}	m = 3	−2 0 1 2+0 1 0 −1 0 1 3+0 1 −2 3+0 1 2+0 −1 2+0 1 3+0 −1 3+0 1 2+0 −1
9_{17}	m = 3	−2 1 4+0 1 −1 6+0 1 2+0 −1 1 −1 0 1 3+0 1 0 −1 1 0 −1 3+0 −1 1
9_{18}	m = 2	2 2+0 −1 0 2 2−1 2+0 1 −1 −2 −1 0 3
9_{19}	m = 2	2 −2 2+0 −1 2 2+0 1 0 −2 1 0 −1 1 −1
9_{20}	m = 3	1 2+0 −1 3+0 1 2+0 −1 3+0 1 −1 3+0 −1 0 2 4+0 −1 0 1 0 1 −1 3+0 −1
9_{21}	m = 2	−2 2+1 0 2 −3 3+0 1 −1 3+0 2+1
9_{22}	m = 3	−1 2+0 1 3+0 −1 1 3+0 1 0 −1 6+0 −1 2+0 1 −1 2+0 1 −1 0 1 −1 0 −1 2
9_{23}	m = 2	1 −1 3+0 3 2−1 0 −1 2 3−1 0 2
9_{24}	m = 3	1 5+0 1 −1 0 1 4+0 −1 5+0 1 −1 6+0 1 −1 0 −1 3+0 1
9_{25}	m = 2	2 −1 2+0 −1 2 −1 3+0 1 0 −1 1 0 −1
9_{26}	m = 3	−1 6+0 −1 0 1 4+0 −1 1 2+0 1 0 1 −2 2+0 1 0 −1 0 1 3+0 1 2−1 1
9_{27}	m = 3	1 −1 5+0 2 −1 3+0 −1 0 1 3+0 −1 1 0 −1 0 1 3+0 1 −1 0 1 4+0 −1
9_{28}	m = 3	1 −1 5+0 1 6+0 −1 3+0 −1 0 1 −1 6+0 1 −1 3+0 −1 0 1
9_{29}	m = 3	−1 6+0 1 0 −1 4+0 1 0 −1 4+0 1 2+0 1 −1 2+0 1 2+0 1 −1 2+0 −1
9_{30}	m = 3	1 −1 5+0 2 −1 4+0 −1 1 6+0 −1 0 1 −1 1 0 1 −1 0 1 0 −1 2+0 −1
9_{31}	m = 3	1 −1 5+0 1 6+0 1 −1 5+0 1 3+0 1 −1 0 −1 2+0 −1 2+0 1 −1
9_{32}	m = 3	−1 6+0 −1 0 1 4+0 −1 5+0 1 −1 2+0 1 −1 2+0 1 2+0 1 0 2−1 1
9_{33}	m = 3	1 −1 5+0 1 −1 3+0 −1 0 2 3+0 −1 1 0 −1 0 1 3+0 1 −1 0 1 4+0 −1
9_{34}	m = 3	1 −1 5+0 1 4+0 1 0 −1 0 1 4+0 −1 3+0 −1 0 1 −1 3+0 1 −1 0 1
9_{35}	m = 1	3 −2 −1 3
9_{36}	m = 3	−1 6+0 −1 2+0 1 3+0 −1 4+0 1 0 −1 4+0 1 0 −1 0 1 −1 3+0 1

Table II

9_{37}	m = 2	2 3+0 −1 1 2+0 1 2−1 2+0 1 0 −1
9_{38}	m = 2	2 0 2−1 0 2 −1 2+0 −1 2 3−1 0 2
9_{39}	m = 2	1 4+0 −2 0 1 0 1 −2 1 −1 2+1 −2
9_{40}	m = 3	1 −1 5+0 1 4+0 1 0 −1 1 3+0 −1 0 −1 4+0 1 −1 1 4+0 1 −1 1
9_{41}	m = 2	−1 3+0 1 −1 2+0 1 0 2 −1 0 2−1 2
9_{42}	m = 2	3+0 −1 0 −1 2+0 −1 3+0 −1 2+1 0
9_{43}	m = 3	−1 5+0 1 0 −1 4+0 −1 1 6+0 −1 0 1 −1 1 0 1 −1 0 1 0 −1 2+0 −1
9_{44}	m = 2	1 6+0 2+1 2−1 0 −1 1 2+0
9_{45}	m = 2	2 −1 1 0 −1 3+0 2+1 2+0 −1 1 −2 1
9_{46}	m = 1	3 −2 −1 0
9_{47}	m = 3	−1 6+0 1 0 1 −1 2+0 −1 1 0 1 −1 3+0 −1 6+0 −1 1 −1 2+0 1 0 −1
9_{48}	m = 2	−1 4+0 −1 0 1 0 1 −1 1 −1 2+1 −2
9_{49}	m = 2	−1 4+0 −2 0 1 0 1 −2 1 −1 2+1 −2
10_{1}	m = 1	4 0 1 −1
10_{2}	m = 4	−1 8+0 1 3+0 −1 4+0 1 3+0 −1 4+0 1 3+0 −1 1 3+0 1 3+0 −1 3+0 −1 1 3+0 −1 4+0 1 3+0 −1 4+0 1
10_{3}	m = 1	−2 0 1 3
10_{4}	m = 2	1 −1 3+0 1 2+0 −1 0 1 0 1 −1 0 −3
10_{5}	m = 4	−1 3+0 1 4+0 −1 3+0 1 4+0 −1 5+0 1 2+0 −1 5+0 1 2+0 −1 5+0 1 2+0 −1 8+0 1 −1 1 2+0 −1 3+0 1
10_{6}	m = 3	2 2+0 −2 3+0 1 2+0 −1 3+0 1 3+0 −1 0 −1 2 2+0 −1 3+0 1 0 −1 2+0 1 0 −1
10_{7}	m = 2	3 0 −3 2+0 1 2+0 −2 −1 3 2+0 1 2−1
10_{8}	m = 3	−2 5+0 2+1 6+0 1 0 −1 4+0 1 0 −1 0 −1 2+0 1 3+0 −1 2+0 1
10_{9}	m = 4	−1 3+0 1 4+0 −1 8+0 −1 1 4+0 1 2+0 −1 5+0 1 2+0 −1 3+0 1 2+0 −1 0 1 8+0 1 −1 5+0 −1 0 1
10_{10}	m = 2	1 −1 3+0 1 4+0 −3 2 −1 0 3 −3
10_{11}	m = 2	2 2−1 0 −2 2 4+0 1 0 1 −1 0 −2
10_{12}	m = 3	−2 0 2+1 3+0 −1 4+0 2 0 −2 4+0 1 0 −1 6+0 1 −1 1 0 −1 2+0 1
10_{13}	m = 2	−1 1 2+0 1 −2 2+0 1 −1 2 −2 0 1 −2 3
10_{14}	m = 3	2 0 2−1 3+0 1 2+0 −1 0 −1 0 2 5+0 −1 1 2+0 −1 3+0 1 0 −1 2+0 1 0 −1

Table II

10_{15}	m = 3	−1 2+0 1 3+0 −1 4+0 1 0 −1 4+0 1 0 −1 6+0 1 −1 1 0 −1 2+0 2
10_{16}	m = 2	−1 1 3+0 −2 2+0 1 0 −1 0 1 −1 0 2
10_{17}	m = 4	−1 2+0 1 5+0 −1 6+0 1 0 −1 6+0 1 0 −1 8+0 1 0 −1 6+0 1 0 −1 1 0 −1 3+0 1 5+0 −1 2+0 1
10_{18}	m = 2	2 0 −1 0 −1 1 4+0 1 0 1 −1 0 −2
10_{19}	m = 3	1 0 −1 4+0 1 0 −1 4+0 1 3+0 −1 2+0 1 6+0 −2 0 −1 0 1 0 1 −1
10_{20}	m = 2	3 −3 2+0 −2 3 2+0 −1 0 1 0 1 −1 0 −1
10_{21}	m = 3	1 3+0 −1 2+0 1 6+0 2 2−1 2+0 −1 0 1 4+0 −2 0 2 3+0 1 −1 0 −1
10_{22}	m = 3	−2 0 1 4+0 −1 1 3+0 2 0 −2 3+0 1 0 −1 1 6+0 1 −1 3+0 −1 0 1
10_{23}	m = 3	−1 2+0 1 3+0 −1 4+0 1 0 −2 4+0 1 0 −1 6+0 1 −1 1 0 −1 2+0 1
10_{24}	m = 2	2 0 −2 2+0 2 −1 0 −1 −2 3 2+0 1 2−1
10_{25}	m = 3	2 2+0 2−1 2+0 1 6+0 1 0 −1 3+0 −1 1 2+0 2−1 2+0 2 0 −1 2+0 1 0 −1
10_{26}	m = 3	1 0 −1 4+0 1 5+0 −1 1 3+0 −1 0 1 −1 1 0 1 0 −1 0 −2 4+0 1 0 −1
10_{27}	m = 3	−1 5+0 1 −1 6+0 1 0 −1 4+0 2 3−1 1 0 −1 2 3+0 −1 2+0 1
10_{28}	m = 2	−2 3+0 1 −2 3+0 2+1 −1 0 −1 0 1
10_{29}	m = 3	1 2+0 −1 3+0 1 6+0 1 −1 3+0 2−1 2 3+0 1 −1 0 −1 3+0 1 −1 0 −1
10_{30}	m = 2	2 −2 2+0 −1 3 −1 3+0 1 2+0 −1 1 −1
10_{31}	m = 2	−1 1 3+0 −2 2+0 1 −1 2 −2 −1 1 −1 2
10_{32}	m = 3	−1 1 5+0 −1 4+0 1 0 −1 3+0 1 −1 0 1 0 2−1 1 0 −1 2 −1 4+0 −1 2
10_{33}	m = 2	2 −2 2+0 −1 2 3+0 1 −1 2+0 −1 1 −2
10_{34}	m = 2	1 −1 3+0 1 2+0 −1 1 −3 3+0 1 −1
10_{35}	m = 2	1 −1 2+0 −1 2 2+0 −1 0 −2 0 1 −1 0 −1
10_{36}	m = 2	1 −1 3+0 3 −1 3+0 1 2+0 −1 1 −1
10_{37}	m = 2	2 −2 2+0 −1 2 2+0 −1 1 −2 3+0 1 −1
10_{38}	m = 2	−1 3+0 −1 3 2−1 1 −2 2 4+0 1
10_{39}	m = 3	−1 5+0 1 2 −1 4+0 −1 2 0 −1 4+0 1 0 −1 0 −1 2+0 1 3+0 −1 2+0 1

Table II

10_{40}	m = 3	1 5+0 −1 6+0 −2 2+0 2+1 −1 0 −1 0 1 2+0 1 0 −1 0 −1 2+1 0 1 −2
10_{41}	m = 3	1 0 −1 3+0 −1 2 6+0 1 −1 3+0 −1 0 1 2+0 1 −1 2+0 −1 1 −1 1 0 2+1 −2
10_{42}	m = 3	1 5+0 −1 1 6+0 1 2+0 1 −1 1 0 −1 0 2+1 −1 0 1 −2 5+0 1 −1
10_{43}	m = 3	1 0 −1 4+0 1 −1 3+0 −1 0 2 6+0 −1 2+0 1 −1 2+0 −1 0 −1 0 2+1 0 −1
10_{44}	m = 3	1 2+0 −1 2+0 −1 2 −1 5+0 1 4+0 −1 0 1 2+0 1 −1 2+0 −1 3+0 1 −1 0 −1
10_{45}	m = 3	1 0 −1 3+0 −1 2 5+0 −1 1 3+0 1 −1 0 −1 0 1 0 1 −1 0 −1 1 −1 3+1 0 −2
10_{46}	m = 4	−1 5+0 1 2+0 −1 8+0 −1 0 1 6+0 −1 0 1 5+0 1 −1 3+0 1 4+0 −1 3+0 1 4+0 −1 0 1 3+0 −1 2+0 1
10_{47}	m = 4	1 −1 7+0 1 6+0 −1 0 −1 3+0 1 4+0 −1 3+0 1 4+0 −1 5+0 1 2+0 −1 5+0 1 2+0 −1 5+0 1 2+0 −1
10_{48}	m = 4	1 0 −1 6+0 1 0 −1 6+0 1 5+0 −1 2+0 1 8+0 −1 2+0 1 5+0 −1 4+0 −1 0 1 0 −1 3+0 1 2+0 1 0 −1
10_{49}	m = 3	1 0 −1 4+0 1 0 −1 4+0 2 0 3−1 2+0 1 3+0 −1 2+0 2 −1 2+0 −1 2+0 2
10_{50}	m = 3	−1 6+0 −2 0 2 4+0 −1 0 1 2+0 2+1 −2 2+0 1 3+0 −1 0 1 2+0 −1 0 1
10_{51}	m = 3	1 −1 5+0 1 4+0 −1 1 −1 2+0 1 3+0 −2 4+0 1 0 −1 4+0 1 0 −1
10_{52}	m = 3	2 −2 4+0 −1 2 6+0 −1 2+0 1 3+0 −1 3+0 −1 1 0 −1 2+0 1 0 1 0 −1
10_{53}	m = 2	2 −2 2+0 −1 3 3−1 0 2 −1 0 −1 0 2
10_{54}	m = 3	2 −1 5+0 1 6+0 −1 2+0 1 3+0 −1 2+0 1 0 1 0 −1 0 −1 2+0 1 0 −1
10_{55}	m = 2	2 −1 3+0 1 −1 0 3 −1 3+0 1
10_{56}	m = 3	−2 1 0 1 2+0 1 −2 2+0 1 0 1 0 −1 4+0 1 0 −1 6+0 −1 2+0 1 −1 2+0 1
10_{57}	m = 3	1 −1 5+0 1 4+0 −1 1 −1 2+0 2+1 −1 0 −2 0 1 3+0 1 −1 4+0 2+1 −2
10_{58}	m = 2	2 −1 2+0 −1 2 2+0 1 0 −2 1 0 −1 1 −1
10_{59}	m = 3	−2 1 5+0 −1 0 1 2+0 1 0 −1 5+0 1 −1 2+0 1 −1 2+0 1 2−1 1 0 2−1 2
10_{60}	m = 3	1 −1 4+0 −1 2 6+0 1 3+0 −1 2+0 −1 1 0 1 −1 2+0 −1 1 0 1 −1 2+0 −1

Table II

10_{61}	m = 3	−1 2+0 1 3+0 −1 2+0 1 3+0 −1 4+0 1 0 −1 4+0 1 0 −1 3+0 1 −1 0 2
10_{62}	m = 4	−1 3+0 1 4+0 −1 3+0 1 4+0 −1 5+0 1 2+0 −1 5+0 1 2+0 −1 5+0 1 2+0 −1 8+0 1 −1 1 0 −1 4+0 1
10_{63}	m = 2	3 0 −1 −2 0 1 0 −1 2+0 1 0 −2 2+0 3
10_{64}	m = 4	−1 8+0 −1 0 1 6+0 −1 0 1 5+0 1 −1 4+0 1 3+0 −1 8+0 1 0 −1 1 2+0 −1 2+0 1 0 −1 2+0 1 2+0 −1 1
10_{65}	m = 3	−1 2+0 1 3+0 −2 0 1 2+0 1 0 −1 4+0 2 0 −2 2+0 −1 1 2+0 1 −1 1 −1 3+0 1
10_{66}	m = 3	2 2+0 −1 0 −1 0 1 2+0 −1 3+0 1 2+0 −1 3+0 1 2+0 −1 3+0 1 2+0 −1 3+0 2
10_{67}	m = 2	−1 3+0 1 2 0 −1 2+0 1 −1 0 −2 0 3
10_{68}	m = 2	−1 3+0 1 −1 4+0 3 −2 −1 0 −1 2
10_{69}	m = 3	−1 2+0 1 3+0 −1 0 1 4+0 −1 3+0 3+1 −3 2+0 1 −1 2+0 1 2+0 1 −1 0 −1 1
10_{70}	m = 3	1 6+0 1 0 1 −1 0 −1 0 −2 2+1 0 1 2+0 −1 4+0 1 0 −1 3+0 1 2+0 −1
10_{71}	m = 3	−1 6+0 −1 1 3+0 2+1 −2 4+0 −1 1 2 −1 0 −1 1 0 −1 1 0 1 0 2−1 0 1
10_{72}	m = 3	−1 2+0 1 3+0 −1 4+0 1 0 −1 4+0 1 0 −2 1 5+0 −1 4+0 1 −1 1
10_{73}	m = 3	1 −1 5+0 2 −1 3+0 −1 0 1 6+0 1 0 1 −1 3+0 −1 0 1 3+0 1 −1
10_{74}	m = 2	−1 3+0 2+1 0 3−1 2 4+0 2
10_{75}	m = 3	−1 1 4+0 1 −3 1 4+0 1 −1 3+0 1 −1 0 1 3+0 1 2−1 1 3+0 1 0 −1 1
10_{76}	m = 3	−2 2+0 1 3+0 −1 0 1 4+0 −1 0 1 0 1 0 1 −2 2+0 1 3+0 −1 0 1 2+0 −1 0 1
10_{77}	m = 3	1 −1 5+0 1 6+0 −1 2+0 1 3+0 −1 4+0 1 0 −1 0 1 −1 0 1 0 −2
10_{78}	m = 3	2 −1 5+0 1 −1 3+0 −1 0 1 6+0 1 −1 5+0 1 3+0 1 −1 0 −1
10_{79}	m = 4	1 0 −1 6+0 1 0 −1 6+0 1 5+0 −1 2+0 1 4+0 −1 1 2+0 −1 2+0 1 5+0 −1 6+0 1 0 −1 6+0 1 0 −1
10_{80}	m = 3	2 0 2−1 3+0 1 0 −1 3+0 −1 2 0 −1 0 −1 2+0 2 2+0 −1 3+0 1 3+0 −1 2+0 1
10_{81}	m = 3	−1 6+0 −1 5+0 1 −1 6+0 2 3−1 1 2+0 1 0 1 −1 0 −1 0 1
10_{82}	m = 4	−1 8+0 −1 1 5+0 1 0 −1 8+0 1 2+0 −1 5+0 1 2+0 −1 0 1 −1 2+0 1 2+0 −1 0 1 2+0 −1 1 4+0 −1 3+0 1

Table II

10_{83}	m = 3	−2 2+0 2 3+0 −1 4+0 1 0 −1 3+0 2+1 0 −2 3+0 1 −1 0 1 −1 0 −1 0 1 0 1
10_{84}	m = 3	1 −1 5+0 1 4+0 −1 1 −1 5+0 1 −1 3+0 −1 0 1 −2 5+0 1 −1
10_{85}	m = 4	1 2+0 −1 5+0 1 8+0 1 0 −1 6+0 1 0 −1 3+0 −1 2+0 1 5+0 −1 2+0 1 5+0 1 −1 0 −1 4+0 −1 0 2+1 −1
10_{86}	m = 3	−1 0 1 4+0 −2 1 4+0 2 −2 3+0 1 0 −1 1 6+0 1 −1 2+0 1 −1 0 1
10_{87}	m = 3	−1 0 1 4+0 −1 5+0 1 −2 3+0 1 0 −1 1 6+0 1 −1 2+0 1 −1 0 1
10_{88}	m = 3	1 5+0 1 −2 0 1 2+0 −1 1 −1 4+0 1 0 −1 4+0 1 −1 1 4+0 1 −1 1
10_{89}	m = 3	−1 1 2+0 1 2+0 −1 3+0 −1 1 −1 1 4+0 1 0 1 6+0 1 −1 5+0 1
10_{90}	m = 3	1 0 −1 4+0 1 5+0 −1 1 3+0 −1 0 1 −2 0 1 4+0 −1 0 1 −1 2+0 1 −1
10_{91}	m = 4	−1 1 7+0 −1 0 1 6+0 −1 7+0 1 −1 4+0 1 −1 2+0 1 0 −1 6+0 1 0 2−1 0 1 3+0 1 5+0 −1 2+0 1
10_{92}	m = 3	−1 3+0 1 2+0 −1 0 1 4+0 −1 3+0 1 2+0 −2 1 2+0 2 +1 0 −2 0 1 0 −1 2+0 1
10_{93}	m = 3	−1 5+0 1 −2 6+0 1 −1 3+0 −1 0 1 0 2−1 1 −1 0 1 0 1 4+0 1
10_{94}	m = 4	1 0 −1 5+0 −1 1 8+0 1 8+0 −1 4+0 1 −1 2+0 −1 0 1 2+0 1 −1 2+0 −1 0 1 5+0 1 −1 0 −1 0 2+1 3+0 −1
10_{95}	m = 3	1 −1 5+0 1 6+0 −2 1 0 1 2+0 1 −2 2+0 −1 2+1 0 −1 0 1 −1 0 1 0 −1
10_{96}	m = 3	−1 6+0 1 6+0 1 −1 2+0 1 −1 0 1 3+0 1 0 −1 −2 1 2+0 −1 2+1 −1
10_{97}	m = 2	1 3+0 −1 −2 1 0 1 0 −2 1 0 2+1 −2
10_{98}	m = 3	−1 6+0 2 2+0 2−1 1 0 1 6+0 1 −1 2+0 2−1 0 2 0 −1 2+0 −1 0 1
10_{99}	m = 4	−1 8+0 −1 1 7+0 −1 1 4+0 1 2+0 −1 4+0 1 −1 2+0 1 0 −1 2+0 1 −1 2+0 1 0 2−1 0 1 3+0 1 5+0 −1 2+0 1
10_{100}	m = 4	−1 1 7+0 −1 6+0 1 −1 1 2+0 −1 3+0 1 0 1 3+0 2−1 3+0 1 0 −1 6+0 1 5+0 −1 2+0 1 3+0 −1 4+0 1
10_{101}	m = 2	−3 0 3+1 −1 3+0 1 −2 0 1 0 1 −2
10_{102}	m = 3	1 0 −1 4+0 1 5+0 −1 1 3+0 −1 0 1 −2 0 2 4+0 −1 0 1 −1 0 2+1 −2
10_{103}	m = 3	−1 5+0 1 −1 6+0 1 −1 3+0 −1 0 2 0 −2 −1 1 −1 0 1 0 1 2+0 −1 0 2

Table II

10_{104}	m = 4	1 7+0 −1 1 8+0 1 −1 5+0 −1 0 1 4+0 −1 2+0 1 −1 0 1 0 1 −1 3+0 −1 7+0 1 −1 5+0 1 2+0 −1
10_{105}	m = 3	2 −1 4+0 −1 1 4+0 1 2−1 0 1 2+0 1 0 −1 0 1 3+0 1 −2 5+0 1 −1
10_{106}	m = 4	1 8+0 1 −1 5+0 −1 0 1 5+0 −1 2+0 −1 1 3+0 1 0 −1 0 −1 2+0 1 5+0 −1 5+0 1 2+0 −1 6+0 1 0 −1
10_{107}	m = 3	1 6+0 1 −1 5+0 1 6+0 −2 0 1 −1 2+0 1 −1 0 1 −1 0 1 0 −1
10_{108}	m = 3	−1 6+0 −1 1 5+0 −1 1 2+0 1 2+0 −1 2+0 −1 0 1 0 2 −1 0 1 −1 2+0 1
10_{109}	m = 4	−1 2+0 1 5+0 −1 6+0 1 0 −1 6+0 1 0 −1 8+0 1 0 −1 6+0 1 0 −1 1 2+0 −1 2+0 1 4+0 1 −1 2+0 1
10_{110}	m = 3	−1 6+0 −1 6+0 2 2−1 4+0 1 2+0 −1 1 −1 0 1 0 1 0 −1 2+0 1
10_{111}	m = 3	1 5+0 2−1 0 1 4+0 −1 0 1 3+0 1 −2 0 2+1 3+0 −1 2+0 1 0 1 0 −2
10_{112}	m = 4	−1 8+0 −1 1 5+0 1 0 −1 6+0 1 −1 1 0 −1 6+0 1 0 −1 2+0 −1 3+0 1 0 −1 1 5+0 1 5+0 −1 2+0 1
10_{113}	m = 3	1 −1 5+0 1 6+0 −2 0 1 3+0 1 −1 2+0 −1 1 0 1 −2 2+1 0 1 2+0 −1
10_{114}	m = 3	1 0 −1 4+0 2 −1 4+0 −2 2 3+0 −1 0 1 −1 3+0 1 −1 1 −1 2+0 −1 2+0 1 −1
10_{115}	m = 3	−1 6+0 −1 1 5+0 −1 3+0 1 −1 0 1 0 −1 0 1 −1 0 1 −1 3+0 −1 0 2
10_{116}	m = 4	−1 1 7+0 −1 1 7+0 −1 5+0 1 −1 0 1 3+0 −1 0 1 −1 0 1 0 −1 3+0 1 2+0 1 5+0 −1 2+0 1 0 −1 4+0 −1 0 1
10_{117}	m = 3	1 −1 5+0 1 6+0 −2 0 2+1 −1 2+1 −1 2+0 1 3+0 −1 2+0 −1 2+1 0 −2
10_{118}	m = 4	−1 2+0 1 5+0 −1 6+0 1 0 −1 6+0 1 0 −1 5+0 1 −1 0 1 2+0 −1 5+0 1 −1 0 1 2+0 −1 2+0 1 2+0 −1 0 1 0 −1 0 1
10_{119}	m = 3	1 0 −1 4+0 1 5+0 −1 1 6+0 −2 1 2+0 1 −1 1 −2 1 −1 0 2+1 0 −1
10_{120}	m = 2	2 2−1 2+0 2 −1 0 −1 0 2 −1 0 −1 0 2
10_{121}	m = 3	−1 5+0 1 −1 6+0 2 −1 2+0 −1 1 0 1 0 −1 1 0 −1 0 1 2 +0 −1 3+0 1
10_{122}	m = 3	−1 1 5+0 −2 1 3+0 2+1 −2 3+0 1 −1 0 1 −1 0 −1 0 1 0 1 −1 2+0 −1 2+0 1
10_{123}	m = 4	−1 1 7+0 −1 8+0 −1 1 4+0 1 2+0 −1 4+0 1 −1 2+0 1 2+0 −1 2+0 1 −1 0 1 3+0 1 2+0 −1 0 1 0 −1 2+0 1 0 −1 0 1

Table II

10_{124}	m = 4	−1 5+0 1 2+0 −1 8+0 −1 0 1 6+0 −1 0 1 5+0 1 −1 3+0 1 4+0 −1 3+0 1 4+0 −1 0 −1 3+0 1 2+0 −1
10_{125}	m = 3	−1 5+0 2−1 6+0 2 −1 4+0 −1 5+0 −1 0 1 0 1 2+0 −1 0 −1
10_{126}	m = 3	1 5+0 −1 1 4+0 1 0 1 6+0 −1 4+0 1 −1 0 1 3+0 2+1 0
10_{127}	m = 3	0 −1 0 1 3+0 2 0 2−1 3+0 1 2+0 −1 1 5+0 −1 3+0 1 2+0 −1 3+0 1
10_{128}	m = 3	−1 1 5+0 −1 4+0 −1 0 −2 0 1 0 1 −1 0 −1 0 1 0 1 2 0 −2 5+0 1 −1
10_{129}	m = 2	2 0 −1 2 2+1 2+0 −1 3+0 1 2−1 0
10_{130}	m = 2	0 −1 2+0 −1 0 2 0 1 2 2+0 2−1 2 −1
10_{131}	m = 2	0 −1 2+0 −1 2+0 2 0 2+1 0 1 2 2+0
10_{132}	m = 2	3+0 −1 1 3+0 −1 0 1 2+0 −1 2+0
10_{133}	m = 2	1 4+0 1 2+0 −1 0 1 0 2−1 1 −1
10_{134}	m = 3	−1 5+0 1 −1 6+0 −2 0 1 3+0 1 −1 2+0 −1 1 0 1 −2 2+1 0 1 2+0 −1
10_{135}	m = 2	−1 3+0 −1 1 3+0 2+1 0 2−2 −1 −3
10_{136}	m = 2	−1 3+0 1 −1 2+0 1 −1 0 2+1 0 1 0
10_{137}	m = 2	1 −1 2+0 −1 1 −1 0 −1 1 −1 1 2 −3 0 −2
10_{138}	m = 3	1 −1 4+0 −1 7+0 1 3+0 −1 2+0 −1 1 0 1 −1 2+0 −1 1 0 1 −1 2+0 −1
10_{139}	m = 4	−1 2+0 1 5+0 −1 6+0 1 0 −1 6+0 1 0 −1 8+0 −1 8+0 −1 0 1 0 −1 0 1 0 1 −1 0 −1 1 2+0 1 2+0 −1
10_{140}	m = 2	2+1 2+0 1 4+0 2+1 0 1 −1 0 −1
10_{141}	m = 3	1 6+0 −1 4+0 1 2+0 −1 0 −1 2+1 0 −1 2+0 2+1 2+0 1 3+0 2−1 2+0
10_{142}	m = 3	−1 6+0 −1 0 1 4+0 −1 0 1 3+0 1 −1 2+0 1 3+0 −1 0 −1 2+0 1 0 −2
10_{143}	m = 3	3+0 −1 0 1 −1 1 6+0 1 3+0 1 −1 2+1 2+0 2 −1 2+1 −1 0 −1 1 2−1 1 0
10_{144}	m = 2	2−1 2 2+0 2 0 −1 2 2−1 0 −1 2+0 1
10_{145}	m = 2	1 0 1 0 −1 1 2+0 1 −1 2+1 2 −3 0 2
10_{146}	m = 2	−1 3+0 2−1 0 2+1 −1 2 −1 0 2 −1 0
10_{147}	m = 2	−1 1 3+0 −1 2 0 1 2 −4 2+0 1 −2 −1
10_{148}	m = 3	−1 6+0 1 6+0 1 4+0 −1 2+1 2+0 −1 2+0 −1 0 1 2 0 −1 2+1 −2
10_{149}	m = 3	4+0 −1 0 −1 1 4+0 1 0 1 5+0 −1 1 2+0 −1 9+0 −1 1

Table II

10_{150}	m = 3	−1 0 1 3+0 1 −1 0 −1 3+0 1 −1 5+0 −1 1 2+0 −1 2+0 1 −1 2+1 0 −1 2+0 −1
10_{151}	m = 3	−1 6+0 −1 5+0 1 −1 7+0 −1 1 −1 1 2+0 1 0 1 −1 0 1 0 −1
10_{152}	m = 4	1 2+0 −1 5+0 1 −1 7+0 1 6+0 −1 0 1 4+0 1 −1 2+0 1 0 −1 6+0 1 0 −1 6+0 1 5+0 −1 2+0 1
10_{153}	m = 3	−2 2+0 2+1 2+0 1 0 −1 2+0 1 −1 4+0 1 7+0 1 0 −1 3+0 −1 2+0 1
10_{154}	m = 3	−1 6+0 −1 5+0 1 −1 6+0 −2 0 1 −1 1 0 1 −1 0 1 −1 0 1 0 −1
10_{155}	m = 3	4+0 −1 2+0 −1 4+0 −1 5+0 −1 3+1 2+0 3−1 −2 5+0 −1 2 1
10_{156}	m = 3	1 6+0 1 6+0 −1 0 1 3+0 1 3+0 1 −1 0 1 −1 2+0 1 0 −1 0 1
10_{157}	m = 3	−1 6+0 −1 4+0 −1 1 −1 1 6+0 −1 1 −2 1 −1 1 −3 2 −1 1 0 2+1 0
10_{158}	m = 3	−1 1 5+0 −1 4+0 −1 0 −1 0 1 0 1 −1 0 1 3+0 1 2 0 2−1 3+0 −1 0 1
10_{159}	m = 3	1 5+0 2−1 6+0 1 3+0 −2 −1 0 1 0 3−1 1 −1 3+0 −1 1 −2 −1 0
10_{160}	m = 3	1 −1 5+0 −1 5+0 1 −1 3+0 −1 1 0 −1 3+0 −1 2+1 −1 3+0 −1 0 1 −1
10_{161}	m = 3	1 6+0 1 4+0 2−1 1 3+0 1 0 −1 1 3+0 1 0 −1 1 2+0 −2 2+1 −1 1
10_{162}	m = 2	−1 3+0 −1 1 2+0 −1 2+1 0 2 −2 −1 3
10_{163}	m = 3	1 0 −1 4+0 −1 2 4+0 1 −1 3+0 −1 0 1 −1 3+0 1 −1 1 −1 2+0 −1 2+0 1 −1
10_{164}	m = 2	−1 5+0 1 0 −1 2+1 3 −2 1 5 6
10_{165}	m = 2	−2 0 1 0 1 2+0 −1 0 1 −2 2+0 −1 1 0

Table III contains the invariant $\lambda(\zeta)$ computed by G. Wenzel and U. Lüdicke. It is given for prime numbers p with $p \mid T_r$, $p \nmid T_{r-1}$ (see Table I), ζ is a primitive p-th root of unity. (Compare 14.11.)

The sequences printed are $a_1, a_2, \ldots, a_{\frac{p-1}{2}}$ computed for the knot indicated and its mirror image where $\lambda(\zeta) = \sum_{k=1}^{p-1} a_k \zeta^k$, $a_k = a_{p-k}$. From the class $[\lambda(\zeta)]$ always a lexicographically first (and unique) was chosen. If the two sequences do not coincide the knot is shown to be non-amphicheiral by this invariant.

The following formulae allow to compute the linking number v_{ij} and μ_{ij} of the regular and irregular dihedral branched coverings $\hat{R}_p$ and $\hat{I}_p$, see Section 14 C:

$$2v_{0j} = a_j - \frac{1}{p} \sum_{k=1}^{p-1} a_k,$$

$$\mu_{ij} = 2v_{0j}, \quad \mu_{ij} = v_{0,i-j} + v_{0,i+j}.$$

A blank in the table indicates that either no admissible prime p exists or that no result was obtained due to computer overflow. Table III contains $\lambda(\zeta)$ for knots with less than ten crossings. It was computed, though, for knots with ten crossings, but the material seemed to be too voluminous to be included here.

Table III

Knot : 3_1 p = 3

6				
−6				

Knot: 4_1 p = 5

−2	2			
−2	2			

Knot: 5_1 p = 5

10	10			
−10	−10			

Knot: 5_2 p = 7

2	6	6		
−6	−6	−2		

Knot: 6_1 p = 3

−6				
6				

Knot: 6_2 p = 11

2	6	2	6	6
−6	−6	−6	−2	−2

Knot: 6_3 p = 13

−2	−2	2	−2	2	2
−2	−2	2	−2	2	2

Knot: 7_1 p = 7

14	14	14		
−14	−14	−14		

Knot: 7_2 p = 11

2	2	6	6	6
−6	−6	−2	−6	−2

Table III

Knot: 7_3 p = 13

−10	−10	−10	−10	−6	−6
6	10	6	10	10	10

Knot: 7_4 p = 3

6
−6

Knot: 7_4 p = 5

−14	−6
6	14

Knot: 7_5 p = 17

6	6	10	10	6	10	10	10
−10	−10	−10	−10	−6	−10	−6	−6

Knot: 7_6 p = 19

2	2	2	6	6	6	2	6	6
−6	−6	−6	−2	−6	−6	−2	−2	−2

Knot: 7_7 p = 3

−18
18

Knot: 7_7 p = 7

2	2	10
−10	−2	−2

Knot: 8_1 p = 13

−2	−2	−2	2	2	2
−2	−2	2	2	−2	2

Knot: 8_2 p = 17

6	10	6	10	6	10	10	10
−10	−10	−10	−10	−10	−6	−6	−6

Knot: 8_3 p = 17

−2	−2	−2	2	2	−2	2	2
−2	−2	−2	2	2	−2	2	2

Knot: 8_4 p = 19

2	2	6	2	6	6	2	6	6
−6	−6	−6	−6	−2	−6	−2	−2	−2

Knot: 8_5 p = 3

−12
12

Knot: 8_5 p = 7

−6	6	14
−14	6	−6

Table III

Knot: 8_6 p = 23

2	2	2	6	6	2	2	6	6	6	6
−6	−6	−6	−6	−2	−6	−2	−2	−6	−2	−2

Knot: 8_7 p = 23

−6	−6	−6	−6	−2	−6	−2	−6	−2	−2	−2
2	2	6	2	2	6	6	2	6	6	6

Knot: 8_8 p = 5

6	14
−14	−6

Knot: 8_9 p = 5

−2	2
−2	2

Knot: 8_{10} p = 3

0
0

Knot: 8_{11} p = 3

−18
18

Knot: 8_{12} p = 29

−2	−2	−2	−2	2	−2	2	−2	2	2	−2	2	2	2
−2	−2	−2	−2	2	−2	2	−2	2	2	−2	2	2	2

Knot: 8_{13} p = 29

−2	−2	−2	−2	−2	2	2	2	2	−2	−2	2	2	2
−2	−2	−2	2	−2	−2	−2	2	2	−2	2	2	2	2

Knot: 8_{14} p = 31

2	2	2	6	2	2	6	6	2	2	6	6	6	6
−6	−6	−6	−6	−6	−6	−2	−2	−2	−2	−6	−6	−2	−2
6													
−2													

Knot: 8_{15} p = 3

12
−12

Knot: 8_{15} p = 11

10	18	22	30	30
−30	−22	−10	−30	−18

Knot: 8_{16} p = 5

18	42
−42	−18

Table III

Knot: 8_{16} p = 7

−42	−2	−26
2	26	42

Knot: 8_{17} p = 37

−6	6	−2	−2	−2	6	2	−6	2	−2	6	−6	2	2	6	−6	−2
−6	6	−2	−2	−2	6	2	−6	2	−2	6	−6	2	2	6	−6	−2
2																
2																

Knot: 8_{18} p = 5

−4	4
−4	4

Knot: 8_{19} p = 3

−12
12

Knot: 8_{20} p = 3

0
0

Knot: 8_{21} p = 3

12
−12

Knot: 8_{21} p = 5

14	26
−26	−14

Knot: 9_1 p = 3

18
−18

Knot: 9_2 p = 3

6
−6

Knot: 9_2 p = 5

−2	2
−2	2

Knot: 9_3 p = 19

−14	−14	−14	−14	−14	−14	−10	−10	−10
10	14	10	14	10	14	14	14	14

Knot: 9_4 p = 3

6
−6

Table III

Knot: 9_4 p = 7

10	14	18
−18	−10	−14

Knot: 9_5 p = 23

−6	−6	−6	−6	−2	−2	−2	−6	−6	−2	−2
2	2	2	6	2	2	6	6	6	6	6

Knot: 9_6 p = 3

18
−18

Knot: 9_7 p = 29

6	6	6	6	10	10	10	6	6	10	10	10
−10	−10	−10	−10	−6	−10	−10	−10	−6	−6	−6	−10
10	10										
−6	−6										

Knot: 9_8 p = 31

2	2	2	2	6	6	2	2	6	6	6	6	2	6
−6	−6	−6	−6	−6	−2	−2	−6	−6	−6	−2	−2	−2	−2
6													
−2													

Knot: 9_9 p = 31

10	10	10	14	14	10	10	14	14	14	10
−14	−14	−14	−14	−14	−14	−10	−14	−14	−10	−10
14	14	14	14							
−14	−10	−10	−10							

Knot: 9_{10} p = 3

18
−18

Knot: 9_{10} p = 11

−18	−10	−18	−10	−10
10	10	10	18	18

Knot: 9_{11} p = 3

−18
18

Knot: 9_{11} p = 11

−10	−6	−6	−2	2
−2	10	2	6	6

Knot: 9_{12} p = 5

14	26
−26	−14

Table III

Knot: 9_{12} p = 7

2	2	10
−10	−2	−2

Knot: 9_{13} p = 37

−10	−10	−10	−10	−10	−10	−6	−10	−6	−10	−6	−6
6	6	6	6	10	10	6	6	6	10	10	10

−10	−6	−10	−6	−6	−6
6	10	10	10	10	10

Knot: 9_{14} p = 37

−2	−2	−2	2	−2	−2	−2	2	2	−2	−2	2	2	−2	2	2	2
−2	−2	−2	−2	−2	−2	−2	2	2	2	2	2	−2	−2	2	2	2

2
2

Knot: 9_{15} p = 3

−18
18

Knot: 9_{15} p = 13

−14	−2	−10	−6	−10	−10
2	6	10	10	10	14

Knot: 9_{16} p = 3

−12
12

Knot: 9_{16} p = 13

−10	−10	−2	2	10	10
−10	2	10	−10	10	−2

Knot: 9_{17} p = 3

−30
30

Knot: 9_{17} p = 13

6	6	6	6	14	14
−14	−6	−14	−6	−6	−6

Knot: 9_{18} p = 41

6	6	6	10	6	6	6	10	10	6	6	10	10	6	10
−10	−10	−10	−10	−10	−10	−10	−10	−6	−6	−6	−6	−6	−10	−10

10	10	10	10	10
−10	−6	−6	−6	−6

Knot: 9_{19} p = 41

−2	−2	−2	−2	2	−2	−2	2	−2	2	−2	−2	2
−2	−2	−2	−2	−2	−2	2	−2	2	−2	2	2	2

−2	2	2	2	2	2	2
2	−2	2	−2	2	2	2

Table III

Knot: 9_{20} p = 41

6	6	6	6	6	10	10	10	6	6	6	10	10
−10	−10	−10	−10	−10	−6	−10	−10	−10	−10	−6	−6	−6

10	10	10	6	10	10	10
−10	−10	−6	−6	−6	−6	−6

Knot: 9_{21} p = 43

−6	−6	−6	−6	−6	−6	−2	−6	−2	−6	−2	−6
2	2	2	2	6	2	2	2	6	6	2	2

−2	−2	−6	−2	−6	−2	−2	−2	−2
6	6	6	6	2	6	6	6	6

Knot: 9_{22} p = 43

−2	−2	−2	−2	2	2	2	6	10	10	14	14	18	18
−26	−2	−18	−10	−10	−22	2	−26	2	−26	−2	−18	−14	−6

22	22	22	26	26	26	26
−22	2	−26	2	−22	−2	−14

Knot: 9_{23} p = 3

18
−18

Knot: 9_{23} p = 5

−18	−2
2	18

Knot: 9_{24} p = 3

0
0

Knot: 9_{24} p = 5

−2	2
−2	2

Knot: 9_{25} p = 47

6	6	6	6	10	10	10	14	14	18	18	22	22
−34	−14	−18	−30	−6	−34	−14	−18	−30	−6	−34	−10	−22

22	26	30	30	30	34	34	34	34	34
−30	−6	−34	−10	−22	−26	−6	−34	−10	−22

Knot: 9_{26} p = 47

−6	−6	−6	−6	−2	−6	−6	−6	−6	−2	−2	−6	−6
2	2	2	2	2	2	6	2	6	2	6	2	6

−6	−2	−2	−2	−6	−2	−2	−2	−2	−2
6	6	6	2	6	2	6	6	6	6

Knot: 9_{27} p = 7

−6	−6	−2
2	6	6

Table III

Knot: 9_{28} p = 3

12
−12

Knot: 9_{28} p = 17

6	6	14	14	18	26	26	26
−26	−18	−6	−26	−14	−6	−26	−14

Knot: 9_{29} p = 3

30
−30

Knot: 9_{29} p = 17

−10	6	−10	6	−6	6	2	6
−6	−6	−6	−6	−2	6	10	10

Knot: 9_{30} p = 53

2	2	2	2	2	6	6	6	10	10	14	14	14
−30	−10	−14	−26	−2	−30	−2	−22	−18	−6	−30	−2	−26
18	18	22	22	26	26	26	26	30	30	30	30	30
−10	−14	−26	−2	−30	−6	−22	−18	−6	−30	−2	−26	−14

Knot: 9_{31} p = 5

22	38
−38	−22

Knot: 9_{31} p = 11

−14	2	−6	2	−6
−2	−2	6	6	14

Knot: 9_{32} p = 59

−10	−10	−6	−6	−2	−2	2	−2	−6	−6	−6	−2	−2	−2
−2	2	6	6	10	2	6	6	6	6	−2	6	6	2
2	−2	−2	2	2	−2	−6	−2	−10	−10	−6	−6		
2	2	10	2	−2	2	6	10	2	6	10	2		
−6	−6	−6											
2	−2	6											

Knot: 9_{33} p = 61

−6	−2	2	−2	−6	−2	−2	−6	2	2	−2	−6
−6	−2	−6	2	2	−2	−2	6	−2	−2	2	2
2	−2	2	2	2	−2	2	2	2	6	−2	−2
2	−2	6	2	6	2	2	2	6	−6	2	−2
2	6	−2	6	6	−2						
2	−6	−2	−2	−2	−2						

Knot: 9_{34} p = 3

−42/5
42/5

Table III

Knot: 9_{34} p = 23

−1498/277	−1022/277	206/277	−366/277	−250/277	−214/277
−206/277	214/277	526/277	438/277	146/277	250/277
−802/277	−146/277	−526/277	−878/277	−438/277	
1022/277	1498/277	366/277	802/277	878/277	

Knot: 9_{35}

Knot: 9_{36} p = 37

−6	−6	−6	−2	−2	−2	2	6	6	10	10	14	18	18
−22	−2	−6	−18	6	−22	2	−6	−18	6	−22	2	−10	−14
22	22	22	22										
6	−22	2	−10										

Knot: 9_{37} p = 5

−2	2
−2	2

Knot: 9_{38} p = 3

42
−42

Knot: 9_{38} p = 19

−6	6	−6	10	−2	10	6	10	10
−10	−10	−6	6	6	2	−10	−10	−6

Knot: 9_{39} p = 5

−22	−18
18	22

Knot: 9_{39} p = 11

−242/23	−142/23	−82/23	−190/23	−70/23
70/23	242/23	190/23	142/23	82/23

Knot: 9_{40} p = 3

12
−12

Knot: 9_{41}

Knot: 9_{42} p = 7

2	14	26
−26	−2	−14

Knot: 9_{43} p = 13

−6	−2	6	14	18	22
−22	6	−18	2	−14	−6

Knot: 9_{44} p = 17

2	6	10	14	18	26	30	30
−30	−10	−14	−26	−2	−30	−6	−18

Table III

Knot: 9_{45} p = 23

6	6	10	14	18	22	26	30	30	34	34
−34	−10	−26	−22	−14	−30	−6	−34	−6	−30	−18

Knot: 9_{46}

Knot: 9_{47}

Knot: 9_{48}

Knot: 9_{49}

Appendix D: Knot Projections 0_1–9_{49}

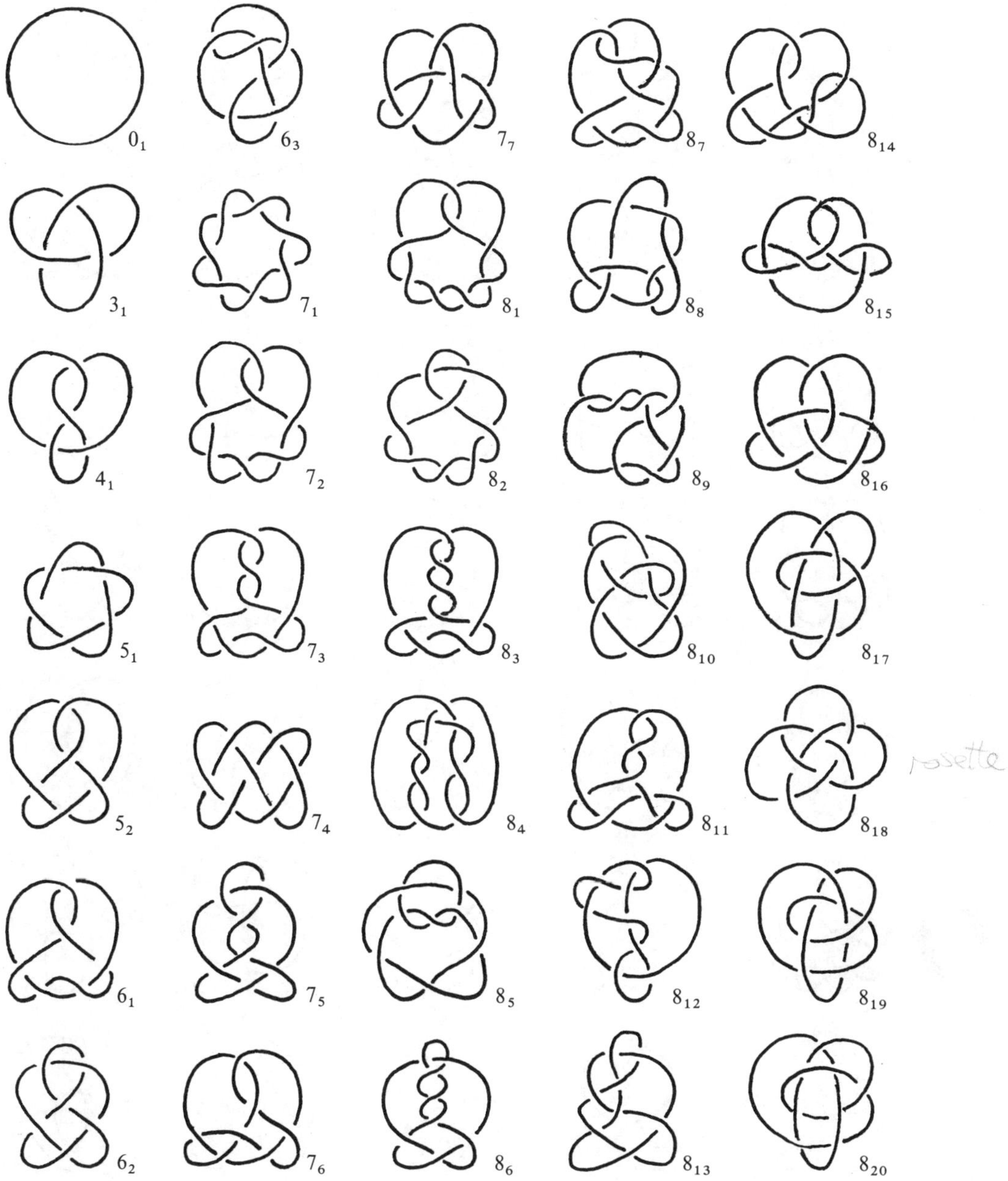

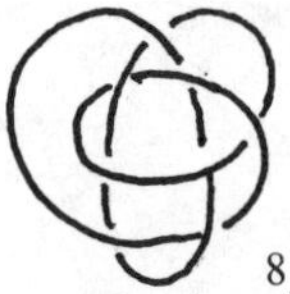
8_{21}

9_8

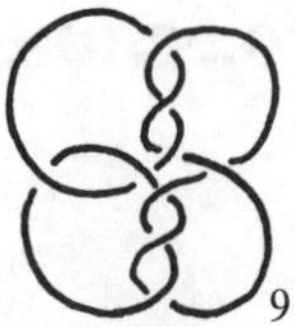
9_{16}

9_{24}

9_{32}

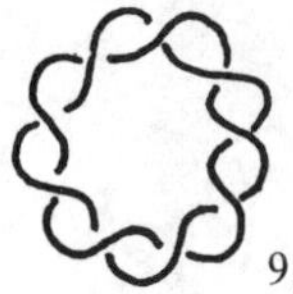
9_1

9_9

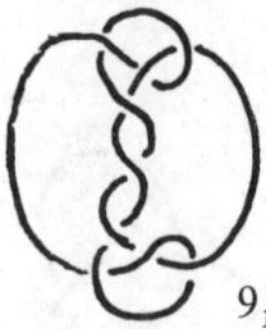
9_{17}

9_{25}

9_{33}

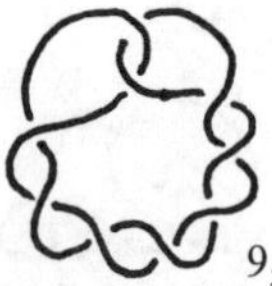
9_2

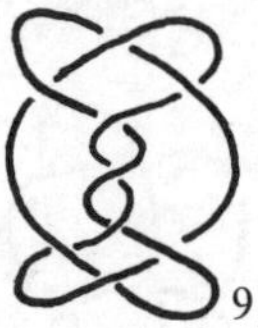
9_{10}

9_{18}

9_{26}

9_{34}

9_3

9_{11}

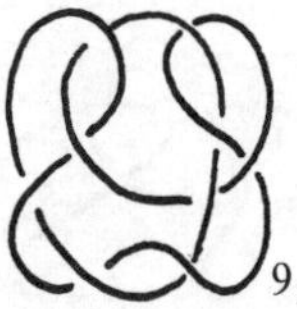
9_{19}

9_{27}

9_{35}

9_4

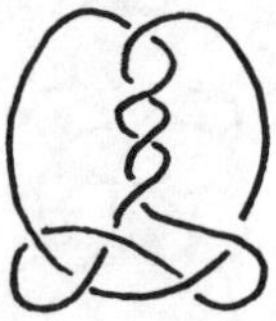
9_{12}

9_{20}

9_{28}

9_{36}

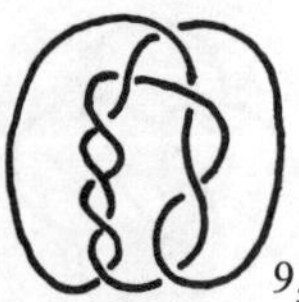
9_5

9_{13}

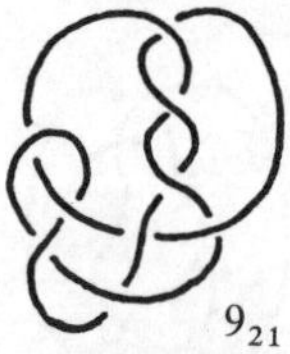
9_{21}

9_{29}

9_{37}

9_6

9_{14}

9_{22}

9_{30}

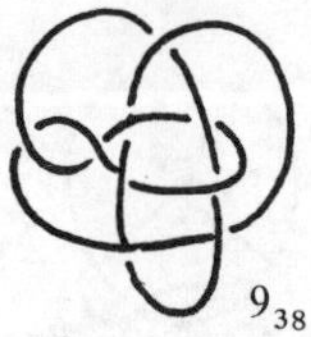
9_{38}

9_7

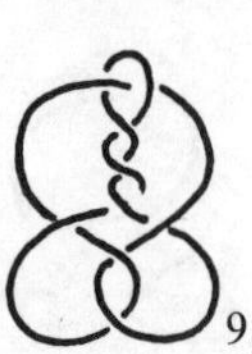
9_{15}

9_{23}

9_{31}

9_{39}

9_{40}

9_{42}

9_{44}

9_{46}

9_{48}

9_{41}

9_{43}

9_{45}

9_{47}

9_{49}

Bibliography

In addition to the usual data each title contains one or more code numbers indicating the particular fields the paper belongs to (e.g., ⟨K 16⟩, knot groups; ⟨M⟩, 3-dimensional topology).

A complete list of these code numbers and the corresponding fields is given on page 381.

In addition, on pages 382–392 there are listed, for each code, all items in the bibliography having this code number.

A'Campo, N., 1973: *Sur la monodromie des singularités isolées d'hypersurfaces complexes.* Invent. math., **20** (1973), 147–169 ⟨K 32, K 34⟩

Akbulut, S., 1977: *On 2-dimensional homology classes of 4-manifolds.* Math. Proc. Cambridge Phil. Soc., **82** (1977), 99–106 ⟨K 33, K 50⟩

Akbulut, S.; H. King, 1981: *All knots are algebraic.* Comment. Math. Helv., **56** (1981), 339–351 ⟨K 12, K 32, K 60⟩

Alexander, J. W., 1920: *Note on Riemann spaces.* Bull. Amer. Math. Soc., **26** (1920), 370–372 ⟨K 21⟩

Alexander, J. W., 1923: *On the deformation of an n-cell.* Proc. Nat. Acad. Sci. USA, **9** (1923), 406–407 ⟨B, M⟩

Alexander, J. W., 1923': *A lemma on systems of knotted curves.* Proc. Nat. Acad. Sci. USA, **9** (1923), 93–95 ⟨K 12⟩

Alexander, J. W., 1924: *An example of a simply connected surface bounding a region that is not simply connected.* Proc. Nat. Acad. Sci. USA, **10** (1924), 8–10

Alexander, J. W., 1924': *On the subdivision of a 3-space by a polyhedron.* Proc. Nat. Acad. Sci. USA, **10** (1924), 6–8 ⟨M⟩

Alexander, J. W., 1928: *Topological invariants of knots and links.* Trans. Amer. Math. Soc., **30** (1928), 275–306 ⟨K 12⟩

Alexander, J. W., 1932: *Some problems in topology.* Verhandl. Internat. Mathematiker-Kongress Zürich, **1** (1932), 249–257 ⟨K 11⟩

Alexander, J. W.; G. B. Briggs, 1927: *On types of knotted curves.* Ann. of Math., (2) **28** (1927), 562–586 ⟨K 13⟩

Alford, W. R., 1962: *Some "nice" wild 2-spheres in E^3.* In: Top. 3-manifolds, Proc. 1961 Top. Inst. Univ. Georgia (ed. M. K. Fort, jr). pp 29–30, Englewood Cliffs, N. J.: Prentice-Hall ⟨K 55⟩

Alford, W. R., 1970: *Complements of minimal spanning surfaces of knots are not unique.* Ann. of Math., **91** (1970), 419–424 ⟨K 15⟩

Almgren, F. J., jr.; W. P. Thurston, 1977: *Examples of unknotted curves which bound only surfaces of high genus within their curve hull.* Ann. of Math., **105** (1977), 527–538 ⟨K 15⟩

Ammann, A., 1982: *Sur les nœuds représentable comme tresses à trois brins.* Publ. Centre Rech. Math. Pures (I), (Neuchâtel), **17** (1982), 21–33 ⟨K 30⟩

Anderson, G. A., 1983: *Unlinking Λ-homology spheres.* Houston J. Math., **8** (1983), 147–151 ⟨K 60⟩

Andrews, J. J.; M. L. Curtis, 1959: *Knotted 2-spheres in the 4-sphere.* Ann. of Math., **70** (1959), 565–571 ⟨K 61⟩

Andrews, J.; F. Dristy, 1964: *The Minkowski units of ribbon knots.* Proc. Amer. Math. Soc., **15** (1964), 856–864 ⟨K 27, K 35⟩

Andrews, J. S.; S. J. Lomonaco, 1969: *The second homology group of spun 2-spheres in 4-space.* Bull. Amer. Math. Soc., **75** (1969), 169–171 ⟨K 61⟩

Antoine, L., 1921: *Sur l'homéomorphie de deux figures et de leurs voisinages.* J. Math. pure appl., (8) **4** (1921), 221–325 ⟨K 55⟩

Appel, K. I., 1974: *On the conjugacy problem for knot groups.* Math. Z., **138** (1974), 273–294 ⟨K 16, K 29⟩

Appel, K. I.; P. E. Schupp, 1972: *The conjugacy problem for the group of any tame alternating knot is solvable.* Proc. Amer. Math. Soc., **33** (1972), 329–336 ⟨K 16, K 29⟩

Appel, K. I.; P. E. Schupp, 1983: *Artin groups and infinite Coxeter groups.* Invent. math., **72** (1983), 201–220 ⟨K 40⟩

Arnol'd, V. I., 1969: Кольцо когомологии

группы крашеных кос. Мат. заметки, **5** (1969), 227–231, Engl. transl.: *The cohomological ring of the colored braid groups.* Math. Notes Acad. Sci. USSR, **5** (1969), 227–232 ⟨K 40⟩

Arnol'd, V.I., 1970: О некоторых топологических инвариантах алгбраических функций. Труды моск. мат. обш., **21** (1970), 27–46, Engl. transl.: *On some topological invariants of algebraic functions.* Trans. Moscow Math. Soc., **21** (1971), 30–52 ⟨K 40⟩

Arnol'd, V.I., 1970′: Топологические инвариаты алгебраичесних функций. II. Функц. анализ прил., **4:2** (1970), 1–9, Engl. transl.: *Topological invariants of algebraic functions. II.* Functional Analysis Appl., **4** (1970), 91–98 ⟨K 40⟩

Artin, E., 1925: *Theorie der Zöpfe.* Abh. Math. Sem. Univ. Hamburg, **4** (1925), 47–72 ⟨K 40⟩

Artin, E., 1947: *Theory of braids.* Ann. of Math., (2) **48** (1947), 101–126 ⟨K 40⟩

Artin, E., 1947′: *Braids and permutations.* Ann. of Math., (2) **48** (1947), 643–649 ⟨K 40⟩

Asano, K.; Y. Marumuto; T. Yanagana, 1981: *Ribbon knots and ribbon disks.* Osaka J. Math., **18** (1981), 161–174 ⟨K 30⟩

Asano, K.; K. Yoshikawa, 1981: *On polynomial invariants of fibred 2-knots.* Pacific J. Math., **98** (1981), 267–269 ⟨K 61⟩

Ashley, C.W., (1944): *The Ashley book of knots.* New York: Doubleday and Co. ⟨K 12, K 13⟩

Aumann, R.J., 1956: *Asphericity of alternating knots.* Ann. of Math., (2) **64** (1956), 374–392 ⟨K 16, K 31⟩

Bailey, J.L., 1977: *Alexander invariants of links.* Ph.D. Thesis, Univ. British Columbia, Vancouver ⟨K 25, K 40⟩

Bailey, J.; D. Rolfsen, 1977: *An unexpected surgery construction of a lens space.* Pacific J. Math., **71** (1977), 295–298 ⟨K 21⟩

Banchoff, T., 1976: *Self linking numbers of space polygons.* Indiana Univ. Math. J., **25** (1976), 1171–1188 ⟨K 12⟩

Bankwitz, C., 1930: *Über die Torsionszahlen der alternierenden Knoten.* Math. Ann., **103** (1930), 145–161 ⟨K 25, K 31⟩

Bankwitz, C., 1930′: *Über die Fundamentalgruppe des inversen Knotens und des gerichteten Knotens.* Ann. of. Math., **31** (1930), 129–130 ⟨K 16, K 23⟩

Bankwitz, C., 1930″: *Über die Torsionszahlen der zyklischen Überlagerungsräume des Kontenaußenraumes.* Ann. of Math., **31** (1930), 131–133 ⟨K 20⟩

Bankwitz, C., 1935: *Über Knoten und Zöpfe in gleichsinniger Verdrillung.* Math. Z., **40** (1935), 588–591 ⟨K 30, K 40⟩

Bankwitz, C.; H.G. Schumann, 1934: *Über Viergeflechte.* Abh. Math. Sem. Univ. Hamburg, **10** (1934), 263–284 ⟨K 35, K 30⟩

Bayer, E., 1980: *S-équivalence et congruence de matrices de Seifert: Une conjecture de Trotter.* Invent. math., **56** (1980), 97–99 ⟨K 60⟩

Bayer, E., 1980′: *Factorization is not unique for higher dimensional knots.* Comment. Math. Helv., **55** (1980), 583–592 ⟨K 60⟩

Bayer, E., 1983′: *Definite hermitian forms and the cancellation of simple knots.* Archiv. Math., **40** (1983), 182–185 ⟨K 27, K 60⟩

Bayer, E.; J.A. Hillman; C. Kearton, 1981: *The factorization of simple knots.* Math. Proc. Cambridge Phil. Soc., **90** (1981), 495–506 ⟨K 60⟩

Bayer, E.; F. Michel, 1979: *Finitude du nombre des classes d'isomorphisme des structures isometriques entières.* Comment. Math. Helv., **54** (1979), 378–396 ⟨K 60⟩

Bayer-Fluckinger, E., 1983: *Higher dimensional simple knots and minimal Seifert surfaces.* Comment. Math. Helv., **58** (1983), 646–656 ⟨K 60⟩

Bayer-Fluckinger, E.; N.W. Stoltzfus, 1983: *Indecomposable knots and concordance.* Math. Proc. Cambridge Phil. Soc., **93** (1983), 495–501 ⟨K 60⟩

Bedient, R.E., 1984; *Double branched covers and pretzel knots.* Pacific J. Math., **112** (1984), 265–272 ⟨K 20, K 35⟩

Berge, C., 1970: *Graphs and Hypergraphs.* Amsterdam-London: North-Holland Publ. Comp. ⟨X⟩

Bing, R.H., 1956: *A simple closed curve that pierces no disk.* J. de Math. Pures Appl., (9) **35** (1956), 337–343 ⟨K 55⟩

Bing, R.H., 1958: *Necessary and sufficient conditions that a 3-manifold be S^3.* Ann. of Math., **68** (1958), 17–37 ⟨M⟩

Bing, R.H., (1983): *The geometric topology of 3-manifolds.* Amer. Math. Soc. Colloqu. Publ. **40**. Providence, Rh.I.: Amer. Math. Soc. ⟨K 11, K 55, M⟩

✓ Bing, R.; V. Klee, 1964: *Every simple closed curve in E^3 is unknotted in E^4.* J. London Math. Soc., **39** (1964), 86–94 ⟨K 12, B⟩

Bing, R.H.; J.M. Martin, 1971: *Cubes with knotted holes.* Trans. Amer. Math. Soc., **155** (1971), 217–231 ⟨K 17, K 19, K 30⟩

Birman, J.S., 1969: *On braid groups.* Commun. Pure Appl. Math., **22** (1969), 41–72 ⟨K 40, F⟩

Birman, J.S., 1969′: *Mapping class groups and their relationship to braid groups.* Com. Pure Appl. Math., **22** (1969), 213–238 ⟨K 40, F⟩

Birman, J.S., 1969″: *Non-conjugate braids can define isotopic knots.* Commun. Pure Appl. Math., **22** (1969), 239–242 ⟨K 40⟩

Birman, J., 1973: *Plat presentations for link groups.* Commun. Pure Appl. Math., **26** (1973), 673–678 ⟨K 16, K 30⟩

Birman, J., 1973′: *An inverse function theorem for free groups.* Proc. Amer. Math. Soc., **41** (1973), 634–638 ⟨G⟩

Birman, J.S., (1974): *Braids, links, and mapping class groups.* Ann. Math. Studies **82**. Princeton, N.J.: Princeton Univ. Press ⟨K 11, K 40, F, G⟩

Birman, J.S., 1976: *On the stable equivalence of plat representations of knots and links.* Canad. J. Math., **28** (1976), 264–290 ⟨K 12, K 30⟩

Birman, J.S., 1979: *A representation theorem for fibered knots.* In: Top. Low-Dim. Manifolds, Second Sussex Conf. 1977 (ed. R. Fenn). Lecture Notes in Math., **722** (1979), 1–8. Berlin-Heidelberg-New York: Springer Verlag ⟨K 16, K 18⟩

Birman, J.S.; J.M. Montesinos, 1980: *On minimal Heegaard splittings.* Michigan Math. J., **27** (1980), 47–57 ⟨M⟩

Birman, J.S.; R.F. Williams, 1983: *Knotted periodic orbits in dynamical systems. I: Lorenz's equations.* Topology, **22** (1983), 47–82 ⟨K 59⟩

Birman, J.S.; R.F. Williams, 1983′: *Knotted periodic orbits in dynamical systems. II: Knot holders for fibered knots.* Amer. Math. Soc. Contemp. Math., **20** (1983), 1–60 ⟨K 18, K 59⟩

Blanchfield, R.C., 1957: *Intersection theory of manifolds with operators with applications to knot theory.* Ann. of Math., **65** (1957), 340–356 ⟨K 26, A⟩

Blanchfield, R.C.; R.H. Fox, 1951: *Invariants of self-linking.* Ann. of Math., **53** (1951), 556–564 ⟨K 25, K 59⟩

Blankinship, W.A., 1951: *Generalization of a construction of Antoine.* Ann. of Math., **53** (1951), 276–297 ⟨K 55⟩

Blankinship, W.A.; R.H. Fox, 1950: *Remarks on certain pathological open subsets of 3-space and their fundamental groups.* Proc. Amer. Math. Soc., **1** (1950), 618–624 ⟨K 55⟩

Bleiler, D., 1983: *Doubly prime knots.* Amer. Math. Soc. Contemporary Math., **20** (1983), 61–64 ⟨K 17, 35⟩

Boardman, J., 1964: *Some embeddings of 2-spheres in 4-manifolds.* Proc. Cambridge Phil. Soc., **60** (1964), 354–356 ⟨K 61⟩

Bohnenblust, F., 1947: *The algebraical braid group.* Ann. of Math., **48** (1947), 127–136 ⟨K 40, G⟩

Boileau, C.M., 1979: *Inversibilité des nœuds de Montesinos.* These 3ème cycle, Univ. de Paris-Sud, Orsay ⟨K 23, K 35⟩

Boileau, C.M., 1982: *Groupe des symmetries des nœuds de bretzel et de Montesinos.* Publ. Genève (unpublished) ⟨K 23, K 35⟩

Boileau, C.M., 1984: *Nœuds rigidement inversibles.* (Preprint) Genève ⟨K 23, K 35⟩

Boileau, M.; M. Rost; H. Zieschang, 1984: *On Heegaard decompositions of torus knot exteriors.* (in preparation) ⟨K 16, K 59⟩

Boileau, M.; L. Siebenmann, 1980: *A planar classification of pretzel knots and Montesinos knots.* Prépublications Orsay 1980 ⟨K 35⟩

Boileau, M.; C. Weber, 1983: *Le problème de J. Milnor sur le nombre gordien des nœuds algébriques.* In: Nœuds, tresses et singularités. Comp. Rend. Sem. Plans-sur-Bex (ed. C. Weber), Monographie No. 31 de L'Enseign. Math., **31** (1983), 49–98. Genève: Univ. de Genève ⟨K 29, K 32⟩

Boileau, M.; H. Zieschang, 1983: *Genre de Heegaard d'une variété de dimension 3 et générateurs de son groupe fondamental.* C.R. Acad. Sci. Paris, **296-I** (1983), 925–928 ⟨K 16, K 20, K 32, M⟩

Boileau, M.; H. Zieschang, 1984: *Nombre de ponts et générateurs méridiens des entrelacs de Montesinos.* Comment. Math. Helv. (to appear) ⟨K 16, K 30, K 35⟩

Boileau, M.; B. Zimmermann, 1984: *Symmetries of Montesinos links.* (to appear) ⟨K 22, K 23, K 35⟩

Bonahon, F., 1979: *Involutions et fibrés de Seifert dans les variétés de dimension 3.* Thèse de 3e cycle, Orsay ⟨K 20, M⟩

Bonahon, F., 1983: *Ribbon fibred knots, cobordism of surface diffeomorphisms and pseudo-Anosov diffeomorphisms.* Math. Proc. Cambridge Phil. Soc., **94** (1983), 235–251 ⟨K 18, K 35⟩

Bonahon, F.; L. Siebenmann, 1984: *Algebraic knots.* Proc. Bangor Conf. 1979, London Math. Soc. Lecture Notes (to appear) ⟨K 17, K 23, K 29, K 35, K 30⟩

Bonahon, F.; L. Siebenmann, 1984′: *Equivariant characteristic varieties in dimension 3.* (à paraître) ⟨M⟩

Borsuk, K., 1947: *An example of a simple arc in space whose projection in every plane has interior points.* Fund. Math., **34** (1947), 272–277 ⟨K 55⟩

Borsuk, K., 1948: *Sur la courbure totale des courbes fermées.* Ann. Soc. Polonaise Math., **20** (1948), 251–265 ⟨K 38⟩

Bothe, H.G., 1974: *Are neighbourhoods of curves in 3-manifolds embeddable in E^3?* Bull. Acad.

Polonaise Sci., Ser. math., astr. et phys., **22** (1974), 53–59 ⟨K 12, M⟩

Bothe, H.G., 1981: *Homogeneously wild curves and infinite knot products*. Fund. Math., **113** (1981), 91–111 ⟨K 12, K 17, K 55⟩

Bothe, H.G., 1981′: *Homogeneously embedded simple closed curves and the position of certain minimal sets in differentiable dynamics*. Geometric Topology, Proc. Int. Conf. Warzawa 1978, 51–57 ⟨K 59⟩

Bott, R.; J.P. Mayberry, 1954: *Matrices and trees*. In: Economic Activity Analysis (1954) (ed. D. Morgenstern), pp. 391–400. New York: Wiley ⟨X⟩

Bozhügük, M.E., 1978: *On 3-sheeted covering spaces of (3,4)-Turk's head knot*. Colloquia Math. Soc. János Bolyai 23, Topology, Budapest ⟨K 20, K 30⟩

Bozhügük, M.E., 1982: *On three sheeted branched covering spaces of (3,2)-Turk's head knot*. J. Fac. Sci. Kavadencz Techn. Univ., Ser. MA, **3** (1982), 21–25 ⟨K 20, K 35⟩

Brakes, W.R., 1980: *On certain non-trivial ribbon knots*. Math. Proc. Cambridge Phil. Soc., **87** (1980), 207–211 ⟨K 35⟩

Brakes, W.R., 1980′: *Manifolds with multiple knot-surgery descriptions*. Math. Proc. Cambridge Phil. Soc., **87** (1980), 443–448 ⟨K 21⟩

Brauner, K., 1928: *Zur Geometrie der Funktionen zweier komplexer Veränderlicher. II. Das Verhalten der Funktionen in der Umgebung ihrer Verzweigungsstellen*. Abh. Math. Sem. Univ. Hamburg, **6** (1928), 1–55 ⟨K 12, 32, 34⟩

Brieskorn, E., 1970: *Die Monodromie der isolierten Singularitäten von Hyperflächen*. Manuscr. Math., **2** (1970), 103–161 ⟨K 32, K 34⟩

Brieskorn, E., 1973: *Sur les groupes de tresses* (d'après V.I. Arnol'd). Sém. Bourbaki 1971/72 No. 401. Lect. Notes in Math. **317** (1973), 21–44, Berlin-Heidelberg-New York: Springer ⟨K40⟩

Brieskorn, E.; K. Saito, 1972: *Artin-Gruppen und Coxeter-Gruppen*. Invent. math., **17** (1972), 245–270 ⟨K 40, G⟩

Brode, R., 1981: *Über wilde Knoten und ihre "Anzahl"*. Diplomarbeit. Ruhr-Universität Bochum ⟨K 55⟩

Brody, E.J., 1960: *The topological classification of lens spaces*. Ann. of Math., **71** (1960), 163–184 ⟨K 21, M⟩

Brown, E.M.; R.H. Crowell, 1965: *Deformation retractions of 3-manifolds into their boundaries*. Ann. of Math., **82** (1965), 445–458 ⟨K 16, M⟩

Brown, E.M.; R.H. Crowell, 1966: *The augmentation subgroup of a link*. J. Math. Mech., **15** (1966), 1065–1074 ⟨K 16, K 50⟩

Brown, M., 1962: *Locally flat imbeddings of topological manifolds*. Ann. of Math., **75** (1962), 331–341 ⟨K 50, B⟩

Brunn, H., 1892: *Topologische Betrachtungen*. Zeitschrift Math. Phys., **37** (1892), 106–116 ⟨K 12⟩

Brunn, H., 1892′: *Über Verkettung*. S.-B. Math.-Phys. Kl. Bayer. Akad. Wiss., **22** (1892), 77–99 ⟨K 12, K 35⟩

Brunn, H., 1897: *Über verknotete Kurven*. Verh. Math.-Kongr. Zürich 1897, 256–259 ⟨K 12, K 35⟩

Brusotti, L., 1936: *Le trecce di Artin nella topologia proviettiva ad affine*. Scritti Mat. Off. a Luigi Berzolari (1936), 101–118 ⟨K 40⟩

Bullett, S., 1981: *Braid orientations and Stiefel-Whitney classes*. Quart. J. Math. Oxford, (2) **32** (1981), 267–285 ⟨K 40⟩

Burau, W., 1933: *Über Zopfinvarianten*. Abh. Math. Sem. Univ. Hamburg, **9** (1933), 117–124 ⟨K 40⟩

Burau, W., 1933′: *Kennzeichnung der Schlauchknoten*. Abh. Math. Sem. Univ. Hamburg, **9** (1933), 125–133 ⟨K 17, K 35⟩

Burau, W., 1934: *Kennzeichnung der Schlauchverkettungen*. Abh. Math. Sem. Univ. Hamburg, **10** (1934), 285–297 ⟨K 17, K 35, K 50⟩

Burau, W., 1936: *Über Verkettungsgruppen*. Abh. Math. Sem. Univ. Hamburg, **11** (1936), 171–178 ⟨K 16, K 50⟩

Burau, W., 1936: *Über Zopfgruppen und gleichsinnig verdrillte Verkettungen*. Abh. Math. Sem. Univ. Hamburg, **11** (1936), 179–186 ⟨K 40, K 50⟩

Burde, G., 1963: *Zur Theorie der Zöpfe*. Math. Ann., **151** (1963), 101–107 ⟨K 40⟩

Burde, G., 1964: *Über Normalisatoren der Zopfgruppe*. Abh. Math. Sem. Univ. Hamburg, **27** (1964), 97–115 ⟨K 40⟩

Burde, G., 1966: *Alexanderpolynome Neuwirthscher Knoten*. Topology, **5** (1966), 321–330 ⟨K 18, K 26⟩

Burde, G., 1967: *Darstellungen von Knotengruppen*. Math. Ann., **173** (1967), 24–33 ⟨K 28⟩

Burde, G., 1969: *Dualität in Gruppen Neuwirthscher Knoten*. Arch. Math., **20** (1969), 186–189 ⟨K 16, K 18, K 25⟩

Burde, G., 1970: *Darstellungen von Knotengruppen und eine Knoteninvariante*. Abh. Math. Sem. Univ. Hamb., **35** (1970), 107–120 ⟨K 28⟩

Burde, G., 1971: *On branched coverings of S^3*. Canad. J. Math., **23** (1971), 84–89 ⟨K 20⟩

Burde, G., 1975: *Verschlingungsinvarianten von Knoten und Verkettungen mit zwei Brücken*. Math. Z., **145** (1975), 235–242 ⟨K 30⟩

Burde, G., 1978: *Über periodische Knoten*. Archiv Math., **30** (1978), 487–492 ⟨K 22⟩

Burde, G., 1984: *Über das Geschlecht und die Faserbarkeit von Montesinos Knoten.* Abh. Math. Sem. Univ. Hamburg, **54** (1984), 199–226 ⟨K 15, K 18, K 35⟩

Burde, G., 1984': *Das Alexanderpolynom der Knoten mit zwei Brücken.* Archiv Math., **44** (1985), 180–189 ⟨K 18, K 26, K 30⟩

Burde, G.; K. Murasugi, 1970: *Links and Seifert fiber spaces.* Duke Math. J., **37** (1970), 89–93 ⟨K 16, K 20, K 50⟩

Burde, G.; H. Zieschang, 1966: *Eine Kennzeichnung der Torusknoten.* Math. Ann., **167** (1966), 169–176 ⟨K 16, K 35⟩

Burde, G.; H. Zieschang, 1967: *Neuwirthsche Knoten und Flächenabbildungen.* Abh. Math. Sem. Univ. Hamburg, **31** (1967), 239–246 ⟨K 18⟩

Burger, E., 1950: *Über Gruppen mit Verschlingungen.* J. reine angew. Math., **188** (1950), 193–200 ⟨K 16, K 25⟩

van Buskirk, J., 1966: *Braid groups of compact 2-manifolds with elements of finite order.* Trans. Amer. Math. Soc., **122** (1966), 81–97 ⟨K 40, F⟩

van Buskirk, J. M., 1983: *A class of negative-amphicheiral knots and their Alexander polynomials.* Rocky Mountain J. Math., **13** (1983), 413–422 ⟨K 23, K 26⟩

Caffarelli, L. A., 1975: *Surfaces of minimum capacity for a knot.* Ann. Scuola Normale Sup. Pisa, (IV) **2** (1975), 497–505 ⟨K 38⟩

Călugăreanu, G., 1959: *L'intégrale de Gauss et l'analyse des nœuds tridimensionnels.* Revue Roumaine Math. Pures Appl., **4** (1959), 5–20 ⟨K 38⟩

Călugăreanu, G., 1961: *Un théorème élémentaire sur les nœuds.* C.R. Acad. Sci. Paris, **252-I** (1961), 2172–2173 ⟨K 12⟩

Călugăreanu, G., 1961': *Sur les classes d'isotopie des nœuds tridimensionnels et leurs invariants.* Czechoslovak. Math. J., **11** (1961), 588–625 ⟨K 12, K 38⟩

Călugăreanu, G., 1961'': *O teoremă asupra înlantuirilor tridimensionale de curbe închise.* Comun. Acad. Repl. Pop. Romîne, **9** (1961), 829–832 ⟨K 12, K 38⟩

Călugăreanu, G., 1962: *O teopemă asupra traversărilor unui nod.* Studia Univ. Babeş-Bolyai, Ser. Math. Phys., **7** (1962), 39–43 ⟨K 14, K 59⟩

Călugăreanu, G., 1962': *Un théorème sur les traversées d'un nœud.* Revue Roumaine Math. Pures Appl., **7** (1962), 565–569 ⟨K 14, K 59⟩

Călugăreanu, G., 1965: *Considérations directes sur la génération des nœuds. (I).* Revue Roumaine Math. Pures Appl., **10** (1965), 389–403 ⟨K 14⟩

Călugăreanu, G., 1967: *Considérations directes sur la génération des nœuds. (II).* Studia Univ. Babeş-Bolyai (Cluj), Ser. Math.-Phys., **2** (1967), 25–30 ⟨K 14⟩

Călugăreanu, G., 1968: *Sur un choix intrinsèque des générateurs du groupe d'un nœud.* Revue Roumaine Math. Pure Appl., **13** (1968), 19–23 ⟨K 16⟩

Călugăreanu, G., 1969: *Sur les relations du groupe d'un nœud.* Revue Roumaine Math. Pure Appl., **14** (1969), 753–757 ⟨K 16⟩

Călugăreanu, G., 1970: *Points de vue sur la théorie des nœuds.* L'Enseign. Mathém., **16** (1970), 97–110 ⟨K 12⟩

Călugăreanu, G., 1970': *Nœuds et cercles topologiques sur les surfaces fermées.* Mathematica (Cluj), **12** (1970), 223–226 ⟨K 12, K 15⟩

Călugăreanu, G., 1973: *Sur une conjecture de M.L.P. Neuwirth relative aux groupes des nœuds.* Mathematica (Cluj), **15** (1973), 149–156 ⟨K 16⟩

Cannon, J. W.; C. D. Feustel, 1976: *Essential annuli and Moebius bands in M^3.* Trans. Amer. Math. Soc., **215** (1976), 219–239 ⟨M⟩

Cappell, S., 1976: *A splitting theorem for manifolds.* Invent. math., **33** (1976), 69–170 ⟨M⟩

Cappell, S. E.; J. L. Shaneson, 1975: *Invariants of 3-manifolds.* Bull. Amer. Math. Soc., **81** (1975), 559–562 ⟨M⟩

Cappell, S. E.; J. L. Shaneson, 1976: *There exist inequivalent knots with the same complement.* Ann. of Math., **103** (1976), 349–353 ⟨K 60⟩

Cappell, S. E.; J. L. Shanesson, 1978: *A note on the Smith conjecture.* Topology, **17** (1978), 105–107

Cappell, S.; J. L. Shaneson, 1980: *Link cobordism.* Comment. Math. Helv., **55** (1980), 20–49 ⟨K 24⟩

Casson, A. J.; C. McA. Gordon, 1978: *On slice knots in dimension three.* Algebr. Geom. Top. (Stanford 1976) II (ed. R. J. Milgram). Proc. Sympos. Pure Math. **32**, 39–53. Providence, R.I.: Amer. Math. Soc. ⟨K 33⟩

Casson, A. J.; C. McA. Gordon, 1983: *A loop theorem for duality spaces and fibred ribbon knots.* Invent. math., **74** (1983), 119–137 ⟨K 18, K 35⟩

Caudron, A., 1981: *Classification des nœuds et des enlacements.* Prépublications Univ. Paris-Sud, Orsay ⟨K 12, K 13, K 21⟩

Cayley, A., 1878: *On the theory of groups.* Amer. J. Math., **1** (1878), 50–52 ⟨G⟩

Cayley, A., 1978': *The theory of groups.* Amer. J. Math., **1** (1978), 174–176 ⟨G⟩

César de Sá, E., 1979: *A link calculus for 4-mani-*

folds. In: Topology Low-Dim. Manifolds, Second Sussex Conf. (ed. R. Fenn). Lecture Notes in Math., **722** (1979), 16–30. Berlin-Heidelberg-New York: Springer-Verlag ⟨K 60⟩

Chang, B.C. (= Jiang, B.), 1973: *Some theorems about knot groups*. Indiana Univ. Math. J., **22** (1973), 801–812 ⟨K 16, K 35⟩

Chang, B.C. (= Jiang, B.), 1972: *Which abelian groups can be fundamental groups of regions in euclidean spaces?* Bull. Amer. Math. Soc., **78** (1972), 470–473 ⟨K 16⟩

Chang, B.C. (= Jiang, B.), 1974: *Which abelian groups can be fundamental groups of regions in euclidean spaces?* Canad. J. Math., **26** (1974), 7–18 ⟨K 16⟩

Chen, K.I., 1951: *Integration in free groups*. Ann. of Math., **54** (1951), 147–162 ⟨K 25, G⟩

Chen, K.I., 1952: *Commutator calculus and link invariants*. Proc. Amer. Math. Soc., **3** (1952), 44–55 ⟨K 16, K 25, G⟩

Chen, K.I., 1952′: *Isotopy invariants of links*. Ann. of Math., **56** (1952), 343–353 ⟨K 25, K 50⟩

Chow, K.-N., 1948: *On the algebraical braid groups*. Ann. of Math., **49** (1948), 654–658 ⟨K 40, G⟩

Clark, B.E., 1978: *Surgery on links containing a cable sublink*. Proc. Amer. Math. Soc., **72** (1978), 587–592 ⟨K 21, K 50⟩

Clark, B.E., 1978′: *Crosscaps and knots*. Intern. J. Math. & Math. Sci., **1** (1978), 113–123 ⟨K 12⟩

Clark, B., 1980: *The Heegaard genus of manifolds obtained by surgery on links and knots*. Internat. J. Math. & Math. Sci., **3** (1980), 583–589 ⟨K 21⟩

Clark, B.E., 1982: *Longitudinal surgery on composite knots*. Proc. Conf. Topology Blacksburg, VA 1981, Vol. 6 No. 1 (1982), 25–30 ⟨K 17, K 21⟩

Clark, B.E.; V.P. Schneider, 1984: *All knots are metric*. Math. Z. **187**, (1984), 269–271 ⟨K 59⟩

Cochran, D.S., 1970: *Links with Alexander polynomial zero*. Ph.D. thesis. Dartmouth College ⟨K 23, K 50⟩

Cochran, D.S.; R.H. Crowell, 1970: *$H_2(G')$ for tamely embedded graphs*. Quart. J. Math. Oxford, (2) **21** (1970), 25–27 ⟨K 25⟩

Cochran, T., 1983: *Ribbon knots in S^4*. J. London Math. Soc., (2) **28** (1983), 563–576 ⟨K 61⟩

Cochran, T., 1984: *Slice links in S^4*. Trans. Amer. Math. Soc., **285** (1984), 389–400 ⟨K 33, K 61⟩

Cohen, D.I.A., 1967: *On representations of the braid group*. J. Algebra, **7** (1967), 145–151 ⟨K 40⟩

Cohen, R.L., 1979: *The geometry of $\Omega^2 S^3$ and braid orientations*. Invent. math., **54** (1979), 53–67 ⟨K 40⟩

Collins, D.J., 1978: *Presentations of the amalgamted free product of two infinite cycles*. Math. Ann., **237** (1978), 233–241 ⟨K 16, G⟩

Connor, P.E.; F. Raymond, 1970: *Actions of compact Lie groups on aspherical manifolds*. In: Top. of Manifolds, Proc. Inst. Univ. Georgia, Athens, Ga, 1969 (eds. J.C. Cantrell and C.H. Edwards jr.), 227–264. Chicago: Markham ⟨A⟩

Connor, P.E.; F. Raymond, 1977: *Deforming homotopy equivalences to homeomorphisms in aspherical manifolds*. Bull. Amer. Math. Soc., **83** (1977), 36–85 ⟨A⟩

Conway, J., 1970: *An enumeration of knots and links and some of their related properties*. Computational problems in Abstract Algebra, Proc. Conf. Oxford 1967 (ed. J. Leech), 329–358. New York: Pergamon Press ⟨K 12, K 29⟩

Conway, J.H.; C.McA. Gordon, 1975: *A group to classify knots*. Bull. London Math. Soc., **7** (1975), 84–86 ⟨K 12, K 29⟩

Cooper, D., 1982: *The universal abelian cover of a link*. Low-Dim. Top. (Bangor, 1979). London Math. Soc. Lecture Note Ser., **48** (1982), 51–56 ⟨K 20⟩

Coray, D.; F. Michel, 1983: *Knot cobordism and amphicheirality*. Comment. Math. Helv., **58** (1983), 601–616 ⟨K 23, K 24⟩

Cossey, J.; I.M.S. Dey; S. Meskin, 1971: *Subgroups of knot groups*. Math. Z., **121** (1971), 99–103 ⟨K 16⟩

Crowell, R.H., 1959: *Genus of alternating link types*. Ann. of Math., **69** (1959), 258–275 ⟨K 15, K 31⟩

Crowell, R.H., 1959′: *Non-alternating links*. Illinois J. Math., **3** (1959), 101–120 ⟨K 35, K 50⟩

Crowell, R.H., 1959″: *On the van Kampen theorem*. Pacific J. Math., **9** (1959), 43–50 ⟨A⟩

Crowell, R.H., 1961: *Corresponding group and module sequences*. Nagoya Math. J., **19** (1961), 27–40 ⟨K 25, G⟩

Crowell, R.H., 1963: *The group G'/G'' of a knot group G*. Duke Math. J., **30** (1963), 349–354 ⟨K 16, K 25⟩

Crowell, R.H., 1964: *On the annihilator of a knot module*. Proc. Amer. Math. Soc., **15** (1964), 696–700 ⟨K 25⟩

Crowell, R.H., 1965: *Torsion in link modules*. J. Math. Mech., **14** (1965), 289–298 ⟨K 25⟩

Crowell, R.H., 1970: *H_2 of subgroups of knot groups*. Illinois J. Math., **14** (1970), 665–673 ⟨K 16⟩

Crowell, R.H., 1971: *The derived module of a homomorphism*. Adv. Math., **6** (1971), 210–238 ⟨K 25⟩

Crowell, R.H.; R.H. Fox, (1963): *Introduction to knot theory*. New York: Ginn and Co., or: Grad. Texts Math. **57**, Berlin-Heidelberg -New York: Springer Verlag 1977 ⟨K 11⟩

Crowell, R.H.; D. Strauss, 1969: *On the elementary ideals of link modules*. Trans. Amer. Math. Soc., **143** (1969), 93–109 ⟨K 25, K 50⟩

Crowell, R.H.; H.F. Trotter, 1963: *A class of pretzel knots*. Duke Math. J., **30** (1963), 373–377 ⟨K 35⟩

Culler, M.; P.B. Shalen, 1984: *Bounded, separating, incompressible surfaces in knot manifolds*. Invent. math., **75** (1984), 537–545 ⟨K 16, K 15, M⟩

Dahm, D.M., 1962: *A generalization of braid theory*. Ph.D. Thesis. Princeton ⟨K 40⟩

Davis, P.J. 1979: *Circulant matrices*. New York–London–Sidney: John Wiley & Sons ⟨X⟩

Debrunner, H., 1961: *Links of Brunnian type*. Duke Math. J., **28** (1961), 17–23 ⟨K 35, K 50⟩

Dehn, M., 1910: *Über die Topologie des dreidimensionalen Raumes*. Math. Ann., **69** (1910), 137–168 ⟨M⟩

Dehn, M., 1914: *Die beiden Kleeblattschlingen*. Math. Ann., **102** (1914), 402–413 ⟨K 35⟩

Dehn, M., 1938: *Die Gruppe der Abbildungsklassen*. Acta Math., **69** (1938), 135–206 ⟨F⟩

Deligne, P., 1972: *Les immeubles des groupes de tresses généralisés*. Invent. math., **17** (1972), 273–302 ⟨K 40⟩

Ding, Ch.-H., 1963: *On the total curvature of curves, II*. Chinese Math., **4** (1963), 553–560 ⟨K 38⟩

Dowker, C.H.; M.B. Thistlethwaite, 1982: *On the classification of knots*. C.R. Math. Rep. Acad. Sci. Canada, **4** (1982), 129–131 ⟨K 14, K 29⟩

Dowker, C.H.; M.B. Thistlethwaite, 1983: *Classification of knot projections*. Topology Appl., **16** (1983), 19–31 ⟨K 14, K 29⟩

Doyle, P.H., 1973: *Fundamental groups*. Quart. J. Math. Oxford, (2) **24** (1973), 397–398 ⟨K 16, K 55⟩

Dror, E., 1975: *Homology circles and knot complements*. Topology, **14** (1975), 279–289 ⟨K 60, A⟩

Dugopoiski, M.J., 1982: *A new solution to the word problem in the fundamental groups of alternating knots and links*. Trans. Amer. Math. Soc., **272** (1982), 375–382 ⟨K 16, K 29, K 31⟩

Durfee, A.H., 1974: *Fibered knots and algebraic singularities*. Topology, **13** (1974), 47–59 ⟨K 18, K 34⟩

Durfee, A.H., 1975: *The characteristic polynomial of the monodromy*. Pacific J. Math., **59** (1975), 21–26 ⟨K 34⟩

Durfee, A.H.; L.R. Kauffman, 1975: *Periodicity of branched cyclic covers*. Math. Ann., **218** (1975), 157–174 ⟨K 20, K 60⟩

Durfee, A.H.; H.B. Lawson, 1972: *Fibered knots and foliations of highly connected manifolds*. Invent. math., **12** (1972), 203–215 ⟨K 60⟩

Dyck, W., 1882: *Gruppentheoretische Studien*. Math. Ann., **20** (1882), 1–44 ⟨G⟩

Dyer, E.; A.T. Vasques, 1973: *The asphericity of higher dimensional knots*. Canad. J. Math., **25** (1973), 1132–1136 ⟨K 60⟩

Dyer, J.L., 1980: *The algebraic braid groups are torsion-free: an algebraic proof*. Math. Z., **172** (1980), 157–160 ⟨K 40⟩

Dyer, J.L.; E.K. Grossman, 1981: *The automorphism groups of the braid groups*. Amer. J. Math., **103** (1981), 1151–1169 ⟨K 40⟩

Eckmann, B., 1976: *Aspherical manifolds and higher-dimensional knots*. Comment. Math. Helv., **51** (1976), 93–98 ⟨K 60⟩

Edmonds, A.L.; C. Livingston, 1983: *Group actions on fibred three manifolds*. Comment. Math. Helvetici, **58** (1983), 529–542 ⟨K 18, M⟩

Edwards, C.H., 1962: *Concentric tori and tame curves in S^3*. In: Top. 3-manifolds, Proc. 1961 Top. Inst. Univ. Georgia (ed. M.K. Fort jr.), pp. 39–41. Englewood Cliffs, N.J.: Prentice-Hall ⟨K 12, M⟩

Edwards, C.H., 1964: *Concentricity in 3-manifolds*. Trans. Amer. Math. Soc., **113** (1964), 406–423 ⟨M⟩

Eilenberg, S., 1936: *Sur les courbes sans nœuds*. Fund. Math., **28** (1936), 233–242 ⟨K 12⟩

Eisner, J.R., 1977: *Knots with infinitely many minimal spanning surfaces*. Trans. Amer. Math. Soc., **229** (1977), 329–349 ⟨K 15⟩

Eisner, J.R., 1977′: *Addendum to "Knots with infinitely many minimal spanning surfaces"*. Trans. Amer. Math. Soc., **233** (1977), 367–369 ⟨K 15⟩

Epstein, D.B.A., 1960: *Linking spheres*. Proc. Cambridge Phil. Soc., **56** (1960), 215–219 ⟨K 60⟩

Epstein, D.B.A., 1961: *Projective planes in 3-manifolds*. Proc. London Math. Soc., **11** (1969), 469–484 ⟨M⟩

Erle, D., 1969: *Quadratische Formen als Invarianten von Einbettungen der Kodimension 2*. Topology, **8** (1969), 99–114 ⟨K 27, K 60⟩

Erle, D., 1969′: *Die quadratische Form eines Knotens und ein Satz über Knotenmannigfaltigkeiten.* J. reine angew. Math., **236** (1969), 174–218 ⟨K 27⟩

Fadell, E., 1962: *Homotopy groups of configuration spaces und the string problem of Dirac.* Duke Math. J., **29** (1962), 231–242 ⟨K 40⟩

Fadell, E.; J. van Buskirk, 1961: *On the braid groups of E^2 and S^2.* Bull. Amer. Math. Soc., **67** (1961), 211–213 ⟨K 40⟩

Fadell, E.; J. van Buskirk, 1962: *The braid groups on E^2 and S^2.* Duke Math. J., **29** (1962), 248–257 ⟨K 40⟩

Fadell, E.; L. Neuwirth, 1962: *Configuration spaces.* Math. Scand., **10** (1962), 111–118 ⟨K 40⟩

Farber, M.Š., 1975: Коэффициенты зацепления и двумерные узлы. Доклады Акад. Наук СССР, **222** (1975), 299–301 Engl. transl.: *Linking coefficients and two-dimensional knots.* Soviet. Math. Doklady, **16** (1975), 647–650 ⟨K 60, K 61⟩

Farber, M.Š., 1977: Двойственность в бесконечном циклическом накрытии и четномериые узлы. Известия Акад. Наук СССР, сер. мат., **41** (1977), 794–828, Engl. transl.: *Duality in an infinite cyclic covering and even-dimensional knots.* Math. USSR-Izvestia, **11** (1977), 749–781 ⟨K 60⟩

Farber, M.Š., 1978: Классификация некоторых узлов коразмерности два. Доклады Ан СССР, **240** (1978), 32–35, Engl. transl.: *Classification of some knots of codimension two.* Soviet Math. Dokl, **19** (1978), 555–558 ⟨K 60⟩

Farber, M.S., 1980: *Isotopy types of knots of codimension two.* Trans. Amer. Math. Soc., **261** (1980), 185–209 ⟨K 60⟩

Farber, M. Š., 1980′: Тип узла и его дополнение. (*Type of a knot and its complement.)* Doklady Acad. Sci. Aserbaya. SSR. **36**, (1980), 7–11 ⟨K 60⟩

Farber, M. Š., 1981: Задания модулей узлов (*Presentations for knot modules*). Isvestia Acad. Sci. Aserbaya. SSR, Ser. phys.-tech. math. sci., 1981 No 2, 105–111 ⟨K 25, K 60⟩

Farber, M.Š., 1981′: Функторы в категории модулей узлов (*Functors in the category of knot modules*). Izvestia Acad. Sci. Aserbaya. SSR, Ser. phys.-tech. math. sci., 1981 No 3, 94–100 ⟨K 25, K 60⟩

Farber, M.S., 1981″: Стабильная классификация узлов. Доклады Акад. Наук СССР, **258** (1981), 1318–1321, Engl. transl.: *Stable classification of knots.* Soviet. Math. Doklady, **23** (1981), 685–688 ⟨K 12, K 60⟩

Farber, M.Š., 1981‴: Классификация стабильиых узлов. Мат. сб., **115** (1981), 223–262, Engl. transl.: *Classification of stably fibred knots.* Math. USSR-Sb., **43** (1982), 199–234 ⟨K 18, K 60⟩

Farber, M.Š., 1981^IV: Стабильная классификация сферчуеских узлов (*A stable classification of spherical knots*). Bull. Acad. Sci. Georgian SSR, **104** (1981), 285–288 ⟨K 12, K 60⟩

Farber, M.Š. 1983: Классификация простых узлов (*Classification of simple knots*), Успехи Mam. Hayk, **38:5** (1983), 59–106 ⟨K 15, K 25, K 60⟩

Farber, M.Š., 1984: *An algebraic classification of some even-dimensional spherical knots.* I. Trans. Amer. Math. Soc., **281** (1984), 507–527 ⟨K 60⟩

Farber, M.S., 1984′: *An algebraic classification of some even-dimensional spherical knots.* II. Trans. Amer. Math. Soc., **281** (1984), 529–570 ⟨K 60⟩

Farber, M.Š., 1984″: Отображения в окружность с минимальным числом критических точек и многомерные узлы. (*Mappings to the circle with a minimal number of critical points and multidimensional knots.*) Doklady AN USSR, **276** (1984), 43–46 ⟨K 60⟩

Fary, I., 1949: *Sur la courbure totale d'une courbe gauche faisant un* nœud. Bull. Soc. Math. France, **77** (1949), 128–138 ⟨K 38⟩

Fenchel, W., 1948: *Estensiono di gruppi descontinui e transformazioni periodiche delle superficie.* Rend. Acc. Naz. Lincei (Sc. fis-mat e nat), **5** (1948), 326–329 ⟨F⟩

Fenchel, W., 1950: *Bemarkingen om endelige gruppen af abbildungsklasser.* Mat. Tidsschrift B (1950), 90–95 ⟨F⟩

Fenn, R. (ed.), 1979: *Topology of Low-dimensional Manifolds.* Proc. Second Sussex Conf. 1977, Lect. Notes Math. **722** *(1979).* Berlin-Heidelberg-New York: Springer Verlag ⟨K 11⟩

Fenn, R.; C. Rourke, 1979: *On Kirby's calculus of links.* Topology, **18** (1979), 1–15 ⟨K 12⟩

Feustel, C.D., 1966: *Homotopic arcs are isotopic.* Proc. Amer. Math. Soc., **17** (1966), 891–896 ⟨M⟩

Feustel, C.D., 1972: *A splitting theorem for closed orientable 3-manifolds.* Topology, **11** (1972), 151–158 ⟨M⟩

Feustel, C.D., 1976: *On the torus theorem and its applications.* Trans. Amer. Math. Soc., **217** (1976), 1–43 ⟨M⟩

Feustel, C.D., 1976′: *On the torus theorem for closed manifolds.* Trans. Amer. Math. Soc., **217** (1976), 45–57 ⟨M⟩

Feustel, C.D.; W. Whitten, 1978: *Groups and complements of knots*. Canad. J. Math., **30** (1978), 1284–1295 ⟨K 19⟩

Fintushel, R.; R.J. Stern, 1980: *Constructing lens spaces by surgery on knots*. Math. Z., **175** (1980), 33–51 ⟨K 17, K 21⟩

Fisher, G.M., 1960: *On the group of all homeomorphisms of a manifold*. Trans. Amer. Math. Soc., **97** (1960), 193–212 ⟨F, M⟩

Flapan, E., 1983: *Infinitely periodic knots*. (preprint), Univ. Wisconsin, Madison ⟨K 22⟩

Floyd, W.; A. Hatcher, 1984: *Incompressible surfaces in 2-bridge link complements*. (to appear) ⟨K 30, K 35⟩

Fox, R.H., 1948: *On the imbedding of polyhedra in 3-space*. Ann. of Math., **49** (1948), 462–470 ⟨M⟩

Fox, R.H., 1949: *A remarkable simple closed curve*. Ann. of Math., **50** (1949), 264–265 ⟨K 55⟩

Fox, R.H., 1950: *On the total curvature of some tame knots*. Ann. of Math., **52** (1950), 258–260 ⟨K 38⟩

Fox, R.H., 1952: *On the complementary domains of a certain pair of inequivalent knots*. Indag. Math., **14** (1952), 37–40 ⟨K 19⟩

Fox, R.H., 1952′: *Recent development of knot theory at Princeton*. Proc. Internat. Congress Math. Cambridge 1950, vol. **2**, pp. 453–457 ⟨K 11⟩

Fox, R.H., 1953: *Free differential calculus. I. Derivation in the free group ring*. Ann. of Math., **57** (1953), 547–560 ⟨G⟩

Fox, R.H., 1954: *Free differential calculus. II. The isomorphism problem*. Ann. of Math., **59** (1954), 196–210 ⟨G⟩

Fox, R.H., 1956: *Free differential calculus. III. Subgroups*. Ann. of. Math., **64** (1956), 407–419 ⟨K 20, G⟩

Fox, R.H., 1957: *Covering spaces with singularities*. Lefschetz symposium. Princeton Math. Series **12** (1957), 243–257. Princeton, N.J.: Princeton Univ. Press ⟨A⟩

Fox, R.H., 1958: *On knots whose points are fixed under a periodic transformation of the 3-sphere*. Osaka Math. J., **10** (1958), 31–35 ⟨K 22⟩

Fox, R.H., 1958′: *Congruence classes of knots*. Osaka Math. J., **10** (1958), 37–41 ⟨K 26, K 59⟩

Fox, R.H., 1960: *The homology characters of the cyclic coverings of the knots of genus one*. Ann. of Math., **71** (1960), 187–196 ⟨K 20⟩

Fox, R.H., 1960′: *Free differential calculus, V. The Alexander matrices reexamined*. Ann. of Math., **71** (1960), 408–422 ⟨K 25, G⟩

Fox, R.H., 1962: *A quick trip through knot theory*. In: Top. 3-manifolds, Proc. 1961 Top. Inst. Univ. Georgia (ed. M.K. Fort, jr.), pp. 120–167. Englewood Cliffs, N.J.: Prentice-Hall ⟨K 11⟩

Fox, R.H., 1962′: *Construction of simply connected 3-manifolds*. In: Top. 3-manifolds, Proc. 1961 Top. Institut Univ. Georgia (ed. M.K. Fort, jr.), pp. 213–216. Englewood Cliffs, N.J.: Prentice-Hall ⟨K 21, M⟩

Fox, R.H., 1962″: *Some problems in knot theory*. In: Top. 3-manifolds, Proc. 1961 Top. Inst. Georgia (ed. M.K. Fort jr.), pp. 168–176. Englewood Cliffs, N.J.: Prentice-Hall ⟨K 11⟩

Fox, R.H., 1962‴: *Knots and periodic transformations*. In: Top. 3-manifolds, Proc. 1961 Top. Inst. Univ. Georgia (ed. M.K. Fort jr.), pp. 177–182. Englewood Cliffs, N.J.: Prentice-Hall ⟨K 22⟩

Fox, R.H., 1966: *Rolling*. Bull. Amer. Math. Soc., **72** (1966), 162–164 ⟨K 61⟩

Fox, R.H., 1967: *Two theorems about periodic transformations of the 3-sphere*. Michigan Math. J., **14** (1967), 331–334 ⟨K 22⟩

Fox, R.H., 1970: *Metacyclic invariants of knots and links*. Canad. J. Math., **22** (1970), 193–207 ⟨K 25⟩

Fox, R.H., 1972: *A note on branched cyclic coverings of spheres*. Rev. Mat. Hisp.-Am., (4) **32** (1972), 158–166 ⟨K 20⟩

Fox, R.H., 1973: *Characterization of slices and ribbons*. Osaka J. Math., **10** (1973), 69–76 ⟨K 35, K 33⟩

Fox, R.H.; E. Artin, 1948: *Some wild cells and spheres in three-dimensional space*. Ann. of Math., **49** (1948), 979–990 ⟨K 55⟩

Fox, R.H.; O.G. Harrold, 1962: *The Wilder arcs*. In: Top. 3-manifolds, Proc. 1961 Top. Inst. Univ. Georgia (ed. M.K. Fort jr.), pp. 184–187. Englewood Cliffs, N.J.: Prentice-Hall ⟨K 55⟩

Fox, R.H.; J.W. Milnor, 1957: *Singularities of 2-spheres in 4-space and equivalence of knots*. Bull. Amer. Math. Soc., **63** (1957), 406 ⟨K 34⟩

Fox, R.H.; J. Milnor, 1966: *Singularities of 2-spheres in 4-space and cobordism of knots*. Osaka J. Math., **3**, 257–267 ⟨K 24, K 34⟩

Fox, R.H.; L. Neuwirth, 1962: *The braid groups*. Math. Scand., **10** (1962), 119–126 ⟨K 40⟩

Fox, R.H.; N.F. Smythe, 1964: *An ideal class invariants of knots*. Proc. Amer. Math. Soc., **15** (1964), 707–709 ⟨K 25⟩

Fox, R.H.; G. Torres, 1954: *Dual presentations of the group of a knot*. Ann. of Math., **59** (1954), 211–218 ⟨K 16, K 25⟩

Francis, G.K., 1983: *Drawing Seifert surfaces that fiber the figure-8 knot complement in S^3 over S^1*. Amer. Math. Monthly, **90** (1983), 589–599 ⟨K 15, K 18⟩

Frankl, F.; L. Pontrjagin, 1930: *Ein Knotensatz mit Anwendung auf die Dimensionstheorie*. Math. Ann., **102** (1930), 785–789 ⟨K 15⟩

Franks, J.M., 1981: *Knots, links, and symbolic dynamics*. Ann. of Math., **113** (1981), 529–552 ⟨K 59⟩

Franz, W., 1935: *Über die Torsion einer Überdeckung*. J. reine angew. Math., **173** (1935), 245–254 ⟨A, M⟩

Franz, W., (1965): *Topology. II. Algebraische Topologie*. Sammlung Göschen, Berlin 1965: de Gruyter ⟨A⟩

Fröhlich, KW., 1936: *Über ein spezielles Transformationsproblem bei einer besonderen Klasse von Zöpfen*. Monatsh. Math. Phys., **44** (1936), 225–237 ⟨K 40⟩

Fuks, D.B., 1970: Когомологии групп кос mod. 2. Функц. анализ прил., **8** (1970) 62–73, Engl. transl.: *Cohomologies of group COS mod 2*. Funct. Anal. appl., **4:2** (1970), 143–151 ⟨K 40⟩

Fukuhara, S., 1983: *On framed link groups*. Tokyo J. Math., **4** (1983), 307–318 ⟨K 21⟩

Fukuhara, S., 1984: *On an invariant of homology lens spaces*. J. Math. Soc. Japan, **36** (1984), 259–277 ⟨K 21, M⟩

Funcke, K., 1975: *Nicht frei äquivalente Darstellungen von Knotengruppen mit einer definierenden Relation*. Math. Z., **141** (1975), 205–217 ⟨K 16, K 30⟩

Funcke, K., 1978: *Geschlecht von Knoten mit zwei Brücken und die Faserbarkeit ihrer Außenräume*. Math. Z., **159** (1978), 3–24 ⟨K 15, K 18, K 29, K 30⟩

Furusawa, F.; M. Sakuma, 1983: *Dehn surgery on symmetric knots*. Math. Sem. Notes Kobe Univ., **11** (1983), 179–198 ⟨K 21, K 23⟩

Gabai, D., 1983: *The Murasugi sum is a natural geometric operation*. Amer. Math. Soc. Contemporary Math., **20** (1983), 131–143 ⟨K 15, K 18⟩

Gabai, D., 1983′: *Foliations and the topology of 3-manifolds*. J. Diff. Geom., **18** (1983), 445–503 ⟨K 15, K 59, M⟩

Gabai, D., 1984: *Foliations and genera of links*. Topology, **23** (1984), 381–400 ⟨K 15, K 59, M⟩

Gabai, D., 1984′: *The Murasugi sum is a natural geometric operation. II*. Amer. Math. Soc. Contemporary Math., (to appear) ⟨K 15, K8⟩

Gamst, J., 1967: *Linearisierung von Gruppendaten mit Anwendungen auf Knotengruppen*. Math. Z., **97** (1967), 291–302 ⟨K 25, G⟩

Garside, F.A., 1969: *The braid group and other groups*. Quart. J. Math. Oxford, (2) **20** (1969), 235–254 ⟨K 40, G⟩

Gassner, B.J., 1961: *On braid groups*. Abh. Math. Sem. Univ. Hamburg, **25** (1961), 10–22 ⟨K 40⟩

Gauss, K.F., 1833: *Zur mathematischen Theorie der electrodynamischen Wirkungen*. Werke Königl. Gesell. Wiss. Göttingen 1877, vol. **5**, p. 605 ⟨K 38⟩

Giffen, C., 1966: *The generalized Smith conjecture*. Amer. J. Math., **88** (1966), 187–198 ⟨K 22, M⟩

Giffen, C.H., 1967: *On transformations of the 3-sphere fixing a knot*. Bull. Amer. Math. Soc., **73** (1967), 913–914 ⟨K 22⟩

Giffen, C.H., 1967′: *Cyclic branched coverings of doubled curves in 3-manifolds*. Illinois J. Math., **11** (1967), 644–646 ⟨K 20⟩

Giffen, C.H., 1976: *New results on link equivalence relations*. (preprint) ⟨K 50⟩

Giffen, C.H., 1979: *Link concordance implies link homotopy*. Math. Scand., **45** (1979), 243–254 ⟨K 24⟩

Giller, C.A., 1982: *A family of links and the Conway calculus*. Trans. Amer. Math. Soc., **270** (1982), 75–109 ⟨K 12, K 35⟩

Giller, C.A., 1982′: *Towards a classical knot theory for surfaces in R^4*. Illinois J. Math., **26** (1982), 591–631 ⟨K 60⟩

Gillette, R.; J. van Buskirk, 1968: *The word problem and consequences for the braid groups and mapping class groups of the 2-sphere*. Trans. Amer. Math. Soc., **131** (1968), 277–296 ⟨K 29, K 40, F⟩

Gilmer, P.M., 1982: *On the slice genus of knots*. Invent. math., **66** (1982), 191–197 ⟨K 12, K 15, K 33⟩

Gilmer, P.M., 1983: *Slice knots in S^3*. Quart. J. Math. Oxford, (2) **34** (1983), 305–322 ⟨K 33⟩

Gilmer, P.M., 1984: *Ribbon concordance and a partial order on S-equivalence classes*. (preprint) ⟨K 24⟩

Gilmer, P.M., 1984′: *On the ribbon genus of knots*. (preprint) ⟨K 12, K 15, K 35⟩

Gluck, H., 1961: *The embedding of two-spheres in the four-sphere*. Bull. Amer. Math. Soc., **67** (1961), 586–589 ⟨K 61⟩

Gluck, H., 1961′: *Orientable surfaces in four-space*. Bull. Amer. Math. Soc., **67** (1961), 590–592 ⟨K 60⟩

Gluck, H., 1962: *Tangled manifolds*. Ann. of Math., **76** (1962), 62–72 ⟨K 59, M⟩

Gluck, H., 1963: *Unknotting S^1 in S^4*. Bull. Amer. Math. Soc., **69** (1963), 91–94 ⟨K 12, K 60⟩

Goblirsch, R.P., 1959: *On decompositions of 3-space by linkages*. Proc. Amer. Math. Soc., **10** (1959), 728–730 ⟨K 59⟩

Goeritz, L., 1932: *Die Heegaard-Diagramme des*

Torus. Abh. math. Sem. Hamb. Univ., **9** (1932), 187–188 ⟨F, M⟩

Goeritz, L., 1933: *Knoten und quadratische Formen*. Math. Z., **36** (1933), 647–654 ⟨K 27⟩

Goeritz, L., 1934: *Die Betti'schen Zahlen der zyklischen Überlagerungsräume der Knotenaussenräume*. Amer. J. Math., (2) **56** (1934), 194–198 ⟨K 20⟩

Goeritz, L., 1934': *Bemerkungen zur Knotentheorie*. Abh. Math. Sem. Univ. Hamburg, **10** (1934), 201–210 ⟨K 27⟩

Goldberg, Ch. H., 1973: *An exact sequence of braid groups*. Math. Scand., **33** (1973), 68–82 ⟨K 40⟩

Goldsmith, D. L., 1974: *Homotopy of braids – an answer to a question of E. Artin*. Top. Conf. Virginia Polytechn. Inst. and State Univ. (eds R. F. Dickman jr., P. Fletcher), Lect. Notes in Math. **375** (1974), 91–96, Berlin-Heidelberg-New York: Springer Verlag ⟨K 40⟩

Goldsmith, D. L., 1974': *Motions of links in the 3-sphere*. Bull. Amer. Math. Soc., **80** (1974), 62–66 ⟨K 59⟩

Goldsmith, D. L., 1975: *Symmetric fibered links*. In: Knots, Groups and 3-manifolds. Ann. Math. Stud. **84** (1975) (ed. L. P. Neuwirth), 3–23. Princeton, N. J.: Princeton Univ. Press ⟨K 18, K 23⟩

Goldsmith, D. L., 1978: *A linking invariant of classical link concordance*. In: Knot Theory (ed. J. C. Hausmann). Lect. Notes in Math. **685** (1978), 135–170. Berlin-Heidelberg-New York: Springer Verlag ⟨K 24⟩

Goldsmith, D. L., 1979: *Concordance implies homotopy for classical links in M^3*. Comment. Math. Helv., **54** (1979), 347–355 ⟨K 24⟩

Goldsmith, D. L., 1982: *Motions of links in the 3-sphere*. Math. Scand., **50** (1982), 167–205 ⟨K 59⟩

Goldsmith, D. L.; L. H. Kauffman, 1978: *Twist spinning revisited*. Trans. Amer. Math. Soc., **239** (1978), 229–251 ⟨K 35, K 60⟩

Gomez-Larrañage, J. C., 1982: *Totally knotted knots are prime*. Math. Proc. Cambridge Phil. Soc., **91** (1982), 467–472 ⟨K 17, K 35⟩

Gonzáles-Acuña, F., 1970: *Dehn's construction on knots*. Bol. Soc. Mat. Mexicana, **15** (1970), 58–79 ⟨K 21⟩

Gonzáles-Acuña, F., 1975: *Homomorphs of knot groups*. Ann. of Math., **102** (1975), 373–377 ⟨K 16⟩

Gonzáles-Acuña, F.; J. M. Montesinos, 1978: *Ends of knot groups*. Ann. of Math., **108** (1978), 91–96 ⟨K 16⟩

Gonzáles-Acuña, F.; J. M. Montesinos, 1982: *Embedding knots in trivial knots*. Bull. London Math. Soc., **14** (1982), 238–240 ⟨K 60⟩

Gonzáles-Acuña, F.; J. M. Montesinos, 1983: *Quasiaspherical knots with infinitely many ends*. Comment. Math. Helv., **58** (1983), 257–263 ⟨K 60⟩

Goodrick, R. E., 1969: *A note on Seifert circles*. Proc. Amer. Math. Soc., **21** (1969), 615–617 ⟨K 12, K 15⟩

Goodrick, R. E., 1970: *Numerical invariants of knots*. Illinois J. Math., **14** (1970), 414–418 ⟨K 12⟩

Goodrick, R. E., 1972: *Two bridge knots are alternating knots*. Pacific J. Math., **40** (1972), 561–564 ⟨K 30, K 31, K 35⟩

Gordon, C. McA., 1971: *A short proof of a theorem of Plans on the homology of the branched cyclic coverings of a knot*. Bull. Amer. Math. Soc., **77** (1971), 85–87 ⟨K 20⟩

Gordon, C. McA., 1972: *Knots whose branched cyclic coverings have periodic homology*. Trans. Amer. Math. Soc., **168** (1972), 357–370 ⟨K 20, K 35⟩

Gordon, C. McA., 1972': *Twist-spun torus knots*. Proc. Amer. Math. Soc., **32** (1972), 319–322 ⟨K 35⟩

Gordon, C. McA., 1973: *Some higher-dimensioned knots with the same homotopy groups*. Quart. J. Math. Oxford, (2) **24** (1973), 411–422 ⟨K 60⟩

Gordon, C. M., 1975: *Knots, homology spheres and contractible 4-manifolds*. Topology, **14** (1975), 151–172 ⟨K 22, K 33, K 59⟩

Gordon, C. McA., 1976: *Knots in the 4-sphere*. Comment. Math. Helv., **39** (1976), 585–596 ⟨K 61⟩

Gordon, C. McA., 1976': *A note on spun knots*. Proc. Amer. Math. Soc., **58** (1976), 361–362 ⟨K 35⟩

Gordon, C. McA., 1977: *Uncountably many stably trivial strings in codimension two*. Quart. J. Math. Oxf., (2) **28** (1977), 369–379 ⟨K 60⟩

Gordon, C. McA., 1978: *Some aspects of classical knot theory*. In: Knot theory (ed. J. C. Hausmann). Lect. Notes in Math. **685** (1978), 1–60. Berlin-Heidelberg-New York: Springer Verlag ⟨K 11⟩

Gordon, C. McA., 1981: *Homology of groups of surfaces in the 4-sphere*. Math. Proc. Cambridge Phil. Soc., **89** (1981), 113-117 ⟨K 60⟩

Gordon, C. McA., 1981': *Ribbon concordance of knots in the 3-sphere*. Math. Ann., **257** (1981), 157–170 ⟨K 24⟩

Gordon, C. McA., 1983: *Dehn surgery and satellite knots*. Trans. Amer. Math. Soc., **275** (1983), 687–708 ⟨K 17, K 21⟩

Gordon, C. McA.; R. A. Litherland, 1978: *On the signature of a link*. Invent. math., **47** (1978), 53–69 ⟨K 27⟩

Gordon, C. McA.; R.A. Litherland, 1979: *On the Smith conjecture for homotopy 3-spheres*. Notices Amer. Math. Soc., **26** (1979), A-252, Abstract 764–G13 ⟨K 22, M⟩

Gordon, C. McA.; R.A. Litherland, 1979′: *On a theorem of Murasugi*. Pacific J. Math., **82** (1979), 69–74 ⟨K 27⟩

Gordon, C. McA.; R.A. Litherland, K. Murasugi, 1981: *Signatures of covering links*. Canad. J. Math., **33** (1981), 381–394 ⟨K 22, K 27⟩

Gorin, E.L.; V.Ya. Lin, 1969: Алгебраические уравнения с непрерывными коэффициентами и некоторые вопросы алгебраической теории кос. Мат. сб., **78** (1969) 579–610, Engl. transl.: *Algebraic equations with continuous coefficients and some problems of the algebraic theory of braids*. Math. USSR-Sbornik, **7** (1969), 569–596 ⟨K 32, K 40⟩

Gorin, E.L.; V.Ya. Lin, 1969′: Группа кос и алгебраические уравнения с непрерывными коэффициентами (*The braid group and algebraic equations with continuous coefficients.*). Uspehi Math. Nauk, **24:2** (1969), 225–226 ⟨K 32, K 40⟩

Gorjunov, V.V., 1981: Когомологии групп кос серий *C* и Д. Труды моск. мат. обш., **42** (1981), 234–242, Engl. transl.: *Cohomology of braid groups of the series C and D*. Trans. Moscow Math. Soc. 1982:2, 233–241 ⟨K 40⟩

Gramain, A., 1977: *Sur le groupe fondamental de l'espace des n*œuds. Ann. Inst. Fourier, Grenoble, **27** (1977), 29–44 ⟨K 59⟩

Graeub, W., 1950: *Die semilinearen Abbildungen*. Sitz.-Ber. Heidelberger Akad. Wiss., Math. Nat. Kl. 1950, 205–272 ⟨B⟩

Grayson, M.A., 1983: *The orbit space of a Kleinian group: Riley's modest example*. Math. Comput., **40** (1983), 633–646 ⟨K 28, K 59, M⟩

Gurso, G.G., 1984: Система образуюших для некоторых злементов групп кос. (*Systems of generators for some elements of the braid groups.*) Isvestia AN USSR, ser. math., **48** (1984), 479–519 ⟨K 40⟩

Gustafson, R.F., 1981: *A simple genus one knot with incompessible spanning surface of arbitrarily high genus*. Pacific J. Math., **96** (1981), 81–98 ⟨K 59⟩

Gutiérrez, M.A., 1971: *Homology of knot groups: I. Groups with deficiency one*. Bol. Soc. Mat. Mex., **16** (1971), 58–63 ⟨K 16, K 60⟩

Gutiérrez, M.A., 1972: *An exact sequence calculation for the second homotopy of a knot*. Proc. Amer. Math. Soc., **32** (1972), 571–577 ⟨K 60⟩

Gutiérrez, M.A., 1972′: *On knot modules*. Invent. math., **17** (1972), 329–335 ⟨K 25, 60⟩

Gutiérrez, M.A., 1972″: *Secondary invariants for links*. Rev. Columbiana Mat., **6** (1972), 106–115 ⟨K 50⟩

Gutiérrez, M.A., 1972‴: *Boundary links and an unlinking theorem*. Trans. Amer. Math. Soc., **171** (1972), 491–499 ⟨K 60⟩

Gutiérrez, M.A., 1973: *Unlinking up to cobordism*. Bull. Amer. Math. Soc., **79** (1973), 1299–1302 ⟨K 24, K 60⟩

Gutiérrez, M.A., 1973′: *An exact sequence calculation for the second homotopy of a knot. II*. Proc. Amer. Math. Soc., **40** (1973), 327–330 ⟨K 16, K 35⟩

Gutiérrez, M.A., 1974: *Polynomial invariants of boundary links*. Rev. Colombiana Mat., **8** (1974), 97–109 ⟨K 15, K 26, K 50⟩

Gutiérrez, M.A., 1978: *On the Seifert manifold of a 2-knot*. Trans. Amer. Math. Soc., **240** (1978), 287–294 ⟨K 61⟩

Guitérrez, M.A., 1979: *Homology of knot groups. III. Knots in* S^6. Proc. London Math. Soc., (3) **39** (1979), 469–487 ⟨K 60⟩

Gutiérrez, M.A., 1980: *Homology of knot groups. II. Free products.* (to appear) ⟨K 16, K 60⟩

Hacon, D., 1976: *Iterated torus knots*. Math. Proc. Cambridge Phil. Soc., **80** (1976), 57–60 ⟨K 35⟩

Haefliger, A., 1962: *Knotted (4k-1)-spheres in 6k-space*. Ann. of Math., **75** (1962), 452–466 ⟨K 60⟩

Haefliger, A., 1962′: *Differentiable links*. Topology, **1** (1962), 241–244 ⟨K 60⟩

Haefliger, A., 1963: *Plongement differentiable dans le domaine stable*. Comment. Math. Helv., **37** (1963), 155–176 ⟨K 60⟩

Haefliger, A.; K. Steer, 1965: *Symmetry of linking coefficients*. Comment. Math. Helv., **39** (1965), 259–270 ⟨K 60⟩

Hafer, E., 1974: *Darstellung von Verkettungsgruppen und einen Invariante der Verkettungstypen*. Abh. Math. Sem. Univ. Hamburg, **40** (1974), 176–186 ⟨K 28⟩

Haken, W., 1961: *Theorie der Normalflächen*. Acta Math., **105** (1961), 245–375 ⟨M⟩

Haken, W., 1962: *Über das Homöomorphieproblem der 3-Mannigfaltigkeiten. I*. Math. Z., **80** (1962), 89–120 ⟨M⟩

Hammer, G., 1963: *Ein Verfahren zur Bestimmung von Begleitknoten*. Math. Z., **81** (1963), 395–413 ⟨K 17, K 29⟩

Hanner, O., 1983: *Knots which cannot be untied*. Normat, **31** (1983), 78–84 ⟨K 12⟩

Harer, J., 1982: *How to construct all fibered knots and links*. Topology, **21** (1982), 268–280 ⟨K 18⟩

Harer, J., 1983: *Representing elements of $\pi_1(M)^3$ by fibered knots.* Math. Proc. Cambridge Phil. Soc., **92** (1982), 133–138 ⟨K 18⟩

Harrold, O.G., 1962: *Combinatorial structures, local unknottedness, and local peripheral unknottedness.* Top. 3-manifolds, Proc. 1961 Top. Inst. Univ. Georgia (ed. M.K. Fort, jr.), pp. 71–83. Englewood Cliffs, N.J.: Prentice-Hall ⟨K 60⟩

Harrold, O.G., 1973: *Locally unknotted sets in three-space.* Yokohama Math. J., **21** (1973), 47–60 ⟨K 59⟩

Harrold, O.G., 1981: *A remarkable simple closed curve revisited.* Proc. Amer. Math. Soc., **81** (1981), 133–136 ⟨K 55⟩

Hartley, R.; K. Murasugi, 1978: *Homology invariants.* Canad. J. Math., **30** (1978), 655–670 ⟨K20, K28, A⟩

Hartley, R., 1979: *Metabelian representations of knot groups.* Pacific J. Math., **82** (1979), 93–104 ⟨K 28⟩

Hartley, R.I., 1979′: *On two-bridged knots polynomials.* J. Austral. Math. Soc., **28** (1979), 241–249 ⟨K 26, K 30⟩

Hartley, R., 1980: *On the classification of three-braid links.* Abh. Math. Sem. Univ. Hamburg, **50** (1980), 108–117 ⟨K 35, K 40⟩

Hartley, R., 1980′: *Knots and involutions.* Math. Z., **171** (1980), 175–185 ⟨K 22⟩

Hartley, R.I., 1980″: *Twisted amphicheiral knots.* Math. Ann., **252** (1980), 103–109 ⟨K 35⟩

Hartley, R., 1980‴: *Invertible amphicheiral knots.* Math. Ann., **252** (1980), 103–109 ⟨K 35⟩

Hartley, R., 1981: *Knots with free periods.* Canad. J. Math., **33** (1981), 91–102 ⟨K 23⟩

Hartley, R., 1983: *Lifting group homomorphisms.* Pacific J. Math., **105** (1983), 311–320 ⟨K 26, K 28⟩

Hartley, R., 1983′: *Identifying non-invertible knots.* Topology, **22** (1983), 137–145 ⟨K 13, K 23⟩

Hartley, R., 1983″: *The Conway potential function for links.* Comment. Math. Helv., **58** (1983), 365–378 ⟨K 12, K 29⟩

Hartley, R.; A. Kawauchi, 1979: *Polynomials of amphicheiral knots.* Math. Ann., **243** (1979), 63–70 ⟨K 23, K 26⟩

Hartley, R.; K. Murasugi, 1977: *Covering linkage invariants.* Canad. J. Math., **29** (1977), 1312–1339 ⟨K 20, K 28⟩

Hashizume, Y., 1958: *On the uniqueness of the decomposition of a link.* Osaka Math. J., **10** (1958), 283–300 ⟨K 17⟩

Hashizume, Y.; F. Hosokawa, 1958: *On symmetric skew unions of knots.* Proc. Japan Acad., **34** (1958), 87–91 ⟨K 17⟩

Hass, J., 1983: *The geometry of the slice-ribbon problem.* Math. Proc. Cambridge Phil. Soc., **94** (1983), 101–108 ⟨K 33⟩

Hatcher, A., 1983: *Hyperbolic structures of arithmetic type on some link complements.* J. London Math. Soc., **27** (1983), 345–355 ⟨K 38⟩

Hatcher, A.; W. Thurston, 1980: *A presentation of the mapping class group of a closed orientable surface.* Topology, **19** (1980), 221–237 ⟨F⟩

Hausmann, J.-C., 1978: *Nœuds antisimples.* In: Knot Theory (ed. J.-C. Hausmann). Lect. Notes in Math. **685** (1978), 171–202. Berlin-Heidelberg-New York: Springer ⟨K 60⟩

Hausmann, J.C.; M. Kervaire, 1978: *Sous-groupes dérivés des groupes de nœuds.* L'Enseign. Math., **24** (1978), 111–123 ⟨K 60⟩

Hausmann, J.C.; M. Kervaire, 1978′: *Sur le centre des groupes de nœuds multidimensionels.* C.R. Acad. Sci. Paris, 287-I (1978), 699–702 ⟨K 60, K 16⟩

Hempel, J., 1962: *Construction of orientable 3-manifolds.* Top. 3-manifolds, Proc. 1961 Top. Inst. Univ. Georgia (ed. M.K. Fort, jr.), pp. 207–212. Englewood Cliffs, N.J.: Prentice-Hall ⟨K 21⟩

Hempel, J., 1964: *A simply-connected 3-manifold is S^3 if it is the sum of solid torus and the complement of a torus knot.* Proc. Amer. Math. Soc., **15** (1964), 154–158 ⟨K 19, K 35⟩

Hempel, J., (1976): *3-manifolds.* Ann. of Math. Studies, **86** (1976). Princeton, N.J.: Princeton Univ. Press ⟨M⟩

Hempel, J., 1984: *Homology of coverings.* Pacific J. Math., **112** (1984), 83–114 ⟨K 20, M⟩

Henninger, H., 1978: *Geschlossene Zöpfe und Darstellungen.* Dissertation. Frankfurt ⟨K 28, K 40⟩

Higman, G., 1948: *A theorem on linkages.* Quart. J. Math. Oxford, **19** (1948), 117–122 ⟨K 16, K 50⟩

Hilden, H.M., 1975: *Generators for two subgroups related to the braid groups.* Pacific J. Math., **59** (1975), 475–486 ⟨K 40⟩

Hilden, H.M., 1976: *Three-fold branched coverings of S^3.* Amer. J. of Math., **98** (1976), 989–997 ⟨K 20⟩

Hilden, H.M.; M.T. Lozano; J.M. Montesinos, 1983: *Universal knots.* Bull. Amer. Math. Soc., **8** (1983), 449–450 ⟨K 20⟩

Hilden, H.M.; M.T. Lozano; J.M. Montesinos, 1984: *On knots that are universal.* (preprint) ⟨K 20⟩

Hilden, H.M.; J.M. Montesinos; T. Thickstun, 1976: *Closed oriented 3-manifolds as 3-fold branched coverings of S^3 of special type.* Pacific J. Math., **65** (1976), 65–76 ⟨K 20⟩

Hillman, J. A., 1977: *A non-homology boundary link with zero Alexander polynomial.* Bull. Austr. Math. Soc., **16** (1977), 229–236 ⟨K 26, K 50⟩

Hillman, J. A., 1977′: *High dimensional knot groups which are not two-knot groups.* Bull. Austr. Math. Soc., **16** (1977), 449–462 ⟨K 60⟩

Hillman, J. A., 1978: *Longitudes of a link and principality of an Alexander ideal.* Proc. Amer. Math. Soc., **72** (1978), 370–374 ⟨K 25, K 50⟩

Hillman, J. A., 1978′: *Alexander ideals and Chen groups.* Bull. London Math. Soc., **10** (1978), 105–110 ⟨K 25⟩

Hillman, J. A., 1980: *Orientability, asphericity and two-knots.* Houston J. Math., **6** (1980), 67–76 ⟨K 61⟩

Hillman, J. A., 1980′: *Spanning links by non-orientable surfaces.* Quart. J. Math. Oxford, (2) **31** (1980), 169–179 ⟨K 15⟩

Hillman, J. A., 1980″: *Trivializing ribbon links by Kirby moves.* Bull. Austr. Math. Soc., **21** (1980), 21–28 ⟨K 35⟩

Hillman, J. A., 1981: *The Torres conditions are insufficient.* Math. Proc. Cambridge Phil. Soc., **89** (1981), 19–22 ⟨K 26⟩

Hillman, J. A., (1981′): *Alexander ideals of links.* Lect. Notes in Math. **895** (1981). Berlin-Heidelberg-New York: Springer ⟨K 11, 25, 50⟩

Hillman, J. A., 1981″: *Finite knot modules and the factorization of certain simple knots.* Math. Ann., **257** (1981), 261–274 ⟨K 25, K 60⟩

Hillman, J. A., 1981‴: *A link with Alexander module free which is not a homology boundary link.* J. Pure Appl. Algebra, **20** (1981), 1–5 ⟨K 25, K 35⟩

Hillman, J. A., 1981^{IV}: *New proofs of two theorems on periodic knots.* Archiv Math., **37** (1981), 457–461 ⟨K 20⟩

Hillman, J. A., 1981^{V}: *Aspherical four-manifolds and the centres of two-knot groups.* Comment. Math. Helv., **56** (1981), 465–473. Corrigend. ibid., **58** (1983), 166 ⟨K 61⟩

Hillman, J. A., 1982: *Alexander polynomials, annihilator ideals, and the Steinitz-Fox-Smythe invariant.* Proc. London Math. Soc., (3) **45** (1982), 31–48 ⟨K 25, K 26⟩

Hillman, J. A., 1983: *On the Alexander polynomial of a cyclically periodic knot.* Proc. Amer. Math. Soc., **89** (1983), 155–156 ⟨K 22, K 26⟩

Hillman, J. A., 1984: *Links with infinitely many semifree periods are trivial.* Archiv Math., **42** (1984), 568–572 ⟨K 22⟩

Hillman, J. A., 1984′: *Factorization of Kojima knots and hyperbolic concordance of Levine pairings.* Houston Math. J., **10** (1984), 187–194 ⟨K 17, K 60⟩

Hilton, P. J.; S. Wylie, (1960): *Homology theory. An introduction to algebraic topology.* Cambridge: Cambridge Univ. Press ⟨A⟩

Hirsch, U.; W. D. Neumann, 1975: *On cyclic branched coverings of spheres.* Math. Ann., **215** (1975), 289–291 ⟨K 20⟩

Hirschhorn, P. S., 1979: *On the "stable" homotopy type of knot complements.* Illinois J. Math., **23** (1979), 101–134 ⟨K 59⟩

Hirschhorn, P. S., 1980: *Link complements and coherent group rings.* Illinois J. Math., **24** (1980), 159–163 ⟨K 60⟩

Hirschhorn, P.; J. G. Ratcliffe, 1980: *A simple proof of the algebraic unknotting of spheres in codimension two.* Amer. J. Math., **102** (1980), 489–491 ⟨K 60⟩

Hirzebruch, F.; K. H. Mayer, (1968): *O(n)-Mannigfaltigkeiten, exotische Sphären und Singularitäten.* Lect. Notes in Math. **57** (1968), Berlin-Heidelberg-New York: Springer Verlag ⟨K 34, K 59, K 60⟩

Hitt, L. R., 1977: *Examples of higher dimensional slice knots which are not ribbon knots.* Proc. Amer. Math. Soc., **77** (1977), 291–297 ⟨K 60⟩

Hitt, L. R.; D. W. Summers, 1982: *There exist arbitrary many different disks with the same exterior.* Proc. Amer. Math. Soc., **86** (1982), 148–150

Hodgson, C. D., 1981: *Involutions and isotopies.* Master-thesis, Univ. Melbourne ⟨M⟩

Holmes, R.; N. Smythe, 1966: *Algebraic invariants of isotopy of links.* Amer. J. Math., **88** (1966), 646–654 ⟨K 25, K 59⟩

Homma, T., 1954: *On the existence of unknotted polygons on 2-manifolds in E^3.* Osaka Math. J., **6** (1954), 129–134 ⟨K 59⟩

Homma, T.; M. Ochiai, 1978: *On relations of Heegaard diagrams and knots.* Math. Sem. Notes Kobe Univ, **6** (1978), 383–393 ⟨K 29, K 35⟩

Hosokawa, F., 1958: *On ∇-polynomials of links.* Osaka Math. J., **10** (1958), 273–282 ⟨K 26, K 50⟩

Hosokawa, F., 1967: *A concept of cobordism between links.* Ann. of Math., **86** (1967), 362–373

Hosokawa, F.; A. Kawauchi, 1979: *Proposals for unknotted surfaces in four-spaces.* Osaka J. Math., **16** (1979), 233–248 ⟨K 60⟩

Hosokawa, F.; S. Kinoshita, 1960: *On the homology group of branched cyclic covering spaces of links.* Osaka Math. J., **12** (1960), 331–335 ⟨K 20⟩

Hosokawa, F.; T. Maeda, S. Suzuki, 1979: *Numerical invariants of surfaces in 4-space.* Math. Sem. Notes Kobe Univ., **7** (1979), 409–420 ⟨K 60⟩

Hotz, G., 1959: *Ein Satz über Mittellinien*. Archiv Math., **10** (1959), 314–320 ⟨K 12, K 14⟩

Hotz, G., 1960: *Arkadenfadendarstellung von Knoten und eine neue Darstellung der Knotengruppe*. Abh. Math. Sem. Univ. Hamburg, **24** (1960), 132–148 ⟨K 12, K 14⟩

Hu, S., (1959): *Homotopy theory*. London: Acad. Press Inc. ⟨A⟩

Husch, L. S., 1969: *On piecewise linear unknotting of a polyhedra*. Yokohama Math. J., **17** (1969), 87–92 ⟨G⟩

Ikegamyi, G.; D. Rolfsen, 1971: *A note for knots and flows on 3-manifolds*. Proc. Japan Acad., **47** (1971), 29–30 ⟨K 59⟩

Jaco, W. H.; P. B. Shalen, (1979): *Seifert fibered spaces in 3-manifolds*. Memoirs Amer. Math. Soc., **21** No. 220 (1979), viii + 192. Providence, Rh. I.: Amer. Math. Soc. ⟨M⟩

Jänich, K., 1966: *Differenzierbare Mannigfaltigkeiten mit Rand als Orbiträume differenzierbarer G-Mannigfaltigkeiten ohne Rand*. Topology, **5** (1966), 301–320 ⟨K 59, K 60⟩

Jänich, K., (1968): *Differenzierbare G-Mannigfaltigkeiten*. Lect. Notes in Math. **59** (1968). Berlin-Heidelberg-New York: Springer Verlag ⟨K 59, K 60⟩

Jiang, B. (= Chang, B.), 1981: *A simple proof that the concordance group of algebraic slice knots is infinitely generated*. Proc. Amer. Math. J., **83** (1981), 181–192 ⟨K 24, K 32, K 33⟩

Jiang, B. (= Chang, B.), 1984: *Fixed points and braids*. Invent. math., **75** (1984), 69–74 ⟨K 40, A, F⟩

Jiang, B. (= Chang, B.), 1985: *Fixed points and braids, II*. Math. Ann. (to appear) ⟨K 40, A, F⟩

Johannson, K., (1979): *Homotopy equivalence of 3-manifolds with boundaries*. Lecture Notes in Math. **761** (1979). Berlin-Heidelberg-New York: Springer Verlag ⟨M⟩

Johannson, K., 1985: *On the mapping class group of knot spaces*. (preprint) ⟨K 59, M⟩

Johnson, D., 1980: *Homomorphism of knot groups*. Proc. Amer. Math. Soc., **78** (1980), 135–138 ⟨K 16⟩

Jones, B. W., 1950: *The arithmetic theory of quadratic forms*. Carus Math. Monogr. Nr. **10** (1950). Math. Ass. Amer. John Wiley and Sons ⟨X⟩

Joyce, D., 1982: *A classifying invariant of knots, the knot quandle*. J. Pure Appl. Algebra, **23** (1982), 37–65 ⟨K 12, K 16⟩

Kähler, E., 1929: *Über die Verzweigung einer algebraischen Funktion zweier Veränderlichen in der Umgebung einer singulären Stelle*. Math. Z., **30** (1929), 188–204 ⟨K 34⟩

Kamishima, Y.; K. B. Lee; F. Raymond, 1983: *The Seifert construction and its application to infranilmanifolds*. Quart. J. Math. Oxford, (2) **34** (1983), 433–452 ⟨A⟩

van Kampen, E. R., 1933: *On the connection between the fundamental groups of some related spaces*. Amer. J. Math., **55** (1933), 261–267 ⟨A⟩

Kanenobu, T., 1979: *The augmentation subgroup of a pretzel link*. Math. Sem. Notes Kobe Univ., **7** (1979), 363–384 ⟨K 25, K 35, K 50⟩

Kanenobu, T., 1980: *2-knot groups with elements of finite order*. Math. Sem. Notes Kobe Univ., **8** (1980), 557–560 ⟨K 16, K 61⟩

Kanenobu, T., 1981: *Module d'Alexander des nœuds fibres et polynome des Hosokawa des lacements fibres*. Math. Sem. Notes Kobe Univ., **9** (1981), 75–84 ⟨K 18, K 25, K 50⟩

Kanenobu, T., 1981′: *A note on 2-fold branched covering spaces of S^3*. Math. Ann., **256** (1981), 449–452 ⟨K 17, K 20⟩

Kanenobu, T., 1983: *Groups of higher-dimensional satellite knots*. J. Pure Appl. Algebra, **28** (1983), 179–188 ⟨K 17, K 60⟩

Kanenobu, T., 1983′: *Fox's 2-spheres are twist spun knots*. Mem. Fac. Sci. Kyusha Univ., Ser. A., **37** (1983), 81–86 ⟨K 35, K 61⟩

Kanenobu, T., 1984: *Alexander polynomials of two-bridged links*. J. Austr. Math. Soc., **36** (1984), 59–68 ⟨K 26, K 35⟩

Kaplan, S. J., 1982: *Twisting to algebraically slice knots*. Pacific J. Math., **102** (1982), 55–59 ⟨K 32, K 33⟩

Kauffman, L., 1974: *Branched coverings, open books and knot periodicity*. Topology, **13** (1974), 143–160 ⟨K 20, K 21, K 22, K 60⟩

Kauffman, L. H., 1974′: *Products of knots*. Bull. Amer. Math. Soc., **80** (1974), 1104–1107 ⟨K 60⟩

Kauffman, L. H., 1974″: *An invariant of link concordance*. In: Top. Conf. Virginia Polytechn. Inst. and State Univ. 1973 (eds. R. F. Dickman, jr., P. Fletcher). Lect. Notes in Math., **375** (1974), 153–157. Berlin-Heidelberg-New York: Springer Verlag ⟨K 24⟩

Kauffman, L. H., 1974‴: *Link manifolds*. Michigan J. Math., **21** (1974), 33–44 ⟨K 59, K 60⟩

Kauffman, L. H., 1981: *The Conway polynomial*. Topology, **20** (1981), 101–108 ⟨K 12, K 26⟩

Kauffman, L. H., (1983): *Formal knot theory*. Math. Notes **30**. Princeton, N.J.: Princeton Univ. Press ⟨K 15, K 26, K 31⟩

Kauffman, L.H., 1983′: *Combinatorics and knot theory*. Amer. Math. Soc. Contemporary Math., **20** (1983), 181–200 ⟨K15, K26, K31⟩

Kauffman, L.H.; W.D. Neumann, 1977: *Products of knots, branched fibrations and sums of singularities*. Topology, **16** (1977), 369–393 ⟨K 34, K 60⟩

Kauffman, L.H.; L.R. Taylor, 1976: *Signature of links*. Trans. Amer. Math. Soc., **216** (1976), 351–365 ⟨K 27⟩

Kawauchi, A., 1977: *On quadratic forms of 3-manifolds*. Invent. math., **43** (1977), 177–198 ⟨K 27⟩

Kawauchi, A., 1978: *On the Alexander polynomials of cobordant links*. Osaka J. Math., **15** (1978), 151–159 ⟨K 24, K 26⟩

Kawauchi, A., 1979: *The invertibility problem on amphicheiral excellent knots*. Proc. Japan Acad. Sci., Ser. A Math. Sci., **55** (1979), 399–402 ⟨K 23, K 35⟩

Kawauchi, A., 1980: *On links not cobordant to split links*. Topology, **19** (1980), 321–334 ⟨K 24, K 50⟩

Kawauchi, A., 1982: *On the Rochlin invariants of Z_2-homology 3-spheres with cyclic actions*. Japan. J. Math., **8** (1982), 217–258 ⟨K 22⟩

Kawauchi, A., 1984: *On the Robertello invariants of proper links*. Osaka J. Math., 21 (1984), 81–90 ⟨K 25, K 50⟩

Kawauchi, A.; T. Kobayashi; M. Sakuma, 1984: *On 3-manifolds with no periodic maps*. (preprint) ⟨K 22⟩

Kawauchi, A.; S. Kojima, 1980: *Algebraic classification of linking pairings on 3-manifolds*. Math. Ann., **253** (1980), 29–42 ⟨K 59⟩

Kawauchi, A.; T. Matumuto, 1980: *An estimate of infinite cyclic coverings and knot theory*. Pacific J. Math., **90**, 99–103 ⟨K 20, K 60⟩

Kawauchi, A.; H. Murakami; K. Sugishita, 1983: *On the T-genus of knot cobordism*. Proc. Japan Acad. Sci., Ser. A Math. Sci, **59** (1983), 91–93 ⟨K 24⟩

Kearton, C., 1973: *Classification of simple knots by Blanchfield duality*. Bull. Amer. Math. Soc., **79** (1973), 962–955 ⟨K 60⟩

Kearton, C., 1973′: *Noninvertible knots of codimension 2*. Proc. Amer. Math. Soc., **40** (1973), 274–276 ⟨K 60⟩

Kearton, C., 1975: *Presentations of n-knots*. Trans. Amer. Math. Soc., **202** (1975), 123–140 ⟨K 60⟩

Kearton, C., 1975′: *Blanchfield duality and simple knots*. Trans. Amer. Math. Soc., 202 (1975), 141–160 ⟨K 60⟩

Kearton, C., 1975″: *Simple knots which are doubly-nullcobordant*. Proc. Amer. Math. Soc., 52 (1975), 471–472 ⟨K 24, K 60⟩

Kearton, C., 1975‴: *Cobordism of knots and Blanchfield duality*. J. London Math. Soc., (2) 10 (1975), 406–408 ⟨K 24, K 25⟩

Kearton, C., 1978: *Attempting to classify knot modules and their hermitean pairings*. In: Knot Theory (ed. J.-C. Hausmann). Lect. Notes in Math. **685** (1978), 227–242. Berlin-Heidelberg-New York: Springer Verlag ⟨K 25⟩

Kearton, C., 1979: *Signatures of knots and the free differential calculus*. Quart. J. Math. Oxford, (2) **30** (1979), 157–182 ⟨K 27⟩

Kearton, C., 1979′: Factorization is not unique for 3-knots. Indiana Univ. Math. J., **28** (1979), 451–452 ⟨K 17, K 60⟩

Kearton, C., 1979″: The Milnor signatures of compound knots. Proc. Amer. Math. Soc., 76 (1979), 157–160 ⟨K 17, K 27⟩

Kearton, C., 1981: *Hermitian signature and double-nullcobordism of knots*. J. London Math. Soc., (2) **23** (1981), 563–576 ⟨K 24, K 27, K 33⟩

Kearton, C., 1982: *A remarkable 3-knot*. Bull. London Math. Soc., 14 (1982), 387–398 ⟨K 60⟩

Kearton, C., 1983: *Spinning, factorization of knots, and cyclic group actions on spheres*. Archiv Math., 40 (1983), 361–363 ⟨K 17, K 60⟩

Kearton, C., 1983′: *Some non-fibred 3-knots*. Bull. London Math. Soc., **15** (1983), 365–367 ⟨K 60⟩

Kearton, C., 1983″: *An algebraic classification of certain simple even-dimensional knots*. Trans. Amer. Math. Soc., **276** (1983), 1–53 ⟨K 60⟩

Kearton, C., 1984: *Simple spun knots*. Topology, **23** (1984), 91–95 ⟨K 60⟩

Kearton, C.; S.M.J. Wilson, 1981: *Cyclic group actions on odd dimensional spheres*. Comment. Math. Helv., **56** (1981), 615–626 ⟨K 22, K 60⟩

Kerckhoff, S.P., 1980: *The Nielsen realization problem*. Bull. Amer. Math. Soc., (2) **2** (1980), 452–454 ⟨F⟩

Kerckhoff, S.P., 1983: *The Nielsen realization problem*. Ann. of Math., **117** (1983), 235–265 ⟨F⟩

Kervaire, M., 1965: *Les nœuds de dimensions supérieures*. Bull. Soc. Math. France, **93** (1965), 225–271 ⟨K 60⟩

Kervaire, M.A., 1971: *Knot cobordism in codimension 2*. In: Manifolds Amsterdam 1970. Lect. Notes in Math. **197** (1971), 83–105. Berlin-Heidelberg-New York: Springer Verlag ⟨K 24, K 60⟩

Kervaire, J.; J. Milnor, 1961: *On 2-spheres in 4-manifolds*. Proc. Nat. Acad. USA, **47** (1961), 1651–1657 ⟨K 61⟩

Kervaire, M.A.; C. Weber, 1978: *A survey of multidimensional knots*. In: Knot theory (ed.

J.-C. Haussmann). Proc., Plans-sur-Bex Switzerland 1977. Lect. Notes in Math. **685** (1978), 61–134. Berlin-Heidelberg-New York: Springer Verlag ⟨K 11, K 60⟩

Kidwell, M. E., 1978: *On the Alexander polynomials of certain three-component links.* Proc. Amer. Math. Soc., **71** (1978), 351–354 ⟨K 26, K 50⟩

Kidwell, M. E., 1978′: *Alexander polynomials of links of small order.* Illinois J. Math., **22** (1978), 459–475 ⟨K 26, K 50⟩

Kidwell, M. E., 1979: *On the Alexander polynomials of alternating two-component links.* Intern. J. Math. & Math. Sci., **2** (1979), 229–237 ⟨K 26, K 50⟩

Kidwell, M. E., 1982: *Relations between the Alexander polynomial and summit power of a closed braid.* Math. Sem. Notes Kobe, **10** (1982), 387–409 ⟨K 26, K 40⟩

Kinoshita, S., 1957: *On Wendt's theorem on knots.* Osaka Math. J., **9** (1957), 61–66 ⟨K 14, K 20⟩

Kinoshita, S., 1957′: *Notes on knots and periodic transformations.* Proc. Japan Acad., **33** (1957), 359–362 ⟨K 20, K 22⟩

Kinoshita, S., 1958: *On Wendt's theorem of knots. II.* Osaka Math. J., **10** (1958), 259–261 ⟨K 14, K 20, K 25⟩

Kinoshita, S., 1958′: *On knots and periodic transformations.* Osaka Math. J., **10** (1958), 43–52 ⟨K 20, K 22⟩

Kinoshita, S., 1958″: *Alexander polynomials as isotopy invariants. I.* Osaka Math. J., **10** (1958), 263–271 ⟨K 26, K 61⟩

Kinoshita, S., 1959: *Alexander polynomials as isotopy invariants. II.* Osaka Math. J., **11** (1959), 91–94 ⟨K 26, K 59⟩

Kinoshita, S., 1961: *On the Alexander polynomials of 2-spheres in a 4-sphere.* Ann. of Math., **74** (1961), 518–531 ⟨K 26, K 61⟩

Kinoshita, S., 1962: *A note on the genus of a knot.* Proc. Am. Math. Soc., **13** (1962), 451 ⟨K 15⟩

Kinoshita, S., 1962′: *On quasi translations in 3-space.* In: Top. 3-manifolds, Proc. 1961 Top. Inst. Univ. Georgia (ed. M. K. Fort, jr.), pp. 223–226. Englewood Cliffs, N. J.: Prentice Hall 1962 ⟨K 55⟩

Kinoshita, S., 1967: *On irregular branched coverings of a kind of knots.* Notices Amer. Math. Soc., **14** (1967), 924 ⟨K 20⟩

Kinoshita, S.-I., 1972: *On elementary ideals of polyhedra in the 3-sphere.* Pacific J. Math., **42** (1972), 89–98 ⟨K 25, K 60⟩

Kinoshita, S.-I., 1973: *On elementary idals of θ-curves in the 3-sphere and 2-links in the 4-sphere.* Pacific J. Math., **49** (1973), 127–134 ⟨K 25, K 61⟩

Kinoshita, S., 1980: *On the distribution of Alexander polynomials of alternating knots and links.* Proc. Amer. Math. Soc., **79** (1980), 644–648 ⟨K 26, K 31⟩

Kinoshita, S.-I., 1980′: *The homology of a branched cyclic cover.* (preprint) ⟨K 20⟩

Kinoshita, S.; H. Terasaka, 1957: *On unions of knots.* Osaka Math. J., **9** (1957), 131–153 ⟨K 17⟩

Kirby, R., 1978: *A calculus for framed links in S^3.* Invent. math., **45** (1978), 35–56 ⟨K 59⟩

Kirby, R., 1978′: *Problems in low dimensional topology.* In: Alg. Geom. Topology (Stanford 1976) II (ed. R. J. Milgram). Proc. Symp. Pure Math. **32**, 273–312. Providence, R. I.: Amer. Math. Soc. ⟨K 11, M⟩

Kirby, R. C.; W. B. R. Lickorish, 1979: *Prime knots and concordance.* Math. Proc. Cambridge Phil. Soc., **86** (1979), 437–441 ⟨K 17, K 24⟩

Kirby, R.; P. Melwin, 1978: *Slice knots and property R.* Invent. math., **45** (1978), 57–59 ⟨K 19, K 33⟩

Klassen, G. I., 1970: К вопросу об эквивалентности узлов и зацеплений *(On the question of the equivalence of knots and links)*. Tul. Gos. Ped. Inst. Ucep. Zap. Math. Kaf. Vys. Geometri i Algebra (1970), 161–167 ⟨K 40⟩

Kneser, M.; D. Puppe, 1953: *Quadratische Formen und Verschlingungsinvarianten von Knoten.* Math. Z., **58** (1953), 376–384 ⟨K 27⟩

Knigge, E.: *Über periodische Verkettungen.* Dissertation, Frankfurt 1981 ⟨K 22, K 50⟩

Kobel'skij, V. L., 1982: Изотопическая классификация нечетномерных простых зацеплений коразмерности два. Известия Акад. Наук СССР, сер. мат., **46** (1982), 983–993, Engl. transl.: *Isotopic classification of odd-dimensional simple links of codimension two.* Math. USSR-Izvestia **21** (1983), 281–290 ⟨K 60⟩

Kojima, S.; M. Yamasaki, 1979: *Some new invariants of links.* Invent. math., **54** (1979), 213–228 ⟨K 24, K 50⟩

Kondu, H., 1979: *Knots of unknotting number 1 and their Alexander polynomials.* Osaka J. Math., **16** (1979), 551–559 ⟨K 26, K 35⟩

Krishnamurthz, E. V.; S. K. Sen, 1973: *Algorithm line-notation for the representation of knots.* Proc. Indian Acad. Sci., A **77** (1973), 51–61 ⟨K 14, K 29⟩

Krötenheerdt, O., 1964: *Über einen speziellen Typ alternierender Knoten.* Math. Ann., **153** (1964), 270–284 ⟨K 31⟩

Krötenheerdt, O.; S. Veit, 1976: *Zur Theorie massiver Knoten.* Beitr. Algebra und Geometrie, **5** (1976), 61–74 ⟨K 31, K 35⟩

Kuiper, N. H.; W. Meeks III, 1984: *Total curva-*

ture for knotted surfaces. IHES (preprint) ⟨K 38, K 60⟩

Kuono, M., 1983: *The irreducibility of 2-fold branched covering spaces of 3-manifolds*. Math. Sem. Notes Kobe Univ., **11** (1983), 205–220 ⟨K 20, M⟩

Kyle, R.H., 1954: *Branched covering spaces and the quadratic forms of links*. Ann. of Math., **59** (1954), 539–548 ⟨K 20, K 27⟩

Kyle, R.H., 1955: *Embeddings of Möbius bands in 3-dimensional space*. Proc. Royal Irish Acad., **A-57** (1955), 131–136 ⟨K 12, K 15⟩

Kyle, R.H., 1959: *Branched covering spaces and the quadratic forms of links. II*. Ann. of Math., **69** (1959), 686–699 ⟨K 20, K 27⟩

Ladegaillerie, Y., 1976: *Groupes de tresses et problème des mots dans les groupes de tresses*. Bull. Sci. Math., **100** (1976), 255–267 ⟨K 29, K 40⟩

Lambert, H.W., 1969: *Mapping cubes with holes onto cubes with handles*. Illinois. J. Math., **13** (1959), 606–615 ⟨K 17, M⟩

Lambert, H.W., 1970: *A 1-linked link whose longitudes lie in the second commutator subgroup*. Trans. Amer. Math. Soc., 147 (1970), 261–269 ⟨K 16, K 50⟩

Lambert, H., 1977: *Links which are unknottable by maps*. Pacific J. Math., **65** (1977), 109–112 ⟨K 59⟩

Lambert, H., 1977′: *Longitude surgery of genus 1 knots*. Proc. Amer. Math. Soc., **63** (1977), 359-362 ⟨K 21, K 35⟩

Langevin, R.; H. Rosenberg, 1976: *On curvature integrals and knots*. Topology, **15** (1976), 405–416 ⟨K 38⟩

Lashof, R.K.; J.L. Shaneson, 1969: *Classification of knots in codimension two*. Bull. Amer. Math. Soc., **75** (1969), 171–175 ⟨K 60⟩

Laudenbach, F., 1979: *Une remarque sur certains nœuds de* $S^1 \times S^2$. Compositio Math., **38** (1979), 77–82 ⟨K 15, K 59⟩

Laufer, H.B., 1971: *Some numerical link invariants*. Topology, **10** (1971), 119–131 ⟨K 25⟩

Lê Dũng Trans, 1972: *Sur les nœuds algébriques*. Compositio Math., **25** (1972), 281–321 ⟨K 32⟩

Lee, K.B.; F. Raymond, 1984: *Geometric realization of group extensions by the Seifert construction*. Adv. Math. (to appear) ⟨M⟩

Levine, J., 1965: *A characterization of knot polynomials*. Topology, **4** (1965), 135–141 ⟨K 26, K 60⟩

Levine, J., 1965′: *A classification of differentiable knots*. Ann. of Math., **82** (1965), 15–51 ⟨K 60⟩

Levine, J., 1965″: *Unknotting spheres in codimension two*. Topology, **4** (1965), 9–16 ⟨K 60⟩

Levine, J., 1966: *Polynomial invariants of knots of codimension two*. Ann. of. Math., **84** (1966), 537–554 ⟨K 26, K 60⟩

Levine, J., 1967: *A method for generating link polynomials*. Amer. J. Math., **89** (1967), 69–84 ⟨K 26, K 50, K 60⟩

Levine, J., 1969: *Knot cobordism groups in codimension two*. Comment. Math. Helv., **44** (1969), 229–244 ⟨K 24, K 60⟩

Levine, J., 1970: *An algebraic classification of some knots of codimension two*. Comment. Math. Helv., **45** (1970), 185–198 ⟨K 60⟩

Levine, J., 1971: *The role of the Seifert matrix in knot theory*. Acta Congr. Intern. Math. 1970, **2** (1971), 95–98. Paris: Gauthier-Villars ⟨K 25, K 60⟩

Levine, J., 1975: *Knot modules*. In: Ann. Math. Studies **84** (1975), 25–34 (ed. L.P. Neuwirth). Princeton, N.J.: Princeton Univ. Press ⟨K 11, K 25⟩

Levine, J., 1977: *Knot modules. I*. Trans. Amer. Math. Soc., **229** (1977), 1–50 ⟨K 25, K 60⟩

Levine, J., 1978: *Some results on higher dimensional knot groups*. In: Knot Theory (ed. J.-C. Haussmann). Proc., Plans-sur-Bex, Switzerland 1977. Lect. Notes in Math. **685** (1978), 243–269. Berlin-Heidelberg-New York: Springer Verlag ⟨K 60⟩

Levine, J.P., (1980): *Algebraic structure of knot modules*. Lect. Notes in Math. **772** (1980), Berlin-Heidelberg-New York: Springer Verlag ⟨K 11, K 25⟩

Levine, J., 1982: *The module of a 2-component link*. Comment. Math. Helv., **57** (1982), 377–399 ⟨K 25, K 50⟩

Levine, J., 1983: *Doubly slice knots and doubled disk knots*. Michigan J. Math., **30** (1983), 249–256 ⟨K 33, K 35⟩

Levine, J.P., 1983′: *Localization of link modules*. Amer. Math. Soc. Contemporary Math., **20** (1983), 213–229 ⟨K 25,K 50⟩

Levinson, H., 1973: *Decomposable braids and linkages*. Trans. Amer. Math. Soc., **178** (1973), 111–126 ⟨K 40, K 50⟩

Levinson, H., 1975: *Decomposable braids as subgroups of braid groups*. Trans. Amer. Math. Soc., **202** (1975), 51–55 ⟨K 40⟩

Liang, C.-C., 1975: *Semifree involutions on sphere knots*. Michigan Math. J., **22** (1975), 161–163 ⟨K 60⟩

Liang, C.-C., 1976: *Browder-Livesay index invariant and equivariant knots*. Michigan Math. J., **23** (1976), 321–323 ⟨K 60⟩

Liang, C.-C., 1977: *Involutions fixing codimension two knots*. Pacific J. Math., **73** (1977), 125–129 ⟨K 60⟩

Liang, C.-C., 1977′: *An algebraic classification of*

some links of codimension two. Proc. Amer. Math. Soc., **67** (1977), 147–151 ⟨K 60⟩

Liang, C.-C., 1978: *Knots fixed by $\mathbb{Z}_p$-actions, and periodic links*. Math. Ann., **233** (1978), 49–54 ⟨K 22, K 60⟩

Libgober, A., 1980: *Levine's formula in knot theory and quadratic reciprocity law*. L'Enseign. Math., **26** (1980), 323–331 ⟨K 60⟩

Libgober, A., 1980′: *Alexander polynomials of plane algebraic curves and cyclic multiple planes*. (preprint) ⟨K 26, K 32⟩

Libgober, A., 1983: *Alexander modules of plane algebraic curves*. Amer. Math. Soc. Contemporary Math., **20** (1983), 231–247 ⟨K 25, K 32, K 60⟩

Lickorish, W.B.R., 1962: *A representation of orientable conbinatorial 3-manifolds*. Ann. of Math., **76** (1962), 531–540 ⟨K 21, M⟩

Lickorish, W.B.R., 1964: *A finite set of generators for the homeotpy group of a 2-manifold*. Proc. Cambridge Phil. Soc., **60** (1964), 769–778 ⟨F⟩

Lickorish, W.B.R., 1966: *A finite set of generators for the homeotopy group of a 2-manifold (corrigendum)*. Proc. Cambridge Phil. Soc., **62** (1966), 679–681 ⟨F⟩

Lickorish, W.B.R., 1977: *Surgery on knots*. Proc. Amer. Math. Soc., **60** (1977)., 296–298 ⟨K 21⟩

Lickorish, R.W.B., 1979: *Shake-slice knots*. In: Topology Low-Dim. Manifolds, Second Sussex Conf. 1977, Proc., Lect. Notes in Math. **722** (1979), 67–70, Berlin-Heidelberg-New York: Springer Verlag ⟨K 33⟩

Lickorish, W.B.R., 1981: *Prime knots and tangles*. Trans. Amer. Math. Soc., **267** (1981), 321–332 ⟨K 12, K 17⟩

Lin, V.Ya., 1972: О представлениях группы кос перестановками (*Representations of the braid group by permutations*). Uspehi Math. Nauk, **27:3** (1972), 192 ⟨K 40⟩

Lin, V.Ya., 1974: Представления кос перестановками (*Representations of braids by permutations*). Uspehi Math. Nauk, **29:1** (1974), 173–174 ⟨K 40⟩

Lin, V.Ya., 1979: Косы Артина и связдннные с ними группы и пространства. Итоги. А-Т-Г, **17** (1983), 159–227, Engl. transl.: *Artin braids and the groups and spaces connected with them*. J. Soviet. Math., **18** (1982), 736–788 ⟨K 11, K 40⟩

Lines, D., 1979: *Cobordisme de nœuds classiques fibrés et leur monodromies*. Monogr. L'Enseign. Math., **31** (1983), 147–173 ⟨K 24⟩

Lines, D.; C. Weber, 1983: *Nœuds rationnels fibres algébraiquement cobordants à zero*. Topology, **22** (1983), 267–283 ⟨K 24, K 35⟩

Lipschutz, S., 1961: *On a finite matrix representation of the braid group*. Archiv Math., **12** (1961), 7–12 ⟨K 40, G⟩

Lipschutz, S., 1963: *Note on a paper by Shepperd on the braid group*. Proc. Amer. Math. Soc., **14** (1963), 225–227 ⟨K 40, G⟩

Listing, J.B., 1847: *Vorstudien zur Topologie*. Göttinger Studien 1847 ⟨K 12⟩

Litherland, R.A., 1979: *Deforming twist-spun knots*. Trans. Amer. math. Soc., **250** (1979), 311–331 ⟨K 17⟩

Litherland, R.A., 1979′: *Surgery on knots in solid tori*. Proc. London math. Soc., (3) **39** (1979), 130–146 ⟨K 19, K 21⟩

Litherland, R.A., 1979″: *Slicing doubles of knots in homology 3-spheres*. Invent. Math., **54** (1979), 69–74 ⟨K 17, K 21⟩

Litherland, R.A., 1979‴: *Signatures of iterated torus knots*. In: Topology Low-Dim. Manifolds Second Sussex Conf. 1977 (ed. R. Fenn). Lect. Notes in Math. **722** (1979), 71–84. Berlin-Heidelberg-New York: Springer ⟨K 27, 35⟩

Litherland, R.A., 1980: *Surgery on knots in solid tori. II*. J. London Math. Soc., **22** (1980), 559–569 ⟨K 19, K 21⟩

Litherland, R.A., 1981: *The second cohomology of the group of a knotted surface*. Quart. J. Math. Oxford, (2) **32** (1981), 425–434 ⟨K 60⟩

Little, C.N., 1885: *On knots, with a census for order ten*. Trans. Conn. Acad. Sci., **18** (1885), 374–378 ⟨K 12⟩

Little, C.N., 1889: *Non-alternate ± knots, of orders eight or nine*. Trans. Royal Soc. Edinburgh, **35** (1889), 663–664 ⟨K 12⟩

Little, C.N., 1890: *Alternate ± knots of order 11*. Trans. Roy. Soc. Edingburgh, **36** (1890), 253–255 ⟨K 121⟩

Little, C.N., 1900: *Non-alternate ± knots*. Trans. Roy. Soc. Edinburgh, **39** (1900), 771–778 ⟨K 12⟩

Little, J.A., 1978: *Spaces with positive torsion*. Ann. di Mat. Pura Appl., (4) **116** (1978, 57–86 ⟨K 38⟩

Livingston, C., 1981: *Homology cobordisms of 3-manifolds, knot cocordance, and prime knots*. Pacific J. Math., **94** (1981), 193–206 ⟨K 17, K 24⟩

Livingston, C., 1982: *Surfaces bounding the unlink*. Michigan Math. J., **29** (1982), 289–298 ⟨K 15⟩

Livingston, C., 1982′: *More 3-manifolds with multiple knot-surgery and branched-cover descriptions*. Math. Proc. Cambridge Phil. Soc., **91** (1982), 473–475 ⟨K 20, K 21⟩

Livingston, C., 1983: *Knots which are not concordant to their inverses*. Quart. J. Math. Oxford, (2) **34** (1983), 323–328 ⟨K 23, K 24⟩

Livingston, C.; P. Melvin, 1983: *Algebraic knots are algebraically dependent*. Proc. Amer. Math. Soc., **87** (1983), 179–180 ⟨K 32⟩

Lomonaco, S.J., 1967: *An algebraic theory of local knottedness. I*. Trans. Amer. Math. Soc., **129** (1967), 322–343 ⟨K 12, M⟩

Lomonaco, S.J., jr., 1969: *The second homology group of a spun knot*. Topology, **8** (1969), 95–98 ⟨K 35, K 61⟩

Lomonaco, S.J., jr., 1975: *The third homotopy group of some higher dimensional knots*. Ann. Math. Studies **84** (1975), 35–45 (ed. L.P. Neuwirth). Princeton, N.J.: Princeton Univ. Press ⟨K 60⟩

Lomonaco, S.J., 1981: *The homotopy groups of knots. I. How to compute the algebraic 2-type*. Pacific J. Math., **95** (1981), 349–390 ⟨K 16, K 60⟩

Lomonaco, S.J., 1983: *Five dimensional knot theory*. Amer. Math. Soc. Contemporary Math., **20** (1983), 249–270 ⟨K 60⟩

Long, D.D., 1984: *Strongly plus-amphicheiral knots are algebraically slice*. Math. Proc. Cambridge Phil. Soc., **95** (1984), 309–312 ⟨K 22, K 33⟩

Lozano, M.T., 1983: *Arcbodies*. Math. Proc. Cambridge Phil. Soc., **94** (1983), 253–260 ⟨K 20⟩

Lüdicke, U., 1978: *Darstellungen der Verkettungsgruppe und zyklische Knoten*. Dissertation. Frankfurt/Main ⟨K 22, K 28⟩

Lüdicke, U., 1979: *Zyklische Knoten*. Archiv. Math., **32** (1979), 588–599 ⟨K 22⟩

Lüdicke, U., 1980: *Darstellungen von Verkettungsgruppen*. Abh. Math. Sem. Univ. Hamburg, **50** (1980), 232–237 ⟨K 28⟩

Lüdicke, U., 1984: *9_{25} has no period 3*. C.R. Math. Rep. Acad. Sci. Canada **VI** No. 3, (1984) 157 ⟨K 22⟩

Lyndon, R.C.; P.E. Schupp, (1977): *Combinatorial group theory*. Ergebn. Math. Grenzgeb. **89**. Berlin-Heidelberg-N.Y: Springer ⟨G⟩

Lyon, H.C., 1971: *Incompressible surfaces in knot spaces*. Trans. Amer. Math. Soc., **157** (1971), 53–62 ⟨K 15⟩

Lyon, H.C., 1972: *Knots without unknotted incompressible spanning surfaces*. Proc. Amer. Math. Soc., **35** (1972), 617–620 ⟨K 15⟩

Lyon, H.C., 1974: *Simple knots with unique spanning surfaces*. Topology, **13** (1974), 275–279 ⟨K 15⟩

Lyon, H.C., 1974′: *Simple knots without minimal surfaces*. Proc. Amer. Math. Soc., **43** (1974), 449–454 ⟨K 15⟩

Lyon, H.C., 1980: *Torus knots in the complement of links and surfaces*. Michigan Math. J., **27** (1980), 39–46

Maclachlan, C., 1978: *On representations of Artin's braid group*. Michigan Math. J., **25** (1978), 235–244 ⟨K 40⟩

MacLane, S., (1963): *Homology*. Berlin-Göttingen-Heidelberg: Springer Verlag ⟨A⟩

Maeda, T., 1977: *On the groups with Wirtinger presentations*. Math. Sem. Notes Kobe, **5** (1977), 347–358 ⟨K 16, G⟩

Maeda, T., 1977′: *On a composition of knot groups. II. Algebraic bridge index*. Math. Sem. Notes Kobe Univ., **5** (1977), 457–464 ⟨K 16, K 60⟩

Maeda, T., 1978: *A unique decomposition for knot-like groups*. Math. Sem. Notes Kobe Univ., **6** (1978), 567–602 ⟨K 16, K 60⟩

Maeda, T., 1979: *Numerical invariants of surfaces in 4-space*. Math. Sem. Notes Kobe, **7** (1979), 409–420 ⟨K 61⟩

Maeda, T.; K. Murasugi, 1983: *Covering linkage invariants and Fox's problem 13*. Amer. Math. Soc. Contemporary Math., **20** (1983), 271–283 ⟨K 20⟩

Magnus, W., 1931: *Untersuchungen über einige unendliche diskontinuierliche Gruppen*. Math. Ann., **105** (1931), 52–74 ⟨G⟩

Magnus, W., 1934: *Über Automorphismen von Fundamentalgruppen berandeter Flächen*. Math. Ann., **109** (1934), 617–646 ⟨F⟩

Magnus, W., 1972: *Braids and Riemann surfaces*. Commun. Pure Appl. Math., **25** (1972), 151–161 ⟨K 40, F⟩

Magnus, W., 1973: *Braid groups: a survey*. Proc. 2nd Int. Conf. of Groups (ed. M.F. Newman). Canberra 1973. Lect. Notes in Math. **372** (1974), 463–487. Berlin-Heidelberg-New York: Springer Verlag ⟨K 11, K 40⟩

Magnus, W.; A. Karrass; D. Solitar, (1966): *Combinatorial group theory: presentations of groups in terms of generators and relations*. N.Y: Interscience Publ. Wiley & Sons ⟨G⟩

Magnus, W.; A. Peluso, 1967: *On knot groups*. Commun. Pure Appl. Math., **20** (1967), 749–770 ⟨K 16⟩

Magnus, W.; A. Peluso, 1969: *On a theorem of V.I. Arnol'd*. Commun. Pure Appl. Math., **22** (1969), 683–692 ⟨K 40, F⟩

Makanin, G.S., 1968: Проблема сопряженности в группе кос. Докпады Акад. Наук СССР, **182** (1968), 495–496, Engl. transl.: *The conjugacy problem in the braid groups*. Soviet Math. Doklady, **9** (1968), 1156–1157 ⟨K 40⟩

Makanin, G.S., 1971: О нормализаторах группы кос. Мат. сб., **86** (1971), 171–179, Engl. transl.: *On normalizers in the braid groups*. Math. USSR-Sbornik, **15** (1971), 167–175 ⟨K 40⟩

Markoff, A.A., 1936: Über die freie Äquivalenz der geschlossenen Zöpfe. Recueil Math. Moskau, **1** (43) (1936), 73–78 ⟨K 40⟩

Markov, A.A., (1945): Основы алгебраической теории кос (*Foundations of the algebraic theory of braids*). Trudy Math. Inst. Steklov **16** (1945), 1–54 ⟨K 40⟩

Martin, R.J., 1974: *Determining knot types from diagrams of knots*. Pacific J. Math., **51** (1974), 241–249 ⟨K 12⟩

Marumuto, Y., 1977: *Relations between some conjectures in knot theory*. Math. Sem. Notes Kobe Univ., **5** (1977), 377–388 ⟨K 19⟩

Marumoto, Y., 1984: *A class of higher dimensional knots*. J. Fac. Educ. Saga Univ., **31** (1984), 177–185 ⟨K 60⟩

Massey, W.S., (1967): *Algebraic Topology: An Introduction*. Harbrace College Mathematics Series. New York-Chicago-San Francisco-Los Angeles: Harcourt, Brace & World, Inc. ⟨A⟩

Massey, W.S., (1980): *Singular Homology Theory*. Berlin-Heidelberg-New York: Springer Verlag ⟨A⟩

Massey, W.S., 1980′: *Completion of link modules*. Duke Math. J., **47** (1980), 399–420 ⟨K 25⟩

Massey, W.S.; L. Traldi, 1981: *Links with free groups are trivial*. Proc. Amer. Math. Soc., **82** (1981), 155–156 ⟨K 16, K 50⟩

Mathieu, Y.; B. Vincent, 1975: *Apropos des groupes de nœuds qui sont des produits libres amalgamés non triviaux*. C.R. Acad. Sci. Paris, **280-A** (1975), 1045–1047 ⟨K 16⟩

Matveev, S.V., 1981: Построение точного апгебраического цнварцхнта узла (*Construction of a complete algebraic knot invariant*). Celabrinsk Univ. 1981, 14 p. ⟨K 12, K 29⟩

Matveev, S.V., 1982: Дистрибутивные группоиды в теории узлов. Мат. сб., **119** (1982), 78–88, Engl. transl.: *Distributive gruppoids in knot theory*. Math. USSR-Sbornik, **47** (1984), 73–83 ⟨K 12⟩

Mayberry, J.P.; K. Murasugi, 1982: *Torsion-groups of abelian coverings of links*. Trans. Amer. Math. Soc., **271** (1982), 143–173 ⟨K 20, K 50⟩

Mayland, E.J., 1972: *On residually finite knot groups*. Trans. Amer. Math. Soc., **168** (1972), 221–232 ⟨K 16⟩

Mayland, E.J., jr., 1974: *Two-bridge knots have residually finite groups*. Proc. Second Intern. Conf. Theory of Groups (ed. M.F. Newman) Canberra 1973. Lect. Notes in Math. **372** (1974), 488–493, Berlin-Heidelberg-New York: Springer Verlag ⟨K 16, K 30⟩

Mayland, E.J., 1975: *The residual finiteness of the groups of classical knots*. Proc. Geometric Topology Conf., Park City, Utah (eds. L.C. Glaser, R.B. Rushin). Lecture Notes in Math. **438** (1975), 339–342. Berlin-Heidelberg-New York: Springer Verlag ⟨K 16⟩

Mayland, E.J., jr., 1975′: *The residual finiteness of the classical knot groups*. Candian J. Math., **17** (1975), 1092–1099 ⟨K 16⟩

Mayland, E.J., jr., 1977: *A class of two-bridge knots with property-P*. Proc. Amer. Math. Soc., **64** (1977), 365–369 ⟨K 19, K 30⟩

Mayland, E.J.; K. Murasugi, 1976: *On a structural property of the groups of alternating links*. Canad. J. Math., **28** (1976), 568–588 ⟨K 16, K 31⟩

McCallum, W.A., 1976: *The higher homotopy groups of the p-spun trefoil knot*. Glasgow Math. J., **17** (1976), 44–46 ⟨K 60⟩

McCool, J., 1975: *Some finitely presented subgroups of the automorphism group of a free group*. J. Algebra, **35** (1975), 205–213 ⟨F⟩

McPherson, J.M., 1969: *On the nullity and enclosure genus of wild knots*. Trans. Amer. Math. Soc., **144** (1969), 545–555 ⟨K 25, K 55⟩

McPherson, J.M., 1970: *Wild knots and arcs in a 3-manifold*. In: Top. of Manifolds, Proc. Inst. Univ. Georgia, Athens, Ga 1969, 176–178 (eds. J.C. Cantrell, C.H. Edwards, jr.). Chicago: Markham Publ. Comp. ⟨K 55⟩

McPherson, J.M., 1971: *A family of non-invertible prime links*. Bull. Austr. Math. Soc., **4** (1971), 105–108 ⟨K 23, K 55⟩

McPherson, J.M., 1971′: *A family of non-invertible prime links. Corrigendum*. Bull. Austr. Math. Soc., **5** (1971), 141–143 ⟨K 23, K 50⟩

McPherson, J.M., 1971″: *A sufficient condition for an arc to be nearly polyhedral*. Proc. Amer. Math. Soc., **28** (1971), 229–*33* ⟨K 55⟩

McPherson, J.M., 1973: *The nullity of a wild knot in a compact 3-manifold*. J. Austr. Math. Soc., **16** (1973), 262–271 ⟨K 25, K 55⟩

McPherson, J.M., 1973′: *Wild arcs in three-space. II. An invariant of non-oriented local type*. Pacific J. Math., **44** (1973), 619–635 ⟨K 55⟩

McPherson, J.M., 1973″: *Wild arcs in three-space. I. Families of Fox-Artin arcs*. Pacific J. Math., **45** (1973), 585–598 ⟨K 55⟩

Meeks, W.H. III.; S.T. Yau, 1980: *Topology of three dimensional manifolds and the embedding problem in minimal surface theory*. Ann. of Math., **112** (1980), 441–484 ⟨M⟩

Mehta, M.L., 1980: *On a relation between torsion numbers and Alexander matrix of a knot*. Bull. Soc. math. France, **108** (1980), 81–94 ⟨K 25⟩

Menasco, W.W., 1983: *Polyhedra representation*

of link complements. Amer. Math. Soc. Contemporary Math., **20** (1983) 305–325 ⟨K 50, B⟩

Menasco, W., 1984: *Closed incompressible surfaces in alternating knot and link complements*. Topology, **23** (1984), 37–44 ⟨K 19, K 31, M⟩

Menasco, W. W., 1984′: *Determining incompressibility of surfaces in alternating knot and link complements*. (preprint) ⟨K 15, K 29⟩

Michel, F., 1980: *Inversibilité des nœuds et idéaux ambigues*. C. R. Acad. Sci. Paris, **290-A** (1980), 909–912 ⟨K 60⟩

Michel, F., 1980′: *Nœuds algébraiquement cobordants à zero*. Prépublications Orsay ⟨K 60⟩

Michel, F., 1983: *Formes de Seifert et singularités isolées*. Monogr. L'Enseigm. Math., **31** (1983), 175–190 ⟨K 32, K 60⟩

Millett, K. C., 1980: *Smooth families of knots*. Houston J. Math., **6** (1980), 85–111 ⟨K 60⟩

Milnor, J. W., 1950: *On the total curvature of knots*. Ann. of Math., **52** (1950), 248–257 ⟨K 38⟩

Milnor, J., 1953: *On the total curvatures of closed space curves*. Math. Scand., **1** (1953), 289–296 ⟨K 38⟩

Milnor, J., 1954: *Link groups*. Ann. of Math., **59** (1954), 177–195 ⟨K 16, K 50⟩

Milnor, J., 1957: *Isotopy of links*. Lefschety symposium (eds. R.H. Fox, D.C. Spencer, W. Tucker). Princeton Math. Ser. **12** (1957), 280–306. Princeton, N.J.: Princeton Univ. Press ⟨K 12, K 55⟩

Milnor, J., 1962: *A unique decomposition theorem for 3-manifolds*. Amer. J. Math., **84** (1962), 1–7 ⟨K 17, M⟩

Milnor, J. W., 1962′: *A duality theorem for Reidemeister torsion*. Ann. of Math., **76** (1962), 137–147 ⟨K 38, M⟩

Milnor, J., 1964: *Most knots are wild*. Fund. Math., **54** (1964), 335–338 ⟨K 55⟩

Milnor, J. W., (1968): *Singular points of complex hypersurfaces*. Ann. of Math. Studies **61**. Princeton, N.J.: Princeton Univ. press ⟨K 34⟩

Milnor, J. W., 1968′: *Infinite cyclic covers*. In: Conf. Topology of Manifolds 1968 (ed. J.G. Hocking), pp. 115–133. Boston-London-Sydney: Prindle, Weber and Schmdit ⟨K 20⟩

Milnor, J. W., 1975: *On the 3-dimensional Brieskorn manifolds $M(p, q, r)$*. In: Knots, groups and 3-manifolds (ed. L.P. Neuwirth). Ann. Math. Studies **84** (1975), 175–225. Princeton, N.J.: Princeton Univ. Press ⟨K 20⟩

Milnor, J. W.; R. H. Fox, 1966: *Singularities of 2-spheres in 4-space and cobordism of knots*. Osaka J. Math., **3** (1966), 257–267 ⟨K 24, K 34⟩

Minkus, J., (1982): *The branched cyclic coverings of 2-bridge knots and links*. Memoirs Amer. Math. Soc. **35** Nr. 255 (1982), 69 p.. Providence, Rh. I.: Amer. Math. Soc. ⟨K 20, K 30⟩

Moise, E. E., 1952: *Affine structures in 3-manifolds. V. The triangulation theorem and Hauptvermutung*. Ann. of Math., **57** (1952), 547–560 ⟨M⟩

Moise, E. E., 1954: *Affine structures in 3-manifolds. VII. Invariance of the knot-types; local tame imbedding*. Ann. of Math., **59** (1954), 159–170 ⟨K 12, M⟩

Moise, E., 1962: *Periodic homeomorphisms of the 3-sphere*. Illinois J. Math., **6** (1962), 206–225 ⟨K 22⟩

Moise, E. E., (1977): *Geometric Topology in Dimensions 2 and 3*. Graduate Texts in Math. **47**. Berlin-Heidelberg-N.Y: Springer ⟨F, M⟩

Moishezon, B., 1981: *Stable branch curves and braid monodromics*. Algebraic Geometry, in: Proc. Midwest Alg. geom. Conf., Univ. Illinois Chicago Circle 1980 (eds. A. Libgober, P. Wagreich). Lect. Notes in Math. **862** (1981), 107–192. Berlin-Heidelberg-New York: Springer Verlag ⟨K 20, K 40⟩

Moishezon, B., 1983: *Algebraic surfaces and the arithmetic of braids. I.* In: Arithmetic and Geometry II (ed. M. Artin, J. Tate), Progress Math. **36** (1983), Boston-Basel-Stuttgart: Birkhäuser ⟨K 40⟩

Montesinos, J. M., 1973: *Una familia infinita de nudos representados no separables*. Revista Math. Hisp.-Amer., (IV) **33** (1973), 32–35 ⟨K 20, K 28⟩

Montesinos, J. M., 1973′: *Variedades de Seifert que son recubridores ciclicos ramificedos de dos hojas*. Bol. Soc. Mat. Mexicana, **18** (1973), 1–32 ⟨K 20, M⟩

Montesinos, J., 1974: *A representation of closed, orientable 3-manifolds as 3-fold branched coverings of S^3*. Bull. Amer. Math. Soc., **80** (1974), 845–846 ⟨K 20, M⟩

Montesinos, J., 1975: *Surgery on links and double branched covers of S^3*. In: Knots, groups and 3-manifolds (ed. L.P. Neuwirth), Ann. Math. Studies **84** (1975), 227–259. Princeton, N.J.: Princeton Univ. Press ⟨K 20, K 21⟩

Montesinos, J. M., 1976: *Minimal plat representations of prime knots and links are not unique*. Canad. J. Math., **28** (1976), 161–167 ⟨K 12, K 17⟩

Montesinos, J. M., 1976′: *Three-manifolds as 3-fold branched coverings of S^3*. Quart. J. Math. Oxford, (2) **27** (1976), 85–94 ⟨K 20⟩

Montesinos, J. M., 1979: *Revêtements ramifiés de nœuds, espaces fibrés de Seifert et scindements de Heegaard*. Prépublications Orsay ⟨K 20, K 35⟩

Montesinos, J.M., 1980: *A note on 3-fold branched coverlings of* S^3. Math. Proc. Cambridge Phil. Soc., **88** (1980), 321–325 ⟨K 20⟩

Montesinos, J.M., 1983: *Representing 3-manifolds by a universal branching set*. Math. Proc. Cambridge Phil. Soc. **94** (1983), 109–133 ⟨K 20⟩

Montesinos, J.M., 1984′: *On twins in the four-sphere. I*. Quart. J. Math. Oxford, (to appear) ⟨K 61⟩

Montesinos, J.M., 1984″: *On twins in the four-space. II*. (preprint) ⟨K 61⟩

Montesinos, J.M.; W. Whitten, 1984: *Constructions of two-fold branched covering spaces*. (preprint) ⟨K 20, K 23⟩

Montgomery, D.; H. Samelson, 1955: *A theorem on fixed points of involutions in* S^3. Canad. J. Math., **7** (1955), 208–220 ⟨K 22⟩

Moran, S., 1981: *The Alexander matrix of a knot*. Arch. Math., **36** (1981), 125–132 ⟨K 25⟩

Moran, S., (1983): *The mathematical theory of knots and braids. An introduction*. North-Holland Math. Studies 82. Amsterdam-New York: North-Holland Publ. Comp. ⟨K 11, K 12, K 40⟩

Morgan, J.W.; D.P. Sullivan, 1974: *The transversality characteristic class and linking cycles in surgery theory*. Ann. of Math., **99** (1974), 463–544 ⟨K 21⟩

Morgan, J.W.; H. Bass, (1984): *The Smith conjecture*. Acad. Press, Inc. ⟨K 11, K 20, K 22, M⟩

Morikawa, O., 1981: *A class of 3-bridge knots. I*. Math. Sem. Notes Kobe Univ., **9** (1981), 349–369 ⟨K 30, K 35⟩

Morikawa, O., 1982: *A class of 3-bridge knots. II*. Yokahama Math. J., **30** (1982), 53–72 ⟨K 30, K 35⟩

Morton, H.R., 1976: *A criterion for an embedded surface in* $\mathbb{R}^3$ *to be unknotted*. (preprint) ⟨K 18⟩

Morton, H.R., 1978: *Infinitely many fibered knots having the same Alexander polynomial*. Topology, **17** (1978), 101–104 ⟨K 18, K 26⟩

Morton, H.R., 1979: *Closed braids which are not prime knots*. Math. Proc. Cambridge Phil. Soc., **86** (1979), 422–426 ⟨K 17, K 40⟩

Morton, H.R., 1983: *An irreducible 4-string braid with unknotted closure*. Math. Proc. Cambridge Phil. Soc., **93** (1983), 259–261 ⟨K 35, K 40⟩

Morton, H.R., 1983′: *Fibred knots with a given Alexander polynomial*. In: Nœuds, tresses et singularités. Comp. Rend. Sem. Plans-sur-Bex (ed. C. Weber). Monogr. N. 31 de L'Enseign. Math. **31** (1983), 207–222 Genève: Univ. de Genève ⟨K 18, K 26⟩

Morton, H.R., 1984: *Alexander polynominals of closed 3-braids*. Math. Proc. Cambridge Phil. Soc., **96** (1984), 295–299 ⟨K 26, K 40⟩

Morton, H.R.; D.M.Q. Mond, 1982: *Closed curves with no quadrisecants*. Topology, **21** (1982), 235–243 ⟨K 12⟩

Moser, L., 1971: *Elementary surgery along a torus knot*. Pacific J. Math., **38** (1971), 737–745 ⟨K 21⟩

Moser, L.F., 1974: *On the impossibility of obtaining* $S^2 \times S^1$ *by elementary surgery along a knot*. Pacific J. Math., **53** (1974), 519–523 ⟨K 21⟩

Mostow, G.D., 1968: *Quasi-conformal mappings in n-space and the rigidity of hyperbolic space forms*. Publ. Inst. Hautes Etudes Sci., **34** (1968), 55–104 ⟨X⟩

Motter, W.L., 1976: *Homology of regular coverings of spun CW pairs with applications to knot theory*. Proc. Amer. Math. Soc., **58** (1976), 331–338 ⟨K 20, K 35⟩

Murasugi, K., 1958: *On the genus of the alternating knot. I*. J. Math. Soc. Japan, **10** (1958), 94–105 ⟨K 15, K 31⟩

Murasugi, K., 1958′: *On the genus of the alternating knot. II*. J. Math. Soc. Japan, **10** (1958), 235–248 ⟨K 15, K 31⟩

Murasugi, K., 1958″: *On the Alexander polynomials of the alternating knot*. Osaka Math. J., **10** (1958), 181–189 ⟨K 26, K 31⟩

Murasugi, K., 1960: *On alternating knots*. Osaka Math. J., **12** (1960), 277–303 ⟨K 31⟩

Murasugi, K., 1961: *Remarks on torus knots*. Proc. Japan Acad., **37** (1961), 222 ⟨K 16, K 35⟩

Murasugi, K., 1961′: *Remarks on knots with two bridges*. Proc. Japan Acad., **37** (1961), 294–297 ⟨K 30⟩

Murasugi, K., 1961″: *On the definition of the knot matrix*. Proc. Japan Acad., **37** (1961), 220–221 ⟨K 12, K 26⟩

Murasugi, K., 1962: *Non-amphicheirality of the special alternating links*. Proc. Amer. Math. Soc., **13** (1962), 771–776 ⟨K 23, K 31, K 50⟩

Murasugi, K., 1963: *On a certain subgroup of the group of an alternating link*. Amer. J. Math., **85** (1963), 544–550 ⟨K 16, K 25, K 31, K 50⟩

Murasugi, K., 1964: *The center of a group with one defining relation*. Math. Ann., **155** (1964), 246–251 ⟨G⟩

Murasugi, K., 1965: *On a certain numerical invariant of link types*. Trans. Amer. Math. Soc., **117** (1965), 387–422 ⟨K 27⟩

Murasugi, K., 1965′: *On the center of the group of a link*. Proc. Amer. Math. Soc., **16** (1965), 1052–1057 (Erreta: Proc. Amer. Math. Soc. **18** (1967), 1142) ⟨K 16⟩

Murasugi, K., 1965'': *Remarks on rosette knots.* Math. Ann., **158** (1965), 290–292 ⟨K 27, 31⟩

Murasugi, K., 1965''': *On the Minkowski unit of slice links.* Trans. Amer. Math. Soc., **114** (1965), 377–383 ⟨K 27, K 33⟩

Murasugi, K., 1966: *On Milnor's invariants for links.* Trans. Amer. Math. Soc., **124** (1966), 94–110 ⟨K 26, K 50⟩

Murasugi, K., 1969: *The Arf invariant for knot types.* Proc. Amer. Math. Soc., **21** (1969), 69–72 ⟨K 25⟩

Murasugi, K., 1970: *On Milnor's invariant for links. II. The Chen group.* Trans. Amer. Math. Soc., **148** (1970), 41–61 ⟨K 26, K 50⟩

Murasugi, K., 1970': *On the signature of links.* Topology, **9** (1970), 283–298 ⟨K 27, K 50⟩

Murasugi, K., 1971: *On periodic knots.* Comment. Math. Helv., **46** (1971), 162–174 ⟨K 18, K 22, K 26, K 30⟩

Murasugi, K., 1971': *The commutator subgroups of the alternating knot groups.* Proc. Amer. Math. Soc., **28** (1971), 237–241 ⟨K 16, K 31⟩

Murasugi, K., (1974): *On closed 3-braids.* Memoirs Amer. Math. Soc. No. **151** (1974), 124 pp. Providence, Rh. I.: Amer. Math. Soc. ⟨K 11, K 16, K 20, K 25, K 27, K 40, K 30⟩

Murasugi, K., 1974': *On the divisibility of knot groups.* Pacific J. Math., **52** (1974), 491–503 ⟨K 16, K 18⟩

Murasugi, K., 1977: *On a group that cannot be the group of a 2-knot.* Proc. Amer. Math. Soc., **64** (1977), 154–155 ⟨K 16, K 61⟩

Murasugi, K., 1980: *On dihedral coverings of S^3.* C. R. Math. Rep. Acad. Sci. Canada, Vol. **II**, No.2 (1980), 99–102 ⟨K 20⟩

Murasugi, K., 1980': *On symmetries of knots.* Tsukuba J. Math., **4** (1980), 331–347 ⟨K 22⟩

Murasugi, K., 1982: *Seifert fibre spaces and braid groups.* Proc. London Math. Soc., (3) **44** (1982), 71–84 ⟨K 40, M⟩

Murasugi, K., 1983: *Signatures and Alexander polynomials of two bridge knots.* Math. Repts. Acad. Sci. Canad., **5** (1983), 133–136 ⟨K 26, K 27, K 30⟩

Murasugi, K., 1984: *On the Arf invariant of links.* Math. Proc. Cambridge Phil. Soc., **95** (1984), 61–69 ⟨K 25, K 50⟩

Murasugi, K., 1984': *Nilpotent coverings of links and Milnor's invariant.* Proc. Sussex Conf. Low-dim. Topology 1982 (ed. R. Fenn); (to appear) ⟨K 20⟩

Murasugi, K.; R. S. D. Thomas, 1972: *Isotopic closed nonconjugate braids.* Proc. Amer. Math. Soc., **33** (1972), 137–138 ⟨K 40⟩

Myers, R., 1982: *Simple knots in compact, orientable 3-manifolds.* Trans. Amer. Math. Soc., **273** (1982), 75–91 ⟨K 59, M⟩

Nakagawa, Y., 1975: *A new class of knots with property P.* Publ. Res. Inst. Math. Sci. Kyoto Univ., **10** (1975), 445–455 ⟨K 19⟩

Nakagawa, Y., 1976: *On the Alexander polynomials of slice links.* Math. Sem. Notes Kobe Univ., **4** (1976), 217–224 ⟨K 26, K 33, K 50⟩

Nakagawa, Y., 1976': *Elementary disks and their equivalences.* Quart. J. Math. Oxford, (2) **27** (1976), 355–369 ⟨K 15⟩

Nakagawa, Y., 1978: *On the Alexander polynomials of slice links.* Osaka J. Math., **15** (1978), 161–182 ⟨K 26, K 33, K 50⟩

Nakagawa, Y., 1981: *Genus of pretzel links $(2p_1, \ldots, 2p_\mu)$.* Math. Sem. Notes Kobe Univ., **9** (1981), 387–402 ⟨ K 30, K 35, K 50,⟩

Nakagawa, Y.; Y. Nakanishi, 1981: *Prime links, concordance and Alexander invariants. II.* Math. Sem. Kobe Univ., **9** (1981), 403–440 ⟨K 17, K 24, K 26⟩

Nakanishi, Y., 1980: *A surgical view of Alexander invariants of links.* Math. Sem. Notes Kobe Univ., **8** (1980), 199–218 ⟨K 21, K 26⟩

Nakanishi, Y., 1980': *Prime links, concordance and Alexander invariants.* Math. Sem. Kobe Univ., **8** (1980), 561–568 ⟨K 17, K 24, K 26⟩

Nakanishi, Y., 1981: *A note on unknotting number.* Math. Sem. Notes Kobe Univ., **9** (1981), 99–108 ⟨K 15, K 24, K 59⟩

Nakanishi, Y., 1981': *Primeness of links.* Math. Sem. Notes Kobe Univ., **9** (1981), 415–440 ⟨K 24, K 25, K 50⟩

Nakanishi, Y., 1983: *Prime and simple links.* Math. Sem. Notes Kobe Univ., **11** (1983), 249–256 ⟨K 14, K 17, K 50⟩

Nakanishi, Y., 1983': *Unknotting numbers and knot diagrams with the minimum crossings.* Math. Sem. Notes Kobe Univ., **11** (1983), 257–258 ⟨K 14⟩

Nakanishi, Y.; Y. Nakagowa, 1982: *On ribbon knots.* Math. Sem. Notes Kobe Univ., **10** (1982), 423–430 ⟨K 60, K 61⟩

Nejinskii, V. M., 1976: Вычисление некоторых групп в теории зацеплений *(Calculation of some groups in the theory of links).* Notes sci. sem. Leningrad sec. Acad. Sci. USSR, **66** (1976), 177–179 ⟨K 12, K 50⟩

Neukirch, J., 1981: *Zöpfe und Galoisgruppen.* Abh. Math. Sem. Univ. Hamburg, **51** (1981), 98–119 ⟨K 40⟩

Neuwirth, L., 1960: *The algebraic determination of the genus of a knot.* Amer. J. Math., **82** (1960), 791–798 ⟨K 15, K 16⟩

Neuwirth, L., 1961: *A note on torus knots and links determined by their groups.* Duke Math. J., **28** (1961), 545–551 ⟨K 16, K 35⟩

Neuwirth, L., 1961': *The algebraic determination of the topological type of the complement of a knot*. Proc. Amer. Math. Soc., **12** (1961), 904–906 ⟨K 16, K 18⟩

Neuwirth, L., 1963: *A remark on knot groups with a center*. Proc. Amer. Math. Soc., **14** (1963), 378–379 ⟨K 16, K 18⟩

Neuwirth, L., 1963′: *On Stallings fibrations*. Proc. Amer. Math. Soc., **14** (1963), 380–381 ⟨K 16, K 18⟩

Neuwirth, L., 1963″: *A topological classification of certain 3-manifolds*. Bull. Amer. Math. Soc., **59** (1963), 372–375 ⟨M⟩

Neuwirth, L., 1963‴: *Interpolating manifolds for knots in S^3*. Topology, **2** (1963), 359–365 ⟨K 16⟩

Neuwirth, L., (1965): *Knot Groups*. Ann. Math. Studies **56**. Princeton, N.J.: Princeton Univ. Press ⟨K 11, K 16, K 18⟩

Neuwirth, L.P., 1974: *The status of some problems related to knot groups*. In: Topology Conference Virginia Polytechn. Inst. and State Univ. (eds. R.F. Dickman, P. Fletcher). Lect. Notes in Math. **375** (1974), 208–230. Berlin-Heidelberg-New York: Springer Verlag ⟨K 11, K 16⟩

Neuzil, J.P., 1973: *Embedding the dunce hat in S^4*. Topology, **12** (1973), 411–415 ⟨K 12, K 61⟩

Newman, M.H.A., 1942: *On a string problem of Dirac*. J. London Math. Soc., **17** (1942), 173–177 ⟨K 40⟩

Newman, M.H.A.; J.H.C. Whitehead, 1937: *On the group of a certain linkage*. Quart. J. Math. Oxford, **8** (1937), 14–21 ⟨K 16, K 35, K 55⟩

Nielsen, J., 1918: *Die Isomorphismen der allgemeinen, unendlichen Gruppe mit zwei Erzeugenden*. Math. Ann., **78** (1918), 385–397 ⟨G⟩

Nielsen, J., 1921: *Om Regning med ikke kommutative Faktoren og dens Anvendelse i Gruppenteorien*. Mat. Tidsskr. B (1921), 77–94 ⟨G⟩

Nielsen, J., 1927: *Untersuchungen zur Topologie der geschlossenen zweiseitigen Flächen*. Acta Math., **50** (1927), 189–358 ⟨F⟩

Nielsen, J., 1937: *Die Struktur periodischer Transformationen von Flächen*. Det. Kgl. Dansk Vidensk. Selskab. Mat. fys. Meddelerer, **15** (1937),1–77 ⟨F⟩

Nielsen, J., 1942: *Abbildungsklassen endlicher Ordnung*. Acta Math., **75** (1942), 23–115 ⟨F⟩

Nielsen, J., 1984: *Collected Work*. Basel-New York-Stuttgart: Birkhäuser ⟨F⟩

Noga, D., 1967: *Über den Außenraum von Produktknoten und die Bedeutung der Fixgruppe*. Math. Z., **101** (1967), 131–141 ⟨K 17, K 19⟩

Norman, R.A., 1969: *Dehn's Lemma for certain 4-manifolds*. Invent. math., **7** (1969), 143–147 ⟨K 59⟩

Norwood, F.H., 1982: *Every two generator knot is prime*. Proc. Amer. Math. Soc., **86** (1982), 143–147 ⟨K 16, K 17⟩

Ochiai, M., 1978: *Dehn's surgery along 2-bridge knots*. Yokohama Math. J., **26** (1978), 69–75 ⟨K 21, K 40⟩

Oertel, U., 1984: *Closed incompressible surfaces in complements of star links*. Pacific J. Math., **111** (1984), 209–230 ⟨K 15⟩

Ore, O., 1951: *Some studies on cyclic determinants*. Duke Math. J., **18** (1951), 343–371 ⟨X⟩

Orlik, P., (1972): *Seifert manifolds*. Lect. Notes in Math. **291** (1972). Berlin-Heidelberg-New York: Springer-Verlag ⟨M⟩

Orlik, P.; E. Vogt; H. Zieschang, 1967: *Zur Topologie gefaserter dreidimensionaler Mannigfaltigkeiten*. Topology, **6** (1967), 49–64 ⟨M⟩

Osborne, R.P., 1981: *Knots with Heegaard genus 2 complements are invertible*. Proc. Amer. Math. Soc., **81** (1981), 501–506 ⟨K 23⟩

Otal, J.-P., 1982: *Présentations en ponts du nœud trivial*. C.R. Acad. Sc. Paris, **294-I**, 553–556 (1982) ⟨K 30, K 35⟩

Pannwitz, E., 1983: *Eine elementargeometrische Eigenschaft von Verschlingungen und Knoten*. Math. Ann., **108** (1933), 629–672 ⟨K 14⟩

Papakyriakopoulos, C.D., 1955: *On the ends of knot groups*. Ann. of Math., **62** (1955), 293–299 ⟨K 16⟩

Papakyriakopoulos, C.D., 1957: *On solid tori*. Proc. London Math. Soc., **7** (1957), 281–299 ⟨M⟩

Papakyriakopoulos, C.D., 1957′: *On Dehn's lemma and the asphericity of knots*. Ann. of Math., **66** (1957), 1–26 ⟨K 16, M⟩

Papakyriakopoulos, C.D., 1958: *Some problems on 3-dimensional manifolds*. Bull. Amer. Math. Soc., **64** (1958), 317–335 ⟨K 11⟩

Penney, D.E., 1969: *Generalized Brunnian links*. Duke Math. J., **36** (1960), 31–32 ⟨K 35⟩

Penney, D.E., 1972: *Establishing isomorphisms between tame prime knots in E^3*. Pacific J. Math., **40** (1972), 675–680 ⟨K 12, K 29⟩

Perko, K.A., 1974: *On coverings of knots*. Glasnik Mat., **9** (1974), 141–145 ⟨K 20⟩,

Perko, K.A., jr., 1976: *On dihedral covering spaces of knots*. Invent. math., **34** (1976), 77–84 ⟨K 20, K 27,K 30⟩

Perko, A.P., 1979: *On 10-crossing knots*. Portugalliae Math., **38** (1979), 5–9 ⟨K 13⟩

Perko, K.A., 1982: *Invariants of 11-crossing knots*. Prépublications Orsay ⟨K 13⟩

Perron, B., 1982: *Le nœud «huit» est algebraique réel*. Invent. math., **65** (1982), 441–451 ⟨K 32⟩

Perron, O., (1954): *Die Lehre von den Kettenbrüchen. I. II.* Stuttgart: Teubner ⟨X⟩

Plans, A., 1953: *Aportacion al estudio de los grupos de homologia de los recubrimientos cicicos ramificados correspondiente a un nudo.* Rev. Real Acad. Cienc. Exact., Fisica y Nat. Madrid, **47** (1953), 161–193 ⟨K 20⟩

Plans, A., 1957: *Aportación a la homotopia de sistemas de nudos.* Revista Mat. Hisp.-Amer., (4) **17** (1957), 224–237 ⟨K 16⟩

Plotnick, S., 1982: *Embedding homology 3-spheres in S^5.* Pacific J. Math., **101** (1982), 147–151 ⟨K 60⟩

Plotnick, S.P., 1983: *Infinitely many disk knots with the same exterior.* Math. Proc. Cambridge Phil. Soc., **98** (1983), 67–72 ⟨K 60, K 61⟩

Plotnick, S.P., 1983′: *The homotopy type of four dimensional knot complements.* Math. Z., **183** (1983), 447–471 ⟨K 60⟩

Plotnick, S.P., 1984: *Fibered knots in S^4-twisting, spinning, rolling, surgery and branching.* In: Four manifold theory, Amer. Math. Soc. Summer Conf., UNH 1982. Amer. Math. Soc. Contemporary Math. ⟨K 61⟩

Plotnick, S.P.; A.I. Suciu, 1984: *k-invariants of knotted 2-spheres.* (preprint) Columbia Univ. ⟨K 61⟩

Poenaru, V., 1971: *An note on the generators for the fundamental group of the complement of a submanifold of codimension 2.* Topology, **10** (1971), 47–52 ⟨K 60⟩

Popov, S.L., 1972: Заузливание стягиваемых полиэдров в $\mathbb{R}^4$. Mat. сб., **89** (1972), 323–330, Engl. transl.: *Knotting of contractable two-dimensional polyhedra in $\mathbb{R}^4$.* Math. USSR-Sborniki, **18** (1972), 333–341 ⟨K 61⟩

Przytycki J.H., 1983: *Incompressibility of surfaces after Dehn surgery.* Michigan Math. J., **30** (1983), 289–308 ⟨K 21, M⟩

Puppe, S.D., 1952: *Minkowskische Einheiten und Verschlingungsinvarianten von Knoten.* Math. Z., **56** (1952), 33–48 ⟨K 25, K 27⟩

Quách, Châm Vân, 1979: *Polynôme d'Alexander des nœuds fibrés.* C.R. Acad. Sci. Paris, **289** A (1979), 375–377 ⟨K 18, K 26⟩

Quách, Thi Câm Vân, 1983: *On a theorem on partially summing tangles by Lickorish.* Math. Proc. Cambridge Phil. Soc., **93** (1983), 63–66 ⟨K 12, K 17⟩

Quách, Thi Câm Vân, 1983′: *On a realization of prime tangles and knots.* Canad. J. Math., **35** (1983), 311–323 ⟨K 12, K 17, K 32⟩

Quách, Thi Cân, Vân; C. Weber, 1979: *Une famille infinie de nœuds fibrés cobordants à zéro et ayant même polynôme.* Comment Math. Helv., **54** (1979), 562–566 ⟨K 18, K 26⟩

Rabin, M.O., 1958′: *Recursive unsolvability of group theoretic problems.* Ann. of Math., **67** (1958), 172–194 ⟨K 29, G⟩

Rapaport, E.S., 1960: *On the commutator subgroup of a knot group.* Ann. of Math., **71** (1960), 157–162 ⟨K 16⟩

Rapaport Strasser, E., 1975: *Knot-like groups.* In: Knots, groups and 3-manifolds (ed. L.P. Neuwirth). Ann. Math. Studies **84** (1975), 119–133. Princeton, N.J.: Princeton Univ. Press ⟨K 16⟩

Ratcliffe, J.G., 1981: *On the ends of higher dimensioned knot groups,* J. Pure Appl. Algebra, **20** (1981), 317–324 ⟨K 16, K 60⟩

Ratcliffe, J.G., 1983: *A fibered knot in a homology 3-sphere whose group is nonclassical.* Amer. Math. Soc. Contemporary Math., **20** (1983), 327–339 ⟨K 16, K 18⟩

Reeve, J.E., 1955: *A summary of results in the topological classification of plane algebroid singularities.* Rendiconti Sem. Mat. Torino, **14** (1955), 159–187 ⟨K 34⟩

Reidemeister, K., 1926: *Knoten und Gruppen.* Abh. Math. Sem. Univ. Hamburg, **5** (1927), 7–23 ⟨K 16⟩

Reidemeister, K., 1926′: *Elementare Begründung der Knotentheorie.* Abh. Math. Sem. Univ. Hamburg, **5** (1927), 24–32 ⟨K 12, K 14⟩

Reidemeister, K., 1928: *Über Knotengruppen.* Abh. Math. Sem. Univ. Hamburg, **6** (1928), 56–64 ⟨K 16⟩

Reidemeister, K., 1929: *Knoten und Verkettungen.* Math. Z., **29** (1929), 713–729 ⟨K 16, K 20⟩

Reidemeister, K., 1932: *Knotentheorie.* Ergebn. Math. Grenzgeb., Bd. **1**; Berlin: Springer-Verlag ⟨K 11, K 16, K 25⟩

Reidemeister, K., 1933: *Zur dreidimensionalen Topologie.* Abh. Math. Sem. Univ. Hamburg, **9** (1933), 189–194 ⟨M⟩

Reidemeister, K., 1984: *Homotopiegruppen von Komplexen.* Abh. Math. Sem. Univ. Hamburg, 11 (1934), 211–215 ⟨A⟩

Reidemeister, K., 1935: *Homotopieringe und Linsenräume.* Abh. Math. Sem. Univ. Hamburg, **11** (1935), 102–109 ⟨A, M⟩

Reidemeister, K., 1935′: *Überdeckungen von Komplexen.* J. reine angew. Math. **173** (1935), 164–173 ⟨A⟩

Reidemeister, K., 1960: *Knoten und Geflechte.* Nachr. Akad. Wiss. Göttingen, math.-phys. Kl. 1960, Nr. 5, 105–115 ⟨K 12⟩

Reidemeister, K.; H.G. Schumann, 1934: *L-Polynome von Verkettungen.* Abh. Math. Sem. Univ. Hamburg, **10** (1934), 256–262 ⟨K 25⟩

Reyner, S.W., 1970: *Metacyclic invariants of knots and links.* Canad. J. Math., **22** (1970),

193–201 (Corrigendum by R.H. Fox: Canadian J. Math., **25** (1973), 1000–1001) ⟨K 20⟩

de Rham, G., 1967: *Introduction aux polynomes d'un nœud.* L'Enseign. Math., **13** (1967), 187–195 ⟨K 26⟩

Rice, P.M., 1968: *Killing knots.* Proc. Amer. Math. Soc., **19** (1968), 254 ⟨K 14⟩

Rice, P.M., 1971: *Equivalence of Alexander matrices.* Math. Ann., **193** (1971), 65–75 ⟨K 25⟩

Riley, R., 1971′: *Homomorphisms of knot groups on finite groups.* Math. Comput., **25** (1971), 603–619 ⟨K 28⟩

Riley, R., 1972: *Parabolic representations of knot groups.* Proc. London Math. Soc., **24** (1972), 217–242 ⟨K 28⟩

Riley, R., 1972′: *A finiteness theorem for alternating links.* J. London Math. Soc., (2) **5** (1972), 263–266 ⟨K 26, K 31⟩

Riley, R., 1974: *Hecke invariants of knot groups.* Glasgow Math. J., **15** (1974), 17–26 ⟨K 28⟩

Riley, R., 1974′: *Knots with parabolic property P.* Quart. J. Math. Oxford, (2) **25** (1974), 273–283 ⟨K 19, K 28⟩

Riley, R., 1975: *Parabolic representations of knot groups. II.* Proc. London Math. Soc., **31** (1975), 495–512 ⟨K 28⟩

Riley, R., 1975′: *Discrete parabolic representations of link groups.* Mathematika, **22** (1975), 141–150 ⟨K 28⟩

Riley, R., 1975″: *A quadratic parabolic group.* Math. Proc. Cambridge Phil. Soc., **77** (1975), 281–288 ⟨K 28, K 59⟩

Riley, R., 1977: *Automorphisms of excellent link groups.* (preprint) ⟨K 16, K 28⟩

Riley, R., 1979: *An elliptical path from parabolic representations to hyperbolic structures.* In: Topology Low-Dim. Manifolds, Second Sussex Conf. 1977 (ed. R. Fenn). Lect. Notes in Math. **722** (1979), 99–133. Berlin-Heidelberg-New York: Springer Verlag ⟨K 28, K 59⟩

Riley, R., 1983: *Applications of a computer implementation of Poincaré's theorem on fundamental polyhedra.* Math. Comput., **40** (1983), 607–632 ⟨K 28, K 59, M⟩

Riley, R., 1984: *Nonabelian representations of 2-bridge knot groups.* Quart. J. Math. Oxford, (2) **35**, (1984) 191–208 ⟨K 28, K 30⟩

Robertello, R.A., 1965: *An invariant of knot cobordism.* Commun. Pure Appl. Math., **18** (1965), 543–555 ⟨K 24⟩

Roeling, L.G., 1971: *On certain links in 3-manifolds.* Michigan Math. J., **18** (1971), 99–101 ⟨K 21⟩

Rolfsen, D., 1972: *Isotopy of links in codimension two.* J. Indian Math. Soc., **36** (1972), 263–278 ⟨K 12, K 24, K 50⟩

Rolfsen, D., 1974: *Some counterexample in link theory.* Canad. J. Math., **26** (1974), 978–984 ⟨K 50, K 60⟩

Rolfsen, D., 1975: *A surgical view of Alexander's polynomial.* In: Proc. Geometric Topology Conf., Park City, Utah 1974 (eds. L.C. Glaser, T.B. Rushing). Lect. Notes in Math., **438** (1975), 415–423. Berlin-Heidelberg- New York: Springer Verlag ⟨K 21, K 26⟩

Rolfsen, D., 1975′: *Localized Alexander invariants and isotopy of links.* Ann. of Math., **101** (1975), 1–19 ⟨K 26, K 60⟩

Rolfsen, D., (1976): *Knots and links.* Berkeley, CA: Publish or Perish, Inc. ⟨K 11, K 13⟩

Roseman, D., 1974: *Woven knots are spun knots.* Osaka J. Math., **11** (1974), 307–312 ⟨K 35⟩

Rost, M.; H. Zieschang, 1984: *Meridional generators and plat presentations of torus links.* (to appear) ⟨K 16, K 35⟩

Ruberman, D., 1983: *Doubly slice knots and the Casson-Gordon invariants.* Trans. Amer. Math. Soc., **279** (1983), 569–588 ⟨K 33⟩

Rudolph, L., 1982: *Non-trivial positive braids have positive signature.* Topology, **21** (1982), 325–327 ⟨K 27, K 33, K 40⟩

Rudolph, L., 1983: *Algebraic functions and closed braids.* Topology, **22** (1983), 191–202 ⟨K 32, K 40⟩

Rudolph, L., 1983′: *Braided surfaces and Seifert ribbons for closed braids.* Comment. Math. Helv., **58** (1983), 1–37 ⟨K 15, K 40⟩

Rushing, T.B., (1973): *Topological embeddings.* New York-London: Academic Press ⟨B⟩

Sakai, S., 1958: *A generalization of symmetric unions of knots.* Bull. Educational Fac. Shizuoka Univ., **9** (1958), 117–121 ⟨K 17⟩

Sakai, T., 1977: *A remark on the Alexander polynomials of knots.* Math. Sem. Notes Kobe Univ., **5** (1977), 451–456 ⟨K 26⟩

Sakai, T., 1983: *On the generalization of union of knots.* Hokkaido Math. J., **12** (1983), 129–146 ⟨K 17⟩

Sakai, T., 1983′: *Polynomials of invertible knots.* Math. Ann., **266** (1983), 229–232 ⟨K 23, K 26⟩

Sakuma, M., 1979: *The homology groups of abelian coverings of links.* Math. Sem. Notes Kobe Univ., **7** (1979), 515–530 ⟨K 20, K 25⟩

Sakuma, M., 1981: *Surface bundles over S^1 which are 2-fold branched cyclic coverings of S^3.* Math. Sem. Notes Kobe Univ., **9** (1981), 159–180 ⟨K 20⟩

Sakuma, M., 1981′: *On the polynomials of periodic links.* Math. Ann., **257** (1981), 487–494 ⟨K 23, K 26⟩

Sakuma, M., 1981″: *Periods of composite links.* Math. Sem. Notes Kobe Univ., **9** (1981), 445–452 ⟨K 17, K 23⟩

Sakuma, M., 1982: *On regular coverings of links.* Math. Ann., **260** (1982), 303–315 ⟨K 20⟩

Sakuma, M., 1984: *Homolgy cobordisms and 3-manifolds with no periodic maps.* (preprint) Osaka City Univ. ⟨K 22⟩

Sato, N. A., 1978: *Algebraic invariants of links of codimension two.* Ph. D. Thesis. Brandeis Univ. ⟨K 25, K 60⟩

Sato, N., 1981: *Alexander modules of sublinks and an invariant of classical link concordance.* Illinois J. Math., **25** (1981), 508–519 ⟨K 24, K 25, K 50⟩

Sato, N. A., 1981′: *Free coverings and modules of boundary links.* Trans. Amer. Math. Soc., **264** (1981), 499–505 ⟨K 60⟩

Sato, N. A., 1981″: *Algebraic invariants of boundary links.* Trans. Amer. Math. Soc., **265** (1981), 359–374 ⟨K 60⟩

Scharlemann, M., 1977: *The fundamental group of fibered knot cobordisms.* Math. Ann., **225** (1977), 243–251 ⟨K 24, K 35⟩

Scharlemann, M., 1984: *Tunnel number one knots are doubly prime.* (preprint) ⟨K 17, K 59⟩

Schaufele, C. B., 1966: *A note on link groups.* Bull. Amer. Math. Soc., **72** (1966), 107–110 ⟨K 16⟩

Schaufele, C. B., 1967: *Kernels of free abelian representations of a link group.* Proc. Amer. Math. Soc., **18** (1967), 535–539 ⟨K 28⟩

Schaufele, C. B., 1967′: *The commutator group of a doubled knot.* Duke Math. J., **34** (1967), 677–682 ⟨K 16, K 35⟩

Schmid, J., 1963: *Über eine Klasse von Verkettungen.* Math. Z., **81** (1963), 187–205 ⟨K 12, K 14, K 50⟩

Schreier, O., 1924: *Über die Gruppen $A^a B^b = 1$.* Abh. Math. Sem. Univ. Hamburg, **3** (1924), 167–169 ⟨G⟩

Schubert, H., 1949: *Die eindeutige Zerlegbarkeit eines Knoten in Primknoten.* Sitzungsber. Akad. Wiss. Heidelberg, math.-nat. Kl. 1949, 3. Abh., 57–104 ⟨K 17⟩

Schubert, H., 1953: *Knoten und Vollringe.* Acta Math., **90** (1953), 131–286 ⟨K 17⟩

Schubert, H., 1954: Über eine numerische Knoteninvariante. Math. Z., **61** (1954), 245–288 ⟨K 30⟩

Schubert, H., 1956: *Knoten mit zwei Brücken.* Math. Z., **65** (1956), 133–170 ⟨K 30⟩

Schubert, H., 1961: *Bestimmung der Primfaktorzerlegung von Verkettungen.* Math. Z., **76** (1961), 116–148 ⟨K 17, K 29, K 50⟩

Schubert, H.; K. Soltsien, 1964: *Isotopie von Flächen in einfachen Knoten.* Abh. Math. Sem. Univ. Hamburg, **27** (1964), 116–123 ⟨K 15, K 29⟩

Scott, G. P., 1970: *Braid groups and the group of homomorphisms of a surface.* Proc. Cambridge Phil. Soc., **68** (1970), 605–617 ⟨K 40, F⟩

Seifert, H., 1932: *Homologiegruppen berandeter dreidimensionaler Mannigfaltigkeiten.* Math. Z., **35** (1932), 609–611 ⟨M⟩

Seifert, H., 1933: *Topologie dreidimensionaler gefaserter Räume.* Acta Math., **60** (1933), 147–238 ⟨M⟩

Seifert, H., 1933′: *Verschlingungsinvarianten.* Sitzungsber. Preuss. Akad. Wiss. Berlin, **26** (1933), 811–828 ⟨K 20, K 25⟩

Seifert, H., 1934: *Über das Geschlecht von Knoten.* Math. Ann., **110** (1934), 571–592 ⟨K 15, K 25⟩

Seifert, H., 1936: *Die Verschlingungsinvarianten der zyklischen Knotenüberlagerungen.* Abh. Math. Sem. Univ. Hamburg, **11** (1936), 84–101 ⟨K 20, K 25⟩

Seifert, H., 1936′: *La théorie des nœuds.* L'Enseign. Math., **35** (1936), 201–212 ⟨K 11⟩

Seifert, H., 1949: *Schlingknoten.* Math. Z., **52** (1949), 62–80 ⟨K 17⟩

Seifert, H., 1950: *On the homology invariants of knots.* Quart. J. Math. Oxford, (2) **1** (1950), 23–32 ⟨K 15, K 26⟩

Seifert, H.; W. Threlfall, (1934): *Lehrbuch der Topologie.* Leipzig: Teubner ⟨A, B, M⟩

Seifert, H.; W. Threlfall, 1950: *Old and new results on knots.* Canad. J. Math., **2** (1950), 1–15 ⟨K 11⟩

Shapiro, A.; J. H. C. Whitehead, 1958: *A proof and extension of Dehn's lemma.* Bull. Amer. Math. Soc., **64** (1958), 174–178 ⟨M⟩

Shepperd, J. A. H., 1962: *Braids which can be plaited with their threads tied together at an end.* Proc. Royal Soc., **A-265** (1962), 229–244 ⟨K 40⟩

Shibuya, T., 1974: *Some relation among various numerical invariants for links.* Osaka J. Math., **11** (1974), 313–322 ⟨K 12⟩

Shibuya, T., 1977: *On links with disconnected spanning surfaces.* Math. Sem. Notes Kobe Univ., **5** (1977), 435–442 ⟨K 50⟩

Shibuya, T., 1980: *On the cobordism of compound knots.* Math. Sem. Notes Kobe Univ., **8** (1980), 331–337 ⟨K 24, K 33⟩

Shibuya, T., 1982: *On knot types of compound knots.* Math. Sem. Notes Kobe, **10** (1982), 507–513 ⟨K 17⟩

Shibuya, T., 1984: *On boundary links and weak boundary links.* (preprint) ⟨K 50⟩

Shilepsky, A. C., 1973: *Homogeneity by isotopy for simple closed curves.* Duke Math. J., **40** (1973), 463–472 ⟨K 55⟩

Shinohara, Y., 1971: *On the signature of knots and links.* Trans. Amer. Math. Soc., **156** (1971), 273–285 ⟨K 27⟩

Shinohara, Y., 1971′: *Higher dimensional knots in tubes.* Trans. Amer. Math. Soc., **161** (1971), 35–49 ⟨K 60⟩

Shinohara, Y., 1976: *On the signature of a link with two bridges.* Kwansei Gakuin Univ. Annual Stud., **25** (1976), 111–119 ⟨K 27, K 30⟩

Shinohara, Y., D.W. Sumners, 1972: *Homology invariants of cyclic coverings with applications to links.* Trans. Amer. Math. Soc., **163** (1972), 101–121 ⟨K 20, K 25⟩

Siebenmann, L., 1975: *Exercices sur les nœuds rationnels.* Polycopie, Orsay ⟨K 32⟩

Sikkema, C.D., 1972: *Pseudo-isotopies of arcs and knots.* Proc. Amer. Math. Soc., **31** (1972), 615–616 ⟨K 55⟩

Simon, J., 1970: *Some classes of knots with property P.* In: Top. of Manifolds (eds. J.C. Cantrell and C.H. Edwards, jr.), Proc. Inst. Univ. Georgia, Athens, GA (1969), 195–199. Chicago: Markham Publ. Comp. ⟨K 17, K 19⟩

Simon, J., 1971: *On knots with nontrivial interpolating manifolds.* Trans. Amer. Math. Soc., **160** (1971), 467–473 ⟨K 19⟩

Simon, J., 1973: *An algebraic classification of knots in S^3.* Ann. of Math., **97** (1973), 1–13 ⟨K 12, K 19⟩

Simon, J., 1976: *Roots and centralizers of peripheral elements in knot groups.* Math. Ann., **222** (1976), 205–209 ⟨K 16, K 17⟩

Simon, J., 1976′: *On the problems of determing knots by their complements and knot complements by their groups.* Proc. Amer. Math. Soc., **57** (1976), 140–142 ⟨K 19⟩

Simon, J., 1976″: Fibered knots in homotopy 3-spheres. Proc. Amer. Math. Soc., **58** (1976), 325–328 ⟨K 18, M⟩

Simon, J., 1976‴: *Compactification of covering spaces of compact 3-manifolds.* Michigan Math. J., **23** (1976), 245–256 ⟨K 20, K 35⟩

Simon, J., 1980: *Wirtinger approximations and the knot groups of F^n in S^{n+2}.* Pacific J. Math., **90** (1980), 177–190 ⟨K 16, G⟩

Simon, J., 1980′: *How many knots may have the same group?* Proc. Amer. Math. Soc., **80** (1980), 162–166 ⟨K 19⟩

Sinde, V.M., 1975: Коммутанты групп Артина, (*The derived groups of Artin groups.*) Uspehi Math. Nauk, **30 : 5** (1975), 207–208 ⟨K 40⟩

Sinde, V.M., 1977: Некоторые гомоморфизмы групп Артина серии B_n и D_n B группь тех же серий B и D. (*Some homomorphisms of the Artin groups of the series B_n and D_n into groups of the same series B and D.*) Uspehi Mat. Nauk, **32 : 1** (1977), 189–190 ⟨K 40⟩

Singer, J., 1933: *Three-dimensional manifolds and their Heegard diagrams.* Trans. Amer. Math. Soc., **35** (1933), 88–111 ⟨M⟩

Smith, P.A., 1934: *A theorem on fixed points for periodic transformations.* Ann. of Math., **35** (1934), 572–578 ⟨A, B⟩

Smythe, N., 1966: *Boundary links.* Topology Seminar Wisconsin, 1965 (eds. R.H. Bing, R.J. Bean). Ann. of Math. Studies **60** (1966), 69–72. Princeton, N.J.: Princeton Univ. Press, ⟨K 50⟩

Smythe, N., 1967: *Isotopic invariants of links and the Alexander matrix.* Amer. J. Math., **89** (1967), 693–704 ⟨K 25, K 59⟩

Smythe, N., 1967′: *Trivial knots with arbitrary projection.* J. Austr. Math. Soc., **7** (1967), 481–489 ⟨K 12, K 35⟩

Smythe, N., 1970: *Topological invariants of isotopy of links. I.* Amer. J. Math., **92** (1970), 86–98 ⟨K 50⟩

Smythe, N., 1970′: *n-linking and n-splitting.* Amer. J. Math., **92** (1970), 272–282 ⟨K 50⟩

Smythe, N.F., 1979: *The Burau representation of the braid group is pairwise free.* Archiv Math., **32** (1979), 309–317 ⟨K 40⟩

Soltsien, K., 1965: *Bestimmung von Schlingknoten.* Abh. Math. Sem. Univ. Hamburg, **28** (1965), 234–249 ⟨K 17, K 29⟩

Soma, T., 1981: *The Gromov invariant of links.* Invent. math., **64** (1981), 445–454 ⟨K 38⟩

Soma, T., 1984: *Hyperbolic, fibred links and fibre-concordance.* Math. Proc. Cambridge Phil. Soc., **96** (1984), 283–294 ⟨K 18, K 21, K 24, M⟩

Soma, T., 1984′: *A homotopy 3-sphere and 3-fold branched covers of S^3.* (preprint) ⟨K 20⟩

Sosinskii, A.B., 1965: Многомерные топологические узлы. Доклады Акад. Наук СССР, **163** (1965), 1326–1329, Engl. transl.: *Multidimensional knots.* Soviet Math. Doklady **6** (1965), 1119–1122 ⟨K 60⟩

Sosinskii, A.B., 1967: Гомотопии дополнений к узлам. Доклады Акад. Наук СССР, **176** (1967), 1258–1261, Engl. transl.: *Homotopy of knot complements.* Soviet Math. Doklady **8** (1967), 1324–1328 ⟨K 60⟩

Sosinskii, A.B., 1970: Разложения узлов. Мат. сб., **81** (1970), 145–158, Engl. transl.: *Decompositions of knots.* Math. USSR-Sbornik, **10** (1970), 139–150 ⟨K 60⟩

Spanier, E.H., (1966): *Algebraic topology.* New York: McGraw-Hill Book Comp. ⟨A⟩

Stallings, J., 1962: *On fibering certain 3-manifolds.* In: Top. 3-manifolds, Proc. 1961 Top.

Inst. Univ. Georgia (ed. M.K. Fort, jr.), pp. 95–100. Englewood Cliffs, N.J.: Prentice-Hall ⟨K 18, M⟩

Stallings, J., 1963: *On topologically unknotted spheres*. Ann. of Math., **77** (1963), 490–503 ⟨K 60⟩

Stallings, J.R., 1978: *Construction of fibered knots and links*. Algebr. Geom. Top. Stanford/Calif. 1976 II (ed. R.J. Milgram), Proc. Symp. Pure Math., **32**, 55–60. Providence, R.I.: Amer. Math. Soc. ⟨K 18⟩

Stebe, P., 1968: *Residual finiteness of a class of knot groups*. Commun. Pure Appl. Math., **21** (1968), 563–583 ⟨K 16, K 28⟩

Stillwell, J., 1979: *The compound crossing number of a knot*. Austral. Math. Soc. Gaz., **6** (1979), 1–10 ⟨K 59⟩

Stillwell, J., (1980): *Classical topology and combinatorial group theory*. Grad. Texts Math. **72**. Berlin-Heidelberg-New York: Springer Verlag ⟨K 11, G⟩

Stöcker, R.; H. Zieschang, (1985): *Algebraische Topologie*. Stuttgart: Teubner-Verlag ⟨A⟩

Stoel, T.B., 1962: An attempt to distinguish certain knots of ten und eleven crossings. Princeton senior thesis. ⟨K 12⟩

Stoltzfus, N., (1977): *Unravelling the integral knot concordance group*. Memoirs Amer. Math. Soc. **12** (1977), no. 192. Englewood Cliffs, Rh.I.: Amer. Math. Soc. ⟨K 24, K 60⟩

Stoltzfus, N.W., 1978: *Algebraic computations of the integral concordance and double null concordance group of knots*. In: Knot Theory (ed. J.-C. Hausmann). Proc., Plans-sur-Bex, Switzerland 1977. Lecture Notes in Math. **685** (1978), 274–290, Berlin-Heidelberg-New York: Springer Verlag ⟨K 24, K 60⟩

Stoltzfus, N.W., 1979: *Equivariant concordance of invariant knots*. Trans. Amer. Math. Soc., **254** (1979), 1–45 ⟨K 24, K 60⟩

Stysnev, V.B., 1978: Извлечение корня в группе кос. Известия Акад. Наук СССР, сер. мат., **42** (1978), 1120–1131, Engl. transl.: *The extension of a root in a braid group*. Math. USSR-Izvestya, **13** (1979), 405–416 ⟨K 40⟩

Sumners, D.W., 1971: *H^2 of the commutator subgroup of a knot group*. Proc. Amer. Math. Soc., **28** (1971), 319–320 ⟨K 25⟩

Sumners, D.W., 1972: *Polynomial invariants and the integral homology of coverings of knots and links*. Invent. math., **15** (1972), 78–90 ⟨K 20, K 25⟩

Sumners, D.W., 1974: *On the homology of finite cyclic coverings of higher-dimensional links*. Proc. Amer. Math. Soc., **46** (1974), 143–149 ⟨K 20, K 25, K 60⟩

Sumners, D.W., 1975: *Smooth $\mathbb{Z}_p$-actions on spheres which leave points pointwise fixed*. Trans. Amer. Math. Soc., **205** (1975), 193–203 ⟨K 22, K 60⟩

Sumners, D.W.; Woods, J.M., 1977: *The monodromy of reducible curves*. Invent. math., **40** (1977), 107–141 ⟨K 26, K 32⟩

Suzuki, S., 1969: *On the knot associated with the solid torus*. Osaka J. Math., **6** (1969), 475–483 ⟨K 15, K 26, K 61⟩

Suzuki, S., 1974: *On a complexity of a surface in 3-sphere*. Osaka J. Math., **11** (1974), 113–127 ⟨K 59⟩

Suzuki, S., 1976: *Knotting problems of 2-spheres in the 4-sphere*. Math. Sem. Notes Kobe Univ., **4** (1976), 241–371 ⟨K 61⟩

Suzuki, S., 1984: *Alexander ideals of graphs in the 3-sphere,* Tokyo J. Math., **7** (1984), 233–247 ⟨K 26⟩

Swarup, G.A., 1973: *On incompressible surfaces in the complement of knots*. J. Indian Math. Soc., **37** (1973), 9–24 ⟨K 15⟩

Swarup, G.A., 1974: *Addendum to "On incompressible surfaces in the complement of knots"*. J. Indian. Math. Soc., **38** (1974), 411–413 ⟨K 15⟩

Swarup, G.A., 1975: *An unknotting criterion*. J. Pure Appl. Algebra, **6** (1975), 291–296 ⟨K 60⟩

Swarup, G.A., 1980: *Cable knots in homotopy 3-spheres*. Quart. J. Math. Oxford, (2) **31** (1980), 97–104 ⟨K 19, K 35⟩

Tait, P.G., 1898: *On Knots I. II. III.* Scientific Papers, I. 273–437, 1877–1885, London: Cambridge Univ. Press 1898 ⟨K 12, K 13⟩

Takahashi, M., 1977: *Two knots with the same 2-fold branched covering space*, Yokohama Math. J., **25** (1977), 91–99 ⟨K 20⟩

Takahashi, M., 1978: *An alternative proof of Birman-Hilden-Viros's theorem*. Tsukuba J. Math., **2** (1978), 17–34 ⟨K 20⟩

Takahashi, M., (1981): *Two-bridge knots have property P*. Memoirs Amer. Math. Soc., **29** No. 239 (1981). Providence, Rh.I.: Amer. Math. Soc. ⟨K 19, K 35⟩

Takahashi, M.; Ochiai, M., 1982: *Heegaard diagrams of torus bundles over S^1*. Comment. Math. Univ. Sancti Pauli, **31** (1982), 63–69 ⟨K 20, M⟩

Takase, R., 1963: *Note on orientable surfaces in 4-space*. Proc. Japan Acad., **39** (1963), 424 ⟨K 60⟩

Tamura, I., 1983: *Fundamental theorems in global knot theory. I*. Proc. Japan Acad., **59** Ser. A (1983), 446–448 ⟨K 60⟩

Tamura, I., 1983′: *Fundamental theorems in*

global knot theory. II. Proc. Japan Acad., **59** Ser. A (1983), 481–483 ⟨K 60⟩

Taylor, L. R., 1979: *On the genera of knots.* In: Topology Low-Dim. Manifolds (ed. R. Fenn), Second Sussex Conf. 1977. Lect. Notes Math. **772** (1979), 144–154. Berlin-Heidelberg-New York: Springer Verlag ⟨K 15⟩

Terasaka, H., 1959: *On null-equivalent knots.* Osaka J. Math., **11** (1959), 95–113 ⟨K 26, K 35⟩

Terasaka, H., 1960: *On the non-triviality of some kinds of knots.* Osaka J. Math., **12** (1960), 113–144 ⟨K 17, K 26, K 31⟩

Terasaka, H., 1960: *Musubime no riron (Theory of knots).* (Japanese) Sugaku, **12** (1960), 1–20 ⟨K 12⟩

Terasaka, H.; F. Hosokawa, 1961: *On the unknotted sphere S^2 in E^4.* Osaka J. Math., **13** (1961), 265–270 ⟨K 61⟩

Thomas, R. S. D., 1971: *Computed topological equivalence of partially closed braids.* Proc. 25 Summer Meeting, Canadian Math. Congr., Thunder Bay 1971, 564–584 ⟨K 40⟩

Thomas, R. S. D., 1975: *The structure of the fundamental braids.* Quart. J. Math. Oxford, (2) **26** (1975), 283–288 ⟨K 40⟩

Thomas, R. S. D., 1975′: *Partially closed braids.* Canad. Math. Bull., **17** (1975), 99–107 ⟨K 40⟩

Thomas, R. S. D.; B. T. Paley, 1974: *Garside's braid-conjugacy solution implemented.* Utilitas Math., **6** (1974), 321–335 ⟨K 40⟩

Threlfall, W., 1949: *Knotengruppen und Homologieinvarianten.* Sitzungsber. Heidelberger Akad. Wiss., Math.-naturw. Kl., 1949, 8. Abh., 357–370 ⟨K 26⟩

Thurston, W. P., 1982: *Three dimensional manifolds, Kleinian groups and hyperbolid geometry.* Bull. Amer. Math. Loc., **6** (1982), 357–381 ⟨K 11, M⟩

Thurston, W. P., (1984): *The geometry and topology of 3-manifolds.* (to appear) Princeton, N.J.: Princeton Univ. Press ⟨M⟩

Tietze, H., 1908: *Über die topologischen Invarianten mehrdimensionaler Mannigfaltigkeiten.* Monatsh. Math. Phys., **19** (1908), 1–118 ⟨K 55⟩

Tietze, H., (1942): *Ein Kapitel Topologie. Zur Einführung in die Lehre von den verknoteten Linien.* Hamburger Math. Einzelschriften, **36** (1942). Leipzig-Berlin: Teubner ⟨K 11⟩

Torres, G., 1951: *Sobre las superficies orientables extensibles en nudos.* Bol. Soc. Mat. Mexicana, **8** (1951), 1–14 ⟨K 15⟩

Torres, G., 1953: *On the Alexander polynomial.* Ann. of Math., **57** (1953), 57–89 ⟨K 26⟩

Torres, G.; R. H. Fox, 1954: *Dual presentations of the group of a knot.* Ann. of Math., **59** (1954), 211–218 ⟨K 16, K 26⟩

Trace, B., 1983: *On the Reidemeister moves of a classical knot.* Proc. Amer. Math. Soc., **89** (1983), 722–724 ⟨K 14⟩

Traldi, L., 1980: *On the determinantal ideals of link modules and a generalization of Torres' second relation.* Ph.d. thesis. Yale Univ. ⟨K 25⟩

Traldi, L., 1982: *The determinantal ideals of link modules. I.* Pacific J. Math., **101** (1982), 215–222 ⟨K 25, K 50⟩

Traldi, L., 1982′: *A generalization of Torres' second relation.* Trans. Amer. Math. Soc., **269** (1982), 593–610 ⟨K 25, K 50⟩

Traldi, L., 1983: *Linking numbers and the elementary ideals of links.* Trans. Amer. Math. Soc., **275** (1983), 309–318 ⟨K 25, K 50⟩

Traldi, L., 1983′: *The determinantal ideals of link modules. II.* Pacific J. Math., **109** (1983), 237–245 ⟨K 25, K 50⟩

Traldi, L., 1984: *Milnor's invariants and the elementary ideals of links.* (preprint) ⟨K 25, K 50⟩

Traldi, L.; Sakuma, M., 1983: *Linking numbers and the groups of links.* Math. Sem. Notes Kobe Univ., **11** (1983), 119–132 ⟨K 16, K 50⟩

Treybig, L. B., 1968: *A characterization of the double point structure of the projection of a polygonal knot in regular position.* Trans. Amer. Math. Soc., **130** (1968), 223–247 ⟨K 12⟩

Treybig, L. B., 1971: *An approach to the polygonal knot problem using projections and isotopies.* Trans. Amer. Math. Soc., **158** (1971), 409–421 ⟨K 12, K 29⟩

Treybig, L. B., 1971′: *Concerning a bound problem in knot theory.* Trans. Amer. Math. Soc., **158** (1971), 423–436 ⟨K 12, K 29⟩

Tristram, A. G., 1969: *Some cobordism invariants for links.* Proc. Cambridge Phil. Soc., **66** (1969), 251–264 ⟨K 24⟩

Trotter, H. F., 1961: *Periodic automorphism of groups and knots.* Duke Math. J., **28** (1961), 553–557 ⟨K 22, K 26⟩

Trotter, H. F., 1962: *Homology of group systems with applications to knot theory.* Ann. of. Math., **76** (1962), 464–498 ⟨K 16, K 20, K 25⟩

Trotter, H., 1964: *Non-invertible knots exist.* Topology, **2** (1964), 341–358 ⟨K 23, K 35⟩

Trotter, H. F., 1973: *On S-equivalence of Seifert matrices.* Invent. math., **20** (1973), 173–207 ⟨K 25, K 27⟩

Trotter, H. F., 1975: *Some knots spanned by more than one unknotted surface of minimal genus.* In: Knots, groups and 3-manifolds (ed. L. P. Neuwirth). Ann. Math. Studies **84** (1975),

51–62. Princeton, N.J.: Princeton Univ. Press ⟨K 15⟩
Tuler, R., 1981: *On the linking number of a 2-bridge link*. Bull. London Math. Soc., **13** (1981), 540–544 ⟨K 30, K 35, K 50⟩
Turaev, V.G., 1975: Многочлен Александера трехмерного многообразия. Мат. сб., **97** (1975), 341–359, Engl. transl.: *The Alexander polynomial of a three-dimensional manifold*. Math. USSR-Sbornik, **26** (1975), 313–329 ⟨K 26, M⟩
Turaev, V.G., 1976: Кручение Рейдемейстера и мнгогочлен Александера. Мат. сб., **101** (1976), 252–270, Engl. transl.: *Reidemeister torsion and the Alexander polynomial*. Math. USSR-Sbornik, **30** (1976), 221–237 ⟨K 26, M⟩
Turaev, V.G., 1978: *Framed braids and representations for 3-manifolds*. Preprints Steklov Math. Inst., Leningrad Department Acad. Sci. USSR, Leningrad ⟨K 21, K 40⟩
Turaev, V.G., 1981: Многоместные обобщения формы Зейферта классического узла. Мат. сб., **116** (1981), 370–397, Engl. transl.: *Multiplace generalizations of the Seifert form of a classical knot*. Math. USSR-Sbornik, **44** (1983), 335–361 ⟨K 25, K 26, K 27, K 59⟩

Vainshtein, F.V., 1978: Когомологии групп. кос. (*Cohomology of braid groups*.) Funct. Anal. appl., **12** : **2** (1978), 135–137 ⟨K 40⟩
Viro, O.Ya., 1972: Зацепления, двулистные разветвленные накрытия и косы. Мат. сб., **87** (1972), 216–228, Engl. transl.: *Linkings, two-sheeted branched coverings and braids*. Math. USSR-Sbornik, **16** (1972), 223–236 ⟨K 20, K 40⟩
Viro, O.Ya., 1973: Разветвленные накрытия многообразий с краем и инвариинты зацеплений. I. Известия Акад. Наук СССР, сер. мат., **37** (1973), 1241–1258, Engl. transl.: *Branched coverings of manifolds with boundary, and invariants of links*. Math. USSR-Izvestia, **7** (1973), 1239–1356 ⟨K 20⟩
Viro, O.Ya., 1973′: Локальное заузливание подмногообраий. Мат. сб., **90** (1973), 173–183, Engl. transl.: *Local knotting of submanifolds*. Math. USSR-Sbornik, **19** (1973), 166–176 ⟨K 60⟩
Viro, O.Ya., 1973″: *Twofold branched coverings of the 3-sphere*. In: Research on Topology (ed. A.A. Ivanov). Mat. Inst. Steklov, Leningr. Sect. Acad. Sci. USSR (1973), 6–39. Leningrad: Nauka ⟨K 20⟩
Viro, O.Ya., 1976: Непроектирующиеся изотопии и узлы с гомеоморфными накрывающими (*Non projectible isotopies and knots with homeomorphic coverings*). Notes Sci. Sem. Leningrad Sec. Acad. Sci. USSR, **66** (1976), 144–147 ⟨K 20, K 60⟩
Vogt, R., 1978: *Cobordismus von Knoten*. In: Knot Theory (ed. J.C. Hausmann). Proc., Plans-sur-Bex, Switzerland 1977. Lect. Notes in Math. **685** (1978), 218–226. Berlin-Heidelberg-New York: Springer Verlag ⟨K 24⟩

van der Waerden, B.L., 1955: *Algebra II*. Berlin-Göttingen-Heidelberg: Springer Verlag ⟨X⟩
Wajnryb, B., 1983: *A simple presentation for the mapping class group of an orientable surface*. Israel J. Math., **45** (1983), 157–174 ⟨F⟩
Waldhausen, F., 1967: *Gruppen mit Zentrum und 3-dimensionale Mannigfaltigkeiten*. Topology, **6** (1967), 505–517 ⟨M⟩
Waldhausen, F., 1968: *On irreducible 3-manifolds which are sufficiently large*. Ann. of Math., **87** (1968), 56–88 ⟨M⟩
Waldhausen, F., 1968′: *Heegaard-Zerlegungen der 3-Sphäre*. Topology, **7** (1968), 195–203 ⟨M⟩
Waldhausen; F., 1969: *Über Involutionen der 3-Sphäre*. Topology, **8** (1969), 81–91 ⟨K 22, M⟩
Wallace, A.H., 1960: *Modifications and cobounding manifolds*. Canad. J. Math., **12** (1960), 503–528 ⟨K 21⟩
Weber, C., 1978: *Torsion dans les modules d'Alexander*. In: Knot Theory (ed. J.-C. Hausmann). Proc., Plans-sur-Bex, Switzerland 1977. Lect. Notes in Math. **685** (1978), 300–308. Berlin-Heidelberg-New York: Springer Verlag ⟨K 25, K 60⟩
Weber, C., 1979: *Sur une formule de R.H. Fox concernant l'homologie des revêtements cycliques*. L'Enseign. Math., **25** (1979), 261–271 ⟨K 20⟩
Weber, C., 1982: *Des nœuds classiques aux nœuds en grand dimensions*. Actualités math., Acta Ge Conf. Group. Math. Exper. Latina Luxembourg 1981, (1982), 197–211 ⟨K 12, K 60⟩
Weber, C., 1984: *La démonstration de J. Levine des theorèmes de A. Plans*. Algebraic Topology Aarhus 1982, Proc. (ed. I. Madson, B. Oliver). Lecture Notes in Math. **1051** (1984), 315–330. Berlin-Heidelberg-New York: Springer Verlag ⟨K 20⟩
Weber, C., 1984′: *Sur le module d'Alexander des nœuds satellites*. (a paraître) ⟨K 17, K 25⟩
Weber-Michel, F., 1979: *Finitude du nombre des classes d'isomorphisme de structures isométriques entières avec polynome minimal irréductible*. These, Univ. Geneve ⟨K 60⟩
Weinbaum, C.M., 1971: *The word and conjugacy*

problems for the knot group of any tame, prime, alternating knot. Proc. Amer. Math. Soc., **30** (1971), 22–26 ⟨K 16, K 29⟩

Weinberg, N. M., 1939: О свободной эквивалентности кос (*Sur l'équivalence libre des tresses fermées*). C. R. (Doklady) Acad. Sci. USSR., **23** (1939), 215–216 ⟨K 40⟩

Wendt, H., 1937: *Die gordische Auflösung von Knoten*. Math. Z., **42** (1937), 680–696 ⟨K 12, K 14⟩

Wenzel, G., 1978: *Die Längskreisinvariante und Brezelknoten*. Diss. Frankfurt/M. ⟨K 35⟩

Wenzel, C., 1979: *Über eine Klasse von Brezelknoten*. Monatsh. Math., **88** (1979), 69–79 ⟨K 26, K 35⟩

Weyl, H., 1940: *Algebraic theory of numbers*, Princeton, N. J.: Princeton Univ. Press ⟨X⟩

Whitehead, J. H. C., 1935: *A certain region in euclidean 3-space*. Proc. Nat. Acad. Sci. USA, **21** (1935), 364–366 ⟨K 55⟩

Whitehead, J. H. C., 1935′: *A certain open manifold whose group is unity*. Quart. J. Math. Oxford, **6** (1935), 268–279 ⟨K 55⟩

Whitehead, J. H. C., 1937: *On doubled knots*. J. London Math. Soc., **12** (1937), 63–71 ⟨K 17⟩

Whitehead, J. H. C., 1958: *On 2-spheres in 3-manifolds*. Bull. Amer. Math. Soc., **64** (1958), 161–166 ⟨M⟩

Whittemore, A., 1973: *On representations of the group of Listing's knot by subgroups of SL (2,C)*. Proc. Amer. Math. Soc., **40** (1973), 378–382 ⟨K 16, K 35⟩

Whitten, W. C., jr., 1969: *Symmetries of links*. Trans. Amer. Math. Soc., **135** (1969), 213–222 ⟨K 22, K 50⟩

Whitten, W. C., 1969′: A pair of non-invertible links. Duke Math. J., **36** (1969), 695–698 ⟨K 23, K 50⟩

Whitten, W. C., 1970: *On noninvertible links with invertible proper sublinks*. Proc. Amer. Math. Soc., **26** (1970), 341–346 ⟨K 23, K 50⟩

Whitten, W., 1970′: *Some intricate noninvertible links*. Bull. Amer. Math. Soc., **76** (1970), 1100–1102 ⟨K 23, K 50⟩

Whitten, W., 1971: *On prime noninvertible links*. Bull. Austr. Math. Soc., **5** (1971), 127–130 ⟨K 23, K 50⟩

Whitten, W., 1972: *Surgically transforming links into noninvertible knots*. Bull. Amer. Math. Soc., **78** (1972), 99–103 ⟨K 21, K 23, K 50⟩

Whitten, W., 1972′: *Fibered knots through T-surgery*. Proc. Amer. Math. Soc., **34** (1972), 293–298 ⟨K 18, K 21⟩

Whitten, W., 1972″: *Surgically transforming links into invertible knots*. Amer. J. Math., **94** (1972), 1269–1281 ⟨K 21, K 23, K 50⟩

Whitten, W., 1972‴: *Imbedding fibered knot groups*. Amer. J. Math., **94** (1972), 771–776 ⟨K 18⟩

Whitten, W., 1973: *Isotopy types of knot spanning surfaces*. Topology, **12** (1973), 373–380 ⟨K 15⟩

Whitten, C. W., 1974: *Characterization of knots and links*. Bull. Amer. Math. Soc., **80** (1974), 1265–1270 ⟨K 19⟩

Whitten, W., 1974′: *Algebraic and geometric characterizations of knots*. Invent. math., **26** (1974), 259–270 ⟨K 16, K 19⟩

Whitten, W., 1976: *A classification of un splittable-link complements*. Michigan Math. J., **23** (1976). 261–266 ⟨K 19⟩

Whitten, W., 1981: *Inverting double knots*. Pacific J. Math., **97** (1981), 209–216 ⟨K 17, K 23, K 35⟩

Williams, R. F., 1983: *Lorenz knots are prime*. (preprint) ⟨K 59⟩

Yajima, T., 1962: *On the fundamental groups of knotted 2-manifolds in the 4-space*. Osaka Math. J., **13** (1962), 63–71 ⟨K 16, K 60⟩

Yajima, T., 1964: *On simply knotted spheres in* $\mathbb{R}^4$. Osaka J. Math., **1** (1964), 133–152 ⟨K 61⟩

Yajima, T., 1969: *On a characterization of knot groups of some spheres in* $\mathbb{R}^4$. Osaka J. Math., **6** (1969), 435–446 ⟨K 16, K 61⟩

Yajima, T., 1970: *Wirtinger representations of knot groups*. Proc. Japan Acad., **46** (1970), 997–1000 ⟨K 16⟩

Yajima, T.; Kinoshita, S., 1957: *On the graphs of knots*. Osaka Math. J., **9** (1957), 155–163 ⟨K 12, K 14⟩

Yamamoto, Y., 1978: *Amida diagrams and Seifert matrices of positive iterated torus knots*. Proc. Japan Acad., A **8** (1978), 256–262 ⟨K 25, K 35⟩

Yanagawa, T., 1964: *Brunnian systems of 2-spheres in 4-space*. Osaka J. Math., **1** (1964), 127–132 ⟨K 61⟩

Yanagawa, T., 1969: *On Ribbon 2-knots. I. The 3-manifold bounded by the 2-knots*. Osaka J. Math., **6** (1969), 447–464 ⟨K 61⟩

Yanagawa, T., 1969′: *On Ribbon 2-knots. II. The second homotopy group of the complementary domain*. Osaka J. Math., **6** (1969), 465–474 ⟨K 61⟩

Yanagawa, T., 1970: *On ribbon 2-knots. III. On the unknotting ribbon 2-knots in* S^4. Osaka J. Math., **7** (1970), 165–172 ⟨K 61⟩

Yokoyama, K., 1977: *On links with property P**. Yokohama Math. J., **25** (1977), 71–84 ⟨K 19⟩

Yoshikawa, K., 1981: *On fibering a class of n-knots*. Math. Sem. Notes Kobe Univ., **9** (1981), 241–245 ⟨K 18, K 60⟩

Yoshikawa, K., 1982: *On a 2-knot with non-trivial center*. Bull. Austr. Math. Soc., **25** (1982), 321–326 ⟨K 61⟩

Zariski, O., 1935: *Algebraic surfaces*. In: Ergebn. Math. Grenzgeb., Bd. **3**, No. 5. Berlin: Springer-Verlag (reprinted: New York: Chelsea 1948) ⟨K 32⟩

Zeeman, E. C., 1960: Unknotting spheres. Ann. of Math., **72** (1960), 350–361 ⟨K 60⟩

Zeeman, E. C., 1960′: *Linking spheres*. Abh. Math. Sem. Univ. Hamburg, **24** (1960), 149–153 ⟨K 60⟩

Zeeman, E. C., 1960‴: *Unknotting spheres in five dimensions*. Bull. Amer. Math. Soc., **66** (1960), 198 ⟨K 60⟩

Zeeman, E. C., 1962: *Unknotting 3-spheres in six dimensions*. Proc. Amer. Math. Soc., **13** (1962), 753–757 ⟨K 60⟩

Zeeman, E. C., 1962′: *Isotopies and knots in manifolds*. In: Top. 3-manifolds, Proc. 1961 Top. Inst. Univ. Georgia (ed. M. K. Fort, jr.), pp. 187–198. Englewood Cliffs, N.J.: Prentice-Hall ⟨K 60⟩

Zeeman, E., 1963: *Unknotting combinatorial balls*. Ann. of Math., **78** (1963), 501–520 ⟨K 61⟩

Zeeman, E. C., 1965: *Twisting spun knots*. Trans. Amer. Math. Soc., **115** (1965), 471–495 ⟨K 33, K 60⟩

Zieschang, H., 1962: *Über Worte* $S_1^{a_1} S_2^{a_2} \dots S_q^{a_q}$ *in einer freien Gruppe mit p freien Erzeugenden*. Math. Ann., **147** (1962), 143–153 ⟨G⟩

Zieschang, H. (= Cišang, H.), 1963: К одной проблеме Нейвирта о группах узлов. Доклады Акад. Наук СССР, **153** (1983), 1017–1019, Engl. transl.: *On a problem of Neuwirth concerning knot groups*. Soviet Math. Doklady, **4** (1963), 1781–1783 ⟨K 16⟩

Zieschang, H., 1965: *Über einfache Kurvensysteme auf einer Vollbrezel vom Geschlecht 2*. Abh. Math. Sem. Univ. Hamburg, **26** (1963), 237–247 ⟨K 35⟩

Zieschang, H., 1966: Дискретные группы движений плоскости и плоские групповые образы (*Diskrete Bewegungsgruppen der Ebene und ebene Gruppenbilder*). Uspehi Math. Nauk, **21 : 3** (1966), 195–212 ⟨F⟩

Zieschang, H., 1967: Теорема Нильсена, некоторые ее приложения и обошения (*A theorem of Nielsen, some of its applications and generalizations)*. Proc. IV Allunion Top. Conf. 1963. Taschkent: FAN UsbSSR ⟨F, M⟩

Zieschang, H., 1970: *Über die Nielsensche Kürzungsmethode in freien Produkten mit Amalgam*. Invent. math., **10** (1970), 4–37 ⟨G⟩

Zieschang, H., 1971: *On extensions of fundamental groups of surfaces and related groups*. Bull. Amer. Math. Soc., **77** (1971), 1116–1119 ⟨F⟩

Zieschang, H., 1974: *Addendum to "On extensions of fundamental groups of surfaces and related groups"*. Bull. Amer. Math. Soc., **80** (1974), 366–367 ⟨F⟩

Zieschang, H., 1977: *Generators of the free product with amalgamation of two infinite cyclic groups*. Math. Ann., **227** (1977), 195–221 ⟨K 16⟩

Zieschang, H., (1981): *Finite groups of mapping classes of surfaces*. Lecture Notes in Math. **875** (1981). Berlin-Heidelberg-New York: Springer Verlag ⟨F, M⟩

Zieschang, H., 1984: *Classification of Montesinos knots*. In: Topology, Proc. Leningrad 1982 (ed. L. D. Faddeev + A. A. Mal'cev), Lecture Notes in Math. **1060** (1984), 378–389, Berlin-Heidelberg-New York: Springer Verlag ⟨K 20, K 35⟩

Zieschang, H.; E. Vogt; H.-D. Coldewey, (1970): Flächen und ebene diskontinuierliche Gruppen. Lecture Notes in Math. **122** (1970). Berlin-Heidelberg-New York: Springer Verlag ⟨F, G⟩

Zieschang, H., E. Vogt; H.-D. Coldewey, (1980): *Surfaces and Planar Discontinuous Groups*. Lect. Notes in Math. **835** (1980). Berlin-Heidelberg-New York: Springer Verlag ⟨F, G⟩

Zieschang, H.; Zimmermann, B., 1982: *Über Erweiterungen von* $\mathbb{Z}$ *und* $\mathbb{Z}_2 * \mathbb{Z}_2$ *durch nichteuklidische kristallographische Gruppen*. Math. Ann., **259** (1982), 29–51 ⟨M⟩

Zimmermann, B., 1977: *Endliche Erweiterungen nichteuklidischer kristallographischer Gruppen*. Math. Ann., **231** (1977), 187–192 ⟨F⟩

Zimmermann, B., 1982: *Das Nielsensche Realisierungsproblem für hinreichend große 3-Mannigfaltigkeiten*. Math. Z., **180** (1982), 349–359 ⟨M⟩

Supplement

Titles are not quoted in the List of Authors According to Codes.

Artin, E., 1950: *The theory of braids*. Amer. Sci., **38** (1950), 112–119 ⟨K40⟩

Bleiler, S., 1984: *A note on unknotting number*. Math. Proc. Cambridge Phil. Soc., **96** (1984), 469–471 ⟨K14, K29⟩

Bleiler, S.; Scharlemann, M., 1985: *Property P and strongly invertible knots.* (preprint) ⟨K19, K20⟩

Cochran, T. D., 1984′: *On an invariant of link cobordism in dimension four*. Topology Appl., **18** (1984), 97–108 ⟨K24, K61⟩

Cochran, T., 1984″: *Embedding 4-manifolds in* S^5. Topology, **23** (1984), 257–269 ⟨K60⟩

Cowan, T. M., 1974: *The theory of braids and the analysis of impossible figures*. J. Math. Psychol., **11** (1974), 190–192 ⟨K59⟩

Flapan, E., 1985: *Infinitely periodic knots*. Canad. J., **37** (1985), 17–28 ⟨K22⟩

Fukuhara, S., 1985: *Homology lens spaces obtained by surgery on knots*. (preprint) ⟨K21, K26⟩

Hatcher, A.; Thurston, W., 1985: *Incompressible surfaces in 2-bridge knot complements*. Invent. math., **79** (1985), 225–246 ⟨K15, K30⟩

Havas, G.; L. G. Kovács, 1984: *Distinguishing eleven crossing knots*. In: Computational group theory (ed: M. D. Atkinson), Proc. London Math. Soc. Symp. 1982, 367–373. London: Academic Press (1984) ⟨K28⟩

Hillman, J. A., 1984″: *Simple locally flat 3-knots*. Bull. London Math. Soc., **16** (1984), 599–602 ⟨K60⟩

Ishigaki, M., 1985: *Genus of pretzel link*. (preprint) ⟨K15, K35⟩

Jones, V. F. R., 1985: *A polynomial invariant for knots via von Neumann algebra*. Bull. Amer. Math. Soc., **12** (1985), 103–111 ⟨K28, K40, K59⟩

Kanenobu, T., 1984′: *Fibred links of genus zero whose monodromy is the identity*. Kobe J. Math., **1** (1984), 31–41 ⟨K18, K50⟩

Kawauchi, A.; T. Shibuya; S. Suzuki, 1982: *Descriptions on surfaces in four space, I: Normal form*. Math. Sem. Notes Kobe Univ., **10** (1982), 75–125 ⟨K35, K59⟩

Kawauchi, A.; T. Shibuya; S. Suzuki, 1983: *Descriptions on surfaces in four space, II: Singularities and cross-sectional links*, Math. Sem. Notes Kobe Univ., **11** (1983), 31–69 ⟨K33,59⟩

Kojima, S., 1985: *Determining knots by branched coverings*. preprint ⟨K20⟩

Kwasik, S., 1984: *On invariant knots*. Math. Proc. Cambridge Phil. Soc., **94** (1984), 473–475 ⟨K60⟩

Mandelbaum, R.; B. Moishezon, 1983: *Numerical invariants of links in 3-manifolds*. Amer. Math. Soc. Contemporary Math., **20** (1983), 285–304 ⟨K59⟩

Matumoto, T., 1984: *On a weakly unknotted 2-sphere in a simply-connected 4-manifold.* Osaka J. Math., **21** (1984), 489–492

Morton, H. R., 1985: *Threading knot diagrams*. (preprint) ⟨K14, K40⟩

Murakami, H., 1983: *The Arf invariant and the Conway polynomial of a link*. Math. Sem. Notes Kobe Univ., **11** (1983), 335–344 ⟨K26, K27, K50⟩

Murakami, H.; K. Sugishita, 1984: *Triple points and knot cobodism*. Kobe J. Math., **1** (1984), 1–16 ⟨K24, K33⟩

Myers, R., 1983: *Homology cobordisms, link concordances, and hyperbolic 3-manifolds*. Trans. Amer. Math. Soc., **278** (1983), 271–288 ⟨K24, M⟩

Negami, S., 1984: *The minimum crossing of 3-bridge links*. Osaka J. Math., **21** (1984), 477–487 ⟨K14, K30⟩

Negami, S.; K. Okita, 1985: *The splittability and triviality of 3-bridge links*. (preprint) ⟨K30, K50⟩

Pizer, A., 1984: *Matrices over group rings which are Alexander matrices*. Osaka J. Math., **21** (1984), 461–472 ⟨K25⟩

Pizer, A., 1984′: *Non reversible knots exist*. Kobe J. Math., **1** (1984), 23–29 ⟨K23, K35⟩

Riley, R., 1982: *Seven excellent knots*. In: Low-dimensional topology, Proc. Conf., Bangor 1979, Vol. 1 (ed.: R. Brown, T. L. Thickstun), 81–151 Cambridge: Cambridge Phil. Soc. (1982) ⟨K30, K35⟩

Rudolph, L., 1985: *Special positions for surfaces bounded by closed braids*. (preprint MSRI 02512-85) ⟨K15⟩

Saito, M., 1983: *Minimal number of saddle points of properly embedded surfaces in the 4-ball*. Math. Sem. Notes Kobe Univ., **11** (1983), 345–348 ⟨K35⟩

Sakuma, M., 1985: *On strongly invertible knots*. (preprint) ⟨K22, K23, K35⟩

Sakuma, M., 1985′: *Non-free-periodicity of amphicheiral hyperbolic knots*. (preprint) ⟨K22, K23, K35⟩

Sakuma, M., 1985″: *Uniqueness of symmetries of knots*. (preprint) ⟨K22, K23⟩

Shibuya, T., 1983: *On compound links*. Math. Sem. Notes Kobe Univ., **11** (1983), 349–361 ⟨K17, K24, K26, K27, K50⟩

Soma, T., 1983: *Simple links and tangles*. Tokyo J. Math., **6** (1983), 65–73 ⟨K24, K35⟩

Suzuki, S., 1984′: *Almost unknotted θ_n-curves in the 3-sphere*. Kobe J. Math., **1** (1984), 19–22 ⟨K59⟩

Traldi, L., 1983″: *Some properties of the determinantal ideals of link modules*. Math. Sem. Notes Kobe Univ., **11** (1983), 363–380 ⟨K25⟩

Traldi, L., 1984′: *Milnor's invariants and the completions of link modules*. Trans. Amer. Math. Soc., **284** (1984), 401–429 ⟨K25, K26, K50⟩

Traldi, L., 1985: *On the Goeritz matrix of a link*. Math. Z., **188** (1985), 203–213 ⟨K20, K25, K50⟩

Turaev, V.G., 1985: Кручение Райдемайстера в теории узлов (*Reidemeister torsion in knot theory*). Uspehi Math. Nauk (to appear) ⟨K26, K59, A⟩

Turaev, V.G., 1985′: *Classification of oriented Montesinos links by means of invariants of spin structures*. Preprint Steklov Math. Inst. Leninrad Dept. AN USSR ⟨K35, K59⟩

Varopoulos, N.Th., 1985: *Brownian motion can see a knot*. Math. Proc. Cambridge Phil. Soc., **99** (1985), 299–309 ⟨K59⟩

Whitten, W., 1985: *Knot complements and groups*. (preprint) ⟨K16, K19⟩

Yamamoto, M., 1982: *Lower bound for the unknotting numbers of certain torus knots*. Proc. Amer. Math. Soc., **86** (1982), 519–524 ⟨K29, K35, K59⟩

Yamamoto, M., 1983: *Infinitely many fibred links having the same Alexander polynomial*. Math. Sem. Notes Kobe Univ., **11** (1983), 387–389 ⟨K18, K26, K50⟩

Yamamoto, M., 1984: *Classification of isolated algebraic singularities by their Alexander polynomials*. Topology, **23** (1984), 277–287 ⟨K26, K32⟩

List of code numbers

A algebraic topology
B geometric topology
F surface theory, Fuchsian groups
G combinatorial group theory
K knot theory
M 3-dimensional topology
X further fields

Knot Theory

K 11 books, survey articles
K 12 general theory of knots and links
K 13 tables
K 14 elementary geometric constructions
K 15 surfaces spanned by knots, genus of knots
K 16 knot groups
K 17 companion knots, product knots etc.
K 18 fibred knots
K 19 Property P and related problems
K 20 knots and 3-manifolds: branched coverings
K 21 knots and 3-manifolds: surgery
K 22 knots and periodic maps of 3-manifolds
K 23 symmetries of knots and links
K 24 knot cobordisms
K 25 the Alexander module
K 26 the Alexander polynomial
K 27 quadratic forms and signatures of knots and links
K 28 representations of knot groups
K 29 algorithmic questions
K 30 2-bridge knots, bridge number
K 31 alternating knots
K 32 algebraic knots
K 33 slice knots
K 34 singularities and knots
K 35 further special knots
K 38 differential geometric properties of knots (curvature, integral invariants)
K 40 braids
K 50 links (special articles on links with more than one component)
K 55 wild knots
K 59 properties of 1-knots not classified above
K 60 higher dimensional knots
K 61 $S^2 \subset S^4$

List of Authors According to Codes

K 11 books, survey articles

Alexander 1932
Bing 1983
Birman 1974
Crowell-Fox 1963
Fenn 1979
Fox 1952′, 1962, 1962″
Gordon 1978
Hillman 1981′
Kervaire – Weber 1978
Kirby 1978′
Levine 1975, 1980
Lin 1979
Magnus 1973
Moran 1983
Morgan – Bass 1984
Murasugi 1974
Neuwirth 1965, 1974
Papakyriakopoulos 1958
Reidemeister 1932
Rolfsen 1976
Seifert 1936′
Seifert-Threlfall 1950
Stillwell 1980
Thurston 1982
Tietze 1942

K 12 general theory of knots and links

Akbuiut-King 1981
Alexander 1923′, 1928
Ashley 1944
Banchoff 1976
Bing-Klee 1964
Birman 1976
Bothe 1974, 1981
Brauner 1928
Brunn 1892, 1892′, 1897
Calugareanu 1961, 1961′, 1961″, 1970, 1970′
Caudron 1981
Clark 1978′
Conway 1970
Conway-Gordon 1975
Edwards 1962
Eilenberg 1936
Farber 1981″, 1981^{IV}
Fenn-Rourke 1979
Giller 1982
Gilmer 1982, 1984′
Gluck 1963
Goodrick 1969, 1970
Hanner 1983
Hartley 1983″
Hotz 1959, 1960
Joyce 1982
Kauffman 1981
Kyle 1955
Lickorish 1981
Listing 1847
Little 1885, 1889, 1890, 1900
Lomonaco 1967
Martin 1974
Matveev 1981, 1982
Milnor 1957
Moise 1954
Montesinos 1976
Moran 1983
Morton-Mond 1982
Murasugi 1961″
Nejinskii 1976
Neuzil 1973
Penney 1972
Quach 1983, 1983′
Reidemeister 1926′, 1960
Rolfsen 1972
Shibuya 1974
Simon 1973
Smythe 1967′
Schmid 1963
Stoel 1962
Tait 1898
Terasaka 1960″
Treybig 1968, 1971, 1971′
Turaev 1981
Weber 1982
Wendt 1937
Yajima-Kinoshita 1957

K 13 tables

Alexander-Briggs 1927
Ashley 1944
Caudron 1981
Hartley 1983′
Perko 1979, 1982
Rolfsen 1976
Tait 1898

K 14 elementary geometric constructions

Calugareanu 1962, 1962′, 1965, 1967
Dowker-Thistlethwaite 1982, 1983
Hotz 1959, 1960
Kinoshita 1957, 1958
Krishnamurthz-Sen 1973
Nakanishi 1983, 1983′
Pannwitz 1983
Reidemeister 1926′
Rice 1968
Schmid 1963
Trace 1983
Wendt 1937
Yajima-Kinoshita 1957

K 15 surfaces spanned by knots, genus of knots

Alford 1970
Almgren-Thurston 1977
Burde 1984
Calugareanu 1970′
Crowell 1959
Culler-Shalen 1984
Eisner 1977, 1977′
Farber 1983
Francis 1983
Frankl-Pontrjagin 1930
Funcke 1978
Gabai 1983, 1983′, 1984, 1984′
Gilmer 1982, 1984′
Goodrick 1969
Gutierrez 1974
Hillman 1980′
Kauffman 1983, 1983′
Kinoshita 1962
Kyle 1955
Laudenbach 1979
Livingston 1982
Lyon 1971, 1972, 1974, 1974′
Menasco 1984′
Murasugi 1958, 1958′
Nakagawa 1976′
Nakanishi 1981
Neuwirth 1960
Oertel 1984
Rudolph 1983′
Seifert 1934, 1950
Suzuki 1969
Swarup 1973, 1974
Schubert-Soltsien 1964
Taylor 1979
Torres 1951
Trotter 1975
Whitten 1973

K 16 knot groups

Appel 1974
Appel-Schupp 1972
Aumann 1956
Bankwitz 1930′
Birman 1973, 1979
Boileau-Rost-Zieschang 1984
Boileau-Zieschang 1983, 1984
Brown-Crowell 1965, 1966
Burau 1936
Burde 1969
Burde-Murasugi 1970
Burde-Zieschang 1966
Burger 1950
Calugareanu 1968, 1969, 1973
Chang 1972, 1973, 1974
Chen 1952
Collins 1978
Cossey-Dey-Meskin 1971
Crowell 1963, 1970
Culler-Shalen 1984
Doyle 1973
Dugopolski 1982
Fox-Torres 1954
Funcke 1975
Gonzales-Acuna 1975
Gonzales-Acuna-Montesinos 1978
Gutierrez 1971, 1973′, 1980
Hausmann-Kervaire 1978′
Higman 1948
Johnson 1980
Joyce 1982
Kanenobu 1980
Lambert 1970
Lomonaco 1981
Maeda 1977, 1977′, 1978
Magnus-Peluso 1967
Massey-Traldi 1981
Mathieu-Vincent 1975
Mayland 1972, 1974, 1975, 1975′
Mayland-Murasugi 1976
Milnor 1954
Murasugi 1961, 1963, 1965, 1971′, 1974, 1974′, 1977
Neuwirth 1960, 1961, 1961′, 1963, 1963′, 1963‴, 1965, 1974
Newman-Whitehead 1937
Norwood 1982
Papakyriakopoulos 1955, 1957′
Plans 1957

Rapaport 1960
Rapaport Strasser 1975
Ratcliffe 1981
Reidemeister 1926, 1928, 1929, 1932
Riley 1977
Rost-Zieschang 1984
Simon 1976, 1980
Schaufele 1966, 1967′
Stebe 1968
Torres-Fox 1954
Traldi-Sakuma 1983
Trotter 1962
Weinbaum 1971
Whittemore 1973
Whitten 1974′
Yajima 1969, 1970
Zieschang 1963, 1977

K 17 companion knots, producted knots etc.

Bing-Martin 1971
Bleiler 1983
Bonahon-Siebenmann 1984
Bothe 1981
Burau 1933′, 1934
Clark 1982
Fintushel-Stern 1980
Gomez-Larranage 1982
Gordon 1983
Hammer 1963
Hashizume 1958
Hillman 1984′
Kanenobu 1981′, 1983
Kearton 1979′, 1979″, 1983
Kinoshita-Terasaka 1957
Kirby-Lickorish 1979
Lambert 1969
Lickorish 1981
Litherland 1979, 1979″
Livingston 1981
Lyon 1980
Milnor 1962
Montesinos 1976
Morton 1979
Nakagawa-Nakanishi 1981
Nakanishi 1980′, 1983
Noga 1967
Norwood 1982
Quach 1983, 1983′
Sakai 1958, 1983
Sakuma 1981″
Scharlemann 1984
Seifert 1949
Shibuya 1982
Simon 1976
Soltsien 1965
Schubert 1949, 1953, 1961
Terasaka 1960
Weber 1984′
Whitehead 1937
Whitten 1981

K 18 fibred knots

Birman 1979
Birman-Williams 1984
Bonahon 1983
Burde 1966, 1969, 1984, 1985
Burde-Zieschang 1967
Casson-Gordon 1983
Durfee 1974
Edmonds-Livingston 1983
Farber 1981‴
Francis 1983
Funcke 1978
Gabai 1983, 1984′
Goldsmith 1975
Harer 1982, 1983
Kanenobu 1981
Morton 1976, 1978, 1983′
Murasugi 1971, 1974′
Neuwirth 1961′, 1963, 1963′, 1965
Quach 1979
Quach-Weber 1979
Ratcliffe 1983
Simon 1976″
Soma 1984
Stallings 1962, 1978
Whitten 1972′, 1972‴
Yoshikawa 1981

K 19 Property P and related problems

Bing-Martin 1971
Feustel-Whitten 1978
Fox 1952
Hempel 1964
Kirby-Melwin 1978
Litherland 1979′, 1980
Marumuto 1977
Mayland 1977
Menasco 1984
Nakagawa 1975
Noga 1967
Riley 1974′
Simon 1970, 1973, 1976′, 1980′
Swarup 1980
Takahashi 1981
Whitten 1974, 1974′, 1976
Yokoyama 1977

K 20 knots and 3-manifolds: branched coverings

Bankwitz 1930″
Bankwitz 1930″
Boileau-Zieschang 1983
Bonahon 1979
Bozhueyuek 1978, 1982
Burde 1971
Burde-Murasugi 1970
Cooper 1982
Durfee-Kauffman 1975
Fox 1956, 1960, 1972
Giffen 1967′
Goeritz 1934
Gordon 1971, 1972
Hartley-Murasugi 1977, 1978
Hempel 1984
Hilden 1976
Hilden-Lozano-Montesinos 1983, 1984
Hilden-Montesinos-Thickstun 1976
Hirsch-Neumann 1975
Hosokawa-Kinoshita 1960
Kanenobu 1981′
Kauffman 1974, 1974″
Kawauchi-Matumuto 1980
Kinoshita 1957, 1957′, 1958, 1958′, 1967, 1980
Kuono 1983
Kyle 1954, 1959
Livingston 1982′
Lozano 1983
Maeda-Murasugi 1983
Mayberry-Murasugi 1982
Milnor 1968′, 1975
Minkus 1982
Moishezon 1981
Montesinos 1973, 1973′, 1974, 1975, 1976′, 1979, 1980, 1984
Montesinos-Whitten 1984
Morgan-Bass 1984
Motter 1976
Murasugi 1974, 1980, 1984′
Perko 1974, 1976
Plans 1953
Reidemeister 1929
Reyner 1970
Sakuma 1979, 1981, 1982
Seifert 1933′, 1936
Shinohara-Sumners 1972
Simon 1976‴
Soma 1984
Sumners 1972, 1974
Takahashi 1977, 1978
Takahashi-Ochiai 1982
Trotter 1962
Viro 1972, 1973, 1973″, 1976
Weber 1979, 1980, 1984
Zieschang 1984

K 21 knots and 3-manifolds: surgery

Alexander 1920
Bailey-Rolfsen 1977
Brakes 1980′
Brody 1960
Caudron 1981
Clark 1978, 1980, 1982
Fintushel-Stern 1980
Fox 1962′
Fukuhara 1983, 1984
Furusawa-Sakuma 1983
Gonzales-Acuna 1970
Gordon 1983
Hempel 1962
Kauffman 1974
Lambert 1977′
Lickorish 1962, 1977
Litherland 1979′, 1979″, 1980
Livingston 1982′
Montesinos 1975
Morgan-Sullivan 1974
Moser 1971, 1974
Nakanishi 1980
Ochiai 1978
Przytycki 1983
Roeling 1971
Rolfsen 1975
Soma 1984
Wallace 1960
Whitten 1972, 1972′, 1972″
Zieschang 1967

K 22 knots and periodic maps of 3-manifolds

Boileau-Zimmermann 1984
Burde 1978
Flapan 1983
Fox 1958, 1962‴, 1967
Giffen 1966, 1967
Gordon 1975
Gordon-Litherland 1979
Gordon-Litherland-Murasugi 1981
Hartley 1980′
Hillman 1981^{IV}, 1983, 1984
Kauffman 1974, 1974″
Kawauchi 1982
Kawauchi-Kobayashi-Sakuma 1984
Kearton-Wilson 1981

Kinoshita 1957′, 1958′
Knigge 1981
Long 1984
Lüdicke 1978, 1979, 1984
Moise 1962
Montgomery-Samelson 1955
Morgan-Bass 1984
Murasugi 1971, 1980′
Sakuma 1984
Sumners 1975
Trotter 1961
Waldhausen 1969
Whitten 1969

K 23 symmetries of knots and links

Bankwitz 1930′
Boileau 1979, 1982, 1984
Boileau-Zimmermann 1984
Bonahon-Siebenmann 1984
von Buskirk 1983
Cochran 1970
Coray-Michel 1983
Furusawa-Sakuma 1983
Goldsmith 1975
Hartley 1980‴, 1981, 1983′
Hartley-Kawauchi 1979
Kawauchi 1979
Livingston 1983
McPherson 1971, 1971′
Montesinos-Whitten 1984
Murasugi 1962
Osborne 1981
Sakai 1983′
Sakuma 1981′, 1981″
Trotter 1964
Whitten 1969′, 1970, 1970′, 1971, 1972, 1972″, 1981

K 24 knot cobordism

Cappell-Shaneson 1980
Coray-Michel 1983
Fox-Milnor 1966
Giffen 1979
Gilmer 1984
Goldsmith 1978, 1979
Gordon 1981′
Gutierrez 1973
Hosakawa 1967
Jiang, B., 1981
Kauffman 1974″
Kawauchi 1978, 1980
Kawauchi-Murakami-Sugishita 1983
Kearton 1975″, 1975‴,1981
Kervaire 1971
Kirby-Lickorish 1979
Kojima-Yamasaki 1979
Levine 1969
Lines 1983
Lines-Weber 1983
Livingston 1981, 1983
Milnor-Fox 1966
Nakagawa-Nakanishi 1981
Nakanishi 1980′, 1981, 1981′
Robertello 1965
Rolfsen 1972
Sato 1981
Scharlemann 1977
Shibuya 1980
Soma 1984
Stoltzfus 1977, 1978, 19
Tristram 1969
Vogt 1978

K 25 Alexander module

Bailey 1977
Bankwitz 1930
Bedient 1984
Blanchfield-Fox 1951
Burde 1969
Burger 1950
Chen 1951, 1952, 1952′
Cochran-Crowell 1970
Crowell 1961, 1963, 1964, 1965, 1971
Crowell-Strauss 1969
Farber 1981, 1983
Fox 1960′, 1970
Fox-Smythe 1964
Fox-Torres 1954
Gamst 1967
Gutierrez 1972′
Hillman 1978, 1978′, 1981′, 1981″, 1981‴, 1982
Holmes-Smythe 1966
Kanenobu 1979, 1981
Kawauchi 1984
Kearton 1975‴, 1978
Kinoshita 1958, 1972, 1973
Laufer 1971
Levine 1971, 1975, 1977, 1980, 1982, 1983
Libgober 1983
Massey 1980, 1980′
McPherson 1969, 1973
Mehta 1980
Moran 1981
Murasugi 1963, 1969, 1974, 1984
Nakanishi 1981′
Puppe 1952
Reidemeister 1932
Reidemeister-Schumann 1934
Rice 1971

Sakuma 1979
Sato 1978, 1981
Seifert 1933′, 1934, 1936
Shinohara-Sumners 1972
Smythe 1967
Sumners 1971, 1972, 1974
Traldi 1980, 1982, 1982′, 1983, 1983′, 1984
Trotter 1962, 1973
Turaev 1981
Weber 1978, 1984′
Yamamoto 1978

K 26 Alexander polynomial

Blanchfield 1957
Burde 1966, 1985
von Buskirk 1983
Fox 1958′
Gutierrez 1974
Hartley 1979′, 1983, 1983′
Hartley-Kawauchi 1979
Hillman 1977, 1981, 1982, 1983
Hosokawa 1958
Kanenobu 1984
Kauffman 1981, 1983
Kawauchi 1978
Kidwell 1978, 1978′, 1979, 1982
Kinoshita 1958″, 1959, 1961, 1980
Kondu 1979
Levine 1965, 1966, 1967
Libgober 1980′
Morton 1978, 1983′, 1984
Murasugi 1958″, 1961″, 1966, 1970, 1971, 1983
Nakagawa 1976, 1978
Nakagawa-Nakanishi 1981
Nakanishi 1980, 1980′
Quach 1979
Quach-Weber 1979
de Rham 1967
Riley 1972′
Rolfson 1975, 1975′
Sakai 1977, 1983′
Sakuma 1981′
Seifert 1950
Sumners-Woods 1977
Suzuki 1969, 1984
Terasaka 1959, 1960
Threlfall 1949
Torres 1953
Torres-Fox 1954
Trotter 1961
Turaev 1975, 1976, 1981
Wenzel 1979

K 27 quadratic forms and signatures of knots and links

Andrews-Dristy 1964
Bayer 1983′
Erle 1969, 1969′
Goeritz 1933, 1934′
Gordon-Litherland 1978, 1979′
Gordon-Litherland-Murasugi 1981
Kauffman-Taylor 1976
Kawauchi 1977
Kearton 1979, 1979″, 1981
Kneser-Puppe 1953
Kyle 1954, 1959
Litherland 1979‴
Murasugi 1965, 1965′, 1965″, 1970′, 1974, 1983
Perko 1976
Puppe 1952
Rudolph 1982
Shinohara 1971, 1976, 1976′
Trotter 1973
Turaev 1981

K 28 representations of knot groups

Burde 1967, 1970
Grayson 1983
Hafer 1974
Hartley 1979, 1983
Hartley-Murasugi 1977, 1978
Henninger 1978
Lüdicke 1978, 1980
Montesinos 1973
Riley 1971, 1972, 1974, 1974′, 1975, 1975′, 1975″, 1977, 1979, 1983, 1984
Schaufele 1967
Stebe 1968

K 29 algorithmic questions

Appel 1974
Appel-Schupp 1972
Boileau-Weber 1983
Bonahon-Siebenmann 1984
Conway 1970
Conway-Gordon 1975
Dowker-Thistlethwaite 1982, 1983
Dugopolski 1982
Funcke 1978
Gillette-van Buskirk 1968
Hammer 1963
Hartley 1983″

Homma-Ochiai 1978
Krishnamurthz-Sen 1973
Ladegaillerie 1976
Matveev 1981
Menasco 1984′
Penney 1972
Rabin 1958′
Soltsien 1965
Schubert 1961
Schubert-Soltsien 1964
Treybig 1971, 1971′
Turaev 1978
Weinbaum 1971

K 30 2-bridge knots, bridge number

Ammann 1982
Bankwitz-Schumann 1934
Birman 1973, 1976
Boileau-Zieschang 1984
Bonahon-Siebenmann 1984
Burde 1975, 1984, 1985′
Floyd-Hatcher 1984
Funcke 1975, 1978
Goodrick 1972
Hartley 1979′
Mayland 1974, 1977
Minkus 1982
Morikawa 1981, 1982
Murasugi 1961′, 1971, 1974, 1983
Nakagawa 1981
Otal 1982
Perko 1976
Riley 1984
Shinohara 1976
Schubert 1954, 1956
Tuler 1981

K 31 alternating knots

Aumann 1956
Bankwitz 1930
Crowell 1959
Dugopolski 1982
Goodrick 1972
Kauffman 1983, 1983′
Kinoshita 1980
Krötenheerdt 1964
Krötenheerdt-Veit 1976
Mayland-Murasugi 1976
Menasco 1984
Murasugi 1958, 1958′, 1958″, 1960, 1962, 1963, 1965′, 1971′
Riley 1972′
Terasaka 1960

K 32 algebraic knots

A'Campo 1973
Akbulut-King 1981
Boileau-Weber 1983
Boileau-Zieschang 1983
Brauner 1928
Brieskorn 1970
Gorin-Lin 1969, 1969′
Jiang 1981
Kaplan 1982
Le Dung Trans 1972
Libgober 1980′, 1983
Livingston-Melvin 1983
Michel 1983
Perron 1982
Quach 1983′
Rudolph 1983
Siebenmann 1975
Sumners-Woods 1977
Zariski 1935

K 33 slice knots

Akbulut 1977
Casson-Gordon 1978
Cochran 1984
Fox 1973
Gilmer 1982, 1983
Gordon 1975
Hass 1983
Jiang 1981
Kaplan 1982
Kearton 1981
Kirby-Melwin 1978
Levine 1983
Lickorish 1979
Long 1984
Murasugi 1965″
Nakagawa 1976, 1978
Ruberman 1983
Rudolph 1982
Shibuya 1980
Zeeman 1965

K 34 singularities and knots

A'Campo 1973
Brauner 1928
Brieskorn 1970
Durfee 1974, 1975
Fox-Milnor 1957, 1966
Hirzebruch-Mayer 1968
Kaehler 1929
Kauffman-Neumann 1977
Milnor 1968
Milnor-Fox 1966
Reeve 1955

K 35 further special knots

Andrews-Dristy 1964
Asano-Marumuto-Yanagana 1981
Bankwitz-Schumann 1934
Bedient 1984
Bing-Martin 1971
Bleiler 1983
Boileau 1979, 1982
Boileau-Siebenmann 1980
Boileau-Zieschang 1984
Boileau-Zimmermann 1984
Bonahon 1983
Bonahon-Siebenmann 1984
Bozhueyuek 1978, 1982
Brakes 1980
Brunn 1892′, 1897
Burau 1933′, 1934
Burde 1985
Burde-Zieschang 1966
Casson-Gordon 1983
Chang 1973
Crowell 1959′
Crowell-Trotter 1963
Debrunner 1961
Dehn 1914
Floyd-Hatcher 1984
Fox 1973
Giller 1982
Gilmer 1984′
Goldsmith-Kauffman 1978
Gomez-Larranage 1982
Goodrick 1972
Gordon 1972, 1972′, 1976′
Gutierrez 1973′
Hacon 1976
Hartley 1980, 1980″
Hempel 1964
Hillman 1980″, 1981‴
Homma-Ochiai 1978
Kanenobu 1979, 1984
Kawauchi 1979
Kondu 1979
Krötenheerdt-Veit 1976
Lambert 1977′
Levine 1983
Lines-Weber 1983
Litherland 1979‴
Lomonaco 1969
Montesinos 1979
Morikawa 1981, 1982
Morton 1983
Motter 1976
Murasugi 1961
Nakagawa 1981
Neuwirth 1961
Newman-Whitehead 1937
Otal 1982
Penney 1969
Roseman 1974
Rost-Zieschang 1984
Scharlemann 1977
Schaufele 1967′
Simon 1976‴
Smythe 1967′
Swarup 1980
Takahashi 1981
Terasaka 1959
Trotter 1964
Tuler 1981
Wenzel 1978, 1979
Whittemore 1973
Whitten 1981
Yamamoto 1978
Zieschang 1963′, 1984

K 38 differential geometric properties of knots (curvature, integral invariants)

Borsuk 1948
Caffarelli 1975
Calugareanu 1959, 1961′, 1961″
Ding 1963
Fary 1949
Fox 1950
Gauss 1833
Hatcher 1983
Kuiper-Meeks III 1984
Langevin-Rosenberg 1976
Little 1978
Milnor 1950, 1953, 1962′
Soma 1981

K 40 braids

Appel-Schupp 1983
Arnol'd 1969, 1970, 1970′
Artin 1925, 1947, 1947′
Bankwitz 1935
Birman 1969, 1969′, 1969″, 1974
Bohnenblust 1947
Brieskorn 1973
Brieskorn-Saito 1972
Brusotti 1936
Bullett 1981
Burau 1933, 1936′
Burde 1963, 1964
van Buskirk 1966
Chow 1948
Cohen, D.I.A. 1967
Cohen, R.L. 1979
Dahm 1962
Deligne 1972

Dyer 1980
Dyer-Grossman 1981
Fadell 1962
Fadell-van Buskirk 1961, 1962
Fadell-Neuwirth 1962
Fox-Neuwirth 1962
Froehlich 1936
Fuks 1970
Garside 1969
Gassner 1961
Gillette-van Buskirk 1968
Goldberg 1973
Goldsmith 1974
Gorin-Lin 1969, 1969′
Gorjunov 1981
Gurso 1984
Hartley 1980
Henninger 1978
Hilden 1975
Jiang 1984, 1985
Kidwell 1982
Klassen 1970
Ladegaillerie 1976
Levinson 1973, 1975
Lin 1972, 1974, 1979
Lipschutz 1961, 1963
Maclachlan 1978
Magnus 1972, 1973
Magnus-Peluso 1969
Makanin 1968, 1971
Markoff 1936, 1945
Moishezon 1981, 1983
Moran 1983
Morton 1979, 1983, 1984
Murasugi 1974, 1982
Murasugi-Thomas 1972
Neukirch 1981
Newman 1942
Ochiai 1978
Rudolph 1982, 1983, 1983′
Scott 1970
Shepperd 1962
Sinde 1975, 1977
Smythe 1979
Stysnev 1978
Thomas 1971, 1975, 1975′
Thomas-Paley 1974
Turaev 1978
Vainshtein 1978
Viro 1972
Weinberg 1939

K 50 links

Bailey 1977
Brown-Crowell 1966
Burau 1934, 1936, 1936′
Burde-Murasugi 1970
Chen 1952′
Clark 1978
Cochran 1970
Crowell 1959′
Crowell-Strauss 1969
Debrunner 1961
Giffen 1976
Gutierrez 1972″, 1974
Higman 1948
Hillman 1977, 1978, 1981′
Hosokawa 1958
Kanenobu 1979, 1981
Kawauchi 1980, 1984
Kidwell 1978, 1978′, 1979
Knigge 1981
Kojima-Yamasaki 1979
Lambert 1970
Levine 1967, 1982
Levinson 1973
Massey-Traldi 1981
Mayberry-Murasugi 1982
McPherson 1971′
Menasco, 1983
Milnor 1954
Murasugi 1962, 1963, 1966, 1970, 1970′, 1984
Nakagawa 1976, 1978, 1981
Nakanishi 1981′, 1983
Nejinskii 1976
Rolfsen 1972, 1974
Sato 1981
Shibuya 1977, 1984
Smythe 1966, 1970, 1970′
Schmid 1963
Schubert 1961
Traldi 1982, 1982′, 1983, 1983′, 1984
Traldi-Sakuma 1983
Tuler 1981
Whitten 1969, 1969′, 1970, 1970′, 1971, 1972

K 55 wild knots

Alexander 1924
Alford 1962
Antoine 1921
Bing 1956, 1983
Blankinship 1951
Blankinship-Fox 1950
Borsuk 1947
Bothe 1981
Brode 1981
Doyle 1973
Fox 1949
Fox-Artin 1948

Fox-Harrold 1962
Harrold 1981
Kinoshita 1962′
McPherson 1969, 1970, 1971, 1971″, 1973, 1973′, 1973″
Milnor 1957, 1964
Newman-Whitehead 1937
Shilepsky 1973
Sikkema 1972
Tietze 1908
Whitehead 1935, 1935′

K 59 properties of 1-knots not classified above

Birman-Williams 1983, 1984
Blanchfield-Fox 1951
Boileau-Rost-Zieschang 1984
Bothe 1981′
Calugareanu 1962, 1962′
Clark 1984
Fox 1958′
Franks 1981
Gabai 1983′, 1984
Gluck 1962
Goblirsch 1959
Goldsmith 1974′, 1982
Gordon 1975
Gramain 1977
Grayson 1983
Gustafson 1981
Harrold 1973
Hirschhorn 1979
Hirzebruch-Mayer 1968
Holmes-Smythe 1966
Homma 1954
Ikegamyi-Rolfsen 1971
Jaenich 1966, 1968
Johannson 1985
Kauffman 1974′
Kawauchi-Kojima 1980
Kinoshita 1959
Kirby 1978
Lambert 1977
Laudenbach 1979
Myers 1982
Nakanishi 1981
Norman 1969
Riley 1975″, 1979, 1983
Smythe 1967
Suzuki 1974
Stillwell 1979
Turaev 1981
Williams 1983

K 60 higher dimensional knots

Akbulut-King 1981
Anderson 1983
Bayer 1980′, 1983′
Bayer-Fluckiger 1983
Bayer-Hillman-Kearton 1981
Bayer-Michel 1979
Bayer-Fluckiger-Stoltzfus 1983
Brown 1962
Cappell-Shaneson 1976
Cesar de Sa 1979
Dror 1975
Durfee-Kauffman 1975
Durfee-Lawson 1972
Dyer-Vasques 1973
Eckmann 1976
Epstein 1960
Erle 1969
Farber 1975, 1977, 1978, 1980, 1980′, 1981, 1981′, 1981″, 1981‴, 1981^{IV}, 1983, 1984, 1984′, 1984″
Giller 1982′
Gluck 1961′, 1963
Goldsmith-Kauffman 1978
Gonzales-Acuna-Montesinos 1982, 1983
Gordon 1973, 1977, 1981
Gutierrez 1971, 1972, 1972′, 1972‴, 1973, 1979, 1980
Haefliger 1962, 1962′, 1963
Haefliger-Steer 1965
Harrold 1962
Hausmann 1978
Hausmann-Kervaire 1978, 1978′
Hillman 1977′, 1981″, 1984′
Hirschhorn 1980
Hirschhorn-Ratcliffe 1980
Hirzebruch-Mayer 1968
Hitt 1977
Hitt-Summers 1982
Hosokawa-Kawauchi 1979
Hosokawa-Maeda-Suzuki 1979
Jaenich 1966, 1968
Kanenobu 1983
Kauffman 1974, 1974′, 1974‴
Kauffman-Neumann 1977
Kawauchi-Matumuto 1980
Kearton 1973, 1973′, 1975, 1975′, 1975″, 1979′, 1982, 1983, 1983′, 1983″, 1984
Kearton-Wilson 1981
Kervaire 1965, 1971
Kervaire-Weber 1978
Kinoshita 1972
Kobel'skij 1982
Kuiper-Meeks III 1984

Lashof-Shaneson 1969
Levine 1965, 1965′, 1965″, 1966, 1967, 1969, 1970, 1971, 1977, 1978
Liang 1975, 1976, 1977, 1977′
Libgober 1980, 1983
Litherland 1981
Lomonaco 1975, 1981
Maeda 1977′, 1978
Marumoto 1984
McCallum 1976
Michel 1980, 1980′, 1983
Millett 1980
Nakanishi-Nakagowa 1982
Plotnick 1982
Ratcliffe 1981
Rolfsen 1974, 1975′
Sato 1978, 1981′, 1981″
Shinohara 1971′
Sosinskii 1965, 1967, 1970
Sumners 1974, 1975
Swarup 1975
Stallings 1963
Stoltzfus 1977, 1978, 1979
Takase 1963
Tamura 1983, 1983′
Viro 1973′, 1976
Weber 1978, 1982
Weber-Michel 1979
Yoshikawa 1981
Zeeman 1960, 1960′, 1960‴, 1962, 1962′, 1965

K 61 $S^2 \subset S^4$

Andrews-Curtis 1959
Andrews-Lomonaco 1969
Asano-Yoshikawa 1981
Boardman 1964
Cochran 1983, 1984
Farber 1975, 1977
Fox 1966
Gluck 1961
Gordon 1976
Gutierrez 1978
Hillman 1980, 1981^V
Kanenobu 1980, 1983′
Kearton 1984
Kervaire-Milnor 1961
Kinoshita 1958″, 1961, 1973
Lomonaco 1969
Maeda 1979
Montesinos 1984′, 1984″
Murasugi 1977
Nakanishi-Nakagowa 1982
Neuzil 1973
Plotnick 1983, 1983′
Plotnick-Suciu 1984
Poenaru 1971
Popov 1972
Suzuki 1969, 1976
Terasaka-Hosokawa 1961
Yajima 1964, 1969
Yanagawa 1964, 1969, 1969′, 1970
Yoshikawa 1982
Zeeman 1963

Glossary of Notations

General Notations

$\sim$	homologous
$\simeq$	homotopic
$\cong$	homeomorphic or isomorphic
$\oplus$	direct sum
$\times$	cartesian or direct product
$\ltimes$	semidirect product
$*$	free product
$*_C$	free product with amalgamated subgroup C
$\bar{X}$	closure of X
$\mathring{X}$	interior of X
$\partial X = \dot{X}$	boundary of X
p.l.	piecewise linear
$\mathbb{Z}, \mathbb{Q}, \mathbb{R}, \mathbb{C}$	integral, rational, real, complex numbers
S^n	n-sphere
$E^n (E^2 = E)$	euclidean n-space
B^n, D^n	n-ball (n-cell)
$I = [0, 1]$	unit interval
$\chi(X)$	Euler characteristic of X
$\mathfrak{Z}$	free cyclic group
$n\mathfrak{Z} (\subset \mathfrak{Z})$	subgroup of $\mathfrak{Z}$ of index $[\mathfrak{Z}: n\mathfrak{Z}] = n$.
$\mathfrak{Z}_n$	cyclic group of order n
$\mathfrak{S}_n$	symmetric (group on n elements (group of permutations)
$\mathfrak{F}_n$	free group of rank n
$\mathbb{Z}\mathfrak{G}$	group ring (algebra) of the group $\mathfrak{G}$
$I\mathfrak{G}$	augmentation ideal of $\mathbb{Z}\mathfrak{G}$
$[a, b]$	commutator $a^{-1}b^{-1}ab$
$\mathfrak{G}' = \mathfrak{G}^{(1)} = [\mathfrak{G}, \mathfrak{G}]$	commutator subgroup of $\mathfrak{G}$

$\mathfrak{G}^{(n)} = [\mathfrak{G}^{(n-1)}, \mathfrak{G}^{(n-1)}]$	n-th commutator subgroup
$\mathfrak{G} = \langle s_1, s_2, .. \mid r_1, r_2, .. \rangle = \langle s \mid r \rangle$	presentation of $\mathfrak{G}$
$\langle a_1, a_2, .. \rangle$	group, generated by $a_1, a_2, \ldots$
$\overline{\langle a_1, a_2, \ldots \rangle}$	normal closure of $\langle a_1, a_2, \ldots \rangle$
$\mathfrak{U} \lhd \mathfrak{G}, \mathfrak{G} \rhd \mathfrak{U}$	$\mathfrak{U}$ normal subgroup of $\mathfrak{G}$
$a = (a_i)$	vector a with components a_i
A^T	transpose of the matrix A
$\lvert A \rvert = \det A$	determinant of the matrix A
$\lvert \mathfrak{G} \rvert$	order of the group $\mathfrak{G}$
$\lvert a \rvert$	order of the element $a \in \mathfrak{G}$
$x^a = a^{-1}xa$	conjugate of x by a
$\lvert x \rvert$	absolute value of x
$K[t]$	polynomial algebra over K
$K(a)$	extension field of K by adjoining a
δ_{jk}	Kronecker symbol
$\varphi: X \to Y$, $X \ni x \mapsto \varphi(x) \in Y$, $\varphi(x) = x^{\varphi}$	mapping φ
$\psi\varphi = \psi \circ \varphi$, $(x^{\varphi})^{\psi} = x^{\psi\varphi}$	combined mapping (first φ, then ψ)
$\varphi_*, \varphi^*, \varphi_\#$	induced mapping on homology, cohomology, homotopy groups
$\Rightarrow$	logical implication
$\Leftrightarrow$	logical equivalence
$\square$	end of proof

Special Notations

The numbers are those of the pages where the notations are explained.

a_i^+, a_i^-	103–106
$\mathfrak{b}(a, b)$	183
$\mathfrak{B}$	244
$\mathfrak{B}_n$	140
$C = \overline{S^3 - V}$	29
C_n, C_∞	49
C^*	51
$\hat{C}_n$	114
$\mathfrak{C}$	201
$\mathfrak{C}^+$	241
$\mathfrak{F}^{(i)}$	147
$F = (f_{ik})$	104
$(\mathfrak{G}, \mathscr{m}, \ell), (\mathfrak{G}, \mathfrak{P})$	38
$E_1(t), E_k(A), E_k(t)$	109, 110
$I_p, \hat{I}_p$	250
$\mathfrak{J}_n$	147
$I\mathfrak{G}$	123
$\mathfrak{k}$	3
$\hat{\mathfrak{k}}, \tilde{\mathfrak{k}}$	20
$\mathfrak{k}^*, -\mathfrak{k}$	15
$\mathfrak{k}^{(q)}$	257
ℓ	19
$\mathscr{m}$	19
$\mathfrak{m}(e_0; \beta_1/\alpha_1, \ldots, \beta_r/\alpha_r)$	196
$M(t)$	102
$\mathfrak{p}(p, q, r)$	119
R_p	244
$\hat{R}_p$	250
$srg(S^3, \mathfrak{k}, r/n)$	274
$\mathfrak{t}(a, b)$	44
$v_{jk} = lk(a_j^-, a_k)$	104
V^T	104
$V = V(\mathfrak{k}), U(\mathfrak{k})$	29
$\gamma_p: \mathfrak{G} \to \mathfrak{B}$	244, 246
$\gamma_p^*: \mathfrak{G} \to \mathfrak{Z}_2 \ltimes \mathfrak{Z}_p$	243, 246
$\Gamma, \Gamma_\alpha, \Gamma_\beta, \Gamma_\alpha^*$	16, 225
$\varepsilon_i(P)$	222
$\Delta(t), \Delta_k(t)$	109
$\varepsilon: \mathbb{Z}\mathfrak{G} \to \mathbb{Z}$	123
$\nabla(t)$	131
$\nabla_{\mathfrak{k}}(z)$	191
$\theta(A)$	16
λ	257
$\lambda(\zeta)$	248
$[\lambda(\zeta)]$	248–255, 329–339
μ	1
$\mu_{ij} = lk(\mathfrak{k}_i', \mathfrak{k}_j')$	254, 330
$\nu_{ij} = lk(\mathfrak{k}_i, \mathfrak{k}_j)$	252, 330
$\varrho_\lambda(t)$	259
$\sigma(\mathfrak{k})$	219
σ_i, σ_i^{-1}	141
$\Omega_{\mathfrak{k}}(t)$	236
$\Omega_1, \Omega_2, \Omega_3$	9, 13
$[a_1, \ldots, a_n]$	196
$\dfrac{\partial}{\partial S_i}$	124
$\#$	19
$\doteq$	109
$\prec, \triangleq$	152
$\boxed{\alpha, \beta}$	196

Author Index

Alexander 5, 6, 12, 26, 27, 118, 157, 158, 163, 178, 206, 266, 307
Arnol'd 162
Artin 2, 3, 22, 27, 140, 144, 146, 152, 155, 156, 161, 162
Aumann 17

Bankwitz 15, 185, 189, 208, 233, 234
Bayer 99
Bing 110, 272, 274, 276, 278, 280, 299
Birman 125, 139, 157, 158, 161, 162, 177, 178
Boileau 181, 196, 205, 207, 208
Bonahon 15, 181, 195, 196, 205, 207, 208
Bott 225, 226, 303, 306
Brauner 47
Brode 3
Brody 185
Brown 5, 53, 62, 65
Brunn 27
Burau 158, 160
Burde 8, 10, 70, 73, 75, 77, 78, 87, 112, 113, 156, 170, 195, 208, 254, 255, 267

Cannon 299
Cayley 47
Conner 202
Conway 112, 191, 310
Coxeter 275
Crowell XII, 17, 53, 62, 65, 109, 112, 131, 135, 193, 225, 233, 234, 238, 307
Culler 300

Dehn 13, 15, 47, 73, 87, 172, 308
Dyck 47

Erle 212, 230, 237

Fadell 139, 151, 155, 162
Fenchel 78
Feustel 286, 297, 299, 300
Fisher 5
Flapan 264
Fox, R. H. XII, 2, 3, 24, 25, 27, 47, 109, 112, 123, 130, 131, 135, 151, 152, 170, 173, 242, 256, 266, 273, 274, 307
Franz 135
Fröhlich 157
Funcke 181, 195, 208

Garside 139, 157, 162
Goeritz 177, 211, 231, 237
Gordon 230, 234, 235, 237, 264, 300
Graeub 5, 7, 67, 307

Hacon 26
Hafer 249
Haken 99, 308
Hartley 15, 181, 195, 208, 237, 249, 250, 252, 254, 255, 266, 267, 310
Hashizume 96, 99
Hatcher 178
Henninger 249, 268
Hilden 162, 163, 174, 178
Hillman XII, 99, 131, 135, 264, 266
Hosokawa 99, 131

Jaco 113, 205, 308
Johannson 113, 205, 300
Jones 219, 235, 302

Kamishima 202
van Kampen 307
Kanenobu 113
Kauffman 235
Kawauchi 15
Kearton 99
Kerckhoff 78
Kervaire 157
Kinoshita 16, 17, 99, 170, 268
Kneser 231, 235
Knigge 264

Lee 202
Levine 112, 131
Lickorish 172
Litherland 230, 234, 235, 237, 264, 300
Luecke 300
Lüdicke 264, 269, 310, 319, 329

Magnus 267
Makanin 157, 162
Markov 158
Martin 113, 272, 274, 276, 278, 280, 299
Mayberry 225, 226, 303, 306
Mayland 208
McCool 178
Metha 310
Milnor 1, 3, 12, 24, 25, 26, 27, 99, 212, 237

Moise 5, 46, 90
Montesinos 173, 174, 178, 181, 195, 208
Morton 113
Mostow 205
Murasugi 25, 77, 87, 151, 156, 161, 193, 212, 219, 220, 221, 223, 225, 228, 230, 235, 236, 237, 249, 250, 251, 254, 255, 260, 264, 267, 310

Neiss 252
Neuwirth XII, 52, 61, 65, 75, 77, 87, 139, 151, 152, 155, 162, 229
Nielsen XI, 43, 66, 73, 77, 78, 79
Noga 280, 299

Pannwith 1, 11
Papakyriakopoulos XI, 13, 39, 46, 47, 66, 200, 308
Peluso 267
Perko 253, 254, 255, 310
Plans 117
Puppe 231, 237

Quach 113

Raymond 202
Reidemeister XII, 4, 8, 13, 18, 41, 61, 121, 135, 185, 237, 250, 255, 266, 268, 310
Riley 47, 267
Rolfsen XII, 18, 71, 157, 308, 310

Sakuma 264
Schreier 47, 87, 161
Schubert 18, 19, 20, 23, 27, 92, 93, 99, 173, 181, 185, 208, 274, 292, 296, 297, 307, 310
Schumann 185, 189, 208
Seifert 18, 27, 77, 102, 118, 173, 181, 195, 196, 208, 220, 221, 230, 237, 244, 250, 266, 307
Serre 245
Shalen 113, 205, 300
Shapiro 308
Siebenmann 15, 181, 195, 205, 208
Simon 286, 287, 298, 300
Singer 41
Smith 86
Stallings 65, 68, 75, 293, 308
Strauss 131, 135

Terasaka 17, 99, 268
Thickstun 178
Thomas 161
Thurston 47, 113, 178, 205, 300
Tietze 5
Torres 131
Trace 10
Trotter 15, 181, 212, 230, 237, 263, 266

Wajnryb 178
Waldhausen 38, 39, 41, 47, 70, 75, 77, 87, 155, 271, 273, 289, 295, 298, 299, 308, 309
Wenzel 329
Whitehead 20, 271, 299, 308
Whitten 93, 203, 297, 300
Wirtinger 31, 47

Yajima 16

Zieschang 70, 73, 75, 77, 78, 86, 87, 113, 196, 202
Zimmermann 78, 181, 196, 202, 205, 208

Index

Pages in italics refer to definitions.

Alexander matrix *107*, 110, 126, 133
– module *102*, 107, 118, 128, 130
– polynomial *109*–113, 116, 128, *130*–132, 191, 228, 237, 241, 259–266, 311–318
– trick 6
algorithm, Conway 191
–, generalized euclidean 187, 190
arc, spanning 284
annihilator 120
aspherical, asphericity *46*, 173, 199
associated braid automorphism 143
augmentation homomorphism 123
– ideal 123

band projection 102
basis, associated 212
Betti number 306
Borromean links 132
boundary parallel 284
braid *22*, 139–162
–, closed *23*, 156
–, elementary *141*, 145–146
–, fundamental 162
–, normal form of a 149
–, pure 147
– automorphism *143*–147
– group *140*–141, 147–152, 155
– substitution in $\mathfrak{S}_n$ 166
braids, isotopic *22, 139*
bridge-number *23*, 92, 99, 170, 172
– presentation *23*, 24

centre of a knot group 56–57, 77
characteristic μ_j 33
chess-board, colouring 16
chord (four-fold) 21
commutator subgroup of a knot group 53–61, 65–67, 239
companion see knot, companion
complement of a knot, see knot complement
configuration space *152*–156
congruence of Murasugi 261
conjugacy problem in $\mathfrak{T}_n$ 157
continued fractions 187, 196, 208, 209
covering, branched *114*–117, 162–179
–, cyclic 49–52, 85, 113–118, 211, 240, 244
–, 3-fold branched 174–176, 179
–, two-fold branched 172–173, 183, 197, 311–318
Coxeter group 275
crossing 8
– number 183
cube with a knotted hole 278
curvature, total 12
cutting along a surface 50

decomposing spheres 94, 95
decomposition of fibred knots 97
– of knots 91
– of links 96
deformation 5
Dehn's lemma 55, 66, *308*
derivation *123*–125
–, partial *124*, 136
determinant of a knot *233*, 235
diagram, reduced, of $\mathfrak{b}$ (α, β) *182*, 208
–, special, see projection, special
– of a knot 9
dissection, normal *143*–144
double point 8

elementary divisor 306
– ideal *109*, 126, 128, 130, 132, 306
equiform group 240
equivalence, A- 213
–, combinatorial 5
– of braids *22, 139, 156*
– of knots *3*, 9
– of knot diagrams 9
– of matrices 213
equivalent, s- 219, *235*
–, S- 220
essential 284
exceptional point 79

factor knot 257
factor of a knot *19*, 94
Fibonacci polynomial 191
fibration, locally finite 65
frame of a braid 22
fundamental formula 124

genus, canonical *18*, 228
– of a knot *18*, 20, 57, 65, 73, 90, 193, 194, 228
Goeritz form, matrix 231
graph, α- 225
– matrix *225*, 303
– of a knot *16*, 225–226, 303
group of a knot, see knot group

half-plat 179
handlebody 40
Heegaard genus *170*, 173
– splitting (decomposition, diagram) *41*–42, 169–174
– splitting, standard 44
homology of a knot 29, 33, 102–137, 211, 215
$H_1 (C_\infty)$, $H_1 (C_\infty, \partial C_\infty)$ 107, 126, 215, 218
$H_1 (\tilde{X}, \tilde{X}_o)$ 122, 123, 125
$H_2 (\hat{C}_n)$ 115–117, 133, 233
homotopy chain 122
incompressible 56
index, branching *114*, 164
index $\varepsilon_i(P)$ 222
– $\theta(P)$ *16*, 222, 230
infinite region 16
intersection matrix *106*, 212
irreducible 3-manifold 68
isotopic, isotopy (ambient) 1, 2, 3
– by moves 5

Jacobian 126

knot 1, *3*
–, algebraic 26
–, alternating *15*, 189, 226–230, 238, 310–318
–, amphicheiral *15*, 40, 45, 70, 100, 203, 219, 249, 310–318
–, braid-like 62
–, cable *20*, 282, *285*-296, 300
–, clover leaf, see knot, trefoil
–, companion *20*, 37, 118
–, composite 19, *91*
–, corresponding to an arc 89
–, doubled *20*, 120, 136, 281
–, factor *257*, 259
–, fibred *68*, 65–75, 77, 97–99, 113, 193, 194, 227, 228
–, four-, figure eight *15*, 35, 40, 71, 112, 170, 194, 243, 248, 254, 276
–, granny 273
–, invertible *15*, 40, 44, 70, 184, 203, 218, 310-–318
–, iterated torus 26
–, Listing's see four-knot
–, mirrored *15*, 194, 218
–, Montesinos *196*–207, 209
–, non-alternating *15*, 238
–, non-amphicheiral 329–339
–, non-invertible 181, 203
–, oriented 4
–, periodic *256*–266
–, pretzel 63, *119*, 265, 269
–, prime *91*–96, 209
–, ribbon 25
–, rosette 266 [8_{18}]
–, satellite *20*, 37, 58–61, 118, 120, 280
–, slice *24*, 25
–, square 273
–, tame 3
–, torus 20, 26, *44*–46, 57, 77–87, 92, 128, 133, 135, 227, 238, 264, 267, 268, 274
–, trefoil *2*, 15, 20, 25, 34, 70, 73, 112, 127, 133, 170, 179, 194, 231, 265
–, trivial *2*, 13, 90, 91, 112
–, twist 271–273, 276
–, 2-bridge *24*, 36, 91, 170, 181–185, 189, 192–194, 208, 253–255, 311–318
–, wild 2, *3*
– complement *29*, 46, 65–75, 286
– diagram, see projection
– group *31*–37, 42, 45, 49–68, 92, 157, 286
– manifold 274
– projection *9*, 340–342
– type 274
knots, product of *19*, 89–100, 112, 218, 267, 280, 285, 296–300
knotted arc 89
knottedness 11
$K(\pi,1)$-space 46

lens space *87*, 183
link 1
–, invertible 203
–, Montesinos *196*–207, 209
–, splittable *11*, 131
–, Whitehead 271
– group 157
linking number 19, 250
– numbers lk $(\mathfrak{t}_i, \mathfrak{t}_j)$ 250–255, 330–339
– numbers, dihedral 252
locally flat 24
longitude *19*, 29–31, 37
longitudinal invariant *248*, 329–339
loop theorem 39, 52, *308*.

mapping class 145
– – group 177–178, 204–207
meridian *19*, 29–31
metabelian 239
–, k-step 239
Minkowski units 237
mirror-image of a knot, see knot, mirrored
move, Δ-, Δ-process *4*, 6–8, 139
multiplicity μ 1

Murasugi knot matrix 220–223
– product 229

orbifold 202
orbit manifold 77
order of a knot *8*, 233

pattern *20*, 37, 118
period of a knot *256*, 311–318
peripheral (group) system *38*, 268, 272, 274
permutation of a braid 22
plat *24*, 143
–, 4-*24*, 185–193
polynomial, Conway 112, *191*, 236–237
–, Hosokawa *131*, 160, 191, 228, 237
potential function, Conway *191*, 236–237
presentation, Dehn 48
–, Wirtinger 33
process, Δ- 4
product of knots, see knots, product
projection, regular *8*, 233
–, special *220*–227, 231
proper embedding 284
Property P *39*, 274–284

quadratic form of Gordon-Litherland 237
– – of Trotter 217, *218*, 219
quotient of a continued fraction 187

region, α-, β- *16*, 220–225
Reidemeister moves 9
representation, Burau *158*–159, 162
–, dihedral *243*, 246
–, metabelian *239*–244
–, metacyclic *241*–243, 254
–, Riley- 267
–, trivial 239
root of a tree 303

satellite, see knot, satellite
Seifert cycle 17
– cycle of first (second) kind 228
– fibred manifold 77–79, 197
– matrix *104*, 106, 112, 209, *212*, 213, 225, 236, 319–329
– matrix, reduced *213*, 217, 220, 223, 319–329
– surface *17*, 52, 65–67, 102, 209, 211, 220, 221, 225–230
semigroup of knots 94
set, branching *114*, 164
signature 302
– of a knot 209, *219*, 223, 235, 311–318
similar homeomorphisms 69
Smith conjecture 309
sphere theorem 46, *308*
surgery on a knot 274
symmetric union 268
symmetries of knots *15*, 202–207, 255–266, 311–318

tangle, circular 269
–, m- 99
–, m-rational 99, 196
theorem, Grushko 97
–, matrix tree- 226
– of Alexander 163, 307
– of Alexander-Schönflies 5
– of Bott-Mayberry 303
– of Dehn-Lickorish 172
– of Feustel 286
– of Nielsen 78, 79
– of Seifert-Van Kampen 307
– of Smith 86
– of Stallings 68
– of Waldhausen 308
Torres-conditions 131
torsion (of 2-bridge knot) *183*, 310–318
– number 306, 311–318
tree, rooted *226*, 304
trefoil see knot, trefoil
twist, Dehn *171*–172

union of knots 268
unknot(ted) 2

valuation 225
Viergeflecht = 4-plat *24*, 185

Wirtinger class 241
– presentation, see presentation, Wirtinger